EMOTIONAL INTELLIGENCE

&

WORKING WITH EMOTIONAL INTELLIGENCE

DANIEL GOLEMAN Ph.D., is the author of the international bestsellers *Emotional Intelligence*, *Working with Emotional Intelligence*, *Destructive Emotions* and *Focus*, and is co-author of *Primal Leadership*. Nominated twice for the Pulitzer Prize for his journalistic work covering the brain and behavioural sciences published in the *New York Times*, he is currently co-chair of the Consortium for Research on Emotional Intelligence at Rutgers University and a Fellow of the American Association for the Advancement of Science.

BY THE SAME AUTHOR

Vital Lies, Simple Truths
The Meditative Mind
Emotional Intelligence
Working with Emotional Intelligence
Primal Leadership
(Co-author)
Focus

EMOTIONAL INTELLIGENCE

WHY IT CAN MATTER MORE THAN IQ

&

WORKING WITH EMOTIONAL INTELLIGENCE

Daniel Goleman

BLOOMSBURY

LONDON · NEW DELHI · NEW YORK · SYDNEY

Emotional Intelligence first published in Great Britain 1996
Copyright © 1995 by Daniel Goleman

Illustration of brain on page 19 is adapted from '*Emotional Memory and the Brain*' by Joseph E. LeDoux. Copyright © 1994 by Scientific America, Inc. All rights reserved. Artist: Roberto Osti.

Working with Emotional Intelligence first published in Great Britain 1998
Copyright © 1998 by Daniel Goleman

This paperback edition published 2004
Copyright © 2004 by Daniel Goleman

The moral right of the author has been asserted

Bloomsbury Publishing Plc, 50 Bedford Square, London WC1B 3DP

Bloomsbury is a trademark of Bloomsbury Publishing Plc

A CIP catalogue record for this book
is available from the British Library

ISBN 978 0 7475 7456 9

18

Printed and bound by CPI Group (UK) Ltd, Croydon, CR0 4YY

www.bloomsbury.com/danielgoleman

EMOTIONAL INTELLIGENCE

For Tara, wellspring of emotional wisdom

Contents

PART FIVE

EMOTIONAL LITERACY

Aristotle's Challenge

Anyone can become angry—that is easy. But to be angry with the right person, to the right degree, at the right time, for the right purpose, and in the right way—this is not easy.

ARISTOTLE, *The Nicomachean Ethics*

It was an unbearably steamy August afternoon in New York City, the kind of sweaty day that makes people sullen with discomfort. I was heading back to a hotel, and as I stepped onto a bus up Madison Avenue I was startled by the driver, a middle-aged black man with an enthusiastic smile, who welcomed me with a friendly, "Hi! How you doing?" as I got on, a greeting he proffered to everyone else who entered as the bus wormed through the thick midtown traffic. Each passenger was as startled as I, and, locked into the morose mood of the day, few returned his greeting.

But as the bus crawled uptown through the gridlock, a slow, rather magical transformation occurred. The driver gave a running monologue for our benefit, a lively commentary on the passing scene around us: there was a terrific sale at that store, a wonderful exhibit at this museum, did you hear about the new movie that just opened at that cinema down the block? His delight in the rich possibilities the city offered was infectious. By the time people got off the bus, each in turn had shaken off the sullen shell they had entered with, and when the driver shouted out a "So long, have a great day!" each gave a smiling response.

The memory of that encounter has stayed with me for close to twenty years. When I rode that Madison Avenue bus, I had just finished my own doctorate in psychology—but there was scant attention paid in the psychology of the day to just how such a transformation could happen. Psychological science knew little or nothing of the mechanics of emotion. And yet, imagining the spreading virus of good feeling that must have rippled through the city, starting from passengers on his bus, I saw that this bus driver was an urban peacemaker of sorts, wizardlike in his power to transmute the sullen irritability that seethed in his passengers, to soften and open their hearts a bit.

In stark contrast, some items from this week's paper:

• At a local school, a nine-year-old goes on a rampage, pouring paint over school desks, computers, and printers, and vandalizing a car in the school parking lot. The reason: some third-grade classmates called him a "baby" and he wanted to impress them.

• Eight youngsters are wounded when an inadvertent bump in a crowd of teenagers milling outside a Manhattan rap club leads to a shoving match, which ends when one of those affronted starts shooting a .38 caliber automatic handgun into the crowd. The report notes that such shootings over seemingly minor slights, which are perceived as acts of disrespect, have become increasingly common around the country in recent years.

• For murder victims under twelve, says a report, 57 percent of the murderers are their parents or stepparents. In almost half the cases, the parents say they were "merely trying to discipline the child." The fatal beatings were prompted by "infractions" such as the child blocking the TV, crying, or soiling diapers.

• A German youth is on trial for murdering five Turkish women and girls in a fire he set while they slept. Part of a neo-Nazi group, he tells of failing to hold jobs, of drinking, of blaming his hard luck on foreigners. In a barely audible voice, he pleads, "I can't stop being sorry for what we've done, and I am infinitely ashamed."

Each day's news comes to us rife with such reports of the disintegration of civility and safety, an onslaught of mean-spirited impulse running amok. But the news simply reflects back to us on a larger scale a creeping sense of emotions out of control in our own lives and in those of the people around us. No one is insulated from this erratic tide of outburst and regret; it reaches into all of our lives in one way or another.

The last decade has seen a steady drumroll of reports like these, portraying an uptick in emotional ineptitude, desperation, and recklessness in our families, our communities, and our collective lives. These years have chronicled surging rage and despair, whether in the quiet loneliness of latchkey kids left with a TV for a babysitter, or in the pain of children abandoned, neglected, or abused, or in the ugly intimacy of marital violence. A spreading emotional malaise can be read in numbers showing a jump in depression around the world, and in the reminders of a surging tide of aggression—

teens with guns in schools, freeway mishaps ending in shootings, disgruntled ex-employees massacring former fellow workers. *Emotional abuse, drive-by shooting,* and *post-traumatic stress* all entered the common lexicon over the last decade, as the slogan of the hour shifted from the cheery "Have a nice day" to the testiness of "Make my day."

This book is a guide to making sense of the senselessness. As a psychologist, and for the last decade as a journalist for *The New York Times*, I have been tracking the progress of our scientific understanding of the realm of the irrational. From that perch I have been struck by two opposing trends, one portraying a growing calamity in our shared emotional life, the other offering some hopeful remedies.

WHY THIS EXPLORATION NOW

The last decade, despite its bad news, has also seen an unparalleled burst of scientific studies of emotion. Most dramatic are the glimpses of the brain at work, made possible by innovative methods such as new brain-imaging technologies. They have made visible for the first time in human history what has always been a source of deep mystery: exactly how this intricate mass of cells operates while we think and feel, imagine and dream. This flood of neurobiological data lets us understand more clearly than ever how the brain's centers for emotion move us to rage or to tears, and how more ancient parts of the brain, which stir us to make war as well as love, are channeled for better or worse. This unprecedented clarity on the workings of emotions and their failings brings into focus some fresh remedies for our collective emotional crisis.

I have had to wait till now before the scientific harvest was full enough to write this book. These insights are so late in coming largely because the place of feeling in mental life has been surprisingly slighted by research over the years, leaving the emotions a largely unexplored continent for scientific psychology. Into this void has rushed a welter of self-help books, well-intentioned advice based at best on clinical opinion but lacking much, if any, scientific basis. Now science is finally able to speak with authority to these urgent and perplexing questions of the psyche at its most irrational, to map with some precision the human heart.

This mapping offers a challenge to those who subscribe to a narrow view of intelligence, arguing that IQ is a genetic given that cannot be changed by life experience, and that our destiny in life is largely fixed by these aptitudes. That argument ignores the more challenging question: What *can* we change that will help our children fare better in life? What factors are at play, for example, when people of high IQ flounder and those of modest IQ do surprisingly well? I would argue that the difference quite often lies in the abilities called here *emotional intelligence,* which include self-control, zeal and persistence, and the ability to motivate oneself. And these skills, as we shall see, can be taught to children, giving them a better chance to use whatever intellectual potential the genetic lottery may have given them.

Beyond this possibility looms a pressing moral imperative. These are times when the fabric of society seems to unravel at ever-greater speed, when selfishness, violence, and a meanness of spirit seem to be rotting the goodness of our communal lives. Here the argument for the importance of emotional intelligence hinges on the link between sentiment, character, and moral instincts. There is growing evidence that fundamental ethical stances in life stem from underlying emotional capacities. For one, impulse is the medium of emotion; the seed of all impulse is a feeling bursting to express itself in action. Those who are at the mercy of impulse—who lack self-control—suffer a moral deficiency: The ability to control impulse is the base of will and character. By the same token, the root of altruism lies in empathy, the ability to read emotions in others; lacking a sense of another's need or despair, there is no caring. And if there are any two moral stances that our times call for, they are precisely these, self-restraint and compassion.

OUR JOURNEY

In this book I serve as a guide in a journey through these scientific insights into the emotions, a voyage aimed at bringing greater understanding to some of the most perplexing moments in our own lives and in the world around us. The journey's end is to understand what it means—and how—to bring intelligence to emotion. This understanding itself can help to some degree; bringing cognizance to the realm of feeling has an effect something like the impact of an observer at the quantum level in physics, altering what is being observed.

Our journey begins in Part One with new discoveries about the brain's emotional architecture that offer an explanation of those most baffling moments in our lives when feeling overwhelms all rationality. Understanding the interplay of brain structures that rule our moments of rage and fear—or passion and joy—reveals much about how we learn the emotional habits that can undermine our best intentions, as well as what we can do to subdue our more destructive or self-defeating emotional impulses. Most important, the neurological data suggest an opportunity for shaping our children's emotional habits.

The next major stop on our journey, Part Two of this book, is in seeing how neurological givens play out in the basic flair for living called *emotional intelligence:* being able, for example, to rein in emotional impulse; to read another's innermost feelings; to handle relationships smoothly—as Aristotle put it, the rare skill "to be angry with the right person, to the right degree, at the right time, for the right purpose, and in the right way." (Readers who are not drawn to neurological detail may want to proceed directly to this section.)

This expanded model of what it means to be "intelligent" puts emotions at the center of aptitudes for living. Part Three examines some key differences this aptitude makes: how these abilities can preserve our most prized relationships, or their lack corrode them; how the market forces that are reshaping our worklife are putting an unprecedented premium on emotional intelligence for on-the-job success; and how toxic emotions put our physical health at as much risk as does chain-smoking, even as emotional balance can help protect our health and well-being.

Our genetic heritage endows each of us with a series of emotional set points that determines our temperament. But the brain circuitry involved is extraordinarily malleable; temperament is not destiny. As Part Four shows, the emotional lessons we learn as children at home and at school shape the emotional circuits, making us more adept—or inept—at the basics of emotional intelligence. This means that childhood and adolescence are critical for setting down the essential emotional habits that will govern our lives.

Part Five explores what hazards await those who, in growing to maturity, fail to master the emotional realm—how deficiencies in emotional intelligence heighten a spectrum of risks, from depression or a life of violence to eating disorders and drug abuse. And it documents how pioneering schools are teaching children the emotional and social skills they need to keep their lives on track.

Perhaps the most disturbing single piece of data in this book comes from a massive survey of parents and teachers and shows a worldwide trend for the present generation of children to be more troubled emotionally than the last: more lonely and depressed, more angry and unruly, more nervous and prone to worry, more impulsive and aggressive.

If there is a remedy, I feel it must lie in how we prepare our young for life. At present we leave the emotional education of our children to chance, with ever more disastrous results. One solution is a new vision of what schools can do to educate the whole student, bringing together mind and heart in the classroom. Our journey ends with visits to innovative classes that aim to give children a grounding in the basics of emotional intelligence. I can foresee a day when education will routinely include inculcating essential human competencies such as self-awareness, self-control, and empathy, and the arts of listening, resolving conflicts, and cooperation.

In *The Nicomachean Ethics,* Aristotle's philosophical enquiry into virtue, character, and the good life, his challenge is to manage our emotional life with intelligence. Our passions, when well exercised, have wisdom; they guide our thinking, our values, our survival. But they can easily go awry, and do so all too often. As Aristotle saw, the problem is not with emotionality, but with the *appropriateness* of emotion and its expression. The question is, how can we bring intelligence to our emotions—and civility to our streets and caring to our communal life?

PART ONE

THE EMOTIONAL BRAIN

1

What Are Emotions For?

It is with the heart that one sees rightly; what is essential is invisible to the eye.

ANTOINE DE SAINT-EXUPÉRY,
The Little Prince

Ponder the last moments of Gary and Mary Jane Chauncey, a couple completely devoted to their eleven-year-old daughter Andrea, who was confined to a wheelchair by cerebral palsy. The Chauncey family were passengers on an Amtrak train that crashed into a river after a barge hit and weakened a railroad bridge in Louisiana's bayou country. Thinking first of their daughter, the couple tried their best to save Andrea as water rushed into the sinking train; somehow they managed to push Andrea through a window to rescuers. Then, as the car sank beneath the water, they perished.[1]

Andrea's story, of parents whose last heroic act is to ensure their child's survival, captures a moment of almost mythic courage. Without doubt such incidents of parental sacrifice for their progeny have been repeated countless times in human history and prehistory, and countless more in the larger course of evolution of our species.[2] Seen from the perspective of evolutionary biologists, such parental self-sacrifice is in the service of "reproductive success" in passing on one's genes to future generations. But from the perspective of a parent making a desperate decision in a moment of crisis, it is about nothing other than love.

As an insight into the purpose and potency of emotions, this exemplary act of parental heroism testifies to the role of altruistic love—and every other emotion we feel—in human life.[3] It suggests that our deepest feelings, our passions and longings, are essential guides, and that our species owes much of its existence to their power in human affairs. That power is extraordinary: Only a potent love—the urgency of saving a cherished child—could lead a parent to override the impulse for personal survival. Seen from the intellect, their self-sacrifice was arguably irrational; seen from the heart, it was the only choice to make.

Sociobiologists point to the preeminence of heart over head at such crucial moments when they conjecture about why evolution has given emotion such a central role in the human psyche. Our emotions, they say, guide us in facing predicaments and tasks too important to leave to intellect alone—danger, painful loss, persisting toward a goal despite frustrations, bonding with a mate, building a family. Each emotion offers a distinctive readiness to act; each points us in a direction that has worked well to handle the recurring challenges of human life.[4] As these eternal situations were repeated and repeated over our evolutionary history, the survival value of our emotional repertoire was attested to by its becoming imprinted in our nerves as innate, automatic tendencies of the human heart.

A view of human nature that ignores the power of emotions is sadly shortsighted. The very name *Homo sapiens*, the thinking species, is misleading in light of the new appreciation and vision of the place of emotions in our lives that science now offers. As we all know from experience, when it comes to shaping our decisions and our actions, feeling counts every bit as much—and often more—than thought. We have gone too far in emphasizing the value and import of the purely rational—of what IQ measures—in human life. Intelligence can come to nothing when the emotions hold sway.

WHEN PASSIONS OVERWHELM REASON

It was a tragedy of errors. Fourteen-year-old Matilda Crabtree was just playing a practical joke on her father: she jumped out of a closet and yelled "Boo!" as her parents came home at one in the morning from visiting friends.

But Bobby Crabtree and his wife thought Matilda was staying with friends that night. Hearing noises as he entered the house, Crabtree reached for his .357 caliber pistol and went into Matilda's bedroom to investigate. When his daughter jumped from the closet, Crabtree shot her in the neck. Matilda Crabtree died twelve hours later.[5]

One emotional legacy of evolution is the fear that mobilizes us to protect our family from danger; that impulse impelled Bobby Crabtree to get his gun and search his house for the intruder he thought was prowling there. Fear primed Crabtree to shoot before he could fully register what he was shooting at, even before he could recognize his daughter's voice. Automatic reactions of this sort have become etched in our nervous system, evolutionary biologists presume, because for a long and crucial period in human prehistory they made the difference between survival and death. Even more important, they mattered for the main task of evolution: being able to bear progeny who would carry on these very genetic predispositions—a sad irony, given the tragedy at the Crabtree household.

But while our emotions have been wise guides in the evolutionary long run, the new realities civilization presents have arisen with such rapidity that the slow march of evolution cannot keep up. Indeed, the first laws and proclamations of ethics—the Code of Hammurabi, the Ten Commandments of the Hebrews, the Edicts of Emperor Ashoka—can be read as attempts to harness, subdue, and domesticate emotional life. As Freud described in *Civilization and Its Discontents,* society has had to enforce from without rules meant to subdue tides of emotional excess that surge too freely within.

Despite these social constraints, passions overwhelm reason time and again. This given of human nature arises from the basic architecture of mental life. In terms of biological design for the basic neural circuitry of emotion, what we are born with is what worked best for the last 50,000 human generations, not the last 500 generations—and certainly not the last five. The slow, deliberate forces of evolution that have shaped our emotions have done their work over the course of a million years; the last 10,000 years— despite having witnessed the rapid rise of human civilization and the explosion of the human population from five million to five billion—have left little imprint on our biological templates for emotional life.

For better or for worse, our appraisal of every personal encounter and our responses to it are shaped not just by our rational judgments or our personal history, but also by our distant ancestral past. This leaves us with sometimes tragic propensities, as witness the sad events at the Crabtree household. In short, we too often confront postmodern dilemmas with an emotional repertoire tailored to the urgencies of the Pleistocene. That predicament is at the heart of my subject.

Impulses to Action

One early spring day I was driving along a highway over a mountain pass in Colorado, when a snow flurry suddenly blotted out the car a few lengths ahead of me. As I peered ahead I couldn't make out anything; the swirling snow was now a blinding whiteness. Pressing my foot on the brake, I could feel anxiety flood my body and hear the thumping of my heart.

The anxiety built to full fear: I pulled over to the side of the road, waiting for the flurry to pass. A half hour later the snow stopped, visibility returned, and I continued on my way—only to be stopped a few hundred yards down the road, where an ambulance crew was helping a passenger in a car that had rear-ended a slower car in front; the collision blocked the highway. If I had continued driving in the blinding snow, I probably would have hit them.

The caution fear forced on me that day may have saved my life. Like a rabbit frozen in terror at the hint of a passing fox—or a protomammal hiding from a marauding dinosaur—I was overtaken by an internal state that compelled me to stop, pay attention, and take heed of a coming danger.

All emotions are, in essence, impulses to act, the instant plans for handling life that evolution has instilled in us. The very root of the word *emotion* is *motere,* the Latin verb "to move," plus the prefix "e-" to connote "move away," suggesting that a tendency to act is implicit in every emotion. That emotions lead to actions is most obvious in watching animals or children; it is only in "civilized" adults we so often find the great anomaly in the animal kingdom, emotions—root impulses to act—divorced from obvious reaction.[6]

In our emotional repertoire each emotion plays a unique role, as revealed by their distinctive biological signatures (see Appendix A for details on "basic" emotions). With new methods to peer into the body and brain, researchers are discovering more physiological details of how each emotion prepares the body for a very different kind of response:[7]

- With *anger* blood flows to the hands, making it easier to grasp a weapon or strike at a foe; heart rate increases, and a rush of hormones such as adrenaline generates a pulse of energy strong enough for vigorous action.

- With *fear* blood goes to the large skeletal muscles, such as in the legs, making it easier to flee—and making the face blanch as blood is shunted away from it (creating the feeling that the blood "runs cold"). At the same time, the body freezes, if only for a moment, perhaps allowing time to gauge whether hiding might be a better reaction. Circuits in the brain's emotional centers trigger a flood of hormones that put the body on general alert, making it edgy and ready for action, and attention fixates on the threat at hand, the better to evaluate what response to make.

- Among the main biological changes in *happiness* is an increased activity in a brain center that inhibits negative feelings and fosters an increase in available energy, and a quieting of those that generate worrisome thought. But there is no particular shift in physiology save a quiescence, which makes the body recover more quickly from the biological arousal of upsetting emotions. This configuration offers the body a general rest, as well as readiness and enthusiasm for whatever task is at hand and for striving toward a great variety of goals.

• *Love,* tender feelings, and sexual satisfaction entail parasympathetic arousal—the physiological opposite of the "fight-or-flight" mobilization shared by fear and anger. The parasympathetic pattern, dubbed the "relaxation response," is a bodywide set of reactions that generates a general state of calm and contentment, facilitating cooperation.

• The lifting of the eyebrows in *surprise* allows the taking in of a larger visual sweep and also permits more light to strike the retina. This offers more information about the unexpected event, making it easier to figure out exactly what is going on and concoct the best plan for action.

• Around the world an expression of *disgust* looks the same, and sends the identical message: something is offensive in taste or smell, or metaphorically so. The facial expression of disgust—the upper lip curled to the side as the nose wrinkles slightly—suggests a primordial attempt, as Darwin observed, to close the nostrils against a noxious odor or to spit out a poisonous food.

• A main function for *sadness* is to help adjust to a significant loss, such as the death of someone close or a major disappointment. Sadness brings a drop in energy and enthusiasm for life's activities, particularly diversions and pleasures, and, as it deepens and approaches depression, slows the body's metabolism. This introspective withdrawal creates the opportunity to mourn a loss or frustrated hope, grasp its consequences for one's life, and, as energy returns, plan new beginnings. This loss of energy may well have kept saddened—and vulnerable—early humans close to home, where they were safer.

These biological propensities to act are shaped further by our life experience and our culture. For instance, universally the loss of a loved one elicits sadness and grief. But how we show our grieving—how emotions are displayed or held back for private moments—is molded by culture, as are which particular people in our lives fall into the category of "loved ones" to be mourned.

The protracted period of evolution when these emotional responses were hammered into shape was certainly a harsher reality than most humans endured as a species after the dawn of recorded history. It was a time when few infants survived to childhood and few adults to thirty years, when predators could strike at any moment, when the vagaries of droughts and floods meant the difference between starvation and survival. But with the coming of agriculture and even the most rudimentary human societies, the odds for survival began to change dramatically. In the last ten thousand years, when these advances took hold throughout the world, the ferocious pressures that had held the human population in check eased steadily.

Those same pressures had made our emotional responses so valuable for survival; as they waned, so did the goodness of fit of parts of our emotional repertoire. While in the ancient past a hair-trigger anger may have offered a crucial edge for survival, the availability of automatic weaponry to thirteen-year-olds has made it too often a disastrous reaction.[8]

Our Two Minds

A friend was telling me about her divorce, a painful separation. Her husband had fallen in love with a younger woman at work, and suddenly announced he was leaving to live with the other woman. Months of bitter wrangling over house, money, and custody of the children followed. Now, some months later, she was saying that her independence was appealing to her, that she was happy to be on her own. "I just don't think about him anymore—I really don't care," she said. But as she said it, her eyes momentarily welled up with tears.

That moment of teary eyes could easily pass unnoted. But the empathic understanding that someone's watering eyes means she is sad despite her words to the contrary is an act of comprehending just as surely as is distilling meaning from words on a printed page. One is an act of the emotional mind, the other of the rational mind. In a very real sense we have two minds, one that thinks and one that feels.

These two fundamentally different ways of knowing interact to construct our mental life. One, the rational mind, is the mode of comprehension we are typically conscious of: more prominent in awareness, thoughtful, able to ponder and reflect. But alongside that there is another system of knowing: impulsive and powerful, if sometimes illogical—the emotional mind. (For a more detailed description of the characteristics of the emotional mind, see Appendix B.)

The emotional/rational dichotomy approximates the folk distinction between "heart" and "head"; knowing something is right "in your heart" is a different order of conviction—somehow a deeper kind of certainty—than thinking so with your rational mind. There is a steady gradient in the ratio of rational-to-emotional control over the mind; the more intense the feeling, the more dominant the emotional mind becomes—and the more ineffectual the rational. This is an arrangement that seems to stem from eons of evolutionary advantage to having emotions and intuitions guide our instantaneous response in situations where our lives are in peril—and where pausing to think over what to do could cost us our lives.

These two minds, the emotional and the rational, operate in tight harmony for the most part, intertwining their very different ways of knowing to guide us through the world. Ordinarily there is a balance between emotional and rational minds, with emotion feeding into and informing the operations of the rational mind, and the rational mind refining and sometimes vetoing the inputs of the emotions. Still, the emotional and rational minds are semi-independent faculties, each, as we shall see, reflecting the operation of distinct, but interconnected, circuitry in the brain.

In many or most moments these minds are exquisitely coordinated; feelings are essential to thought, thought to feeling. But when passions surge the balance tips: it is the emotional mind that captures the upper hand, swamping the rational mind. The sixteenth-century humanist Erasmus of Rotterdam wrote in a satirical vein of this perennial tension between reason and emotion:[9]

> Jupiter has bestowed far more passion than reason—you could calculate the ratio as 24 to one. He set up two raging tyrants in opposition to Reason's solitary power: anger and lust. How far Reason can prevail against the combined forces of these two the common life of man makes quite clear. Reason does the only thing she can and shouts herself hoarse, repeating formulas of virtue, while the other two bid her go hang herself, and are increasingly noisy and offensive, until at last their Ruler is exhausted, gives up, and surrenders.

HOW THE BRAIN GREW

To better grasp the potent hold of the emotions on the thinking mind—and why feeling and reason are so readily at war—consider how the brain evolved. Human brains, with their three pounds or so of cells and neural juices, are about triple the size of those in our nearest cousins in evolution, the nonhuman primates. Over millions of years of evolution, the brain has grown from the bottom up, with its higher centers developing as elaborations of lower, more ancient parts. (The growth of the brain in the human embryo roughly retraces this evolutionary course.)

The most primitive part of the brain, shared with all species that have more than a minimal nervous system, is the brainstem surrounding the top of the spinal cord. This root brain regulates basic life functions like breathing and the metabolism of the body's other organs, as well as controlling stereotyped reactions and movements. This primitive brain cannot be said to think or learn; rather it is a set of preprogrammed regulators that keep the body running as it should and reacting in a way that ensures survival. This brain reigned supreme in the Age of the Reptiles: Picture a snake hissing to signal the threat of an attack.

From the most primitive root, the brainstem, emerged the emotional centers. Millions of years later in evolution, from these emotional areas evolved the thinking brain or "neocortex," the great bulb of convoluted tissues that make up the top layers. The fact that the thinking brain grew from the emotional reveals much about the relationship of thought to feeling; there was an emotional brain long before there was a rational one.

The most ancient root of our emotional life is in the sense of smell, or, more precisely, in the olfactory lobe, the cells that take in and analyze smell. Every living entity, be it nutritious, poisonous, sexual partner, predator or prey, has a distinctive molecular signature that can be carried in the wind. In those primitive times smell commended itself as a paramount sense for survival.

From the olfactory lobe the ancient centers for emotion began to evolve, eventually growing large enough to encircle the top of the brainstem. In its rudimentary stages, the olfactory center was composed of little more than thin layers of neurons gathered to analyze smell. One layer of cells took in what was smelled and sorted it out into the relevant categories: edible or toxic, sexually available, enemy or meal. A second layer of cells sent reflexive messages throughout the nervous system telling the body what to do: bite, spit, approach, flee, chase.[10]

With the arrival of the first mammals came new, key layers of the emotional brain. These, surrounding the brainstem, look roughly like a bagel with a bite taken out at the bottom where the brainstem nestles into them. Because this part of the brain rings and borders the brainstem, it was called the "limbic" system, from "limbus," the Latin word for "ring." This new neural territory added emotions proper to the brain's repertoire.[11] When we are in the grip of craving or fury, head-over-heels in love or recoiling in dread, it is the limbic system that has us in its grip.

As it evolved, the limbic system refined two powerful tools: learning and memory. These revolutionary advances allowed an animal to be much smarter in its choices for survival, and to fine-tune its responses to adapt to hanging demands rather than having invariable and automatic reactions. If a food led to sickness, it could be avoided next time. Decisions like knowing what to eat and what to spurn were still determined largely through smell; the connections between the olfactory bulb and the limbic system now took on the tasks of making distinctions among smells and recognizing them, comparing a present smell with past ones, and so discriminating good from bad. This was done by the "rhinencephalon," literally, the "nose brain," a part of the limbic wiring, and the rudimentary basis of the neocortex, the thinking brain.

About 100 million years ago the brain in mammals took a great growth spurt. Piled on top of the thin two-layered cortex—the regions that plan, comprehend what is sensed, coordinate movement—several new layers of brain cells were added to form the neocortex. In contrast to the ancient brain's two-layered cortex, the neocortex offered an extraordinary intellectual edge.

The *Homo sapiens* neocortex, so much larger than in any other species, has added all that is distinctly human. The neocortex is the seat of thought; it contains the centers that put together and comprehend what the senses perceive. It adds to a feeling what we think about it—and allows us to have feelings about ideas, art, symbols, imaginings.

In evolution the neocortex allowed a judicious fine-tuning that no doubt has made enormous advantages in an organism's ability to survive adversity, making it more likely that its progeny would in turn pass on the genes that contain that same neural circuitry. The survival edge is due to the neocortex's talent for strategizing, long-term planning, and other mental wiles. Beyond that, the triumphs of art, of civilization and culture, are all fruits of the neocortex.

This new addition to the brain allowed the addition of nuance to emotional life. Take love. Limbic structures generate feelings of pleasure and sexual desire—the emotions that feed sexual passion. But the addition of the neocortex and its connections to the limbic system allowed for the mother-child bond that is the basis of the family unit and the long-term commitment to childrearing that makes human development possible. (Species that have no neocortex, such as reptiles, lack maternal affection; when their young hatch, the newborns must hide to avoid being cannibalized.) In humans the protective bond between parent and child allows much of maturation to go on over the course of a long childhood—during which the brain continues to develop.

As we proceed up the phylogenetic scale from reptile to rhesus to human, the sheer mass of the neocortex increases; with that increase comes a geometric rise in the interconnections in brain circuitry. The larger the number of such connections, the greater the range of possible responses. The neocortex allows for the subtlety and complexity of emotional life, such as the ability to have feelings *about* our feelings. There is more neocortex-to-limbic system in primates than in other species—and vastly more in humans—suggesting why we are able to display a far greater range of reactions to our emotions, and more nuance. While a rabbit or rhesus has a restricted set of typical responses to fear, the larger human neocortex allows a far more nimble repertoire—including calling 999. The more complex the social system, the more essential is such flexibility—and there is no more complex social world than our own.[12]

But these higher centers do not govern all of emotional life; in crucial matters of the heart—and most especially in emotional emergencies—they can be said to defer to the limbic system. Because so many of the brain's higher centers sprouted from or extended the scope of the limbic area, the emotional brain plays a crucial role in neural architecture. As the root from which the newer brain grew, the emotional areas are intertwined via myriad connecting circuits to all parts of the neocortex. This gives the emotional centers immense power to influence the functioning of the rest of the brain—including its centers for thought.

2

Anatomy of an Emotional Hijacking

Life is a comedy for those who think and a tragedy for those who feel.

Horace Walpole

It was a hot August afternoon in 1963, the same day that the Rev. Martin Luther King, Jr., gave his "I Have a Dream" speech to a civil rights march on Washington. On that day Richard Robles, a seasoned burglar who had just been paroled from a three-year sentence for the more than one hundred break-ins he had pulled to support a heroin habit, decided to do one more. He wanted to renounce crime, Robles later claimed, but he desperately needed money for his girlfriend and their three-year-old daughter.

The apartment he broke into that day belonged to two young women, twenty-one-year-old Janice Wylie, a researcher at *Newsweek* magazine, and twenty-three-year-old Emily Hoffert, a grade-school teacher. Though Robles chose the apartment on New York's swanky Upper East Side to burglarize because he thought no one would be there, Wylie was home. Threatening her with a knife, Robles tied her up. As he was leaving, Hoffert came home. To make good his escape, Robles began to tie her up, too.

As Robles tells the tale years later, while he was tying up Hoffert, Janice Wylie warned him he would not get away with this crime: She would remember his face and help the police track him down. Robles, who had promised himself this was to have been his last burglary, panicked at that, completely losing control. In a frenzy, he grabbed a soda bottle and clubbed the women until they were unconscious, then, awash in rage and fear, he slashed and stabbed them over and over with a kitchen knife. Looking back on that moment some twenty-five years later, Robles lamented, "I just went bananas. My head just exploded."

To this day Robles has lots of time to regret those few minutes of rage unleashed. At this writing he is still in prison, some three decades later, for what became known as the "Career Girl Murders."

Such emotional explosions are neural hijackings. At those moments, evidence suggests, a center in the limbic brain proclaims an emergency, recruiting the rest of the brain to its urgent agenda. The hijacking occurs in an instant, triggering this reaction crucial moments before the neocortex, the thinking brain, has had a chance to glimpse fully what is happening, let alone decide if it is a good idea. The hallmark of such a hijack is that once the moment passes, those so possessed have the sense of not knowing what came over them.

These hijacks are by no means isolated, horrific incidents that lead to brutal crimes like the Career Girl Murders. In less catastrophic form—but not necessarily less intense—they happen to us with fair frequency. Think back to the last time you "lost it," blowing up at someone—your spouse or child, or perhaps the driver of another car—to a degree that later, with some reflection and hindsight, seemed uncalled for. In all probability, that, too, was such a hijacking, a neural takeover which, as we shall see, originates in the amygdala, a center in the limbic brain.

Not all limbic hijackings are distressing. When a joke strikes someone as so uproarious that their laughter is almost explosive, that, too, is a limbic response. It is at work also in moments of intense joy: When Dan Jansen, after several heartbreaking failures to capture an Olympic Gold Medal for speed skating (which he had vowed to do for his dying sister), finally won the Gold in the 1,000-meter race in the 1994 Winter Olympics in Norway, his wife was so overcome by the excitement and happiness that she had to be rushed to emergency physicians at rinkside.

- THE SEAT OF ALL PASSION

In humans the amygdala (from the Greek word for "almond") is an almond-shaped cluster of interconnected structures perched above the brainstem, near the bottom of the limbic ring. There are two amygdalas, one on each side of the brain, nestled toward the side of the head. The human amygdala is relatively large compared to that in any of our closest evolutionary cousins, the primates.

The hippocampus and the amygdala were the two key parts of the primitive "nose brain" that, in evolution, gave rise to the cortex and then the neocortex. To this day these limbic structures do much or most of the brain's learning and remembering; the amygdala is the specialist for emotional matters. If the amygdala is severed from the rest of the brain, the result is a striking inability to gauge the emotional significance of events; this condition is sometimes called "affective blindness."

Lacking emotional weight, encounters lose their hold. One young man whose amygdala had been surgically removed to control severe seizures became completely uninterested in people, preferring to sit in isolation with no human contact. While he was perfectly capable of conversation, he no longer recognized close friends, relatives, or even his mother, and remained impassive in the face of their anguish at his indifference. Without an amygdala he seemed to have lost all recognition of feeling, as well as any feeling about feelings.[1] The amygdala acts as a storehouse of emotional memory, and thus of significance itself; life without the amygdala is a life stripped of personal meanings.

More than affection is tied to the amygdala; all passion depends on it. Animals that have their amygdala removed or severed lack fear and rage, lose the urge to compete or cooperate, and no longer have any sense of their place in their kind's social order; emotion is blunted or absent. Tears, an emotional signal unique to humans, are triggered by the amygdala and a nearby structure, the cingulate gyrus; being held, stroked, or otherwise comforted soothes these same brain regions, stopping the sobs. Without an amygdala, there are no tears of sorrow to soothe.

Joseph LeDoux, a neuroscientist at the Center for Neural Science at New York University, was the first to discover the key role of the amygdala in the emotional brain.[2] LeDoux is part of a fresh breed of neuroscientists who draw on innovative methods and technologies that bring a previously unknown level of precision to mapping the brain at work, and so can lay bare mysteries of mind that earlier generations of scientists have found impenetrable. His findings on the circuitry of the emotional brain overthrow a long-standing notion about the limbic system, putting the amygdala at the center of the action and placing other limbic structures in very different roles.[3]

LeDoux's research explains how the amygdala can take control over what we do even as the thinking brain, the neocortex, is still coming to a decision.

As we shall see, the workings of the amygdala and its interplay with the neocortex are at the heart of emotional intelligence.

THE NEURAL TRIPWIRE

Most intriguing for understanding the power of emotions in mental life are those moments of impassioned action that we later regret, once the dust has settled; the question is how we so easily become so irrational. Take, for example, a young woman who drove two hours to Boston to have brunch and spend the day with her boyfriend. During brunch he gave her a present she'd been wanting for months, a hard-to-find art print brought back from Spain. But her delight dissolved the moment she suggested that after brunch they go to a matinee of a movie she'd been wanting to see and her friend stunned her by saying he couldn't spend the day with her because he had softball practice. Hurt and incredulous, she got up in tears, left the cafe, and, on impulse, threw the print in a garbage can. Months later, recounting the incident, it's not walking out she regrets, but the loss of the print.

It is in moments such as these—when impulsive feeling overrides the rational—that the newly discovered role for the amygdala is pivotal. Incoming signals from the senses let the amygdala scan every experience for trouble. This puts the amygdala in a powerful post in mental life, something like a psychological sentinel, challenging every situation, every perception, with but one kind of question in mind, the most primitive: "Is this something I hate? That hurts me? Something I fear?" If so—if the moment at hand somehow draws a "Yes"—the amygdala reacts instantaneously, like a neural tripwire, telegraphing a message of crisis to all parts of the brain.

In the brain's architecture, the amygdala is poised something like an alarm company where operators stand ready to send out emergency calls to the fire department, police, and a neighbor whenever a home security system signals trouble.

When it sounds an alarm of, say, fear, it sends urgent messages to every major part of the brain: it triggers the secretion of the body's fight-or-flight hormones, mobilizes the centers for movement, and activates the cardiovascular system, the muscles, and the gut.[4] Other circuits from the amygdala signal the secretion of emergency dollops of the hormone norepinephrine to heighten the reactivity of key brain areas, including those that make the senses more alert, in effect setting the brain on edge. Additional signals from the amygdala tell the brainstem to fix the face in a fearful expression, freeze unrelated movements the muscles had underway, speed heart rate and raise blood pressure, slow breathing. Others rivet attention on the source of the fear, and prepare the muscles to react accordingly. Simultaneously, cortical memory systems are shuffled to retrieve any knowledge relevant to the emergency at hand, taking precedence over other strands of thought.

And these are just part of a carefully coordinated array of changes the amygdala orchestrates as it commandeers areas throughout the brain (for a more detailed account, see Appendix C). The amygdala's extensive web of neural connections allows it, during an emotional emergency, to capture and drive much of the rest of the brain—including the rational mind.

THE EMOTIONAL SENTINEL

A friend tells of having been on vacation in England, and eating brunch at a canalside cafe. Taking a stroll afterward along the stone steps down to the canal, he suddenly saw a girl gazing at the water, her face frozen in fear. Before he knew quite why, he had jumped in the water—in his coat and tie. Only once he was in the water did he realize that the girl was staring in shock at a toddler who had fallen in—whom he was able to rescue.

What made him jump in the water before he knew why? The answer, very likely, was his amygdala.

In one of the most telling discoveries about emotions of the last decade, LeDoux's work revealed how the architecture of the brain gives the amygdala a privileged position as an emotional sentinel, able to hijack the brain.[5] His research has shown that sensory signals from eye or ear travel first in the brain to the thalamus, and then—across a single synapse—to the amygdala; a second signal from the thalamus is routed to the neocortex—the thinking brain. This branching allows the amygdala to begin to respond *before* the neocortex, which mulls information through several levels of brain circuits before it fully perceives and finally initiates its more finely tailored response.

LeDoux's research is revolutionary for understanding emotional life because it is the first to work out neural pathways for feelings that bypass the neocortex. Those feelings that take the direct route through the amygdala include our most primitive and potent; this circuit does much to explain the power of emotion to overwhelm rationality.

The conventional view in neuroscience had been that the eye, ear, and other sensory organs transmit signals to the thalamus, and from there to

sensory processing areas of the neocortex, where the signals are put together
into objects as we perceive them. The signals are sorted for meanings so that
the brain recognizes what each object is and what its presence means. From
the neocortex, the old theory held, the signals are sent to the limbic brain, and
from there the appropriate response radiates out through the brain and the
rest of the body. That is the way it works much or most of the time—but
LeDoux discovered a smaller bundle of neurons that leads directly from the
thalamus to the amygdala, in addition to those going through the larger path
of neurons to the cortex. This smaller and shorter pathway—something like a
neural back alley—allows the amygdala to receive some direct inputs from
the senses and start a response *before* they are fully registered by the neocortex.

This discovery overthrows the notion that the amygdala must depend
entirely on signals from the neocortex to formulate its emotional reactions.
The amygdala can trigger an emotional response via this emergency route
even as a parallel reverberating circuit begins between the amygdala and
neocortex. The amygdala can have us spring to action while the slightly
slower—but more fully informed—neocortex unfolds its more refined plan
for reaction.

LeDoux overturned the prevailing wisdom about the pathways traveled by
emotions through his research on fear in animals. In a crucial experiment he
destroyed the auditory cortex of rats, then exposed them to a tone paired
with an electric shock. The rats quickly learned to fear the tone, even though
the sound of the tone could not register in their neocortex. Instead, the sound
took the direct route from ear to thalamus to amygdala, skipping all higher
avenues. In short, the rats had learned an emotional reaction without any
higher cortical involvement: The amygdala perceived, remembered, and
orchestrated their fear independently.

"Anatomically the emotional system can act independently of the neocortex," LeDoux told me. "Some emotional reactions and emotional memories can be formed without any conscious, cognitive participation at all." The
amygdala can house memories and response repertoires that we enact without quite realizing why we do so because the shortcut from thalamus to
amygdala completely bypasses the neocortex. This bypass seems to allow
the amygdala to be a repository for emotional impressions and memories that
we have never known about in full awareness. LeDoux proposes that it is the
amygdala's subterranean role in memory that explains, for example, a startling experiment in which people acquired a preference for oddly shaped

FIGHT OR FLIGHT RESPONSE:
Heart rate and blood pressure increase. Large muscles prepare for quick action.

A visual signal first goes from the retina to the thalamus, where it is translated into the language of the brain. Most of the message then goes to the visual cortex, where it is analyzed and assessed for meaning and appropriate response; if that response is emotional, a signal goes to the amygdala to activate the emotional centers. But a smaller portion of the original signal goes straight from the thalamus to the amygdala in a quicker transmission, allowing a faster (though less precise) response. Thus the amygdala can trigger an emotional response before the cortical centers have fully understood what is happening.

geometric figures that had been flashed at them so quickly that they had no conscious awareness of having seen them at all![6]

Other research has shown that in the first few milliseconds of our perceiving something we not only unconsciously comprehend what it is, but decide whether we like it or not; the "cognitive unconscious" presents our awareness with not just the identity of what we see, but an opinion about it.[7] Our emotions have a mind of their own, one which can hold views quite independently of our rational mind.

THE SPECIALIST IN EMOTIONAL MEMORY

Those unconscious opinions are emotional memories; their storehouse is the amygdala. Research by LeDoux and other neuroscientists now seems to suggest that the hippocampus, which has long been considered the key structure of the limbic system, is more involved in registering and making sense of perceptual patterns than with emotional reactions. The hippocampus's main input is in providing a keen memory of context, vital for emotional meaning; it is the hippocampus that recognizes the differing significance of, say, a bear in the zoo versus one in your backyard.

While the hippocampus remembers the dry facts, the amygdala retains the emotional flavor that goes with those facts. If we try to pass a car on a two-lane highway and narrowly miss having a head-on collision, the hippocampus retains the specifics of the incident, like what stretch of road we were on, who was with us, what the other car looked like. But it is the amygdala that everafter will send a surge of anxiety through us whenever we try to pass a car in similar circumstances. As LeDoux put it to me, "The hippocampus is crucial in recognizing a face as that of your cousin. But it is the amygdala that adds you don't really like her."

The brain uses a simple but cunning method to make emotional memories register with special potency: the very same neurochemical alerting systems that prime the body to react to life-threatening emergencies by fighting or fleeing also stamp the moment in memory with vividness.[8] Under stress (or anxiety, or presumably even the intense excitement of joy) a nerve running from the brain to the adrenal glands atop the kidneys triggers a secretion of the hormones epinephrine and norepinephrine, which surge through the body priming it for an emergency. These hormones activate receptors on the vagus nerve; while the vagus nerve carries messages from the brain to regulate the heart, it also carries signals back into the brain, triggered by epinephrine and norepinephrine. The amygdala is the main site in the brain where these signals go; they activate neurons within the amygdala to signal other brain regions to strengthen memory for what is happening.

This amygdala arousal seems to imprint in memory most moments of emotional arousal with an added degree of strength—that's why we are more likely, for example, to remember where we went on a first date, or what we were doing when we heard the news that the space shuttle *Challenger* had exploded. The more intense the amygdala arousal, the stronger the imprint; the experiences that scare or thrill us the most in life are among our most indelible memories. This means that, in effect, the brain has two memory systems, one for ordinary facts and one for emotionally charged ones. A special system for emotional memories makes excellent sense in evolution, of course, ensuring that animals would have particularly vivid memories of what threatens or pleases them. But emotional memories can be faulty guides to the present.

OUT-OF-DATE NEURAL ALARMS

One drawback of such neural alarms is that the urgent message the amygdala sends is sometimes, if not often, out-of-date—especially in the fluid social world we humans inhabit. As the repository for emotional memory, the amygdala scans experience, comparing what is happening now with what happened in the past. Its method of comparison is associative: when one key element of a present situation is similar to the past, it can call it a "match"—which is why this circuit is sloppy: it acts before there is full confirmation. It frantically commands that we react to the present in ways that were imprinted long ago, with thoughts, emotions, reactions learned in response to events perhaps only dimly similar, but close enough to alarm the amygdala.

Thus a former army nurse, traumatized by the relentless flood of ghastly wounds she once tended in wartime, is suddenly swept with a mix of dread, loathing, and panic—a repeat of her battlefield reaction triggered once again, years later, by the stench when she opens a closet door to find her toddler had stashed a stinking diaper there. A few spare elements of the situation is all that need seem similar to some past danger for the amygdala to trigger its emergency proclamation. The trouble is that along with the emotionally charged memories that have the power to trigger this crisis response can come equally outdated ways of responding to it.

The emotional brain's imprecision in such moments is added to by the fact that many potent emotional memories date from the first few years of life, in the relationship between an infant and its caretakers. This is especially true for traumatic events, like beatings or outright neglect. During this early period of life other brain structures, particularly the hippocampus, which is crucial for narrative memories, and the neocortex, seat of rational thought, have yet to become fully developed. In memory, the amygdala and hippocampus work hand-in-hand; each stores and retrieves its special information independently. While the hippocampus retrieves information, the amygdala determines if that information has any emotional valence. But the amygdala, which matures very quickly in the infant's brain, is much closer to fully formed at birth.

LeDoux turns to the role of the amygdala in childhood to support what has long been a basic tenet of psychoanalytic thought: that the interactions of life's earliest years lay down a set of emotional lessons based on the attunement and upsets in the contacts between infant and caretakers.[9] These emotional lessons are so potent and yet so difficult to understand from the vantage point of adult life because, believes LeDoux, they are stored in the amygdala as rough, wordless blueprints for emotional life. Since these earliest emotional memories are established at a time before infants have words for their experience, when these emotional memories are triggered in later life there is no matching set of articulated thoughts about the response that takes us over. One reason we can be so baffled by our emotional outbursts, then, is that they often date from a time early in our lives when things were bewildering and we did not yet have words for comprehending events. We may have the chaotic feelings, but not the words for the memories that formed them.

WHEN EMOTIONS ARE FAST AND SLOPPY

It was somewhere around three in the morning when a huge object came crashing through the ceiling in a far corner of my bedroom, spilling the contents of the attic into the room. In a second I leapt out of bed and ran out of the room, terrified the entire ceiling would cave in. Then, realizing I was safe, I cautiously peered back in the bedroom to see what had caused all the damage—only to discover that the sound I had taken to be the ceiling caving in was actually the fall of a tall pile of boxes my wife had stacked in the corner the day before while she sorted out her closet. Nothing had fallen from the attic: there was no attic. The ceiling was intact, and so was I.

My leap from bed while half-asleep—which might have saved me from injury had it truly been the ceiling falling—illustrates the power of the amygdala to propel us to action in emergencies, vital moments before the neocortex has time to fully register what is actually going on. The emergency route from eye or ear to thalamus to amygdala is crucial: it saves time in an emergency, when an instantaneous response is required. But this circuit from thalamus to amygdala carries only a small portion of sensory messages, with the majority taking the main route up to the neocortex. So what registers in the amygdala via this express route is, at best, a rough signal, just enough for a warning. As LeDoux points out, "You don't need to know exactly what something is to know that it may be dangerous."[10]

The direct route has a vast advantage in brain time, which is reckoned in thousandths of a second. The amygdala in a rat can begin a response to a perception in as little as twelve milliseconds—twelve thousandths of a second. The route from thalamus to neocortex to amygdala takes about twice as long. Similar measurements have yet to be made in the human brain, but the rough ratio would likely hold.

In evolutionary terms, the survival value of this direct route would have been great, allowing a quick-response option that shaves a few critical milliseconds in reaction time to dangers. Those milliseconds could well have saved the lives of our protomammalian ancestors in such numbers that this arrangement is now featured in every mammalian brain, including yours and mine. In fact, while this circuit may play a relatively limited role in human mental life, largely restricted to emotional crises, much of the mental life of birds, fish, and reptiles revolves around it, since their very survival depends on constantly scanning for predators or prey. "This primitive, minor brain system in mammals is the main brain system in non-mammals," says LeDoux. "It offers a very rapid way to turn on emotions. But it's a quick-and-dirty process; the cells are fast, but not very precise."

Such imprecision in, say, a squirrel, is fine, since it leads to erring on the side of safety, springing away at the first sign of anything that might signal a looming enemy, or springing toward a hint of something edible. But in human emotional life that imprecision can have disastrous consequences for our relationships, since it means, figuratively speaking, we can spring at or away from the wrong thing—or person. (Consider, for example, the waitress who dropped a tray of six dinners when she glimpsed a woman with a huge, curly mane of red hair—exactly like the woman her ex-husband had left her for.)

Such inchoate emotional mistakes are based on feeling prior to thought. LeDoux calls it "precognitive emotion," a reaction based on neural bits and pieces of sensory information that have not been fully sorted out and integrated into a recognizable object. It's a very raw form of sensory information, something like a neural *Name That Tune,* where, instead of snap judgments of melody being made on the basis of just a few notes, a whole perception is grasped on the basis of the first few tentative parts. If the amygdala senses a sensory pattern of import emerging, it jumps to a conclusion, triggering its reactions before there is full confirming evidence—or any confirmation at all.

Small wonder we can have so little insight into the murk of our more explosive emotions, especially while they still hold us in thrall. The amygdala can react in a delirium of rage or fear before the cortex knows what is going on because such raw emotion is triggered independent of, and prior to, thought.

THE EMOTIONAL MANAGER

A friend's six-year-old daughter Jessica was spending her first night ever sleeping over at a playmate's, and it was unclear who was more nervous about it, mother or daughter. While the mother tried not to let Jessica see the intense anxiety she felt, her tension peaked near midnight that night, as she was getting ready for bed and heard the phone ring. Dropping her toothbrush, she raced to the phone, her heart pounding, images of Jessica in terrible distress racing through her mind.

The mother snatched the receiver, and blurted, "Jessica!" into the phone—only to hear a woman's voice say, "Oh, I think this must be a wrong number. . . ."

At that, the mother recovered her composure, and in a polite, measured tone, asked, "What number were you calling?"

While the amygdala is at work in priming an anxious, impulsive reaction, another part of the emotional brain allows for a more fitting, corrective response. The brain's damper switch for the amygdala's surges appears to lie at the other end of a major circuit to the neocortex, in the prefrontal lobes just behind the forehead. The prefrontal cortex seems to be at work when someone is fearful or enraged, but stifles or controls the feeling in order to deal more effectively with the situation at hand, or when a reappraisal calls for a completely different response, as with the worried mother on the phone. This neocortical area of the brain brings a more analytic or appropriate response to our emotional impulses, modulating the amygdala and other limbic areas.

Ordinarily the prefrontal areas govern our emotional reactions from the start. The largest projection of sensory information from the thalamus, remember, goes not to the amygdala, but to the neocortex and its many centers for taking in and making sense of what is being perceived; that information and our response to it is coordinated by the prefrontal lobes, the seat of planning and organizing actions toward a goal, including emotional ones. In the neocortex a cascading series of circuits registers and analyzes that information, comprehends it, and, through the prefrontal lobes, orchestrates a reaction. If in the process an emotional response is called for, the prefrontal lobes dictate it, working hand-in-hand with the amygdala and other circuits in the emotional brain.

This progression, which allows for discernment in emotional response, is the standard arrangement, with the significant exception of emotional emergencies. When an emotion triggers, within moments the prefrontal lobes perform what amounts to a risk/benefit ratio of myriad possible reactions, and bet that one of them is best.[11] For animals, when to attack, when to run. And for we humans . . . when to attack, when to run—and also, when to placate, persuade, seek sympathy, stonewall, provoke guilt, whine, put on a facade of bravado, be contemptuous—and so on, through the whole repertoire of emotional wiles.

The neocortical response is slower in brain time than the hijack mechanism because it involves more circuitry. It can also be more judicious and considered, since more thought precedes feeling. When we register a loss and become sad, or feel happy after a triumph, or mull over something someone has said or done and then get hurt or angry, the neocortex is at work.

Just as with the amygdala, absent the workings of the prefrontal lobes, much of emotional life would fall away; lacking an understanding that something merits an emotional response, none comes. This role of the prefrontal lobes in emotions has been suspected by neurologists since the advent in the 1940s of that rather desperate—and sadly misguided—surgical "cure" for mental illness: the prefrontal lobotomy, which (often sloppily) removed part of the prefrontal lobes or otherwise cut connections between the prefrontal cortex and the lower brain. In the days before any effective medications for mental illness, the lobotomy was hailed as the answer to grave emotional distress—sever the links between the prefrontal lobes and the rest of the brain, and patients' distress was "relieved." Unfortunately, the cost was that most of patients' emotional lives seemed to vanish, too. The key circuitry had been destroyed.

Emotional hijackings presumably involve two dynamics: triggering of the amygdala and a failure to activate the neocortical processes that usually keep emotional response in balance—or a recruitment of the neocortical zones to the emotional urgency.[12] At these moments the rational mind is swamped by the emotional. One way the prefrontal cortex acts as an efficient manager of emotion—weighing reactions before acting—is by dampening the signals for activation sent out by the amygdala and other limbic centers—something like a parent who stops an impulsive child from grabbing and tells the child to ask properly (or wait) for what it wants instead.[13]

The key "off" switch for distressing emotion seems to be the left prefrontal lobe. Neuropsychologists studying moods in patients with injuries to parts of the frontal lobes have determined that one of the tasks of the left frontal lobe is to act as a neural thermostat, regulating unpleasant emotions. The right prefrontal lobes are a seat of negative feelings like fear and aggression, while the left lobes keep those raw emotions in check, probably by inhibiting the right lobe.[14] In one group of stroke patients, for example, those whose lesions were in the left prefrontal cortex were prone to catastrophic worries and fears; those with lesions on the right were "unduly cheerful"; during neurological exams they joked around and were so laid back they clearly did not care how well they did.[15] And then there was the case of the happy husband: a man whose right prefrontal lobe had been partially removed in surgery for a brain malformation. His wife told physicians that after the operation he underwent a dramatic personality change, becoming less easily upset and, she was happy to say, more affectionate.[16]

The left prefrontal lobe, in short, seems to be part of a neural circuit that can switch off, or at least dampen down, all but the strongest negative surges of emotion. If the amygdala often acts as an emergency trigger, the left prefrontal lobe appears to be part of the brain's "off" switch for disturbing emotion: the amygdala proposes, the prefrontal lobe disposes. These prefrontal-limbic connections are crucial in mental life far beyond fine-tuning emotion; they are essential for navigating us through the decisions that matter most in life.

HARMONIZING EMOTION AND THOUGHT

The connections between the amygdala (and related limbic structures) and the neocortex are the hub of the battles or cooperative treaties struck between head and heart, thought and feeling. This circuitry explains why emotion is so crucial to effective thought, both in making wise decisions and in simply allowing us to think clearly.

Take the power of emotions to disrupt thinking itself. Neuroscientists use the term "working memory" for the capacity of attention that holds in mind the facts essential for completing a given task or problem, whether it be the ideal features one seeks in a house while touring several prospects, or the elements of a reasoning problem on a test. The prefrontal cortex is the brain region responsible for working memory.[17] But circuits from the limbic brain to the prefrontal lobes mean that the signals of strong emotion—anxiety, anger, and the like—can create neural static, sabotaging the ability of the prefrontal lobe to maintain working memory. That is why when we are emotionally upset we say we "just can't think straight"—and why continual emotional distress can create deficits in a child's intellectual abilities, crippling the capacity to learn.

These deficits, if more subtle, are not always tapped by IQ testing, though they show up through more targeted neuropsychological measures, as well as in a child's continual agitation and impulsivity. In one study, for example, primary school boys who had above-average IQ scores but nevertheless were doing poorly in school were found via these neuropsychological tests to have impaired frontal cortex functioning.[18] They also were impulsive and anxious, often disruptive and in trouble—suggesting faulty prefrontal control over their limbic urges. Despite their intellectual potential, these are the children at highest risk for problems like academic failure, alcoholism, and criminality—not because their intellect is deficient, but because their control over their emotional life is impaired. The emotional brain, quite separate from those cortical areas tapped by IQ tests, controls rage and compassion alike. These emotional circuits are sculpted by experience throughout childhood—and we leave those experiences utterly to chance at our peril.

Consider, too, the role of emotions in even the most "rational" decision-making. In work with far-reaching implications for understanding mental life, Dr. Antonio Damasio, a neurologist at the University of Iowa College of Medicine, has made careful studies of just what is impaired in patients with damage to the prefrontal-amygdala circuit.[19] Their decision-making is terribly flawed—and yet they show no deterioration at all in IQ or any cognitive ability. Despite their intact intelligence, they make disastrous choices in business and their personal lives, and can even obsess endlessly over a decision so simple as when to make an appointment.

Dr. Damasio argues that their decisions are so bad because they have lost access to their *emotional* learning. As the meeting point between thought and emotion, the prefrontal-amygdala circuit is a crucial doorway to the repository for the likes and dislikes we acquire over the course of a lifetime. Cut off from emotional memory in the amygdala, whatever the neocortex mulls over no longer triggers the emotional reactions that have been associated with it in the past—everything takes on a gray neutrality. A stimulus, be it a favorite pet or a detested acquaintance, no longer triggers either attraction or aversion; these patients have "forgotten" all such emotional lessons because they no longer have access to where they are stored in the amygdala.

Evidence like this leads Dr. Damasio to the counter-intuitive position that feelings are typically *indispensable* for rational decisions; they point us in the proper direction, where dry logic can then be of best use. While the world often confronts us with an unwieldy array of choices (How should you invest your retirement savings? Whom should you marry?), the emotional learning that life has given us (such as the memory of a disastrous investment or a painful breakup) sends signals that streamline the decision by eliminating some options and highlighting others at the outset. In this way, Dr. Damasio argues, the emotional brain is as involved in reasoning as is the thinking brain.

The emotions, then, matter for rationality. In the dance of feeling and thought the emotional faculty guides our moment-to-moment decisions, working hand-in-hand with the rational mind, enabling—or disabling—thought itself. Likewise, the thinking brain plays an executive role in our emotions—except in those moments when emotions surge out of control and the emotional brain runs rampant.

In a sense we have two brains, two minds—and two different kinds of intelligence: rational and emotional. How we do in life is determined by both—it is not just IQ, but *emotional* intelligence that matters. Indeed, intellect cannot work at its best without emotional intelligence. Ordinarily the complementarity of limbic system and neocortex, amygdala and prefrontal lobes, means each is a full partner in mental life. When these partners interact well, emotional intelligence rises—as does intellectual ability.

This turns the old understanding of the tension between reason and feeling on its head: it is not that we want to do away with emotion and put reason in its place, as Erasmus had it, but instead find the intelligent balance of the two. The old paradigm held an ideal of reason freed of the pull of emotion. The new paradigm urges us to harmonize head and heart. To do that well in our lives means we must first understand more exactly what it means to use emotion intelligently.

PART TWO

THE NATURE OF EMOTIONAL INTELLIGENCE

3

When Smart Is Dumb

Exactly why David Pologruto, a high-school physics teacher, was stabbed with a kitchen knife by one of his star students is still debatable. But the facts as widely reported are these:

Jason H., a sophomore and straight-A student at a Coral Springs, Florida, high school, was fixated on getting into medical school. Not just any medical school—he dreamt of Harvard. But Pologruto, his physics teacher, had given Jason an 80 on a quiz. Believing the grade—a mere B—put his dream in jeopardy, Jason took a butcher knife to school and, in a confrontation with Pologruto in the physics lab, stabbed his teacher in the collarbone before being subdued in a struggle.

A judge found Jason innocent, temporarily insane during the incident—a panel of four psychologists and psychiatrists swore he was psychotic during the fight. Jason claimed he had been planning to commit suicide because of the test score, and had gone to Pologruto to tell him he was killing himself because of the bad grade. Pologruto told a different story: "I think he tried to completely do me in with the knife" because he was infuriated over the bad grade.

After transferring to a private school, Jason graduated two years later at the top of his class. A perfect grade in regular classes would have given him a straight-A, 4.0 average, but Jason had taken enough advanced courses to raise his grade-point average to 4.614—way beyond A+. Even as Jason graduated with highest honors, his old physics teacher, David Pologruto, complained that Jason had never apologized or even taken responsibility for the attack.[1]

The question is, how could someone of such obvious intelligence do something so irrational—so downright dumb? The answer: Academic intelligence has little to do with emotional life. The brightest among us can founder on the shoals of unbridled passions and unruly impulses; people with high IQs can be stunningly poor pilots of their private lives.

One of psychology's open secrets is the relative inability of grades, IQ, or SAT scores, despite their popular mystique, to predict unerringly who will succeed in life. To be sure, there is a relationship between IQ and life circumstances for large groups as a whole: many people with very low IQs end up in menial jobs, and those with high IQs tend to become well-paid— but by no means always.

There are widespread exceptions to the rule that IQ predicts success— many (or more) exceptions than cases that fit the rule. At best, IQ contributes about 20 percent to the factors that determine life success, which leaves 80 percent to other forces. As one observer notes, "The vast majority of one's ultimate niche in society is determined by non-IQ factors, ranging from social class to luck."[2]

Even Richard Herrnstein and Charles Murray, whose book *The Bell Curve* imputes a primary importance to IQ, acknowledge this; as they point out, "Perhaps a freshman with an SAT math score of 500 had better not have his heart set on being a mathematician, but if instead he wants to run his own business, become a U.S. Senator or make a million dollars, he should not put aside his dreams. . . . The link between test scores and those achievements is dwarfed by the totality of other characteristics that he brings to life."[3]

My concern is with a key set of these "other characteristics," *emotional intelligence:* abilities such as being able to motivate oneself and persist in the face of frustrations; to control impulse and delay gratification; to regulate one's moods and keep distress from swamping the ability to think; to empathize and to hope. Unlike IQ, with its nearly one-hundred-year history of research with hundreds of thousands of people, emotional intelligence is a new concept. No one can yet say exactly how much of the variability from person to person in life's course it accounts for. But what data exist suggest it can be as powerful, and at times more powerful, than IQ. And while there are those who argue that IQ cannot be changed much by experience or education, I will show in Part Five that the crucial emotional competencies can indeed be learned and improved upon by children—if we bother to teach them.

EMOTIONAL INTELLIGENCE AND DESTINY

I remember the fellow in my own class at Amherst College who had attained five perfect 800 scores on the SAT and other achievement tests he took before entering. Despite his formidable intellectual abilities, he spent most of his time hanging out, staying up late, and missing classes by sleeping until noon. It took him almost ten years to finally get his degree.

IQ offers little to explain the different destinies of people with roughly equal promises, schooling, and opportunity. When ninety-five Harvard students from the classes of the 1940s—a time when people with a wider spread of IQ were at Ivy League schools than is presently the case—were followed into middle age, the men with the highest test scores in college were not particularly successful compared to their lower-scoring peers in terms of salary, productivity, or status in their field. Nor did they have the greatest life satisfaction, nor the most happiness with friendships, family, and romantic relationships.[4]

A similar follow-up in middle age was done with 450 boys, most sons of immigrants, two thirds from families on welfare, who grew up in Somerville, Massachusetts, at the time a "blighted slum" a few blocks from Harvard. A third had IQs below 90. But again IQ had little relationship to how well they had done at work or in the rest of their lives; for instance, 7 percent of men with IQs under 80 were unemployed for ten or more years, but so were 7 percent of men with IQs over 100. To be sure, there was a general link (as there always is) between IQ and socioeconomic level at age forty-seven. But childhood abilities such as being able to handle frustrations, control emotions, and get on with other people made the greater difference.[5]

Consider also data from an ongoing study of eighty-one valedictorians and salutatorians from the 1981 class in Illinois high schools. All, of course, had the highest grade-point averages in their schools. But while they continued to achieve well in college, getting excellent grades, by their late twenties they had climbed to only average levels of success. Ten years after graduating from high school, only one in four were at the highest level of young people of comparable age in their chosen profession, and many were doing much less well.

Karen Arnold, professor of education at Boston University, one of the researchers tracking the valedictorians, explains, "I think we've discovered the 'dutiful'—people who know how to achieve in the system. But valedictorians struggle as surely as we all do. To know that a person is a valedictorian is to know only that he or she is exceedingly good at achievement as measured by grades. It tells you nothing about how they react to the vicissitudes of life."[6]

And that is the problem: academic intelligence offers virtually no preparation for the turmoil—or opportunity—life's vicissitudes bring. Yet even though a high IQ is no guarantee of prosperity, prestige, or happiness in life, our schools and our culture fixate on academic abilities, ignoring *emotional* intelligence, a set of traits—some might call it character—that also matters immensely for our personal destiny. Emotional life is a domain that, as surely as math or reading, can be handled with greater or lesser skill, and requires its unique set of competencies. And how adept a person is at those is crucial to understanding why one person thrives in life while another, of equal intellect, dead-ends: emotional aptitude is a *meta-ability,* determining how well we can use whatever other skills we have, including raw intellect.

Of course, there are many paths to success in life, and many domains in which other aptitudes are rewarded. In our increasingly knowledge-based society, technical skill is certainly one. There is a children's joke: "What do you call a nerd fifteen years from now?" The answer: "Boss." But even among "nerds" emotional intelligence offers an added edge in the workplace, as we shall see in Part Three. Much evidence testifies that people who are emotionally adept—who know and manage their own feelings well, and who read and deal effectively with other people's feelings—are at an advantage in any domain of life, whether romance and intimate relationships or picking up the unspoken rules that govern success in organizational politics. People with well-developed emotional skills are also more likely to be content and effective in their lives, mastering the habits of mind that foster their own productivity; people who cannot marshal some control over their emotional life fight inner battles that sabotage their ability for focused work and clear thought.

A DIFFERENT KIND OF INTELLIGENCE

To the casual observer, four-year-old Judy might seem a wallflower among her more gregarious playmates. She hangs back from the action at playtime, staying on the margins of games rather than plunging into the center. But Judy is actually a keen observer of the social politics of her preschool classroom, perhaps the most sophisticated of her playmates in her insights into the tides of feeling within the others.

Her sophistication is not apparent until Judy's teacher gathers the four-year-olds around to play what they call the Classroom Game. The Classroom Game—a dollhouse replica of Judy's own preschool classroom, with stick figures who have for heads small photos of the students and teachers—is a test of social perceptiveness. When Judy's teacher asks her to put each girl and boy in the part of the room they like to play in most—the art corner, the blocks corner, and so on—Judy does so with complete accuracy. And when asked to put each boy and girl with the children they like to play with most, Judy shows she can match best friends for the entire class.

Judy's accuracy reveals that she has a perfect social map of her class, a level of perceptiveness exceptional for a four-year-old. These are the skills that, in later life, might allow Judy to blossom into a star in any of the fields where "people skills" count, from sales and management to diplomacy.

That Judy's social brilliance was spotted at all, let alone this early, was due to her being a student at the Eliot-Pearson Preschool on the campus of Tufts University, where Project Spectrum, a curriculum that intentionally cultivates a variety of kinds of intelligence, was then being developed. Project Spectrum recognizes that the human repertoire of abilities goes far beyond the three R's, the narrow band of word-and-number skills that schools traditionally focus on. It acknowledges that capacities such as Judy's social perceptiveness are talents that an education can nurture rather than ignore or even frustrate. By encouraging children to develop a full range of the abilities that they will actually draw on to succeed, or use simply to be fulfilled in what they do, school becomes an education in life skills.

The guiding visionary behind Project Spectrum is Howard Gardner, a psychologist at the Harvard School of Education.[7] "The time has come," Gardner told me, "to broaden our notion of the spectrum of talents. The single most important contribution education can make to a child's development is to help him toward a field where his talents best suit him, where he will be satisfied and competent. We've completely lost sight of that. Instead we subject everyone to an education where, if you succeed, you will be best suited to be a college professor. And we evaluate everyone along the way according to whether they meet that narrow standard of success. We should spend less time ranking children and more time helping them to identify their natural competencies and gifts, and cultivate those. There are hundreds and hundreds of ways to succeed, and many, many different abilities that will help you get there."[8]

If anyone sees the limits of the old ways of thinking about intelligence, it is Gardner. He points out that the glory days of the IQ tests began during World War I, when two million American men were sorted out through the first mass paper-and-pencil form of the IQ test, freshly developed by Lewis Terman, a psychologist at Stanford. This led to decades of what Gardner calls the "IQ way of thinking": "that people are either smart or not, are born that way, that there's nothing much you can do about it, and that tests can tell you if you are one of the smart ones or not. The SAT test for college admissions is based on the same notion of a single kind of aptitude that determines your future. This way of thinking permeates society."

Gardner's influential 1983 book *Frames of Mind* was a manifesto refuting the IQ view; it proposed that there was not just one, monolithic kind of intelligence that was crucial for life success, but rather a wide spectrum of intelligences, with seven key varieties. His list includes the two standard academic kinds, verbal and mathematical-logical alacrity, but it goes on to include the spatial capacity seen in, say, an outstanding artist or architect; the kinesthetic genius displayed in the physical fluidity and grace of a Martha Graham or Magic Johnson; and the musical gifts of a Mozart or YoYo Ma. Rounding out the list are two faces of what Gardner calls "the personal intelligences": interpersonal skills, like those of a great therapist such as Carl Rogers or a world-class leader such as Martin Luther King, Jr., and the "intrapsychic" capacity that could emerge, on the one hand, in the brilliant insights of Sigmund Freud, or, with less fanfare, in the inner contentment that arises from attuning one's life to be in keeping with one's true feelings.

The operative word in this view of intelligences is *multiple:* Gardner's model pushes way beyond the standard concept of IQ as a single, immutable factor. It recognizes that the tests that tyrannized us as we went through school—from the achievement tests that sorted us out into those who would be shunted toward technical schools and those destined for college, to the SATs that determined what, if any, college we would be allowed to attend— are based on a limited notion of intelligence, one out of touch with the true range of skills and abilities that matter for life over and beyond IQ.

Gardner acknowledges that seven is an arbitrary figure for the variety of intelligences; there is no magic number to the multiplicity of human talents. At one point, Gardner and his research colleagues had stretched these seven to a list of twenty different varieties of intelligence. Interpersonal intelligence, for example, broke down into four distinct abilities: leadership, the ability to nurture relationships and keep friends, the ability to resolve conflicts, and skill at the kind of social analysis that four-year-old Judy excels at.

This multifaceted view of intelligence offers a richer picture of a child's ability and potential for success than the standard IQ. When Spectrum students were evaluated on the Stanford-Binet Intelligence Scale—once the gold standard of IQ tests—and again by a battery designed to measure Gardner's spectrum of intelligences, there was no significant relationship between children's scores on the two tests.[9] The five children with the highest IQs (from 125 to 133) showed a variety of profiles on the ten strengths measured by the Spectrum test. For example, of the five "smartest" children according to the IQ tests, one was strong in three areas, three had strengths in two areas, and one "smart" child had just one Spectrum strength. Those strengths were scattered: four of these children's strengths were in music, two in the visual arts, one in social understanding, one in logic, two in language. None of the five high-IQ kids were strong in movement, numbers, or mechanics; movement and numbers were actually weak spots for two of these five.

Gardner's conclusion was that "the Stanford-Binet Intelligence Scale did not predict successful performance across or on a consistent subset of Spectrum activities." On the other hand, the Spectrum scores give parents and teachers clear guidance about the realms that these children will take a spontaneous interest in, and where they will do well enough to develop the passions that could one day lead beyond proficiency to mastery.

Gardner's thinking about the multiplicity of intelligence continues to evolve. Some ten years after he first published his theory, Gardner gave these nutshell summaries of the personal intelligences:

> *Inter*personal intelligence is the ability to understand other people: what motivates them, how they work, how to work cooperatively with them. Successful salespeople, politicians, teachers, clinicians, and religious leaders are all likely to be individuals with high degrees of interpersonal intelligence. *Intra*personal intelligence . . . is a correlative ability, turned inward. It is a capacity to form an accurate, veridical model of oneself and to be able to use that model to operate effectively in life.[10]

In another rendering, Gardner noted that the core of interpersonal intelligence includes the "capacities to discern and respond appropriately to the moods, temperaments, motivations, and desires of other people." In intrapersonal intelligence, the key to self-knowledge, he included "access to one's own feelings and the ability to discriminate among them and draw upon them to guide behavior."[11]

SPOCK VS. DATA: WHEN COGNITION IS NOT ENOUGH

There is one dimension of personal intelligence that is broadly pointed to, but little explored, in Gardner's elaborations: the role of emotions. Perhaps this is so because, as Gardner suggested to me, his work is so strongly informed by a cognitive-science model of mind. Thus his view of these intelligences emphasizes cognition—the *understanding* of oneself and of others in motives, in habits of working, and in putting that insight into use in conducting one's own life and getting along with others. But like the kinesthetic realm, where physical brilliance manifests itself nonverbally, the realm of the emotions extends, too, beyond the reach of language and cognition.

While there is ample room in Gardner's descriptions of the personal intelligences for insight into the play of emotions and mastery in managing them, Gardner and those who work with him have not pursued in great detail the role of *feeling* in these intelligences, focusing more on cognitions *about* feeling. This focus, perhaps unintentionally, leaves unexplored the rich sea of emotions that makes the inner life and relationships so complex, so compelling, and so often puzzling. And it leaves yet to be plumbed both the sense in which there is intelligence *in* the emotions and the sense in which intelligence can be brought *to* emotions.

Gardner's emphasis on the cognitive elements in the personal intelligences reflects the zeitgeist of psychology that has shaped his views. Psychology's overemphasis on cognition even in the realm of emotion is, in part, due to a quirk in the history of that science. During the middle decades of this century academic psychology was dominated by behaviorists in the mold of B. F. Skinner, who felt that only behavior that could be seen objectively, from the outside, could be studied with scientific accuracy. The behaviorists ruled all inner life, including emotions, out-of-bounds for science.

Then, with the coming in the late 1960s of the "cognitive revolution," the focus of psychological science turned to how the mind registers and stores information, and the nature of intelligence. But emotions were still off-limits. Conventional wisdom among cognitive scientists held that intelligence entails a cold, hard-nosed processing of fact. It is hyperrational, rather like *Star Trek*'s Mr. Spock, the archetype of dry information bytes unmuddied by feeling, embodying the idea that emotions have no place in intelligence and only muddle our picture of mental life.

The cognitive scientists who embraced this view have been seduced by the computer as the operative model of mind, forgetting that, in reality, the brain's wetware is awash in a messy, pulsating puddle of neurochemicals, nothing like the sanitized, orderly silicon that has spawned the guiding metaphor for mind. The predominant models among cognitive scientists of how the mind processes information have lacked an acknowledgment that rationality is guided by—and can be swamped by—feeling. The cognitive model is, in this regard, an impoverished view of the mind, one that fails to explain the Sturm und Drang of feelings that brings flavor to the intellect. In order to persist in this view, cognitive scientists themselves have had to ignore the relevance for their models of mind of their personal hopes and fears, their marital squabbles and professional jealousies—the wash of feeling that gives life its flavor and its urgencies, and which in every moment biases exactly how (and how well or poorly) information is processed.

The lopsided scientific vision of an emotionally flat mental life—which has guided the last eighty years of research on intelligence—is gradually changing as psychology has begun to recognize the essential role of feeling in thinking. Rather like the Spockish character Data in *Star Trek: The Next Generation,* psychology is coming to appreciate the power and virtues of emotions in mental life, as well as their dangers. After all, as Data sees (to his own dismay, could he feel dismay), his cool logic fails to bring the right *human* solution. Our humanity is most evident in our feelings; Data seeks to feel, knowing that something essential is missing. He wants friendship, loyalty; like the Tin Man in *The Wizard of Oz,* he lacks a heart. Lacking the lyrical sense that feeling brings, Data can play music or write poetry with technical virtuosity, but not feel its passion. The lesson of Data's yearning for yearning itself is that the higher values of the human heart—faith, hope, devotion, love—are missing entirely from the coldly cognitive view. Emotions enrich; a model of mind that leaves them out is impoverished.

When I asked Gardner about his emphasis on thoughts about feelings, or metacognition, more than on emotions themselves, he acknowledged that he tended to view intelligence in a cognitive way, but told me, "When I first wrote about the personal intelligences, I *was* talking about emotion, especially in my notion of intrapersonal intelligence—one component is emotionally tuning in to yourself. It's the visceral-feeling signals you get that are essential for interpersonal intelligence. But as it has developed in practice, the theory of multiple intelligence has evolved to focus more on metacognition"—that is, awareness of one's mental processes—"rather than on the full range of emotional abilities."

Even so, Gardner appreciates how crucial these emotional and relationship abilities are in the rough-and-tumble of life. He points out that "many people with IQs of 160 work for people with IQs of 100, if the former have poor intrapersonal intelligence and the latter have a high one. And in the day-to-day world no intelligence is more important than the interpersonal. If you don't have it, you'll make poor choices about who to marry, what job to take, and so on. We need to train children in the personal intelligences in school."

CAN EMOTIONS BE INTELLIGENT?

To get a fuller understanding of just what such training might be like, we must turn to other theorists who are following Gardner's intellectual lead—most notably a Yale psychologist, Peter Salovey, who has mapped in great detail the ways in which we can bring intelligence to our emotions.[12] This endeavor is not new; over the years even the most ardent theorists of IQ have occasionally tried to bring emotions within the domain of intelligence, rather than seeing "emotion" and "intelligence" as an inherent contradiction in terms. Thus E. L. Thorndike, an eminent psychologist who was also influential in popularizing the notion of IQ in the 1920s and 1930s, proposed in a *Harper's Magazine* article that one aspect of emotional intelligence, "social" intelligence—the ability to understand others and "act wisely in human relations"—was itself an aspect of a person's IQ. Other psychologists of the time took a more cynical view of social intelligence, seeing it in terms of skills for manipulating other people—getting them to do what you want, whether they want to or not. But neither of these formulations of social intelligence held much sway with theorists of IQ, and by 1960 an influential textbook on intelligence tests pronounced social intelligence a "useless" concept.

But personal intelligence would not be ignored, mainly because it makes both intuitive and common sense. For example, when Robert Sternberg, another Yale psychologist, asked people to describe an "intelligent person," practical people skills were among the main traits listed. More systematic research by Sternberg led him back to Thorndike's conclusion: that social intelligence is both distinct from academic abilities and a key part of what makes people do well in the practicalities of life. Among the practical intelligences that are, for instance, so highly valued in the workplace is the kind of sensitivity that allows effective managers to pick up tacit messages.[13]

In recent years a growing group of psychologists has come to similar conclusions, agreeing with Gardner that the old concepts of IQ revolved around a narrow band of linguistic and math skills, and that doing well on IQ tests was most directly a predictor of success in the classroom or as a professor but less and less so as life's paths diverged from academe. These psychologists—Sternberg and Salovey among them—have taken a wider view of intelligence, trying to reinvent it in terms of what it takes to lead life successfully. And that line of enquiry leads back to an appreciation of just how crucial "personal" or emotional intelligence is.

Salovey subsumes Gardner's personal intelligences in his basic definition of emotional intelligence, expanding these abilities into five main domains:[14]

1. *Knowing one's emotions.* Self-awareness—recognizing a feeling *as it happens*—is the keystone of emotional intelligence. As we will see in Chapter 4, the ability to monitor feelings from moment to moment is crucial to psychological insight and self-understanding. An inability to notice our true feelings leaves us at their mercy. People with greater certainty about their feelings are better pilots of their lives, having a surer sense of how they really feel about personal decisions from whom to marry to what job to take.

2. *Managing emotions.* Handling feelings so they are appropriate is an ability that builds on self-awareness. Chapter 5 will examine the capacity to soothe oneself, to shake off rampant anxiety, gloom, or irritability—and the consequences of failure at this basic emotional skill. People who are poor in this ability are constantly battling feelings of distress, while those who excel in it can bounce back far more quickly from life's setbacks and upsets.

3. *Motivating oneself.* As Chapter 6 will show, marshaling emotions in the service of a goal is essential for paying attention, for self-motivation and mastery, and for creativity. Emotional self-control—delaying gratification and stifling impulsiveness—underlies accomplishment of every sort. And being able to get into the "flow" state enables outstanding performance of all kinds. People who have this skill tend to be more highly productive and effective in whatever they undertake.

4. *Recognizing emotions in others.* Empathy, another ability that builds on emotional self-awareness, is the fundamental "people skill." Chapter 7 will investigate the roots of empathy, the social cost of being emotionally tone-deaf, and the reasons empathy kindles altruism. People who are empathic are more attuned to the subtle social signals that indicate what others need or want. This makes them better at callings such as the caring professions, teaching, sales, and management.

5. *Handling relationships.* The art of relationships is, in large part, skill in managing emotions in others. Chapter 8 looks at social competence and incompetence, and the specific skills involved. These are the abilities that undergird popularity, leadership, and interpersonal effectiveness. People

who excel in these skills do well at anything that relies on interacting smoothly with others; they are social stars.

Of course, people differ in their abilities in each of these domains; some of us may be quite adept at handling, say, our own anxiety, but relatively inept at soothing someone else's upsets. The underlying basis for our level of ability is, no doubt, neural, but as we will see, the brain is remarkably plastic, constantly learning. Lapses in emotional skills can be remedied: to a great extent each of these domains represents a body of habit and response that, with the right effort, can be improved on.

IQ AND EMOTIONAL INTELLIGENCE: PURE TYPES

IQ and emotional intelligence are not opposing competencies, but rather separate ones. We all mix intellect and emotional acuity; people with a high IQ but low emotional intelligence (or low IQ and high emotional intelligence) are, despite the stereotypes, relatively rare. Indeed, there is a slight correlation between IQ and some aspects of emotional intelligence—though small enough to make clear these are largely independent entities.

Unlike the familiar tests for IQ, there is, as yet, no single paper-and-pencil test that yields an "emotional intelligence score" and there may never be one. Although there is ample research on each of its components, some of them, such as empathy, are best tested by sampling a person's actual ability at the task—for example, by having them read a person's feelings from a video of their facial expressions. Still, using a measure for what he calls "ego re-silience" which is quite similar to emotional intelligence (it includes the main social and emotional competences), Jack Block, a psychologist at the University of California at Berkeley, has made a comparison of two theoretical pure types: people high in IQ versus people high in emotional aptitudes.[15] The differences are telling.

The high-IQ pure type (that is, setting aside emotional intelligence) is almost a caricature of the intellectual, adept in the realm of mind but inept in the personal world. The profiles differ slightly for men and women. The high-IQ male is typified—no surprise—by a wide range of intellectual interests and abilities. He is ambitious and productive, predictable and dogged, and untroubled by concerns about himself. He also tends to be critical and condescending, fastidious and inhibited, uneasy with sexuality and sensual experience, unexpressive and detached, and emotionally bland and cold.

By contrast, men who are high in emotional intelligence are socially poised, outgoing and cheerful, not prone to fearfulness or worried rumination. They have a notable capacity for commitment to people or causes, for taking responsibility, and for having an ethical outlook; they are sympathetic and caring in their relationships. Their emotional life is rich, but appropriate; they are comfortable with themselves, others, and the social universe they live in.

Purely high-IQ women have the expected intellectual confidence, are fluent in expressing their thoughts, value intellectual matters, and have a wide range of intellectual and aesthetic interests. They also tend to be introspective, prone to anxiety, rumination, and guilt, and hesitate to express their anger openly (though they do so indirectly).

Emotionally intelligent women, by contrast, tend to be assertive and express their feelings directly, and to feel positive about themselves; life holds meaning for them. Like the men, they are outgoing and gregarious, and express their feelings appropriately (rather than, say, in outbursts they later regret); they adapt well to stress. Their social poise lets them easily reach out to new people; they are comfortable enough with themselves to be playful, spontaneous, and open to sensual experience. Unlike the women purely high in IQ, they rarely feel anxious or guilty, or sink into rumination.

These portraits, of course, are extremes—all of us mix IQ and emotional intelligence in varying degrees. But they offer an instructive look at what each of these dimensions adds separately to a person's qualities. To the degree a person has both cognitive and emotional intelligence, these pictures merge. Still, of the two, emotional intelligence adds far more of the qualities that make us more fully human.

4

Know Thyself

A belligerent samurai, an old Japanese tale goes, once challenged a Zen master to explain the concept of heaven and hell. But the monk replied with scorn, "You're nothing but a lout—I can't waste my time with the likes of you!"

His very honor attacked, the samurai flew into a rage and, pulling his sword from its scabbard, yelled, "I could kill you for your impertinence."

"That," the monk calmly replied, "is hell."

Startled at seeing the truth in what the master pointed out about the fury that had him in its grip, the samurai calmed down, sheathed his sword, and bowed, thanking the monk for the insight.

"And that," said the monk, "is heaven."

The sudden awakening of the samurai to his own agitated state illustrates the crucial difference between being caught up in a feeling and becoming aware that you are being swept away by it. Socrates's injunction "Know thyself" speaks to this keystone of emotional intelligence: awareness of one's own feelings as they occur.

It might seem at first glance that our feelings are obvious; more thoughtful reflection reminds us of times we have been all too oblivious to what we really felt about something, or awoke to these feelings late in the game. Psychologists use the rather ponderous term *metacognition* to refer to an awareness of thought process, and *metamood* to mean awareness of one's own emotions. I prefer the term *self-awareness,* in the sense of an ongoing attention to one's internal states.[1] In this self-reflexive awareness mind observes and investigates experience itself, including the emotions.[2]

This quality of awareness is akin to what Freud described as an "evenly hovering attention," and which he commended to those who would do psychoanalysis. Such attention takes in whatever passes through awareness with impartiality, as an interested yet unreactive witness. Some psycho-analysts call it the "observing ego," the capacity of self-awareness that allows the analyst to monitor his own reactions to what the patient is saying, and which the process of free association nurtures in the patient.[3]

Such self-awareness would seem to require an activated neocortex, partic-ularly the language areas, attuned to identify and name the emotions being aroused. Self-awareness is not an attention that gets carried away by emotions, overreacting and amplifying what is perceived. Rather, it is a neutral mode that maintains self-reflectiveness even amidst turbulent emotions. William Styron seems to be describing something like this faculty of mind in writing of his deep depression, telling of a sense "of being accompanied by a second self— a wraithlike observer who, not sharing the dementia of his double, is able to watch with dispassionate curiosity as his companion struggles."[4]

At its best, self-observation allows just such an equanimous awareness of passionate or turbulent feelings. At a minimum, it manifests itself simply as a slight stepping-back from experience, a parallel stream of consciousness that is "meta": hovering above or beside the main flow, aware of what is happen-ing rather than being immersed and lost in it. It is the difference between, for example, being murderously enraged at someone and having the self-reflexive thought "This is anger I'm feeling" even as you are enraged. In terms of the neural mechanics of awareness, this subtle shift in mental activity presumably signals that neocortical circuits are actively monitoring the emo-tion, a first step in gaining some control. This awareness of emotions is the fundamental emotional competence on which others, such as emotional self-control, build.

Self-awareness, in short, means being "aware of both our mood and our thoughts about that mood," in the words of John Mayer, a University of New Hampshire psychologist who, with Yale's Peter Salovey, is a coformulator of the theory of emotional intelligence.[5] Self-awareness can be a nonreactive, nonjudgmental attention to inner states. But Mayer finds that this sensibility also can be less equanimous; typical thoughts bespeaking emotional self-awareness include "I shouldn't feel this way," "I'm thinking good things to cheer up," and, for a more restricted self-awareness, the fleeting thought "Don't think about it" in reaction to something highly upsetting.

Although there is a logical distinction between being aware of feelings and acting to change them, Mayer finds that for all practical purposes the two usually go hand-in-hand: to recognize a foul mood is to want to get out of it. This recognition, however, is distinct from the efforts we make to keep from acting on an emotional impulse. When we say "Stop that!" to a child whose anger has led him to hit a playmate, we may stop the hitting, but the anger still simmers. The child's thoughts are still fixated on the trigger for the anger— "But he stole my toy!"—and the anger continues unabated. Self-awareness has a more powerful effect on strong, aversive feelings: the realization "This is anger I'm feeling" offers a greater degree of freedom—not just the option not to act on it, but the added option to try to let go of it.

Mayer finds that people tend to fall into distinctive styles for attending to and dealing with their emotions:[6]

• *Self-aware*. Aware of their moods as they are having them, these people understandably have some sophistication about their emotional lives. Their clarity about emotions may undergird other personality traits: they are autonomous and sure of their own boundaries, are in good psychological health, and tend to have a positive outlook on life. When they get into a bad mood, they don't ruminate and obsess about it, and are able to get out of it sooner. In short, their mindfulness helps them manage their emotions.

• *Engulfed*. These are people who often feel swamped by their emotions and helpless to escape them, as though their moods have taken charge. They are mercurial and not very aware of their feelings, so that they are lost in them rather than having some perspective. As a result, they do little to try to escape bad moods, feeling that they have no control over their emotional life. They often feel overwhelmed and emotionally out of control.

• *Accepting*. While these people are often clear about what they are feeling, they also tend to be accepting of their moods, and so don't try to change them. There seem to be two branches of the accepting type: those who are usually in good moods and so have little motivation to change them, and people who, despite their clarity about their moods, are susceptible to bad ones but accept them with a laissez-faire attitude, doing nothing to change them despite their distress—a pattern found among, say, depressed people who are resigned to their despair.

THE PASSIONATE AND THE INDIFFERENT

Imagine for a moment that you're on an airplane flying from New York to San Francisco. It's been a smooth flight, but as you approach the Rockies the pilot's voice comes over the plane intercom. "Ladies and gentlemen, there's some turbulence ahead. Please return to your seats and fasten your seatbelts." And then the plane hits the turbulence, which is rougher than you've ever endured—the airplane is tossed up and down and side to side like a beach ball in the waves.

The question is, what do you do? Are you the kind of person who buries yourself in your book or magazine, or continues watching the movie, tuning out the turbulence? Or are you likely to take out the emergency card and review the precautions, or watch the flight attendants to see if they show signs of panic, or strain to hear the engines to see if there's anything worrisome?

Which of these responses comes more naturally to us is a sign of our favored attentional stance under duress. The airplane scenario itself is an item from a psychological test developed by Suzanne Miller, a psychologist at Temple University, to assess whether people tend to be vigilant, attending carefully to every detail of a distressing predicament, or, in contrast, deal with such anxious moments by trying to distract themselves. These two attentional stances toward distress have very different consequences for how people experience their own emotional reactions. Those who tune in under duress can, by the very act of attending so carefully, unwittingly amplify the magnitude of their own reactions—especially if their tuning in is devoid of the equanimity of self-awareness. The result is that their emotions seem all the more intense. Those who tune out, who distract themselves, notice less about their own reactions, and so minimize the experience of their emotional response, if not the size of the response itself.

At the extremes, this means that for some people emotional awareness is overwhelming, while for others it barely exists. Consider the college student who, one evening, spotted a fire that had broken out in his dorm, went to get a fire extinguisher, and put the fire out. Nothing unusual—except that on his way to get the extinguisher and then on the way back to the fire, he walked instead of running. The reason? He didn't feel there was any urgency.

This story was told to me by Edward Diener, a University of Illinois at Urbana psychologist who has been studying the *intensity* with which people experience their emotions.[7] The college student stood out in his collection of case studies as one of the least intense Diener had ever encountered. He was, essentially, a man without passions, someone who goes through life feeling little or nothing, even about an emergency like a fire.

By contrast, consider a woman at the opposite end of Diener's spectrum. When she once lost her favorite pen, she was distraught for days. Another time she was so thrilled on seeing an ad for a big sale on women's shoes at an expensive store that she dropped what she was doing, hopped in her car, and drove three hours to the store in Chicago.

Diener finds that women, in general, feel both positive and negative emotions more strongly than do men. And, sex differences aside, emotional life is richer for those who notice more. For one thing, this enhanced emotional sensitivity means that for such people the least provocation unleashes emotional storms, whether heavenly or hellish, while those at the other extreme barely experience any feeling even under the most dire circumstances.

THE MAN WITHOUT FEELINGS

Gary infuriated his fiancée, Ellen, because even though he was intelligent, thoughtful, and a successful surgeon, Gary was emotionally flat, completely unresponsive to any and all shows of feeling. While Gary could speak brilliantly of science and art, when it came to his feelings—even for Ellen— he fell silent. Try as she might to elicit some passion from him, Gary was impassive, oblivious. "I don't naturally express my feelings," Gary told the therapist he saw at Ellen's insistence. When it came to emotional life, he added, "I don't know what to talk about; I have no strong feelings, either positive or negative."

Ellen was not alone in being frustrated by Gary's aloofness; as he confided to his therapist, he was unable to speak openly about his feelings with anyone in his life. The reason: He did not know what he felt in the first place. So far as he could tell, he had no angers, no sadnesses, no joys.[8]

As his own therapist observes, this emotional blankness makes Gary and others like him colorless, bland: "They bore everybody. That's why their wives send them into treatment." Gary's emotional flatness exemplifies what psychiatrists call *alexithymia,* from the Greek *a-* for "lack," *lexis* for "word," and *thymos* for "emotion." Such people lack words for their feelings. Indeed, they seem to lack feelings altogether, although this may actually be because of their inability to *express* emotion rather than from an absence of emotion altogether. Such people were first noticed by psychoanalysts puzzled by a class of patients who were untreatable by that method because they reported no feelings, no fantasies, and colorless dreams—in short, no inner emotional life to talk about at all.[9] The clinical features that mark alexithymics include having difficulty describing feelings—their own or anyone else's—and a sharply limited emotional vocabulary.[10] What's more, they have trouble discriminating among emotions as well as between emotion and bodily sensation, so that they might tell of having butterflies in the stomach, palpitations, sweating, and dizziness—but they would not know they are feeling anxious.

"They give the impression of being different, alien beings, having come from an entirely different world, living in the midst of a society which is dominated by feelings," is the description given by Dr. Peter Sifneos, the Harvard psychiatrist who in 1972 coined the term *alexithymia*.[11] Alexithymics rarely cry, for example, but if they do their tears are copious. Still, they are bewildered if asked what the tears are all about. One patient with alexithymia was so upset after seeing a movie about a woman with eight children who was dying of cancer that she cried herself to sleep. When her therapist suggested that perhaps she was upset because the movie reminded her of her own mother, who was in actuality dying of cancer, the woman sat motionless, bewildered and silent. When her therapist then asked her how she felt at that moment, she said she felt "awful," but couldn't clarify her feelings beyond that. And, she added, from time to time she found herself crying, but never knew exactly what she was crying about.[12]

And that is the nub of the problem. It is not that alexithymics never feel, but that they are unable to know—and especially unable to put into words—precisely what their feelings are. They are utterly lacking in the fundamental skill of emotional intelligence, self-awareness—knowing what we are feeling as emotions roil within us. Alexithymics belie the common-sense notion that it is perfectly self-evident what we are feeling: they haven't a clue. When something—or more likely, someone—does move them to feeling, they find the experience baffling and overwhelming, something to avoid at all costs. Feelings come to them, when they come at all, as a befuddling bundle of distress; as the patient who cried at the movie put it, they feel "awful," but can't say exactly which *kind* of awful it is they feel.

This basic confusion about feelings often seems to lead them to complain of vague medical problems when they are actually experiencing emotional distress—a phenomenon known in psychiatry as *somaticizing,* mistaking an emotional ache for a physical one (and different from a psychosomatic disease, in which emotional problems cause genuine medical ones). Indeed, much of the psychiatric interest in alexithymics is in weeding them out from among those who come to doctors seeking help, for they are prone to lengthy—and fruitless—pursuit of a medical diagnosis and treatment for what is actually an emotional problem.

While no one can as yet say for sure what causes alexithymia, Dr. Sifneos proposes a disconnection between the limbic system and the neocortex, particularly its verbal centers, which fits well with what we are learning about the emotional brain. Patients with severe seizures who had that connection surgically severed to relieve their symptoms, notes Sifneos, became emotionally flat, like people with alexithymia, unable to put their feelings into words and suddenly devoid of fantasy life. In short, though the circuits of the emotional brain may react with feelings, the neocortex is not able to sort out these feelings and add the nuance of language to them. As Henry Roth observed in his novel *Call It Sleep* about this power of language, "If you could put words to what you felt, it was yours." The corollary, of course, is the alexithymic's dilemma: having no words for feelings means not making the feelings your own.

IN PRAISE OF GUT FEELING

Elliot's tumor, growing just behind his forehead, was the size of a small orange; surgery removed it completely. Although the surgery was declared a success, afterward people who knew him well said that Elliot was no longer Elliot—he had undergone a drastic personality change. Once a successful corporate lawyer, Elliot could no longer hold a job. His wife left him. Squandering his savings in fruitless investments, he was reduced to living in a spare bedroom at his brother's home.

There was a puzzling pattern to Elliot's problem. Intellectually he was as bright as ever, but he used his time terribly, getting lost in minor details; he seemed to have lost all sense of priority. Reprimands made no difference; he was fired from a succession of legal jobs. Though extensive intellectual tests found nothing wrong with Elliot's mental faculties, he went to see a neurologist anyway, hoping that discovery of a neurological problem might get him the disability benefits to which he felt he was entitled. Otherwise the conclusion seemed to be that he was just a malingerer.

Antonio Damasio, the neurologist Elliot consulted, was struck by one element missing from Elliot's mental repertoire: though nothing was wrong with his logic, memory, attention, or any other cognitive ability, Elliot was virtually oblivious to his feelings about what had happened to him.[13] Most strikingly, Elliot could narrate the tragic events of his life with complete dispassion, as though he were an onlooker to the losses and failures of his past—without a note of regret or sadness, frustration or anger at life's unfairness. His own tragedy brought him no pain; Damasio felt more upset by Elliot's story than did Elliot himself.

The source of this emotional unawareness, Damasio concluded, was the removal, along with the brain tumor, of part of Elliot's prefrontal lobes. In effect, the surgery had severed ties between the lower centers of the emotional brain, especially the amygdala and related circuits, and the thinking abilities of the neocortex. Elliot's thinking had become computerlike, able to make every step in the calculus of a decision, but unable to assign *values* to differing possibilities. Every option was neutral. And that overly dispassionate reasoning, suspected Damasio, was the core of Elliot's problem: too little awareness of his own feelings about things made Elliot's reasoning faulty.

The handicap showed up even in mundane decisions. When Damasio tried to choose a time and date for the next appointment with Elliot, the result was a muddle of indecisiveness: Elliot could find arguments for and against every date and time that Damasio proposed, but could not choose among them. At the rational level, there were perfectly good reasons for objecting to or accepting virtually every possible time for the appointment. But Elliot lacked any sense of how he *felt* about any of the times. Lacking that awareness of his own feelings, he had no preferences at all.

One lesson from Elliot's indecisiveness is the crucial role of feeling in navigating the endless stream of life's personal decisions. While strong feelings can create havoc in reasoning, the *lack* of awareness of feeling can also be ruinous, especially in weighing the decisions on which our destiny largely depends: what career to pursue, whether to stay with a secure job or switch to one that is riskier but more interesting, whom to date or marry, where to live, which apartment to rent or house to buy—and on and on through life. Such decisions cannot be made well through sheer rationality; they require gut feeling, and the emotional wisdom garnered through past experiences. Formal logic alone can never work as the basis for deciding whom to marry or trust or even what job to take; these are realms where reason without feeling is blind.

The intuitive signals that guide us in these moments come in the form of limbic-driven surges from the viscera that Damasio calls "somatic markers"—literally, gut feelings. The somatic marker is a kind of automatic alarm, typically calling attention to a potential danger from a given course of action. More often than not these markers steer us *away* from some choice that experience warns us against, though they can also alert us to a golden opportunity. We usually do not, at that moment, recall what specific experiences formed this negative feeling; all we need is the signal that a given potential course of action could be disastrous. Whenever such a gut feeling rises up, we can immediately drop or pursue that avenue of consideration with greater confidence, and so pare down our array of choices to a more manageable decision matrix. The key to sounder personal decision-making, in short: being attuned to our feelings.

PLUMBING THE UNCONSCIOUS

Elliot's emotional vacuity suggests that there may be a spectrum of people's ability to sense their emotions as they have them. By the logic of neuroscience, if the absence of a neural circuit leads to a deficit in an ability, then the relative strength or weakness of that same circuit in people whose brains are intact should lead to comparable levels of competence in that same ability. In terms of the role of prefrontal circuits in emotional attunement, this suggests that for neurological reasons some of us may more easily detect the stirring of fear or joy than do others, and so be more emotionally self-aware.

It may be that a talent for psychological introspection hinges on this same circuitry. Some of us are naturally more attuned to the emotional mind's special symbolic modes: metaphor and simile, along with poetry, song, and fable, are all cast in the language of the heart. So too are dreams and myths, in which loose associations determine the flow of narrative, abiding by the logic of the emotional mind. Those who have a natural attunement to their own heart's voice—the language of emotion—are sure to be more adept at articulating its messages, whether as a novelist, songwriter, or psychotherapist. This inner attunement should make them more gifted in giving voice to the "wisdom of the unconscious"—the felt meanings of our dreams and fantasies, the symbols that embody our deepest wishes.

Self-awareness is fundamental to psychological insight; this is the faculty that much of psychotherapy means to strengthen. Indeed, Howard Gardner's model for intrapsychic intelligence is Sigmund Freud, the great mapper of the psyche's secret dynamics. As Freud made clear, much of emotional life is unconscious; feelings that stir within us do not always cross the threshold into awareness. Empirical verification of this psychological axiom comes, for instance, from experiments on unconscious emotions, such as the remarkable finding that people form definite likings for things they do not even realize they have seen before. Any emotion can be—and often is— unconscious.

The physiological beginnings of an emotion typically occur before a person is consciously aware of the feeling itself. For example, when people who fear snakes are shown pictures of snakes, sensors on their skin will detect sweat breaking out, a sign of anxiety, though they say they do not feel any fear. The sweat shows up in such people even when the picture of a snake is presented so rapidly that they have no conscious idea of what, exactly, they just saw, let alone that they are beginning to get anxious. As such pre-conscious emotional stirrings continue to build, they eventually become strong enough to break into awareness. Thus there are two levels of emotion, conscious and unconscious. The moment of an emotion coming into aware-ness marks its registering as such in the frontal cortex.[14]

Emotions that simmer beneath the threshold of awareness can have a powerful impact on how we perceive and react, even though we have no idea they are at work. Take someone who is annoyed by a rude encounter early in the day, and then is peevish for hours afterward, taking affront where none is intended and snapping at people for no real reason. He may well be oblivious to his continuing irritability and will be surprised if someone calls attention to it, though it stews just out of his awareness and dictates his curt replies. But once that reaction is brought into awareness—once it registers in the cortex—he can evaluate things anew, decide to shrug off the feelings left earlier in the day, and change his outlook and mood. In this way emotional self-awareness is the building block of the next fundamental of emotional intelligence: being able to shake off a bad mood.

5

Passion's Slaves

Thou hast been . . .
A man that Fortune's buffets and rewards
Has taken with equal thanks. . . . Give me that man
That is not passion's slave, and I will wear him
In my heart's core, aye, in my heart of hearts
As I do thee. . . .

—HAMLET TO HIS FRIEND HORATIO

A sense of self-mastery, of being able to withstand the emotional storms that the buffeting of Fortune brings rather than being "passion's slave," has been praised as a virtue since the time of Plato. The ancient Greek word for it was *sophrosyne*, "care and intelligence in conducting one's life; a tempered balance and wisdom," as Page DuBois, a Greek scholar, translates it. The Romans and the early Christian church called it *temperantia*, temperance, the restraining of emotional excess. The goal is balance, not emotional suppression: every feeling has its value and significance. A life without passion would be a dull wasteland of neutrality, cut off and isolated from the richness of life itself. But, as Aristotle observed, what is wanted is *appropriate* emotion, feeling proportionate to circumstance. When emotions are too muted they create dullness and distance; when out of control, too extreme and persistent, they become pathological, as in immobilizing depression, overwhelming anxiety, raging anger, manic agitation.

Indeed, keeping our distressing emotions in check is the key to emotional well-being; extremes—emotions that wax too intensely or for too long—undermine our stability. Of course, it is not that we should feel only one kind of emotion; being happy all the time somehow suggests the blandness of those smiley-face badges that had a faddish moment in the 1970s. There is much to be said for the constructive contribution of suffering to creative and spiritual life; suffering can temper the soul.

Downs as well as ups spice life, but need to be in balance. In the calculus of the heart it is the ratio of positive to negative emotions that determines the sense of well-being—at least that is the verdict from studies of mood in which hundreds of men and women have carried beepers that reminded them at random times to record their emotions at that moment.[1] It is not that people need to avoid unpleasant feelings to feel content, but rather that stormy feelings not go unchecked, displacing all pleasant moods. People who have strong episodes of anger or depression can still feel a sense of well-being if they have a countervailing set of equally joyous or happy times. These studies also affirm the independence of emotional from academic intelligence, finding little or no relationship between grades or IQ and people's emotional well-being.

Just as there is a steady murmur of background thoughts in the mind, there is a constant emotional hum; beep someone at six A.M. or seven P.M. and he will always be in some mood or other. Of course, on any two mornings someone can have very different moods; but when people's moods are averaged over weeks or months, they tend to reflect that person's overall sense of well-being. It turns out that for most people, extremely intense feelings are relatively rare; most of us fall into the gray middle range, with mild bumps in our emotional roller coaster.

Still, managing our emotions is something of a full-time job: much of what we do—especially in our free time—is an attempt to manage mood. Everything from reading a novel or watching television to the activities and companions we choose can be a way to make ourselves feel better. The art of soothing ourselves is a fundamental life skill; some psychoanalytic thinkers, such as John Bowlby and D. W. Winnicott, see this as one of the most essential of all psychic tools. The theory holds that emotionally sound infants learn to soothe themselves by treating themselves as their caretakers have treated them, leaving them less vulnerable to the upheavals of the emotional brain.

As we have seen, the design of the brain means that we very often have little or no control over *when* we are swept by emotion, nor over *what* emotion it will be. But we can have some say in *how long* an emotion will last. The issue arises not with garden-variety sadness, worry, or anger; normally such moods pass with time and patience. But when these emotions are of great intensity and linger past an appropriate point, they shade over into their distressing extremes—chronic anxiety, uncontrollable rage, depression. And, at their most severe and intractable, medication, psychotherapy, or both may be needed to lift them.

In these times, one sign of the capacity for emotional self-regulation may be recognizing when chronic agitation of the emotional brain is too strong to be overcome without pharmacologic help. For example, two thirds of those who suffer from manic-depression have never been treated for the disorder. But lithium or newer medications can thwart the characteristic cycle of paralyzing depression alternating with manic episodes that mix chaotic elation and grandiosity with irritation and rage. One problem with manic-depression is that while people are in the throes of mania they often feel so overly confident that they see no need for help of any kind despite the disastrous decisions they are making. In such severe emotional disorders psychiatric medication offers a tool for managing life better.

But when it comes to vanquishing the more usual range of bad moods, we are left to our own devices. Unfortunately, those devices are not always effective—at least such is the conclusion reached by Diane Tice, a psychologist at Case Western Reserve University, who asked more than four hundred men and women about the strategies they used to escape foul moods, and how successful those tactics were for them.[2]

Not everyone agrees with the philosophical premise that bad moods should be changed; there are, Tice found, "mood purists," the 5 percent or so of people who said they never try to change a mood since, in their view, all emotions are "natural" and should be experienced just as they present themselves, no matter how dispiriting. And then there were those who regularly sought to get into unpleasant moods for pragmatic reasons: physicians who needed to be somber to give patients bad news; social activists who nurtured their outrage at injustice so as to be more effective in battling it; even a young man who told of working up his anger to help his little brother with playground bullies. And some people were positively Machiavellian about manipulating moods—witness the bill collectors who purposely worked themselves into a rage in order to be all the firmer with deadbeats.[3] But these rare purposive cultivations of unpleasantness aside, most everyone complained of being at the mercy of their moods. People's track records at shaking bad moods were decidedly mixed.

THE ANATOMY OF RAGE

Say someone in another car cuts dangerously close to you as you are driving on the freeway. If your reflexive thought is "That son of a bitch!" it matters immensely for the trajectory of rage whether that thought is followed by more thoughts of outrage and revenge: "He could have hit me! That bastard—I can't let him get away with that!" Your knuckles whiten as you tighten your hold on the steering wheel, a surrogate for strangling his throat. Your body mobilizes to fight, not run—leaving you trembling, beads of sweat on your forehead, your heart pounding, the muscles in your face locked in a scowl. You want to kill the guy. Then, should a car behind you honk because you have slowed down after the close call, you are apt to explode in rage at that driver too. Such is the stuff of hypertension, reckless driving, even freeway shootings.

Contrast that sequence of building rage with a more charitable line of thought toward the driver who cut you off: "Maybe he didn't see me, or maybe he had some good reason for driving so carelessly, such as a medical emergency." That line of possibility tempers anger with mercy, or at least an open mind, short-circuiting the buildup of rage. The problem, as Aristotle's challenge to have only *appropriate* anger reminds us, is that more often than not our anger surges out of control. Benjamin Franklin put it well: "Anger is never without a reason, but seldom a good one."

There are, of course, different kinds of anger. The amygdala may well be a main source of the sudden spark of rage we feel at the driver whose carelessness endangers us. But the other end of the emotional circuitry, the neocortex, most likely foments more calculated angers, such as cool-headed revenge or outrage at unfairness or injustice. Such thoughtful angers are those most likely, as Franklin put it, to "have good reasons" or seem to.

Of all the moods that people want to escape, rage seems to be the most intransigent; Tice found anger is the mood people are worst at controlling. Indeed, anger is the most seductive of the negative emotions; the self-righteous inner monologue that propels it along fills the mind with the most convincing arguments for venting rage. Unlike sadness, anger is energizing, even exhilarating. Anger's seductive, persuasive power may in itself explain why some views about it are so common: that anger is uncontrollable, or that, at any rate, it *should not* be controlled, and that venting anger in "catharsis" is all to the good. A contrasting view, perhaps a reaction against the bleak picture of these other two, holds that anger can be prevented entirely. But a careful reading of research findings suggests that all these common attitudes toward anger are misguided, if not outright myths.[4]

The train of angry thoughts that stokes anger is also potentially the key to one of the most powerful ways to defuse anger: undermining the convictions that are fueling the anger in the first place. The longer we ruminate about what has made us angry, the more "good reasons" and self-justifications for being angry we can invent. Brooding fuels anger's flames. But seeing things differently douses those flames. Tice found that reframing a situation more positively was one of the most potent ways to put anger to rest.

The Rage "Rush"

That finding squares well with the conclusions of University of Alabama psychologist Dolf Zillmann, who, in a lengthy series of careful experiments, has taken precise measure of anger and the anatomy of rage.[5] Given the roots of anger in the fight wing of the fight-or-flight response, it is no surprise that Zillmann finds that a universal trigger for anger is the sense of being endangered. Endangerment can be signaled not just by an outright physical threat but also, as is more often the case, by a symbolic threat to self-esteem or dignity: being treated unjustly or rudely, being insulted or demeaned, being frustrated in pursuing an important goal. These perceptions act as the instigating trigger for a limbic surge that has a dual effect on the brain. One part of that surge is a release of catecholamines, which generate a quick, episodic rush of energy, enough for "one course of vigorous action," as Zillmann puts it, "such as in fight or flight." This energy surge lasts for minutes, during which it readies the body for a good fight or a quick flight, depending on how the emotional brain sizes up the opposition.

Meanwhile, another amygdala-driven ripple through the adrenocortical branch of the nervous system creates a general tonic background of action readiness, which lasts much longer than the catecholamine energy surge. This generalized adrenal and cortical excitation can last for hours and even days, keeping the emotional brain in special readiness for arousal, and becoming a foundation on which subsequent reactions can build with particular quickness. In general, the hair-trigger condition created by adrenocortical arousal explains why people are so much more prone to anger if they have already been provoked or slightly irritated by something else. Stress of all sorts creates adrenocortical arousal, lowering the threshold for what provokes anger. Thus someone who has had a hard day at work is especially vulnerable to becoming enraged later at home by something—the kids being too noisy or messy, say—that under other circumstances would not be powerful enough to trigger an emotional hijacking.

Zillmann comes to these insights on anger through careful experimentation. In a typical study, for example, he had a confederate provoke men and
women who had volunteered by making snide remarks about them. The
volunteers then watched a pleasant or upsetting film. Later the volunteers
were given the chance to retaliate against the confederate by giving an
evaluation they thought would be used in a decision whether or not to hire
him. The intensity of their retaliation was directly proportional to how
aroused they had gotten from the film they had just watched; they were
angrier after seeing the unpleasant film, and gave the worst ratings.

Anger Builds on Anger

Zillmann's studies seem to explain the dynamic at work in a familiar domestic
drama I witnessed one day while shopping. Down the supermarket aisle
drifted the emphatic, measured tones of a young mother to her son, about
three: "Put . . . it . . . back!"

"But I *want* it!" he whined, clinging more tightly to a Ninja Turtles cereal
box.

"Put it back!" Louder, her anger taking over.

At that moment the baby in her shopping cart seat dropped the jar of jelly she
had been mouthing. When it shattered on the floor the mother yelled, "That's
it!" and, in a fury, slapped the baby, grabbed the three-year-old's box and
slammed it onto the nearest shelf, scooped him up by the waist, and rushed
down the aisle, the shopping cart careening perilously in front, the baby now
crying, her son, his legs dangling, protesting, "Put me *down,* put me *down!*"

Zillmann has found that when the body is already in a state of edginess,
like the mother's, and something triggers an emotional hijacking, the subsequent emotion, whether anger or anxiety, is of especially great intensity. This
dynamic is at work when someone becomes enraged. Zillmann sees escalating anger as "a sequence of provocations, each triggering an excitatory
reaction that dissipates slowly." In this sequence every successive anger-
provoking thought or perception becomes a minitrigger for amygdala-driven
surges of catecholamines, each building on the hormonal momentum of
those that went before. A second comes before the first has subsided, and a
third on top of those, and so on; each wave rides the tails of those before,
quickly escalating the body's level of physiological arousal. A thought that
comes later in this buildup triggers a far greater intensity of anger than one
that comes at the beginning. Anger builds on anger; the emotional brain heats
up. By then rage, unhampered by reason, easily erupts in violence.

At this point people are unforgiving and beyond being reasoned with; their thoughts revolve around revenge and reprisal, oblivious to what the consequences may be. This high level of excitation, Zillmann says, "fosters an illusion of power and invulnerability that may inspire and facilitate aggression" as the enraged person, "failing cognitive guidance," falls back on the most primitive of responses. The limbic urge is ascendant; the rawest lessons of life's brutality become guides to action.

Balm for Anger

Given this analysis of the anatomy of rage, Zillmann sees two main ways of intervening. One way of defusing anger is to seize on and challenge the thoughts that trigger the surges of anger, since it is the original appraisal of an interaction that confirms and encourages the first burst of anger, and the subsequent reappraisals that fan the flames. Timing matters; the earlier in the anger cycle the more effective. Indeed, anger can be completely short-circuited if the mitigating information comes before the anger is acted on.

The power of understanding to deflate anger is clear from another of Zillmann's experiments, in which a rude assistant (a confederate) insulted and provoked volunteers who were riding an exercise bike. When the volunteers were given the chance to retaliate against the rude experimenter (again, by giving a bad evaluation they thought would be used in weighing his candidacy for a job) they did so with an angry glee. But in one version of the experiment another confederate entered after the volunteers had been provoked, and just before the chance to retaliate; she told the provocative experimenter he had a phone call down the hall. As he left he made a snide remark to her too. But she took it in good spirits, explaining after he left that he was under terrible pressures, upset about his upcoming graduate orals. After that the irate volunteers, when offered the chance to retaliate against the rude fellow, chose not to; instead they expressed compassion for his plight.

Such mitigating information allows a reappraisal of the anger-provoking events. But there is a specific window of opportunity for this de-escalation. Zillmann finds it works well at moderate levels of anger; at high levels of rage it makes no difference because of what he calls "cognitive incapacitation"—in other words, people can no longer think straight. When people were already highly enraged, they dismissed the mitigating information with "That's just too bad!" or "the strongest vulgarities the English language has to offer," as Zillmann put it with delicacy.

Cooling Down

> Once when I was about 13, in an angry fit, I walked out of the house vowing I would never return. It was a beautiful summer day, and I walked far along lovely lanes, till gradually the stillness and beauty calmed and soothed me, and after some hours I returned repentant and almost melted. Since then when I am angry, I do this if I can, and find it the best cure.

The account is by a subject in one of the very first scientific studies of anger, done in 1899.[6] It still stands as a model of the second way of de-escalating anger: cooling off physiologically by waiting out the adrenal surge in a setting where there are not likely to be further triggers for rage. In an argument, for instance, that means getting away from the other person for the time being. During the cooling-off period, the angered person can put the brakes on the cycle of escalating hostile thought by seeking out distractions. Distraction, Zillmann finds, is a highly powerful mood-altering device, for a simple reason: It's hard to stay angry when we're having a pleasant time. The trick, of course, is to get anger to cool to the point where someone can *have* a pleasant time in the first place.

Zillmann's analysis of the ways anger escalates and de-escalates explains many of Diane Tice's findings about the strategies people commonly say they use to ease anger. One such fairly effective strategy is going off to be alone while cooling down. A large proportion of men translate this into going for a drive—a finding that gives one pause when driving (and, Tice told me, inspired her to drive more defensively). Perhaps a safer alternative is going for a long walk; active exercise also helps with anger. So do relaxation methods such as deep breathing and muscle relaxation, perhaps because they change the body's physiology from the high arousal of anger to a low-arousal state, and perhaps too because they distract from whatever triggered the anger. Active exercise may cool anger for something of the same reason: after high levels of physiological activation during the exercise, the body rebounds to a low level once it stops.

But a cooling-down period will not work if that time is used to pursue the train of anger-inducing thought, since each such thought is in itself a minor trigger for more cascades of anger. The power of distraction is that it stops that angry train of thought. In her survey of people's strategies for handling anger, Tice found that distractions by and large help calm anger: TV, movies, reading, and the like all interfere with the angry thoughts that stoke rage. But,

Tice found, indulging in treats such as shopping for oneself and eating do not have much effect; it is all too easy to continue with an indignant train of thought while cruising a shopping mall or devouring a piece of chocolate cake.

To these strategies add those developed by Redford Williams, a psychiatrist at Duke University who sought to help hostile people, who are at higher risk for heart disease, to control their irritability.[7] One of his recommendations is to use self-awareness to catch cynical or hostile thoughts as they arise, and write them down. Once angry thoughts are captured this way, they can be challenged and reappraised, though, as Zillmann found, this approach works better before anger has escalated to rage.

The Ventilation Fallacy

As I settle into a New York City cab, a young man crossing the street stops in front of the cab to wait for traffic to clear. The driver, impatient to start, honks, motioning for the young man to move out of the way. The reply is a scowl and an obscene gesture.

"You son of a bitch!" the driver yells, making threatening lunges with the cab by hitting the accelerator and brake at the same time. At this lethal threat, the young man sullenly moves aside, barely, and smacks his fist against the cab as it inches by into traffic. At this, the driver shouts a foul litany of expletives at the man.

As we move along the driver, still visibly agitated, tells me, "You can't take any shit from anyone. You gotta yell back—at least it makes you feel better!"

Catharsis—giving vent to rage—is sometimes extolled as a way of handling anger. The popular theory holds that "it makes you feel better." But, as Zillmann's findings suggest, there is an argument against catharsis. It has been made since the 1950s, when psychologists started to test the effects of catharsis experimentally and, time after time, found that giving vent to anger did little or nothing to dispel it (though, because of the seductive nature of anger, it may *feel* satisfying).[8] There may be some specific conditions under which lashing out in anger does work: when it is expressed directly to the person who is its target, when it restores a sense of control or rights an injustice, or when it inflicts "appropriate harm" on the other person and gets him to change some grievous activity without retaliating. But because of the incendiary nature of anger, this may be easier to say than to do.[9]

Tice found that ventilating anger is one of the worst ways to cool down: outbursts of rage typically pump up the emotional brain's arousal, leaving people feeling more angry, not less. Tice found that when people told of times they had taken their rage out on the person who provoked it, the net effect was to prolong the mood rather than end it. Far more effective was when people first cooled down, and then, in a more constructive or assertive manner, confronted the person to settle their dispute. As I once heard Chogyam Trungpa, a Tibetan teacher, reply when asked how best to handle anger: "Don't suppress it. But don't act on it."

SOOTHING ANXIETY: WHAT, ME WORRY?

> Oh, no! The muffler sounds bad. . . . What if I have to take it to the shop? . . . I can't afford the expense. . . . I'd have to draw the money from Jamie's college fund. . . . What if I can't afford his tuition? . . . That bad school report last week. . . . What if his grades go down and he can't get into college? . . . Muffler sounds bad. . . .

And so the worrying mind spins on in an endless loop of low-grade melodrama, one set of concerns leading on to the next and back again. The above specimen is offered by Lizabeth Roemer and Thomas Borkovec, Pennsylvania State University psychologists, whose research on worrying—the heart of all anxiety—has raised the topic from neurotic's art to science.[10] There is, of course, no hitch when worry works; by mulling over a problem—that is, employing constructive reflection, which can look like worrying—a solution can appear. Indeed, the reaction that underlies worry is the vigilance for potential danger that has, no doubt, been essential for survival over the course of evolution. When fear triggers the emotional brain, part of the resulting anxiety fixates attention on the threat at hand, forcing the mind to obsess about how to handle it and ignore anything else for the time being. Worry is, in a sense, a rehearsal of what might go wrong and how to deal with it; the task of worrying is to come up with positive solutions for life's perils by anticipating dangers before they arise.

The difficulty is with chronic, repetitive worries, the kind that recycle on and on and never get any nearer a positive solution. A close analysis of chronic worry suggests that it has all the attributes of a low-grade emotional hijacking: the worries seem to come from nowhere, are uncontrollable, generate a steady hum of anxiety, are impervious to reason, and lock the worrier into a single, inflexible view of the worrisome topic. When this same cycle of worry intensifies and persists, it shades over the line into full-blown neural hijackings, the anxiety disorders: phobias, obsessions and compulsions, panic attacks. In each of these disorders worry fixates in a distinct fashion; for the phobic, anxieties rivet on the feared situation; for the obsessive, they fixate on preventing some feared calamity; in panic attacks, the worries can focus on a fear of dying or on the prospect of having the attack itself.

In all these conditions the common denominator is worry run amok. For example, a woman being treated for obsessive-compulsive disorder had a series of rituals that took most of her waking hours: forty-five-minute showers several times daily, washing her hands for five minutes twenty or more times a day. She would not sit down unless she first swabbed the seat with rubbing alcohol to sterilize it. Nor would she touch a child or an animal—both were "too dirty." All these compulsions were stirred by her underlying morbid fear of germs; she worried constantly that without her washing and sterilizing she would catch a disease and die.[11]

A woman being treated for "generalized anxiety disorder"—the psychiatric nomenclature for being a constant worrier—responded to the request to worry aloud for one minute this way:

> I might not do this right. This may be so artificial that it won't be an indication of the real thing and we need to get at the real thing. . . . Because if we don't get at the real thing, I won't get well. And if I don't get well I'll never be happy.[12]

In this virtuoso display of worrying about worrying, the very request to worry for one minute had, within a few short seconds, escalated to contemplation of a lifelong catastrophe: "I'll never be happy." Worries typically follow such lines, a narrative to oneself that jumps from concern to concern and more often than not includes catastrophizing, imagining some terrible tragedy. Worries are almost always expressed in the mind's ear, not its eye—that is, in words, not images—a fact that has significance for controlling worry.

Borkovec and his colleagues began to study worrying per se when they were trying to come up with a treatment for insomnia. Anxiety, other researchers have observed, comes in two forms: *cognitive,* or worrisome thoughts, and *somatic,* the physiological symptoms of anxiety, such as sweating, a racing heart, or muscle tension. The main trouble with insomniacs, Borkovec found, was not the somatic arousal. What kept them up were intrusive thoughts. They were chronic worriers, and could not stop worrying, no matter how sleepy they were. The one thing that worked in helping them get to sleep was getting their minds off their worries, focusing instead on the sensations produced by a relaxation method. In short, the worries could be stopped by shifting attention away.

Most worriers, however, can't seem to do this. The reason, Borkovec believes, has to do with a partial payoff from worrying that is highly reinforcing to the habit. There is, it seems, something positive in worries: worries are ways to deal with potential threats, with dangers that may come one's way. The work of worrying—when it succeeds—is to rehearse what those dangers are, and to reflect on ways to deal with them. But worry doesn't work all that well. New solutions and fresh ways of seeing a problem do not typically come from worrying, especially chronic worry. Instead of coming up with solutions to these potential problems, worriers typically simply ruminate on the danger itself, immersing themselves in a low-key way in the dread associated with it while staying in the same rut of thought. Chronic worriers worry about a wide range of things, most of which have almost no chance of happening; they read dangers into life's journey that others never notice.

Yet chronic worriers tell Borkovec that worrying helps them, and that their worries are self-perpetuating, an endless loop of angst-ridden thought. Why should worry become what seems to amount to a mental addiction? Oddly, as Borkovec points out, the worry habit is reinforcing in the same sense that superstitions are. Since people worry about many things that have a very low probability of actually occurring—a loved one dying in a plane crash, going bankrupt, and the like—there is, to the primitive limbic brain at least, something magical about it. Like an amulet that wards off some anticipated evil, the worry psychologically gets the credit for preventing the danger it obsesses about.

The Work of Worrying

She had moved to Los Angeles from the Midwest, lured by a job with a publisher. But the publisher was bought by another soon after, and she was left without a job. Turning to freelance writing, an erratic marketplace, she found herself either swamped with work or unable to pay her rent. She often had to ration phone calls, and for the first time was without health insurance. This lack of coverage was particularly distressing: she found herself catastrophizing about her health, sure every headache signaled a brain tumor, picturing herself in an accident whenever she had to drive somewhere. She often found herself lost in a long reverie of worry, a medley of distress. But, she said, she found her worries almost addictive.

Borkovec discovered another unexpected benefit to worrying. While people are immersed in their worried thoughts, they do not seem to notice the subjective sensations of the anxiety those worries stir—the speedy heartbeat, the beads of sweat, the shakiness—and as the worry proceeds it actually seems to suppress some of that anxiety, at least as reflected in heart rate. The sequence presumably goes something like this: The worrier notices something that triggers the image of some potential threat or danger; that imagined catastrophe in turn triggers a mild attack of anxiety. The worrier then plunges into a long series of distressed thoughts, each of which primes yet another topic for worry; as attention continues to be carried along by this train of worry, focusing on these very thoughts takes the mind off the original catastrophic image that triggered the anxiety. Images, Borkovec found, are more powerful triggers for physiological anxiety than are thoughts, so immersion in thoughts, to the exclusion of catastrophic images, partially alleviates the experience of being anxious. And, to that extent, the worry is also reinforced, as a halfway antidote to the very anxiety it evoked.

But chronic worries are self-defeating too in that they take the form of stereotyped, rigid ideas, not creative breakthroughs that actually move toward solving the problem. This rigidity shows up not just in the manifest content of worried thought, which simply repeats more or less the same ideas over and over. But at a neurological level there seems to be a cortical rigidity, a deficit in the emotional brain's ability to respond flexibly to changing circumstance. In short, chronic worry works in some ways, but not in other, more consequential ones: it eases some anxiety, but never solves the problem.

The one thing that chronic worriers cannot do is follow the advice they are most often given: "Just stop worrying" (or, worse, "Don't worry—be happy"). Since chronic worries seem to be low-grade amygdala episodes, they come unbidden. And, by their very nature, they persist once they arise in the mind. But after much experimentation, Borkovec discovered some simple steps that can help even the most chronic worrier control the habit.

The first step is self-awareness, catching the worrisome episodes as near their beginning as possible—ideally, as soon as or just after the fleeting catastrophic image triggers the worry-anxiety cycle. Borkovec trains people in this approach by first teaching them to monitor cues for anxiety, especially learning to identify situations that trigger worry, or the fleeting thoughts and images that initiate the worry, as well as the accompanying sensations of anxiety in the body. With practice, people can identify the worries at an earlier and earlier point in the anxiety spiral. People also learn relaxation

methods that they can apply at the moment they recognize the worry beginning, and practice the relaxation method daily so they will be able to use it on
the spot, when they need it the most.

The relaxation method, though, is not enough in itself. Worriers also need
to actively challenge the worrisome thoughts; failing this, the worry spiral
will keep coming back. So the next step is to take a critical stance toward their
assumptions: Is it very probable that the dreaded event will occur? Is it
necessarily the case that there is only one or no alternative to letting it
happen? Are there constructive steps to be taken? Does it really help to run
through these same anxious thoughts over and over?

This combination of mindfulness and healthy skepticism would, presumably, act as a brake on the neural activation that underlies low-grade anxiety.
Actively generating such thoughts may prime the circuitry that can inhibit the
limbic driving of worry; at the same time, actively inducing a relaxed state
counters the signals for anxiety the emotional brain is sending throughout
the body.

Indeed, Borkovec points out, these strategies establish a train of mental
activity that is incompatible with worry. When a worry is allowed to repeat
over and over unchallenged, it gains in persuasive power; challenging it by
contemplating a range of equally plausible points of view keeps the one
worried thought from being naively taken as true. Even some people whose
worrying is serious enough to qualify for a psychiatric diagnosis have been
relieved of the worrying habit this way.

On the other hand, for people with worries so severe they have flowered
into phobia, obsessive-compulsive disorder, or panic disorder, it may be
prudent—indeed, a sign of self-awareness—to turn to medication to inter-
rupt the cycle. A retraining of the emotional circuitry through therapy is still
called for, however, in order to lessen the likelihood that anxiety disorders
will recur when medication is stopped.[13]

MANAGING MELANCHOLY

The single mood people generally put most effort into shaking is sadness;
Diane Tice found that people are most inventive when it comes to trying to
escape the blues. Of course, not all sadness should be escaped; melancholy,
like every other mood, has its benefits. The sadness that a loss brings has
certain invariable effects: it closes down our interest in diversions and pleasures, fixes attention on what has been lost, and saps our energy for starting

new endeavors—at least for the time being. In short, it enforces a kind of reflective retreat from life's busy pursuits, and leaves us in a suspended state to mourn the loss, mull over its meaning, and, finally, make the psychological adjustments and new plans that will allow our lives to continue.

Bereavement is useful; full-blown depression is not. William Styron renders an eloquent description of "the many dreadful manifestations of the disease," among them self-hatred, a sense of worthlessness, a "dank joylessness" with "gloom crowding in on me, a sense of dread and alienation and, above all, a stifling anxiety."[14] Then there are the intellectual marks: "confusion, failure of mental focus and lapse of memories," and, at a later stage, his mind "dominated by anarchic distortions," and "a sense that my thought processes were engulfed by a toxic and unnameable tide that obliterated any enjoyable response to the living world." There are the physical effects: sleeplessness, feeling as listless as a zombie, "a kind of numbness, an enervation, but more particularly an odd fragility," along with a "fidgety restlessness." Then there is the loss of pleasure: "Food, like everything else within the scope of sensation, was utterly without savor." Finally, there was the vanishing of hope as the "gray drizzle of horror" took on a despair so palpable it was like physical pain, a pain so unendurable that suicide seemed a solution.

In such major depression, life is paralyzed; no new beginnings emerge. The very symptoms of depression bespeak a life on hold. For Styron, no medication or therapy helped; it was the passing of time and the refuge of a hospital that finally cleared away the despondency. But for most people, especially those with less severe cases, psychotherapy can help, as can medication—Prozac is the treatment of the hour, but there are more than a dozen other compounds offering some help, especially for major depression.

My focus here is the far more common sadness that at its upper limits becomes, technically speaking, a "subclinical depression"—that is, ordinary melancholy. This is a range of despondency that people can handle on their own, if they have the internal resources. Unfortunately, some of the strategies most often resorted to can backfire, leaving people feeling worse than before. One such strategy is simply staying alone, which is often appealing when people are feeling down; more often than not, however, it only adds a sense of loneliness and isolation to the sadness. That may partly explain why Tice found the most popular tactic for battling depression is socializing— going out to eat, to a ballgame or movie; in short, doing something with friends or family. That works well if the net effect is to get the person's mind off his sadness. But it simply prolongs the mood if he uses the occasion just to mull over what put him in the funk.

Indeed, one of the main determinants of whether a depressed mood will persist or lift is the degree to which people ruminate. Worrying about what's depressing us, it seems, makes the depression all the more intense and prolonged. In depression, worry takes several forms, all focusing on some aspect of the depression itself—how tired we feel, how little energy or motivation we have, for instance, or how little work we're getting done. Typically none of this reflection is accompanied by any concrete course of action that might alleviate the problem. Other common worries include "isolating yourself and thinking about how terrible you feel, worrying that your spouse might reject you because you are depressed, and wondering whether you are going to have another sleepless night," says Stanford psychologist Susan Nolen-Hoeksma, who has studied rumination in depressed people.[15]

Depressed people sometimes justify this kind of rumination by saying they are trying to "understand themselves better"; in fact, they are priming the feelings of sadness without taking any steps that might actually lift their mood. Thus in therapy it might be perfectly helpful to reflect deeply on the causes of a depression, if that leads to insights or actions that will change the conditions that cause it. But a passive immersion in the sadness simply makes it worse.

Rumination can also make the depression stronger by creating conditions that are, well, more depressing. Nolen-Hoeksma gives the example of a saleswoman who gets depressed and spends so many hours worrying about it that she doesn't get around to important sales calls. Her sales then decline, making her feel like a failure, which feeds her depression. But if she reacted to depression by trying to distract herself, she might well plunge into the sales calls as a way to get her mind off the sadness. Sales would be less likely to decline, and the very experience of making a sale might bolster her self-confidence, lessening the depression somewhat.

Women, Nolen-Hoeksma finds, are far more prone to ruminate when they are depressed than are men. This, she proposes, may at least partly explain the fact that women are diagnosed with depression twice as often as are men. Of course, other factors may come into play, such as women being more open to disclosing their distress or having more in their lives to be depressed about. And men may drown their depression in alcoholism, for which their rate is about twice that of women.

Cognitive therapy aimed at changing these thought patterns has been found in some studies to be on a par with medication for treating mild clinical depression, and superior to medication in preventing the return of mild depression. Two strategies are particularly effective in the battle.[16] One is to learn to challenge the thoughts at the center of rumination—to question their validity and think of more positive alternatives. The other is to purposely schedule pleasant, distracting events.

One reason distraction works is that depressing thoughts are automatic, intruding on one's state of mind unbidden. Even when depressed people try to suppress their depressing thoughts, they often cannot come up with better alternatives; once the depressive tide of thought has started, it has a powerful magnetic effect on the train of association. For example, when depressed people were asked to unscramble jumbled six-word sentences, they were much better at figuring out the depressing messages ("The future looks very dismal") than the upbeat ones ("The future looks very bright").[17]

The tendency for depression to perpetuate itself shades even the kinds of distractions people choose. When depressed people were given a list of upbeat or ponderous ways to get their minds off something sad, such as the funeral of a friend, they picked more of the melancholy activities. Richard Wenzlaff, the University of Texas psychologist who did these studies, concludes that people who are already depressed need to make a special effort to get their attention on something that is completely upbeat, being careful not to inadvertently choose something—a tearjerker movie, a tragic novel—that will drag their mood down again.

Mood-lifters

Imagine that you're driving on an unfamiliar, steep, and winding road through fog. Suddenly a car pulls out of a driveway only a few feet in front of you, too close for you to stop in time. Your foot slams the brake to the floor and you go into a skid, your car sliding into the side of the other one. You see that the car is full of youngsters, a carpool on the way to preschool—just before the explosion of glass shattering and metal bending into metal. Then, out of the sudden silence after the collision, you hear a chorus of crying. You manage to run to the other car, and see that one of the children is lying motionless. You are flooded with remorse and sadness over this tragedy. . . .

Such heart-wrenching scenarios were used to get volunteers upset in one of Wenzlaff's experiments. The volunteers then tried to keep the scene out of their minds while they jotted notes about the stream of their thoughts for nine minutes. Each time the thought of the disturbing scene intruded into their minds, they made a check mark as they wrote. While most people thought about the upsetting scene less and less as time went on, those volunteers who were more depressed actually showed a pronounced *increase* in intruding thoughts of the scene as time passed, and even made oblique references to it in the thoughts that were supposed to be distractions from it.

What's more, the depression-prone volunteers used other distressing thoughts to distract themselves. As Wenzlaff told me, "Thoughts are associated in the mind not just by content, but by mood. People have what amounts to a set of bad-mood thoughts that come to mind more readily when they are feeling down. People who get depressed easily tend to create very strong networks of association between these thoughts, so that it is harder to suppress them once some kind of bad mood is evoked. Ironically, depressed people seem to use one depressing topic to get their minds off another, which only stirs more negative emotions."

Crying, one theory holds, may be nature's way of lowering levels of the brain chemicals that prime distress. While crying can sometimes break a spell of sadness, it can also leave the person still obsessing about the reasons for despair. The idea of a "good cry" is misleading: crying that reinforces rumination only prolongs the misery. Distractions break the chain of sadness-maintaining thinking; one of the leading theories of why electroconvulsive therapy is effective for the most severe depressions is that it causes a loss of short-term memory—patients feel better because they can't remember why they were so sad. At any rate, to shake garden-variety sadness, Diane Tice found, many people reported turning to distractions such as reading, TV and movies, video games and puzzles, sleeping, and daydreams such as planning a fantasy vacation. Wenzlaff would add that the most effective distractions are ones that will shift your mood—an exciting sporting event, a funny movie, an uplifting book. (A note of caution here: Some distractors in themselves can perpetuate depression. Studies of heavy TV watchers have found that, after watching TV, they are generally more depressed than before they started!)

Aerobic exercise, Tice found, is one of the more effective tactics for lifting mild depression, as well as other bad moods. But the caveat here is that the mood-lifting benefits of exercise work best for the lazy, those who usually do not work out very much. For those with a daily exercise routine, whatever mood-changing benefits it offers were probably strongest when they first took up the exercise habit. In fact, for habitual exercisers there is a reverse effect on mood: they start to feel bad on those days when they skip their workout. Exercise seems to work well because it changes the physiological state the mood evokes: depression is a low-arousal state, and aerobics pitches the body into high arousal. By the same token, relaxation techniques, which put the body into a low-arousal state, work well for anxiety, a high-arousal state, but not so well for depression. Each of these approaches seems to work to break the cycle of depression or anxiety because it pitches the brain into a level of activity incompatible with the emotional state that has had it in its grip.

Cheering oneself up through treats and sensual pleasures was another fairly popular antidote to the blues. Common ways people soothed themselves when depressed ranged from taking hot baths or eating favorite foods, to listening to music or having sex. Buying oneself a gift or treat to get out of a bad mood was particularly popular among women, as was shopping in general, even if only window-shopping. Among those in college, Tice found that eating was three times as common a strategy for soothing sadness among women than men; men, on the other hand, were five times as likely to turn to drinking or drugs when they felt down. The trouble with overeating or alcohol as antidotes, of course, is that they can easily backfire: eating to excess brings regret; alcohol is a central nervous system depressant, and so only adds to the effects of depression itself.

A more constructive approach to mood-lifting, Tice reports, is engineering a small triumph or easy success: tackling some long-delayed chore around the house or getting to some other duty they've been wanting to clear up. By the same token, lifts to self-image also were cheering, even if only in the form of getting dressed up or putting on makeup.

One of the most potent—and, outside therapy, little used—antidotes to depression is seeing things differently, or *cognitive reframing*. It is natural to bemoan the end of a relationship and to wallow in self-pitying thoughts such as the conviction that "this means I'll always be alone," but it's sure to thicken the sense of despair. However, stepping back and thinking about the ways the relationship wasn't so great, and ways you and your partner were mismatched—in other words, seeing the loss differently, in a more positive light—is an antidote to the sadness. By the same token, cancer patients, no matter how serious their condition, were in better moods if they were able to bring to mind another patient who was in even worse shape ("I'm not so bad off—at least I can walk"); those who compared themselves to healthy people were the most depressed.[18] Such downward comparisons are surprisingly cheering: suddenly what had seemed quite dispiriting doesn't look all that bad.

Another effective depression-lifter is helping others in need. Since depression feeds on ruminations and preoccupations with the self, helping others lifts us out of those preoccupations as we empathize with people in pain of their own. Throwing oneself into volunteer work—coaching Little League, being a Big Brother, feeding the homeless—was one of the most powerful mood-changers in Tice's study. But it was also one of the rarest.

Finally, at least some people are able to find relief from their melancholy in turning to a transcendent power. Tice told me, "Praying, if you're very religious, works for all moods, especially depression."

REPRESSORS: UPBEAT DENIAL

"He kicked his roommate in the stomach . . ." the sentence begins. It ends, ". . . but he meant to turn on the light."

That transformation of an act of aggression into an innocent, if slightly implausible, mistake is repression captured *in vivo*. It was composed by a college student who had volunteered for a study of *repressors,* people who habitually and automatically seem to blot emotional disturbance from their awareness. The beginning fragment "He kicked his roommate in the stomach . . ." was given to this student as part of a sentence-completion test. Other tests showed that this small act of mental avoidance was part of a larger pattern in his life, a pattern of tuning out most emotional upset.[19] While at first researchers saw repressors as a prime example of the inability to feel emotion—cousins of alexithymics, perhaps—current thinking sees them as quite proficient in regulating emotion. They have become so adept at buffering themselves against negative feelings, it seems, that they are not even aware of the negativity. Rather than calling them repressors, as has been the custom among researchers, a more apt term might be *unflappables*.

Much of this research, done principally by Daniel Weinberger, a psychologist now at Case Western Reserve University, shows that while such people may seem calm and imperturbable, they can sometimes seethe with physiological upsets they are oblivious to. During the sentence-completion test, volunteers were also being monitored for their level of physiological arousal. The repressors' veneer of calm was belied by the agitation of their bodies: when faced with the sentence about the violent roommate and others like it, they gave all the signs of anxiety, such as a racing heart, sweating, and climbing blood pressure. Yet when asked, they said they felt perfectly calm.

This continual tuning-out of emotions such as anger and anxiety is not uncommon: about one person in six shows the pattern, according to Weinberger. In theory, children might learn to become unflappable in any of several ways. One might be as a strategy for surviving a troubling situation such as having an alcoholic parent in a family where the problem itself is denied. Another might be having a parent or parents who are themselves repressors and so pass on the example of perennial cheerfulness or a stiff upper lip in the face of disturbing feelings. Or the trait may simply be inherited temperament. While no one can say as yet just how such a pattern begins in life, by the time repressors reach adulthood they are cool and collected under duress.

The question remains, of course, as to just how calm and cool they actually are. Can they really be unaware of the physical signs of distressing emotions, or are they simply feigning calm? The answer to that has come from clever research by Richard Davidson, a University of Wisconsin psychologist and an early collaborator with Weinberger. Davidson had people with the unflappable pattern free-associate to a list of words, most neutral, but several with hostile or sexual meanings that stir anxiety in almost everyone. And, as their bodily reactions revealed, they had all the physiological signs of distress in response to the loaded words, even though the words they associated to almost always showed an attempt to sanitize the upsetting words by linking them to an innocent one. If the first word was "hate," the response might be "love."

Davidson's study took advantage of the fact that (in right-handed people) a key center for processing negative emotion is in the right half of the brain, while the center for speaking is in the left. Once the right hemisphere recognizes that a word is upsetting, it transmits that information across the corpus callosum, the great divide between the brain's halves, to the speech center, and a word is spoken in response. Using an intricate arrangement of lenses, Davidson was able to display a word so that it was seen in only half of the visual field. Because of the neural wiring of the visual system, if the display was to the left half of the visual field, it was recognized first by the right half of the brain, with its sensitivity to distress. If the display was to the right half of the visual field, the signal went to the left side of the brain without being assessed for upset.

When the words were presented to the right hemisphere, there was a lag in the time it took the unflappables to utter a response—but only if the word they were responding to was one of the upsetting ones. They had *no* time lag in the speed of their associations to *neutral* words. The lag showed up *only* when the words were presented to the right hemisphere, not to the left. In short, their unflappableness seems due to a neural mechanism that slows or interferes with the transfer of upsetting information. The implication is that they are *not* faking their lack of awareness about how upset they are; their brain is keeping that information from them. More precisely, the layer of mellow feeling that covers over such disturbing perceptions may well be due to the workings of the left prefrontal lobe. To his surprise, when Davidson measured activity levels in their prefrontal lobes, they had a decided predominance of activity on the left—the center for good feeling—and less on the right, the center for negativity.

These people "present themselves in a positive light, with an upbeat mood," Davidson told me. "They deny that stress is upsetting them and show a pattern of left frontal activation while just sitting at rest that is associated with positive feelings. This brain activity may be the key to their positive claims, despite the underlying physiological arousal that looks like distress." Davidson's theory is that, in terms of brain activity, it is energy-demanding work to experience distressing realities in a positive light. The increased physiological arousal may be due to the sustained attempt by the neural circuitry to maintain positive feelings or to suppress or inhibit any negative ones.

In short, unflappableness is a kind of upbeat denial, a positive dissociation—and, possibly, a clue to neural mechanisms at play in the more severe dissociative states that can occur in, say, post-traumatic stress disorder. When it is simply involved in equanimity, says Davidson, "it seems to be a successful strategy for emotional self-regulation" though with an unknown cost to self-awareness.

6

The Master Aptitude

Just once in my life have I been paralyzed by fear. The occasion was a calculus exam during my freshman year in college for which I somehow had managed not to study. I still remember the room I marched to that spring morning with feelings of doom and foreboding heavy in my heart. I had been in that lecture hall for many classes. This morning, though, I noticed nothing through the windows and did not see the hall at all. My gaze shrank to the patch of floor directly in front of me as I made my way to a seat near the door. As I opened the blue cover of my exam book, there was the thump in my ears of heartbeat, there was the taste of anxiety in the pit of my stomach.

I looked at the exam questions once, quickly. Hopeless. For an hour I stared at that page, my mind racing over the consequences I would suffer. The same thoughts repeated themselves over and over, a tape loop of fear and trembling. I sat motionless, like an animal frozen in mid-move by curare. What strikes me most about that dreadful moment was how constricted my mind became. I did not spend the hour in a desperate attempt to patch together some semblance of answers to the test. I did not daydream. I simply sat fixated on my terror, waiting for the ordeal to finish.[1]

That narrative of an ordeal by terror is my own; it is to this day for me the most convincing evidence of the devastating impact of emotional distress on mental clarity. I now see that my ordeal was most likely a testament to the power of the emotional brain to overpower, even paralyze, the thinking brain.

The extent to which emotional upsets can interfere with mental life is no news to teachers. Students who are anxious, angry, or depressed don't learn; people who are caught in these states do not take in information efficiently or deal with it well. As we saw in Chapter 5, powerful negative emotions twist attention toward their own preoccupations, interfering with the attempt to focus elsewhere. Indeed, one of the signs that feelings have veered over the line into the pathological is that they are so intrusive they overwhelm all other thought, continually sabotaging attempts to pay attention to whatever other task is at hand. For the person going through an upsetting divorce—or the child whose parents are—the mind does not stay long on the comparatively trivial routines of the work or school day; for the clinically depressed, thoughts of self-pity and despair, hopelessness and helplessness, override all others.

When emotions overwhelm concentration, what is being swamped is the mental capacity cognitive scientists call "working memory," the ability to hold in mind all information relevant to the task at hand. What occupies working memory can be as mundane as the digits that compose a telephone number or as complicated as the intricate plot lines a novelist is trying to weave together. Working memory is an executive function par excellence in mental life, making possible all other intellectual efforts, from speaking a sentence to tackling a knotty logical proposition.[2] The prefrontal cortex executes working memory—and, remember, is where feelings and emotions meet.[3] When the limbic circuitry that converges on the prefrontal cortex is in the thrall of emotional distress, one cost is in the effectiveness of working memory: we can't think straight, as I discovered during that dread calculus exam.

On the other hand, consider the role of positive motivation—the marshaling of feelings of enthusiasm, zeal, and confidence—in achievement. Studies of Olympic athletes, world-class musicians, and chess grand masters find their unifying trait is the ability to motivate themselves to pursue relentless training routines.[4] And, with a steady rise in the degree of excellence required to be a world-class performer, these rigorous training routines now increasingly must begin in childhood. At the 1992 Olympics, twelve-year-old members of the Chinese diving team had put in as many total lifetime practice dives as had members of the American team in their early twenties—the Chinese divers started their rigorous training at age four. Likewise, the best violin virtuosos of the twentieth century began studying their instrument at around age five; international chess champions started on the game at an average age of seven, while those who rose only to national prominence started at ten. Starting earlier offers a lifetime edge: the top violin students at the best music academy in Berlin, all in their early twenties, had put in ten thousand total hours' lifetime practice, while the second-tier students averaged around seventy-five hundred hours.

What seems to set apart those at the very top of competitive pursuits from others of roughly equal ability is the degree to which, beginning early in life, they can pursue an arduous practice routine for years and years. And that doggedness depends on emotional traits—enthusiasm and persistence in the face of setbacks—above all else.

The added payoff for life success from motivation, apart from other innate abilities, can be seen in the remarkable performance of Asian students in American schools and professions. One thorough review of the evidence suggests that Asian-American children may have an average IQ advantage over whites of just two or three points.[5] Yet on the basis of the professions, such as law and medicine, that many Asian-Americans end up in, as a group they behave as though their IQ were much higher—the equivalent of an IQ of 110 for Japanese-Americans and of 120 for Chinese-Americans.[6] The reason seems to be that from the earliest years of school, Asian children work harder than whites. Sanford Dorenbusch, a Stanford sociologist who studied more than ten thousand high-school students, found that Asian-Americans spent 40 percent more time doing homework than did other students. "While most American parents are willing to accept a child's weak areas and emphasize the strengths, for Asians, the attitude is that if you're not doing well, the answer is to study later at night, and if you still don't do well, to get up and study earlier in the morning. They believe that anyone can do well in school with the right effort." In short, a strong cultural work ethic translates into higher motivation, zeal, and persistence—an emotional edge.

To the degree that our emotions get in the way of or enhance our ability to think and plan, to pursue training for a distant goal, to solve problems and the like, they define the limits of our capacity to use our innate mental abilities, and so determine how we do in life. And to the degree to which we are motivated by feelings of enthusiasm and pleasure in what we do— or even by an optimal degree of anxiety—they propel us to accomplishment. It is in this sense that emotional intelligence is a master aptitude, a capacity that profoundly affects all other abilities, either facilitating or interfering with them.

IMPULSE CONTROL: THE MARSHMALLOW TEST

Just imagine you're four years old, and someone makes the following proposal: If you'll wait until after he runs an errand, you can have two marshmallows for a treat. If you can't wait until then, you can have only one—but you can have it right now. It is a challenge sure to try the soul of any four-year-old, a microcosm of the eternal battle between impulse and restraint, id and ego, desire and self-control, gratification and delay. Which of these choices a child makes is a telling test; it offers a quick reading not just of character, but of the trajectory that child will probably take through life.

There is perhaps no psychological skill more fundamental than resisting impulse. It is the root of all emotional self-control, since all emotions, by their very nature, lead to one or another impulse to act. The root meaning of the word *emotion,* remember, is "to move." The capacity to resist that impulse to act, to squelch the incipient movement, most likely translates at the level of brain function into inhibition of limbic signals to the motor cortex, though such an interpretation must remain speculative for now.

At any rate, a remarkable study in which the marshmallow challenge was posed to four-year-olds shows just how fundamental is the ability to restrain the emotions and so delay impulse. Begun by psychologist Walter Mischel during the 1960s at a preschool on the Stanford University campus and involving mainly children of Stanford faculty, graduate students, and other employees, the study tracked down the four-year-olds as they were graduating from high school.[7]

Some four-year-olds were able to wait what must surely have seemed an endless fifteen to twenty minutes for the experimenter to return. To sustain themselves in their struggle they covered their eyes so they wouldn't have to stare at temptation, or rested their heads in their arms, talked to themselves, sang, played games with their hands and feet, even tried to go to sleep. These plucky preschoolers got the two-marshmallow reward. But others, more impulsive, grabbed the one marshmallow, almost always within seconds of the experimenter's leaving the room on his "errand."

The diagnostic power of how this moment of impulse was handled became clear some twelve to fourteen years later, when these same children were tracked down as adolescents. The emotional and social difference between the grab-the-marshmallow preschoolers and their gratification-delaying peers was dramatic. Those who had resisted temptation at four were now, as adolescents, more socially competent: personally effective, self-assertive, and better able to cope with the frustrations of life. They were less likely to go to pieces, freeze, or regress under stress, or become rattled and disorganized when pressured; they embraced challenges and pursued them instead of giving up even in the face of difficulties; they were self-reliant and confident, trustworthy and dependable; and they took initiative and plunged into projects. And, more than a decade later, they were still able to delay gratification in pursuit of their goals.

The third or so who grabbed for the marshmallow, however, tended to have fewer of these qualities, and shared instead a relatively more troubled psychological portrait. In adolescence they were more likely to be seen as shying away from social contacts; to be stubborn and indecisive; to be easily upset by frustrations; to think of themselves as "bad" or unworthy; to regress or become immobilized by stress; to be mistrustful and resentful about not "getting enough"; to be prone to jealousy and envy; to overreact to irritations with a sharp temper, so provoking arguments and fights. And, after all those years, they still were unable to put off gratification.

What shows up in a small way early in life blossoms into a wide range of social and emotional competences as life goes on. The capacity to impose a delay on impulse is at the root of a plethora of efforts, from staying on a diet to pursuing a medical degree. Some children, even at four, had mastered the basics: they were able to read the social situation as one where delay was beneficial, to pry their attention from focusing on the temptation at hand, and to distract themselves while maintaining the necessary perseverance toward their goal—the two marshmallows.

Even more surprising, when the tested children were evaluated again as they were finishing high school, those who had waited patiently at four were far superior *as students* to those who had acted on whim. According to their parents' evaluations, they were more academically competent: better able to put their ideas into words, to use and respond to reason, to concentrate, to make plans and follow through on them, and more eager to learn. Most astonishingly, they had dramatically higher scores on their SAT tests. The third of children who at four grabbed for the marshmallow most eagerly had an average verbal score of 524 and quantitative (or "math") score of 528; the third who waited longest had average scores of 610 and 652, respectively—a 210-point difference in total score.[8]

At age four, how children do on this test of delay of gratification is twice as powerful a predictor of what their SAT scores will be as is IQ at age four; IQ becomes a stronger predictor of SAT only after children learn to read.[9] This suggests that the ability to delay gratification contributes powerfully to intellectual potential quite apart from IQ itself. (Poor impulse control in childhood is also a powerful predictor of later delinquency, again more so than IQ.[10]) As we shall see in Part Five, while some argue that IQ cannot be changed and so represents an unbendable limitation on a child's life potential, there is ample evidence that emotional skills such as impulse control and accurately reading a social situation *can* be learned.

What Walter Mischel, who did the study, describes with the rather infelicitous phrase "goal-directed self-imposed delay of gratification" is perhaps the essence of emotional self-regulation: the ability to deny impulse in the service of a goal, whether it be building a business, solving an algebraic equation, or pursuing the Stanley Cup. His finding underscores the role of emotional intelligence as a meta-ability, determining how well or how poorly people are able to use their other mental capacities.

FOUL MOODS, FOULED THINKING

I worry about my son. He just started playing on the varsity football team, so he's bound to get an injury sometime. It's so nerve-wracking to watch him play that I've stopped going to his games. I'm sure my son must be disappointed that I'm not watching him play, but it's simply too much for me to take.

The speaker is in therapy for anxiety; she realizes that her worry is interfering with leading the kind of life she would like.[11] But when it comes time to make a simple decision, such as whether to watch her son play football, her mind floods with thoughts of disaster. She is not free to choose; her worries overwhelm her reason.

As we have seen, worry is the nub of anxiety's damaging effect on mental performance of all kind. Worry, of course, is in one sense a useful response gone awry—an overly zealous mental preparation for an anticipated threat. But such mental rehearsal is disastrous cognitive static when it becomes trapped in a stale routine that captures attention, intruding on all other attempts to focus elsewhere.

Anxiety undermines the intellect. In a complex, intellectually demanding, and high-pressure task such as that of air traffic controllers, for example, having chronically high anxiety is an almost sure predictor that a person will eventually fail in training or in the field. The anxious are more likely to fail even given superior scores on intelligence tests, as a study of 1,790 students in training for air traffic control posts discovered.[12] Anxiety also sabotages academic performance of all kinds: 126 different studies of more than 36,000 people found that the more prone to worries a person is, the poorer their academic performance, no matter how measured—grades on tests, grade-point average, or achievement tests.[13]

When people who are prone to worry are asked to perform a cognitive task such as sorting ambiguous objects into one of two categories, and narrate what is going through their mind as they do so, it is the negative thoughts—"I won't be able to do this," "I'm just no good at this kind of test," and the like—that are found to most directly disrupt their decision-making. Indeed, when a comparison group of nonworriers was asked to worry on purpose for fifteen minutes, their ability to do the same task deteriorated sharply. And when the worriers were given a fifteen-minute relaxation session—which reduced their level of worrying—before trying the task, they had no problem with it.[14]

Test anxiety was first studied scientifically in the 1960s by Richard Alpert, who confessed to me that his interest was piqued because as a student his nerves often made him do poorly on tests, while his colleague, Ralph Haber, found that the pressure before an exam actually helped him to do better.[15] Their research, among other studies, showed that there are two kinds of anxious students: those whose anxiety undoes their academic performance, and those who are able to do well despite the stress—or, perhaps, because of it.[16] The irony of test anxiety is that the very apprehension about doing well on the test that, ideally, can motivate students like Haber to study hard in preparation and so do well can sabotage success in others. For people who are too anxious, like Alpert, the pretest apprehension interferes with the clear thinking and memory necessary to study effectively, while during the test it disrupts the mental clarity essential for doing well.

The number of worries that people report while taking a test directly predicts how poorly they will do on it.[17] The mental resources expended on one cognitive task—the worrying—simply detract from the resources available for processing other information; if we are preoccupied by worries that we're going to flunk the test we're taking, we have that much less attention to expend on figuring out the answers. Our worries become self-fulfilling prophecies, propelling us toward the very disaster they predict.

People who are adept at harnessing their emotions, on the other hand, can use anticipatory anxiety—about an upcoming speech or test, say—to motivate themselves to prepare well for it, thereby doing well. The classical literature in psychology describes the relationship between anxiety and performance, including mental performance, in terms of an upside-down U. At the peak of the inverted U is the optimal relationship between anxiety and performance, with a modicum of nerves propelling outstanding achievement. But too little anxiety—the first side of the U—brings about apathy or too little motivation to try hard enough to do well, while too much anxiety—the other side of the U—sabotages any attempt to do well.

A mildly elated state—*hypomania,* as it is technically called—seems optimal for writers and others in creative callings that demand fluidity and imaginative diversity of thought; it is somewhere toward the peak of that inverted U. But let that euphoria get out of control to become outright mania, as in the mood swings of manic-depressives, and the agitation undermines the ability to think cohesively enough to write well, even though ideas flow freely—indeed, much too freely to pursue any one of them far enough to produce a finished product.

Good moods, while they last, enhance the ability to think flexibly and with more complexity, thus making it easier to find solutions to problems, whether intellectual or interpersonal. This suggests that one way to help someone think through a problem is to tell them a joke. Laughing, like elation, seems to help people think more broadly and associate more freely, noticing relationships that might have eluded them otherwise—a mental skill important not just in creativity, but in recognizing complex relationships and foreseeing the consequences of a given decision.

The intellectual benefits of a good laugh are most striking when it comes to solving a problem that demands a creative solution. One study found that people who had just watched a video of television bloopers were better at solving a puzzle long used by psychologists to test creative thinking.[18] In the test people are given a candle, matches, and a box of tacks and asked to attach the candle to a corkboard wall so it will burn without dripping wax on the floor. Most people given this problem fall into "functional fixedness," thinking about using the objects in the most conventional ways. But those who had just watched the funny film, compared to others who had watched a film on math or who exercised, were more likely to see an alternative use for the box holding the tacks, and so come up with the creative solution: tack the box to the wall and use it as a candleholder.

Even mild mood changes can sway thinking. In making plans or decisions people in good moods have a perceptual bias that leads them to be more expansive and positive in their thinking. This is partly because memory is state-specific, so that while in a good mood we remember more positive events; as we think over the pros and cons of a course of action while feeling pleasant, memory biases our weighing of evidence in a positive direction, making us more likely to do something slightly adventurous or risky, for example.

By the same token, being in a foul mood biases memory in a negative direction, making us more likely to contract into a fearful, overly cautious decision. Emotions out of control impede the intellect. But, as we saw in Chapter 5, we can bring out-of-control emotions back into line; this emotional competence is the master aptitude, facilitating all other kinds of intelligence. Consider some cases in point: the benefits of hope and optimism, and those soaring moments when people outdo themselves.

PANDORA'S BOX AND POLLYANNA: THE POWER OF POSITIVE THINKING

College students were posed the following hypothetical situation:

> Although you set your goal of getting a B, when your first exam score, worth 30% of your final grade is returned, you have received a D. It is now one week after you have learned about the D grade. What do you do?[19]

Hope made all the difference. The response by students with high levels of hope was to work harder and think of a range of things they might try that could bolster their final grade. Students with moderate levels of hope thought of several ways they might up their grade, but had far less determination to pursue them. And, understandably, students with low levels of hope gave up on both counts, demoralized.

The question is not just theoretical, however. When C. R. Snyder, the University of Kansas psychologist who did this study, compared the actual academic achievement of freshman students high and low on hope, he discovered that hope was a better predictor of their first-semester grades than were their scores on the SAT, a test supposedly able to predict how students will fare in college (and highly correlated with IQ). Again, given roughly the same range of intellectual abilities, emotional aptitudes make the critical difference.

Snyder's explanation: "Students with high hope set themselves higher goals and know how to work hard to attain them. When you compare students of equivalent intellectual aptitude on their academic achievements, what sets them apart is hope."[20]

As the familiar legend has it, Pandora, a princess of ancient Greece, was given a gift, a mysterious box, by gods jealous of her beauty. She was told she must never open the gift. But one day, overcome by curiosity and temptation,

Pandora lifted the lid to peek in, letting loose in the world the grand afflictions—disease, malaise, madness. But a compassionate god let her close the box just in time to capture the one antidote that makes life's misery bearable: hope.

Hope, modern researchers are finding, does more than offer a bit of solace amid affliction; it plays a surprisingly potent role in life, offering an advantage in realms as diverse as school achievement and bearing up in onerous jobs. Hope, in a technical sense, is more than the sunny view that everything will turn out all right. Snyder defines it with more specificity as "believing you have both the will and the way to accomplish your goals, whatever they may be."

People tend to differ in the general degree to which they have hope in this sense. Some typically think of themselves as able to get out of a jam or find ways to solve problems, while others simply do not see themselves as having the energy, ability, or means to accomplish their goals. People with high levels of hope, Snyder finds, share certain traits, among them being able to motivate themselves, feeling resourceful enough to find ways to accomplish their objectives, reassuring themselves when in a tight spot that things will get better, being flexible enough to find different ways to get to their goals or to switch goals if one becomes impossible, and having the sense to break down a formidable task into smaller, manageable pieces.

From the perspective of emotional intelligence, having hope means that one will not give in to overwhelming anxiety, a defeatist attitude, or depression in the face of difficult challenges or setbacks. Indeed, people who are hopeful evidence less depression than others as they maneuver through life in pursuit of their goals, are less anxious in general, and have fewer emotional distresses.

OPTIMISM: THE GREAT MOTIVATOR

Americans who follow swimming had high hopes for Matt Biondi, a member of the U.S. Olympic Team in 1988. Some sportswriters were touting Biondi as likely to match Mark Spitz's 1972 feat of taking seven gold medals. But Biondi finished a heartbreaking third in his first event, the 200-meter freestyle. In his next event, the 100-meter butterfly, Biondi was inched out for the gold by another swimmer who made a greater effort in the last meter.

Sportscasters speculated that the defeats would dispirit Biondi in his successive events. But Biondi rebounded from defeat and took a gold medal in his next five events. One viewer who was not surprised by Biondi's come-back was Martin Seligman, a psychologist at the University of Pennsylvania, who had tested Biondi for optimism earlier that year. In an experiment done with Seligman, the swimming coach told Biondi during a special event meant to showcase Biondi's best performance that he had a worse time than was actually the case. Despite the downbeat feedback, when Biondi was asked to rest and try again, his performance—actually already very good—was even better. But when other team members who were given a false bad time—and whose test scores showed they were pessimistic—tried again, they did even worse the second time.[21]

Optimism, like hope, means having a strong expectation that, in general, things will turn out all right in life, despite setbacks and frustrations. From the standpoint of emotional intelligence, optimism is an attitude that buffers people against falling into apathy, hopelessness, or depression in the face of tough going. And, as with hope, its near cousin, optimism pays dividends in life (providing, of course, it is a realistic optimism; a too-naive optimism can be disastrous).[22]

Seligman defines optimism in terms of how people explain to themselves their successes and failures. People who are optimistic see a failure as due to something that can be changed so that they can succeed next time around, while pessimists take the blame for failure, ascribing it to some lasting characteristic they are helpless to change. These differing explanations have profound implications for how people respond to life. For example, in reaction to a disappointment such as being turned down for a job, optimists tend to respond actively and hopefully, by formulating a plan of action, say, or seeking out help and advice; they see the setback as something that can be remedied. Pessimists, by contrast, react to such setbacks by assuming there is nothing they can do to make things go better the next time, and so do nothing about the problem; they see the setback as due to some personal deficit that will always plague them.

As with hope, optimism predicts academic success. In a study of five hundred members of the incoming freshman class of 1984 at the University of Pennsylvania, the students' scores on a test of optimism were a better predictor of their actual grades freshman year than were their SAT scores or their high-school grades. Said Seligman, who studied them, "College entrance exams measure talent, while explanatory style tells you who gives up. It is the combination of reasonable talent and the ability to keep going in the face of defeat that leads to success. What's missing in tests of ability is motivation. What you need to know about someone is whether they will keep going when things get frustrating. My hunch is that for a given level of intelligence, your actual achievement is a function not just of talent, but also of the capacity to stand defeat."[23]

One of the most telling demonstrations of the power of optimism to motivate people is a study Seligman did of insurance salesmen with the MetLife company. Being able to take a rejection with grace is essential in sales of all kinds, especially with a product like insurance, where the ratio of noes to yeses can be so discouragingly high. For this reason, about three quarters of insurance salesmen quit in their first three years. Seligman found that new salesmen who were by nature optimists sold 37 percent more insurance in their first two years on the job than did pessimists. And during the first year the pessimists quit at twice the rate of the optimists.

What's more, Seligman persuaded MetLife to hire a special group of applicants who scored high on a test for optimism but failed the normal screening tests (which compared a range of their attitudes to a standard profile based on answers from agents who have been successful). This special group outsold the pessimists by 21 percent in their first year, and 57 percent in the second.

Just why optimism makes such a difference in sales success speaks to the sense in which it is an emotionally intelligent attitude. Each no a salesperson gets is a small defeat. The emotional reaction to that defeat is crucial to the ability to marshal enough motivation to continue. As the noes mount up, morale can deteriorate, making it harder and harder to pick up the phone for the next call. Such rejection is especially hard to take for a pessimist, who interprets it as meaning, "I'm a failure at this; I'll never make a sale"—an interpretation that is sure to trigger apathy and defeatism, if not depression. Optimists, on the other hand, tell themselves, "I'm using the wrong approach," or "That last person was just in a bad mood." By seeing not themselves but something in the situation as the reason for their failure, they can change their approach in the next call. While the pessimist's mental set leads to despair, the optimist's spawns hope.

One source of a positive or negative outlook may well be inborn temperament; some people by nature tend one way or the other. But as we shall also see in Chapter 14, temperament can be tempered by experience. Optimism and hope—like helplessness and despair—can be learned. Underlying both is an outlook psychologists call *self-efficacy,* the belief that one has mastery over the events of one's life and can meet challenges as they come up. Developing a competency of any kind strengthens the sense of self-efficacy, making a person more willing to take risks and seek out more demanding challenges. And surmounting those challenges in turn increases the sense of self-efficacy. This attitude makes people more likely to make the best use of whatever skills they may have—or to do what it takes to develop them.

Albert Bandura, a Stanford psychologist who has done much of the research on self-efficacy, sums it up well: "People's beliefs about their abilities have a profound effect on those abilities. Ability is not a fixed property; there is a huge variability in how you perform. People who have a sense of self-efficacy bounce back from failures; they approach things in terms of how to handle them rather than worrying about what can go wrong."[24]

FLOW: THE NEUROBIOLOGY OF EXCELLENCE

A composer describes those moments when his work is at its best:

> You yourself are in an ecstatic state to such a point that you feel as though you almost don't exist. I've experienced this time and again. My hand seems devoid of myself, and I have nothing to do with what is happening. I just sit there watching in a state of awe and wonderment. And it just flows out by itself.[25]

His description is remarkably similar to those of hundreds of diverse men and women—rock climbers, chess champions, surgeons, basketball players, engineers, managers, even filing clerks—when they tell of a time they outdid themselves in some favored activity. The state they describe is called "flow" by Mihaly Csikszentmihalyi, the University of Chicago psychologist who has collected such accounts of peak performance during two decades of research.[26] Athletes know this state of grace as "the zone," where excellence becomes effortless, crowd and competitors disappearing into a blissful, steady absorption in the moment. Diane Roffe-Steinrotter, who captured a gold medal in skiing at the 1994 Winter Olympics, said after she finished her turn at ski racing that she remembered nothing about it but being immersed in relaxation: "I felt like a waterfall."[27]

Being able to enter flow is emotional intelligence at its best; flow represents perhaps the ultimate in harnessing the emotions in the service of performance and learning. In flow the emotions are not just contained and channeled, but positive, energized, and aligned with the task at hand. To be caught in the ennui of depression or the agitation of anxiety is to be barred from flow. Yet flow (or a milder microflow) is an experience almost everyone enters from time to time, particularly when performing at their peak or stretching beyond their former limits. It is perhaps best captured by ecstatic lovemaking, the merging of two into a fluidly harmonious one.

That experience is a glorious one: the hallmark of flow is a feeling of spontaneous joy, even rapture. Because flow feels so good, it is intrinsically rewarding. It is a state in which people become utterly absorbed in what they are doing, paying undivided attention to the task, their awareness merged with their actions. Indeed, it interrupts flow to reflect too much on what is happening—the very thought "I'm doing this wonderfully" can break the feeling of flow. Attention becomes so focused that people are aware only of the narrow range of perception related to the immediate task, losing track of time and space. A surgeon, for example, recalled a challenging operation during which he was in flow; when he completed the surgery he noticed some rubble on the floor of the operating room and asked what had happened. He was amazed to hear that while he was so intent on the surgery part of the ceiling had caved in—he hadn't noticed at all.

Flow is a state of self-forgetfulness, the opposite of rumination and worry: instead of being lost in nervous preoccupation, people in flow are so absorbed in the task at hand that they lose all self-consciousness, dropping the small preoccupations—health, bills, even doing well—of daily life. In this sense moments of flow are egoless. Paradoxically, people in flow exhibit a masterly control of what they are doing, their responses perfectly attuned to the changing demands of the task. And although people perform at their peak while in flow, they are unconcerned with how they are doing, with thoughts of success or failure—the sheer pleasure of the act itself is what motivates them.

There are several ways to enter flow. One is to intentionally focus a sharp attention on the task at hand; a highly concentrated state is the essence of flow. There seems to be a feedback loop at the gateway to this zone: it can require considerable effort to get calm and focused enough to begin the task—this first step takes some discipline. But once focus starts to lock in, it takes on a force of its own, both offering relief from emotional turbulence and making the task effortless.

Entry to this zone can also occur when people find a task they are skilled at, and engage in it at a level that slightly taxes their ability. As Csikszentmihalyi told me, "People seem to concentrate best when the demands on them are a bit greater than usual, and they are able to give more than usual. If there is too little demand on them, people are bored. If there is too much for them to handle, they get anxious. Flow occurs in that delicate zone between boredom and anxiety."[28]

The spontaneous pleasure, grace, and effectiveness that characterize flow are incompatible with emotional hijackings, in which limbic surges capture the rest of the brain. The quality of attention in flow is relaxed yet highly focused. It is a concentration very different from straining to pay attention when we are tired or bored, or when our focus is under siege from intrusive feelings such as anxiety or anger.

Flow is a state devoid of emotional static, save for a compelling, highly motivating feeling of mild ecstasy. That ecstasy seems to be a by-product of the attentional focus that is a prerequisite of flow. Indeed, the classic literature of contemplative traditions describes states of absorption that are experienced as pure bliss: flow induced by nothing more than intense concentration.

Watching someone in flow gives the impression that the difficult is easy; peak performance appears natural and ordinary. This impression parallels what is going on within the brain, where a similar paradox is repeated: the most challenging tasks are done with a minimum expenditure of mental energy. In flow the brain is in a "cool" state, its arousal and inhibition of neural circuitry attuned to the demand of the moment. When people are engaged in activities that effortlessly capture and hold their attention, their brain "quiets down" in the sense that there is a lessening of cortical arousal.[29] That discovery is remarkable, given that flow allows people to tackle the most challenging tasks in a given domain, whether playing against a chess master or solving a complex mathematical problem. The expectation would be that such challenging tasks would require *more* cortical activity, not less. But a key to flow is that it occurs only within reach of the summit of ability, where skills are well-rehearsed and neural circuits are most efficient.

A strained concentration—a focus fueled by worry—produces increased cortical activation. But the zone of flow and optimal performance seems to be an oasis of cortical efficiency, with a bare minimum of mental energy expended. That makes sense, perhaps, in terms of the skilled practice that allows people to get into flow: having mastered the moves of a task, whether a physical one such as rock climbing or a mental one such as computer programming, means that the brain can be more efficient in performing them. Well-practiced moves require much less brain effort than do ones just being learned, or those that are still too hard. Likewise, when the brain is working less efficiently because of fatigue or nervousness, as happens at the end of a long, stressful day, there is a blurring of the precision of cortical effort, with too many superfluous areas being activated—a neural state experienced as being highly distracted.[30] The same happens in boredom. But when the brain is operating at peak efficiency, as in flow, there is a precise relation between the active areas and the demands of the task. In this state even hard work can seem refreshing or replenishing rather than draining.

LEARNING AND FLOW: A NEW MODEL FOR EDUCATION

Because flow emerges in the zone in which an activity challenges people to the fullest of their capacities, as their skills increase it takes a heightened challenge to get into flow. If a task is too simple, it is boring; if too challenging, the result is anxiety rather than flow. It can be argued that mastery in a craft or skill is spurred on by the experience of flow—that the motivation to get better and better at something, be it playing the violin, dancing, or gene-splicing, is at least in part to stay in flow while doing it. Indeed, in a study of two hundred artists eighteen years after they left art school, Csikszentmihalyi found that it was those who in their student days had savored the sheer joy of painting itself who had become serious painters. Those who had been motivated in art school by dreams of fame and wealth for the most part drifted away from art after graduating.

Csikszentmihalyi concludes: "Painters must want to paint above all else. If the artist in front of the canvas begins to wonder how much he will sell it for, or what the critics will think of it, he won't be able to pursue original avenues. Creative achievements depend on single-minded immersion."[31]

Just as flow is a prerequisite for mastery in a craft, profession, or art, so too with learning. Students who get into flow as they study do better, quite apart from their potential as measured by achievement tests. Students in a special Chicago high school for the sciences—all of whom had scored in the top 5 percent on a test of math proficiency—were rated by their math teachers as high or low achievers. Then the way these students spent their time was monitored, each student carrying a beeper that signaled them at random times during the day to write down what they were doing and what their mood was. Not surprisingly, the low achievers spent only about fifteen hours a week studying at home, much less than the twenty-seven hours a week of homework done by their high-achieving peers. The low achievers spent most of the hours during which they were not studying in socializing, hanging out with friends and family.

When their moods were analyzed, a telling finding emerged. Both the high and low achievers spent a great deal of time during the week being bored by activities, such as TV watching, that posed no challenge to their abilities. Such, after all, is the lot of teenagers. But the key difference was in their experience of studying. For the high achievers, studying gave them the pleasing, absorbing challenge of flow 40 percent of the hours they spent at it. But for the low achievers, studying produced flow only 16 percent of the time; more often than not, it yielded anxiety, with the demands outreaching their abilities. The low achievers found pleasure and flow in socializing, not in studying. In short, students who achieve up to the level of their academic potential and beyond are more often drawn to study because it puts them in flow. Sadly, the low achievers, by failing to hone the skills that would get them in flow, both forfeit the enjoyment of study and run the risk of limiting the level of intellectual tasks that will be enjoyable to them in the future.[32]

Howard Gardner, the Harvard psychologist who developed the theory of multiple intelligences, sees flow, and the positive states that typify it, as part of the healthiest way to teach children, motivating them from inside rather than by threat or promise of reward. "We should use kids' positive states to draw them into learning in the domains where they can develop competencies," Gardner proposed to me. "Flow is an internal state that signifies a kid is engaged in a task that's right. You have to find something you like and stick to it. It's when kids get bored in school that they fight and act up, and when they're overwhelmed by a challenge that they get anxious about their schoolwork. But you learn at your best when you have something you care about and you can get pleasure from being engaged in."

The strategy used in many of the schools that are putting Gardner's model of multiple intelligences into practice revolves around identifying a child's profile of natural competencies and playing to the strengths as well as trying to shore up the weaknesses. A child who is naturally talented in music or movement, for example, will enter flow more easily in that domain than in those where she is less able. Knowing a child's profile can help a teacher fine-tune the way a topic is presented to a child and offer lessons at the level—from remedial to highly advanced—that is most likely to provide an optimal challenge. Doing this makes learning more pleasurable, neither fearsome nor a bore. "The hope is that when kids gain flow from learning, they will be emboldened to take on challenges in new areas," says Gardner, adding that experience suggests this is the case.

More generally, the flow model suggests that achieving mastery of any skill or body of knowledge should ideally happen naturally, as the child is drawn to the areas that spontaneously engage her—that, in essence, she loves. That initial passion can be the seed for high levels of attainment, as the child comes to realize that pursuing the field—whether it be dance, math, or music—is a source of the joy of flow. And since it takes pushing the limits of one's ability to sustain flow, that becomes a prime motivator for getting better and better; it makes the child happy. This, of course, is a more positive model of learning and education than most of us encountered in school. Who does not recall school at least in part as endless dreary hours of boredom punctuated by moments of high anxiety? Pursuing flow through learning is a more humane, natural, and very likely more effective way to marshal emotions in the service of education.

That speaks to the more general sense in which channeling emotions toward a productive end is a master aptitude. Whether it be in controlling impulse and putting off gratification, regulating our moods so they facilitate rather than impede thinking, motivating ourselves to persist and try, try again in the face of setbacks, or finding ways to enter flow and so perform more effectively—all bespeak the power of emotion to guide effective effort.

7

The Roots of Empathy

Back to Gary, the brilliant but alexithymic surgeon who so distressed his fiancée, Ellen, by being oblivious not only to his own feelings but to hers as well. Like most alexithymics, he lacked empathy as well as insight. If Ellen spoke of feeling down, Gary failed to sympathize; if she spoke of love, he changed the subject. Gary would make "helpful" critiques of things Ellen did, not realizing these criticisms made her feel attacked, not helped.

Empathy builds on self-awareness; the more open we are to our own emotions, the more skilled we will be in reading feelings.[1] Alexithymics like Gary, who have no idea what they feel themselves, are at a complete loss when it comes to knowing what anyone else around them is feeling. They are emotionally tone-deaf. The emotional notes and chords that weave through people's words and actions—the telling tone of voice or shift in posture, the eloquent silence or telltale tremble—go by unnoted.

Confused about their own feelings, alexithymics are equally bewildered when other people express their feelings to them. This failure to register another's feelings is a major deficit in emotional intelligence, and a tragic failing in what it means to be human. For all rapport, the root of caring, stems from emotional attunement, from the capacity for empathy.

That capacity—the ability to know how another feels—comes into play in a vast array of life arenas, from sales and management to romance and parenting, to compassion and political action. The absence of empathy is also telling. Its lack is seen in criminal psychopaths, rapists, and child molesters.

People's emotions are rarely put into words; far more often they are expressed through other cues. The key to intuiting another's feelings is in the ability to read nonverbal channels: tone of voice, gesture, facial expression, and the like. Perhaps the largest body of research on people's ability to read such nonverbal messages is by Robert Rosenthal, a Harvard psychologist, and his students. Rosenthal devised a test of empathy, the PONS (Profile of Nonverbal Sensitivity), a series of videotapes of a young woman expressing feelings ranging from loathing to motherly love.[2] The scenes span the spectrum from a jealous rage to asking forgiveness, from a show of gratitude to a seduction. The video has been edited so that in each portrayal one or more channels of nonverbal communication are systematically blanked out; in addition to having the words muffled, for example, in some scenes all other cues but the facial expression are blocked. In others, only the body movements are shown, and so on, through the main nonverbal channels of communication, so that viewers have to detect emotion from one or another specific nonverbal cue.

In tests with over seven thousand people in the United States and eighteen other countries, the benefits of being able to read feelings from nonverbal cues included being better adjusted emotionally, more popular, more outgoing, and—perhaps not surprisingly—more sensitive. In general, women are better than men at this kind of empathy. And people whose performance improved over the course of the forty-five-minute test—a sign that they have a talent for picking up empathy skills—also had better relationships with the opposite sex. Empathy, it should be no surprise to learn, helps with romantic life.

In keeping with findings about other elements of emotional intelligence, there was only an incidental relationship between scores on this measure of empathic acuity and SAT or IQ scores or school achievement tests. Empathy's independence from academic intelligence has been found too in testing with a version of the PONS designed for children. In tests with 1,011 children, those who showed an aptitude for reading feelings nonverbally were among the most popular in their schools, the most emotionally stable.[3] They also did better in school, even though, on average, their IQs were not higher than those of children who were less skilled at reading nonverbal messages— suggesting that mastering this empathic ability smooths the way for classroom effectiveness (or simply makes teachers like them more).

Just as the mode of the rational mind is words, the mode of the emotions is nonverbal. Indeed, when a person's words disagree with what is conveyed via his tone of voice, gesture, or other nonverbal channel, the emotional truth is in *how* he says something rather than in *what* he says. One rule of thumb used in communications research is that 90 percent or more of an emotional message is nonverbal. And such messages—anxiety in someone's tone of voice, irritation in the quickness of a gesture—are almost always taken in unconsciously, without paying specific attention to the nature of the message, but simply tacitly receiving it and responding. The skills that allow us to do this well or poorly are also, for the most part, learned tacitly.

HOW EMPATHY UNFOLDS

The moment Hope, just nine months old, saw another baby fall, tears welled up in her own eyes and she crawled off to be comforted by her mother, as though it were she who had been hurt. And fifteen-month-old Michael went to get his own teddy bear for his crying friend Paul; when Paul kept crying, Michael retrieved Paul's security blanket for him. Both these small acts of sympathy and caring were observed by mothers trained to record such incidents of empathy in action.[4] The results of the study suggest that the roots of empathy can be traced to infancy. Virtually from the day they are born infants are upset when they hear another infant crying—a response some see as the earliest precursor of empathy.[5]

Developmental psychologists have found that infants feel sympathetic distress even before they fully realize that they exist apart from other people. Even a few months after birth, infants react to a disturbance in those around them as though it were their own, crying when they see another child's tears. By one year or so, they start to realize the misery is not their own but someone else's, though they still seem confused over what to do about it. In research by Martin L. Hoffman at New York University, for example, a one-year-old brought his own mother over to comfort a crying friend, ignoring the friend's mother, who was also in the room. This confusion is seen too when one-year-olds imitate the distress of someone else, possibly to better comprehend what they are feeling; for example, if another baby hurts her fingers, a one-year-old might put her own fingers in her mouth to see if she hurts, too. On seeing his mother cry, one baby wiped his own eyes, though they had no tears.

Such *motor mimicry,* as it is called, is the original technical sense of the word *empathy* as it was first used in the 1920s by E. B. Titchener, an American psychologist. This sense is slightly different from its original introduction into English from the Greek *empatheia,* "feeling into," a term used initially by theoreticians of aesthetics for the ability to perceive the subjective experience of another person. Titchener's theory was that empathy stemmed from a sort of physical imitation of the distress of another, which then evokes the same feelings in oneself. He sought a word that would be distinct from *sympathy,* which can be felt for the general plight of another with no sharing whatever of what that other person is feeling.

Motor mimicry fades from toddlers' repertoire at around two and a half years, at which point they realize that someone else's pain is different from their own, and are better able to comfort them. A typical incident, from a mother's diary:

> A neighbor's baby cries . . . and Jenny approaches and tries to give him some cookies. She follows him around and begins to whimper to herself. She then tries to stroke his hair, but he pulls away. . . . He calms down, but Jenny still looks worried. She continues to bring him toys and to pat his head and shoulders.[6]

At this point in their development toddlers begin to diverge from one another in their overall sensitivity to other people's emotional upsets, with some, like Jenny, keenly aware and others tuning out. A series of studies by Marian Radke-Yarrow and Carolyn Zahn-Waxler at the National Institute of Mental Health showed that a large part of this difference in empathic concern had to do with how parents disciplined their children. Children, they found, were more empathic when the discipline included calling strong attention to the distress their misbehavior caused someone else: "Look how sad you've made her feel" instead of "That was naughty." They found too that children's empathy is also shaped by seeing how others react when someone else is distressed; by imitating what they see, children develop a repertoire of empathic response, especially in helping other people who are distressed.

THE WELL-ATTUNED CHILD

Sarah was twenty-five when she gave birth to twin boys, Mark and Fred. Mark, she felt, was more like herself; Fred was more like his father. That perception may have been the seed of a telling but subtle difference in how she treated each boy. When the boys were just three months old, Sarah would often try to catch Fred's gaze, and when he would avert his face, she would try to catch his eye again; Fred would respond by turning away more emphatically. Once she would look away, Fred would look back at her, and the cycle of pursuit and aversion would begin again—often leaving Fred in tears. But with Mark, Sarah virtually never tried to impose eye contact as she did with Fred. Instead Mark could break off eye contact whenever he wanted, and she would not pursue.

A small act, but telling. A year later, Fred was noticeably more fearful and dependent than Mark; one way he showed his fearfulness was by breaking off eye contact with other people, as he had done with his mother at three months, turning his face down and away. Mark, on the other hand, looked people straight in the eye; when he wanted to break off contact, he'd turn his head slightly upward and to the side, with a winning smile.

The twins and their mother were observed so minutely when they took part in research by Daniel Stern, a psychiatrist then at Cornell University School of Medicine.[7] Stern is fascinated by the small, repeated exchanges that take place between parent and child; he believes that the most basic lessons of emotional life are laid down in these intimate moments. Of all such moments, the most critical are those that let the child know her emotions are met with empathy, accepted, and reciprocated, in a process Stern calls *attunement*. The twins' mother was attuned with Mark, but out of emotional synch with Fred. Stern contends that the countlessly repeated moments of attunement or misattunement between parent and child shape the emotional expectations adults bring to their close relationships—perhaps far more than the more dramatic events of childhood.

Attunement occurs tacitly, as part of the rhythm of relationship. Stern has studied it with microscopic precision through videotaping hours of mothers with their infants. He finds that through attunement mothers let their infants know they have a sense of what the infant is feeling. A baby squeals with delight, for example, and the mother affirms that delight by giving the baby a gentle shake, cooing, or matching the pitch of her voice to the baby's squeal. Or a baby shakes his rattle, and she gives him a quick shimmy in response. In such an interaction the affirming message is in the mother more or less matching the baby's level of excitement. Such small attunements give an infant the reassuring feeling of being emotionally connected, a message that Stern finds mothers send about once a minute when they interact with their babies.

Attunement is very different from simple imitation. "If you just imitate a baby," Stern told me, "that only shows you know what he did, not how he felt. To let him know you sense how he feels, you have to play back his inner feelings in another way. Then the baby knows he is understood."

Making love is perhaps the closest approximation in adult life to this intimate attunement between infant and mother. Lovemaking, Stern writes, "involves the experience of sensing the other's subjective state: shared desire, aligned intentions, and mutual states of simultaneously shifting arousal," with lovers responding to each other in a synchrony that gives the tacit sense of deep rapport.[8] Lovemaking is, at its best, an act of mutual empathy; at its worst it lacks any such emotional mutuality.

THE COSTS OF MISATTUNEMENT

Stern holds that from repeated attunements an infant begins to develop a sense that other people can and will share in her feelings. This sense seems to emerge at around eight months, when infants begin to realize they are separate from others, and continues to be shaped by intimate relationships throughout life. When parents are misattuned to a child it is deeply upsetting. In one experiment, Stern had mothers deliberately over- or underrespond to their infants, rather than matching them in an attuned way; the infants responded with immediate dismay and distress.

Prolonged absence of attunement between parent and child takes a tremendous emotional toll on the child. When a parent consistently fails to show any empathy with a particular range of emotion in the child—joys, tears, needing to cuddle—the child begins to avoid expressing, and perhaps even feeling, those same emotions. In this way, presumably, entire ranges of emotion can begin to be obliterated from the repertoire for intimate relations, especially if through childhood those feelings continue to be covertly or overtly discouraged.

By the same token, children can come to favor an unfortunate range of emotion, depending on which moods are reciprocated. Even infants "catch" moods: Three-month-old babies of depressed mothers, for example, mirrored their mothers' moods while playing with them, displaying more feelings of anger and sadness, and much less spontaneous curiosity and interest, compared to infants whose mothers were not depressed.[9]

One mother in Stern's study consistently underreacted to her baby's level of activity; eventually her baby learned to be passive. "An infant treated that way learns, when I get excited I can't get my mother to be equally excited, so I may as well not try at all," Stern contends. But there is hope in "reparative" relationships: "Relationships throughout life—with friends or relatives, for example, or in psychotherapy—continually reshape your working model of relationships. An imbalance at one point can be corrected later; it's an ongoing, lifelong process."

Indeed, several theories of psychoanalysis see the therapeutic relationship as providing just such an emotional corrective, a reparative experience of attunement. *Mirroring* is the term used by some psychoanalytic thinkers for the therapist's reflecting back to the client an understanding of his inner state, just as an attuned mother does with her infant. The emotional synchrony is unstated and outside conscious awareness, though a patient may bask in the sense of being deeply acknowledged and understood.

The lifetime emotional costs of lack of attunement in childhood can be great—and not just for the child. A study of criminals who committed the cruelest and most violent crimes found that the one characteristic of their early lives that set them apart from other criminals was that they had been shuttled from foster home to foster home, or raised in orphanages—life histories that suggest emotional neglect and little opportunity for attunement.[10]

While emotional neglect seems to dull empathy, there is a paradoxical result from intense, sustained emotional abuse, including cruel, sadistic threats, humiliations, and plain meanness. Children who endure such abuse can become hyperalert to the emotions of those around them, in what amounts to a post-traumatic vigilance to cues that have signaled threat. Such an obsessive preoccupation with the feelings of others is typical of psychologically abused children who in adulthood suffer the mercurial, intense emotional ups and downs that are sometimes diagnosed as "borderline personality disorder." Many such people are gifted at sensing what others around them are feeling, and it is quite common for them to report having suffered emotional abuse in childhood.[11]

THE NEUROLOGY OF EMPATHY

As is so often the case in neurology, reports of quirky and bizarre cases were among the early clues to the brain basis of empathy. A 1975 report, for instance, reviewed several cases in which patients with certain lesions in the right area of the frontal lobes had a curious deficit: they were unable to understand the emotional message in people's tone of voice, though they were perfectly able to understand their words. A sarcastic "Thanks," a grateful "Thanks," and an angry "Thanks" all had the same neutral meaning for them. By contrast, a 1979 report spoke of patients with injuries in other parts of the right hemisphere who had a very different gap in their emotional perception. These patients were unable to express their own emotions through their tone of voice or by gesture. They knew what they felt, but they simply could not convey it. All these cortical brain regions, the various authors noted, had strong connections to the limbic system.

These studies were reviewed as background to a seminal paper by Leslie

Brothers, a psychiatrist at the California Institute of Technology, on the biology of empathy.[12] Reviewing both neurological findings and comparative studies with animals, Brothers points to the amygdala and its connections to the association area of the visual cortex as part of the key brain circuitry underlying empathy.

Much of the relevant neurological research is from work with animals, especially nonhuman primates. That such primates display empathy—or "emotional communication," as Brothers prefers to say—is clear not just from anecdotal accounts, but also from studies such as the following: Rhesus monkeys were trained first to fear a certain tone by hearing it while they received an electric shock. Then they learned to avoid the electric shock by pushing a lever whenever they heard the tone. Next, pairs of these monkeys were put in separate cages, their only communication being through closed-circuit TV, which allowed them to see pictures of the face of the other monkey. The first monkey, but not the second, then heard the dreaded tone sound, which brought a look of fear to its face. At that moment, the second monkey, seeing fear on the face of the first, pushed the lever that prevented the shock—an act of empathy, if not of altruism.

Having established that nonhuman primates do indeed read emotions from the faces of their peers, researchers gently inserted long, fine-tipped electrodes into the brains of monkeys. These electrodes allowed the recording of activity in a single neuron. Electrodes tapping neurons in the visual cortex and in the amygdala showed that when one monkey saw the face of another, that information led to a neuron firing first in the visual cortex, then in the amygdala. This pathway, of course, is a standard route for information that is emotionally arousing. But what is surprising about results from such studies is that they have also identified neurons in the visual cortex that seem to fire *only* in response to specific facial expressions or gestures, such as a threatening opening of the mouth, a fearful grimace, or a docile crouch. These neurons are distinct from others in the same region that recognize familiar faces. This would seem to mean that the brain is designed from the beginning to respond to specific emotional expressions—that is, empathy is a given of biology.

Another line of evidence for the key role of the amygdala-cortical pathway in reading and responding to emotions, Brothers suggests, is research in which monkeys in the wild had the connections to and from the amygdala and cortex severed. When they were released back to their troops, these monkeys were able to contend with ordinary tasks such as feeding themselves and climbing trees. But the unfortunate monkeys had lost all sense of how to respond emotionally to other monkeys in their band. Even when one made a friendly approach, they would run away, and eventually lived as isolates, shunning contact with their own troop.

The very regions of the cortex where the emotion-specific neurons concentrate are also, Brothers notes, those with the heaviest connection to the amygdala; reading emotion involves the amygdala-cortical circuitry, which has a key role in orchestrating the appropriate responses. "The survival value of such a system is obvious" for nonhuman primates, notes Brothers. "The perception of another individual's approach should give rise to a specific pattern of [physiological response]—and very quickly—tailored to whether the intent is to bite, to have a quiet grooming session, or to copulate."[13]

A similar physiological basis for empathy in us humans is suggested in research by Robert Levenson, a University of California at Berkeley psychologist who has studied married couples trying to guess what their partner is feeling during a heated discussion.[14] His method is simple: the couple is videotaped and their physiological responses measured while talking over some troubling issue in their marriage—how to discipline the kids, spending habits, and the like. Each partner reviews the tape and narrates what he or she was feeling from moment to moment. Then the partner reviews the tape a second time, now trying to read the *other's* feelings.

The most empathic accuracy occurred in those husbands and wives *whose own physiology tracked that of the spouse* they were watching. That is, when their partner had an elevated sweat response, so did they; when their partner had a drop in heart rate, their heart slowed. In short, their body mimicked the subtle, moment-to-moment physical reactions of their spouse. If the viewer's physiological patterns simply repeated their own during the original interaction, they were very poor at surmising what their partner was feeling. Only when their bodies were in synch was there empathy.

This suggests that when the emotional brain is driving the body with a strong reaction—the heat of anger, say—there can be little or no empathy. Empathy requires enough calm and receptivity so that the subtle signals of feeling from another person can be received and mimicked by one's own emotional brain.

EMPATHY AND ETHICS: THE ROOTS OF ALTRUISM

"Never send to know for whom the bell tolls; it tolls for thee" is one of the most famous lines in English literature. John Donne's sentiment speaks to the heart of the link between empathy and caring: another's pain is one's own. To feel with another is to care. In this sense, the opposite of *empathy* is *antipathy*. The empathic attitude is engaged again and again in moral judgments, for moral dilemmas involve potential victims: Should you lie to keep from hurting a friend's feelings? Should you keep a promise to visit a sick friend or accept a last-minute invitation to a dinner party instead? When should a life-support system be kept going for someone who would otherwise die?

These moral questions are posed by the empathy researcher Martin Hoffman, who argues that the roots of morality are to be found in empathy, since it is empathizing with the potential victims—someone in pain, danger, or deprivation, say—and so sharing their distress that moves people to act to help them.[15] Beyond this immediate link between empathy and altruism in personal encounters, Hoffman proposes that the same capacity for empathic affect, for putting oneself in another's place, leads people to follow certain moral principles.

Hoffman sees a natural progression in empathy from infancy onward. As we have seen, at one year of age a child feels in distress herself when she sees another fall and start to cry; her rapport is so strong and immediate that she puts her thumb in her mouth and buries her head in her mother's lap, as if she herself were hurt. After the first year, when infants become more aware that they are distinct from others, they actively try to soothe another crying infant, offering them their teddy bears, for example. As early as the age of two, children begin to realize that someone else's feelings differ from their own, and so they become more sensitive to cues revealing what another actually feels; at this point they might, for example, recognize that another child's pride might mean that the best way to help them deal with their tears is not to call undue attention to them.

By late childhood the most advanced level of empathy emerges, as children are able to understand distress beyond the immediate situation, and to see that someone's condition or station in life may be a source of chronic distress. At this point they can feel for the plight of an entire group, such as the poor, the oppressed, the outcast. That understanding, in adolescence, can buttress moral convictions centered on wanting to alleviate misfortune and injustice.

Empathy underlies many facets of moral judgment and action. One is "empathic anger," which John Stuart Mill described as "the natural feeling of retaliation . . . rendered by intellect and sympathy applicable to . . . those hurts which wound us through wounding others"; Mill dubbed this the "guardian of justice." Another instance in which empathy leads to moral action is when a bystander is moved to intervene on behalf of a victim; the research shows that the more empathy a bystander feels for the victim, the more likely it is that she will intervene. There is some evidence that the level of empathy people feel shades their moral judgments as well. For example, studies in Germany and the United States found that the more empathic people are, the more they favor the moral principle that resources should be allocated according to people's need.[16]

LIFE WITHOUT EMPATHY: THE MIND OF THE MOLESTER, THE MORALS OF THE SOCIOPATH

Eric Eckardt was involved in an infamous crime: the bodyguard of skater Tonya Harding, Eckardt had arranged to have thugs attack Nancy Kerrigan, Harding's archrival for the 1994 women's Olympic figure skating gold medal. In the attack, Kerrigan's knee was battered, sidelining her during crucial training months. But when Eckardt saw the image of a sobbing Kerrigan on television, he had a sudden rush of remorse, and sought out a friend to bare his secret, beginning the sequence that led to the arrest of the attackers. Such is the power of empathy.

But it is typically, and tragically, lacking in those who commit the most mean-spirited of crimes. A psychological fault line is common to rapists, child molesters, and many perpetrators of family violence alike: they are incapable of empathy. This inability to feel their victims' pain allows them to tell themselves lies that encourage their crime. For rapists, the lies include "Women really want to be raped" or "If she resists, she's just playing hard to get"; for molesters, "I'm not hurting the child, just showing love" or "This is just another form of affection"; for physically abusive parents, "This is just good discipline." These self-justifications are all collected from what people being treated for these problems say they have told themselves as they were brutalizing their victims, or preparing to do so.

The blotting out of empathy as these people inflict damage on victims is almost always part of an emotional cycle that precipitates their cruel acts. Witness the emotional sequence that typically leads to a sex crime such as child molestation.[17] The cycle begins with the molester feeling upset: angry, depressed, lonely. These sentiments might be triggered by, say, watching happy couples on TV, and then feeling depressed about being alone. The molester then seeks solace in a favored fantasy, typically about a warm friendship with a child; the fantasy becomes sexual and ends in masturbation. Afterward, the molester feels a temporary relief from the sadness, but the

. lief is short-lived; the depression and loneliness return even more strongly. The molester begins to think about acting out the fantasy, telling himself justifications like "I'm not doing any real harm if the child is not physically hurt" and "If a child really didn't want to have sex with me, she could stop it."

At this point the molester is seeing the child through the lens of the perverted fantasy, not with empathy for what a real child would feel in the situation. That emotional detachment characterizes everything that follows, from the ensuing plan to get a child alone, to the careful rehearsal of what will happen, and then the execution of the plan. All of it is pursued as though the child involved had no feelings of her own; instead the molester projects on her the cooperative attitude of the child in his fantasy. Her feelings— revulsion, fear, disgust—do not register. If they did, it would "ruin" things for the molester.

This utter lack of empathy for their victims is one of the main focuses of new treatments being devised for child molesters and other such offenders. In one of the most promising treatment programs, the offenders read heart-wrenching accounts of crimes like their own, told from the victim's perspective. They also watch videotapes of victims tearfully telling what it was like to be molested. The offenders then write about their own offense from the victim's point of view, imagining what the victim felt. They read this account to a therapy group, and try to answer questions about the assault from the victim's perspective. Finally, the offender goes through a simulated reenactment of the crime, this time playing the role of the victim.

William Pithers, the Vermont prison psychologist who developed this perspective-taking therapy, told me, "Empathy with the victim shifts perception so that the denial of pain, even in one's fantasies, is difficult" and so strengthens the men's motivation to fight their perverse sexual urges. Sex offenders who have been through the program in prison had only half the rate of subsequent offenses after release compared to those who had no such treatment. Without this initial empathy-inspired motivation, none of the rest of treatment will work.

While there may be some small hope for instilling a sense of empathy in offenders such as child molesters, there is much less for another criminal type, the psychopath (more recently called the *sociopath* as a psychiatric diagnosis). Psychopaths are notorious for being both charming and completely without remorse for even the most cruel and heartless acts. Psychopathy, the incapacity to feel empathy or compassion of any sort, or the least twinge of conscience, is one of the more perplexing of emotional defects. The heart of the psychopath's coldness seems to lie in an inability to make anything more than the shallowest of emotional connections. The cruelest of criminals, such as sadistic serial killers who delight in the suffering of their victims before they die, are the epitome of psychopathy.[18]

Psychopaths are also glib liars, willing to say anything to get what they want, and they manipulate their victims' emotions with the same cynicism. Consider the performance of Faro, a seventeen-year-old member of a Los Angeles gang who crippled a mother and her baby in a drive-by shooting, which he described with more pride than remorse. Driving in a car with Leon Bing, who was writing a book about the Los Angeles gangs the Crips and the Bloods, Faro wants to show off. Faro tells Bing he's "gonna look crazy" at the "two dudes" in the next car. As Bing recounts the exchange:

> The driver, sensing that someone is looking at him, glances over at my car. His eyes connect with Faro's, widen for an instant. Then he breaks the contact, looks down, looks away. And there is no mistaking what I saw there in his eyes: It was fear.

Faro demonstrates the look he flashed at the next car for Bing:

> He looks straight at me and everything about his face shifts and changes, as if by some trick of time-lapse photography. It becomes a nightmare face, and it is a scary thing to see. It tells you that if you return his stare, if you challenge this kid, you'd better be able to stand your ground. His look tells you that he doesn't care about anything, not your life and not his.[19]

Of course, in behavior as complex as crime, there are many plausible explanations that do not evoke a biological basis. One might be that a perverse kind of emotional skill—intimidating other people—has survival value in violent neighborhoods, as might turning to crime; in these cases too much empathy might be counterproductive. Indeed, an opportunistic lack of empathy may be a "virtue" in many roles in life, from "bad cop" police interrogator to corporate raider. Men who have been torturers for terrorist states, for example, describe how they learned to dissociate from the feelings of their victims in order to do their "job." There are many routes to manipulativeness.

One of the more ominous ways this absence of empathy may display itself was discovered by accident in a study of the most vicious of wife batterers. The research revealed a physiological anomaly among many of the most violent husbands, who regularly beat up their wives or threaten them with knives or guns: the husbands do so in a cold, calculating state rather than while being carried away by the heat of fury.[20] As their anger mounts, the anomaly emerges: their heart rate *drops,* instead of climbing higher, as is ordinarily the case with mounting fury. This means they are growing physiologically calmer, even as they get more belligerent and abusive. Their violence appears to be a calculated act of terrorism, a method for controlling their wives by instilling fear.

These coolly brutal husbands are a breed apart from most other men who batter their wives. For one, they are far more likely to be violent outside the marriage as well, getting into bar fights and battling with coworkers and other family members. And while most men who become violent with their wives do so impulsively, out of rage after feeling rejected or jealous, or out of fear of abandonment, these calculating batterers will strike out at their wives seemingly for no reason at all—and once they start, nothing she does, including trying to leave, seems to restrain their violence.

Some researchers who study criminal psychopaths suspect their cold manipulativeness, such absence of empathy or caring, can sometimes stem from a neural defect.* A possible physiological basis of heartless psychopathy has been shown in two ways, both of which suggest the involvement of neural pathways to the limbic brain. In one, people's brain waves are measured as they try to decipher words that have been scrambled. The words are flashed very quickly, for just a tenth of a second or so. Most people react differently to emotional words such as *kill* than to neutral words such as *chair:* they can decide more quickly if the emotional word was scrambled, and their brains show a distinctive wave pattern in response to the emotional words, but not the neutral ones. But psychopaths have neither of these responses: their brains do not show the distinctive pattern in response to the emotional words, and they do not respond more quickly to them, suggesting a disruption in circuits between the verbal cortex, which recognizes the word, and the limbic brain, which attaches feeling to it.

---

* A note of caution: If there are biological patterns at play in some kinds of criminality—such as a neural defect in empathy—that does not argue that all criminals are biologically flawed, or that there is some biological marker for crime. A controversy has raged on this issue, and the best consensus is that there is no such biological marker, and certainly no "criminal gene." Even if there is a biological basis for a lack of empathy in some cases, that does not mean all who have it will drift to crime; most will not. A lack of empathy should be factored in with all the other psychological, economic, and social forces that contribute to a vector toward criminality.

Robert Hare, the University of British Columbia psychologist who has done this research, interprets these results as meaning that psychopaths have a shallow understanding of emotional words, a reflection of their more general shallowness in the affective realm. The callousness of psychopaths, Hare believes, is based in part on another physiological pattern he discovered in earlier research, one that also suggests an irregularity in the workings of the amygdala and related circuits: psychopaths about to receive an electrical shock show no sign of the fear response that is normal in people about to experience pain.[21] Because the prospect of pain does not trigger a surge of anxiety, Hare contends that psychopaths lack concern about future punishment for what they do. And because they themselves do not feel fear, they have no empathy—or compassion—for the fear and pain of their victims.

8

The Social Arts

As so often happens to five-year-olds with younger siblings, Len has lost all
patience with Jay, his two-and-a-half-year-old brother, who is making a mess
of the Lego blocks they've been playing with. Carried away by a wave of
rage, Len bites Jay, who breaks into tears. Their mother, hearing Jay's pained
yelp, bustles over and scolds Len, ordering him to put away those objects of
contention, the Lego blocks. At this—what surely must seem a gross miscar-
riage of justice—Len bursts out crying. Still peeved, his mother refuses to
console him.

But Len is proffered comfort from an unlikely source: Jay, who, although
the original injured party, is now so concerned by his older brother's tears
that he undertakes a campaign to calm Len down. The exchange goes
something like this:[1]

"Len, don't," Jay implores. "Stop crying, mate. Stop it crying."

But Len still cries. His direct plea a failure, Jay beseeches their mother on
Len's behalf: "Len crying, Mummy! Len crying. Look. Me show you. Len
crying."

And then, turning to Len, Jay adopts a mothering mode, patting his weep-
ing brother as he reassures him in soothing tones, "Look, Len. No go on
crying."

Len's sobs continue, despite the comforting. So Jay turns to another tactic,
lending a helping hand in putting away the Lego blocks in their bag, with a
friendly, "Ah, Len. I put it back for Lennie, hey?"

Even so, the tears continue. The ever-ingenious Jay tries yet another
strategy, distraction. Showing his brother a toy car, Jay tries to draw his
attention away from the minor tragedy that has just befallen him. "There's this
man in here. What's this, Len? What's this, Len?"

Len takes no interest. He's inconsolable; his tears know no end. Losing her patience with him, his mother resorts to that classic parental threat, "Do you want me to smack you?" to which Len responds with a wavering, "No."

"Then just stop it, please," says his mother firmly, if a bit exasperatedly. Through his sobs, Len manages a pathetic, gasping, "I'm trying to."

Which prompts Jay's final stratagem: borrowing his mother's firmness and voice of authority, he threatens, "Stop crying, Len. Smack your bottom!"

This microdrama reveals the remarkable emotional sophistication that a toddler of just thirty months can bring to bear in trying to manage someone else's emotions. In his urgent attempts to soothe his brother, Jay is able to draw on a large repertoire of tactics, ranging from a simple plea, to seeking an ally in his mother (no help, she), to physically comforting him, to lending a helping hand, to distraction, threats, and direct commands. No doubt Jay relies on an arsenal that has been tried with him in his own moments of distress. No matter. What counts is that he can readily put them to use in a pinch even at this very young age.

Of course, as every parent of young children knows, Jay's display of empathy and soothing is by no means universal. It is perhaps as likely that a child his age will see a sibling's upset as a chance for vengeance, and so do whatever it takes to make the upset even worse. The same skills can be used to tease or torment a sibling. But even that mean-spiritedness bespeaks the emergence of a crucial emotional aptitude: the ability to know another's feelings and to act in a way that further shapes those feelings. Being able to manage emotions in someone else is the core of the art of handling relationships.

To manifest such interpersonal power, toddlers must first reach a benchmark of self-control, the beginnings of the capacity to damp down their own anger and distress, their impulses and excitement—even if that ability usually falters. Attunement to others demands a modicum of calm in oneself. Tentative signs of this ability to manage their own emotions emerge around this same period: toddlers begin to be able to wait without wailing, to argue or cajole to get their way rather than using brute force—even if they don't always choose to use this ability. Patience emerges as an alternative to tantrums, at least occasionally. And signs of empathy emerge by age two; it was Jay's empathy, the root of compassion, that drove him to try so hard to cheer up his sobbing brother, Len. Thus handling emotions in someone else—the fine art of relationships—requires the ripeness of two other emotional skills, self-management and empathy.

With this base, the "people skills" ripen. These are the social competences that make for effectiveness in dealings with others; deficits here lead to ineptness in the social world or repeated interpersonal disasters. Indeed, it is precisely the lack of these skills that can cause even the intellectually brightest to founder in their relationships, coming off as arrogant, obnoxious, or insensitive. These social abilities allow one to shape an encounter, to mobilize and inspire others, to thrive in intimate relationships, to persuade and influence, to put others at ease.

SHOW SOME EMOTION

One key social competence is how well or poorly people express their own feelings. Paul Ekman uses the term *display rules* for the social consensus about which feelings can be properly shown when. Cultures sometimes vary tremendously in this regard. For example, Ekman and colleagues in Japan studied the facial reactions of students to a horrific film about ritual circumcisions of teenage Aborigines. When the Japanese students watched the film with an authority figure present, their faces showed only the slightest hints of reaction. But when they thought they were alone (though they were being taped by a secret camera) their faces twisted into vivid mixes of anguished distress, dread, and disgust.

There are several basic kinds of display rules.[2] One is *minimizing* the show of emotion—this is the Japanese norm for feelings of distress in the presence of someone in authority, which the students were following when they masked their upset with a poker face. Another is *exaggerating* what one feels by magnifying the emotional expression; this is the ploy used by the six-year-old who dramatically twists her face into a pathetic frown, lips quivering, as she runs to complain to her mother about being teased by her older brother. A third is *substituting* one feeling for another; this comes into play in some Asian cultures where it is impolite to say no, and positive (but false) assurances are given instead. How well one employs these strategies, and knows when to do so, is one factor in emotional intelligence.

We learn these display rules very early, partly by explicit instruction. An education in display rules is imparted when we instruct a child not to seem disappointed, but to smile and say thank you instead, when Grandpa has given a dreadful but well-meant birthday present. This education in display rules, though, is more often through modeling: children learn to do what they see done. In educating the sentiments, emotions are both the medium and the message. If a child is told to "smile and say thank you" by a parent who is, at that moment, harsh, demanding, and cold—who hisses the message instead of warmly whispering it—the child is more likely to learn a very different lesson, and in fact respond to Grandpa with a frown and a curt, flat "Thank you." The effect on Grandpa is very different: in the first case he's happy (though misled); in the second he's hurt by the mixed message.

Emotional displays, of course, have immediate consequences in the impact they make on the person who receives them. The rule being learned by the child is something like, "Mask your real feelings when they will hurt someone you love; substitute a phony, but less hurtful feeling instead." Such rules for expressing emotions are more than part of the lexicon of social propriety; they dictate how our own feelings impact on everyone else. To follow these rules well is to have optimal impact; to do so poorly is to foment emotional havoc.

Actors, of course, are artists of the emotional display; their expressiveness is what evokes response in their audience. And, no doubt, some of us come into life as natural actors. But partly because the lessons we learn about display rules vary according to the models we've had, people differ greatly in their adeptness.

EXPRESSIVENESS AND EMOTIONAL CONTAGION

It was early in the Vietnam War, and an American platoon was hunkered down in some rice paddies, in the heat of a firefight with the Vietcong. Suddenly a line of six monks started walking along the elevated berms that separated paddy from paddy. Perfectly calm and poised, the monks walked directly toward the line of fire.

"They didn't look right, they didn't look left. They walked straight through," recalls David Busch, one of the American soldiers. "It was really strange, because nobody shot at 'em. And after they walked over the berm, suddenly all the fight was out of me. It just didn't feel like I wanted to do this anymore, at least not that day. It must have been that way for everybody, because everybody quit. We just stopped fighting."[3]

The power of the monks' quietly courageous calm to pacify soldiers in the heat of battle illustrates a basic principle of social life: Emotions are contagious. To be sure, this tale marks an extreme. Most emotional contagion is far more subtle, part of a tacit exchange that happens in every encounter. We transmit and catch moods from each other in what amounts to a subterranean economy of the psyche in which some encounters are toxic, some nourishing. This emotional exchange is typically at a subtle, almost imperceptible level; the way a salesperson says thank you can leave us feeling ignored, resented, or genuinely welcomed and appreciated. We catch feelings from one another as though they were some kind of social virus.

We send emotional signals in every encounter, and those signals affect those we are with. The more adroit we are socially, the better we control the signals we send; the reserve of polite society is, after all, simply a means to ensure that no disturbing emotional leakage will unsettle the encounter (a social rule that, when brought into the domain of intimate relationships, is stifling). Emotional intelligence includes managing this exchange; "popular" and "charming" are terms we use for people whom we like to be with because their emotional skills make us feel good. People who are able to help others soothe their feelings have an especially valued social commodity; they are the souls others turn to when in greatest emotional need. We are all part of each other's tool kit for emotional change, for better or for worse.

Consider a remarkable demonstration of the subtlety with which emotions pass from one person to another. In a simple experiment two volunteers filled out a checklist about their moods at the moment, then simply sat facing each other quietly while waiting for an experimenter to return to the room. Two minutes later she came back and asked them to fill out a mood checklist again. The pairs were purposely composed of one partner who was highly expressive of emotion and one who was deadpan. Invariably the mood of the one who was more expressive of emotions had been transferred to the more passive partner.[4]

How does this magical transmission occur? The most likely answer is that we unconsciously imitate the emotions we see displayed by someone else, through an out-of-awareness motor mimicry of their facial expression, gestures, tone of voice, and other nonverbal markers of emotion. Through this imitation people re-create in themselves the mood of the other person—a low-key version of the Stanislavsky method, in which actors recall gestures, movements, and other expressions of an emotion they have felt strongly in the past in order to evoke those feelings once again.

The day-to-day imitation of feeling is ordinarily quite subtle. Ulf Dimberg, a Swedish researcher at the University of Uppsala, found that when people view a smiling or angry face, their own faces show evidence of that same mood through slight changes in the facial muscles. The changes are evident through electronic sensors but are typically not visible to the naked eye.

When two people interact, the direction of mood transfer is from the one who is more forceful in expressing feelings to the one who is more passive. But some people are particularly susceptible to emotional contagion; their innate sensitivity makes their autonomic nervous system (a marker of emotional activity) more easily triggered. This lability seems to make them more impressionable; sentimental commercials can move them to tears, while a quick chat with someone who is feeling cheerful can buoy them (it also may make them more empathic, since they are more readily moved by someone else's feelings).

John Cacioppo, the social psychophysiologist at Ohio State University who has studied this subtle emotional exchange, observes, "Just seeing someone express an emotion can evoke that mood, whether you realize you mimic the facial expression or not. This happens to us all the time—there's a dance, a synchrony, a transmission of emotions. This mood synchrony determines whether you feel an interaction went well or not."

The degree of emotional rapport people feel in an encounter is mirrored by how tightly orchestrated their physical movements are as they talk—an index of closeness that is typically out of awareness. One person nods just as the other makes a point, or both shift in their chairs at the same moment, or one leans forward as the other moves back. The orchestration can be as subtle as both people rocking in swivel chairs at the same rhythm. Just as Daniel Stern found in watching the synchrony between attuned mothers and their infants, the same reciprocity links the movements of people who feel emotional rapport.

This synchrony seems to facilitate the sending and receiving of moods, even if the moods are negative. For example, in one study of physical synchrony, women who were depressed came to a laboratory with their romantic partners, and discussed a problem in their relationship. The more synchrony between the partners at the nonverbal level, the worse the depressed women's partners felt after the discussion—they had caught their girlfriends' bad moods.[5] In short, whether people feel upbeat or down, the more physically attuned their encounter, the more similar their moods will become.

The synchrony between teachers and students indicates how much rapport they feel; studies in classrooms show that the closer the movement coordination between teacher and student, the more they felt friendly, happy, enthused, interested, and easygoing while interacting. In general, a high level of synchrony in an interaction means the people involved like each other. Frank Bernieri, the Oregon State University psychologist who did these studies, told me, "How awkward or comfortable you feel with someone is at some level physical. You need to have compatible timing, to coordinate your movements, to feel comfortable. Synchrony reflects the depth of engagement between the partners; if you're highly engaged, your moods begin to mesh, whether positive or negative."

In short, coordination of moods is the essence of rapport, the adult version of the attunement a mother has with her infant. One determinant of interpersonal effectiveness, Cacioppo proposes, is how deftly people carry out this emotional synchrony. If they are adept at attuning to people's moods, or can easily bring others under the sway of their own, then their interactions will go more smoothly at the emotional level. The mark of a powerful leader or performer is being able to move an audience of thousands in this way. By the same token, Cacioppo points out that people who are poor at receiving and sending emotions are prone to problems in their relationships, since people often feel uncomfortable with them, even if they can't articulate just why this is so.

Setting the emotional tone of an interaction is, in a sense, a sign of dominance at a deep and intimate level: it means driving the emotional state of the other person. This power to determine emotion is akin to what is called in biology a *zeitgeber* (literally, "time-grabber"), a process (such as the day-night cycle or the monthly phases of the moon) that entrains biological rhythms. For a couple dancing, the music is a bodily zeitgeber. When it comes to personal encounters, the person who has the more forceful expressivity—or the most power—is typically the one whose emotions entrain the other. Dominant partners talk more, while the subordinate partner watches the other's face more—a setup for the transmission of affect. By the same token, the forcefulness of a good speaker—a politician or an evangelist, say—works to entrain the emotions of the audience.[6] That is what we mean by, "He had them in the palm of his hand." Emotional entrainment is the heart of influence.

THE RUDIMENTS OF SOCIAL INTELLIGENCE

It's recess at a preschool, and a band of boys is running across the grass. Reggie trips, hurts his knee, and starts crying, but the other boys keep right on running—save for Roger, who stops. As Reggie's sobs subside Roger reaches down and rubs his own knee, calling out, "I hurt my knee, too!"

Roger is cited as having exemplary interpersonal intelligence by Thomas Hatch, a colleague of Howard Gardner at Spectrum, the school based on the concept of multiple intelligences.[7] Roger, it seems, is unusually adept at recognizing the feelings of his playmates and making rapid, smooth connections with them. It was only Roger who noticed Reggie's plight and pain, and only Roger who tried to provide some solace, even if all he could offer was rubbing his own knee. This small gesture bespeaks a talent for rapport, an emotional skill essential for the preservation of close relationships, whether in a marriage, a friendship, or a business partnership. Such skills in preschoolers are the buds of talents that ripen through life.

Roger's talent represents one of four separate abilities that Hatch and Gardner identify as components of interpersonal intelligence:

• *Organizing groups*—the essential skill of the leader, this involves initiating and coordinating the efforts of a network of people. This is the talent seen in theater directors or producers, in military officers, and in effective heads of organizations and units of all kinds. On the playground, this is the child who takes the lead in deciding what everyone will play, or becomes team captain.

• *Negotiating solutions*—the talent of the mediator, preventing conflicts or resolving those that flare up. People who have this ability excel in deal-making, in arbitrating or mediating disputes; they might have a career in diplomacy, in arbitration or law, or as middlemen or managers of takeovers. These are the kids who settle arguments on the playing field.

• *Personal connection*—Roger's talent, that of empathy and connecting. This makes it easy to enter into an encounter or to recognize and respond fittingly to people's feelings and concerns—the art of relationship. Such people make good "team players," dependable spouses, good friends or business partners; in the business world they do well as salespeople or managers, or can be excellent teachers. Children like Roger get along well with virtually everyone else, easily enter into playing with them, and are happy doing so. These children tend to be best at reading emotions from facial expressions and are most liked by their classmates.

• *Social analysis*—being able to detect and have insights about people's feelings, motives, and concerns. This knowledge of how others feel can lead to an easy intimacy or sense of rapport. At its best, this ability makes one a competent therapist or counselor—or, if combined with some literary talent, a gifted novelist or dramatist.

Taken together, these skills are the stuff of interpersonal polish, the necessary ingredients for charm, social success, even charisma. Those who are adept in social intelligence can connect with people quite smoothly, be astute in reading their reactions and feelings, lead and organize, and handle the disputes that are bound to flare up in any human activity. They are the natural leaders, the people who can express the unspoken collective sentiment and articulate it so as to guide a group toward its goals. They are the kind of people others like to be with because they are emotionally nourishing—they leave other people in a good mood, and evoke the comment, "What a pleasure to be around someone like that."

These interpersonal abilities build on other emotional intelligences. People who make an excellent social impression, for example, are adept at monitoring their own expression of emotion, are keenly attuned to the ways others are reacting, and so are able to continually fine-tune their social performance, adjusting it to make sure they are having the desired effect. In that sense, they are like skilled actors.

However, if these interpersonal abilities are not balanced by an astute sense of one's own needs and feelings and how to fulfill them, they can lead to a hollow social success—a popularity won at the cost of one's true satisfaction. Such is the argument of Mark Snyder, a University of Minnesota psychologist who has studied people whose social skills make them first-rate social chameleons, champions at making a good impression.[8] Their psychological credo might well be a remark by W. H. Auden, who said that his private image of himself "is very different from the image which I try to create in the minds of others in order that they may love me." That trade-off can be made if social skills outstrip the ability to know and honor one's own feelings: in order to be loved—or at least liked—the social chameleon will seem to be whatever those he is with seem to want. The sign that someone falls into this pattern, Snyder finds, is that they make an excellent impression, yet have few stable or satisfying intimate relationships. A more healthy pattern, of course, is to balance being true to oneself with social skills, using them with integrity.

Social chameleons, though, don't mind in the least saying one thing and doing another, if that will win them social approval. They simply live with the discrepancy between their public face and their private reality. Helena Deutsch, a psychoanalyst, called such people the "as-if personality," shifting personas with remarkable plasticity as they pick up signals from those around them. "For some people," Snyder told me, "the public and private person meshes well, while for others there seems to be only a kaleidoscope of changing appearances. They are like Woody Allen's character Zelig, madly trying to fit in with whomever they are with."

Such people try to scan someone for a hint as to what is wanted from them before they make a response, rather than simply saying what they truly feel. To get along and be liked, they are willing to make people they dislike think they are friendly with them. And they use their social abilities to mold their actions as disparate social situations demand, so that they may act like very different people depending on whom they are with, swinging from bubbly sociability, say, to reserved withdrawal. To be sure, to the extent that these traits lead to effective impression management, they are highly prized in certain professions, notably acting, trial law, sales, diplomacy, and politics.

Another, perhaps more crucial kind of self-monitoring seems to make the difference between those who end up as anchorless social chameleons, trying to impress everyone, and those who can use their social polish more in keeping with their true feelings. That is the capacity to be true, as the saying has it, "to thine own self," which allows acting in accord with one's deepest feelings and values no matter what the social consequences. Such emotional integrity could well lead to, say, deliberately provoking a confrontation in order to cut through duplicity or denial—a clearing of the air that a social chameleon would never attempt.

THE MAKING OF A SOCIAL INCOMPETENT

There was no doubt Cecil was bright; he was a college-trained expert in foreign languages, superb at translating. But there were crucial ways in which he was completely inept. Cecil seemed to lack the simplest social skills. He would muff a casual conversation over coffee, and fumble when having to pass the time of day; in short, he seemed incapable of the most routine social exchange. Because his lack of social grace was most profound when he was around women, Cecil came to therapy wondering if perhaps he had "homosexual tendencies of an underlying nature," as he put it, though he had no such fantasies.

The real problem, Cecil confided to his therapist, was that he feared that nothing he could say would be of any interest to anybody. This underlying fear only compounded a profound paucity of social graces. His nervousness during encounters led him to snicker and laugh at the most awkward moments, even though he failed to laugh when someone said something genuinely funny. Cecil's awkwardness, he confided to his therapist, went back to childhood; all his life he had felt socially at ease only when he was with his older brother, who somehow helped ease things for him. But once he left home, his ineptitude was overwhelming; he was socially paralyzed.

The tale is told by Lakin Phillips, a psychologist at George Washington University, who proposes that Cecil's plight stems from a failure to learn in childhood the most elementary lessons of social interaction:

> What could Cecil have been taught earlier? To speak directly to others when spoken to; to initiate social contact, not always wait for others; to carry on a conversation, not simply fall back on yes or no or other one-word replies; to express gratitude toward others, to let another person walk before one in passing through a door; to wait until one is served something . . . to thank others, to say "please," to share, and all the other elementary interactions we begin to teach children from age 2 onward.[9]

Whether Cecil's deficiency was due to another's failure to teach him such rudiments of social civility or to his own inability to learn is unclear. But whatever its roots, Cecil's story is instructive because it points up the crucial nature of the countless lessons children get in interaction synchrony and the unspoken rules of social harmony. The net effect of failing to follow these rules is to create waves, to make those around us uncomfortable. The function of these rules, of course, is to keep everyone involved in a social exchange at ease; awkwardness spawns anxiety. People who lack these skills are inept not just at social niceties, but at handling the emotions of those they encounter; they inevitably leave disturbance in their wake.

We all have known Cecils, people with an annoying lack of social graces—people who don't seem to know when to end a conversation or phone call and who keep on talking, oblivious to all cues and hints to say good-bye; people whose conversation centers on themselves all the time, without the least interest in anyone else, and who ignore tentative attempts to refocus on another topic; people who intrude or ask "nosy" questions. These derailments of a smooth social trajectory all bespeak a deficit in the rudimentary building blocks of interaction.

Psychologists have coined the term *dyssemia* (from the Greek *dys-* for "difficulty" and *semes* for "signal") for what amounts to a learning disability in the realm of nonverbal messages; about one in ten children has one or more problems in this realm.[10] The problem can be in a poor sense of personal space, so that a child stands too close while talking or spreads their belongings into other people's territory; in interpreting or using body language poorly; in misinterpreting or misusing facial expressions by, say, failing to make eye contact; or in a poor sense of prosody, the emotional quality of speech, so that they talk too shrilly or flatly.

Much research has focused on spotting children who show signs of social deficiency, children whose awkwardness makes them neglected or rejected by their playmates. Apart from children who are spurned because they are bullies, those whom other children avoid are invariably deficient in the rudiments of face-to-face interaction, particularly the unspoken rules that govern encounters. If children do poorly in language, people assume they are not very bright or poorly educated; but when they do poorly in the nonverbal rules of interaction, people—especially playmates—see them as "strange," and avoid them. These are the children who don't know how to join a game gracefully, who touch others in ways that make for discomfort rather than camaraderie—in short, who are "off." They are children who have failed to master the silent language of emotion, and who unwittingly send messages that create uneasiness.

As Stephen Nowicki, an Emory University psychologist who studies children's nonverbal abilities, put it, "Children who can't read or express emotions well constantly feel frustrated. In essence, they don't understand what's going on. This kind of communication is a constant subtext of everything you do; you can't stop showing your facial expression or posture, or hide your tone of voice. If you make mistakes in what emotional messages you send, you constantly experience that people react to you in funny ways—you get rebuffed and don't know why. If you're thinking you're acting happy but actually seem too hyper or angry, you find other kids getting angry at you in turn, and you don't realize why. Such kids end up feeling no sense of control over how other people treat them, that their actions have no impact on what happens to them. It leaves them feeling powerless, depressed, and apathetic."

Apart from becoming social isolates, such children also suffer academically. The classroom, of course, is as much a social situation as an academic one; the socially awkward child is as likely to misread and misrespond to a teacher as to another child. The resulting anxiety and bewilderment can themselves interfere with their ability to learn effectively. Indeed, as tests of children's nonverbal sensitivity have shown, those who misread emotional cues tend to do poorly in school compared to their academic potential as reflected in IQ tests.[11]

"WE HATE YOU": AT THE THRESHOLD

Social ineptitude is perhaps most painful and explicit when it comes to one of the more perilous moments in the life of a young child: being on the edge of a group at play you want to join. It is a moment of peril, one when being liked or hated, belonging or not, is made all too public. For that reason that crucial moment has been the subject of intense scrutiny by students of child development, revealing a stark contrast in approach strategies used by popular children and by social outcasts. The findings highlight just how crucial it is for social competence to notice, interpret, and respond to emotional and interpersonal cues. While it is poignant to see a child hover on the edge of others at play, wanting to join in but being left out, it is a universal predicament. Even the most popular children are sometimes rejected—a study of second and third graders found that 26 percent of the time the most well liked children were rebuffed when they tried to enter a group already at play.

Young children are brutally candid about the emotional judgment implicit in such rejections. Witness the following dialogue from four-year-olds in a preschool.[12] Linda wants to join Barbara, Nancy, and Bill, who are playing with toy animals and building blocks. She watches for a minute, then makes her approach, sitting next to Barbara and starting to play with the animals. Barbara turns to her and says, "You can't play!"

"Yes, I can," Linda counters. "I can have some animals, too."

"No, you can't," Barbara says bluntly. "We don't like you today."

When Bill protests on Linda's behalf, Nancy joins the attack: "We hate her today."

Because of the danger of being told, either explicitly or implicitly, "We hate you," all children are understandably cautious on the threshold of approaching a group. That anxiety, of course, is probably not much different from that felt by a grown-up at a cocktail party with strangers who hangs back from a happily chatting group who seem to be intimate friends. Because this moment at the threshold of a group is so momentous for a child, it is also, as one researcher put it, "highly diagnostic . . . quickly revealing differences in social skillfulness."[13]

Typically, newcomers simply watch for a time, then join in very tentatively at first, being more assertive only in very cautious steps. What matters most for whether a child is accepted or not is how well he or she is able to enter into the group's frame of reference, sensing what kind of play is in flow, what out of place.

The two cardinal sins that almost always lead to rejection are trying to take the lead too soon and being out of synch with the frame of reference. But this is exactly what unpopular children tend to do: they push their way into a group, trying to change the subject too abruptly or too soon, or offering their own opinions, or simply disagreeing with the others right away—all apparent attempts to draw attention to themselves. Paradoxically, this results in their being ignored or rejected. By contrast, popular children spend time observing the group to understand what's going on before entering in, and then do something that shows they accept it; they wait to have their status in the group confirmed before taking initiative in suggesting what the group should do.

Let's return to Roger, the four-year-old whom Thomas Hatch spotted exhibiting a high level of interpersonal intelligence.[14] Roger's tactic for entering a group was first to observe, then to imitate what another child was doing, and finally to talk to the child and fully join the activity—a winning strategy. Roger's skill was shown, for instance, when he and Warren were playing at putting "bombs" (actually pebbles) in their socks. Warren asks Roger if he wants to be in a helicopter or an airplane. Roger asks, before committing himself, "Are you in a helicopter?"

This seemingly innocuous moment reveals sensitivity to others' concerns, and the ability to act on that knowledge in a way that maintains the connection. Hatch comments about Roger, "He 'checks in' with his playmate so that they and their play remain connected. I have watched many other children who simply get in their own helicopters or planes and, literally and figuratively, fly away from each other."

EMOTIONAL BRILLIANCE: A CASE REPORT

If the test of social skill is the ability to calm distressing emotions in others, then handling someone at the peak of rage is perhaps the ultimate measure of mastery. The data on self-regulation of anger and emotional contagion suggest that one effective strategy might be to distract the angry person, empathize with his feelings and perspective, and then draw him into an alternative focus, one that attunes him with a more positive range of feeling—a kind of emotional judo.

Such refined skill in the fine art of emotional influence is perhaps best exemplified by a story told by an old friend, the late Terry Dobson, who in the 1950s was one of the first Americans ever to study the martial art aikido in Japan. One afternoon he was riding home on a suburban Tokyo train when a huge, bellicose, and very drunk and begrimed laborer got on. The man, staggering, began terrorizing the passengers: screaming curses, he took a swing at a woman holding a baby, sending her sprawling in the laps of an elderly couple, who then jumped up and joined a stampede to the other end of the car. The drunk, taking a few other swings (and, in his rage, missing), grabbed the metal pole in the middle of the car with a roar and tried to tear it out of its socket.

At that point Terry, who was in peak physical condition from daily eight-hour aikido workouts, felt called upon to intervene, lest someone get seriously hurt. But he recalled the words of his teacher: "Aikido is the art of reconciliation. Whoever has the mind to fight has broken his connection with the universe. If you try to dominate people you are already defeated. We study how to resolve conflict, not how to start it."

Indeed, Terry had agreed upon beginning lessons with his teacher never to pick a fight, and to use his martial-arts skills only in defense. Now, at last, he saw his chance to test his aikido abilities in real life, in what was clearly a legitimate opportunity. So, as all the other passengers sat frozen in their seats, Terry stood up, slowly and with deliberation.

Seeing him, the drunk roared, "Aha! A foreigner! You need a lesson in Japanese manners!" and began gathering himself to take on Terry.

But just as the drunk was on the verge of making his move, someone gave an earsplitting, oddly joyous shout: "Hey!"

The shout had the cheery tone of someone who has suddenly come upon a fond friend. The drunk, surprised, spun around to see a tiny Japanese man, probably in his seventies, sitting there in a kimono. The old man beamed with delight at the drunk, and beckoned him over with a light wave of his hand and a lilting "C'mere."

The drunk strode over with a belligerent, "Why the hell should I talk to you?" Meanwhile, Terry was ready to fell the drunk in a moment if he made the least violent move.

"What'cha been drinking?" the old man asked, his eyes beaming at the drunken laborer.

"I been drinking sake, and it's none of your business," the drunk bellowed.

"Oh, that's wonderful, absolutely wonderful," the old man replied in a warm tone. "You see, I love sake, too. Every night, me and my wife (she's seventy-six, you know), we warm up a little bottle of sake and take it out into the garden, and we sit on an old wooden bench . . ." He continued on about the persimmon tree in his backyard, the fortunes of his garden, enjoying sake in the evening.

The drunk's face began to soften as he listened to the old man; his fists unclenched. "Yeah . . . I love persimmons, too . . . ," he said, his voice trailing off.

"Yes," the old man replied in a sprightly voice, "and I'm sure you have a wonderful wife."

"No," said the laborer. "My wife died. . . ." Sobbing, he launched into a sad tale of losing his wife, his home, his job, of being ashamed of himself.

Just then the train came to Terry's stop, and as he was getting off he turned to hear the old man invite the drunk to join him and tell him all about it, and to see the drunk sprawl along the seat, his head in the old man's lap.

That is emotional brilliance.

PART THREE

EMOTIONAL INTELLIGENCE APPLIED

9

Intimate Enemies

To love and to work, Sigmund Freud once remarked to his disciple Erik Erikson, are the twin capacities that mark full maturity. If that is the case, then maturity may be an endangered way station in life—and current trends in marriage and divorce make emotional intelligence more crucial than ever.

Consider divorce rates. The rate *per year* of divorces has more or less leveled off. But there is another way of calculating divorce rates, one that suggests a perilous climb: looking at the odds that a given newly married couple will have their marriage *eventually* end in divorce. Although the overall rate of divorce has stopped climbing, the *risk* of divorce has been shifting to newlyweds.

The shift gets clearer in comparing divorce rates for couples wed in a given year. For American marriages that began in 1890, about 10 percent ended in divorce. For those wed in 1920, the rate was about 18 percent; for couples married in 1950, 30 percent. Couples that were newly wed in 1970 had a fifty-fifty chance of splitting up or staying together. And for married couples starting out in 1990, the likelihood that the marriage would end in divorce was projected to be close to a staggering 67 percent![1] If the estimate holds, just three in ten of recent newlyweds can count on staying married to their new partner.

It can be argued that much of this rise is due not so much to a decline in emotional intelligence as to the steady erosion of social pressures—the stigma surrounding divorce, or the economic dependence of wives on their husbands—that used to keep couples together in even the most miserable of matches. But if social pressures are no longer the glue that holds a marriage together, then the emotional forces between wife and husband are that much more crucial if their union is to survive.

These ties between husband and wife—and the emotional fault lines that can break them apart—have been assayed in recent years with a precision never seen before. Perhaps the biggest breakthrough in understanding what holds a marriage together or tears it apart has come from the use of sophisticated physiological measures that allow the moment-to-moment tracking of the emotional nuances of a couple's encounter. Scientists are now able to detect a husband's otherwise invisible adrenaline surges and jumps in blood pressure, and to observe fleeting but telling microemotions as they flit across a wife's face. These physiological measures reveal a hidden biological subtext to a couple's difficulties, a critical level of emotional reality that is typically imperceptible to or disregarded by the couple themselves. These measures lay bare the emotional forces that hold a relationship together or destroy it. The fault lines have their earliest beginnings in the differences between the emotional worlds of girls and boys.

HIS MARRIAGE AND HERS: CHILDHOOD ROOTS

As I was entering a restaurant on a recent evening, a young man stalked out the door, his face set in an expression both stony and sullen. Close on his heels a young woman came running, her fists desperately pummeling his back while she yelled, "Goddamn you! Come back here and be nice to me!" That poignant, impossibly self-contradictory plea aimed at a retreating back epitomizes the pattern most commonly seen in couples whose relationship is distressed: She seeks to engage, he withdraws. Marital therapists have long noted that by the time a couple finds their way to the therapy office they are in this pattern of engage-withdraw, with his complaint about her "unreasonable" demands and outbursts, and her lamenting his indifference to what she is saying.

This marital endgame reflects the fact that there are, in effect, two emotional realities in a couple, his and hers. The roots of these emotional differences, while they may be partly biological, also can be traced back to childhood, and to the separate emotional worlds boys and girls inhabit while growing up. There is a vast amount of research on these separate worlds, their barriers reinforced not just by the different games boys and girls prefer, but by young children's fear of being teased for having a "girlfriend" or "boyfriend."[2] One study of children's friendships found that three-year-olds say about half their friends are of the opposite sex; for five-year-olds it's about 20 percent, and by age seven almost no boys or girls say they have a best friend of the opposite sex.[3] These separate social universes intersect little until teenagers start dating.

Meanwhile, boys and girls are taught very different lessons about handling emotions. Parents, in general, discuss emotions—with the exception of anger—more with their daughters than their sons.[4] Girls are exposed to more information about emotions than are boys: when parents make up stories to tell their preschool children, they use more emotion words when talking to daughters than to sons; when mothers play with their infants, they display a wider range of emotions to daughters than to sons; when mothers talk to daughters about feelings, they discuss in more detail the emotional state itself than they do with their sons—though with the sons they go into more detail about the causes and consequences of emotions like anger (probably as a cautionary tale).

Leslie Brody and Judith Hall, who have summarized the research on differences in emotions between the sexes, propose that because girls develop facility with language more quickly than do boys, this leads them to be more experienced at articulating their feelings and more skilled than boys at using words to explore and substitute for emotional reactions such as physical fights; in contrast, they note, "boys, for whom the verbalization of affects is de-emphasized, may become largely unconscious of their emotional states, both in themselves and in others."[5]

At age ten, roughly the same percent of girls as boys are overtly aggressive, given to open confrontation when angered. But by age thirteen, a telling difference between the sexes emerges: Girls become more adept than boys at artful aggressive tactics like ostracism, vicious gossip, and indirect vendettas. Boys, by and large, simply continue being confrontational when angered, oblivious to these more covert strategies.[6] This is just one of many ways that boys—and later, men—are less sophisticated than the opposite sex in the byways of emotional life.

When girls play together, they do so in small, intimate groups, with an emphasis on minimizing hostility and maximizing cooperation, while boys' games are in larger groups, with an emphasis on competition. One key difference can be seen in what happens when games boys or girls are playing get disrupted by someone getting hurt. If a boy who has gotten hurt gets upset, he is expected to get out of the way and stop crying so the game can go on. If the same happens among a group of girls who are playing, the *game stops* while everyone gathers around to help the girl who is crying. This difference between boys and girls at play epitomizes what Harvard's Carol Gilligan points to as a key disparity between the sexes: boys take pride in a lone, tough-minded independence and autonomy, while girls see themselves as part of a web of connectedness. Thus boys are threatened by anything that might challenge their independence, while girls are more threatened by a rupture in their relationships. And, as Deborah Tannen has pointed out in her book *You Just Don't Understand,* these differing perspectives mean that men and women want and expect very different things out of a conversation, with men content to talk about "things," while women seek emotional connection.

In short, these contrasts in schooling in the emotions foster very different skills, with girls becoming "adept at reading both verbal and nonverbal emotional signals, at expressing and communicating their feelings," and boys becoming adept at "minimizing emotions having to do with vulnerability, guilt, fear and hurt".[7] Evidence for these different stances is very strong in the scientific literature. Hundreds of studies have found, for example, that on average women are more empathic than men, at least as measured by the ability to read someone else's unstated feelings from facial expression, tone of voice, and other nonverbal cues. Likewise, it is generally easier to read feelings from a woman's face than a man's; while there is no difference in facial expressiveness among very young boys and girls, as they go through the elementary-school grades boys become less expressive, girls more so. This may partly reflect another key difference: women, on average, experience the entire range of emotions with greater intensity and more volatility than men—in this sense, women *are* more "emotional" than men.[8]

All of this means that, in general, women come into a marriage groomed for the role of emotional manager, while men arrive with much less appreciation of the importance of this task for helping a relationship survive. Indeed, the most important element for women—but not for men—in satisfaction with their relationship reported in a study of 264 couples was the sense that the couple has "good communication."[9] Ted Huston, a psychologist at the University of Texas who has studied couples in depth, observes, "For the wives, intimacy means talking things over, especially talking about the relationship itself. The men, by and large, don't understand what the wives want from them. They say, 'I want to do things with her, and all she wants to do is talk.' " During courtship, Huston found, men were much more willing to spend time talking in ways that suited the wish for intimacy of their wives-to-be. But once married, as time went on the men—especially in more traditional couples—spent less and less time talking in this way with their wives, finding a sense of closeness simply in doing things like gardening together rather than talking things over.

This growing silence on the part of husbands may be partly due to the fact that, if anything, men are a bit Pollyannaish about the state of their marriage, while their wives are attuned to the trouble spots: in one study of marriages, men had a rosier view than their wives of just about everything in their relationship—lovemaking, finances, ties with in-laws, how well they listened to each other, how much their flaws mattered.[10] Wives, in general, are more vocal about their complaints than are their husbands, particularly among unhappy couples. Combine men's rosy view of marriage with their aversion to emotional confrontations, and it is clear why wives so often complain that their husbands try to wiggle out of discussing the troubling things about their relationship. (Of course this gender difference is a generalization, and is not true in every case; a psychiatrist friend complained that in his marriage his wife is reluctant to discuss emotional matters between them, and he is the one who is left to bring them up.)

The slowness of men to bring up problems in a relationship is no doubt compounded by their relative lack of skill when it comes to reading facial expressions of emotions. Women, for example, are more sensitive to a sad expression on a man's face than are men in detecting sadness from a woman's expression.[11] Thus a woman has to be all the sadder for a man to notice her feelings in the first place, let alone for him to raise the question of what is making her so sad.

Consider the implications of this emotional gender gap for how couples handle the grievances and disagreements that any intimate relationship inevitably spawns. In fact, specific issues such as how often a couple has sex, how to discipline the children, or how much debt and savings a couple feels comfortable with are not what make or break a marriage. Rather, it is *how* a couple discusses such sore points that matters more for the fate of their marriage. Simply having reached an agreement about *how* to disagree is key to marital survival; men and women have to overcome the innate gender differences in approaching rocky emotions. Failing this, couples are vulnerable to emotional rifts that eventually can tear their relationship apart. As we shall see, these rifts are far more likely to develop if one or both partners have certain deficits in emotional intelligence.

MARITAL FAULT LINES

Fred: Did you pick up my dry cleaning?

Ingrid: (In a mocking tone) "Did you pick up my dry cleaning." Pick up your own damn dry cleaning. What am I, your maid?

Fred: Hardly. If you were a maid, at least you'd know how to clean.

If this were dialogue from a sitcom, it might be amusing. But this painfully caustic interchange was between a couple who (perhaps not surprisingly) divorced within the next few years.[12] Their encounter took place in a laboratory run by John Gottman, a University of Washington psychologist who has done perhaps the most detailed analysis ever of the emotional glue that binds couples together and the corrosive feelings that can destroy marriages.[13] In his laboratory, couples' conversations are videotaped and then subjected to hours of microanalysis designed to reveal the subterranean emotional currents at play. This mapping of the fault lines that may lead a couple to divorce makes a convincing case for the crucial role of emotional intelligence in the survival of a marriage.

During the last two decades Gottman has tracked the ups and downs of more than two hundred couples, some just newlyweds, others married for decades. Gottman has charted the emotional ecology of marriage with such precision that, in one study, he was able to predict which couples seen in his lab (like Fred and Ingrid, whose discussion of getting the dry cleaning was so acrimonious) would divorce within three years with *94 percent accuracy,* a precision unheard of in marital studies!

The power of Gottman's analysis comes from his painstaking method and the thoroughness of his probes. While the couples talk, sensors record the slightest flux in their physiology; a second-by-second analysis of their facial expressions (using the system for reading emotions developed by Paul Ekman) detects the most fleeting and subtle nuance of feeling. After their session, each partner comes separately to the lab and watches a videotape of the conversation, and narrates his or her secret thoughts during the heated moments of the exchange. The result is akin to an emotional X-ray of the marriage.

An early warning signal that a marriage is in danger, Gottman finds, is harsh criticism. In a healthy marriage husband and wife feel free to voice a complaint. But too often in the heat of anger complaints are expressed in a destructive fashion, as an attack on the spouse's character. For example, Pamela and her daughter went shoe shopping while her husband, Tom, went to a bookstore. They agreed to meet in front of the post office in an hour, and then go to a matinee. Pamela was prompt, but there was no sign of Tom. "Where is he? The movie starts in ten minutes," Pamela complained to her daughter. "If there's a way for your father to screw something up, he will."

When Tom showed up ten minutes later, happy about having run into a friend and apologizing for being late, Pamela lashed out with sarcasm:

"That's okay—it gave us a chance to discuss your amazing ability to screw up every single plan we make. You're so thoughtless and self-centered!"

Pamela's complaint is more than that: it is a character assassination, a critique of the person, not the deed. In fact, Tom had apologized. But for this lapse Pamela brands him as "thoughtless and self-centered." Most couples have moments like this from time to time, where a complaint about something a partner has done is voiced as an attack against the person rather than the deed. But these harsh personal criticisms have a far more corrosive emotional impact than do more reasoned complaints. And such attacks, perhaps understandably, become more likely the more a husband or wife feels their complaints go unheard or ignored.

The differences between complaints and personal criticisms are simple. In a complaint, a wife states specifically what is upsetting her, and criticizes her husband's *action,* not her husband, saying how it made her feel: "When you forgot to pick up my clothes at the cleaner's it made me feel like you don't care about me." It is an expression of basic emotional intelligence: assertive, not belligerent or passive. But in a personal criticism she uses the specific grievance to launch a global attack on her husband: "You're always so selfish and uncaring. It just proves I can't trust you to do anything right." This kind of criticism leaves the person on the receiving end feeling ashamed, disliked, blamed, and defective—all of which are more likely to lead to a defensive response than to steps to improve things.

All the more so when the criticism comes laden with contempt, a particularly destructive emotion. Contempt comes easily with anger; it is usually expressed not just in the words used, but also in a tone of voice and an angry expression. Its most obvious form, of course, is mockery or insult—"jerk," "bitch," "wimp." But just as hurtful is the body language that conveys contempt, particularly the sneer or curled lip that are the universal facial signals for disgust, or a rolling of the eyes, as if to say, "Oh, brother!"

Contempt's facial signature is a contraction of the "dimpler," the muscle that pulls the corners of the mouth to the side (usually the left) while the eyes roll upward. When one spouse flashes this expression, the other, in a tacit emotional exchange, registers a jump in heart rate of two or three beats per minute. This hidden conversation takes its toll; if a husband shows contempt regularly, Gottman found, his wife will be more prone to a range of health problems, from frequent colds and flus to bladder and yeast infections, as well as gastrointestinal symptoms. And when a wife's face shows disgust, a near cousin of contempt, four or more times within a fifteen-minute conversation, it is a silent sign that the couple is likely to separate within four years.

Of course, an occasional show of contempt or disgust will not undo a marriage. Rather, such emotional volleys are akin to smoking and high cholesterol as risk factors for heart disease—the more intense and prolonged, the greater the danger. On the road to divorce, one of these factors predicts the next, in an escalating scale of misery. Habitual criticism and contempt or disgust are danger signs because they indicate that a husband or wife has made a silent judgment for the worse about their partner. In his or her thoughts, the spouse is the subject of constant condemnation. Such negative and hostile thinking leads naturally to attacks that make the partner on the receiving end defensive—or ready to counterattack in return.

The two arms of the fight-or-flight response each represent ways a spouse can respond to an attack. The most obvious is to fight back, lashing out in anger. That route typically ends in a fruitless shouting match. But the alternative response, fleeing, can be more pernicious, particularly when the "flight" is a retreat into stony silence.

Stonewalling is the ultimate defense. The stonewaller just goes blank, in effect withdrawing from the conversation by responding with a stony expression and silence. Stonewalling sends a powerful, unnerving message, something like a combination of icy distance, superiority, and distaste. Stonewalling showed up mainly in marriages that were heading for trouble; in 85 percent of these cases it was the husband who stonewalled in response to a wife who attacked with criticism and contempt.[14] As a habitual response stonewalling is devastating to the health of a relationship: it cuts off all possibility of working out disagreements.

TOXIC THOUGHTS

The children are being rambunctious, and Martin, their father, is getting annoyed. He turns to his wife, Melanie, and says in a sharp tone, "Dear, don't you think the kids could quiet down?"

His actual thought: "She's too easy on the kids."

Melanie, responding to his ire, feels a surge of anger. Her face grows taut, her brows knit in a frown, and she replies, "The kids are having a good time. Anyhow, they'll be going up to bed soon."

Her thought: "There he goes again, complaining all the time."

Martin now is visibly enraged. He leans forward menacingly, his fists clenched, as he says in an annoyed tone, "Should I put them to bed now?"

His thought: "She opposes me in everything. I'd better take over."

Melanie, suddenly frightened by Martin's wrath, says meekly, "No, I'll put them to bed right away."

Her thought: "He's getting out of control—he could hurt the kids. I'd better give in."

These parallel conversations—the spoken and the silent—are reported by Aaron Beck, the founder of cognitive therapy, as an example of the kinds of thinking that can poison a marriage.[15] The real emotional exchange between Melanie and Martin is shaped by their thoughts, and those thoughts, in turn, are determined by another, deeper layer, which Beck calls "automatic thoughts"—fleeting, background assumptions about oneself and the people in one's life that reflect our deepest emotional attitudes. For Melanie the background thought is something like, "He's always bullying me with his anger." For Martin, the key thought is, "She has no right to treat me like this." Melanie feels like an innocent victim in their marriage, and Martin feels righteous indignation at what he feels is unjust treatment.

Thoughts of being an innocent victim or of righteous indignation are typical of partners in troubled marriages, continually fueling anger and hurt.[16] Once distressing thoughts such as righteous indignation become automatic, they are self-confirming: the partner who feels victimized is constantly scanning everything his partner does that might confirm the view that she is victimizing him, ignoring or discounting any acts of kindness on her part that would question or disconfirm that view.

These thoughts are powerful; they trip the neural alarm system. Once the husband's thought of being victimized triggers an emotional hijacking, he will for the time being easily call to mind and ruminate on a list of grievances that remind him of the ways she victimizes him, while not recalling anything she may have done in their entire relationship that would disconfirm the view that he is an innocent victim. It puts his spouse in a no-win situation: even things she does that are intentionally kind can be reinterpreted when viewed through such a negative lens and dismissed as feeble attempts to deny she is a victimizer.

Partners who are free of such distress-triggering views can entertain a more benign interpretation of what is going on in the same situations, and so are less likely to have such a hijacking, or if they do, tend to recover from it more readily. The general template for thoughts that maintain or alleviate distress follows the pattern outlined in Chapter 6 by psychologist Martin Seligman for pessimistic and optimistic outlooks. The pessimistic view is that the partner is inherently flawed in a way that cannot change and that guarantees misery:

"He's selfish and self-absorbed; that's the way he was brought up and that's the way he will always be; he expects me to wait on him hand and foot and he couldn't care less about how I feel." The contrasting optimistic view would be something like: "He's being demanding now, but he's been thoughtful in the past; maybe he's in a bad mood—I wonder if something's bothering him about his work." This is a view that does not write off the husband (or the marriage) as irredeemably damaged and hopeless. Instead it sees a bad moment as due to circumstances that can change. The first attitude brings continual distress; the second soothes.

Partners who take the pessimistic stance are extremely prone to emotional hijackings; they get angry, hurt, or otherwise distressed by things their spouses do, and they stay disturbed once the episode begins. Their internal distress and pessimistic attitude, of course, makes it far more likely they will resort to criticism and contempt in confronting the partner, which in turn heightens the likelihood of defensiveness and stonewalling.

Perhaps the most virulent of such toxic thoughts are found in husbands who are physically violent to their wives. A study of violent husbands by psychologists at Indiana University found that these men think like schoolyard bullies: they read hostile intent into even neutral actions by their wives, and use this misreading to justify to themselves their own violence (men who are sexually aggressive with dates do something similar, viewing the women with suspicion and so disregarding their objections).[17] As we saw in Chapter 7, such men are particularly threatened by perceived slights, rejection, or public embarrassment by their wives. A typical scenario that triggers thoughts "justifying" violence in wife-batterers: "You are at a social gathering and you notice that for the past half hour your wife has been talking and laughing with the same attractive man. He seems to be flirting with her." When these men perceive their wives as doing something suggesting rejection or abandonment, their reactions run to indignation and outrage. Presumably, automatic thoughts like "She's going to leave me" are triggers for an emotional hijacking in which battering husbands respond impulsively, as the researchers put it, with "incompetent behavioral responses"—they become violent.[18]

FLOODING: THE SWAMPING OF A MARRIAGE

The net effect of these distressing attitudes is to create incessant crisis, since they trigger emotional hijackings more often and make it harder to recover from the resulting hurt and rage. Gottman uses the apt term *flooding* for this susceptibility to frequent emotional distress; flooded husbands or wives are so overwhelmed by their partner's negativity and their own reaction to it that they are swamped by dreadful, out-of-control feelings. People who are flooded cannot hear without distortion or respond with clear-headedness; they find it hard to organize their thinking, and they fall back on primitive reactions. They just want things to stop, or want to run or, sometimes, to strike back. Flooding is a self-perpetuating emotional hijacking.

Some people have high thresholds for flooding, easily enduring anger and contempt, while others may be triggered the moment their spouse makes a mild criticism. The technical description of flooding is in terms of heart rate rise from calm levels.[19] At rest, women's heart rates are about 82 beats per minute, men's about 72 (the specific heart rate varies mainly according to a person's body size). Flooding begins at about 10 beats per minute above a person's resting rate; if the heart rate reaches 100 beats per minute (as it easily can do during moments of rage or tears), then the body is pumping adrenaline and other hormones that keep the distress high for some time. The moment of emotional hijacking is apparent from the heart rate: it can jump 10, 20, or even as many as 30 beats per minute within the space of a single heartbeat. Muscles tense; it can seem hard to breathe. There is a swamp of toxic feelings, an unpleasant wash of fear and anger that seems inescapable and, subjectively, takes "forever" to get over. At this point—full hijacking—a person's emotions are so intense, their perspective so narrow, and their thinking so confused that there is no hope of taking the other's viewpoint or settling things in a reasonable way.

Of course, most husbands and wives have such intense moments from time to time when they fight—it's only natural. The problem for a marriage begins when one or another spouse feels flooded almost continually. Then the partner feels overwhelmed by the other partner, is always on guard for an emotional assault or injustice, becomes hypervigilant for any sign of attack, insult, or grievance, and is sure to overreact to even the least sign. If a husband is in such a state, his wife saying, "Honey, we've got to talk," can elicit the reactive thought, "She's picking a fight again," and so trigger flooding. It becomes harder and harder to recover from the physiological arousal, which in turn makes it easier for innocuous exchanges to be seen in a sinister light, triggering flooding all over again.

This is perhaps the most dangerous turning point for marriage, a catastrophic shift in the relationship. The flooded partner has come to think the worst of the spouse virtually all the time, reading everything she does in a negative light. Small issues become major battles; feelings are hurt continually. With time, the partner who is being flooded starts to see any and all problems in the marriage as severe and impossible to fix, since the flooding itself sabotages any attempt to work things out. As this continues it begins to seem useless to talk things over, and the partners try to soothe their troubled feelings on their own. They start leading parallel lives, essentially living in isolation from each other, and feel alone within the marriage. All too often, Gottman finds, the next step is divorce.

In this trajectory toward divorce the tragic consequences of deficits in emotional competences are self-evident. As a couple gets caught in the reverberating cycle of criticism and contempt, defensiveness and stonewalling, distressing thoughts and emotional flooding, the cycle itself reflects a disintegration of emotional self-awareness and self-control, of empathy and the abilities to soothe each other and oneself.

MEN: THE VULNERABLE SEX

Back to gender differences in emotional life, which prove to be a hidden spur to marital meltdowns. Consider this finding: Even after thirty-five or more years of marriage, there is a basic distinction between husbands and wives in how they regard emotional encounters. Women, on average, do not mind plunging into the unpleasantness of a marital squabble nearly so much as do the men in their lives. That conclusion, reached in a study by Robert Levenson at the University of California at Berkeley, is based on the testimony of 151 couples, all in long-lasting marriages. Levenson found that husbands uniformly found it unpleasant, even aversive, to become upset during a marital disagreement, while their wives did not mind it much.[20]

Husbands are prone to flooding at a lower intensity of negativity than are their wives; more men than women react to their spouse's criticism with flooding. Once flooded, husbands secrete more adrenaline into their bloodstream, and the adrenaline flow is triggered by lower levels of negativity on their wife's part; it takes husbands longer to recover physiologically from flooding.[21] This suggests the possibility that the stoic, Clint Eastwood type of male imperturbability may represent a defense against feeling emotionally overwhelmed.

The reason men are so likely to stonewall, Gottman proposes, is to protect themselves from flooding; his research showed that once they began stonewalling, their heart rates dropped by about ten beats per minute, bringing a subjective sense of relief. But—and here's a paradox—once the men started stonewalling, it was the wives whose heart rate shot up to levels signaling high distress. This limbic tango, with each sex seeking comfort in opposing gambits, leads to a very different stance toward emotional confrontations: men want to avoid them as fervently as their wives feel compelled to seek them.

Just as men are far more likely to be stonewallers, so the women are more likely to criticize their husbands.[22] This asymmetry arises as a result of wives pursuing their role as emotional managers. As they try to bring up and resolve disagreements and grievances, their husbands are more reluctant to engage in what are bound to be heated discussions. As the wife sees her husband withdraw from engagement, she ups the volume and intensity of her complaint, starting to criticize him. As he becomes defensive or stonewalls in return, she feels frustrated and angry, and so adds contempt to underscore the strength of her frustration. As her husband finds himself the object of his wife's criticism and contempt, he begins to fall into the innocent-victim or righteous-indignation thoughts that more and more easily trigger flooding. To protect himself from flooding, he becomes more and more defensive or simply stonewalls altogether. But when husbands stonewall, remember, it triggers flooding in their wives, who feel completely stymied. And as the cycle of marital fights escalates it all too easily can spin out of control.

HIS AND HERS: MARITAL ADVICE

Given the grim potential outcome of the differences in how men and women deal with distressing feelings in their relationship, what can couples do to protect the love and affection they feel for each other—in short, what protects a marriage? On the basis of watching interaction in the couples whose marriages have continued to thrive over the years, marital researchers offer specific advice for men and for women, and some general words for both.

Men and women, in general, need different emotional fine-tuning. For men, the advice is not to sidestep conflict, but to realize that when their wife brings up some grievance or disagreement, she may be doing it as an act of love, trying to keep the relationship healthy and on course (although there may well be other motives for a wife's hostility). When grievances simmer, they build and build in intensity until there's an explosion; when they are aired and worked out, it takes the pressure off. But husbands need to realize that anger or discontent is not synonymous with personal attack—their wives' emotions are often simply underliners, emphasizing the strength of her feelings about the matter.

Men also need to be on guard against short-circuiting the discussion by offering a practical solution too early on—it's typically more important to a wife that she feel her husband hears her complaint and empathizes with her *feelings* about the matter (though he need not agree with her). She may hear his offering advice as a way of dismissing her feelings as inconsequential. Husbands who are able to stay with their wives through the heat of anger, rather than dismissing their complaints as petty, help their wives feel heard and respected. Most especially, wives want to have their feelings acknowledged and respected as valid, even if their husbands disagree. More often than not, when a wife feels her view is heard and her feelings registered, she calms down.

As for women, the advice is quite parallel. Since a major problem for men is that their wives are too intense in voicing complaints, wives need to make a purposeful effort to be careful not to attack their husbands—to complain about what they did, but not criticize them as a person or express contempt. Complaints are not attacks on character, but rather a clear statement that a particular action is distressing. An angry personal attack will almost certainly lead to a husband's getting defensive or stonewalling, which will be all the more frustrating, and only escalate the fight. It helps, too, if a wife's complaints are put in the larger context of reassuring her husband of her love for him.

THE GOOD FIGHT

The morning paper offers an object lesson in how not to resolve differences in a marriage. Marlene Lenick had a dispute with her husband, Michael: he wanted to watch the Dallas Cowboys–Philadelphia Eagles game, she wanted to watch the news. As he settled down to watch the game, Mrs. Lenick told him that she had "had enough of that football," went into the bedroom to fetch a .38 caliber handgun, and shot him twice as he sat watching the game in the den. Mrs. Lenick was charged with aggravated assault and freed on a $50,000 bond; Mr. Lenick was listed in good condition, recovering from the bullets that grazed his abdomen and tunneled through his left shoulder blade and neck.[23]

While few marital fights are that violent—or that costly—they offer a prime chance to bring emotional intelligence to marriage. For example, couples in marriages that last tend to stick to one topic, and to give each partner the chance to state their point of view at the outset.[24] But these couples go one important step further: they show each other that they are being listened to. Since feeling heard is often exactly what the aggrieved partner really is after, emotionally an act of empathy is a masterly tension reducer.

Most notably missing in couples who eventually divorce are attempts by either partner in an argument to de-escalate the tension. The presence or absence of ways to repair a rift is a crucial difference between the fights of couples who have a healthy marriage and those of couples who eventually end up divorcing.[25] The repair mechanisms that keep an argument from escalating into a dire explosion are simple moves such as keeping the discussion on track, empathizing, and tension reduction. These basic moves are like an emotional thermostat, preventing the feelings being expressed from boiling over and overwhelming the partners' ability to focus on the issue at hand.

One overall strategy for making a marriage work is not to concentrate on the specific issues—childrearing, sex, money, housework—that couples fight about, but rather to cultivate a couple's shared emotional intelligence, thereby improving the chances of working things out. A handful of emotional competences—mainly being able to calm down (and calm your partner), empathy, and listening well—can make it more likely a couple will settle their disagreements effectively. These make possible healthy disagreements, the "good fights" that allow a marriage to flourish and which overcome the negativities that, if left to grow, can destroy a marriage.[26]

Of course, none of these emotional habits changes overnight; it takes persistence and vigilance at the very least. Couples will be able to make the key changes in direct proportion to how motivated they are to try. Many or most emotional responses triggered so easily in marriage have been sculpted since childhood, first learned in our most intimate relationships or modeled for us by our parents, and then brought to marriage fully formed. And so we are primed for certain emotional habits—overreacting to perceived slights, say, or shutting down at the first sign of a confrontation—even though we may have sworn that we would not act like our parents.

Calming Down

Every strong emotion has at its root an impulse to action; managing those impulses is basic to emotional intelligence. This can be particularly difficult, though, in love relationships, where we have so much at stake. The reactions triggered here touch on some of our deepest needs—to be loved and feel respected, fears of abandonment or of being emotionally deprived. Small wonder we can act in a marital fight as though our very survival were at stake.

Even so, nothing gets resolved positively when husband or wife is in the midst of an emotional hijacking. One key marital competence is for partners to learn to soothe their own distressed feelings. Essentially, this means mastering the ability to recover quickly from the flooding caused by an emotional hijacking. Because the ability to hear, think, and speak with clarity dissolves during such an emotional peak, calming down is an immensely constructive step, without which there can be no further progress in settling what's at issue.

Ambitious couples can learn to monitor their pulse rates every five minutes or so during a troubling encounter, feeling the pulse at the carotid artery a few inches below the earlobe and jaw (people who do aerobic workouts learn to do this easily).[27] Counting the pulse for fifteen seconds and multiplying by four gives the pulse rate in beats per minute. Doing so while feeling calm gives a baseline; if the pulse rate rises more than, say, ten beats per minute above that level, it signals the beginning of flooding. If the pulse climbs this much, a couple needs a twenty-minute break from each other to cool down before resuming the discussion. Although a five-minute break may feel long enough, the actual physiological recovery time is more gradual. As we saw in Chapter 5, residual anger triggers more anger; the longer wait gives the body more time to recover from the earlier arousal.

For couples who, understandably, find it awkward to monitor heart rate during a fight, it is simpler to have a prestated agreement that allows one or another partner to call the time-out at the first signs of flooding in either partner. During that time-out period, cooling down can be helped along by engaging in a relaxation technique or aerobic exercise (or any of the other methods we explored in Chapter 5) that might help the partners recover from the emotional hijacking.

Detoxifying Self-talk

Because flooding is triggered by negative thoughts about the partner, it helps if a husband or wife who is being upset by such harsh judgments tackles them head-on. Sentiments like "I'm not going to take this anymore" or "I don't deserve this kind of treatment" are innocent-victim or righteous-indignation slogans. As cognitive therapist Aaron Beck points out, by catching these thoughts and challenging them—rather than simply being enraged or hurt by them—a husband or wife can begin to become free of their hold.[28]

This requires monitoring such thoughts, realizing that one does not have to believe them, and making the intentional effort to bring to mind evidence or perspectives that put them in question. For example, a wife who feels in the heat of the moment that "he doesn't care about my needs—he's always so selfish" might challenge the thought by reminding herself of a number of things her husband has done that are, in fact, thoughtful. This allows her to reframe the thought as: "Well, he does show he cares about me sometimes, even though what he just did was thoughtless and upsetting to me." The latter formulation opens the possibility of change and a positive resolution; the former only foments anger and hurt.

Nondefensive Listening and Speaking

He: "You're shouting!"

She: "Of course I'm shouting—you haven't heard a word I'm saying. You just don't listen!"

Listening is a skill that keeps couples together. Even in the heat of an argument, when both are seized by emotional hijackings, one or the other, and sometimes both, can manage to listen past the anger, and hear and respond to a partner's reparative gesture. Couples headed for divorce, though, get absorbed in the anger and fixated on the specifics of the issue at hand, not managing to hear—let alone return—any peace offerings that might be implicit in what their partner is saying. Defensiveness in a listener takes the form of ignoring or immediately rebutting the spouse's complaint, reacting to it as though it were an attack rather than an attempt to change behavior. Of course, in an argument what one spouse says is often in the form of an attack, or is said with such strong negativity that it is hard to hear anything other than an attack.

Even in the worst case, it's possible for a couple to purposely edit what they hear, ignoring the hostile and negative parts of the exchange—the nasty tone, the insult, the contemptuous criticism—to hear the main message. For this feat it helps if partners can remember to see each other's negativity as an implicit statement of how important the issue is to them—a demand for attention to be paid. Then if she yells, "Will you *stop* interrupting me, for crissake!" he might be more able to say, without reacting overtly to her hostility, "Okay, go ahead and finish."

The most powerful form of nondefensive listening, of course, is empathy: actually hearing the feelings *behind* what is being said. As we saw in Chapter 7, for one partner in a couple to truly empathize with the other demands that his own emotional reactions calm down to the point where he is receptive enough for his own physiology to be able to mirror the feelings of his partner. Without this physiological attunement, a partner's sense of what the other is feeling is likely to be entirely off base. Empathy deteriorates when one's own feelings are so strong that they allow no physiological harmonizing, but simply override everything else.

One method for effective emotional listening, called "mirroring," is commonly used in marital therapy. When one partner makes a complaint, the other repeats it back in her own words, trying to capture not just the thought, but also the feelings that go with it. The partner mirroring checks with the other to be sure the restatement is on target, and if not, tries again until it is right—something that seems simple, but is surprisingly tricky in execution.[29] The effect of being mirrored accurately is not just feeling understood, but having the added sense of being in emotional attunement. That in itself can sometimes disarm an imminent attack, and goes far toward keeping discussions of grievances from escalating into fights.

The art of nondefensive speaking for couples centers around keeping what is said to a specific complaint rather than escalating to a personal attack. Psychologist Haim Ginott, the grandfather of effective-communication programs, recommended that the best formula for a complaint is "XYZ": "When you did X, it made me feel Y, and I'd rather you did Z instead." For example: "When you didn't call to tell me you were going to be late for our dinner appointment, I felt unappreciated and angry. I wish you'd call to let me know you'll be late" instead of "You're a thoughtless, self-centered bastard," which is how the issue is all too often put in couples' fights. In short, open communication has no bullying, threats, or insults. Nor does it allow for any of the innumerable forms of defensiveness—excuses, denying responsibility, counterattacking with a criticism, and the like. Here again empathy is a potent tool.

Finally, respect and love disarm hostility in marriage, as elsewhere in life. One powerful way to de-escalate a fight is to let your partner know that you can see things from the other perspective, and that this point of view may have validity, even if you do not agree with it yourself. Another is to take responsibility or even apologize if you see you are in the wrong. At a minimum, validation means at least conveying that you are listening, and can acknowledge the emotions being expressed, even if you can't go along with the argument: "I see you're upset." And at other times, when there is no fight going on, validation takes the form of compliments, finding something you genuinely appreciate and voicing some praise. Validation, of course, is a way to help soothe your spouse, or to build up emotional capital in the form of positive feelings.

Practicing

Because these maneuvers are to be called upon during the heat of confrontation, when emotional arousal is sure to be high, they have to be overlearned if they are to be accessible when needed most. This is because the emotional brain engages those response routines that were learned earliest in life during repeated moments of anger and hurt, and so become dominant. Memory and response being emotion-specific, in such moments reactions associated with calmer times are less easy to remember and act on. If a more productive emotional response is unfamiliar or not well practiced, it is extremely difficult to try it while upset. But if a response is practiced so that it has become automatic, it has a better chance of finding expression during emotional crisis. For these reasons, the above strategies need to be tried out and rehearsed during encounters that are not stressful, as well as in the heat of battle, if they are to have a chance to become an acquired first response (or at least a not-too belated second response) in the repertoire of the emotional circuitry. In essence, these antidotes to marital disintegration are a small remedial education in emotional intelligence.

10

Managing with Heart

Melburn McBroom was a domineering boss, with a temper that intimidated those who worked with him. That fact might have passed unremarked had McBroom worked in an office or factory. But McBroom was an airline pilot.

One day in 1978 McBroom's plane was approaching Portland, Oregon, when he noticed a problem with the landing gear. So McBroom went into a holding pattern, circling the field at a high altitude while he fiddled with the mechanism.

As McBroom obsessed about the landing gear, the plane's fuel gauges steadily approached the empty level. But his copilots were so fearful of McBroom's wrath that they said nothing, even as disaster loomed. The plane crashed, killing ten people.

Today the story of that crash is told as a cautionary tale in the safety training of airline pilots.[1] In 80 percent of airline crashes, pilots make mistakes that could have been prevented, particularly if the crew worked together more harmoniously. Teamwork, open lines of communication, cooperation, listening, and speaking one's mind—rudiments of social intelligence—are now emphasized in training pilots, along with technical prowess.

The cockpit is a microcosm of any working organization. But lacking the dramatic reality check of an airplane crash, the destructive effects of miserable morale, intimidated workers, or arrogant bosses—or any of the dozens of other permutations of emotional deficiencies in the workplace—can go largely unnoticed by those outside the immediate scene. But the costs can be read in signs such as decreased productivity, an increase in missed deadlines, mistakes and mishaps, and an exodus of employees to more congenial settings. There is, inevitably, a cost to the bottom line from low levels of emotional intelligence on the job. When it is rampant, companies can crash and burn.

The cost-effectiveness of emotional intelligence is a relatively new idea for business, one some managers may find hard to accept. A study of 250 executives found that most felt their work demanded "their heads but not their hearts." Many said they feared that feeling empathy or compassion for those they worked with would put them in conflict with their organizational goals. One felt the idea of sensing the feelings of those who worked for him was absurd—it would, he said, "be impossible to deal with people." Others protested that if they were not emotionally aloof they would be unable to make the "hard" decisions that business requires—although the likelihood is that they would deliver those decisions more humanely.[2]

That study was done in the 1970s, when the business environment was very different. My argument is that such attitudes are outmoded, a luxury of a former day; a new competitive reality is putting emotional intelligence at a premium in the workplace and in the marketplace. As Shoshona Zuboff, a psychologist at Harvard Business School, pointed out to me, "corporations have gone through a radical revolution within this century, and with this has come a corresponding transformation of the emotional landscape. There was a long period of managerial domination of the corporate hierarchy when the manipulative, jungle-fighter boss was rewarded. But that rigid hierarchy started breaking down in the 1980s under the twin pressures of globalization and information technology. The jungle fighter symbolizes where the corporation has been; the virtuoso in interpersonal skills is the corporate future."[3]

Some of the reasons are patently obvious—imagine the consequences for a working group when someone is unable to keep from exploding in anger or has no sensitivity about what the people around him are feeling. All the deleterious effects of agitation on thinking reviewed in Chapter 6 operate in the workplace too: When emotionally upset, people cannot remember, attend, learn, or make decisions clearly. As one management consultant put it, "Stress makes people stupid."

On the positive side, imagine the benefits for work of being skilled in the basic emotional competences—being attuned to the feelings of those we deal with, being able to handle disagreements so they do not escalate, having the ability to get into flow states while doing our work. Leadership is not domination, but the art of persuading people to work toward a common goal. And, in terms of managing our own career, there may be nothing more essential than recognizing our deepest feelings about what we do—and what changes might make us more truly satisfied with our work.

Some of the less obvious reasons emotional aptitudes are moving to the forefront of business skills reflect sweeping changes in the workplace. Let me make my point by tracking the difference three applications of emotional intelligence make: being able to air grievances as helpful critiques, creating an atmosphere in which diversity is valued rather than a source of friction, and networking effectively.

CRITICISM IS JOB ONE

He was a seasoned engineer, heading a software development project, presenting the result of months of work by his team to the company's vice president for product development. The men and women who had worked long days week after week were there with him, proud to present the fruit of their hard labor. But as the engineer finished his presentation, the vice president turned to him and asked sarcastically, "How long have you been out of graduate school? These specifications are ridiculous. They have no chance of getting past my desk."

The engineer, utterly embarrassed and deflated, sat glumly through the rest of the meeting, reduced to silence. The men and women on his team made a few desultory—and some hostile—remarks in defense of their effort. The vice president was then called away and the meeting broke up abruptly, leaving a residue of bitterness and anger.

For the next two weeks the engineer was obsessed by the vice president's remarks. Dispirited and depressed, he was convinced he would never get another assignment of importance at the company, and was thinking of leaving, even though he enjoyed his work there.

Finally the engineer went to see the vice president, reminding him of the meeting, his critical remarks, and their demoralizing effect. Then he made a carefully worded inquiry: "I'm a little confused by what you were trying to accomplish. I assume you were not just trying to embarrass me—did you have some other goal in mind?"

The vice president was astonished—he had no idea that his remark, which he meant as a throwaway line, had been so devastating. In fact, he thought the software plan was promising, but needed more work—he hadn't meant to dismiss it as utterly worthless at all. He simply had not realized, he said, how poorly he had put his reaction, nor that he had hurt anyone's feelings. And, belatedly, he apologized.[4]

It's a question of feedback, really, of people getting the information essential to keep their efforts on track. In its original sense in systems theory, *feedback* meant the exchange of data about how one part of a system is working, with the understanding that one part affects all others in the system, so that any part heading off course could be changed for the better. In a company everyone is part of the system, and so feedback is the lifeblood of the organization—the exchange of information that lets people know if the job they are doing is going well or needs to be fine-tuned, upgraded, or redirected entirely. Without feedback people are in the dark; they have no idea how they stand with their boss, with their peers, or in terms of what is expected of them, and any problems will only get worse as time passes.

In a sense, criticism is one of the most important tasks a manager has. Yet it's also one of the most dreaded and put off. And, like the sarcastic vice president, too many managers have poorly mastered the crucial art of feedback. This deficiency has a great cost: just as the emotional health of a couple depends on how well they air their grievances, so do the effectiveness, satisfaction, and productivity of people at work depend on how they are told about nagging problems. Indeed, how criticisms are given and received goes a long way in determining how satisfied people are with their work, with those they work with, and with those to whom they are responsible.

The Worst Way to Motivate Someone

The emotional vicissitudes at work in marriage also operate in the workplace, where they take similar forms. Criticisms are voiced as personal attacks rather than complaints that can be acted upon; there are ad hominem charges with dollops of disgust, sarcasm, and contempt; both give rise to defensiveness and dodging of responsibility and, finally, to stonewalling or the embittered passive resistance that comes from feeling unfairly treated. Indeed, one of the more common forms of destructive criticism in the workplace, says one business consultant, is a blanket, generalized statement like "You're screwing up," delivered in a harsh, sarcastic, angry tone, providing neither a chance to respond nor any suggestion of how to do things better. It leaves the person receiving it feeling helpless and angry. From the vantage point of emotional intelligence, such criticism displays an ignorance of the feelings it will trigger in those who receive it, and the devastating effect those feelings will have on their motivation, energy, and confidence in doing their work.

This destructive dynamic showed up in a survey of managers who were asked to think back to times they blew up at employees and, in the heat of the moment, made a personal attack.[5] The angry attacks had effects much like they would in a married couple: the employees who received them reacted most often by becoming defensive, making excuses, or evading responsibility. Or they stonewalled—that is, tried to avoid all contact with the manager who blew up at them. If they had been subjected to the same emotional microscope that John Gottman used with married couples, these embittered employees would no doubt have been shown to be thinking the thoughts of innocent victimhood or righteous indignation typical of husbands or wives who feel unfairly attacked. If their physiology were measured, they would probably also display the flooding that reinforces such thoughts. And yet the managers were only further annoyed and provoked by these responses, suggesting the beginning of a cycle that, in the business world, ends in the employee quitting or being fired—the business equivalent of a divorce.

Indeed, in a study of 108 managers and white-collar workers, inept criticism was ahead of mistrust, personality struggles, and disputes over power and pay as a reason for conflict on the job.[6] An experiment done at Rensselaer Polytechnic Institute shows just how damaging to working relationships a cutting criticism can be. In a simulation, volunteers were given the task of creating an ad for a new shampoo. Another volunteer (a confederate) supposedly judged the proposed ads; volunteers actually received one of two prearranged criticisms. One critique was considerate and specific. But the other included threats and blamed the person's innate deficiencies, with remarks like, "Didn't even try; can't seem to do anything right" and "Maybe it's just lack of talent. I'd try to get someone else to do it."

Understandably, those who were attacked became tense and angry and antagonistic, saying they would refuse to collaborate or cooperate on future projects with the person who gave the criticism. Many indicated they would want to avoid contact altogether—in other words, they felt like stonewalling. The harsh criticism made those who received it so demoralized that they no longer tried as hard at their work and, perhaps most damaging, said they no longer felt capable of doing well. The personal attack was devastating to their morale.

Many managers are too willing to criticize, but frugal with praise, leaving their employees feeling that they only hear about how they're doing when they make a mistake. This propensity to criticism is compounded by managers who delay giving any feedback at all for long periods. "Most problems in an employee's performance are not sudden; they develop slowly over time," J. R. Larson, a University of Illinois at Urbana psychologist, notes. "When the boss fails to let his feelings be known promptly, it leads to his frustration building up slowly. Then, one day, he blows up about it. If the criticism had been given earlier on, the employee would have been able to correct the problem. Too often people criticize only when things boil over, when they get too angry to contain themselves. And that's when they give the criticism in the worst way, in a tone of biting sarcasm, calling to mind a long list of grievances they had kept to themselves, or making threats. Such attacks backfire. They are received as an affront, so the recipient becomes angry in return. It's the worst way to motivate someone."

The Artful Critique

Consider the alternative.

An artful critique can be one of the most helpful messages a manager can send. For example, what the contemptuous vice president could have told the software engineer—but did not—was something like: "The main difficulty at this stage is that your plan will take too long and so escalate costs. I'd like you to think more about your proposal, especially the design specifications for software development, to see if you can figure out a way to do the same job more quickly." Such a message has the opposite impact of destructive criticism: instead of creating helplessness, anger, and rebellion, it holds out the hope of doing better and suggests the beginning of a plan for doing so.

An artful critique focuses on what a person has done and can do rather than reading a mark of character into a job poorly done. As Larson observes, "A character attack—calling someone stupid or incompetent—misses the point. You immediately put him on the defensive, so that he's no longer receptive to what you have to tell him about how to do things better." That advice, of course, is precisely the same as for married couples airing their grievances.

And, in terms of motivation, when people believe that their failures are due to some unchangeable deficit in themselves, they lose hope and stop trying. The basic belief that leads to optimism, remember, is that setbacks or failures are due to circumstances that we can do something about to change them for the better.

Harry Levinson, a psychoanalyst turned corporate consultant, gives the following advice on the art of the critique, which is intricately entwined with the art of praise:

• *Be specific.* Pick a significant incident, an event that illustrates a key problem that needs changing or a pattern of deficiency, such as the inability to do certain parts of a job well. It demoralizes people just to hear that they are doing "something" wrong without knowing what the specifics are so they can change. Focus on the specifics, saying what the person did well, what was done poorly, and how it could be changed. Don't beat around the bush or be oblique or evasive; it will muddy the real message. This, of course, is akin to the advice to couples about the "XYZ" statement of a grievance: say exactly what the problem is, what's wrong with it or how it makes you feel, and what could be changed.

"Specificity," Levinson points out, "is just as important for praise as for criticism. I won't say that vague praise has no effect at all, but it doesn't have much, and you can't learn from it."[7]

• *Offer a solution.* The critique, like all useful feedback, should point to a way to fix the problem. Otherwise it leaves the recipient frustrated, demoralized, or demotivated. The critique may open the door to possibilities and alternatives that the person did not realize were there, or simply sensitize her to deficiencies that need attention—but should include suggestions about how to take care of these problems.

• *Be present.* Critiques, like praise, are most effective face to face and in private. People who are uncomfortable giving a criticism—or offering praise—are likely to ease the burden on themselves by doing it at a distance, such as in a memo. But this makes the communication too impersonal, and robs the person receiving it of an opportunity for a response or clarification.

• *Be sensitive.* This is a call for empathy, for being attuned to the impact of what you say and how you say it on the person at the receiving end. Managers who have little empathy, Levinson points out, are most prone to giving feedback in a hurtful fashion, such as the withering put-down. The net effect of such criticism is destructive: instead of opening the way for a corrective, it creates an emotional backlash of resentment, bitterness, defensiveness, and distance.

Levinson also offers some emotional counsel for those at the receiving end of criticism. One is to see the criticism as valuable information about how to do better, not as a personal attack. Another is to watch for the impulse toward defensiveness instead of taking responsibility. And, if it gets too upsetting, ask to resume the meeting later, after a period to absorb the difficult message and cool down a bit. Finally, he advises people to see criticism as an opportunity to work together with the critic to solve the problem, not as an adversarial situation. All this sage advice, of course, directly echoes suggestions for married couples trying to handle their complaints without doing permanent damage to their relationship. As with marriage, so with work.

DEALING WITH DIVERSITY

Sylvia Skeeter, a former army captain in her thirties, was a shift manager at a Denny's restaurant in Columbia, South Carolina. One slow afternoon a group of black customers—a minister, an assistant pastor, and two visiting gospel singers—came in for a meal, and sat and sat while the waitresses ignored them. The waitresses, recalls Skeeter, "would kind of glare, with their hands on their hips, and then they'd go back to talking among themselves, like a black person standing five feet away didn't exist."

Skeeter, indignant, confronted the waitresses, and complained to the manager, who shrugged off their actions, saying, "That's how they were raised, and there's nothing I can do about it." Skeeter quit on the spot; she is black.

If that had been an isolated incident, this moment of blatant prejudice might have passed unnoted. But Sylvia Skeeter was one of hundreds of people who came forward to testify to a widespread pattern of antiblack prejudice throughout the Denny's restaurant chain, a pattern that resulted in a $54 million settlement of a class-action suit on behalf of thousands of black customers who had suffered such indignities.

The plaintiffs included a detail of seven African-American Secret Service agents who sat waiting for an hour for their breakfast while their white colleagues at the next table were served promptly—as they were all on their way to provide security for a visit by President Clinton to the United States Naval Academy at Annapolis. They also included a black girl with paralyzed legs in Tampa, Florida, who sat in her wheelchair for two hours waiting for her food late one night after a prom. The pattern of discrimination, the class-action suit held, was due to the widespread assumption throughout the Denny's chain—particularly at the level of district and branch manager—that black customers were bad for business. Today, largely as a result of the suit and publicity surrounding it, the Denny's chain is making amends to the black community. And every employee, especially managers, must attend sessions on the advantages of a multiracial clientele.

Such seminars have become a staple of in-house training in companies throughout America, with the growing realization by managers that even if people bring prejudices to work with them, they must learn to act as though they have none. The reasons, over and above human decency, are pragmatic. One is the shifting face of the workforce, as white males, who used to be the dominant group, are becoming a minority. A survey of several hundred American companies found that more than three quarters of new employees were nonwhite—a demographic shift that is also reflected to a large extent in the changing pool of customers.[8] Another reason is the increasing need for international companies to have employees who not only put any bias aside to appreciate people from diverse cultures (and markets) but also turn that appreciation to competitive advantage. A third motivation is the potential fruit of diversity, in terms of heightened collective creativity and entrepreneurial energy.

All this means the culture of an organization must change to foster tolerance, even if individual biases remain. But how can a company do this? The sad fact is that the panoply of one-day, one-video, or single-weekend "diversity training" courses do not really seem to budge the biases of those employees who come to them with deep prejudice against one or another group, whether it be whites biased against blacks, blacks against Asians, or Asians resenting Hispanics. Indeed, the net effect of inept diversity courses—those that raise false expectations by promising too much, or simply create an atmosphere of confrontation instead of understanding—can be to heighten the tensions that divide groups in the workplace, calling even greater attention to these differences. To understand what *can* be done, it helps to first understand the nature of prejudice itself.

The Roots of Prejudice

Dr. Vamik Volkan is a psychiatrist at the University of Virginia now, but he remembers what it was like growing up in a Turkish family on the island of Cyprus, then bitterly contested between Turks and Greeks. As a boy Volkan heard rumors that the local Greek priest's cincture had a knot for each Turkish child he had strangled, and remembers the tone of dismay in which he was told how his Greek neighbors ate pigs, whose meat was considered too filthy to eat in his own Turkish culture. Now, as a student of ethnic conflict, Volkan points to such childhood memories to show how hatreds between groups are kept alive over the years, as each new generation is steeped in hostile biases like these.[9] The psychological price of loyalty to one's own group can be antipathy toward another, especially when there is a long history of enmity between the groups.

Prejudices are a kind of emotional learning that occurs early in life, making these reactions especially hard to eradicate entirely, even in people who as adults feel it is wrong to hold them. "The emotions of prejudice are formed in childhood, while the beliefs that are used to justify it come later," explained Thomas Pettigrew, a social psychologist at the University of California at Santa Cruz, who has studied prejudice for decades. "Later in life you may want to change your prejudice, but it is far easier to change your intellectual beliefs than your deep feelings. Many Southerners have confessed to me, for instance, that even though in their minds they no longer feel prejudice against blacks, they feel squeamish when they shake hands with a black. The feelings are left over from what they learned in their families as children."[10]

The power of the stereotypes that buttress prejudice comes in part from a more neutral dynamic in the mind that makes stereotypes of all kinds self-confirming.[11] People remember more readily instances that support the stereotype while tending to discount instances that challenge it. On meeting at a party an emotionally open and warm Englishman who disconfirms the stereotype of the cold, reserved Briton, for example, people can tell themselves that he's just unusual, or "he's been drinking."

The tenacity of subtle biases may explain why, while over the last forty years or so racial attitudes of American whites toward blacks have become increasingly more tolerant, more subtle forms of bias persist: people disavow racist attitudes while still acting with covert bias.[12] When asked, such people say they feel no bigotry, but in ambiguous situations still act in a biased way—though they give a rationale other than prejudice. Such bias can take the form, say, of a white senior manager—who believes he has no prejudices—rejecting a black job applicant, ostensibly not because of his race but because his education and experience "are not quite right" for the job, while hiring a white applicant with about the same background. Or it might take the form of giving a briefing and helpful tips to a white salesman about to make a call, but somehow neglecting to do the same for a black or Hispanic salesman.

Zero Tolerance for Intolerance

If people's long-held biases cannot be so easily weeded out, what *can* be changed is what they *do* about them. At Denny's, for example, waitresses or branch managers who took it upon themselves to discriminate against blacks were seldom, if ever, challenged. Instead, some managers seem to have encouraged them, at least tacitly, to discriminate, even suggesting policies such as demanding payment for meals in advance from black customers only, denying blacks widely advertised free birthday meals, or locking the doors and claiming to be closed if a group of black customers was coming. As John P. Relman, an attorney who sued Denny's on behalf of the black Secret Service agents, put it, "Denny's management closed their eyes to what the field staff was doing. There must have been some message . . . which freed up the inhibitions of local managers to act on their racist impulses."[13]

But everything we know about the roots of prejudice and how to fight it effectively suggests that precisely this attitude—turning a blind eye to acts of bias—allows discrimination to thrive. To do nothing, in this context, is an act of consequence in itself, letting the virus of prejudice spread unopposed. More to the point than diversity training courses—or perhaps essential to their having much effect—is that the norms of a group be decisively changed by taking an active stance against any acts of discrimination, from the top echelons of management on down. Biases may not budge, but acts of prejudice can be quashed, if the climate is changed. As an IBM executive put it, "We don't tolerate slights or insults in any way; respect for the individual is central to IBM's culture."[14]

If research on prejudice has any lesson for making a corporate culture more tolerant, it is to encourage people to speak out against even low-key acts of discrimination or harassment—offensive jokes, say, or the posting of girlie calendars demeaning to women coworkers. One study found that when people in a group heard someone make ethnic slurs, it led others to do the same. The simple act of naming bias as such or objecting to it on the spot establishes a social atmosphere that discourages it; saying nothing serves to condone it.[15] In this endeavor, those in positions of authority play a pivotal role: their failure to condemn acts of bias sends the tacit message that such acts are okay. Following through with action such as a reprimand sends a powerful message that bias is not trivial, but has real—and negative—consequences.

Here too the skills of emotional intelligence are an advantage, especially in having the social knack to know not just when but *how* to speak up productively against bias. Such feedback should be couched with all the finesse of an effective criticism, so it can be heard without defensiveness. If managers and coworkers do this naturally, or learn to do so, bias incidents are more likely to fall away.

The more effective diversity training courses set a new, organizationwide, explicit ground rule that makes bias in any form out-of-bounds, and so encourages people who have been silent witnesses and bystanders to voice their discomforts and objections. Another active ingredient in diversity courses is perspective-taking, a stance that encourages empathy and tolerance. To the degree that people come to understand the pain of those who feel discriminated against, they are more likely to speak out against it.

In short, it is more practical to try to suppress the expression of bias rather than trying to eliminate the attitude itself; stereotypes change very slowly, if at all. Simply putting people of different groups together does little or nothing to lower intolerance, as witness cases of school desegregation in which intergroup hostility rose rather than decreased. For the plethora of diversity training programs that are sweeping through the corporate world, this means a realistic goal is to change the *norms* of a group for showing prejudice or harassing; such programs can do much to raise into the collective awareness the idea that bigotry or harassment are not acceptable and will not be tolerated. But to expect that such a program will uproot deeply held prejudices is unrealistic.

Still, since prejudices are a variety of emotional learning, relearning *is* possible—though it takes time and should not be expected as the outcome of a one-time diversity training workshop. What can make a difference, though, is sustained camaraderie and daily efforts toward a common goal by people of different backgrounds. The lesson here is from school desegregation: when groups fail to mix socially, instead forming hostile cliques, the negative stereotypes intensify. But when students have worked together as equals to attain a common goal, as on sports teams or in bands, their stereotypes break down—as can happen naturally in the workplace, when people work together as peers over the years.[16]

But to stop at battling prejudice in the workplace is to miss a greater opportunity: taking advantage of the creative and entrepreneurial possibilities that a diverse workforce can offer. As we shall see, a working group of varied strengths and perspectives, if it can operate in harmony, is likely to come to better, more creative, and more effective solutions than those same people working in isolation.

ORGANIZATIONAL SAVVY AND THE GROUP IQ

By the end of the century, a third of the American workforce will be "knowledge workers," people whose productivity is marked by adding value to information—whether as market analysts, writers, or computer programmers. Peter Drucker, the eminent business maven who coined the term "knowledge worker," points out that such workers' expertise is highly specialized, and that their productivity depends on their efforts being coordinated as part of an organizational team: writers are not publishers; computer programmers are not software distributors. While people have always worked in tandem, notes Drucker, with knowledge work, "teams become the work unit rather than the individual himself."[17] And that suggests why emotional intelligence, the skills that help people harmonize, should become increasingly valued as a workplace asset in the years to come.

Perhaps the most rudimentary form of organizational teamwork is the meeting, that inescapable part of an executive's lot—in a boardroom, on a conference call, in someone's office. Meetings—bodies in the same room— are but the most obvious, and a somewhat antiquated, example of the sense in which work is shared. Electronic networks, e-mail, teleconferences, work teams, informal networks, and the like are emerging as new functional entities in organizations. To the degree that the explicit hierarchy as mapped on an organizational chart is the skeleton of an organization, these human touchpoints are its central nervous system.

Whenever people come together to collaborate, whether it be in an executive planning meeting or as a team working toward a shared product, there is a very real sense in which they have a group IQ, the sum total of the talents and skills of all those involved. And how well they accomplish their task will be determined by how high that IQ is. The single most important element in group intelligence, it turns out, is not the average IQ in the academic sense, but rather in terms of emotional intelligence. The key to a high group IQ is social harmony. It is this ability to harmonize that, all other things being equal, will make one group especially talented, productive, and successful, and another—with members whose talent and skill are equal in other regards—do poorly.

The idea that there is a group intelligence at all comes from Robert Sternberg, the Yale psychologist, and Wendy Williams, a graduate student, who were seeking to understand why some groups are far more effective than others.[18] After all, when people come together to work as a group, each brings certain talents—say, a high verbal fluency, creativity, empathy, or technical expertise. While a group can be no "smarter" than the sum total of all these specific strengths, it can be much dumber if its internal workings don't allow people to share their talents. This maxim became evident when Sternberg and Williams recruited people to take part in groups that were given the creative challenge of coming up with an effective advertising campaign for a fictitious sweetener that showed promise as a sugar substitute.

One surprise was that people who were *too* eager to take part were a drag on the group, lowering its overall performance; these eager beavers were too controlling or domineering. Such people seemed to lack a basic element of social intelligence, the ability to recognize what is apt and what inappropriate in give-and-take. Another negative was having deadweight, members who did not participate.

The single most important factor in maximizing the excellence of a group's product was the degree to which the members were able to create a state of internal harmony, which lets them take advantage of the full talent of their members. The overall performance of harmonious groups was helped by having a member who was particularly talented; groups with more friction were far less able to capitalize on having members of great ability. In groups where there are high levels of emotional and social static—whether it be from fear or anger, from rivalries or resentments—people cannot offer their best. But harmony allows a group to take maximum advantage of its most creative and talented members' abilities.

While the moral of this tale is quite clear for, say, work teams, it has a more general implication for anyone who works within an organization. Many things people do at work depend on their ability to call on a loose network of fellow workers; different tasks can mean calling on different members of the network. In effect, this creates the chance for ad hoc groups, each with a membership tailored to offer an optimal array of talents, expertise, and placement. Just how well people can "work" a network—in effect, make it into a temporary, ad hoc team—is a crucial factor in on-the-job success.

Consider, for example, a study of star performers at Bell Labs, the world-famous scientific think tank near Princeton. The labs are peopled by engineers and scientists who are all at the top on academic IQ tests. But within this pool of talent, some emerge as stars, while others are only average in their output. What makes the difference between stars and the others is not their academic IQ, but their *emotional* IQ. They are better able to motivate themselves, and better able to work their informal networks into ad hoc teams.

The "stars" were studied in one division at the labs, a unit that creates and designs the electronic switches that control telephone systems—a highly sophisticated and demanding piece of electronic engineering.[19] Because the work is beyond the capacity of any one person to tackle, it is done in teams that can range from just 5 or so engineers to 150. No single engineer knows enough to do the job alone; getting things done demands tapping other people's expertise. To find out what made the difference between those who were highly productive and those who were only average, Robert Kelley and Janet Caplan had managers and peers nominate the 10 to 15 percent of engineers who stood out as stars.

When they compared the stars with everyone else, the most dramatic finding, at first, was the paucity of differences between the two groups. "Based on a wide range of cognitive and social measures, from standard tests for IQ to personality inventories, there's little meaningful difference in innate abilities," Kelley and Caplan wrote in the *Harvard Business Review*. "As it develops, academic talent was not a good predictor of on-the-job productivity," nor was IQ.

But after detailed interviews, the critical differences emerged in the internal and interpersonal strategies "stars" used to get their work done. One of the most important turned out to be a rapport with a network of key people. Things go more smoothly for the standouts because they put time into cultivating good relationships with people whose services might be needed in a crunch as part of an instant ad hoc team to solve a problem or handle a crisis. "A middle performer at Bell Labs talked about being stumped by a technical problem," Kelley and Caplan observed. "He painstakingly called various technical gurus and then waited, wasting valuable time while calls went unreturned and e-mail messages unanswered. Star performers, however, rarely face such situations because they do the work of building reliable networks before they actually need them. When they call someone for advice, stars almost always get a faster answer."

Informal networks are especially critical for handling unanticipated problems. "The formal organization is set up to handle easily anticipated problems," one study of these networks observes. "But when unexpected problems arise, the informal organization kicks in. Its complex web of social ties form every time colleagues communicate, and solidify over time into surprisingly stable networks. Highly adaptive, informal networks move diagonally and elliptically, skipping entire functions to get things done."[20]

The analysis of informal networks shows that just because people work together day to day they will not necessarily trust each other with sensitive information (such as a desire to change jobs, or resentment about how a manager or peer behaves), nor turn to them in crisis. Indeed, a more sophisticated view of informal networks shows that there are at least three varieties: communications webs—who talks to whom; expertise networks, based on which people are turned to for advice; and trust networks. Being a main node in the expertise network means someone will have a reputation for technical excellence, which often leads to a promotion. But there is virtually no relationship between being an expert and being seen as someone people can trust with their secrets, doubts, and vulnerabilities. A petty office tyrant or micromanager may be high on expertise, but will be so low on trust that it will undermine their ability to manage, and effectively exclude them from informal networks. The stars of an organization are often those who have thick connections on all networks, whether communications, expertise, or trust.

Beyond a mastery of these essential networks, other forms of organizational savvy the Bell Labs stars had mastered included effectively coordinating their efforts in teamwork; being leaders in building consensus; being able to see things from the perspective of others, such as customers or others on a work team; persuasiveness; and promoting cooperation while avoiding conflicts. While all of these rely on social skills, the stars also displayed another kind of knack: taking initiative—being self-motivated enough to take on responsibilities above and beyond their stated job—and self-management in the sense of regulating their time and work commitments well. All such skills, of course, are aspects of emotional intelligence.

There are strong signs that what is true at Bell Labs augurs for the future of all corporate life, a tomorrow where the basic skills of emotional intelligence will be ever more important, in teamwork, in cooperation, in helping people learn together how to work more effectively. As knowledge-based services and intellectual capital become more central to corporations, improving the way people work together will be a major way to leverage intellectual capital, making a critical competitive difference. To thrive, if not survive, corporations would do well to boost their collective emotional intelligence.

11

Mind and Medicine

"Who taught you all this, Doctor?"
The reply came promptly:
"Suffering."

—ALBERT CAMUS, *The Plague*

A vague ache in my groin sent me to my doctor. Nothing seemed un-usual until he looked at the results of a urine test. I had traces of blood in my urine.

"I want you to go to the hospital and get some tests . . . kidney function, cytology . . . ," he said in a businesslike tone.

I don't know what he said next. My mind seemed to freeze at the word *cytology*. Cancer.

I have a foggy memory of his explaining to me when and where to go for diagnostic tests. It was the simplest instruction, but I had to ask him to re-peat it three or four times. *Cytology*—my mind would not leave the word. That one word made me feel as though I had just been mugged at my own front door.

Why should I have reacted so strongly? My doctor was just being thorough and competent, checking the limbs in a diagnostic decision tree. There was a tiny likelihood that cancer was the problem. But this rational analysis was irrelevant at that moment. In the land of the sick, emotions reign supreme; fear is a thought away. We can be so emotionally fragile while we are ailing because our mental well-being is based in part on the illusion of invulnera-bility. Sickness—especially a severe illness—bursts that illusion, attacking the premise that our private world is safe and secure. Suddenly we feel weak, helpless, and vulnerable.

The problem is when medical personnel ignore how patients are reacting *emotionally*, even while attending to their physical condition. This inattention to the emotional reality of illness neglects a growing body of evidence showing that people's emotional states can play a sometimes significant role in their vulnerability to disease and in the course of their recovery. Modern medical care too often lacks emotional intelligence.

For the patient, any encounter with a nurse or physician can be a chance for reassuring information, comfort, and solace—or, if handled unfortunately, an invitation to despair. But too often medical caregivers are rushed or indifferent to patients' distress. To be sure, there are compassionate nurses and physicians who take the time to reassure and inform as well as administer medically. But the trend is toward a professional universe in which institutional imperatives can leave medical staff oblivious to the vulnerabilities of patients, or feeling too pressed to do anything about them. With the hard realities of a medical system increasingly timed by accountants, things seem to be getting worse.

Beyond the humanitarian argument for physicians to offer care along with cure, there are other compelling reasons to consider the psychological and social reality of patients as being within the medical realm rather than separate from it. By now a scientific case can be made that there is a margin of *medical* effectiveness, both in prevention and treatment, that can be gained by treating people's emotional state along with their medical condition. Not in every case or every condition, of course. But looking at data from hundreds and hundreds of cases, there is on average enough increment of medical benefit to suggest that an *emotional* intervention should be a standard part of medical care for the range of serious disease.

Historically, medicine in modern society has defined its mission in terms of curing *disease*—the medical disorder—while overlooking *illness*—the patient's experience of disease. Patients, by going along with this view of their problem, join a quiet conspiracy to ignore how they are reacting emotionally to their medical problems—or to dismiss those reactions as irrelevant to the course of the problem itself. That attitude is reinforced by a medical model that dismisses entirely the idea that mind influences body in any consequential way.

Yet there is an equally unproductive ideology in the other direction: the notion that people can cure themselves of even the most pernicious disease simply by making themselves happy or thinking positive thoughts, or that they are somehow to blame for having gotten sick in the first place. The result of this attitude-will-cure-all rhetoric has been to create widespread confusion and misunderstanding about the extent to which illness can be affected by the mind, and, perhaps worse, sometimes to make people feel guilty for having a disease, as though it were a sign of some moral lapse or spiritual unworthiness.

The truth lies somewhere between these extremes. By sorting through the scientific data, my aim is to clarify the contradictions and replace the nonsense with a clearer understanding of the degree to which our emotions— and emotional intelligence—play a part in health and disease.

THE BODY'S MIND: HOW EMOTIONS MATTER FOR HEALTH

In 1974 a finding in a laboratory at the School of Medicine and Dentistry, University of Rochester, rewrote biology's map of the body: Robert Ader, a psychologist, discovered that the immune system, like the brain, could learn. His result was a shock; the prevailing wisdom in medicine had been that only the brain and central nervous system could respond to experience by changing how they behaved. Ader's finding led to the investigation of what are turning out to be myriad ways the central nervous system and the immune system communicate—biological pathways that make the mind, the emotions, and the body not separate, but intimately entwined.

In his experiment white rats had been given a medication that artificially suppressed the quantity of disease-fighting T cells circulating in their blood. Each time they received the medication, they ate it along with saccharin-laced water. But Ader discovered that giving the rats the saccharin-flavored water alone, without the suppressive medication, still resulted in a lowering of the T-cell count—to the point that some of the rats were getting sick and dying. Their immune system had learned to suppress T cells in response to the flavored water. That just should not have happened, according to the best scientific understanding at the time.

The immune system is the "body's brain," as neuroscientist Francisco Varela, at Paris's Ecole Polytechnique, puts it, defining the body's own sense of self—of what belongs within it and what does not.[1] Immune cells travel in the bloodstream throughout the entire body, contacting virtually every other cell. Those cells they recognize, they leave alone; those they fail to recognize, they attack. The attack either defends us against viruses, bacteria, and cancer or, if the immune cells misidentify some of the body's own cells, creates an autoimmune disease such as allergy or lupus. Until the day Ader made his serendipitous discovery, every anatomist, every physician, and every biologist believed that the brain (along with its extensions throughout the body via the central nervous system) and the immune system were separate entities, neither able to influence the operation of the other. There was no pathway that could connect the brain centers monitoring what the rat tasted with the areas of bone marrow that manufacture T cells. Or so it had been thought for a century.

Over the years since then, Ader's modest discovery has forced a new look at the links between the immune system and the central nervous system. The field that studies this, psychoneuroimmunology, or PNI, is now a leading-edge medical science. Its very name acknowledges the links: *psycho,* or "mind"; *neuro,* for the neuroendocrine system (which subsumes the nervous system and hormone systems); and *immunology,* for the immune system.

A network of researchers is finding that the chemical messengers that operate most extensively in both brain and immune system are those that are most dense in neural areas that regulate emotion.[2] Some of the strongest evidence for a direct physical pathway allowing emotions to impact the immune system has come from David Felten, a colleague of Ader's. Felten began by noting that emotions have a powerful effect on the autonomic nervous system, which regulates everything from how much insulin is secreted to blood-pressure levels. Felten, working with his wife, Suzanne, and other colleagues, then detected a meeting point where the autonomic nervous system directly talks to lymphocytes and macrophages, cells of the immune system.[3]

In electron-microscope studies, they found synapselike contacts where the nerve terminals of the autonomic system have endings that directly abut these immune cells. This physical contact point allows the nerve cells to release neurotransmitters to regulate the immune cells; indeed, they signal back and forth. The finding is revolutionary. No one had suspected that immune cells could be targets of messages from the nerves.

To test how important these nerve endings were in the workings of the immune system, Felten went a step further. In experiments with animals he removed some nerves from lymph nodes and spleen—where immune cells are stored or made—and then used viruses to challenge the immune system. The result: a huge drop in immune response to the virus. His conclusion is that without those nerve endings the immune system simply does not respond as it should to the challenge of an invading virus or bacterium. In short, the nervous system not only connects to the immune system, but is essential for proper immune function.

Another key pathway linking emotions and the immune system is via the influence of the hormones released under stress. The catecholamines (epinephrine and norepinephrine—otherwise known as adrenaline and noradrenaline), cortisol and prolactin, and the natural opiates beta-endorphin and enkephalin are all released during stress arousal. Each has a strong impact on immune cells. While the relationships are complex, the main influence is that while these hormones surge through the body, the immune cells are hampered in their function: stress suppresses immune resistance, at least temporarily, presumably in a conservation of energy that puts a priority on the more immediate emergency, which is more pressing for survival. But if stress is constant and intense, that suppression may become long-lasting.[4]

Microbiologists and other scientists are finding more and more such connections between the brain and the cardiovascular and immune systems—having first had to accept the once-radical notion that they exist at all.[5]

TOXIC EMOTIONS: THE CLINICAL DATA

Despite such evidence, many or most physicians are still skeptical that emotions matter clinically. One reason is that while many studies have found stress and negative emotions to weaken the effectiveness of various immune cells, it is not always clear that the range of these changes is great enough to make a *medical* difference.

Even so, an increasing number of physicians acknowledge the place of emotions in medicine. For instance, Dr. Camran Nezhat, an eminent gynecological laparoscopic surgeon at Stanford University, says, "If someone scheduled for surgery tells me she's panicked that day and does not want to go through with it, I cancel the surgery." Nezhat explains, "Every surgeon knows that people who are extremely scared do terribly in surgery. They bleed too much, they have more infections and complications. They have a harder time recovering. It's much better if they are calm."

The reason is straightforward: panic and anxiety hike blood pressure, and veins distended by pressure bleed more profusely when cut by the surgeon's knife. Excess bleeding is one of the most troublesome surgical complications, one that can sometimes lead to death.

Beyond such medical anecdotes, evidence for the *clinical* importance of emotions has been mounting steadily. Perhaps the most compelling data on the medical significance of emotion come from a mass analysis combining results from 101 smaller studies into a single larger one of several thousand men and women. The study confirms that perturbing emotions are bad for health—to a degree.[6] People who experienced chronic anxiety, long periods of sadness and pessimism, unremitting tension or incessant hostility, relentless cynicism or suspiciousness, were found to have *double* the risk of disease—including asthma, arthritis, headaches, peptic ulcers, and heart disease (each representative of major, broad categories of disease). This order of magnitude makes distressing emotions as toxic a risk factor as, say, smoking or high cholesterol are for heart disease—in other words, a major threat to health.

To be sure, this is a broad statistical link, and by no means indicates that everyone who has such chronic feelings will thus more easily fall prey to a disease. But the evidence for a potent role for emotion in disease is far more extensive than this one study of studies indicates. Taking a more detailed look at the data for specific emotions, especially the big three—anger, anxiety, and depression—makes clearer some specific ways that feelings have medical significance, even if the biological mechanisms by which such emotions have their effect are yet to be fully understood.[7]

When Anger Is Suicidal

A while back, the man said, a bump on the side of his car led to a fruitless and frustrating journey. After endless insurance company red tape and auto body shops that did more damage, he still owed $800. And it wasn't even his fault. He was so fed up that whenever he got into the car he was overcome with disgust. He finally sold the car in frustration. Years later the memories still made the man livid with outrage.

This bitter memory was brought to mind purposely, as part of a study of anger in heart patients at Stanford University Medical School. All the patients in the study had, like this embittered man, suffered a first heart attack, and the question was whether anger might have a significant impact of some kind on their heart function. The effect was striking: while the patients recounted incidents that made them mad, the pumping efficiency of their hearts dropped by five percentage points.[8] Some of the patients showed a drop in pumping efficiency of 7 percent or greater—a range that cardiologists regard as a sign of a myocardial ischemia, a dangerous drop in blood flow to the heart itself.

The drop in pumping efficiency was not seen with other distressing feelings, such as anxiety, nor during physical exertion; anger seems to be the one emotion that does most harm to the heart. While recalling the upsetting incident, the patients said they were only about half as mad as they had been while it was happening, suggesting that their hearts would have been even more greatly hampered during an actual angry encounter.

This finding is part of a larger network of evidence emerging from dozens of studies pointing to the power of anger to damage the heart.[9] The old idea has not held up that a hurried, high-pressure Type-A personality is at great risk from heart disease, but from that failed theory has emerged a new finding: it is hostility that puts people at risk.

Much of the data on hostility has come from research by Dr. Redford Williams at Duke University.[10] For example, Williams found that those physicians who had had the highest scores on a test of hostility while still in medical school were seven times as likely to have died by the age of fifty as were those with low hostility scores—being prone to anger was a stronger predictor of dying young than were other risk factors such as smoking, high blood pressure, and high cholesterol. And findings by a colleague, Dr. John Barefoot at the University of North Carolina, show that in heart patients undergoing angiography, in which a tube is inserted into the coronary artery to measure lesions, scores on a test of hostility correlate with the extent and severity of coronary artery disease.

Of course, no one is saying that anger alone causes coronary artery disease; it is one of several interacting factors. As Peter Kaufman, acting chief of the Behavioral Medicine Branch of the National Heart, Lung, and Blood Institute, explained to me, "We can't yet sort out whether anger and hostility play a causal role in the early development of coronary artery disease, or whether it intensifies the problem once heart disease has begun, or both. But take a twenty-year-old who repeatedly gets angry. Each episode of anger adds an additional stress to the heart by increasing his heart rate and blood pressure. When that is repeated over and over again, it can do damage," especially because the turbulence of blood flowing through the coronary artery with each heartbeat "can cause microtears in the vessel, where plaque develops. If your heart rate is faster and blood pressure is higher because you're habitually angry, then over thirty years that may lead to a faster build-up of plaque, and so lead to coronary artery disease."[11]

Once heart disease develops, the mechanisms triggered by anger affect the very efficiency of the heart as a pump, as was shown in the study of angry memories in heart patients. The net effect is to make anger particularly lethal in those who already have heart disease. For instance, a Stanford University Medical School study of 1,012 men and women who suffered from a first heart attack and then were followed for up to eight years showed that those men who were most aggressive and hostile at the outset suffered the highest rate of second heart attacks.[12] There were similar results in a Yale School of Medicine study of 929 men who had survived heart attacks and were tracked for up to ten years.[13] Those who had been rated as easily roused to anger were three times more likely to die of cardiac arrest than those who were more even-tempered. If they also had high cholesterol levels, the added risk from anger was five times higher.

The Yale researchers point out that it may not be anger alone that heightens the risk of death from heart disease, but rather intense negative emotionality of any kind that regularly sends surges of stress hormones through the body. But overall, the strongest scientific links between emotions and heart disease are to anger: a Harvard Medical School study asked more than fifteen hundred men and women who had suffered heart attacks to describe their emotional state in the hours before the attack. Being angry more than doubled the risk of cardiac arrest in people who already had heart disease; the heightened risk lasted for about two hours after the anger was aroused.[14]

These findings do not mean that people should try to suppress anger when it is appropriate. Indeed, there is evidence that trying to completely suppress such feelings in the heat of the moment actually results in magnifying the body's agitation and may raise blood pressure.[15] On the other hand, as we saw in Chapter 5, the net effect of ventilating anger every time it is felt is simply to feed it, making it a more likely response to any annoying situation. Williams resolves this paradox by concluding that whether anger is expressed or not is less important than whether it is chronic. An occasional display of hostility is not dangerous to health; the problem arises when hostility becomes so constant as to define an antagonistic personal style—one marked by repeated feelings of mistrust and cynicism and the propensity to snide comments and put-downs, as well as more obvious bouts of temper and rage.[16]

The hopeful news is that chronic anger need not be a death sentence: hostility is a habit that can change. One group of heart-attack patients at Stanford University Medical School was enrolled in a program designed to help them soften the attitudes that gave them a short temper. This anger-control training resulted in a second-heart-attack rate 44 percent lower than for those who had not tried to change their hostility.[17] A program designed by Williams has had similar beneficial results.[18] Like the Stanford program, it teaches basic elements of emotional intelligence, particularly mindfulness of anger as it begins to stir, the ability to regulate it once it has begun, and empathy. Patients are asked to jot down cynical or hostile thoughts as they notice them. If the thoughts persist, they try to short-circuit them by saying (or thinking), "Stop!" And they are encouraged to purposely substitute reasonable thoughts for cynical, mistrustful ones during trying situations— for instance, if an elevator is delayed, to search for a benign reason rather than harbor anger against some imagined thoughtless person who may be responsible for the delay. For frustrating encounters, they learn the ability to see things from the other person's perspective—empathy is a balm for anger.

As Williams told me, "The antidote to hostility is to develop a more trusting heart. All it takes is the right motivation. When people see that their hostility can lead to an early grave, they are ready to try."

Stress: Anxiety Out of Proportion and Out of Place

> I just feel anxious and tense all the time. It all started in high school. I was a straight-A student, and I worried constantly about my grades, whether the other kids and the teachers liked me, being prompt for classes—things like that. There was a lot of pressure from my parents to do well in school and to be a good role model. . . . I guess I just caved in to all that pressure, because my stomach problems began in my sophomore year of high school. Since that time, I've had to be really careful about drinking caffeine and eating spicy meals. I notice that when I'm feeling worried or tense my stomach will flare up, and since I'm usually worried about something, I'm always nauseous.[19]

Anxiety—the distress evoked by life's pressures—is perhaps the emotion with the greatest weight of scientific evidence connecting it to the onset of sickness and course of recovery. When anxiety helps us prepare to deal with some danger (a presumed utility in evolution), then it has served us well. But in modern life anxiety is more often out of proportion and out of place— distress comes in the face of situations that we must live with or that are conjured by the mind, not real dangers we need to confront. Repeated bouts of anxiety signal high levels of stress. The woman whose constant worrying primes her gastrointestinal trouble is a textbook example of how anxiety and stress exacerbate medical problems.

In a 1993 review in the *Archives of Internal Medicine* of extensive research on the stress-disease link, Yale psychologist Bruce McEwen noted a broad spectrum of effects: compromising immune function to the point that it can speed the metastasis of cancer; increasing vulnerability to viral infections; exacerbating plaque formation leading to atherosclerosis and blood clotting leading to myocardial infarction; accelerating the onset of Type I diabetes and the course of Type II diabetes; and worsening or triggering an asthma attack.[20] Stress can also lead to ulceration of the gastrointestinal tract, triggering symptoms in ulcerative colitis and in inflammatory bowel disease. The brain itself is susceptible to the long-term effects of sustained stress, including damage to the hippocampus, and so to memory. In general, says McEwen, "evidence is mounting that the nervous system is subject to 'wear and tear' as a result of stressful experiences."[21]

Particularly compelling evidence for the medical impact from distress has come from studies with infectious diseases such as colds, the flu, and herpes. We are continually exposed to such viruses, but ordinarily our immune system fights them off—except that under emotional stress those defenses more often fail. In experiments in which the robustness of the immune system has been assayed directly, stress and anxiety have been found to weaken it, but in most such results it is unclear whether the range of immune weakening is of clinical significance—that is, great enough to open the way to disease.[22] For that reason stronger scientific links of stress and anxiety to medical vulnerability come from prospective studies: those that start with healthy people and monitor first a heightening of distress followed by a weakening of the immune system and the onset of illness.

In one of the most scientifically compelling studies, Sheldon Cohen, a psychologist at Carnegie-Mellon University, working with scientists at a specialized colds research unit in Sheffield, England, carefully assessed how much stress people were feeling in their lives, and then systematically exposed them to a cold virus. Not everyone so exposed actually comes down with a cold; a robust immune system can—and constantly does—resist the cold virus. Cohen found that the more stress in their lives, the more likely people were to catch cold. Among those with little stress, 27 percent came down with a cold after being exposed to the virus; among those with the most stressful lives, 47 percent got the cold—direct evidence that stress itself weakens the immune system.[23] (While this may be one of those scientific results that confirms what everyone has observed or suspected all along, it is considered a landmark finding because of its scientific rigor.)

Likewise, married couples who for three months kept daily checklists of hassles and upsetting events such as marital fights showed a strong pattern: three or four days after an especially intense batch of upsets, they came down with a cold or upper-respiratory infection. That lag period is precisely the incubation time for many common cold viruses, suggesting that being exposed while they were most worried and upset made them especially vulnerable.[24]

The same stress-infection pattern holds for the herpes virus—both the type that causes cold sores on the lip and the type that causes genital lesions. Once people have been exposed to the herpes virus, it stays latent in the body, flaring up from time to time. The activity of the herpes virus can be tracked by levels of antibodies to it in the blood. Using this measure, reactivation of the herpes virus has been found in medical students undergoing year-end exams, in recently separated women, and among people under constant pressure from caring for a family member with Alzheimer's disease.[25]

The toll of anxiety is not just that it lowers the immune response; other research is showing adverse effects on the cardiovascular system. While chronic hostility and repeated episodes of anger seem to put men at greatest risk for heart disease, the more deadly emotion in women may be anxiety and fear. In research at Stanford University School of Medicine with more than a thousand men and women who had suffered a first heart attack, those women who went on to suffer a second heart attack were marked by high levels of fearfulness and anxiety. In many cases the fearfulness took the form of crippling phobias: after their first heart attack the patients stopped driving, quit their jobs, or avoided going out.[26]

The insidious physical effects of mental stress and anxiety—the kind produced by high-pressure jobs, or high-pressure lives such as that of a single mother juggling day care and a job—are being pinpointed at an anatomically fine-grained level. For example, Stephen Manuck, a University of Pittsburgh psychologist, put thirty volunteers through a rigorous, anxiety-riddled ordeal in a laboratory while he monitored the men's blood, assaying a substance secreted by blood platelets called adenosine triphosphate, or ATP, which can trigger blood-vessel changes that may lead to heart attacks and strokes. While the volunteers were under the intense stress, their ATP levels rose sharply, as did their heart rate and blood pressure.

Understandably, health risks seem greatest for those whose jobs are high in "strain": having high-pressure performance demands while having little or no control over how to get the job done (a predicament that gives bus drivers, for instance, a high rate of hypertension). For example, in a study of 569 patients with colorectal cancer and a matched comparison group, those who said that in the previous ten years they had experienced severe on-the-job aggravation were five and a half times more likely to have developed the cancer compared to those with no such stress in their lives.[27]

Because the medical toll of distress is so broad, relaxation techniques—which directly counter the physiological arousal of stress—are being used clinically to ease the symptoms of a wide variety of chronic illnesses. These include cardiovascular disease, some types of diabetes, arthritis, asthma, gastrointestinal disorders, and chronic pain, to name a few. To the degree any symptoms are worsened by stress and emotional distress, helping patients become more relaxed and able to handle their turbulent feelings can often offer some reprieve.[28]

The Medical Costs of Depression

She had been diagnosed with metastatic breast cancer, a return and spread of the malignancy several years after what she had thought was successful surgery for the disease. Her doctor could no longer talk of a cure, and the chemotherapy, at best, might offer just a few more months of life. Understandably, she was depressed—so much so that whenever she went to her oncologist, she found herself at some point bursting out into tears. Her oncologist's response each time: asking her to leave the office immediately.

Apart from the hurtfulness of the oncologist's coldness, did it matter medically that he would not deal with his patient's constant sadness? By the time a disease has become so virulent, it would be unlikely that any emotion would have an appreciable effect on its progress. While the woman's depression most certainly dimmed the quality of her final months, the medical evidence that melancholy might affect the course of cancer is as yet mixed.[29] But cancer aside, a smattering of studies suggest a role for depression in many other medical conditions, especially in worsening a sickness once it has begun. The evidence is mounting that for patients with serious disease who are depressed, it would pay medically to treat their depression too.

One complication in treating depression in medical patients is that its symptoms, including loss of appetite and lethargy, are easily mistaken for signs of other diseases, particularly by physicians with little training in psychiatric diagnosis. That inability to diagnose depression may itself add to the problem, since it means that a patient's depression—like that of the weepy breast-cancer patient—goes unnoticed and untreated. And that failure to diagnose and treat may add to the risk of death in severe disease.

For instance, of 100 patients who received bone marrow transplants, 12 of the 13 who had been depressed died within the first year of the transplant, while 34 of the remaining 87 were still alive two years later.[30] And in patients with chronic kidney failure who were receiving dialysis, those who were diagnosed with major depression were most likely to die within the following two years; depression was a stronger predictor of death than any medical sign.[31] Here the route connecting emotion to medical status was not biological but attitudinal: The depressed patients were much worse about complying with their medical regimens—cheating on their diets, for example, which put them at higher risk.

Heart disease too seems to be exacerbated by depression. In a study of 2,832 middle-aged men and women tracked for twelve years, those who felt a sense of nagging despair and hopelessness had a heightened rate of death from heart disease.[32] And for the 3 percent or so who were most severely depressed, the death rate from heart disease, compared to the rate for those with no feelings of depression, was four times greater.

Depression seems to pose a particularly grave medical risk for heart attack survivors.[33] In a study of patients in a Montreal hospital who were discharged after being treated for a first heart attack, depressed patients had a sharply higher risk of dying within the following six months. Among the one in eight patients who were seriously depressed, the death rate was five times higher than for others with comparable disease—an effect as great as that of major medical risks for cardiac death, such as left ventricular dysfunction or a history of previous heart attacks. Among the possible mechanisms that might explain why depression so greatly increases the odds of a later heart attack are its effects on heart rate variability, increasing the risk of fatal arrhythmias.

Depression has also been found to complicate recovery from hip fracture. In a study of elderly women with hip fracture, several thousand were given psychiatric evaluations on their admission to the hospital. Those who were depressed on admission stayed an average of eight days longer than those with comparable injury but no depression, and were only a third as likely ever to walk again. But depressed women who had psychiatric help for their depression along with other medical care needed less physical therapy to walk again and had fewer rehospitalizations over the three months after their return home from the hospital.

Likewise, in a study of patients whose condition was so dire that they were among the top 10 percent of those using medical services—often because of having multiple illnesses, such as both heart disease and diabetes—about one in six had serious depression. When these patients were treated for the problem, the number of days per year that they were disabled dropped from 79 to 51 for those who had major depression, and from 62 days per year to just 18 in those who had been treated for mild depression.[34]

THE MEDICAL BENEFITS OF POSITIVE FEELINGS

The cumulative evidence for adverse medical effects from anger, anxiety, and depression, then, is compelling. Both anger and anxiety, when chronic, can make people more susceptible to a range of disease. And while depression may not make people more vulnerable to becoming ill, it does seem to impede medical recovery and heighten the risk of death, especially with more frail patients with severe conditions.

But if chronic emotional distress in its many forms is toxic, the opposite range of emotion can be tonic—to a degree. This by no means says that positive emotion is curative, or that laughter or happiness alone will turn the course of a serious disease. The edge positive emotions offer seems subtle, but, by using studies with large numbers of people, can be teased out of the mass of complex variables that affect the course of disease.

The Price of Pessimism—and Advantages of Optimism

As with depression, there are medical costs to pessimism—and corresponding benefits from optimism. For example, 122 men who had their first heart attack were evaluated on their degree of optimism or pessimism. Eight years later, of the 25 most pessimistic men, 21 had died; of the 25 most optimistic, just 6 had died. Their mental outlook proved a better predictor of survival than any medical risk factor, including the amount of damage to the heart in the first attack, artery blockage, cholesterol level, or blood pressure. And in other research, patients going into artery bypass surgery who were more optimistic had a much faster recovery and fewer medical complications during and after surgery than did more pessimistic patients.[35]

Like its near cousin optimism, hope has healing power. People who have a great deal of hopefulness are, understandably, better able to bear up under trying circumstances, including medical difficulties. In a study of people paralyzed from spinal injuries, those who had more hope were able to gain greater levels of physical mobility compared to other patients with similar degrees of injury, but who felt less hopeful. Hope is especially telling in paralysis from spinal injury, since this medical tragedy typically involves a man who is paralyzed in his twenties by an accident and will remain so for the rest of his life. How he reacts emotionally will have broad consequences for the degree to which he will make the efforts that might bring him greater physical and social functioning.[36]

Just why an optimistic or pessimistic outlook should have health consequences is open to any of several explanations. One theory proposes that
pessimism leads to depression, which in turn interferes with the resistance of
the immune system to tumors and infection—an unproven speculation at
present. Or it may be that pessimists neglect themselves—some studies have
found that pessimists smoke and drink more, and exercise less, than optimists, and are generally much more careless about their health habits. Or it
may one day turn out that the physiology of hopefulness is itself somehow
helpful biologically to the body's fight against disease.

With a Little Help From My Friends:
The Medical Value of Relationships

Add the sounds of silence to the list of emotional risks to health—and close
emotional ties to the list of protective factors. Studies done over two decades
involving more than thirty-seven thousand people show that social
isolation—the sense that you have nobody with whom you can share your
private feelings or have close contact—doubles the chances of sickness or
death.[37] Isolation itself, a 1987 report in *Science* concluded, "is as significant
to mortality rates as smoking, high blood pressure, high cholesterol, obesity,
and lack of physical exercise." Indeed, smoking increases mortality risk by a
factor of just 1.6, while social isolation does so by a factor of 2.0, making it a
greater health risk.[38]

Isolation is harder on men than on women. Isolated men were two to three
times more likely to die as were men with close social ties; for isolated
women, the risk was one and a half times greater than for more socially
connected women. The difference between men and women in the impact of
isolation may be because women's relationships tend to be emotionally
closer than men's; a few strands of such social ties for a woman may be more
comforting than the same small number of friendships for a man.

Of course, solitude is not the same as isolation; many people who live on
their own or see few friends are content and healthy. Rather, it is the
subjective sense of being cut off from people and having no one to turn to
that is the medical risk. This finding is ominous in light of the increasing
isolation bred by solitary TV-watching and the falling away of social habits
such as clubs and visits in modern urban societies, and suggests an added
value to self-help groups such as Alcoholics Anonymous as surrogate communities.

The power of isolation as a mortality risk factor—and the healing power of close ties—can be seen in the study of one hundred bone marrow transplant patients.[39] Among patients who felt they had strong emotional support from their spouse, family, or friends, 54 percent survived the transplants after two years, versus just 20 percent among those who reported little such support. Similarly, elderly people who suffer heart attacks, but have two or more people in their lives they can rely on for emotional support, are more than twice as likely to survive longer than a year after an attack than are those people with no such support.[40]

Perhaps the most telling testimony to the healing potency of emotional ties is a Swedish study published in 1993.[41] All the men living in the Swedish city of Göteborg who were born in 1933 were offered a free medical exam; seven years later the 752 men who had come for the exam were contacted again. Of these, 41 had died in the intervening years.

Men who had originally reported being under intense emotional stress had a death rate three times greater than those who said their lives were calm and placid. The emotional distress was due to events such as serious financial trouble, feeling insecure at work or being forced out of a job, being the object of a legal action, or going through a divorce. Having had three or more of these troubles within the year before the exam was a stronger predictor of dying within the ensuing seven years than were medical indicators such as high blood pressure, high concentrations of blood triglycerides, or high serum cholesterol levels.

Yet among men who said they had a dependable web of intimacy—a wife, close friends, and the like—*there was no relationship whatever* between high stress levels and death rate. Having people to turn to and talk with, people who could offer solace, help, and suggestions, protected them from the deadly impact of life's rigors and trauma.

The quality of relationships as well as their sheer number seems key to buffering stress. Negative relationships take their own toll. Marital arguments, for example, have a negative impact on the immune system.[42] One study of college roommates found that the more they disliked each other, the more susceptible they were to colds and the flu, and the more frequently they went to doctors. John Cacioppo, the Ohio State University psychologist who did the roommate study, told me, "It's the most important relationships in your life, the people you see day in and day out, that seem to be crucial for your health. And the more significant the relationship is in your life, the more it matters for your health."[43]

The Healing Power of Emotional Support

In *The Merry Adventures of Robin Hood,* Robin advises a young follower: "Tell us thy troubles and speak freely. A flow of words doth ever ease the heart of sorrows; it is like opening the waste where the mill dam is overfull." This bit of folk wisdom has great merit; unburdening a troubled heart appears to be good medicine. The scientific corroboration of Robin's advice comes from James Pennebaker, a Southern Methodist University psychologist, who has shown in a series of experiments that getting people to talk about the thoughts that trouble them most has a beneficial medical effect.[44] His method is remarkably simple: he asks people to write, for fifteen to twenty minutes a day over five or so days, about, for example, "the most traumatic experience of your entire life," or some pressing worry of the moment. What people write can be kept entirely to themselves if they like.

The net effect of this confessional is striking: enhanced immune function, significant drops in health-center visits in the following six months, fewer days missed from work, and even improved liver enzyme function. Moreover, those whose writing showed most evidence of turbulent feelings had the greatest improvements in their immune function. A specific pattern emerged as the "healthiest" way to ventilate troubling feelings: at first expressing a high level of sadness, anxiety, anger—whatever troubling feelings the topic brought up; then, over the course of the next several days weaving a narrative, finding some meaning in the trauma or travail.

That process, of course, seems akin to what happens when people explore such troubles in psychotherapy. Indeed, Pennebaker's findings suggest one reason why other studies show medical patients given psychotherapy in addition to surgery or medical treatment often fare better *medically* than do those who receive medical treatment alone.[45]

Perhaps the most powerful demonstration of the clinical power of emotional support was in groups at Stanford University Medical School for women with advanced metastatic breast cancer. After an initial treatment, often including surgery, these women's cancer had returned and was spreading through their bodies. It was only a matter of time, clinically speaking, until the spreading cancer killed them. Dr. David Spiegel, who conducted the study, was himself stunned by the findings, as was the medical community: women with advanced breast cancer who went to weekly meetings with others survived *twice as long* as did women with the same disease who faced it on their own.[46]

All the women received standard medical care; the only difference was that some also went to the groups, where they were able to unburden themselves with others who understood what they faced and were willing to listen to their fears, their pain, and their anger. Often this was the only place where the women could be open about these emotions, because other people in their lives dreaded talking with them about the cancer and their imminent death. Women who attended the groups lived for thirty-seven additional months, on average, while those with the disease who did not go to the groups died, on average, in nineteen months—a gain in life expectancy for such patients beyond the reach of any medication or other medical treatment. As Dr. Jimmie Holland, the chief psychiatric oncologist at Sloan-Kettering Memorial Hospital, a cancer treatment center in New York City, put it to me, "Every cancer patient should be in a group like this." Indeed, if it had been a new drug that produced the extended life expectancy, pharmaceutical companies would be battling to produce it.

BRINGING EMOTIONAL INTELLIGENCE TO MEDICAL CARE

The day a routine checkup spotted some blood in my urine, my doctor sent me for a diagnostic test in which I was injected with a radioactive dye. I lay on a table while an overhead X-ray machine took successive images of the dye's progression through my kidneys and bladder. I had company for the test: a close friend, a physician himself, happened to be visiting for a few days and offered to come to the hospital with me. He sat in the room while the X-ray machine, on an automated track, rotated for new camera angles, whirred and clicked; rotated, whirred, clicked.

The test took an hour and a half. At the very end a kidney specialist hurried into the room, quickly introduced himself, and disappeared to scan the X-rays. He didn't return to tell me what they showed.

As we were leaving the exam room my friend and I passed the nephrologist. Feeling shaken and somewhat dazed by the test, I did not have the presence of mind to ask the one question that had been on my mind all morning. But my companion, the physician, did: "Doctor," he said, "my friend's father died of bladder cancer. He's anxious to know if you saw any signs of cancer in the X-rays."

"No abnormalities," was the curt reply as the nephrologist hurried on to his next appointment.

My inability to ask the single question I cared about most is repeated a thousand times each day in hospitals and clinics everywhere. A study of patients in physicians' waiting rooms found that each had an average of three or more questions in mind to ask the physician they were about to see. But when the patients left the physician's office, an average of only one and a half of those questions had been answered.[47] This finding speaks to one of the many ways patients' emotional needs are unmet by today's medicine. Unanswered questions feed uncertainty, fear, catastrophizing. And they lead patients to balk at going along with treatment regimes they don't fully understand.

There are many ways medicine can expand its view of health to include the emotional realities of illness. For one, patients could routinely be offered fuller information essential to the decisions they must make about their own medical care; some services now offer any caller a state-of-the-art computer search of the medical literature on what ails them, so that patients can be more equal partners with their physicians in making informed decisions.[48] Another approach is programs that, in a few minutes' time, teach patients to be effective questioners with their physicians, so that when they have three questions in mind as they wait for the doctor, they will come out of the office with three answers.[49]

Moments when patients face surgery or invasive and painful tests are fraught with anxiety—and are a prime opportunity to deal with the emotional dimension. Some hospitals have developed presurgery instruction for patients that help them assuage their fears and handle their discomforts—for example, by teaching patients relaxation techniques, answering their questions well in advance of surgery, and telling them several days ahead of surgery precisely what they are likely to experience during their recovery. The result: patients recover from surgery an average of two to three days sooner.[50]

Being a hospital patient can be a tremendously lonely, helpless experience. But some hospitals have begun to design rooms so that family members can stay with patients, cooking and caring for them as they would at home—a progressive step that, ironically, is routine throughout the Third World.[51]

Relaxation training can help patients deal with some of the distress their symptoms bring, as well as with the emotions that may be triggering or exacerbating their symptoms. An exemplary model is Jon Kabat-Zinn's Stress Reduction Clinic at the University of Massachusetts Medical Center, which offers a ten-week course in mindfulness and yoga to patients; the emphasis is on being mindful of emotional episodes as they are happening, and on cultivating a daily practice that offers deep relaxation. Hospitals have made instructional tapes from the course available over patients' television sets—a far better emotional diet for the bedridden than the usual fare, soap operas.[52]

Relaxation and yoga are also at the core of the innovative program for treating heart disease developed by Dr. Dean Ornish.[53] After a year of this program, which included a low-fat diet, patients whose heart disease was severe enough to warrant a coronary bypass actually reversed the buildup of artery-clogging plaque. Ornish tells me that relaxation training is one of the most important parts of the program. Like Kabat-Zinn's, it takes advantage of what Dr. Herbert Benson calls the "relaxation response," the physiological opposite of the stress arousal that contributes to such a wide spectrum of medical problems.

Finally, there is the added medical value of an empathic physician or nurse, attuned to patients, able to listen and be heard. This means fostering "relationship-centered care," recognizing that the relationship between physician and patient is itself a factor of significance. Such relationships would be fostered more readily if medical education included some basic tools of emotional intelligence, especially self-awareness and the arts of empathy and listening.[54]

TOWARD A MEDICINE THAT CARES

Such steps are a beginning. But for medicine to enlarge its vision to embrace the impact of emotions, two large implications of the scientific findings must be taken to heart:

1. *Helping people better manage their upsetting feelings—anger, anxiety, depression, pessimism, and loneliness—is a form of disease prevention.* Since the data show that the toxicity of these emotions, when chronic, is on a par with smoking cigarettes, helping people handle them better could potentially have a medical payoff as great as getting heavy smokers to quit. One way to do this that could have broad public-health effects would be to impart most basic emotional intelligence skills to children, so that they become lifelong habits. Another high-payoff preventive strategy would be to teach emotion management to people reaching retirement age, since emotional well-being is one factor that determines whether an older person declines rapidly or thrives. A third target group might be so-called at-risk populations—the very poor, single working mothers, residents of high-crime

neighborhoods, and the like—who live under extraordinary pressure day in and day out, and so might do better medically with help in handling the emotional toll of these stresses.

2. *Many patients can benefit measurably when their psychological needs are attended to along with their purely medical ones.* While it is a step toward more humane care when a physician or nurse offers a distressed patient comfort and consolation, more can be done. But emotional care is an opportunity too often lost in the way medicine is practiced today; it is a blind spot for medicine. Despite mounting data on the medical usefulness of attending to emotional needs, as well as supporting evidence for connections between the brain's emotional center and the immune system, many physicians remain skeptical that their patients' emotions matter clinically, dismissing the evidence for this as trivial and anecdotal, as "fringe," or, worse, as the exaggerations of a self-promoting few.

Though more and more patients seek a more humane medicine, it is becoming endangered. Of course, there remain dedicated nurses and physicians who give their patients tender, sensitive care. But the changing culture of medicine itself, as it becomes more responsive to the imperatives of business, is making such care increasingly difficult to find.

On the other hand, there may be a business advantage to humane medicine: treating emotional distress in patients, early evidence suggests, can save money—especially to the extent that it prevents or delays the onset of sickness, or helps patients heal more quickly. In a study of elderly patients with hip fracture at Mt. Sinai School of Medicine in New York City and at Northwestern University, patients who received therapy for depression in addition to normal orthopedic care left the hospital an average of two days earlier; total savings for the hundred or so patients was $97,361 in medical costs.[55]

Such care also makes patients more satisfied with their physicians and medical treatment. In the emerging medical marketplace, where patients often have the option to choose between competing health plans, satisfaction levels will no doubt enter the equation of these very personal decisions—souring experiences can lead patients to go elsewhere for care, while pleasing ones translate into loyalty.

Finally, medical ethics may demand such an approach. An editorial in the *Journal of the American Medical Association,* commenting on a report that depression increases fivefold the likelihood of dying after being treated for a heart attack, notes: "[T]he clear demonstration that psychological factors like depression and social isolation distinguish the coronary heart disease patients at highest risk means it would be unethical not to start trying to treat these factors."[56]

If the findings on emotions and health mean anything, it is that medical care that neglects how people *feel* as they battle a chronic or severe disease is no longer adequate. It is time for medicine to take more methodical advantage of the link between emotion and health. What is now the exception could—and should—be part of the mainstream, so that a more caring medicine is available to us all. At the least it would make medicine more humane. And, for some, it could speed the course of recovery. "Compassion," as one patient put it in an open letter to his surgeon, "is not mere hand holding. It is good medicine."[57]

PART FOUR

WINDOWS OF OPPORTUNITY

12

The Family Crucible

It's a low-key family tragedy. Carl and Ann are showing their daughter Leslie, just five, how to play a brand-new video game. But as Leslie starts to play, her parents' overly eager attempts to "help" her just seem to get in the way. Contradictory orders fly in every direction.

"To the right, to the right—stop. Stop. Stop!" Ann, the mother, urges, her voice growing more intent and anxious as Leslie, sucking on her lip and staring wide-eyed at the video screen, struggles to follow these directives.

"See, you're not lined up . . . put it to the left! To the left!" Carl, the girl's father, brusquely orders.

Meanwhile Ann, her eyes rolling upward in frustration, yells over his advice, "Stop! Stop!"

Leslie, unable to please either her father or her mother, contorts her jaw in tension and blinks as her eyes fill with tears.

Her parents start bickering, ignoring Leslie's tears. "She's not moving the stick *that* much!" Ann tells Carl, exasperated.

As the tears start rolling down Leslie's cheeks, neither parent makes any move that indicates they notice or care. As Leslie raises her hand to wipe her eyes, her father snaps, "Okay, put your hand back on the stick . . . you wanna get ready to shoot. Okay, put it over!" And her mother barks, "Okay, move it just a teeny bit!"

But by now Leslie is sobbing softly, alone with her anguish.

At such moments children learn deep lessons. For Leslie one conclusion from this painful exchange might well be that neither her parents, nor anyone else, for that matter, cares about her feelings.[1] When similar moments are repeated countless times over the course of childhood they impart some of the most fundamental emotional messages of a lifetime—lessons that can determine a life course. Family life is our first school for emotional learning; in this intimate cauldron we learn how to feel about ourselves and how others will react to our feelings; how to think about these feelings and what choices we have in reacting; how to read and express hopes and fears. This emotional schooling operates not just through the things that parents say and do directly to children, but also in the models they offer for handling their own feelings and those that pass between husband and wife. Some parents are gifted emotional teachers, others atrocious.

There are hundreds of studies showing that how parents treat their children—whether with harsh discipline or empathic understanding, with indifference or warmth, and so on—has deep and lasting consequences for the child's emotional life. Only recently, though, have there been hard data showing that having emotionally intelligent parents is itself of enormous benefit to a child. The ways a couple handles the feelings between them—in addition to their direct dealings with a child—impart powerful lessons to their children, who are astute learners, attuned to the subtlest emotional exchanges in the family. When research teams led by Carole Hooven and John Gottman at the University of Washington did a microanalysis of interactions in couples on how the partners handled their children, they found that those couples who were more emotionally competent in the marriage were also the most effective in helping their children with their emotional ups and downs.[2]

The families were first seen when one of their children was just five years old, and again when the child had reached nine. In addition to observing the parents talk with each other, the research team also watched families (including Leslie's) as the father or mother tried to show their young child how to operate a new video game—a seemingly innocuous interaction, but quite telling about the emotional currents that run between parent and child.

Some mothers and fathers were like Ann and Carl: overbearing, losing patience with their child's ineptness, raising their voices in disgust or exasperation, some even putting their child down as "stupid"—in short, falling prey to the same tendencies toward contempt and disgust that eat away at a marriage. Others, however, were patient with their child's errors, helping the child figure the game out in his or her own way rather than imposing the parents' will. The video game session was a surprisingly powerful barometer of the parents' emotional style.

The three most common emotionally inept parenting styles proved to be:

• *Ignoring feelings altogether.* Such parents treat a child's emotional upset as trivial or a bother, something they should wait to blow over. They fail to use emotional moments as a chance to get closer to the child or to help the child learn lessons in emotional competence.

• *Being too laissez-faire*. These parents notice how a child feels, but hold that however a child handles the emotional storm is fine—even, say, hitting. Like those who ignore a child's feelings, these parents rarely step in to try to show their child an alternative emotional response. They try to soothe all upsets, and will, for instance, use bargaining and bribes to get their child to stop being sad or angry.

• *Being contemptuous, showing no respect for how the child feels.* Such parents are typically disapproving, harsh in both their criticisms and their punishments. They might, for instance, forbid any display of the child's anger at all, and become punitive at the least sign of irritability. These are the parents who angrily yell at a child who is trying to tell his side of the story, "Don't you talk back to me!"

Finally, there are parents who seize the opportunity of a child's upset to act as what amounts to an emotional coach or mentor. They take their child's feelings seriously enough to try to understand exactly what is upsetting them ("Are you angry because Tommy hurt your feelings?") and to help the child find positive ways to soothe their feelings ("Instead of hitting him, why don't you find a toy to play with on your own until you feel like playing with him again?").

In order for parents to be effective coaches in this way, they must have a fairly good grasp of the rudiments of emotional intelligence themselves. One of the basic emotional lessons for a child, for example, is how to distinguish among feelings; a father who is too tuned out of, say, his own sadness cannot help his son understand the difference between grieving over a loss, feeling sad in a sad movie, and the sadness that arises when something bad happens to someone the child cares about. Beyond this distinction, there are more sophisticated insights, such as that anger is so often prompted by first feeling hurt.

As children grow the specific emotional lessons they are ready for—and in need of—shift. As we saw in Chapter 7 the lessons in empathy begin in infancy, with parents who attune to their baby's feelings. Though some emotional skills are honed with friends through the years, emotionally adept parents can do much to help their children with each of the basics of emotional intelligence: learning how to recognize, manage, and harness their feelings; empathizing; and handling the feelings that arise in their relationships.

The impact on children of such parenting is extraordinarily sweeping.[3] The University of Washington team found that when parents are emotionally adept, compared to those who handle feelings poorly, their children—understandably—get along better with, show more affection toward, and have less tension around their parents. But beyond that, these children also are better at handling their own emotions, are more effective at soothing themselves when upset, and get upset less often. The children are also more relaxed *biologically,* with lower levels of stress hormones and other physiological indicators of emotional arousal (a pattern that, if sustained through life, might well augur better physical health, as we saw in Chapter 11). Other advantages are social: these children are more popular with and are better-liked by their peers, and are seen by their teachers as more socially skilled. Their parents and teachers alike rate these children as having fewer behavioral problems such as rudeness or aggressiveness. Finally, the benefits are cognitive; these children can pay attention better, and so are more effective learners. Holding IQ constant, the five-year-olds whose parents were good coaches had higher achievement scores in math and reading when they reached third grade (a powerful argument for teaching emotional skills to help prepare children for learning as well as life). Thus the payoff for children whose parents are emotionally adept is a surprising—almost astounding—range of advantages across, and beyond, the spectrum of emotional intelligence.

HEART START

The impact of parenting on emotional competence starts in the cradle. Dr. T. Berry Brazelton, the eminent Harvard pediatrician, has a simple diagnostic test of a baby's basic outlook toward life. He offers two blocks to an eight-month-old, and then shows the baby how he wants her to put the two blocks together. A baby who is hopeful about life, who has confidence in her own abilities, says Brazelton,

> will pick up one block, mouth it, rub it in her hair, drop it over the side of the table, watching to see whether you will retrieve it for her. When you do, she finally completes the requested task—place the two blocks together. Then she looks up at you with a bright-eyed look of expectancy that says, "Tell me how great I am!"[4]

Babies like these have gotten a goodly dose of approval and encouragement from the adults in their lives; they expect to succeed in life's little challenges. By contrast, babies who come from homes too bleak, chaotic, or neglectful go about the same small task in a way that signals they already expect to fail. It is not that these babies fail to bring the blocks together; they understand the instruction and have the coordination to comply. But even when they do, reports Brazelton, their demeanor is "hangdog," a look that says, "I'm no good. See, I've failed." Such children are likely to go through life with a defeatist outlook, expecting no encouragement or interest from teachers, finding school joyless, perhaps eventually dropping out.

The difference between the two outlooks—children who are confident and optimistic versus those who expect to fail—starts to take shape in the first few years of life. Parents, says Brazelton, "need to understand how their actions can help generate the confidence, the curiosity, the pleasure in learning and the understanding of limits" that help children succeed in life. His advice is informed by a growing body of evidence showing that success in school depends to a surprising extent on emotional characteristics formed in the years before a child enters school. As we saw in Chapter 6, for example, the ability of four-year-olds to control the impulse to grab for a marshmallow predicted a 210-point advantage in their SAT scores fourteen years later.

The first opportunity for shaping the ingredients of emotional intelligence is in the earliest years, though these capacities continue to form throughout the school years. The emotional abilities children acquire in later life build on those of the earliest years. And these abilities, as we saw in Chapter 6, are the essential foundation for all learning. A report from the National Center for Clinical Infant Programs makes the point that school success is not predicted by a child's fund of facts or a precocious ability to read so much as by emotional and social measures: being self-assured and inter-ested; knowing what kind of behavior is expected and how to rein in the impulse to misbehave; being able to wait, to follow directions, and to turn to teachers for help; and expressing needs while getting along with other children.[5]

Almost all students who do poorly in school, says the report, lack one or more of these elements of emotional intelligence (regardless of whether they also have cognitive difficulties such as learning disabilities). The magnitude of the problem is not minor; in some states close to one in five children have to repeat first grade, and then as the years go on fall further behind their peers, becoming increasingly discouraged, resentful, and disruptive.

A child's readiness for school depends on the most basic of all knowledge, *how* to learn. The report lists the seven key ingredients of this crucial capacity—all related to emotional intelligence:[6]

1. *Confidence*. A sense of control and mastery of one's body, behavior, and world; the child's sense that he is more likely than not to succeed at what he undertakes, and that adults will be helpful.

2. *Curiosity*. The sense that finding out about things is positive and leads to pleasure.

3. *Intentionality*. The wish and capacity to have an impact, and to act upon that with persistence. This is related to a sense of competence, of being effective.

4. *Self-control*. The ability to modulate and control one's own actions in age-appropriate ways; a sense of inner control.

5. *Relatedness*. The ability to engage with others based on the sense of being understood by and understanding others.

6. *Capacity to communicate*. The wish and ability to verbally exchange ideas, feelings, and concepts with others. This is related to a sense of trust in others and of pleasure in engaging with others, including adults.

7. *Cooperativeness*. The ability to balance one's own needs with those of others in group activity.

Whether or not a child arrives at school on the first day of kindergarten with these capabilities depends greatly on how much her parents—and preschool teachers—have given her the kind of care that amounts to a "Heart Start," the emotional equivalent of the Head Start programs.

GETTING THE EMOTIONAL BASICS

Say a two-month-old baby wakes up at 3 A.M. and starts crying. Her mother comes in and, for the next half hour, the baby contentedly nurses in her mother's arms while her mother gazes at her affectionately, telling her that she's happy to see her, even in the middle of the night. The baby, content in her mother's love, drifts back to sleep.

Now say another two-month-old baby, who also awoke crying in the wee hours, is met instead by a mother who is tense and irritable, having fallen asleep just an hour before after a fight with her husband. The baby starts to tense up the moment his mother abruptly picks him up, telling him, "Just be quiet—I can't stand one more thing! Come on, let's get it over with." As the baby nurses his mother stares stonily ahead, not looking at him, reviewing her fight with his father, getting more agitated herself as she mulls it over. The baby, sensing her tension, squirms, stiffens, and stops nursing. "That's all you want?" his mother says. "Then don't eat." With the same abruptness she puts him back in his crib and stalks out, letting him cry until he falls back to sleep, exhausted.

The two scenarios are presented by the report from the National Center for Clinical Infant Programs as examples of the kinds of interaction that, if repeated over and over, instill very different feelings in a toddler about himself and his closest relationships.[7] The first baby is learning that people can be trusted to notice her needs and counted on to help, and that she can be effective in getting help; the second is finding that no one really cares, that people can't be counted on, and that his efforts to get solace will meet with failure. Of course, most babies get at least a taste of both kinds of interaction. But to the degree that one or the other is typical of how parents treat a child over the years, basic emotional lessons will be imparted about how secure a child is in the world, how effective he feels, and how dependable others are. Erik Erikson put it in terms of whether a child comes to feel a "basic trust" or a basic mistrust.

Such emotional learning begins in life's earliest moments, and continues throughout childhood. All the small exchanges between parent and child have an emotional subtext, and in the repetition of these messages over the years children form the core of their emotional outlook and capabilities. A little girl who finds a puzzle frustrating and asks her busy mother to help gets one message if the reply is the mother's clear pleasure at the request, and quite another if it's a curt "Don't bother me—I've got important work to do." When such encounters become typical of child and parent, they mold the child's emotional expectations about relationships, outlooks that will flavor her functioning in all realms of life, for better or worse.

The risks are greatest for those children whose parents are grossly inept—immature, abusing drugs, depressed or chronically angry, or simply aimless and living chaotic lives. Such parents are far less likely to give adequate care, let alone attune to their toddler's emotional needs. Simple neglect, studies find, can be more damaging than outright abuse.[8] A survey of maltreated children found the neglected youngsters doing the worst of all: they were the most anxious, inattentive, and apathetic, alternately aggressive and withdrawn. The rate for having to repeat first grade among them was 65 percent.

The first three or four years of life are a period when the toddler's brain grows to about two thirds its full size, and evolves in complexity at a greater rate than it ever will again. During this period key kinds of learning take place more readily than later in life—emotional learning foremost among them.

During this time severe stress can impair the brain's learning centers (and so be damaging to the intellect). Though as we shall see, this can be remedied to some extent by experiences later in life, the impact of this early learning is profound. As one report sums up the key emotional lesson of life's first four years, the lasting consequences are great:

> A child who cannot focus his attention, who is suspicious rather than trusting, sad or angry rather than optimistic, destructive rather than respectful and one who is overcome with anxiety, preoccupied with frightening fantasy and feels generally unhappy about himself—such a child has little opportunity at all, let alone equal opportunity, to claim the possibilities of the world as his own.[9]

HOW TO RAISE A BULLY

Much can be learned about the lifelong effects of emotionally inept parenting—particularly its role in making children aggressive—from longitudinal studies such as one of 870 children from upstate New York who were followed from the time they were eight until they were thirty.[10] The most belligerent among the children—those quickest to start fights and who habitually used force to get their way—were the most likely to have dropped out of school and, by age thirty, to have a record for crimes of violence. They also seemed to be handing down their propensity to violence: their children were, in grade school, just like the troublemakers their delinquent parent had been.

There is a lesson in how aggressiveness is passed from generation to generation. Any inherited propensities aside, the troublemakers as grown-ups acted in a way that made family life a school for aggression. As children, the troublemakers had parents who disciplined them with arbitrary, relentless severity; as parents they repeated the pattern. This was true whether it had been the father or the mother who had been identified in childhood as highly aggressive. Aggressive little girls grew up to be just as arbitrary and harshly punitive when they became mothers as the aggressive boys were as fathers. And while they punished their children with special severity, they otherwise took little interest in their children's lives, in effect ignoring them much of the time. At the same time the parents offered these children a vivid—and violent—example of aggressiveness, a model the children took with them to school and to the playground, and followed throughout life. The parents were not necessarily mean-spirited, nor did they fail to wish the best for their children; rather, they seemed to be simply repeating the style of parenting that had been modeled for them by their own parents.

In this model for violence, these children were disciplined capriciously: if their parents were in a bad mood, they would be severely punished; if their parents were in a good mood, they could get away with mayhem at home. Thus punishment came not so much because of what the child had done, but by virtue of how the parent felt. This is a recipe for feelings of worthlessness and helplessness, and for the sense that threats are everywhere and may strike at any time. Seen in light of the home life that spawns it, such children's combative and defiant posture toward the world at large makes a certain sense, unfortunate though it remains. What is disheartening is how early these dispiriting lessons can be learned, and how grim the costs for a child's emotional life can be.

ABUSE: THE EXTINCTION OF EMPATHY

In the rough-and-tumble play of the day-care center, Martin, just two and a half, brushed up against a little girl, who, inexplicably, broke out crying. Martin reached for her hand, but as the sobbing girl moved away, Martin slapped her on the arm.

As her tears continued Martin looked away and yelled, "Cut it out! *Cut it out!*" over and over, each time faster and louder.

When Martin then made another attempt to pat her, again she resisted. This time Martin bared his teeth like a snarling dog, hissing at the sobbing girl.

Once more Martin started patting the crying girl, but the pats on the back quickly turned into pounding, and Martin went on hitting and hitting the poor little girl despite her screams.

That disturbing encounter testifies to how abuse—being beaten repeatedly, at the whim of a parent's moods—warps a child's natural bent toward empathy.[11] Martin's bizarre, almost brutal response to his playmate's distress is typical of children like him, who have themselves been the victims of beatings and other physical abuse since their infancy. The response stands in stark contrast to toddlers' usual sympathetic entreaties and attempts to console a crying playmate, reviewed in Chapter 7. Martin's violent response to distress at the day-care center may well mirror the lessons he learned at home about tears and anguish: crying is met at first with a peremptory consoling gesture, but if it continues, the progression is from nasty looks and shouts, to hitting, to outright beating. Perhaps most troubling, Martin already seems to lack the most primitive sort of empathy, the instinct to stop aggression against someone who is hurt. At two and a half he displays the budding moral impulses of a cruel and sadistic brute.

Martin's meanness in place of empathy is typical of other children like him who are already, at their tender age, scarred by severe physical and emotional abuse at home. Martin was part of a group of nine such toddlers, ages one to three, witnessed in a two-hour observation at his day-care center. The abused toddlers were compared with nine others at the day-care center from equally impoverished, high-stress homes, but who were not physically abused. The differences in how the two groups of toddlers reacted when another child was hurt or upset were stark. Of twenty-three such incidents, five of the nine nonabused toddlers responded to the distress of a child nearby with concern, sadness, or empathy. But in the twenty-seven instances where the abused children could have done so, not one showed the least concern; instead they reacted to a crying child with expressions of fear, anger, or, like Martin, a physical attack.

One abused little girl, for instance, made a ferocious, threatening face at another who had broken out into tears. One-year-old Thomas, another of the abused children, froze in terror when he heard a child crying across the room; he sat completely still, his face full of fear, back stiffly straight, his tension increasing as the crying continued—as though bracing for an attack himself. And twenty-eight-month-old Kate, also abused, was almost sadistic: picking on Joey, a smaller infant, she knocked him to the ground with her feet, and as he lay there looked tenderly at him and began patting him gently on the back—only to intensify the pats into hitting him harder and harder, ignoring his misery. She kept swinging away at him, leaning in to slug him six or seven times more, until he crawled away.

These children, of course, treat others as they themselves have been treated. And the callousness of these abused children is simply a more extreme version of that seen in children whose parents are critical, threatening, and harsh in their punishments. Such children also tend to lack concern when playmates get hurt or cry; they seem to represent one end of a continuum of coldness that peaks with the brutality of the abused children. As they go on through life, they are, as a group, more likely to have cognitive difficulties in learning, more likely to be aggressive and unpopular with their peers (small wonder, if their preschool toughness is a harbinger of the future), more prone to depression, and, as adults, more likely to get into trouble with the law and commit more crimes of violence.[12]

This failure of empathy is sometimes, if not often, repeated over generations, with brutal parents having themselves been brutalized by their own parents in childhood.[13] It stands in dramatic contrast to the empathy ordinarily displayed by children of parents who are nurturing, encouraging their toddlers to show concern for others and to understand how meanness makes other children feel. Lacking such lessons in empathy, these children seem not to learn it at all.

What is perhaps most troubling about the abused toddlers is how early they seem to have learned to respond like miniature versions of their own abusive parents. But given the physical beatings they received as a sometimes daily diet, the emotional lessons are all too clear. Remember that it is in moments when passions run high or a crisis is upon us that the primitive proclivities of the brain's limbic centers take on a more dominant role. At such moments the habits the emotional brain has learned over and over will dominate, for better or worse.

Seeing how the brain itself is shaped by brutality—or by love—suggests that childhood represents a special window of opportunity for emotional lessons. These battered children have had an early and steady diet of trauma. Perhaps the most instructive paradigm for understanding the emotional learning such abused children have undergone is in seeing how trauma can leave a lasting imprint on the brain—and how even these savage imprints can be mended.

13

Trauma and Emotional Relearning

Som Chit, a Cambodian refugee, balked when her three sons asked her to buy them toy AK-47 machine guns. Her sons—ages six, nine, and eleven—wanted the toy guns to play the game some of the kids at their school called Purdy. In the game, Purdy, the villain, uses a submachine gun to massacre a group of children, then turns it on himself. Sometimes, though, the children have it end differently: it is they who kill Purdy.

Purdy was the macabre reenactment by some of the survivors of the catastrophic events of February 17, 1989, at Cleveland Elementary School in Stockton, California. There, during the school's late-morning recess for first, second, and third graders, Patrick Purdy—who had himself attended those grades at Cleveland Elementary some twenty years earlier—stood at the playground's edge and fired wave after wave of 7.22 mm bullets at the hundreds of children at play. For seven minutes Purdy sprayed bullets toward the playground, then put a pistol to his head and shot himself. When the police arrived they found five children dying, twenty-nine wounded.

In ensuing months, the Purdy game spontaneously appeared in the play of boys and girls at Cleveland Elementary, one of many signs that those seven minutes and their aftermath were seared into the children's memory. When I visited the school, just a short bike ride from the neighborhood near the University of the Pacific where I myself had grown up, it was five months after Purdy had turned that recess into a nightmare. His presence was still palpable, even though the most horrific of the grisly remnants of the shooting—swarms of bullet holes, pools of blood, bits of flesh, skin, and scalp—were gone by the morning after the shooting, washed away and painted over.

By then the deepest scars at Cleveland Elementary were not to the building but to the psyches of the children and staff there, who were trying to carry on with life as usual.[1] Perhaps most striking was how the memory of those few minutes was revived again and again by any small detail that was similar in the least. A teacher told me, for example, that a wave of fright swept through the school with the announcement that St. Patrick's Day was coming; a number of the children somehow got the idea that the day was to honor the killer, Patrick Purdy.

"Whenever we hear an ambulance on its way to the rest home down the street, everything halts," another teacher told me. "The kids all listen to see if it will stop here or go on." For several weeks many children were terrified of the mirrors in the restrooms; a rumor swept the school that "Bloody Virgin Mary," some kind of fantasied monster, lurked there. Weeks after the shooting a frantic girl came running up to the school's principal, Pat Busher, yelling, "I hear shots! I hear shots!" The sound was from the swinging chain on a tetherball pole.

Many children became hypervigilant, as though continually on guard against a repetition of the terror; some boys and girls would hover at recess next to the classroom doors, not daring to venture out to the playground where the killings had occurred. Others would only play in small groups, posting a designated child as lookout. Many continued for months to avoid the "evil" areas, where children had died.

The memories lived on, too, as disturbing dreams, intruding into the children's unguarded minds as they slept. Apart from nightmares repeating the shooting itself in some way, children were flooded with anxiety dreams that left them apprehensive that they too would die soon. Some children tried to sleep with their eyes open so they wouldn't dream.

All of these reactions are well known to psychiatrists as among the key symptoms of post-traumatic stress disorder, or PTSD. At the core of such trauma, says Dr. Spencer Eth, a child psychiatrist who specializes in PTSD in children, is "the intrusive memory of the central violent action: the final blow with a fist, the plunge of a knife, the blast of a shotgun. The memories are intense perceptual experiences—the sight, sound, and smell of gunfire; the screams or sudden silence of the victim; the splash of blood; the police sirens."

These vivid, terrifying moments, neuroscientists now say, become memories emblazoned in the emotional circuitry. The symptoms are, in effect, signs of an overaroused amygdala impelling the vivid memories of a traumatic moment to continue to intrude on awareness. As such, the traumatic memories become mental hair triggers, ready to sound an alarm at the least hint that the dread moment is about to happen once again. This hair-trigger phenomenon is a hallmark of emotional trauma of all kinds, including suffering repeated physical abuse in childhood.

Any traumatizing event can implant such trigger memories in the amygdala: a fire or an auto accident, being in a natural catastrophe such as an earthquake or a hurricane, being raped or mugged. Hundreds of thousands of people each year endure such disasters, and many or most come away with the kind of emotional wounding that leaves its imprint on the brain.

Violent acts are more pernicious than natural catastrophes such as a hurricane because, unlike victims of a natural disaster, victims of violence feel themselves to have been intentionally selected as the target of malevolence. That fact shatters assumptions about the trustworthiness of people and the safety of the interpersonal world, an assumption natural catastrophes leave untouched. Within an instant, the social world becomes a dangerous place, one in which people are potential threats to your safety.

Human cruelties stamp their victims' memories with a template that regards with fear anything vaguely similar to the assault itself. A man who was struck on the back of his head, never seeing his attacker, was so frightened afterward that he would try to walk down the street directly in front of an old lady to feel safe from being hit on the head again.[2] A woman who was mugged by a man who got on an elevator with her and forced her out at knifepoint to an unoccupied floor was fearful for weeks of going into not just elevators, but also the subway or any other enclosed space where she might feel trapped; she ran from her bank when she saw a man put his hand in his jacket as the mugger had done.

The imprint of horror in memory—and the resulting hypervigilance—can last a lifetime, as a study of Holocaust survivors found. Close to fifty years after they had endured semistarvation, the slaughter of their loved ones, and constant terror in Nazi death camps, the haunting memories were still alive. A third said they felt generally fearful. Nearly three quarters said they still became anxious at reminders of the Nazi persecution, such as the sight of a uniform, a knock at the door, dogs barking, or smoke rising from a chimney. About 60 percent said they thought about the Holocaust almost daily, even after a half century; of those with active symptoms, as many as eight in ten still suffered from repeated nightmares. As one survivor said, "If you've been through Auschwitz and you don't have nightmares, then you're not normal."

HORROR FROZEN IN MEMORY

The words of a forty-eight-year-old Vietnam vet, some twenty-four years after enduring a horrifying moment in a faraway land:

> I can't get the memories out of my mind! The images come flooding back in vivid detail, triggered by the most inconsequential things, like a door slamming, the sight of an Oriental woman, the touch of a bamboo mat, or the smell of stir-fried pork. Last night I went to bed, was having a good sleep for a change. Then in the early morning a storm front passed through and there was a bolt of crackling thunder. I awoke instantly, frozen in fear. I am right back in Vietnam, in the middle of the monsoon season at my guard post. I am sure I'll get hit in the next volley and convinced I will die. My hands are freezing, yet sweat pours from my entire body. I feel each hair on the back of my neck standing on end. I can't catch my breath and my heart is pounding. I smell a damp sulfur smell. Suddenly I see what's left of my buddy Troy . . . on a bamboo platter, sent back to our camp by the Vietcong. . . . The next bolt of lightning and clap of thunder makes me jump so much that I fall to the floor.[3]

This horrible memory, vividly fresh and detailed though more than two decades old, still holds the power to induce the same fear in this ex-soldier that he felt on that fateful day. PTSD represents a perilous lowering of the neural setpoint for alarm, leaving the person to react to life's ordinary moments as though they were emergencies. The hijacking circuit discussed in Chapter 2 seems critical in leaving such a powerful brand on memory: the more brutal, shocking, and horrendous the events that trigger the amygdala hijacking, the more indelible the memory. The neural basis for these memories appears to be a sweeping alteration in the chemistry of the brain set in motion by a single instance of overwhelming terror.[4] While the PTSD findings are typically based on the impact of a single episode, similar results can come from cruelties inflicted over a period of years, as is the case with children who are sexually, physically, or emotionally abused.

The most detailed work on these brain changes is being done at the National Center for Post-Traumatic Stress Disorder, a network of research sites based at Veterans' Administration hospitals where there are large pools of those who suffer from PTSD among the veterans of Vietnam and other wars. It is from studies on vets such as these that most of our knowledge of PTSD has come. But these insights apply as well to children who have suffered severe emotional trauma, such as those at Cleveland Elementary.

"Victims of a devastating trauma may never be the same biologically," Dr. Dennis Charney told me.[5] A Yale psychiatrist, Charney is director of clinical neuroscience at the National Center. "It does not matter if it was the incessant terror of combat, torture, or repeated abuse in childhood, or a one-time experience, like being trapped in a hurricane or nearly dying in an auto accident. All uncontrollable stress can have the same biological impact."

The operative word is *uncontrollable*. If people feel there is something they can do in a catastrophic situation, some control they can exert, no matter how minor, they fare far better emotionally than do those who feel utterly helpless. The element of helplessness is what makes a given event *subjectively* overwhelming. As Dr. John Krystal, director of the center's Laboratory of Clinical Psychopharmacology, told me, "Say someone being attacked with a knife knows how to defend himself and takes action, while another person in the same predicament thinks, 'I'm dead.' The helpless person is the one more susceptible to PTSD afterward. It's the feeling that your life is in danger *and there's nothing you can do to escape it*—that's the moment the brain change begins."

Helplessness as the wild card in triggering PTSD has been shown in dozens of studies on pairs of laboratory rats, each in a different cage, each being given mild—but, to a rat, very stressful—electric shocks of identical severity. Only one rat has a lever in its cage; when the rat pushes the lever, the shock stops for both cages. Over days and weeks, both rats get precisely the same amount of shock. But the rat with the power to turn the shocks off comes through without lasting signs of stress. It is only in the helpless one of the pair that the stress-induced brain changes occur.[6] For a child being shot at on a playground, seeing his playmates bleeding and dying—or for a teacher there, unable to stop the carnage—that helplessness must have been palpable.

PTSD AS A LIMBIC DISORDER

It had been months since a huge earthquake shook her out of bed and sent her yelling in panic through the darkened house to find her four-year-old son. They huddled for hours in the Los Angeles night cold under a protective doorway, pinned there without food, water, or light while wave after wave of aftershocks tumbled the ground beneath them. Now, months later, she had largely recovered from the ready panic that gripped her for the first few days afterward, when a door slamming could start her shivering with fear. The one lingering symptom was her inability to sleep, a problem that struck only on those nights her husband was away—as he had been the night of the quake.

The main symptoms of such learned fearfulness—including the most intense kind, PTSD—can be accounted for by changes in the limbic circuitry focusing on the amygdala.[7] Some of the key changes are in the locus ceruleus, a structure that regulates the brain's secretion of two substances called *catecholamines:* adrenaline and noradrenaline. These neurochemicals mobilize the body for an emergency; the same catecholamine surge stamps memories with special strength. In PTSD this system becomes hyperreactive, secreting extra-large doses of these brain chemicals in response to situations that hold little or no threat but somehow are reminders of the original trauma, like the children at Cleveland Elementary School who panicked when they heard an ambulance siren similar to those they had heard at their school after the shooting.

The locus ceruleus and the amygdala are closely linked, along with other limbic structures such as the hippocampus and hypothalamus; the circuitry for the catecholamines extends into the cortex. Changes in these circuits are thought to underlie PTSD symptoms, which include anxiety, fear, hyper-vigilance, being easily upset and aroused, readiness for fight or flight, and the indelible encoding of intense emotional memories.[8] Vietnam vets with PTSD, one study found, had 40 percent fewer catecholamine-stopping receptors than did men without the symptoms—suggesting that their brains had undergone a lasting change, with their catecholamine secretion poorly controlled.[9]

Other changes occur in the circuit linking the limbic brain with the pituitary gland, which regulates release of CRF, the main stress hormone the body secretes to mobilize the emergency fight-or-flight response. The changes lead this hormone to be oversecreted—particularly in the amygdala, hippocampus, and locus ceruleus—alerting the body for an emergency that is not there in reality.[10]

As Dr. Charles Nemeroff, a Duke University psychiatrist, told me, "Too much CRF makes you overreact. For example, if you're a Vietnam vet with PTSD and a car backfires at the mall parking lot, it is the triggering of CRF that floods you with the same feelings as in the original trauma: you start sweating, you're scared, you have chills and the shakes, you may have flashbacks. In people who hypersecrete CRF, the startle response is overactive. For example, if you sneak up behind most people and suddenly clap your hands, you'll see a startled jump the first time, but not by the third or fourth repetition. But people with too much CRF don't habituate: they'll respond as much to the fourth clap as to the first."[11]

A third set of changes occurs in the brain's opioid system, which secretes endorphins to blunt the feeling of pain. It also becomes hyperactive. This neural circuit again involves the amygdala, this time in concert with a region in the cerebral cortex. The opioids are brain chemicals that are powerful numbing agents, like opium and other narcotics that are chemical cousins. When experiencing high levels of opioids ("the brain's own morphine"), people have a heightened tolerance for pain—an effect that has been noted by battlefield surgeons, who found severely wounded soldiers needed lower doses of narcotics to handle their pain than did civilians with far less serious injuries.

Something similar seems to occur in PTSD.[12] Endorphin changes add a new dimension to the neural mix triggered by reexposure to trauma: a *numbing* of certain feelings. This appears to explain a set of "negative" psychological symptoms long noted in PTSD: anhedonia (the inability to feel pleasure) and a general emotional numbness, a sense of being cut off from life or from concern about others' feelings. Those close to such people may experience this indifference as a lack of empathy. Another possible effect may be dissociation, including the inability to remember crucial minutes, hours, or even days of the traumatic event.

The neural changes of PTSD also seem to make a person more susceptible to further traumatizing. A number of studies with animals have found that when they were exposed even to *mild* stress when young, they were far more vulnerable than unstressed animals to trauma-induced brain changes later in life (suggesting the urgent need to treat children with PTSD). This seems a reason that, exposed to the same catastrophe, one person goes on to develop PTSD and another does not: the amygdala is primed to find danger, and when life presents it once again with real danger, its alarm rises to a higher pitch.

All these neural changes offer short-term advantages for dealing with the grim and dire emergencies that prompt them. Under duress, it is adaptive to be highly vigilant, aroused, ready for anything, impervious to pain, the body primed for sustained physical demands, and—for the moment—indifferent to what might otherwise be intensely disturbing events. These short-term advantages, however, become lasting problems when the brain changes so that they become predispositions, like a car stuck in perpetual high gear. When the amygdala and its connected brain regions take on a new setpoint during a moment of intense trauma, this change in excitability—this heightened readiness to trigger a neural hijacking—means all of life is on the verge of becoming an emergency, and even an innocent moment is susceptible to an explosion of fear run amok.

EMOTIONAL RELEARNING

Such traumatic memories seem to remain as fixtures in brain function because they interfere with subsequent learning—specifically, with relearning a more normal response to those traumatizing events. In acquired fear such as PTSD, the mechanisms of learning and memory have gone awry; again, it is the amygdala that is key among the brain regions involved. But in overcoming the learned fear, the neocortex is critical.

Fear conditioning is the name psychologists use for the process whereby something that is not in the least threatening becomes dreaded as it is associated in someone's mind with something frightening. When such frights are induced in laboratory animals, Charney notes, the fears can last for years.[13] The key region of the brain that learns, retains, and acts on this fearful response is the circuit between the thalamus, amygdala, and prefrontal lobe—the pathway of neural hijacking.

Ordinarily, when someone learns to be frightened by something through fear conditioning, the fear subsides with time. This seems to happen through a natural relearning, as the feared object is encountered again in the absence of anything truly scary. Thus a child who acquires a fear of dogs because of being chased by a snarling German shepherd gradually and naturally loses that fear if, say, she moves next door to someone who owns a friendly shepherd, and spends time playing with the dog.

In PTSD spontaneous relearning fails to occur. Charney proposes that this may be due to the brain changes of PTSD, which are so strong that, in effect, the amygdala hijacking occurs every time something even vaguely reminiscent of the original trauma comes along, strengthening the fear pathway. This means that there is never a time when what is feared is paired with a feeling of calm—the amygdala never relearns a more mild reaction. "Extinction" of the fear, he observes, "appears to involve an active learning process," which is itself impaired in people with PTSD, "leading to the abnormal persistence of emotional memories."[14]

But given the right experiences, even PTSD can lift; strong emotional memories, and the patterns of thought and reaction that they trigger, *can* change with time. This relearning, Charney proposes, is cortical. The original fear ingrained in the amygdala does not go away completely; rather, the prefrontal cortex actively suppresses the amygdala's command to the rest of the brain to respond with fear.

"The question is, how quickly do you let go of learned fear?" asks Richard Davidson, the University of Wisconsin psychologist who discovered the role of the left prefrontal cortex as a damper on distress. In a laboratory experiment in which people first learned an aversion to a loud noise—a paradigm for learned fear, and a lower-key parallel of PTSD—Davidson found that people who had more activity in the left prefrontal cortex got over the acquired fear more quickly, again suggesting a cortical role in letting go of learned distress.[15]

REEDUCATING THE EMOTIONAL BRAIN

One of the more encouraging findings about PTSD came from a study of Holocaust survivors, about three quarters of whom were found to have active PTSD symptoms even a half century later. The positive finding was that a quarter of the survivors who once had been troubled by such symptoms no longer had them; somehow the natural events of their lives had counteracted the problem. Those who still had the symptoms showed evidence of the catecholamine-related brain changes typical of PTSD—but those who had recovered had no such changes.[16] This finding, and others like it, hold out the promise that the brain changes in PTSD are not indelible, and that people can recover from even the most dire emotional imprinting—in short, that the emotional circuitry can be reeducated. The good news, then, is that traumas as profound as those causing PTSD can heal, and that the route to such healing is through relearning.

One way this emotional healing seems to occur spontaneously—at least in children—is through such games as Purdy. These games, played over and over again, let children relive a trauma safely, as play. This allows two avenues for healing: on the one hand, the memory repeats in a context of low anxiety, desensitizing it and allowing a nontraumatized set of responses to become associated with it. Another route to healing is that, in their minds, children can magically give the tragedy another, better outcome: sometimes in playing Purdy, the children kill him, boosting their sense of mastery over that traumatic moment of helplessness.

Games like Purdy are predictable in younger children who have been through such overwhelming violence. These macabre games in traumatized children were first noted by Dr. Lenore Terr, a child psychiatrist in San Francisco.[17] She found such games among children in Chowchilla, California—just a little over an hour down the Central Valley from Stockton, where Purdy wreaked such havoc—who in 1973 had been kidnapped as they rode a bus home from a summer day camp. The kidnappers buried the bus, children and all, in an ordeal that lasted twenty-seven hours.

Five years later Terr found the kidnapping still being reenacted in the victims' games. Girls, for example, played symbolic kidnapping games with their Barbie dolls. One girl, who had hated the feeling of other children's urine on her skin as they lay huddled together in terror, washed her Barbie over and over again. Another played Traveling Barbie, in which Barbie travels somewhere—it doesn't matter where—and returns safely, which is the point of the game. A third girl's favorite was a scenario in which the doll is stuck in a hole and suffocates.

While adults who have been through overwhelming trauma can suffer a psychic numbing, blocking out memory of or feeling about the catastrophe, children's psyches often handle it differently. They less often become numb to the trauma, Terr believes, because they use fantasy, play, and daydreams to recall and rethink their ordeals. Such voluntary replays of trauma seem to head off the need for damming them up in potent memories that can later burst through as flashbacks. If the trauma is minor, such as going to the dentist for a filling, just once or twice may be enough. But if it's overwhelming, a child needs endless repetitions, replaying the trauma over and over again in a grim, monotonous ritual.

One way to get at the picture frozen in the amygdala is through art, which itself is a medium of the unconscious. The emotional brain is highly attuned to symbolic meanings and to the mode Freud called the "primary process": the messages of metaphor, story, myth, the arts. This avenue is often used in treating traumatized children. Sometimes art can open the way for children to talk about a moment of horror that they would not dare speak of otherwise.

Spencer Eth, the Los Angeles child psychiatrist who specializes in treating such children, tells of a five-year-old boy who had been kidnapped with his mother by her ex-lover. The man brought them to a motel room, where he ordered the boy to hide under a blanket while he beat the mother to death. The boy was, understandably, reluctant to talk with Eth about the mayhem he had heard and seen while underneath the blanket. So Eth asked him to draw a picture—any picture.

The drawing was of a race-car driver who had a strikingly large pair of eyes, Eth recalls. The huge eyes Eth took to refer to the boy's own daring in peeking at the killer. Such hidden references to the traumatic scene almost always appear in the artwork of traumatized children; Eth has made having such children draw a picture the opening gambit in therapy. The potent memories that preoccupy them intrude in their art just as in their thoughts. Beyond that, the act of drawing is itself therapeutic, beginning the process of mastering the trauma.

EMOTIONAL RELEARNING AND RECOVERY FROM TRAUMA

Irene had gone on a date that ended in attempted rape. Though she had fought off the attacker, he continued to plague her: harassing her with obscene phone calls, making threats of violence, calling in the middle of the night, stalking her and watching her every move. Once, when she tried to get the police to help, they dismissed her problem as trivial, since "nothing had really happened." By the time she came for therapy Irene had symptoms of PTSD, had given up socializing at all, and felt a prisoner in her own house.

Irene's case is cited by Dr. Judith Lewis Herman, a Harvard psychiatrist whose groundbreaking work outlines the steps to recovery from trauma. Herman sees three stages: attaining a sense of safety, remembering the details of the trauma and mourning the loss it has brought, and finally reestablishing a normal life. There is a biological logic to the ordering of these steps, as we shall see: this sequence seems to reflect how the emotional brain learns once again that life need not be regarded as an emergency about to happen.

The first step, regaining a sense of safety, presumably translates to finding ways to calm the too-fearful, too easily triggered emotional circuits enough to allow relearning.[18] Often this begins with helping patients understand that their jumpiness and nightmares, hypervigilance and panics, are part of the symptoms of PTSD. This understanding makes the symptoms themselves less frightening.

Another early step is to help patients regain some sense of control over what is happening to them, a direct unlearning of the lesson of helplessness that the trauma itself imparted. Irene, for example, mobilized her friends and family to form a buffer between her and her stalker, and was able to get the police to intervene.

The sense in which PTSD patients feel "unsafe" goes beyond fears that dangers lurk around them; their insecurity begins more intimately, in the feeling that they have no control over what is happening in their body and to their emotions. This is understandable, given the hair trigger for emotional hijacking that PTSD creates by hypersensitizing the amygdala circuitry.

Medication offers one way to restore patients' sense that they need not be so at the mercy of the emotional alarms that flood them with inexplicable anxiety, keep them sleepless, or pepper their sleep with nightmares. Pharmacologists are hoping one day to tailor medications that will target precisely the effects of PTSD on the amygdala and connected neurotransmitter circuits. For now, though, there are medications that counter only some of these changes, notably the antidepressants that act on the serotonin system, and beta-blockers like propranolol, which block the activation of the sympathetic nervous system. Patients also may learn relaxation techniques that give them the ability to counter their edginess and nervousness. A physiological calm opens a window for helping the brutalized emotional circuitry rediscover that life is not a threat and for giving back to patients some of the sense of security they had in their lives before the trauma happened.

Another step in healing involves retelling and reconstructing the story of the trauma in the harbor of that safety, allowing the emotional circuitry to acquire a new, more realistic understanding of and response to the traumatic memory and its triggers. As patients retell the horrific details of the trauma, the memory starts to be transformed, both in its emotional meaning and in its effects on the emotional brain. The pace of this retelling is delicate; ideally it mimics the pace that occurs naturally in those people who are able to recover from trauma without suffering PTSD. In these cases there often seems to be an inner clock that "doses" people with intrusive memories that relive the trauma, intercut with weeks or months when they remember hardly anything of the horrible events.[19]

This alternation of reimmersion and respite seems to allow for a spontaneous review of the trauma and relearning of emotional response to it. For those whose PTSD is more intractable, says Herman, retelling their tale can sometimes trigger overwhelming fears, in which case the therapist should ease the pace to keep the patient's reactions within a bearable range, one that will not disrupt the relearning.

The therapist encourages the patient to retell the traumatic events as vividly as possible, like a horror home video, retrieving every sordid detail. This includes not just the specifics of what they saw, heard, smelled, and felt, but also their reactions—the dread, disgust, nausea. The goal here is to put the entire memory into words, which means capturing parts of the memory that may have been dissociated and so are absent from conscious recall. By putting sensory details and feelings into words, presumably memories are brought more under control of the neocortex, where the reactions they kindle can be rendered more understandable and so more manageable. The emotional relearning at this point is largely accomplished through reliving the events and their emotions, but this time in surroundings of safety and security, in the company of a trusted therapist. This begins to impart a telling lesson to the emotional circuitry—that security, rather than unremitting terror, can be experienced in tandem with the trauma memories.

The five-year-old who drew the picture of the giant eyes after he witnessed the grisly murder of his mother did not make any more drawings after that first one; instead he and his therapist, Spencer Eth, played games, creating a bond of rapport. Only slowly did he begin to retell the story of the murder, at first in a stereotyped way, reciting each detail exactly the same in each telling. Gradually, though, his narrative became more open and free-flowing, his body less tense as he told it. At the same time his nightmares of the scene came less often, an indication, says Eth, of some "trauma mastery." Gradually their talk moved away from the fears left by the trauma to more of what was happening in the boy's day-to-day life as he adjusted to a new home with his father. And finally the boy was able to talk just about his daily life as the hold of the trauma faded.

Finally, Herman finds that patients need to mourn the loss the trauma brought—whether an injury, the death of a loved one or a rupture in a relationship, regret over some step not taken to save someone, or just the shattering of confidence that people can be trusted. The mourning that ensues while retelling such painful events serves a crucial purpose: it marks the ability to let go of the trauma itself to some degree. It means that instead of being perpetually captured by this moment in the past, patients can start to look ahead, even to hope, and to rebuild a new life free of the trauma's grip. It is as if the constant recycling and reliving of the trauma's terror by the emotional circuitry were a spell that could finally be lifted. Every siren need not bring a flood of fear; every sound in the night need not compel a flashback to terror.

Aftereffects or occasional recurrences of symptoms often persist, says Herman, but there are specific signs that the trauma has largely been overcome. These include reducing the physiological symptoms to a manageable level, and being able to bear the feelings associated with memories of the trauma. Especially significant is no longer having trauma memories erupt at uncontrollable moments, but rather being able to revisit them voluntarily, like any other memory—and, perhaps more important, to put them aside like any other memory. Finally, it means rebuilding a new life, with strong, trusting relationships and a belief system that finds meaning even in a world where such injustice can happen.[20] All of these together are markers of success in reeducating the emotional brain.

PSYCHOTHERAPY AS AN EMOTIONAL TUTORIAL

Fortunately, the catastrophic moments in which traumatic memories are emblazoned are rare during the course of life for most of us. But the same circuitry that can be seen so boldly imprinting traumatic memories is presumably at work in life's quieter moments, too. The more ordinary travails of childhood, such as being chronically ignored and deprived of attention or tenderness by one's parents, abandonment or loss, or social rejection may never reach the fever pitch of trauma, but they surely leave their imprint on the emotional brain, creating distortions—and tears and rages—in intimate relationships later in life. If PTSD can be healed, so can the more muted emotional scars that so many of us bear; that is the task of psychotherapy. And, in general, it is in learning to deal skillfully with these loaded reactions that emotional intelligence comes into play.

The dynamic between the amygdala and the more fully informed reactions of the prefrontal cortex may offer a neuroanatomical model for how psychotherapy reshapes deep, maladaptive emotional patterns. As Joseph LeDoux, the neuroscientist who discovered the amygdala's hair-trigger role in emotional outbursts, conjectures, "Once your emotional system learns something, it seems you never let it go. What therapy does is teach you to control it—it teaches your neocortex how to inhibit your amygdala. The propensity to act is suppressed, while your basic emotion about it remains in a subdued form."

Given the brain architecture that underlies emotional relearning, what seems to remain, even after successful psychotherapy, is a vestigial reaction, a remnant of the original sensitivity or fear at the root of a troubling emotional pattern.[21] The prefrontal cortex can refine or put the brakes on the amygdala's impulse to rampage, but cannot keep it from reacting in the first place. Thus while we cannot decide *when* we have our emotional outbursts, we have more control over *how long* they last. A quicker recovery time from such outbursts may well be one mark of emotional maturity.

Over the course of therapy, what seems to change in the main are the *responses* that people make once an emotional reaction is triggered—but the tendency for the reaction to be triggered in the first place does not disappear entirely. Evidence for this comes from a series of studies of psychotherapy conducted by Lester Luborsky and his colleagues at the University of Pennsylvania.[22] They analyzed the main relationship conflicts that brought dozens of patients into psychotherapy—issues such as a deep craving to be accepted or find intimacy, or a fear of being a failure or being overly dependent. They then carefully analyzed the typical (always self-defeating) responses the patients made when these wishes and fears were activated in their relationships—responses such as being too demanding, which created a backlash of anger or coldness in the other person, or withdrawing in self-defense from an anticipated slight, leaving the other person miffed by the seeming rebuff. During such ill-fated encounters, the patients, understandably, felt flooded by upsetting feelings—hopelessness and sadness, resentment and anger, tension and fear, guilt and self-blame, and so on. Whatever the specific pattern of the patient, it seemed to show up in most every important relationship, whether with a spouse or lover, a child or parent, or peers and bosses at work.

Over the course of long-term therapy, however, these patients made two kinds of changes: their emotional reaction to the triggering events became less distressing, even calm or bemused, and their overt responses became more effective in getting what they truly wanted from the relationship. What did not change, however, was their underlying wish or fear, and the initial twinge of feeling. By the time the patients had but a few sessions left in therapy, the encounters they told about showed they had only half as many negative emotional reactions compared to when they first started therapy, and were twice as likely to get the positive response they deeply desired from the other person. But what did not change at all was the particular sensitivity at the root of these needs.

In brain terms, we can speculate, the limbic circuitry would send alarm signals in response to cues of a feared event, but the prefrontal cortex and related zones would have learned a new, more healthy response. In short, emotional lessons—even the most deeply implanted habits of the heart learned in childhood—can be reshaped. Emotional learning is lifelong.

14

Temperament Is Not Destiny

So much for altering emotional patterns that have been learned. But what about those responses that are givens of our genetic endowment—what of changing the habitual reactions of people who by nature are, say, highly volatile, or painfully shy? This range of the emotional compass falls under the sweep of temperament, the background murmur of feelings that mark our basic disposition. Temperament can be defined in terms of the moods that typify our emotional life. To some degree we each have such a favored emotional range; temperament is a given at birth, part of the genetic lottery that has compelling force in the unfolding of life. Every parent has seen this: from birth a child will be calm and placid or testy and difficult. The question is whether such a biologically determined emotional set can be changed by experience. Does our biology fix our emotional destiny, or can even an innately shy child grow into a more confident adult?

The clearest answer to this question comes from the work of Jerome Kagan, the eminent developmental psychologist at Harvard University.[1] Kagan posits that there are at least four temperamental types—timid, bold, upbeat, and melancholy—and that each is due to a different pattern of brain activity. There are likely innumerable differences in temperamental endowment, each based in innate differences in emotional circuitry; for any given emotion people can differ in how easily it triggers, how long it lasts, how intense it becomes. Kagan's work concentrates on one of these patterns: the dimension of temperament that runs from boldness to timidity.

For decades mothers have been bringing their infants and toddlers to Kagan's Laboratory for Child Development on the fourteenth floor of

Harvard's William James Hall to take part in his studies of child development. It was there that Kagan and his coresearchers noticed early
signs of shyness in a group of twenty-one-month-old toddlers brought for
experimental observations. In free play with other toddlers, some were
bubbly and spontaneous, playing with other babies without the least hesita-
tion. Others, though, were uncertain and hesitant, hanging back, clinging
to their mothers, quietly watching the others at play. Almost four years
later, when these same children were in kindergarten, Kagan's group observed them again. Over the intervening years none of the outgoing children had become timid, while two thirds of the timid ones were still
reticent.

Kagan finds that children who are overly sensitive and fearful grow into
shy and timorous adults; from birth about 15 to 20 percent of children are
"behaviorally inhibited," as he calls them. As infants, these children are timid
about anything unfamiliar. This makes them finicky about eating new foods,
reluctant to approach new animals or places, and shy around strangers. It
also renders them sensitive in other ways—for example, prone to guilt and
self-reproach. These are the children who become paralyzingly anxious in
social situations: in class and on the playground, when meeting new people,
whenever the social spotlight shines on them. As adults, they are prone to be
wallflowers, and morbidly afraid of having to give a speech or perform in
public.

Tom, one of the boys in Kagan's study, is typical of the shy type. At every
measurement through childhood—two, five, and seven years of age—Tom
was among the most timid children. When interviewed at thirteen, Tom was
tense and stiff, biting his lip and wringing his hands, his face impassive,
breaking into a tight smile only when talking about his girlfriend; his answers
were short, his manner subdued.[2] Throughout the middle years of childhood, until about age eleven, Tom remembers being painfully shy, breaking
into a sweat whenever he had to approach playmates. He was also troubled
by intense fears: of his house burning down, of diving into a swimming pool,
of being alone in the dark. In frequent nightmares, he was attacked by
monsters. Though he has felt less shy in the last two years or so, he still feels
some anxiety around other children, and his worries now center on doing
well at school, even though he is in the top 5 percent of his class. The son of a
scientist, Tom finds a career in that field appealing, since its relative solitude
fits his introverted inclinations.

By contrast, Ralph was one of the boldest and most outgoing children at
every age. Always relaxed and talkative, at thirteen he sat back at ease in his

chair, had no nervous mannerisms, and spoke in a confident, friendly tone, as though the interviewer were a peer—though the difference in their ages was twenty-five years. During childhood he had only two short-lived fears—one of dogs, after a big dog jumped on him at age three, and another of flying, when he heard about plane crashes at age seven. Sociable and popular, Ralph has never thought of himself as shy.

The timid children seem to come into life with a neural circuitry that makes them more reactive to even mild stress—from birth, their hearts beat faster than other infants' in response to strange or novel situations. At twenty-one months, when the reticent toddlers were holding back from playing, heart rate monitors showed that their hearts were racing with anxiety. That easily aroused anxiety seems to underlie their lifelong timidity: they treat any new person or situation as though it were a potential threat. Perhaps as a result, middle-aged women who remember having been especially shy in childhood, when compared with their more outgoing peers, tend to go through life with more fears, worries, and guilt, and to suffer more from stress-related problems such as migraine headaches, irritable bowel, and other stomach problems.[3]

THE NEUROCHEMISTRY OF TIMIDITY

The difference between cautious Tom and bold Ralph, Kagan believes, lies in the excitability of a neural circuit centered on the amygdala. Kagan proposes that people like Tom, who are prone to fearfulness, are born with a neurochemistry that makes this circuit easily aroused, and so they avoid the unfamiliar, shy away from uncertainty, and suffer anxiety. Those who, like Ralph, have a nervous system calibrated with a much higher threshold for amygdala arousal, are less easily frightened, more naturally outgoing, and eager to explore new places and meet new people.

An early clue to which pattern a child has inherited is how difficult and irritable she is as an infant, and how distressed she becomes when confronted with something or someone unfamiliar. While about one in five infants falls into the timid category, about two in five have the bold. temperament—at least at birth.

Part of Kagan's evidence comes from observations of cats that are unusually timid. About one in seven housecats has a pattern of fearfulness akin to the timid children's: they draw away from novelty (instead of exhibiting a cat's legendary curiosity), they are reluctant to explore new territory, and they attack only the smallest rodents, being too timid to take on larger ones that their more courageous feline peers would pursue with gusto. Direct brain probes have found that portions of the amygdala are unusually excitable in these timid cats, especially when, for instance, they hear a threatening howl from another cat.

The cats' timidity blossoms at about one month of age, which is the point when their amygdala matures enough to take control of the brain circuitry to approach or avoid. One month in kitten brain maturation is akin to eight months in a human infant; it is at eight or nine months, Kagan notes, that "stranger" fear appears in babies—if the baby's mother leaves a room and there is a stranger present, the result is tears. Timid children, Kagan postulates, may have inherited chronically high levels of norepinephrine or other brain chemicals that activate the amygdala and so create a low threshold of excitability, making the amygdala more easily triggered.

One sign of this heightened sensitivity is that, for example, when young men and women who were quite shy in childhood are measured in a laboratory while exposed to stresses such as harsh smells, their heart rate stays elevated much longer than for their more outgoing peers—a sign that surging norepinephrine is keeping their amygdala excited and, through connected neural circuits, their sympathetic nervous system aroused.[4] Kagan finds that timid children have higher levels of reactivity across the range of sympathetic nervous system indices, from higher resting blood pressure and greater dilation of the pupils, to higher levels of norepinephrine markers in their urine.

Silence is another barometer of timidity. Whenever Kagan's team observed shy and bold children in a natural setting—in their kindergarten classes, with other children they did not know, or talking with an interviewer—the timid children talked less. One timid kindergartener would say nothing when other children spoke to her, and spent most of her day just watching the others play. Kagan speculates that a timid silence in the face of novelty or a perceived threat is a sign of the activity of a neural circuit running between the forebrain, the amygdala, and nearby limbic structures that control the ability to vocalize (these same circuits make us "choke up" under stress).

These sensitive children are at high risk for developing an anxiety disorder such as panic attacks, starting as early as sixth or seventh grade. In one study of 754 boys and girls in those grades, 44 were found to have already suffered at least one episode of panic, or to have had several preliminary symptoms. These anxiety episodes were usually triggered by the ordinary alarms of early adolescence, such as a first date or a big exam—alarms that most children handle without developing more serious problems. But teenagers who were timid by temperament and who had been unusually frightened by new situations got panic symptoms such as heart palpitations, shortness of breath, or a choking feeling, along with the feeling that something horrible was going to happen to them, like going crazy or dying. The researchers believe that while the episodes were not significant enough to rate the psychiatric diagnosis "panic disorder," they signal that these teenagers would be at greater risk for developing the disorder as the years went on; many adults who suffer panic attacks say the attacks began during their teen years.[5]

The onset of the anxiety attacks was closely tied to puberty. Girls with few signs of puberty reported no such attacks, but of those who had gone through puberty about 8 percent said they had experienced panic. Once they have had such an attack, they are prone to developing the dread of a recurrence that leads people with panic disorder to shrink from life.

NOTHING BOTHERS ME: THE CHEERFUL TEMPERAMENT

In the 1920s, as a young woman, my aunt June left her home in Kansas City and ventured on her own to Shanghai—a dangerous journey for a solitary woman in those years. There June met and married a British detective in the colonial police force of that international center of commerce and intrigue. When the Japanese captured Shanghai at the outset of World War II, my aunt and her husband were interned in the prison camp depicted in the book and movie *Empire of the Sun*. After surviving five horrific years in the prison camp, she and her husband had, literally, lost everything. Penniless, they were repatriated to British Columbia.

I remember as a child first meeting June, an ebullient elderly woman whose life had followed a remarkable course. In her later years she suffered a stroke that left her partly paralyzed; after a slow and arduous recovery she was able to walk again, but with a limp. In those years I remember going for an outing with June, then in her seventies. Somehow she wandered off, and after several minutes I heard a feeble yell—June crying for help. She had fallen and could not get up on her own. I rushed to help her up, and as I did so, instead of complaining or lamenting she laughed at her predicament. Her only comment was a lighthearted "Well, at least I can walk again."

By nature, some people's emotions seem, like my aunt's, to gravitate toward the positive pole; these people are naturally upbeat and easygoing, while others are dour and melancholy. This dimension of temperament—

ebullience at one end, melancholy at the other—seems linked to the relative activity of the right and left prefrontal areas, the upper poles of the emotional brain. That insight has emerged largely from the work of Richard Davidson, a University of Wisconsin psychologist. He discovered that people who have greater activity in the left frontal lobe, compared to the right, are by temperament cheerful; they typically take delight in people and in what life presents them with, bouncing back from setbacks as my aunt June did. But those with relatively greater activity on the right side are given to negativity and sour moods, and are easily fazed by life's difficulties; in a sense, they seem to suffer because they cannot turn off their worries and depressions.

In one of Davidson's experiments volunteers with the most pronounced activity in the left frontal areas were compared with the fifteen who showed most activity on the right. Those with marked right frontal activity showed a distinctive pattern of negativity on a personality test: they fit the caricature portrayed by Woody Allen's comedy roles, the alarmist who sees catastrophe in the smallest thing—prone to funks and moodiness, and suspicious of a world they saw as fraught with overwhelming difficulties and lurking dangers. By contrast to their melancholy counterparts, those with stronger left frontal activity saw the world very differently. Sociable and cheerful, they typically felt a sense of enjoyment, were frequently in good moods, had a strong sense of self-confidence, and felt rewardingly engaged in life. Their scores on psychological tests suggested a lower lifetime risk for depression and other emotional disorders.[6]

People who have a history of clinical depression, Davidson found, had lower levels of brain activity in the left frontal lobe, and more on the right, than did people who had never been depressed. He found the same pattern in patients newly diagnosed with depression. Davidson speculates that people who overcome depression have learned to increase the level of activity in their left prefrontal lobe—a speculation awaiting experimental testing.

Though his research is on the 30 percent or so of people at the extremes, just about anyone can be classified by their brain wave patterns as tending toward one or the other type, says Davidson. The contrast in temperament between the morose and the cheerful shows up in many ways, large and small. For example, in one experiment volunteers watched short film clips. Some were amusing—a gorilla taking a bath, a puppy at play. Others, like an instructional film for nurses featuring grisly details of surgery, were quite distressing. The right-hemisphere, somber folks found the happy movies only mildly amusing, but they felt extreme fear and disgust in reaction to the surgical blood and gore. The cheerful group had minimal reactions to the surgery; their strongest reactions were of delight when they saw the upbeat films.

Thus we seem by temperament primed to respond to life in either a negative or a positive emotional register. The tendency toward a melancholy or upbeat temperament—like that toward timidity or boldness—emerges within the first year of life, a fact that strongly suggests it too is genetically determined. Like most of the brain, the frontal lobes are still maturing in the first few months of life, and so their activity cannot be reliably measured until the age of ten months or so. But in infants that young, Davidson found that the activity level of the frontal lobes predicted whether they would cry when their mothers left the room. The correlation was virtually 100 percent: of dozens of infants tested this way, every infant who cried had more brain activity on the right side, while those who did not had more activity on the left.

Still, even if this basic dimension of temperament is laid down from birth, or very nearly from birth, those of us who have the morose pattern are not necessarily doomed to go through life brooding and crotchety. The emotional lessons of childhood can have a profound impact on temperament, either amplifying or muting an innate predisposition. The great plasticity of the brain in childhood means that experiences during those years can have a lasting impact on the sculpting of neural pathways for the rest of life. Perhaps the best illustration of the kinds of experiences that can alter temperament for the better is in an observation that emerged from Kagan's research with timid children.

TAMING THE OVEREXCITABLE AMYGDALA

The encouraging news from Kagan's studies is that not all fearful infants grow up hanging back from life—temperament is not destiny. The overexcitable amygdala can be tamed, with the right experiences. What makes the difference are the emotional lessons and responses children learn as they grow. For the timid child, what matters at the outset is how they are treated by their parents, and so how they learn to handle their natural timidness. Those parents who engineer gradual emboldening experiences for their children offer them what may be a lifelong corrective to their fearfulness.

About one in three infants who come into the world with all the signs of an overexcitable amygdala have lost their timidity by the time they reach kindergarten.[7] From observations of these once-fearful children at home, it is clear that parents, and especially mothers, play a major role in whether an innately timid child grows bolder with time or continues to shy away from novelty and become upset by challenge. Kagan's research team found that some of the mothers held to the philosophy that they should protect their timid toddlers from whatever was upsetting; others felt that it was more important to help their timid child learn how to cope with these upsetting moments, and so adapt to life's small struggles. The protective belief seems to have abetted the fearfulness, probably by depriving the youngsters of opportunities for learning how to overcome their fears. The "learn to adapt" philosophy of childrearing seems to have helped fearful children become braver.

Observations in the homes when the babies were about six months old found that the protective mothers, trying to soothe their infants, picked them up and held them when they fretted or cried, and did so longer than those mothers who tried to help their infants learn to master these moments of upset. The ratio of times the infants were held when calm and when upset showed that the protective mothers held their infants much longer during the upsets than the calm periods.

Another difference emerged when the infants were around one year old: the protective mothers were more lenient and indirect in setting limits for their toddlers when they were doing something that might be harmful, such as mouthing an object they might swallow. The other mothers, by contrast, were emphatic, setting firm limits, giving direct commands, blocking the child's actions, insisting on obedience.

Why should firmness lead to a reduction in fearfulness? Kagan speculates that there is something learned when a baby has his steady crawl toward what seems to him an intriguing object (but to his mother a dangerous one) interrupted by her warning, "Get away from that!" The infant is suddenly forced to deal with a mild uncertainty. The repetition of this challenge hundreds and hundreds of times during the first year of life gives the infant continual rehearsals, in small doses, of meeting the unexpected in life. For fearful children that is precisely the encounter that has to be mastered, and manageable doses are just right for learning the lesson. When the encounter takes place with parents who, though loving, do not rush to pick up and soothe the toddler over every little upset, he gradually learns to manage such moments on his own. By age two, when these formerly fearful toddlers are brought back to Kagan's laboratory, they are far less likely to break out into tears when a stranger frowns at them, or an experimenter puts a blood-pressure cuff around their arm.

Kagan's conclusion: "It appears that mothers who protect their high[ly] reactive infants from frustration and anxiety in the hope of effecting a benevolent outcome seem to exacerbate the infant's uncertainty and produce the opposite effect."[8] In other words, the protective strategy backfires by depriving timid toddlers of the very opportunity to learn to calm themselves in the face of the unfamiliar, and so gain some small mastery of their fears. At the neurological level, presumably, this means their prefrontal circuits missed the chance to learn alternate responses to knee-jerk fear; instead, their tendency for unbridled fearfulness may have been strengthened simply through repetition.

In contrast, as Kagan told me, "Those children who had become less timid by kindergarten seem to have had parents who put gentle pressure on them to be more outgoing. Although this temperamental trait seems slightly harder than others to change—probably because of its physiological basis—no human quality is beyond change."

Throughout childhood some timid children grow bolder as experience continues to mold the key neural circuitry. One of the signs that a timid child will be more likely to overcome this natural inhibition is having a higher level of social competence: being cooperative and getting along with other children; being empathic, prone to giving and sharing, and considerate; and being able to develop close friendships. These traits marked a group of children first identified as having a timid temperament at age four, who shook it off by the time they were ten years old.[9]

By contrast, those timid four-year-olds whose temperament changed little over the same six years tended to be less able emotionally: crying and falling apart under stress more easily; being emotionally inappropriate; being fearful, sulky, or whiny; overreacting to minor frustration with anger; having trouble delaying gratification; being overly sensitive to criticism, or mistrustful. These emotional lapses are, of course, likely to mean their relationships with other children will be troubled, should they be able to overcome their initial reluctance to engage.

By contrast, it is easy to see why the more emotionally competent—though shy by temperament—children spontaneously outgrew their timidity. Being more socially skilled, they were far more likely to have a succession of positive experiences with other children. Even if they were tentative about, say, speaking to a new playmate, once the ice was broken they were able to shine socially. The regular repetition of such social success over many years would naturally tend to make the timid more sure of themselves.

These advances toward boldness are encouraging; they suggest that ever innate emotional patterns can change to some degree. A child who comes into the world easily frightened can learn to be calmer, or even outgoing, in the face of the unfamiliar. Fearfulness—or any other temperament—may be part of the biological givens of our emotional lives, but we are not necessarily limited to a specific emotional menu by our inherited traits. There is a range of possibility even within genetic constraints. As behavioral geneticists observe, genes alone do not determine behavior; our environment, especially what we experience and learn as we grow, shapes how a temperamental predisposition expresses itself as life unfolds. Our emotional capacities are not a given; with the right learning, they can be improved. The reasons for this lie in how the human brain matures.

CHILDHOOD: A WINDOW OF OPPORTUNITY

The human brain is by no means fully formed at birth. It continues to shape itself through life, with the most intense growth occurring during childhood. Children are born with many more neurons than their mature brain will retain; through a process known as "pruning" the brain actually loses the neuronal connections that are less used, and forms strong connections in those synaptic circuits that have been utilized the most. Pruning, by doing away with extraneous synapses, improves the signal-to-noise ratio in the brain by removing the cause of the "noise." This process is constant and quick; synaptic connections can form in a matter of hours or days. Experience, particularly in childhood, sculpts the brain.

The classic demonstration of the impact of experience on brain growth was by Nobel Prize–winners Thorsten Wiesel and David Hubel, both neuroscientists.[10] They showed that in cats and monkeys, there was a critical period during the first few months of life for the development of the synapses that carry signals from the eye to the visual cortex, where those signals are interpreted. If one eye was kept closed during that period, the number of synapses from that eye to the visual cortex dwindled away, while those from the open eye multiplied. If after the critical period ended the closed eye was reopened, the animal was functionally blind in that eye. Although nothing was wrong with the eye itself, there were too few circuits to the visual cortex for signals from that eye to be interpreted.

In humans the corresponding critical period for vision lasts for the first six years of life. During this time normal seeing stimulates the formation of increasingly complex neural circuitry for vision that begins in the eye and ends in the visual cortex. If a child's eye is taped closed for even a few weeks, it can produce a measurable deficit in the visual capacity of that eye. If a child has had one eye closed for several months during this period, and later has it restored, that eye's vision for detail will be impaired.

A vivid demonstration of the impact of experience on the developing brain is in studies of "rich" and "poor" rats.[11] The "rich" rats lived in small groups in cages with plenty of rat diversions such as ladders and treadmills. The "poor" rats lived in cages that were similar but barren and lacking diversions. Over a period of months the neocortices of the rich rats developed far more complex networks of synaptic circuits interconnecting the neurons; the poor rats' neuronal circuitry was sparse by comparison. The difference was so great that the rich rats' brains were heavier, and, perhaps not surprisingly, they were far smarter at solving mazes than the poor rats. Similar experiments with monkeys show these differences between those "rich" and "poor" in experience, and the same effect is sure to occur in humans.

Psychotherapy—that is, systematic emotional relearning—stands as a case in point for the way experience can both change emotional patterns and shape the brain. The most dramatic demonstration comes from a study of people being treated for obsessive-compulsive disorder.[12] One of the more common compulsions is hand washing, which can be done so often, even hundreds of times in a day, that the person's skin cracks. PET scan studies show that obsessive-compulsives have greater than normal activity in the prefrontal lobes.[13]

Half of the patients in the study received the standard drug treatment, fluoxetine (better known by the brand name Prozac), and half got behavior therapy. During the therapy they were systematically exposed to the object of their obsession or compulsion without performing it; patients with hand-washing compulsions were put at a sink, but not allowed to wash. At the same time they learned to question the fears and dreads that spurred them on—for example, that failure to wash would mean they would get a disease and die. Gradually, through months of such sessions, the compulsions faded, just as they did with the medication.

The remarkable finding, though, was a PET scan test showing that the behavior therapy patients had as significant a decrease in the activity of a key part of the emotional brain, the caudate nucleus, as did the patients successfully treated with the drug fluoxetine. Their experience had changed brain function—and relieved symptoms—as effectively as the medication!

CRUCIAL WINDOWS

Of all species we humans take the longest for our brains to fully mature. While each area of the brain develops at a different rate during childhood, the onset of puberty marks one of the most sweeping periods of pruning throughout the brain. Several brain areas critical for emotional life are among the slowest to mature. While the sensory areas mature during early childhood, and the limbic system by puberty, the frontal lobes—seat of emotional self-control, understanding, and artful response—continue to develop into late adolescence, until somewhere between sixteen and eighteen years of age.[14]

The habits of emotional management that are repeated over and over again during childhood and the teenage years will themselves help mold this circuitry. This makes childhood a crucial window of opportunity for shaping lifelong emotional propensities; habits acquired in childhood become set in the basic synaptic wiring of neural architecture, and are harder to change later in life. Given the importance of the prefrontal lobes for managing emotion, the very long window for synaptic sculpting in this brain region may well mean that, in the grand design of the brain, a child's experiences over the years can mold lasting connections in the regulatory circuitry of the emotional brain. As we have seen, critical experiences include how dependable and responsive to the child's needs parents are, the opportunities and guidance a child has in learning to handle her own distress and control impulse, and practice in empathy. By the same token, neglect or abuse, the misattunement of a self-absorbed or indifferent parent, or brutal discipline can leave their imprint on the emotional circuitry.[15]

One of the most essential emotional lessons, first learned in infancy and refined throughout childhood, is how to soothe oneself when upset. For very young infants, soothing comes from caretakers: a mother hears her infant crying, picks him up, holds and rocks him until he calms down. This biological attunement, some theorists propose, helps the child begin to learn how to do the same for himself.[16] During a critical period between ten and eighteen months, the orbitofrontal area of the prefrontal cortex is rapidly forming the connections with the limbic brain that will make it a key on/off switch for distress. The infant who through countless episodes of being soothed is helped along in learning how to calm down, the speculation goes, will have stronger connections in this circuit for controlling distress, and so throughout life will be better at soothing himself when upset.

To be sure, the art of soothing oneself is mastered over many years, and with new means, as brain maturation offers a child progressively more sophisticated emotional tools. Remember, the frontal lobes, so important for regulating limbic impulse, mature into adolescence.[17] Another key circuit that continues to shape itself through childhood centers on the vagus nerve, which at one end regulates the heart and other parts of the body, and at the other sends signals to the amygdala from the adrenals, prompting it to secrete the catecholamines, which prime the fight-or-flight response. A University of Washington team that assessed the impact of childrearing discovered that emotionally adept parenting led to a change for the better in vagus-nerve function.

As John Gottman, the psychologist who led the research, explained, "Parents modify their children's vagal tone"—a measure of how easily triggered the vagus nerve is—"by coaching them emotionally: talking to children about their feelings and how to understand them, not being critical and judgmental, problem-solving about emotional predicaments, coaching them on what to do, like alternatives to hitting, or to withdrawing when you're sad." When parents did this well, children were better able to suppress the vagal activity that keeps the amygdala priming the body with fight-or-flight hormones—and so were better behaved.

It stands to reason that the key skills of emotional intelligence each have critical periods extending over several years in childhood. Each period represents a window for helping that child instill beneficial emotional habits or, if missed, to make it that much harder to offer corrective lessons later in life. The massive sculpting and pruning of neural circuits in childhood may be an underlying reason why early emotional hardships and trauma have such enduring and pervasive effects in adulthood. It may explain, too, why psychotherapy can often take so long to affect some of these patterns—and why, as we've seen, even after therapy those patterns tend to remain as underlying propensities, though with an overlay of new insights and relearned responses.

To be sure, the brain remains plastic throughout life, though not to the spectacular extent seen in childhood. All learning implies a change in the brain, a strengthening of synaptic connection. The brain changes in the patients with obsessive-compulsive disorder show that emotional habits are malleable throughout life, with some sustained effort, even at the neural level. What happens with the brain in PTSD (or in therapy, for that matter) is an analog of the effects all repeated or intense emotional experiences bring, for better or for worse.

Some of the most telling of such lessons come from parent to child. There are very different emotional habits instilled by parents whose attunement means an infant's emotional needs are acknowledged and met or whose discipline includes empathy, on the one hand, or self-absorbed parents who ignore a child's distress or who discipline capriciously by yelling and hitting. Much psychotherapy is, in a sense, a remedial tutorial for what was skewed or missed completely earlier in life. But why not do what we can to prevent that need, by giving children the nurturing and guidance that cultivates the essential emotional skills in the first place?

PART FIVE

EMOTIONAL LITERACY

15

The Cost of Emotional Illiteracy

It began as a small dispute, but had escalated. Ian Moore, a senior at Thomas Jefferson High School in Brooklyn, and Tyrone Sinkler, a junior, had had a falling-out with a buddy, fifteen-year-old Khalil Sumpter. Then they had started picking on him and making threats. Now it exploded.

Khalil, scared that Ian and Tyrone were going to beat him up, brought a .38 caliber pistol to school one morning, and, fifteen feet from a school guard, shot both boys to death at point-blank range in the school's hallway.

The incident, chilling as it is, can be read as yet another sign of a desperate need for lessons in handling emotions, settling disagreements peaceably, and just plain getting along. Educators, long disturbed by schoolchildren's lagging scores in math and reading, are realizing there is a different and more alarming deficiency: emotional illiteracy.[1] And while laudable efforts are being made to raise academic standards, this new and troubling deficiency is not being addressed in the standard school curriculum. As one Brooklyn teacher put it, the present emphasis in schools suggests that "we care more about how well schoolchildren can read and write than whether they'll be alive next week."

Signs of the deficiency can be seen in violent incidents such as the shooting of Ian and Tyrone, growing ever more common in American schools. But these are more than isolated events; the heightening of the turmoil of adolescence and troubles of childhood can be read for the United States—a bellwether of world trends—in statistics such as these:[2]

In 1990, compared to the previous two decades, the United States saw the highest juvenile arrest rate for violent crimes ever; teen arrests for forcible rape had doubled; teen murder rates quadrupled, mostly due to an increase in shootings.[3] During those same two decades, the suicide rate for teenagers tripled, as did the number of children under fourteen who are murder victims.[4]

More, and younger, teenage girls are getting pregnant. As of 1993 the birth-rate among girls ten to fourteen has risen steadily for five years in a row—some call it "babies having babies"—as has the proportion of unwanted teen pregnancies and peer pressure to have sex. Rates of venereal disease among teenagers have tripled over the last three decades.[5]

While these figures are discouraging, if the focus is on African-American youth, especially in the inner city, they are utterly bleak—all the rates are higher by far, sometimes doubled, sometimes tripled or higher. For example, heroin and cocaine use among white youth climbed about 300 percent over the two decades before the 1990s; for African-American youth it jumped to a staggering *13 times* the rate of twenty years before.[6]

The most common cause of disability among teenagers is mental illness. Symptoms of depression, whether major or minor, affect up to one third of teenagers; for girls, the incidence of depression doubles at puberty. The frequency of eating disorders in teenage girls has skyrocketed.[7]

Finally, unless things change, the long-term prospects for today's children marrying and having a fruitful, stable life together are growing more dismal with each generation. As we saw in Chapter 9, while during the 1970s and 1980s the divorce rate was around 50 percent, as we entered the 1990s the rate among newlyweds predicted that two out of three marriages of young people would end in divorce.

AN EMOTIONAL MALAISE

These alarming statistics are like the canary in the coal miner's tunnel whose death warns of too little oxygen. Beyond such sobering numbers, the plight of today's children can be seen at more subtle levels, in day-to-day problems that have not yet blossomed into outright crises. Perhaps the most telling data of all—a direct barometer of dropping levels of emotional competence—are from a national sample of American children, ages seven to sixteen, compar-ing their emotional condition in the mid-1970s and at the end of the 1980s.[8] Based on parents' and teachers' assessments, there was a steady worsening. No one problem stood out; all indicators simply crept steadily in the wrong direction. Children, on average, were doing more poorly in these specific ways:

- *Withdrawal or social problems:* preferring to be alone; being secretive; sulking a lot; lacking energy; feeling unhappy; being overly dependent
- *Anxious and depressed:* being lonely; having many fears and worries; needing to be perfect; feeling unloved; feeling nervous or sad and depressed
- *Attention or thinking problems:* unable to pay attention or sit still; daydreaming; acting without thinking; being too nervous to concentrate; doing poorly on schoolwork; unable to get mind off thoughts
- *Delinquent or aggressive:* hanging around kids who get in trouble; lying and cheating; arguing a lot; being mean to other people; demanding attention; destroying other people's things; disobeying at home and at school; being stubborn and moody; talking too much; teasing a lot; having a hot temper

While any of these problems in isolation raises no eyebrows, taken as a group they are barometers of a sea change, a new kind of toxicity seeping into and poisoning the very experience of childhood, signifying sweeping deficits in emotional competences. This emotional malaise seems to be a universal price of modern life for children. While Americans often decry their problems as particularly bad compared to other cultures', studies around the world have found rates on a par with or worse than in the United States. For example, in the 1980s teachers and parents in the Netherlands, China, and Germany rated children at about the same level of problems as were found for American children in 1976. And some countries had children in worse shape than current U.S. levels, including Australia, France, and Thailand. But this may not remain true for long. The larger forces that propel the downward spiral in emotional competence seem to be picking up speed in the United States relative to many other developed nations.[9]

No children, rich or poor, are exempt from risk; these problems are universal, occurring in all ethnic, racial, and income groups. Thus while children in poverty have the worst record on indices of emotional skills, their *rate* of deterioration over the decades was no worse than for middle-class children or for wealthy children: all show the same steady slide. There has also been a corresponding threefold rise in the number of children who have gotten psychological help (perhaps a good sign, signaling that help is more available), as well as a near doubling of the number of children who have enough emotional problems that they *should* get such help but have not (a bad sign)—from about 9 percent in 1976 to 18 percent in 1989.

Urie Bronfenbrenner, the eminent Cornell University developmental psychologist who did an international comparison of children's well-being, says:

"In the absence of good support systems, external stresses have become so great that even strong families are falling apart. The hecticness, instability, and inconsistency of daily family life are rampant in all segments of our society, including the well-educated and well-to-do. What is at stake is nothing less than the next generation, particularly males, who in growing up are especially vulnerable to such disruptive forces as the devastating effects of divorce, poverty, and unemployment. The status of American children and families is as desperate as ever. . . . We are depriving millions of children of their competence and moral character."[10]

This is not just an American phenomenon but a global one, with worldwide competition to drive down labor costs creating economic forces that press on the family. These are times of financially besieged families in which both parents work long hours, so that children are left to their own devices or the TV baby-sits; when more children than ever grow up in poverty; when the one-parent family is becoming ever more commonplace; when more infants and toddlers are left in day care so poorly run that it amounts to neglect. All this means, even for well-intentioned parents, the erosion of the countless small, nourishing exchanges between parent and child that build emotional competences.

If families no longer function effectively to put all our children on a firm footing for life, what are we to do? A more careful look at the mechanics of specific problems suggests how given deficits in emotional or social competences lay the foundation for grave problems—and how well-aimed correctives or preventives could keep more children on track.

TAMING AGGRESSION

In my elementary school the tough kid was Jimmy, a fourth grader when I was in first grade. He was the kid who would steal your lunch money, take your bike, slug you as soon as talk to you. Jimmy was the classic bully, starting fights with the least provocation, or none at all. We all stood in awe of Jimmy—and we all stood at a distance. Everyone hated and feared Jimmy; no one would play with him. It was as though everywhere he went on the playground an invisible bodyguard cleared kids out of his way.

Kids like Jimmy are clearly troubled. But what may be less obvious is that being so flagrantly aggressive in childhood is a mark of emotional and other troubles to come. Jimmy was in jail for assault by the time he reached sixteen.

The lifelong legacy of childhood aggressiveness in kids like Jimmy has emerged from many studies.[11] As we have seen, the family life of such aggressive children typically includes parents who alternate neglect with harsh and capricious punishments, a pattern that, perhaps understandably, makes the children a bit paranoid or combative.

Not all angry children are bullies; some are withdrawn social outcasts who overreact to being teased or to what they perceive as slights or unfairness. But the one perceptual flaw that unites such children is that they perceive slights where none were intended, imagining their peers to be more hostile toward them than they actually are. This leads them to misperceive neutral acts as threatening ones—an innocent bump is seen as a vendetta—and to attack in return. That, of course, leads other children to shun them, isolating them further. Such angry, isolated children are highly sensitive to injustices and being treated unfairly. They typically see themselves as victims and can recite a list of instances when, say, teachers blamed them for doing something when in fact they were innocent. Another trait of such children is that once they are in the heat of anger they can think of only one way to react: by lashing out.

These perceptual biases can be seen at work in an experiment in which bullies are paired with a more peaceable child to watch videos. In one video, a boy drops his books when another knocks into him, and children standing nearby laugh; the boy who dropped the books gets angry and tries to hit one of those who laughed. When the boys who watched the video talk about it afterward, the bully always sees the boy who struck out as justified. Even more telling, when they have to rate how aggressive the boys were during their discussion of the video, the bullies see the boy who knocked into the other as more combative, and the anger of the boy who struck out as justified.[12]

This jump to judgment testifies to a deep perceptual bias in people who are unusually aggressive: they act on the basis of the assumption of hostility or threat, paying too little attention to what is actually going on. Once they assume threat, they leapfrog to action. For instance, if an aggressive boy is playing checkers with another who moves a piece out of turn, he'll interpret the move as "cheating" without pausing to find out if it had been an innocent mistake. His presumption is of malevolence rather than innocence; his reaction is automatic hostility. Along with the knee-jerk perception of a hostile act is entwined an equally automatic aggression; instead of, say, pointing out to the other boy that he made a mistake, he will jump to accusation, yelling, hitting. And the more such children do this, the more automatic aggression becomes for them, and the more the repertoire of alternatives—politeness, joking—shrinks.

Such children are emotionally vulnerable in the sense that they have a low threshold for upset, getting peeved more often by more things; once upset, their thinking is muddled, so that they see benign acts as hostile and fall back on their overlearned habit of striking out.[13]

These perceptual biases toward hostility are already in place by the early grades. While most children, and especially boys, are rambunctious in kindergarten and first grade, the more aggressive children fail to learn a modicum of self-control by second grade. Where other children have started to learn negotiation and compromise for playground disagreements, the bullies rely more and more on force and bluster. They pay a social price: within two or three hours of a first playground contact with a bully, other children already say they dislike him.[14]

But studies that have followed children from the preschool years into the teenage ones find that up to half of first graders who are disruptive, unable to get along with other kids, disobedient with their parents, and resistant with teachers will become delinquents in their teen years.[15] Of course, not all such aggressive children are on the trajectory that leads to violence and criminality in later life. But of all children, these are the ones most at risk for eventually committing violent crimes.

The drift toward crime shows up surprisingly early in these children's lives. When children in a Montreal kindergarten were rated for hostility and troublemaking, those highest at age five already had far greater evidence of delinquency just five to eight years later, in their early teens. They were about three times as likely as other children to admit they had beaten up someone who had not done anything to them, to have shoplifted, to have used a weapon in a fight, to have broken into or stolen parts from a car, and to have been drunk—and all this before they reached fourteen years of age.[16]

The prototypical pathway to violence and criminality starts with children who are aggressive and hard to handle in first and second grade.[17] Typically, from the earliest school years their poor impulse control also contributes to their being poor students, seen as, and seeing themselves as, "dumb"—a judgment confirmed by their being shunted to special-education classes (and though such children may have a higher rate of "hyperactivity" or learning disorders, by no means all do). Children who on entering school already have learned in their homes a "coercive" style—that is, bullying—are also written off by their teachers, who have to spend too much time keeping the children in line. The defiance of classroom rules that comes naturally to these children means that they waste time that would otherwise be used in learning; their destined academic failure is usually obvious by about third grade. While boys on a trajectory toward delinquency tend to have lower IQ scores than their peers, their impulsivity is more directly at cause: impulsivity in ten-year-old boys is almost three times as powerful a predictor of their later delinquency as is their IQ.[18]

By fourth or fifth grade these kids—by now seen as bullies or just "difficult"—are rejected by their peers and are unable to make friends easily, if at all, and have become academic failures. Feeling themselves friendless, they gravitate to other social outcasts. Between grade four and grade nine they commit themselves to their outcast group and a life of defying the law: they show a fivefold increase in their truancy, drinking, and drug taking, with the biggest boost between seventh and eighth grade. By the middle-school years, they are joined by another type of "late starters," who are attracted to their defiant style; these late starters are often youngsters who are completely unsupervised at home and have started roaming the streets on their own in grade school. In the high-school years this outcast group typically drops out of school in a drift toward delinquency, engaging in petty crimes such as shoplifting, theft, and drug dealing.

(A telling difference emerges in this trajectory between boys and girls. A study of fourth-grade girls who were "bad"—getting in trouble with teachers and breaking rules, but not unpopular with their peers—found that 40 percent had a child by the time they finished the high-school years.[19] That was three times the average pregnancy rate for girls in their schools. In other words, antisocial teenage girls don't get violent—they get pregnant.)

There is, of course, no single pathway to violence and criminality, and many other factors can put a child at risk: being born in a high-crime neighborhood where they are exposed to more temptations to crime and violence, coming from a family under high levels of stress, or living in poverty. But none of these factors makes a life of violent crime inevitable. All things being equal, the psychological forces at work in aggressive children greatly intensify the likelihood of their ending up as violent criminals. As Gerald Patterson, a psychologist who has closely followed the careers of hundreds of boys into young adulthood, puts it, "the anti-social acts of a five-year-old may be prototypic of the acts of the delinquent adolescent."[20]

SCHOOL FOR BULLIES

The bent of mind that aggressive children take with them through life is one that almost ensures they will end up in trouble. A study of juvenile offenders convicted of violent crimes and of aggressive high-school students found a

common mind-set: When they have difficulties with someone, they immediately see the other person in an antagonistic way, jumping to conclusions
about the other person's hostility toward them without seeking any further
information or trying to think of a peaceful way to settle their differences. At
the same time, the negative consequence of a violent solution—a fight,
typically—never crosses their mind. Their aggressive bent is justified in
their mind by beliefs like, "It's okay to hit someone if you just go crazy from
anger"; "If you back down from a fight everyone will think you're a
coward"; and "People who get beaten up badly don't really suffer that
much."[21]

But timely help can change these attitudes and stop a child's trajectory
toward delinquency; several experimental programs have had some success
in helping such aggressive kids learn to control their antisocial bent before it
leads to more serious trouble. One, at Duke University, worked with anger-
ridden grade-school troublemakers in training sessions for forty minutes
twice a week for six to twelve weeks. The boys were taught, for example, to
see how some of the social cues they interpreted as hostile were in fact
neutral or friendly. They learned to take the perspective of other children, to
get a sense of how they were being seen and of what other children might be
thinking and feeling in the encounters that had gotten them so angry. They
also got direct training in anger control through enacting scenes, such as
being teased, that might lead them to lose their temper. One of the key skills
for anger control was monitoring their feelings—becoming aware of their
body's sensations, such as flushing or muscle tensing, as they were getting
angry, and to take those feelings as a cue to stop and consider what to do next
rather than strike out impulsively.

John Lochman, a Duke University psychologist who was one of the
designers of the program, told me, "They'll discuss situations they've been
in recently, like being bumped in the hallway when they think it was on
purpose. The kids will talk about how they might have handled it. One kid
said, for example, that he just stared at the boy who bumped him and told
him not to do it again, and walked away. That put him in the position of
exerting some control and keeping his self-esteem, without starting a fight."

This appeals; many such aggressive boys are unhappy that they lose their
temper so easily, and so are receptive to learning to control it. In the heat of
the moment, of course, such cool-headed responses as walking away or
counting to ten so the impulse to hit will pass before reacting are not
automatic; the boys practice such alternatives in role-playing scenes such as
getting on a bus where other kids are taunting them. That way they can try

out friendly responses that preserve their dignity while giving them an alternative to hitting, crying, or running away in shame.

Three years after the boys had been through the training, Lochman compared these boys with others who had been just as aggressive, but did not have the benefit of the anger-control sessions. He found that, in adolescence, the boys who graduated from the program were much less disruptive in class, had more positive feelings about themselves, and were less likely to drink or take drugs. And the longer they had been in the program, the less aggressive they were as teenagers.

PREVENTING DEPRESSION

Dana, sixteen, had always seemed to get along. But now, suddenly, she just could not relate with other girls, and, more troubling for her, she could not find a way to hold on to boyfriends, even though she slept with them. Morose and constantly fatigued, Dana lost interest in eating, in having fun of any kind; she said she felt hopeless and helpless to do anything to escape her mood, and was thinking of suicide.

The drop into depression had been triggered by her most recent breakup. She said she didn't know how to go out with a boy without getting sexually involved right away—even if she was uncomfortable about it—and that she did not know how to end a relationship even if it was unsatisfying. She went to bed with boys, she said, when all she really wanted to do was get to know them better.

She had just moved to a new school, and felt shy and anxious about making friends with girls there. For instance, she held back from starting conversations, only talking once someone spoke to her. She felt unable to let them know what she was like, and didn't even feel she knew what to say after "Hello, how are you?"[22]

Dana went for therapy to an experimental program for depressed adolescents at Columbia University. Her treatment focused on helping her learn how to handle her relationships better: how to develop a friendship, how to feel more confident with other teens, how to assert limits on sexual closeness, how to be intimate, how to express her feelings. In essence, it was a remedial tutorial in some of the most basic emotional skills. And it worked; her depression lifted.

Particularly in young people, problems in relationships are a trigger for depression. The difficulty is as often in children's relationships with their parents as it is with their peers. Depressed children and teenagers are frequently unable or unwilling to talk about their sadness. They seem unable to label their feelings accurately, showing instead a sullen irritability, impatience, crankiness, and anger—especially toward their parents. This, in turn, makes it harder for their parents to offer the emotional support and guidance the depressed child actually needs, setting in motion a downward spiral that typically ends in constant arguments and alienation.

A new look at the causes of depression in the young pinpoints deficits in two areas of emotional competence: relationship skills, on the one hand, and a depression-promoting way of interpreting setbacks, on the other. While some of the tendency to depression almost certainly is due to genetic destiny, some of that tendency seems due to reversible, pessimistic habits of thought that predispose children to react to life's small defeats—a bad grade, arguments with parents, a social rejection—by becoming depressed. And there is evidence to suggest that the predisposition to depression, whatever its basis, is becoming ever more widespread among the young.

A COST OF MODERNITY: RISING RATES OF DEPRESSION

These millennial years are ushering in an Age of Melancholy, just as the twentieth century became an Age of Anxiety. International data show what seems to be a modern epidemic of depression, one that is spreading side by side with the adoption throughout the world of modern ways. Each successive generation worldwide since the opening of the century has lived with a higher risk than their parents of suffering a major depression—not just sadness, but a paralyzing listlessness, dejection, and self-pity, and an overwhelming hopelessness—over the course of life.[23] And those episodes are beginning at earlier and earlier ages. Childhood depression, once virtually unknown (or, at least, unrecognized) is emerging as a fixture of the modern scene.

Although the likelihood of becoming depressed rises with age, the greatest increases are among young people. For those born after 1955 the likelihood they will suffer a major depression at some point in life is, in many countries, three times or more greater than for their grandparents. Among Americans born before 1905, the rate of those having a major depression over a lifetime was just 1 percent; for those born since 1955, by age twenty-four about 6 percent had become depressed. For those born between 1945 and 1954, the chances of having had a major depression before age thirty-four are ten times greater than for those born between 1905 and 1914.[24] And for each generation the onset of a person's first episode of depression has tended to occur at an ever-earlier age.

A worldwide study of more than thirty-nine thousand people found the same trend in Puerto Rico, Canada, Italy, Germany, France, Taiwan, Lebanon, and New Zealand. In Beirut, the rise of depression tracked political events closely, the upward trends rocketing during periods of civil war. In Germany, for those born before 1914 the rate of depression by age thirty-five is 4 percent; for those born in the decade before 1944 it is 14 percent at age thirty-five. Worldwide, generations that came of age during politically troubled times had higher rates of depression, though the overall upward trend holds apart from any political events.

The lowering into childhood of the age when people first experience depression also seems to hold worldwide. When I asked experts to hazard a guess as to why, there were several theories.

Dr. Frederick Goodwin, then director of the National Institute of Mental Health, speculated, "There's been a tremendous erosion of the nuclear family—a doubling of the divorce rate, a drop in parents' time available to children, and an increase in mobility. You don't grow up knowing your extended family much anymore. The losses of these stable sources of self-identification mean a greater susceptibility to depression."

Dr. David Kupfer, chairman of psychiatry at the University of Pittsburgh medical school, pointed to another trend: "With the spread of industrialization after World War II, in a sense nobody was home anymore. In more and more families there has been growing parental indifference to children's needs as they grow up. This is not a direct cause of depression, but it sets up a vulnerability. Early emotional stressors may affect neuron development, which can lead to a depression when you are under great stress even decades later."

Martin Seligman, the University of Pennsylvania psychologist, proposed: "For the last thirty or forty years we've seen the ascendance of individualism and a waning of larger beliefs in religion, and in supports from the community and extended family. That means a loss of resources that can buffer you against setbacks and failures. To the extent you see a failure as something that is lasting and which you magnify to taint everything in your life, you are prone to let a momentary defeat become a lasting source of hopelessness. But if you have a larger perspective, like a belief in God and an afterlife, and you lose your job, it's just a temporary defeat."

Whatever the cause, depression in the young is a pressing problem. In the United States, estimates vary widely for how many children and teens are depressed in any given year, as opposed to vulnerability over their lifetime. Some epidemiological studies using strict criteria—the official diagnostic symptoms for depression—have found that for boys and girls between ten and thirteen the rate of major depression over the course of a year is as high as 8 or 9 percent, though other studies place it at about half that rate (and some as low as about 2 percent). At puberty, some data suggest, the rate nearly doubles for girls; up to 16 percent of girls between fourteen and sixteen suffer a bout of depression, while the rate is unchanged for boys.[25]

THE COURSE OF DEPRESSION IN THE YOUNG

That depression should not just be treated, but *prevented,* in children is clear from an alarming discovery: Even mild episodes of depression in a child can augur more severe episodes later in life.[26] This challenges the old assumption that depression in childhood does not matter in the long run, since children supposedly "grow out of it." Of course, every child gets sad from time to time; childhood and adolescence are, like adulthood, times of occasional disappointments and losses large and small with the attendant grief. The need for prevention is not for these times, but for those children for whom sadness spirals downward into a gloom that leaves them despairing, irritable, and withdrawn—a far more severe melancholy.

Among children whose depression was severe enough that they were referred for treatment, three quarters had a subsequent episode of severe depression, according to data collected by Maria Kovacs, a psychologist at Western Psychiatric Institute and Clinic in Pittsburgh.[27] Kovacs studied children diagnosed with depression when they were as young as eight years old, assessing them every few years until some were as old as twenty-four.

The children with major depression had episodes lasting about eleven months on average, though in one in six of them it persisted for as long as eighteen months. Mild depression, which began as early as age five in some children, was less incapacitating but lasted far longer—an average of about four years. And, Kovacs found, children who have a minor depression are more likely to have it intensify into major depression—a so-called double depression. Those who develop double depression are much more prone to suffer recurring episodes as the years go on. As children who had an episode of depression grew into adolescence and early adulthood, they suffered from depression or manic-depressive disorder, on average, one year in three.

The cost to children goes beyond the suffering caused by depression itself. Kovacs told me, "Kids learn social skills in their peer relations—for example, what to do if you want something and aren't getting it, seeing how other children handle the situation and then trying it yourself. But depressed kids are likely to be among the neglected children in a school, the ones other kids don't play with much."[28]

The sullenness or sadness such children feel leads them to avoid initiating social contacts, or to look away when another child is trying to engage them—a social signal the other child only takes as a rebuff; the end result is that depressed children end up rejected or neglected on the playground. This lacuna in their interpersonal experience means they miss out on what they would normally learn in the rough-and-tumble of play, and so can leave them social and emotional laggards, with much catching up to do after the depression lifts.[29] Indeed, when depressed children have been compared to those without depression, they have been found to be more socially inept, to have fewer friends, to be less preferred than others as playmates, to be less liked, and to have more troubled relationships with other children.

Another cost to these children is doing poorly in school; depression interferes with their memory and concentration, making it harder to pay attention in class and retain what is taught. A child who feels no joy in anything will find it hard to marshal the energy to master challenging lessons, let alone experience flow in learning. Understandably, the longer children in Kovacs's study were depressed, the more their grades dropped and the poorer they did on achievement tests, so that they were more likely to be held back in school. In fact, there was a direct correlation between the length of time a child had been depressed and his grade-point average, with a steady plummet over the course of the episode. All of this academic rough going, of course, compounds the depression. As Kovacs observes, "Imagine you're already feeling depressed, and you start flunking out of school, and you sit home by yourself instead of playing with other kids."

DEPRESSIONOGENIC WAYS OF THOUGHT

Just as with adults, pessimistic ways of interpreting life's defeats seem to feed the sense of helplessness and hopelessness at the heart of children's depression. That people who are *already* depressed think in these ways has long been known. What has only recently emerged, though, is that children who are most prone to melancholy tend toward this pessimistic outlook *before* they become depressed. This insight suggests a window of opportunity for inoculating them against depression before it strikes.

One line of evidence comes from studies of children's beliefs about their own ability to control what happens in their lives—for example, being able to change things for the better. This is assessed by children's ratings of themselves in such terms as "When I have problems at home I'm better than most kids at helping to solve the problems" and "When I work hard I get good grades." Children who say none of these positive descriptions fits them have little sense that they can do anything to change things; this sense of helplessness is highest in those children who are most depressed.[30]

A telling study looked at fifth and sixth graders in the few days after they received report cards. As we all remember, report cards are one of the greatest sources of elation and despair in childhood. But researchers find a marked consequence in how children assess their role when they get a worse grade than they expected. Those who see a bad grade as due to some personal flaw ("I'm stupid") feel more depressed than those who explain it away in terms of something they could change ("If I work harder on my math homework I'll get a better grade").[31]

Researchers identified a group of third, fourth, and fifth graders whom classmates had rejected, and tracked which ones continued to be social outcasts in their new classes the following year. How the children explained the rejection to themselves seemed crucial to whether they became depressed. Those who saw their rejection as due to some flaw in themselves grew more depressed. But the optimists, who felt that they could do something to change things for the better, were not especially depressed despite the continuing rejection.[32] And in a study of children making the notoriously stressful transition to seventh grade, those who had the pessimistic attitude responded to high levels of hassles at school and to any additional stress at home by becoming depressed.[33]

The most direct evidence that a pessimistic outlook makes children highly susceptible to depression comes from a five-year study of children beginning when they were in third grade.[34] Among the younger children, the strongest predictor that they would become depressed was a pessimistic outlook coupled with a major blow such as parents divorcing or a death in the family, which left the child upset, unsettled, and, presumably, with parents less able to offer a nurturing buffer. As the children grew through the elementary-school years, there was a telling shift in their thinking about the good and bad events of their lives, with the children increasingly ascribing them to their own traits: "I'm getting good grades because I'm smart"; "I don't have many friends because I'm no fun." This shift seems to set in gradually over the third to fifth grades. As this happens those children who develop a pessimistic outlook—attributing the setbacks in their lives to some dire flaw in themselves—begin to fall prey to depressed moods in reaction to setbacks. What's more, the experience of depression itself seems to reinforce these pessimistic ways of thinking, so that even after the depression lifts, the child is left with what amounts to an emotional scar, a set of convictions fed by the depression and solidified in the mind: that he can't do well in school, is unlikable, and can do nothing to escape his own brooding moods. These fixed ideas can make the child all the more vulnerable to another depression down the road.

SHORT-CIRCUITING DEPRESSION

The good news: there is every sign that teaching children more productive ways of looking at their difficulties lowers their risk of depression.* In a study of one Oregon high school, about one in four students had what psychologists call a "low-level depression," not severe enough to say it was beyond ordinary unhappiness as yet.[35] Some may have been in the early weeks or months of what was to become a depression.

In a special after-school class seventy-five of the mildly depressed students learned to challenge the thinking patterns associated with depression, to become more adept at making friends, to get along better with their parents, and to engage in more social activities they found pleasant. By the end of the eight-week program, 55 percent of the students had recovered from their mild depression, while only about a quarter of equally depressed students who were not in the program had begun to pull out of their depression. A year later a quarter of those in the comparison group had gone on to fall into a major depression, as opposed to only 14 percent of students in the depression-prevention program. Though they lasted just eight sessions, the classes seemed to have cut the risk of depression in half.[36]

* In children, unlike adults, medication is not a clear alternative to therapy or preventive education for treating depression; children metabolize medications differently than do adults. Tricyclic antidepressants, often successful with adults, have failed in controlled studies with children to prove better than an inactive placebo drug. Newer depression medications, including Prozac, are as yet untested for use in children. And desipramine, one of the most common (and safest) tricyclics used with adults, has, at this writing, become the focus of FDA scrutiny as a possible cause of death in children.

Similarly promising findings came from a special once-a-week class given to ten- to thirteen-year-old youngsters at odds with their parents and showing some signs of depression. In after-school sessions they learned some basic emotional skills, including handling disagreements, thinking before acting, and, perhaps most important, challenging the pessimistic beliefs associated with depression—for example, resolving to study harder after doing poorly on an exam instead of thinking, "I'm just not smart enough."

"What a child learns in these classes is that moods like anxiety, sadness, and anger don't just descend on you without your having any control over them, but that you can change the way you feel by what you think," points out psychologist Martin Seligman, one of the developers of the twelve-week program. Because disputing the depressing thoughts vanquishes the gathering mood of gloom, Seligman added, "it's an instant reinforcer that becomes a habit."

Again the special sessions lowered depression rates by one half—and did so as long as two years later. A year after the classes ended, just 8 percent of those who participated scored at a moderate-to-severe level on a test of depression, versus 29 percent of children in a comparison group. And after two years, about 20 percent of those in the course were showing some signs of at least mild depression, compared to 44 percent of those in the comparison group.

Learning these emotional skills at the cusp of adolescence may be especially helpful. Seligman observes, "These kids seem to be better at handling the routine teenage agonies of rejection. They seem to have learned this at a crucial window for risk of depression, just as they enter the teen years. And the lesson seems to persist and grow a bit stronger over the course of the years after they learn it, suggesting the kids are actually using it in their day-to-day lives."

Other experts on childhood depression applaud the new programs. "If you want to make a real difference for psychiatric illness like depression, you have to do something before the kids get sick in the first place," Kovacs commented. "The real solution is a psychological inoculation."

EATING DISORDERS

During my days as a graduate student in clinical psychology in the late 1960s, I knew two women who suffered from eating disorders, though I realized this only after many years had passed. One was a brilliant graduate student in mathematics at Harvard, a friend from my undergraduate days; the other was on the staff at M.I.T. The mathematician, though skeletally thin, simply could not bring herself to eat; food, she said, repulsed her. The librarian had an ample figure and was given to bingeing on ice cream, Sara Lee carrot cake, and other desserts; then—as she once confided with some embarrassment— she would secretly go off to the bathroom and make herself vomit. Today the mathematician would be diagnosed with anorexia nervosa, the librarian with bulimia.

In those years there were no such labels. Clinicians were just beginning to comment on the problem; Hilda Bruch, the pioneer in this movement, published her seminal article on eating disorders in 1969.[37] Bruch, puzzled by women who were starving themselves to death, proposed that one of the several underlying causes lay in an inability to label and respond appropriately to bodily urges—notably, of course, hunger. Since then the clinical literature on eating disorders has mushroomed, with a multitude of hypotheses about the causes, ranging from ever-younger girls feeling compelled to compete with unattainably high standards of female beauty, to intrusive mothers who enmesh their daughters in a controlling web of guilt and blame.

Most of these hypotheses suffered from one great drawback: they were extrapolations from observations made during therapy. Far more desirable, from a scientific viewpoint, are studies of large groups of people over a period of several years, to see who among them eventually comes down with the problem. That kind of study allows a clean comparison that can tell, for example, if having controlling parents predisposes a girl to eating disorders. Beyond that, it can identify the cluster of conditions that leads to the problem, and distinguish them from conditions that might seem to be a cause, but which actually are found as often in people without the problem as in those who come for treatment.

When just such a study was done with more than nine hundred girls in the seventh through tenth grades, emotional deficits—particularly a failure to tell distressing feelings from one another and to control them—were found to be key among the factors leading to eating disorders.[38] Even by tenth grade, there were sixty-one girls in this affluent, suburban Minneapolis high school who already had serious symptoms of anorexia or bulimia. The greater the problem, the more the girls reacted to setbacks, difficulties, and minor annoyances with intense negative feelings that they could not soothe, and the less their awareness of what, exactly, they were feeling. When these two emotional tendencies were coupled with being highly dissatisfied with their body, then the outcome was anorexia or bulimia. Overly controlling parents were found not to play a prime role in causing eating disorders. (As Bruch herself had warned, theories based on hindsight were unlikely to be accurate; for example, parents can easily become intensely controlling *in response* to their daughter's eating disorder, out of desperation to help her.) Also judged irrelevant were such popular explanations as fear of sexuality, early onset of puberty, and low self-esteem.

Instead, the causal chain this prospective study revealed began with the effects on young girls of growing up in a society preoccupied with unnatural thinness as a sign of female beauty. Well in advance of adolescence, girls are already self-conscious about their weight. One six-year-old, for example, broke into tears when her mother asked her to go for a swim, saying she'd look fat in a swimsuit. In fact, says her pediatrician, who tells the story, her weight was normal for her height.[39] In one study of 271 young teenagers, half the girls thought they were too fat, even though the vast majority of them were normal in weight. But the Minneapolis study showed that an obsession with being overweight is not in and of itself sufficient to explain why some girls go on to develop eating disorders.

Some obese people are unable to tell the difference between being scared, angry, and hungry, and so lump all those feelings together as signifying hunger, which leads them to overeat whenever they feel upset.[40] Something similar seems to be happening in these girls. Gloria Leon, the University of Minnesota psychologist who did the study of young girls and eating disorders, observed that these girls "have poor awareness of their feelings and body signals; that was the strongest single predictor that they would go on to develop an eating disorder within the next two years. Most children learn to distinguish among their sensations, to tell if they're feeling bored, angry, depressed, or hungry—it's a basic part of emotional learning. But these girls have trouble distinguishing among their most basic feelings. They may have a problem with their boyfriend, and not be sure whether they're angry, or anxious, or depressed—they just experience a diffuse emotional storm that they do not know how to deal with effectively. Instead they learn to make themselves feel better by eating; that can become a strongly entrenched emotional habit."

But when this habit for soothing themselves interacts with the pressures girls feel to stay thin, the way is paved for eating disorders to develop. "At first she might start with binge eating," Leon observes. "But to stay thin she may turn to vomiting or laxatives, or intense physical exertion to undo the weight gain from overeating. Another avenue this struggle to handle emotional confusion can take is for the girl not to eat at all—it can be a way to feel you have at least some control over these overwhelming feelings."

The combination of poor inner awareness and weak social skills means that these girls, when upset by friends or parents, fail to act effectively to soothe either the relationship or their own distress. Instead their upset triggers the eating disorder, whether it be that of bulimia or anorexia, or simply binge eating. Effective treatments for such girls, Leon believes, need to include some remedial instruction in the emotional skills they lack. "Clinicians find," she told me, "that if you address the deficits therapy works better. These girls need to learn to identify their feelings and learn ways to soothe themselves or handle their relationships better, without turning to their maladaptive eating habits to do the job."

ONLY THE LONELY: DROPOUTS

It's a grade-school drama: Ben, a fourth grader with few friends, has just heard from his one buddy, Jason, that they aren't going to play together this lunch period—Jason wants to play with another boy, Chad, instead. Ben, crushed, hangs his head and cries. After his sobs subside, Ben goes over to the lunch table where Jason and Chad are eating.

"I hate your guts!" Ben yells at Jason.

"Why?" Jason asks.

"Because you lied," Ben says, his tone accusatory. "You said this whole week that you were gonna play with me and you lied."

Ben then stalks off to his empty table, crying quietly. Jason and Chad go over to him and try to talk to him, but Ben puts his fingers in his ears, determinedly ignoring them, and runs out of the lunchroom to hide behind the school Dumpster. A group of girls who have witnessed the exchange try to play a peacemaker role, finding Ben and telling him that Jason is willing to play with him too. But Ben will have none of it, and tells them to leave him alone. He nurses his wounds, sulking and sobbing, defiantly alone.[41]

A poignant moment, to be sure; the feeling of being rejected and friendless is one most everyone goes through at some point in childhood or adolescence. But what is most telling about Ben's reaction is his failure to respond to Jason's efforts to repair their friendship, a stance that extends his plight when it might have ended. Such an inability to seize key cues is typical of children who are unpopular; as we saw in Chapter 8, socially rejected children typically are poor at reading emotional and social signals; even when they do read such signals, they may have limited repertoires for response.

Dropping out of school is a particular risk for children who are social rejects. The dropout rate for children who are rejected by their peers is between two and eight times greater than for children who have friends. One study found, for example, that about 25 percent of children who were unpopular in elementary school had dropped out before completing high school, compared to a general rate of 8 percent.[42] Small wonder: imagine spending thirty hours a week in a place where no one likes you.

Two kinds of emotional proclivities lead children to end up as social outcasts. As we have seen, one is the propensity to angry outbursts and to perceive hostility even where none is intended. The second is being timid, anxious, and socially shy. But over and above these temperamental factors, it is children who are "off"—whose awkwardness repeatedly makes people uncomfortable—who tend to be shunted aside.

One way these children are "off" is in the emotional signals they send. When grade schoolers with few friends were asked to match an emotion such as disgust or anger with faces that displayed a range of emotions, they made far more mismatches than did children who were popular. When kindergarteners were asked to explain ways they might make friends with someone or keep from having a fight, it was the unpopular children—the ones others shied away from playing with—who came up with self-defeating answers ("Punch him" for what to do when both children wanted the same toy, for example), or vague appeals for help from a grown-up. And when teenagers were asked to role-play being sad, angry, or mischievous, the more unpopular among them gave the least convincing performances. It is perhaps no surprise that such children come to feel that they are helpless to do any better at making friends; their social incompetence becomes a self-fulfilling prophecy. Instead of learning new approaches to making friends, they simply keep doing the same things that have not worked for them in the past, or come up with even more inept responses.[43]

In the lottery of liking, these children fall short on key emotional criteria: they are not seen as fun to be with, and they don't know how to make another child feel good. Observations of unpopular children at play show, for example, that they are much more likely than others to cheat, sulk, quit when losing, or show off and brag about winning. Of course, most children want to win at a game—but win or lose, most children are able to contain their emotional reaction so that it does not undermine the relationship with the friend they play games with.

While children who are socially tone-deaf—who continually have trouble reading and responding to emotions—end up as social isolates, this does not apply, of course, to children who go through a temporary period of feeling left out. But for those who are continually excluded and rejected, their painful outcast status clings to them as they continue their school years. The consequences of ending up at the social margins are potentially great as a child continues on into adulthood. For one, it is in the cauldron of close friendships and the tumult of play that children refine the social and emotional skills that they will bring to relationships later in life. Children who are excluded from this realm of learning are, inevitably, disadvantaged.

Understandably, those who are rejected report great anxiety and many worries, as well as being depressed and lonely. In fact, how popular a child was in third grade has been shown to be a better predictor of mental-health problems at age eighteen than anything else—teachers' and nurses' ratings, school performance and IQ, even scores on psychological tests.[44] And, as we have seen, in later stages of life people who have few friends and are chronically lonely are at greater risk for medical diseases and an early death.

As psychoanalyst Harry Stack Sullivan pointed out, we learn how to negotiate intimate relations—to work out differences and share our deepest feelings—in our first close friendships with same-sex chums. But children who are socially rejected are only half as likely as their peers to have a best friend during the crucial years of elementary school, and so miss out on one of the essential chances for emotional growth.[45] One friend can make the difference—even when all others turn their backs (and even when that friendship is not all that solid).

COACHING FOR FRIENDSHIP

There is hope for rejected children, despite their ineptness. Steven Asher, a University of Illinois psychologist, has designed a series of "friendship coaching" sessions for unpopular children that has shown some success.[46] Identifying third and fourth graders who were the least liked in their classes, Asher gave them six sessions in how to "make playing games more fun" through being "friendly, fun, and nice." To avoid stigma, the children were told that they were acting as "consultants" to the coach, who was trying to learn what kinds of things make it more enjoyable to play games.

The children were coached to act in ways Asher had found typical of more popular children. For example, they were encouraged to think of alternative suggestions and compromises (rather than fighting) if they disagree about the rules; to remember to talk with and ask questions about the other child while they play; to listen and look at the other child to see how he's doing; to say something nice when the other person does well; to smile and offer help or suggestions and encouragement. The children also tried out these basic social amenities while playing games such as Pick-up Sticks with a classmate, and were coached afterward on how well they did. This minicourse in getting along had a remarkable effect: a year later the children who were coached—all of whom were selected because they were the least-liked in their class—were now solidly in the middle of classroom popularity. None were social stars, but none were rejects.

Similar results have been found by Stephen Nowicki, an Emory University psychologist.[47] His program trains social outcasts to hone their ability to read and respond appropriately to other children's feelings. The children, for example, are videotaped while practicing expression of feelings such as happiness and sadness, and are coached to improve their emotional expressiveness. They then try out their newly honed skills with a child they want to make friends with.

Such programs have reported a 50 to 60 percent success rate in raising the popularity of rejected children. These programs (at least as presently designed) seem to work best for third and fourth graders rather than children in higher grades, and to be more helpful for socially inept children than for highly aggressive ones. But that is all a matter for fine-tuning; the hopeful sign is that many or most rejected children can be brought into the circle of friendship with some basic emotional coaching.

DRINKING AND DRUGS: ADDICTION AS SELF-MEDICATION

Students at the local campus call it *drinking to black*—bingeing on beer to the point of passing out. One of the techniques: attach a funnel to a garden hose, so that a can of beer can be downed in about ten seconds. The method is not an isolated oddity. One survey found that two fifths of male college students down seven or more drinks at a time, while 11 percent call themselves "heavy drinkers." Another term, of course, might be "alcoholics."[48] About half of college men and almost 40 percent of women have at least two binge-drinking episodes in a month.[49]

While in the United States use of most drugs among young people generally tapered off in the 1980s, there is a steady trend toward more alcohol use at ever-younger ages. A 1993 survey found that 35 percent of college women said they drank to get drunk, while just 10 percent did so in 1977; overall, one in three students drinks to get drunk. That poses other risks: 90 percent of all rapes reported on college campuses happened when either the assailant or the victim—or both—had been drinking.[50] Alcohol-related accidents are the leading cause of death among young people between fifteen and twenty-four.[51]

Experimentation with drugs and alcohol might seem a rite of passage for adolescents, but this first taste can have long-lasting results for some. For most alcoholics and drug abusers, the beginnings of addiction can be traced to their teen years, though few of those who so experiment end up as alcoholics or drug abusers. By the time students leave high school, over 90 percent have tried alcohol, yet only about 14 percent eventually become alcoholics; of the millions of Americans who experimented with cocaine, fewer than 5 percent became addicted.[52] What makes the difference?

To be sure, those living in high-crime neighborhoods, where crack is sold on the corner and the drug dealer is the most prominent local model of economic success, are most at risk for substance abuse. Some may end up addicted through becoming small-time dealers themselves, others simply because of the easy access or a peer culture that glamorizes drugs—a factor that heightens the risk of drug use in any neighborhood, even (and perhaps especially) the most well-off. But still the question remains, of the pool of those exposed to these lures and pressures, and who go on to experiment, which ones are most likely to end up with a lasting habit?

One current scientific theory is that those who stay with the habit, becoming increasingly dependent on alcohol or drugs, are using these substances as a medication of sorts, a way to soothe feelings of anxiety, anger, or depression. Through their early experimentation they hit upon a chemical fix, a way to calm the feelings of anxiety or melancholy that have tormented them. Thus of several hundred seventh- and eighth-grade students tracked for two years, it was those who reported higher levels of emotional distress who subsequently went on to have the highest rates of substance abuse.[53] This may explain why so many young people are able to experiment with drugs and drinking without becoming addicted, while others become dependent almost from the start: those most vulnerable to addiction seem to find in the drug or alcohol an instant way to soothe emotions that have distressed them for years.

As Ralph Tarter, a psychologist at the Western Psychiatric Institute and Clinic in Pittsburgh, put it, "For people who are biologically predisposed, the first drink or dose of a drug is immensely reinforcing, in a way others just don't experience. Many recovering drug abusers tell me, 'The moment I took my first drug, I felt normal for the first time.' It stabilizes them physiologically, at least in the short term."[54] That, of course, is the devil's bargain of addiction: a short-term good feeling in exchange for the steady meltdown of one's life.

Certain emotional patterns seem to make people more likely to find emotional relief in one substance rather than another. For example, there are two emotional pathways to alcoholism. One starts with someone who was high-strung and anxious in childhood, who typically discovers as a teenager that alcohol will calm the anxiety. Very often they are children—usually sons—of alcoholics who themselves have turned to alcohol to soothe their nerves. One biological marker for this pattern is undersecretion of GABA, a neurotransmitter that regulates anxiety—too little GABA is experienced as a high level of tension. One study found that sons of alcoholic fathers had low levels of GABA and were highly anxious, but when they drank alcohol, their GABA levels rose as their anxiety fell.[55] These sons of alcoholics drink to ease their tension, finding in alcohol a relaxation that they could not seem to get otherwise. Such people may be vulnerable to abusing sedatives as well as alcohol for the same anxiety-reduction effect.

A neuropsychological study of sons of alcoholics who at age twelve showed signs of anxiety such as a heightened heart rate in response to stress, as well as impulsivity, found the boys also had poor frontal lobe functioning.[56] Thus the brain areas that might have helped ease their anxiety or control their impulsiveness brought them less help than in other boys. And since the pre-frontal lobes also handle working memory—which holds in mind the consequences of various routes of action while making a decision—their deficit could support a slide into alcoholism by helping them ignore the long-term drawbacks of drinking, even as they found an immediate sedation from anxiety through alcohol.

This craving for calm seems to be an emotional marker of a genetic susceptibility to alcoholism. A study of thirteen hundred relatives of alcoholics found that the children of alcoholics who were most at risk for becoming alcoholics themselves were those who reported having chronically high levels of anxiety. Indeed, the researchers concluded that alcoholism develops in such people as "self-medication of anxiety symptoms."[57]

A second emotional pathway to alcoholism comes from a high level of agitation, impulsivity, and boredom. This pattern shows up in infancy as being restless, cranky, and hard to handle, in grade school as having the "fidgets," hyperactivity, and getting into trouble, a propensity that, as we have seen, can push such children to seek out friends on the fringe— sometimes leading to a criminal career or the diagnosis of "antisocial personality disorder." Such people (and they are mainly men) have as their main emotional complaint agitation; their main weakness is unrestrained impulsivity; their usual reaction to boredom—which they often feel—is an impulsive search for risk and excitement. As adults, people with this pattern (which may be tied to deficiencies in two other neurotransmitters, serotonin and MAO) find that alcohol can soothe their agitation. And the fact that they can't stand monotony makes them ready to try anything; coupled with their general impulsivity, it makes them prone to abusing an almost random list of drugs besides alcohol.[58]

While depression can drive some to drink, the metabolic effects of alcohol often simply worsen the depression after a short lift. People who turn to alcohol as an emotional palliative do so much more often to calm anxiety than for depression; an entirely different class of drugs soothes the feelings of people who are depressed—at least temporarily. Feeling chronically unhappy puts people at greater risk for addiction to stimulants such as cocaine, which provide a direct antidote to feeling depressed. One study found that more than half the patients being treated at a clinic for cocaine addiction would have been diagnosed with severe depression before they started their habit, and the deeper the preceding depression, the stronger the habit.[59]

Chronic anger may lead to still another kind of susceptibility. In a study of four hundred patients being treated for addiction to heroin and other opioids, the most striking emotional pattern was a lifelong difficulty handling anger and a quickness to rage. Some of the patients themselves said that with opiates they finally felt normal and relaxed.[60]

Though the predisposition to substance abuse may, in many cases, be brain-based, the feelings that drive people to "self-medicate" themselves through drink or drugs can be handled without recourse to medication, as Alcoholics Anonymous and other recovery programs have demonstrated for decades. Acquiring the ability to handle those feelings—soothing anxiety, lifting depression, calming rage—removes the impetus to use drugs or alcohol in the first place. These basic emotional skills are taught remedially in treatment programs for drug and alcohol abuse. It would be far better, of course, if they were learned early in life, well before the habit became established.

NO MORE WARS: A FINAL COMMON PREVENTIVE PATHWAY

Over the last decade or so "wars" have been proclaimed, in turn, on teen pregnancy, dropping out, drugs, and most recently violence. The trouble with such campaigns, though, is that they come too late, after the targeted problem has reached epidemic proportions and taken firm root in the lives of the young. They are crisis intervention, the equivalent of solving a problem by sending an ambulance to the rescue rather than giving an inoculation that would ward off the disease in the first place. Instead of more such "wars," what we need is to follow the logic of prevention, offering our children the skills for facing life that will increase their chances of avoiding any and all of these fates.[61]

My focus on the place of emotional and social deficits is not to deny the role of other risk factors, such as growing up in a fragmented, abusive, or chaotic family, or in an impoverished, crime- and drug-ridden neighborhood. Poverty itself delivers emotional blows to children: poorer children at age five are already more fearful, anxious, and sad than their better-off peers, and have more behavior problems such as frequent tantrums and destroying things, a trend that continues through the teen years. The press of poverty corrodes family life too: there tend to be fewer expressions of parental warmth, more depression in mothers (who are often single and jobless), and a greater reliance on harsh punishments such as yelling, hitting, and physical threats.[62]

But there is a role that emotional competence plays over and above family and economic forces—it may be decisive in determining the extent to which any given child or teenager is undone by these hardships or finds a core of resilience to survive them. Long-term studies of hundreds of children brought up in poverty, in abusive families, or by a parent with severe mental illness show that those who are resilient even in the face of the most grinding hardships tend to share key emotional skills.[63] These include a winning sociability that draws people to them, self-confidence, an optimistic persistence in the face of failure and frustration, the ability to recover quickly from upsets, and an easygoing nature.

But the vast majority of children face such difficulties without these advantages. Of course, many of these skills are innate, the luck of genes—but even qualities of temperament can change for the better, as we saw in Chapter 14. One line of intervention, of course, is political and economic, alleviating the poverty and other social conditions that breed these problems. But apart from these tactics (which seem to move ever lower on the social agenda) there is much that can be offered to children to help them grapple better with such debilitating hardships.

Take the case of emotional disorders, afflictions that about one in two Americans experiences over the course of life. A study of a representative sample of 8,098 Americans found that 48 percent suffered from at least one psychiatric problem during their lifetime.[64] Most severely affected were the 14 percent of people who developed three or more psychiatric problems at once. This group was the most troubled, accounting for 60 percent of all psychiatric disorders occurring at any one time, and 90 percent of the most severe and disabling ones. While they need intensive care now, the optimal approach would be, wherever possible, to prevent these problems in the first place. To be sure, not every mental disorder can be prevented—but there are some, and perhaps many, that can. Ronald Kessler, the University of Michigan sociologist who did the study, told me, "We need to intervene early in life. Take a young girl who has a social phobia in the sixth grade, and starts drinking in junior high school to handle her social anxieties. By her late twenties, when she shows up in our study, she's still fearful, has become both an alcohol and drug abuser, and is depressed because her life is so messed up. The big question is, what could we have done early in her life to have headed off the whole downward spiral?"

The same holds, of course, for dropping out or violence, or most of the litany of perils faced by young people today. Educational programs to prevent one or another specific problem such as drug use and violence have proliferated wildly in the last decade or so, creating a mini-industry within the education marketplace. But many of them—including many of the most slickly marketed and most widely used—have proven to be ineffective. A few, to the chagrin of educators, even seemed to increase the likelihood of the problems they were meant to head off, particularly drug abuse and teen sex.

Information Is Not Enough

An instructive case in point is sexual abuse of children. As of 1993, about two hundred thousand substantiated cases were reported annually in the United States, with that number growing by about 10 percent per year. And while estimates vary widely, most experts agree that between 20 and 30 percent of girls and about half that number of boys are victims of some form of sexual abuse by age seventeen (the figures rise or fall depending on how sexual abuse is defined, among other factors).[65] There is no single profile of a child who is particularly vulnerable to sexual abuse, but most feel unprotected, unable to resist on their own, and isolated by what has happened to them.

With these risks in mind, many schools have begun to offer programs to prevent sexual abuse. Most such programs are tightly focused on basic information about sexual abuse, teaching kids, for example, to know the difference between "good" and "bad" touching, alerting them to the dangers, and encouraging them to tell an adult if anything untoward happens to them. But a national survey of two thousand children found that this basic training was little better than nothing—or actually worse than nothing—in helping children do something to prevent being victimized, whether by a school bully or a potential child molester.[66] Worse, the children who had only such basic programs and who had subsequently become victims of sexual assault were actually *half* as likely to report it afterward than were children who had had no programs at all.

By contrast, children given more comprehensive training—including related emotional and social competences—were better able to protect themselves against the threat of being victimized: they were far more likely to demand to be left alone, to yell or fight back, to threaten to tell, and to actually tell if something bad did happen to them. This last benefit—reporting the abuse—is preventive in a telling sense: many child molesters victimize hundreds of children. A study of child molesters in their forties found that, on average, they had one victim a month since their teenage years. A report on a bus driver and a high-school computer teacher reveals they molested about three hundred children each year between them—yet not one of the children reported the sexual abuse; the abuse came to light only after one of the boys who had been abused by the teacher started to sexually abuse his sister.[67]

Those children who got the more comprehensive programs were three times more likely than those in minimal programs to report abuse. What worked so well? These programs were not one-shot topics, but were given at different levels several times over the course of a child's school career, as part of health or sex education. They enlisted parents to deliver the message to the child along with what was taught in school (children whose parents did this were the very best at resisting threats of sexual abuse).

Beyond that, social and emotional competences made the difference. It is not enough for a child simply to know about "good" and "bad" touching; children need the self-awareness to know when a situation *feels* wrong or distressing long before the touching begins. This entails not just self-awareness, but also enough self-confidence and assertiveness to trust and act on those feelings of distress, even in the face of an adult who may be trying to reassure her that "it's okay." And then a child needs a repertoire of ways to disrupt what is about to happen—everything from running away to threatening to tell. For these reasons, the better programs teach children to stand up for what they want, to assert their rights rather than be passive, to know what their boundaries are and defend them.

The most effective programs, then, supplemented the basic sexual-abuse information with essential emotional and social skills. These programs taught children to find ways to solve interpersonal conflicts more positively, to have more self-confidence, not to blame themselves if something happened, and to feel they had a network of support in teachers and parents whom they could turn to. And if something bad did happen to them, they were far more likely to tell.

The Active Ingredients

Such findings have led to a reenvisioning of what the ingredients of an optimal prevention program should be, based on those that impartial evaluations showed to be truly effective. In a five-year project sponsored by the W. T. Grant Foundation, a consortium of researchers studied this landscape and distilled the active ingredients that seemed crucial to the success of those programs that worked.[68] The list of key skills the consortium concluded should be covered, no matter what specific problem it is designed to prevent, reads like the ingredients of emotional intelligence (see Appendix D for the full list).[69]

The emotional skills include self-awareness; identifying, expressing, and managing feelings; impulse control and delaying gratification; and handling stress and anxiety. A key ability in impulse control is knowing the difference between feelings and actions, and learning to make better emotional decisions by first controlling the impulse to act, then identifying alternative actions and their consequences before acting. Many competences are interpersonal: reading social and emotional cues, listening, being able to resist negative influences, taking others' perspectives, and understanding what behavior is acceptable in a situation.

These are among the core emotional and social skills for life, and include at least partial remedies for most, if not all, of the difficulties I have discussed in this chapter. The choice of specific problems these skills might inoculate against is nearly arbitrary—similar cases for the role of emotional and social competences could have been made for, say, unwanted teen pregnancy or teen suicide.

To be sure, the causes of all such problems are complex, interweaving differing ratios of biological destiny, family dynamics, the politics of poverty, and the culture of the streets. No single kind of intervention, including one targeting emotions, can claim to do the whole job. But to the degree emotional deficits add to a child's risk—and we have seen that they add a great deal—attention must be paid to emotional remedies, not to the exclusion of other answers, but along with them. The next question is, what would an education in the emotions look like?

16
Schooling the Emotions

The main hope of a nation lies in the proper education of its youth.

—Erasmus

It's a strange roll call, going around the circle of fifteen fifth graders sitting Indian-style on the floor. As a teacher calls their names the students respond not with the vacant "Here" standard in schools, but instead call out a number that indicates how they feel; one means low spirits, ten high energy.

Today spirits are high:

"Jessica."

"Ten: I'm jazzed, it's Friday."

"Patrick."

"Nine: excited, a little nervous."

"Nicole."

"Ten: peaceful, happy . . ."

It's a class in Self Science at the Nueva Learning Center, a school retrofitted into what used to be the grand manse of the Crocker family, the dynasty that founded one of San Francisco's biggest banks. Now the building, which resembles a miniature version of the San Francisco Opera House, houses a private school that offers what may be a model course in emotional intelligence.

The subject in Self Science is feelings—your own and those that erupt in relationships. The topic, by its very nature, demands that teachers and students focus on the emotional fabric of a child's life—a focus that is determinedly ignored in almost every other classroom in America. The strategy here includes using the tensions and traumas of children's lives as the topic of the day. Teachers speak to real issues—hurt over being left out, envy, disagreements that could escalate into a schoolyard battle. As Karen Stone McCown, developer of the Self Science Curriculum and director of Nueva, put it, "Learning doesn't take place in isolation from kids' feelings. Being emotionally literate is as important for learning as instruction in math and reading."[1]

Self Science is a pioneer, an early harbinger of an idea that is spreading to schools coast to coast.* Names for these classes range from "social development" to "life skills" to "social and emotional learning." Some, referring to Howard Gardner's idea of multiple intelligences, use the term "personal intelligences." The common thread is the goal of raising the level of social and emotional competence in children as a part of their regular education—not just something taught remedially to children who are faltering and identified as "troubled," but a set of skills and understandings essential for every child.

The emotional-literacy courses have some remote roots in the affective-education movement of the 1960s. The thinking then was that psychological and motivational lessons were more deeply learned if they involved an immediate experience of what was being taught conceptually. The emotional-literacy movement, though, turns the term *affective education* inside out—instead of using affect to educate, it educates affect itself.

More immediately, many of these courses and the momentum for their spread come from an ongoing series of school-based prevention programs, each targeting a specific problem: teen smoking, drug abuse, pregnancy, dropping out, and most recently violence. As we saw in the last chapter, the W. T. Grant Consortium's study of prevention programs found they are far more effective when they teach a core of emotional and social competences, such as impulse control, managing anger, and finding creative solutions to social predicaments. From this principle a new generation of interventions has emerged.

As we saw in Chapter 15, interventions designed to target the specific deficits in emotional and social skills that undergird problems such as aggression or depression can be highly effective as buffers for children. But those well-designed interventions, in the main, have been run by research psychol-

---

* For more information on emotional literacy courses: The Collaborative for the Advancement of Social and Emotional Learning (CASEL), Yale Child Study Center, P.O. Box 207900, 230 South Frontage Road, New Haven, CT 06520-7900.

ogists as experiments. The next step is to take the lessons learned from such highly focused programs and generalize them as a preventive measure for the entire school population, taught by ordinary teachers.

This more sophisticated and more effective approach to prevention includes information about problems such as AIDS, drugs, and the like, at the points in youngsters' lives when they are beginning to face them. But its main, ongoing subject is the core competence that is brought to bear on any of these specific dilemmas: emotional intelligence.

This new departure in bringing emotional literacy into schools makes emotions and social life themselves topics, rather than treating these most compelling facets of a child's day as irrelevant intrusions or, when they lead to eruptions, relegating them to occasional disciplinary trips to the guidance counselor or the principal's office.

The classes themselves may at first glance seem uneventful, much less a solution to the dramatic problems they address. But that is largely because, like good childrearing at home, the lessons imparted are small but telling, delivered regularly and over a sustained period of years. That is how emotional learning becomes ingrained; as experiences are repeated over and over, the brain reflects them as strengthened pathways, neural habits to apply in times of duress, frustration, hurt. And while the everyday substance of emotional literacy classes may look mundane, the outcome—decent human beings—is more critical to our future than ever.

A LESSON IN COOPERATION

Compare a moment from a class in Self Science with the classroom experiences you can recall.

A fifth-grade group is about to play the Cooperation Squares game, in which the students team up to put together a series of square-shaped jigsaw puzzles. The catch: their teamwork is all in silence, with no gesturing allowed.

The teacher, Jo-An Varga, divides the class into three groups, each assigned to a different table. Three observers, each familiar with the game, get an evaluation sheet to assess, for example, who in the group takes the lead in organizing, who is a clown, who disrupts.

The students dump the pieces of the puzzles on the table and go to work. Within a minute or so it's clear that one group is surprisingly efficient as a team; they finish in just a few minutes. A second group of four is engaged in solitary, parallel efforts, each working separately on their own puzzle, but getting nowhere. Then they slowly start to work collectively to assemble their first square, and continue to work as a unit until all the puzzles are solved.

But the third group still struggles, with only one puzzle nearing completion, and even that looking more like a trapezoid than a square. Sean, Fairlie, and Rahman have yet to find the smooth coordination that the other two groups fell into. They are clearly frustrated, frantically scanning the pieces on the table, seizing on likely possibilities and putting them near the partly finished squares, only to be disappointed by the lack of fit.

The tension breaks a bit when Rahman takes two of the pieces and puts them in front of his eyes like a mask; his partners giggle. This will prove to be a pivotal moment in the day's lesson.

Jo-An Varga, the teacher, offers some encouragement: "Those of you who have finished can give one specific hint to those who are still working."

Dagan moseys over to the still-struggling group, points to two pieces that jut out from the square, and suggests, "You've got to move those two pieces around." Suddenly Rahman, his wide face furrowed in concentration, grasps the new gestalt, and the pieces quickly fall into place on the first puzzle, then the others. There's spontaneous applause as the last piece falls into place on the third group's final puzzle.

A POINT OF CONTENTION

But as the class goes on to mull over the object lessons in teamwork they've received, there is another, more intense interchange. Rahman, tall and with a shock of bushy black hair cut into a longish crew cut, and Tucker, the group's observer, are locked in contentious discussion over the rule that you can't gesture. Tucker, his blond hair neatly combed except for a cowlick, wears a baggy blue T-shirt emblazoned with the motto "Be Responsible," which somehow underscores his official role.

"You can *too* offer a piece—that's *not* gesturing," Tucker says to Rahman in an emphatic, argumentative tone.

"But that *is* gesturing," Rahman insists, vehement.

Varga notices the heightened volume and increasingly aggressive staccato of the exchange, and gravitates to their table. This is a critical incident, a spontaneous exchange of heated feeling; it is in moments such as this that the lessons already learned will pay off, and new ones can be taught most profitably. And, as every good teacher knows, the lessons applied in such electric moments will last in students' memories.

"This isn't a criticism—you cooperated very well—but Tucker, try to say what you mean in a tone of voice that doesn't sound so critical," Varga coaches.

Tucker, his voice calmer now, says to Rahman, "You can just put a piece where you think it goes, give someone what you think they need, without gesturing. Just offering."

Rahman responds in an angry tone, "You could have just gone like this"— he scratches his head to illustrate an innocent movement—"and he'd say 'No gesturing!' "

There is clearly more to Rahman's ire than this dispute about what does or does not constitute a gesture. His eyes constantly go to the evaluation sheet Tucker has filled out, which—though it has not yet been mentioned—has actually provoked the tension between Tucker and Rahman. On the evaluation sheet Tucker has listed Rahman's name in the blank for "Who is disruptive?"

Varga, noticing Rahman looking at the offending form, hazards a guess, saying to Tucker, "He's feeling that you used a negative word—*disruptive*— about him. What did you mean?"

"I didn't mean it was a *bad* kind of disruption," says Tucker, now conciliatory.

Rahman isn't buying it, but his voice is calmer, too: "That's a little far-fetched, if you ask me."

Varga emphasizes a positive way of seeing it. "Tucker is trying to say that what could be considered disruptive could also be part of lightening things up during a frustrating time."

"But," Rahman protests, now more matter-of-fact, "*disruptive* is like when we're all concentrating hard on something and if I went like this"—he makes a ridiculous, clowning expression, his eyes bulging, cheeks puffed out— "that would be disruptive."

Varga tries more emotional coaching, telling Tucker, "In trying to help, you didn't mean he was disruptive in a bad way. But you send a different message in how you're talking about it. Rahman is needing you to hear and accept his feelings. Rahman was saying that having negative words like *disruptive* feels unfair. He doesn't like being called that."

Then, to Rahman, she adds, "I appreciate the way you're being assertive in talking with Tucker. You're not attacking. But it's not pleasant to have a label like *disruptive* put on you. When you put those pieces up to your eyes it seems like you were feeling frustrated and wanted to lighten things up. But Tucker called it disruptive because he didn't understand your intent. Is that right?"

Both boys nod assent as the other students finish clearing away the puzzles. This small classroom melodrama is reaching its finale. "Do you feel better?" Varga asks. "Or is this still distressing?"

"Yeah, I feel okay," says Rahman, his voice softer now that he feels heard and understood. Tucker nods, too, smiling. The boys, noticing that everyone else has already left for the next class, turn in unison and dash out together.

POSTMORTEM: A FIGHT THAT DID NOT BREAK OUT

As a new group starts to find their chairs, Varga dissects what has just transpired. The heated exchange and its cooling-down draw on what the boys have been learning about conflict resolution. What typically escalates to conflict begins, as Varga puts it, with "not communicating, making assumptions, and jumping to conclusions, sending a 'hard' message in ways that make it tough for people to hear what you're saying."

Students in Self Science learn that the point is not to avoid conflict completely, but to resolve disagreement and resentment before it spirals into an out-and-out fight. There are signs of these earlier lessons in how Tucker and Rahman handled the dispute. Both, for example, made some effort to express their point of view in a way that would not accelerate the conflict. This assertiveness (as distinct from aggression or passivity) is taught at Nueva from third grade on. It emphasizes expressing feelings forthrightly, but in a way that will not spiral into aggression. While at the beginning of their dispute neither boy was looking at the other, as it went on they began to show signs of "active listening," facing each other, making eye contact, and sending the silent cues that let a speaker know that he is being heard.

By putting these tools into action, helped along by some coaching, "assertiveness" and "active listening" for these boys become more than just empty phrases on a quiz—they become ways of reacting the boys can draw on at those moments when they need them most urgently.

Mastery in the emotional domain is especially difficult because skills need to be acquired when people are usually least able to take in new information and learn new habits of response—when they are upset. Coaching in these moments helps. "Anyone, adult or fifth grader, needs some help being a self-observer when they're so upset," Varga points out. "Your heart is pounding, your hands are sweaty, you're jittery, and you're trying to listen clearly while keeping your own self-control to get through it without screaming, blaming, or clamming up in defensiveness."

For anyone familiar with the rough-and-tumble of fifth-grade boys, what may be most remarkable is that both Tucker and Rahman tried to assert their views without resorting to blaming, name-calling, or yelling. Neither let their feelings escalate to a contemptuous "f—— you!" or a fistfight, nor cut off the other by stalking out of the room. What could have been the seed of a full-fledged battle instead heightened the boys' mastery of the nuances of conflict resolution. How differently it all could have gone in other circumstances. Youngsters daily come to blows—and even worse—over less.

CONCERNS OF THE DAY

At the traditional circle that opens each class in Self Science, the numbers are not always so high as they were today. When they are low—the ones, twos, or threes that indicate feeling terrible—it opens the way for someone to ask, "Do you want to talk about why you feel that way?" And, if the student wants (no one is pressured to talk about things they don't want to), it allows the airing of whatever is so troubling—and the chance to consider creative options for handling it.

The troubles that emerge vary with the grade level. In the lower grades typical ones are teasing, feeling left out, fears. Around sixth grade a new set of concerns emerges—hurt feelings about not being asked on a date, or being left out; friends who are immature; the painful predicaments of the young ("Big kids are picking on me"; "My friends are smoking, and they're always trying to get me to try, too").

These are the topics of gripping import in a child's life, which are aired on the periphery of school—at lunch, on the bus to school, at a friend's house—if at all. More often than not, these are the troubles that children keep to themselves, obsessing about them alone at night, having no one to mull them over with. In Self Science they can become topics of the day.

Each of these discussions is potential grist for the explicit goal of Self Science, which is illuminating the child's sense of self and relationships with others. While the course has a lesson plan, it is flexible so that when moments such as the conflict between Rahman and Tucker occur they can be capitalized on. The issues that students bring up provide the living examples to which students and teachers alike can apply the skills they are learning, such as the conflict-resolution methods that cooled down the heat between the two boys.

THE ABC'S OF EMOTIONAL INTELLIGENCE

In use for close to twenty years, the Self Science curriculum stands as a model for the teaching of emotional intelligence. The lessons sometimes are surprisingly sophisticated; as Nueva's director, Karen Stone McCown, told me, "When we teach about anger, we help kids understand that it is almost always a secondary reaction and to look for what's underneath—are you hurt? jealous? Our kids learn that you always have choices about how you respond to emotion, and the more ways you know to respond to an emotion, the richer your life can be."

A list of the contents of Self Science is an almost point-for-point match with the ingredients of emotional intelligence—and with the core skills recommended as primary prevention for the range of pitfalls threatening children (see Appendix E for the full list).[2] The topics taught include self-awareness, in the sense of recognizing feelings and building a vocabulary for them, and seeing the links between thoughts, feelings, and reactions; knowing if thoughts or feelings are ruling a decision; seeing the consequences of alternative choices; and applying these insights to decisions about such issues as drugs, smoking, and sex. Self-awareness also takes the form of recognizing your strengths and weaknesses, and seeing yourself in a positive but realistic light (and so avoiding a common pitfall of the self-esteem movement).

Another emphasis is managing emotions: realizing what is behind a feeling (for example, the hurt that triggers anger), and learning ways to handle anxieties, anger, and sadness. Still another emphasis is on taking responsibility for decisions and actions, and following through on commitments.

A key social ability is empathy, understanding others' feelings and taking their perspective, and respecting differences in how people feel about things. Relationships are a major focus, including learning to be a good listener and question-asker; distinguishing between what someone says or does and your own reactions and judgments; being assertive rather than angry or passive; and learning the arts of cooperation, conflict resolution, and negotiating compromise.

There are no grades given in Self Science; life itself is the final exam. But at the end of the eighth grade, as students are about to leave Nueva for high school, each is given a Socratic examination, an oral test in Self Science. One question from a recent final: "Describe an appropriate response to help a friend solve a conflict over someone pressuring them to try drugs, or over a friend who likes to tease." Or, "What are some healthy ways to deal with stress, anger, and fear?"

Were he alive today, Aristotle, so concerned with emotional skillfulness, might well approve.

EMOTIONAL LITERACY IN THE INNER CITY

Skeptics understandably will ask if a course like Self Science could work in a less privileged setting, or if it is only possible in a small private school like Nueva, where every child is, in some respect, gifted. In short, can emotional competence be taught where it may be most urgently needed, in the gritty chaos of an inner-city public school? One answer is to visit the Augusta Lewis Troup Middle School in New Haven, which is as far from the Nueva Learning Center socially and economically as it is geographically.

To be sure, the atmosphere at Troup has much of the same excitement about learning—the school is also known as the Troup Magnet Academy of Science and is one of two such schools in the district that are designed to draw fifth- to eighth-grade students from all over New Haven to an enriched science curriculum. Students there can ask questions about the physics of outer space through a satellite-dish hookup to astronauts in Houston or program their computers to play music. But despite these academic amenities, as in many cities, white flight to the New Haven suburbs and to private schools has left Troup's enrollment about 95 percent black and Hispanic.

Just a few short blocks from the Yale campus—and again a distant universe—Troup is in a decaying working-class neighborhood that, in the 1950s, had twenty thousand people employed in nearby factories, from Olin Brass Mills to Winchester Arms. Today that job base has shrunk to under three thousand, shrinking with it the economic horizons of the families who live there. New Haven, like so many other New England manufacturing cities, has sunk into a pit of poverty, drugs, and violence.

It was in response to the urgencies of this urban nightmare that in the 1980s a group of Yale psychologists and educators designed the Social Competence Program, a set of courses that covers virtually the same terrain as the Nueva Learning Center's Self Science curriculum. But at Troup the connection to the topics is often more direct and raw. It is no mere academic exercise when, in the eighth-grade sex education class, students learn how personal decision-making can help them avoid diseases such as AIDS. New Haven has the highest proportion of women with AIDS in the United States; a number of the mothers who send their children to Troup have the disease—and so do some of the students there. Despite the enriched curriculum, students at Troup struggle with all the problems of the inner city; many children have home situations so chaotic, if not horrific, they just cannot manage to get to school some days.

As in all New Haven schools, the most prominent sign that greets a visitor is in the familiar form of a yellow diamond-shaped traffic sign, but reads "Drug-Free Zone." At the door is Mary Ellen Collins, the school's facilitator—an all-purpose ombudsman who sees to special problems as they surface, and whose role includes helping teachers with the demands of the social competence curriculum. If a teacher is unsure of how to teach a lesson, Collins will come to the class to show how.

"I taught in this school for twenty years," Collins says, greeting me. "Look at this neighborhood—I can't see only teaching academic skills anymore, with the problems these kids face just in living. Take the kids here who are struggling because they have AIDS themselves or it's in their homes—I'm not sure they'd say it during the discussion on AIDS, but once a kid knows a teacher will listen to an emotional problem, not just academic ones, the avenue is open to have that conversation."

On the third floor of the old brick school Joyce Andrews is leading her fifth graders through the social competence class they get three times a week. Andrews, like all the other fifth-grade teachers, went to a special summer course in how to teach it, but her exuberance suggests the topics in social competence come naturally to her.

Today's lesson is on identifying feelings; being able to name feelings, and so better distinguish between them, is a key emotional skill. Last night's assignment was to bring in pictures of a person's face from a magazine, name which emotion the face displays, and explain how to tell the person has those feelings. After collecting the assignment, Andrews lists the feelings on the board—sadness, worry, excitement, happiness, and so on—and launches into a fast-paced repartee with the eighteen students who managed to get to school that day. Sitting in four-desk clusters, the students excitedly raise their hands high, straining to catch her eye so they can give their answer.

As she adds *frustrated* to the list on the board, Andrews asks, "How many people ever felt frustrated?" Every hand goes up.

"How do you feel when you're frustrated?"

The answers come in a cascade: "Tired." "Confused." "You can't think right." "Anxious."

As *aggravated* is added to the list, Joyce says, "I know that one—when does a teacher feel aggravated?"

"When everyone is talking," a girl offers, smiling.

Without missing a beat, Andrews passes out a mimeographed worksheet. In one column are faces of boys and girls, each displaying one of the six basic emotions—happy, sad, angry, surprised, afraid, disgusted—and a description of the facial muscle activity underlying each, for example:

AFRAID:

* The mouth is open and drawn back.
* The eyes are open and the inner corners go up.
* The eyebrows are raised and drawn together.
* There are wrinkles in the middle of the forehead.[3]

While they read through the sheet, expressions of fear, anger, surprise, or disgust float over the faces of the kids in Andrews's class as they imitate the pictures and follow the facial-muscle recipes for each emotion. This lesson comes straight from Paul Ekman's research on facial expression; as such, it is taught in most every college introductory psychology course—and rarely, if ever, in grade school. This elementary lesson in connecting a name with a feeling, and the feeling with the facial expression that matches it, might seem so obvious that it need not be taught at all. Yet it may serve as an antidote to surprisingly common lapses in emotional literacy. Schoolyard bullies, remember, often strike out in anger because they misinterpret neutral messages and expressions as hostile, and girls who develop eating disorders fail to distinguish anger from anxiety from hunger.

EMOTIONAL LITERACY IN DISGUISE

With the curriculum already besieged by a proliferation of new topics and agendas, some teachers who understandably feel overburdened resist taking extra time from the basics for yet another course. So an emerging strategy in emotional education is not to create a new class, but to blend lessons on feelings and relationships with other topics already taught. Emotional lessons can merge naturally into reading and writing, health, science, social studies, and other standard courses as well. While in the New Haven schools Life Skills is a separate topic in some grades, in other years the social development curriculum blends into courses such as reading or health. Some of the lessons are even taught as part of math class—notably basic study skills such as how to put aside distractions, motivate yourself to study, and manage your impulses so you can attend to learning.

Some programs in emotional and social skills take no curriculum or class time as a separate subject at all, but instead infiltrate their lessons into the very fabric of school life. One model for this approach—essentially, an invisible emotional and social competence course—is the Child Development Project, created by a team directed by psychologist Eric Schaps. The project, based in Oakland, California, is currently being tried in a handful of schools across the nation, most in neighborhoods that share many of the troubles of New Haven's decaying core.[4]

The project offers a prepackaged set of materials that fit into existing courses. Thus first graders in their reading class get a story, "Frog and Toad Are Friends," in which Frog, eager to play with his hibernating friend Toad, plays a trick on him to get him up early. The story is used as a platform for a class discussion about friendship, and issues such as how people feel when someone plays a trick on them. A succession of adventures brings up topics such as self-consciousness, being aware of a friend's needs, what it feels like to be teased, and sharing feelings with friends. A set curriculum plan offers increasingly sophisticated stories as children go through the elementary and middle-school grades, giving teachers entry points to discuss topics such as empathy, perspective-taking, and caring.

Another way emotional lessons are woven into the fabric of existing school life is through helping teachers rethink how to discipline students who misbehave. The assumption in the Child Development program is that such moments are ripe opportunities to teach children skills that are lacking—impulse control, explaining their feelings, resolving conflicts—and that there are better ways to discipline than coercion. A teacher seeing three first graders pushing to be the first in the lunchroom line might suggest that they each guess a number, and let the winner go first. The immediate lesson is that there are impartial, fair ways to settle such pint-size disputes, while the deeper teaching is that disputes can be negotiated. And since that is an approach those children can take with them to settle other similar disputes ("Me first!" is, after all, epidemic in lower grades—if not through much of life, in one form or another) it has a more positive message than the ubiquitous, authoritarian "Stop that!"

THE EMOTIONAL TIMETABLE

"My friends Alice and Lynn won't play with me."

That poignant grievance is from a third-grade girl at John Muir Elementary School in Seattle. The anonymous sender put it in the "mailbox" in her classroom—actually a specially painted cardboard box—where she and her classmates are encouraged to write in their complaints and problems so the whole class can talk about them and try to think of ways to deal with them. The discussion will not mention the names of those involved; instead the teacher points out that all children share such problems from time to time, and they all need to learn how to handle them. As they talk about how it feels to be left out, or what they might do to be included, they have the chance to try out new solutions to these quandaries—a corrective for the one-track thinking that sees conflict as the only route to solving disagreements.

The mailbox allows flexibility as to exactly which crises and issues will become the subject of the class, for a too-rigid agenda can be out of step with the fluid realities of childhood. As children change and grow the preoccupation of the hour changes accordingly. To be most effective, emotional lessons must be pegged to the development of the child, and repeated at different ages in ways that fit a child's changing understanding and challenges.

One question is how early to begin. Some say the first few years of life are none too soon. The Harvard pediatrician T. Berry Brazelton proposes that many parents can benefit from being coached as emotional mentors to their infants and toddlers, as some home-visit programs do. A strong argument can be made for emphasizing social and emotional skills more systematically in preschool programs such as Head Start; as we saw in Chapter 12, children's readiness to learn depends to a large extent on acquiring some of these basic emotional skills. The preschool years are crucial ones for laying foundation skills, and there is some evidence that Head Start, when run well (an important caveat), can have beneficial long-term emotional and social effects on the lives of its graduates even into their early adult years—fewer drug problems and arrests, better marriages, greater earning power.[5]

Such interventions work best when they track the emotional timetable of development.[6] As the wail of newborns testifies, babies have intense feelings from the moment they are born. But the newborn's brain is far from fully mature; as we saw in Chapter 15, only as its nervous system reaches final development—a process that unfolds according to an innate biological clock over the entire course of childhood and into early adolescence—will the child's emotions ripen completely. The newborn's repertoire of feeling is primitive compared to the emotional range of a five-year-old, which, in turn, is lacking when measured against the fullness of feelings of a teenager. Indeed, adults all too readily fall into the trap of expecting children to have reached a maturity far beyond their years, forgetting that each emotion has its preprogrammed moment of appearance in a child's growth. A four-year-old's braggadocio, for example, might bring a parent's reprimand—and yet the self-consciousness that can breed humility typically does not emerge until age five or so.

The timetable for emotional growth is intertwined with allied lines of development, particularly for cognition, on the one hand, and brain and biological maturation, on the other. As we have seen, emotional capacities such as empathy and emotional self-regulation start to build virtually from infancy. The kindergarten year marks a peak ripening of the "social emotions"—feelings such as insecurity and humility, jealousy and envy, pride and confidence—all of which require the capacity for comparing oneself with others. The five-year-old, on entering the wider social world of school, enters too the world of social comparison. It is not just the external shift that elicits these comparisons, but also the emergence of a cognitive skill: being able to compare oneself to others on particular qualities, whether popularity, attractiveness, or skateboarding talents. This is the age when, for example, having an older sister who gets straight A's can make the younger sister start to think of herself as "dumb" by comparison.

Dr. David Hamburg, a psychiatrist and president of the Carnegie Corporation, which has evaluated some pioneering emotional-education programs, sees the years of transition into grade school and then again into junior high or middle school as marking two crucial points in a child's adjustment.[7] From ages six to eleven, says Hamburg, "school is a crucible and a defining experience that will heavily influence children's adolescence and beyond. A child's sense of self-worth depends substantially on his or her ability to achieve in school. A child who fails in school sets in motion the self-defeating attitudes that can dim prospects for an entire lifespan." Among the essentials for profiting from school, Hamburg notes, are an ability "to postpone gratification, to be socially responsible in appropriate ways, to maintain control over their emotions, and to have an optimistic outlook"—in other words, emotional intelligence.[8]

Puberty—because it is a time of extraordinary change in the child's biology, thinking capacities, and brain functioning—is also a crucial time for emotional and social lessons. As for the teen years, Hamburg observes that "most adolescents are ten to fifteen years old when they are exposed to sexuality, alcohol and drugs, smoking," and other temptations.[9]

The transition to middle school or junior high marks an end to childhood, and is itself a formidable emotional challenge. All other problems aside, as they enter this new school arrangement virtually all students have a dip in self-confidence and a jump in self-consciousness; their very notions of themselves are rocky and in tumult. One of the greatest specific blows is in "social self-esteem"—students' confidence that they can make and keep friends. It is at this juncture, Hamburg points out, that it helps immensely to buttress boys' and girls' abilities to build close relationships and navigate crises in friendships, and to nurture their self-confidence.

Hamburg notes that as students are entering middle school, just on the cusp of adolescence, there is something different about those who have had emotional literacy classes: they find the new pressures of peer politics, the upping of academic demands, and the temptations to smoke and use drugs less troubling than do their peers. They have mastered emotional abilities that, at least for the short term, inoculate them against the turmoil and pressures they are about to face.

TIMING IS ALL

As developmental psychologists and others map the growth of emotions, they are able to be more specific about just what lessons children should be learning at each point in the unfolding of emotional intelligence, what the lasting deficits are likely to be for those who fail to master the right competences at the appointed time, and what remedial experiences might make up for what was missed.

In the New Haven program, for example, children in the youngest grades get basic lessons in self-awareness, relationships, and decision-making. In first grade students sit in a circle and roll the "feelings cube," which has words such as *sad* or *excited* on each side. At their turn, they describe a time they had that feeling, an exercise that gives them more certainty in tying feelings to words and helps with empathy as they hear others having the same feelings as themselves.

By fourth and fifth grade, as peer relationships take on an immense importance in their lives, they get lessons that help their friendships work better: empathy, impulse control, and anger management. The Life Skills class on reading emotions from facial expressions that the Troup school fifth graders were trying, for example, is essentially about empathizing. For impulse control, there is a "stoplight" poster displayed prominently, with six steps:

Red light	1. Stop, calm down, and think before you act.
Yellow light	2. Say the problem and how you feel.
	3. Set a positive goal.
	4. Think of lots of solutions.
	5. Think ahead to the consequences.
Green Light	6. Go ahead and try the best plan.

The stoplight notion is regularly invoked when a child, for example, is about to strike out in anger, or withdraw into a huff at some slight, or burst into tears at being teased, and offers a concrete set of steps for dealing with these loaded moments in a more measured way. Beyond the management of feelings, it points a way to more effective action. And, as a habitual way of handling the unruly emotional impulse—to think before acting from feelings—it can evolve into a basic strategy for dealing with the risks of adolescence and beyond.

In sixth grade the lessons relate more directly to the temptations and pressures for sex, drugs, or drinking that begin to enter children's lives. By ninth grade, as teenagers are confronted with more ambiguous social realities, the ability to take multiple perspectives—your own as well as those of others involved—is emphasized. "If a kid is mad because he saw his girlfriend talking with another guy," says one of the New Haven teachers, "he'd be encouraged to consider what might be going on from their point of view, too, rather than just plunge into a confrontation."

EMOTIONAL LITERACY AS PREVENTION

Some of the most effective programs in emotional literacy were developed as a response to a specific problem, notably violence. One of the fastest-growing of these prevention-inspired emotional literacy courses is the Resolving Conflict Creatively Program, in several hundred New York City public schools and schools across the country. The conflict-resolution course focuses on how to settle schoolyard arguments that can escalate into incidents like the hallway shooting of Ian Moore and Tyrone Sinkler by their classmate at Jefferson High School.

Linda Lantieri, the founder of the Resolving Conflict Creatively Program and director of the Manhattan-based national center for the approach, sees it as having a mission far beyond just preventing fights. She says, "The program shows students that they have many choices for dealing with conflict besides passivity or aggression. We show them the futility of violence while replacing it with concrete skills. Kids learn to stand up for their rights without resorting to violence. These are lifelong skills, not just for those most prone to violence."[10]

In one exercise, students think of a single realistic step, no matter how small, that might have helped settle some conflict they have had. In another students enact a scene in which a big sister trying to do her homework gets fed up with her younger sister's loud rap tape. In frustration the older sister turns off the tape despite the younger one's protests. The class brainstorms ways they might work out the problem that would satisfy both sisters.

One key to the success of the conflict-resolution program is extending it beyond the classroom to the playground and cafeteria, where tempers are more likely to explode. To that end, some students are trained as mediators, a role that can begin in the latter years of elementary school. When tension erupts, students can seek out a mediator to help them settle it. The schoolyard mediators learn to handle fights, taunts and threats, interracial incidents, and the other potentially incendiary incidents of school life.

The mediators learn to phrase their statements in ways that make both parties feel the mediator is impartial. Their tactics include sitting down with those involved and getting them to listen to the other person without interruptions or insults. They have each party calm down and state their position, then have each paraphrase what's been said so it's clear they've really heard. Then they all try to think of solutions that both sides can live with; the settlements are often in the form of a signed agreement.

Beyond the mediation of a given dispute, the program teaches students to think differently about disagreements in the first place. As Angel Perez, trained as a mediator while in grade school, put it, the program "changed my way of thinking. I used to think, hey, if somebody picks on me, if somebody does something to me, the only thing was to fight, do something to get back at them. Since I had this program, I've had a more positive way of thinking. If something's done negative to me, I don't try to do the negative thing back—I try to solve the problem." And he has found himself spreading the approach in his community.

While the focus of Resolving Conflict Creatively is on preventing violence, Lantieri sees it as having a wider mission. Her view is that the skills needed to head off violence cannot be separated from the full spectrum of emotional competence—that, for example, knowing what you are feeling or how to handle impulse or grief is as important for violence prevention as is managing anger. Much of the training has to do with emotional basics such as recognizing an expanded range of feelings and being able to put names to them, and empathizing. When she describes the evaluation results of her program's effects, Lantieri points with as much pride to the increase in "caring among the kids" as to the drops in fights, put-downs, and name-calling.

A similar convergence on emotional literacy occurred with a consortium of psychologists trying to find ways to help youngsters on a trajectory toward a life marked by crime and violence. Dozens of studies of such boys—as we saw in Chapter 15—yielded a clear sense of the path most take, starting from impulsiveness and a quickness to anger in their earliest school years, through becoming social rejects by the end of grade school, to bonding with a circle of others like themselves and beginning crime sprees in the middle-school years. By early adulthood, a large portion of these boys have acquired police records and a readiness for violence.

When it came to designing interventions that might help such boys get off this road to violence and crime, the result was, once again, an emotional-literacy program.[11] One of these, developed by a consortium including Mark Greenberg at the University of Washington, is the PATHS curriculum (PATHS is the acronym for Parents and Teachers Helping Students). While those at risk for a trajectory toward crime and violence are most in need of these lessons, the course is given to all those in a class, avoiding any stigmatizing of a more troubled subgroup.

Still, the lessons are useful for all children. These include, for example, learning in the earliest school years to control their impulses; lacking this ability, children have special trouble paying attention to what is being taught and so fall behind in their learning and grades. Another is recognizing their feelings; the PATHS curriculum has fifty lessons on different emotions, teaching the most basic, such as happiness and anger, to the youngest children, and later touching on more complicated feelings such as jealousy, pride, and guilt. The emotional-awareness lessons include how to monitor what they and those around them are feeling, and—most important for those prone to aggression—how to recognize when someone is actually hostile, as opposed to when the attribution of hostility comes from oneself.

One of the most important lessons, of course, is anger management. The basic premise children learn about anger (and all other emotions as well) is that "all feelings are okay to have," but some reactions are okay and others not. Here one of the tools for teaching self-control is the same "stoplight" exercise used in the New Haven course. Other units help children with their friendships, a counter to the social rejections that can help propel a child toward delinquency.

RETHINKING SCHOOLS: TEACHING BY BEING, COMMUNITIES THAT CARE

As family life no longer offers growing numbers of children a sure footing in life, schools are left as the one place communities can turn to for correctives to children's deficiencies in emotional and social competence. That is not to say that schools alone can stand in for all the social institutions that too often are in or nearing collapse. But since virtually every child goes to school (at least at the outset), it offers a place to reach children with basic lessons for living that they may never get otherwise. Emotional literacy implies an expanded mandate for schools, taking up the slack for failing families in socializing children. This daunting task requires two major changes: that teachers go beyond their traditional mission and that people in the community become more involved with schools.

Whether or not there is a class explicitly devoted to emotional literacy may matter far less than *how* these lessons are taught. There is perhaps no subject where the quality of the teacher matters so much, since how a teacher handles her class is in itself a model, a de facto lesson in emotional competence—or the lack thereof. Whenever a teacher responds to one student, twenty or thirty others learn a lesson.

There is a self-selection in the kind of teacher who gravitates to courses such as these, because not everyone is suited by temperament. To begin with, teachers need to be comfortable talking about feelings; not every teacher is at ease doing so or wants to be. There is little or nothing in the standard education of teachers that prepares them for this kind of teaching. For these reasons, emotional literacy programs typically give prospective teachers several weeks of special training in the approach.

While many teachers may be reluctant at the outset to tackle a topic that seems so foreign to their training and routines, there is evidence that once they are willing to try it, most will be pleased rather than put off. In the New Haven schools, when teachers first learned that they would be trained to teach the new emotional literacy courses, 31 percent said they were reluctant to do so. After a year of teaching the courses, more than 90 percent said they were pleased by them, and wanted to teach them again the following year.

AN EXPANDED MISSION FOR SCHOOLS

Beyond teacher training, emotional literacy expands our vision of the task of schools themselves, making them more explicitly society's agent for seeing that children learn these essential lessons for life—a return to a classic role for education. This larger design requires, apart from any specifics of curriculum, using opportunities in and out of class to help students turn moments of personal crisis into lessons in emotional competence. It also works best when the lessons at school are coordinated with what goes on in children's homes. Many emotional literacy programs include special classes for parents to teach them about what their children are learning, not just to complement what is imparted at school, but to help parents who feel the need to deal more effectively with their children's emotional life.

That way, children get consistent messages about emotional competence in all parts of their lives. In the New Haven schools, says Tim Shriver, director of the Social Competence Program, "if kids get into a beef in the cafeteria, they'll be sent to a peer mediator, who sits down with them and works through their conflict with the same perspective-taking technique they learned in class. Coaches will use the technique to handle conflicts on the playing field. We hold classes for parents in using these methods with kids at home."

Such parallel lines of reinforcement of these emotional lessons—not just in the classroom, but also on the playground; not just in the school, but also in the home—is optimal. That means weaving the school, the parents, and the community together more tightly. It increases the likelihood that what children learned in emotional literacy classes will not stay behind at school, but will be tested, practiced, and sharpened in the actual challenges of life.

Another way in which this focus reshapes schools is in building a campus culture that makes it a "caring community," a place where students feel respected, cared about, and bonded to classmates, teachers, and the school itself.[12] For example, schools in areas such as New Haven, where families are disintegrating at a high rate, offer a range of programs that recruit caring people in the community to get engaged with students whose home life is shaky at best. In the New Haven schools, responsible adults volunteer as mentors, regular companions for students who are foundering and who have few, if any, stable and nurturing adults in their home life.

In short, the optimal design of emotional literacy programs is to begin early, be age-appropriate, run throughout the school years, and intertwine efforts at school, at home, and in the community.

Even though much of this fits neatly into existing parts of the school day, these programs are a major change in any curriculum. It would be naive not to anticipate hurdles in getting such programs into schools. Many parents may feel that the topic itself is too personal a domain for the schools, that such things are best left to parents (an argument that gains credibility to the extent that parents actually *do* address these topics—and is less convincing when they fail to). Teachers may be reluctant to yield yet another part of the school day to topics that seem so unrelated to the academic basics; some teachers may be too uncomfortable with the topics to teach them, and all will need special training to do so. Some children, too, will resist, especially to the extent that these classes are out of synch with their actual concerns, or feel like intrusive impositions on their privacy. And then there is the dilemma of maintaining high quality, and ensuring that slick education marketers do not peddle ineptly designed emotional-competence programs that repeat the disasters of, say, ill-conceived courses on drugs or teen pregnancy.

Given all this, why should we bother to try?

DOES EMOTIONAL LITERACY MAKE A DIFFERENCE?

It's every teacher's nightmare: one day Tim Shriver opened the local paper to read that Lamont, one of his favorite former students, had been shot nine times on a New Haven street, and was in critical condition. "Lamont had been one of the school leaders, a huge—six foot two—and hugely popular line-backer, always smiling," recalls Shriver. "Back then Lamont had enjoyed coming to a leadership club I led, where we would toss around ideas in a problem-solving model known as SOCS."

The acronym is for Situation, Options, Consequence, Solutions—a four-step method: say what the situation is and how it makes you feel; think about your options for solving the problem and what their consequences might be; pick a solution and execute it—a grown-up version of the stoplight method. Lamont, Shriver added, loved brainstorming imaginative but potentially effective ways to handle the pressing dilemmas of high-school life, such as problems with girlfriends and how to avoid fights.

But those few lessons seemed to have failed him after high school. Drifting on the streets in a sea of poverty, drugs, and guns, Lamont at twenty-six lay in a hospital bed, shrouded in bandages, his body riddled with bullet holes. Rushing to the hospital, Shriver found Lamont barely able to talk, his mother and girlfriend huddled over him. Seeing his former teacher, Lamont motioned him to the bedside, and as Shriver leaned over to hear, whispered, "Shrive, when I get out of here, I'm gonna use the SOCS method."

Lamont went through Hillhouse High in the years before the social-development course was given there. Would his life have turned out differently had he benefited from such an education throughout his school years, as children in New Haven public schools do now? The signs point to a possible yes, though no one can ever say for sure.

As Tim Shriver put it, "One thing is clear: the proving ground for social problem-solving is not just the classroom, but the cafeteria, the streets, home." Consider testimony from teachers in the New Haven program. One recounts how a former student, still single, visited and said that she almost certainly would have been an unwed mother by now "if she hadn't learned to stand up for her rights during our Social Development classes."[13] Another teacher recalls how a student's relationship with her mother was so poor that their talks continually ended up as screaming matches; after the girl learned about calming down and thinking before reacting, the mother told her teacher that they could now talk without going "off the deep end." At the Troup school, a sixth grader passed a note to the teacher of her Social Development class; her best friend, the note said, was pregnant, had no one to talk to about what to do, and was planning suicide—but she knew the teacher would care.

A revealing moment came when I was observing a seventh-grade class in social development in the New Haven Schools, and the teacher asked for "someone to tell me about a disagreement they've had recently that ended in a good way."

A plumpish twelve-year-old girl shot up her hand: "This girl was supposed to be my friend and someone said she wanted to fight me. They told me she was going to get me in a corner after school."

But instead of confronting the other girl in anger, she applied an approach encouraged in the class—finding out what is going on before jumping to conclusions: "So I went to the girl and I asked why she said that stuff. And she said she never did. So we never had a fight."

The story seems innocuous enough. Except that the girl who tells the tale had already been expelled from another school for fighting. In the past she attacked first, asked questions later—or not at all. For her to engage a seeming adversary in a constructive way rather than immediately wading into an angry confrontal is a small but real victory.

Perhaps the most telling sign of the impact of such emotional literacy classes are the data shared with me by the principal of this twelve-year-old's school. An unbendable rule there is that children caught fighting are suspended. But as the emotional literacy classes have been phased in over the years there has been a steady drop in the number of suspensions. "Last year," says the principal, "there were 106 suspensions. So far this year—we're up to March—there have been only 26."

These are concrete benefits. But apart from such anecdotes of lives bettered or saved, there is the empirical question of how much emotional literacy classes really matter to those who go through them. The data suggest that although such courses do not change anyone overnight, as children advance through the curriculum from grade to grade, there are discernible improvements in the tone of a school and the outlook—and level of emotional competence—of the girls and boys who take them.

There have been a handful of objective evaluations, the best of which compare students in these courses with equivalent students not taking them, with independent observers rating the children's behavior. Another method is to track changes in the same students before and after the courses based on objective measures of their behavior, such as the number of schoolyard fights or suspensions. Pooling such assessments reveals a widespread benefit for children's emotional and social competence, for their behavior in and out of the classroom, and for their ability to learn (see Appendix F for details):

EMOTIONAL SELF-AWARENESS

- Improvement in recognizing and naming own emotions
- Better able to understand the causes of feelings
- Recognizing the difference between feelings and actions

MANAGING EMOTIONS

- Better frustration tolerance and anger management
- Fewer verbal put-downs, fights, and classroom disruptions
- Better able to express anger appropriately, without fighting
- Fewer suspensions and expulsions
- Less aggressive or self-destructive behavior
- More positive feelings about self, school, and family

- Better at handling stress
- Less loneliness and social anxiety

HARNESSING EMOTIONS PRODUCTIVELY

- More responsible
- Better able to focus on the task at hand and pay attention
- Less impulsive; more self-control
- Improved scores on achievement tests

EMPATHY: READING EMOTIONS

- Better able to take another person's perspective
- Improved empathy and sensitivity to others' feelings
- Better at listening to others

HANDLING RELATIONSHIPS

- Increased ability to analyze and understand relationships
- Better at resolving conflicts and negotiating disagreements
- Better at solving problems in relationships
- More assertive and skilled at communicating
- More popular and outgoing; friendly and involved with peers
- More sought out by peers
- More concerned and considerate
- More "pro-social" and harmonious in groups
- More sharing, cooperation, and helpfulness
- More democratic in dealing with others

One item on this list demands special attention: emotional literacy programs improve children's *academic* achievement scores and school performance. This is not an isolated finding; it recurs again and again in such studies. In a time when too many children lack the capacity to handle their upsets, to listen or focus, to rein in impulse, to feel responsible for their work or care about learning, anything that will buttress these skills will help in their education. In this sense, emotional literacy enhances schools' ability to teach. Even in a time of back-to-basics and budget cuts, there is an argument to be made that these programs help reverse a tide of educational decline and strengthen schools in accomplishing their main mission, and so are well worth the investment.

Beyond these educational advantages, the courses seem to help children better fulfill their roles in life, becoming better friends, students, sons and daughters—and in the future are more likely to be better husbands and wives, workers and bosses, parents, and citizens. While not every boy and girl will acquire these skills with equal sureness, to the degree they do we are all the better for it. "A rising tide lifts all boats," as Tim Shriver put it. "It's not just the kids with problems, but all kids who can benefit from these skills; these are an inoculation for life."

CHARACTER, MORALITY, AND THE ARTS OF DEMOCRACY

There is an old-fashioned word for the body of skills that emotional intelligence represents: *character*. Character, writes Amitai Etzioni, the George Washington University social theorist, is "the psychological muscle that moral conduct requires."[14] And philosopher John Dewey saw that a moral education is most potent when lessons are taught to children in the course of real events, not just as abstract lessons—the mode of emotional literacy.[15]

If character development is a foundation of democratic societies, consider some of the ways emotional intelligence buttresses this foundation. The bedrock of character is self-discipline; the virtuous life, as philosophers since Aristotle have observed, is based on self-control. A related keystone of character is being able to motivate and guide oneself, whether in doing homework, finishing a job, or getting up in the morning. And, as we have seen, the ability to defer gratification and to control and channel one's urges to act is a basic emotional skill, one that in a former day was called will. "We need to be in control of ourselves—our appetites, our passions—to do right by others," notes Thomas Lickona, writing about character education.[16] "It takes will to keep emotion under the control of reason."

Being able to put aside one's self-centered focus and impulses has social benefits: it opens the way to empathy, to real listening, to taking another person's perspective. Empathy, as we have seen, leads to caring, altruism, and compassion. Seeing things from another's perspective breaks down biased stereotypes, and so breeds tolerance and acceptance of differences. These capacities are ever more called on in our increasingly pluralistic society, allowing people to live together in mutual respect and creating the possibility of productive public discourse. These are basic arts of democracy.[17]

Schools, notes Etzioni, have a central role in cultivating character by inculcating self-discipline and empathy, which in turn enable true commitment to civic and moral values.[18] In doing so, it is not enough to lecture children about values: they need to practice them, which happens as children build the essential emotional and social skills. In this sense, emotional literacy goes hand in hand with education for character, for moral development, and for citizenship.

A LAST WORD

As I complete this book some troubling newspaper items catch my eye. One announces that guns have become the number-one cause of death in America, edging out auto accidents. The second says that last year murder rates rose by 3 percent.[19] Particularly disturbing is the prediction in that second article, by a criminologist, that we are in a lull before a "crime storm" to come in the next decade. The reason he gives is that murders by teenagers as young as fourteen and fifteen are on the rise, and that age group represents the crest of a mini baby boom. In the next decade this group will become eighteen- to twenty-four-year-olds, the age at which violent crimes peak in the course of a criminal career. The harbingers are on the horizon: A third article says that in the four years between 1988 and 1992 Justice Department figures show a 68 percent jump in the number of juveniles charged with murder, aggravated assault, robbery, and forcible rape, with aggravated assault alone up 80 percent.[20]

These teenagers are the first generation to have not just guns but automatic weaponry easily available to them, just as their parents' generation was the first to have wide access to drugs. The toting of guns by teenagers means that disagreements that in a former day would have led to fistfights can readily lead to shootings instead. And, as another expert points out, these teenagers "just aren't very good at avoiding disputes."

One reason they are so poor at this basic life skill, of course, is that as a society we have not bothered to make sure every child is taught the essentials of handling anger or resolving conflicts positively—nor have we bothered to teach empathy, impulse control, or any of the other fundamentals of emotional competence. By leaving the emotional lessons children learn to chance, we risk largely wasting the window of opportunity presented by the slow maturation of the brain to help children cultivate a healthy emotional repertoire.

Despite high interest in emotional literacy among some educators, these courses are as yet rare; most teachers, principals, and parents simply do not know they exist. The best models are largely outside the education mainstream, in a handful of private schools and a few hundred public schools. Of course no program, including this one, is an answer to every problem. But given the crises we find ourselves and our children facing, and given the quantum of hope held out by courses in emotional literacy, we must ask ourselves: Shouldn't we be teaching these most essential skills for life to every child—now more than ever?

And if not now, when?

APPENDIX A

What Is Emotion?

A word about what I refer to under the rubric *emotion,* a term whose precise meaning psychologists and philosophers have quibbled over for more than a century. In its most literal sense, the *Oxford English Dictionary* defines *emotion* as "any agitation or disturbance of mind, feeling, passion; any vehement or excited mental state." I take *emotion* to refer to a feeling and its distinctive thoughts, psychological and biological states, and range of propensities to act. There are hundreds of emotions, along with their blends, variations, mutations, and nuances. Indeed, there are many more subtleties of emotion than we have words for.

Researchers continue to argue over precisely which emotions can be considered primary—the blue, red, and yellow of feeling from which all blends come—or even if there are such primary emotions at all. Some theorists propose basic families, though not all agree on them. The main candidates and some of the members of their families:

- *Anger:* fury, outrage, resentment, wrath, exasperation, indignation, vexation, acrimony, animosity, annoyance, irritability, hostility, and, perhaps at the extreme, pathological hatred and violence
- *Sadness:* grief, sorrow, cheerlessness, gloom, melancholy, self-pity, loneliness, dejection, despair, and, when pathological, severe depression
- *Fear:* anxiety, apprehension, nervousness, concern, consternation, misgiving, wariness, qualm, edginess, dread, fright, terror; as a psychopathology, phobia and panic
- *Enjoyment:* happiness, joy, relief, contentment, bliss, delight, amusement, pride, sensual pleasure, thrill, rapture, gratification, satisfaction, euphoria, whimsy, ecstasy, and at the far edge, mania
- *Love:* acceptance, friendliness, trust, kindness, affinity, devotion, adoration, infatuation, *agape*

* *Surprise:* shock, astonishment, amazement, wonder
* *Disgust:* contempt, disdain, scorn, abhorrence, aversion, distaste, revulsion
* *Shame:* guilt, embarrassment, chagrin, remorse, humiliation, regret, mortification, and contrition

To be sure, this list does not resolve every question about how to categorize emotion. For example, what about blends such as jealousy, a variant of anger that also melds sadness and fear? And what of the virtues, such as hope and faith, courage and forgiveness, certainty and equanimity? Or some of the classic vices, feelings such as doubt, complacency, sloth, and torpor—or boredom? There are no clear answers; the scientific debate on how to classify emotions continues.

The argument for there being a handful of core emotions hinges to some extent on the discovery by Paul Ekman, at the University of California at San Francisco, that specific facial expressions for four of them (fear, anger, sadness, enjoyment) are recognized by people in cultures around the world, including preliterate peoples presumably untainted by exposure to cinema or television—suggesting their universality. Ekman showed facial photos portraying expressions with technical precision to people in cultures as remote as the Fore of New Guinea, an isolated Stone Age tribe in the remote highlands, and found people everywhere recognized the same basic emotions. This universality of facial expressions for emotion was probably first noted by Darwin, who saw it as evidence the forces of evolution had stamped these signals in our central nervous system.

In seeking basic principles, I follow Ekman and others in thinking of emotions in terms of families or dimensions, taking the main families—anger, sadness, fear, enjoyment, love, shame, and so on—as cases in point for the endless nuances of our emotional life. Each of these families has a basic emotional nucleus at its core, with its relatives rippling out from there in countless mutations. In the outer ripples are *moods*, which, technically speaking, are more muted and last far longer than an emotion (while it's relatively rare to be in the full heat of anger all day, for example, it is not that rare to be in a grumpy, irritable mood, in which shorter bouts of anger are easily triggered). Beyond moods are *temperaments*, the readiness to evoke a given emotion or mood that makes people melancholy, timid, or cheery. And still beyond such emotional dispositions are the outright *disorders* of emotion such as clinical depression or unremitting anxiety, in which someone feels perpetually trapped in a toxic state.

Hallmarks of the Emotional Mind

Only in recent years has there emerged a scientific model of the emotional mind that explains how so much of what we do can be emotionally driven—how we can be so reasonable at one moment and so irrational the next—and the sense in which emotions have their own reasons and their own logic. Perhaps the two best assessments of the emotional mind are offered independently by Paul Ekman, head of the Human Interaction Laboratory at the University of California, San Francisco, and by Seymour Epstein, a clinical psychologist at the University of Massachusetts.[1] While Ekman and Epstein have each weighed different scientific evidence, together they offer a basic list of the qualities that distinguish emotions from the rest of mental life.[2]

A Quick but Sloppy Response

The emotional mind is far quicker than the rational mind, springing into action without pausing even a moment to consider what it is doing. Its quickness precludes the deliberate, analytic reflection that is the hallmark of the thinking mind. In evolution this quickness most likely revolved around that most basic decision, what to pay attention to, and, once vigilant while, say, confronting another animal, making split-second decisions like, Do I eat this, or does it eat me? Those organisms that had to pause too long to reflect on these answers were unlikely to have many progeny to pass on their slower-acting genes.

Actions that spring from the emotional mind carry a particularly strong sense of certainty, a by-product of a streamlined, simplified way of looking at things that can be absolutely bewildering to the rational mind. When the dust settles, or even in mid-response, we find ourselves thinking, "What did I do that for?"—a sign that the rational mind is awakening to the moment, but not with the rapidity of the emotional mind.

Since the interval between what triggers an emotion and its eruption can be virtually instantaneous, the mechanism that appraises perception must be capable of great speed, even in brain time, which is reckoned in thousandths of a second. This appraisal of the need to act needs to be automatic, so rapid that it never enters conscious awareness.[3] This quick-and-dirty variety of emotional response sweeps over us virtually before we quite know what is happening.

This rapid mode of perception sacrifices accuracy for speed, relying on first impressions, reacting to the overall picture or the most striking aspects. It takes things in at once, as a whole, reacting without taking the time for thoughtful analysis. Vivid elements can determine that impression, outweighing a careful evaluation of the details. The great advantage is that the emotional mind can read an emotional reality (he's angry with me; she's lying; this is making him sad) in an instant, making the intuitive snap judgments that tell us who to be wary of, who to trust, who's in distress. The emotional mind is our radar for danger; if we (or our forebears in evolution) waited for the rational mind to make some of these judgments, we might not only be wrong—we might be dead. The drawback is that these impressions and intuitive judgments, because they are made in the snap of a finger, may be mistaken or misguided.

Paul Ekman proposes that this quickness, in which emotions can overtake us before we are quite aware they have started, is essential to their being so highly adaptive: they mobilize us to respond to urgent events without wasting time pondering whether to react or how to respond. Using the system he developed for detecting emotions from subtle changes in facial expression, Ekman can track microemotions that flit across the face in less than a half second. Ekman and his collaborators have discovered that emotional expressions begin to show up in changes in facial musculature within a few thousandths of a second after the event that triggers the reaction, and that the physiological changes typical of a given emotion—like shunting blood flow and increasing heart rate—also take only fractions of a second to begin. This swiftness is particularly true of intense emotion, like fear of a sudden threat.

Ekman argues that, technically speaking, the full heat of emotion is very brief, lasting just seconds rather than minutes, hours, or days. His reasoning is that it would be maladaptive for an emotion to capture the brain and body for a long time regardless of changing circumstance. If the emotions caused by a single event invariably continued to dominate us after it had passed, and regardless of what else was happening around us, then our feelings would be poor guides to action. For emotions to last longer the trigger must be sustained, in effect continually evoking the emotion, as when the loss of a loved one keeps us mourning. When feelings persist for hours, it is usually as moods, a muted form. Moods set an affective tone, but they are not such strong shapers of how we perceive and act as is the high heat of full emotion.

First Feelings, Second Thoughts

Because it takes the rational mind a moment or two longer to register and respond than it does the emotional mind, the "first impulse" in an emotional situation is the heart's, not the head's. There is also a second kind of emotional reaction, slower than the quick-response, which simmers and brews first in our thoughts before it leads to feeling. This second pathway to triggering emotions is more deliberate, and we are typically quite aware of the thoughts that lead to it. In this kind of emotional reaction there is a more extended appraisal; our thoughts—cognition—play the key role in determining what emotions will be roused. Once we make an appraisal—"that taxi driver is cheating me" or "this baby is adorable," a fitting emotional response follows. In this slower sequence, more fully articulated thought precedes feeling. More complicated emotions, like embarrassment or apprehension over an upcoming exam, follow this slower route, taking seconds or minutes to unfold—these are emotions that follow from thoughts.

By contrast, in the fast-response sequence feeling seems to precede or be simultaneous with thought. This rapid-fire emotional reaction takes over in situations that have the urgency of primal survival. This is the power of such rapid decisions: they mobilize us in an instant to rise to an emergency. Our most intense feelings are involuntary reactions; we cannot decide when they will erupt. "Love," wrote Stendhal, "is like a fever that comes and goes independently of the will." Not just love, but our angers and fears, as well, sweep over us, seeming to happen *to* us rather than being our choice. For that reason they can offer an alibi: "It is the fact that *we cannot choose the emotions which we have*," notes Ekman, that allows people to explain away their actions by saying they were in the grip of emotion.[4]

Just as there are quick and slow paths to emotion—one through immediate perception and the other through reflective thought—there are also emotions which come bidden. One example is intentionally manipulated feeling, the actors' stock-in-trade, like the tears that come when sad memories are intentionally milked for their effect. But actors are simply more skilled than the rest of us at the intentional use of the second pathway to emotion, feeling via thinking. While we cannot easily change what specific emotions a certain kind of thought will trigger, we very often can, and do, choose what to think about. Just as a sexual fantasy can lead to sexual feelings, so can happy memories cheer us up, or melancholy thoughts make us reflective.

But the rational mind usually does not decide what emotions we "should" have. Instead, our feelings typically come to us as a fait accompli. What the rational mind can ordinarily control is the *course* of those reactions. A few exceptions aside, we do not decide *when* to be mad, sad, and so on.

A Symbolic, Childlike Reality

The logic of the emotional mind is *associative;* it takes elements that symbolize a reality, or trigger a memory of it, to be the same as that reality. That is why similes, metaphors, and images speak directly to the emotional mind, as do the arts—novels, film, poetry, song, theater, opera. Great spiritual teachers, like Buddha and Jesus, have touched their disciples' hearts by speaking in the language of emotion, teaching in parables, fables, and stories. Indeed, religious symbol and ritual makes little sense from the rational point of view; it is couched in the vernacular of the heart.

This logic of the heart—of the emotional mind—is well-described by Freud in his concept of "primary process" thought; it is the logic of religion and poetry, psychosis and children, dream and myth (as Joseph Campbell put it, "Dreams are private myths; myths are shared dreams"). The primary process is the key that unlocks the meanings of works like James Joyce's *Ulysses:* In primary process thought, loose associations determine the flow of a narrative; one object symbolizes another; one feeling displaces another and stands for it; wholes are condensed into parts. There is no time, no laws of cause-and-effect. Indeed, there is no such thing as "No" in the primary process; anything is possible. The psychoanalytic method is in part the art of deciphering and unraveling these substitutions in meaning.

If the emotional mind follows this logic and its rules, with one element standing for another, things need not necessarily be defined by their objective identity: what matters is how they are *perceived;* things are as they seem. What something reminds us of can be far more important than what it "is." Indeed, in emotional life, identities can be like a hologram in the sense that a single part evokes a whole. As Seymour Epstein points out, while the rational mind makes logical connections between causes and effects, the emotional mind is indiscriminate, connecting things that merely have similar striking features.[5]

There are many ways in which the emotional mind is childlike, the more so the stronger the emotion grows. One way is *categorical* thinking, where everything is in black and white, with no shades of gray; someone who is mortified about a faux pas might have the immediate thought, "I *always* say the wrong thing." Another sign of this childlike mode is *personalized* thinking, with events perceived with a bias centering on oneself, like the driver who, after an accident, explained that "the telephone pole came straight at me."

This childlike mode is *self-confirming,* suppressing or ignoring memories or facts that would undermine its beliefs and seizing on those that support it. The beliefs of the rational mind are tentative; new evidence can disconfirm one belief and replace it with a new one—it reasons by objective evidence. The emotional mind, however, takes its beliefs to be absolutely true, and so discounts any evidence to the contrary. That is why it is so hard to reason with someone who is emotionally upset: no matter the soundness of your argument from a logical point of view, it carries no weight if it is out of keeping with the emotional conviction of the moment. Feelings are self-justifying, with a set of perceptions and "proofs" all their own.

The Past Imposed on the Present

When some feature of an event seems similar to an emotionally charged memory from the past, the emotional mind responds by triggering the feelings that went with the remembered event. The emotional mind reacts to the present *as though it were the past.*[6] The trouble is that, especially when the appraisal is fast and automatic, we may not realize that what was once the case is no longer so. Someone who has learned, through painful childhood beatings, to react to an angry scowl with intense fear and loathing will have that reaction to some degree even as an adult, when the scowl carries no such threat.

If the feelings are strong, then the reaction that is triggered is obvious. But if the feelings are vague or subtle, we may not quite realize the emotional reaction we are having, even though it is subtly coloring how we react to the moment. Thoughts and reactions at this moment will take on the coloration of thoughts and reactions then, even though it may seem that the reaction is due solely to the circumstance of the moment. Our emotional mind will harness the rational mind to its purposes, so we come up with explanations for our feelings and reactions—rationalizations—justifying them in terms of the present moment, without realizing the influence of the emotional memory. In that sense, we can have no idea of what is actually going on, though we may have the conviction of certainty that we know exactly what is happening. At such moments the emotional mind has entrained the rational mind, putting it to its own uses.

State-specific Reality

The working of the emotional mind is to a large degree *state-specific*, dictated by the particular feeling ascendant at a given moment. How we think and act when we are feeling romantic is entirely different from how we behave when enraged or dejected; in the mechanics of emotion, each feeling has its own distinct repertoire of thought, reactions, even memories. These state-specific repertoires become most predominant in moments of intense emotion.

One sign that such a repertoire is active is selective memory. Part of the mind's response to an emotional situation is to reshuffle memory and options for action so that those most relevant are at the top of the hierarchy and so more readily enacted. And, as we have seen, each major emotion has its hallmark biological signature, a pattern of sweeping changes that entrain the body as that emotion becomes ascendant, and a unique set of cues the body automatically sends out when in its grip.[7]

APPENDIX C

The Neural Circuitry of Fear

The amygdala is central to fear. When a rare brain disease destroyed the amygdala (but no other brain structures) in the patient neurologists call "S.M.," fear disappeared from her mental repertoire. She became unable to identify looks of fear on other people's faces, nor to make such an expression herself. As her neurologist put it, "If someone put a gun to S.M.'s head, she would know intellectually to be afraid but she would not feel afraid as you or I would."

Neuroscientists have mapped the circuitry for fear in perhaps finest detail, though at the present state of this art the full circuitry for none of the emotions is completely surveyed. Fear is an apt case in point for understanding the neural dynamics of emotion. Fear, in evolution, has a special prominence: perhaps more than any other emotion it is crucial for survival. Of course in modern times misplaced fears are the bane of daily life, leaving us suffering from frets, angst, and garden variety worries—or at pathological extreme, from panic attacks, phobias, or obsessive-compulsive disorder.

Say you're alone one night at home, reading a book, when suddenly you hear a crash in another room. What happens in your brain over the next moments offers a window into the neural circuitry of fear, and the role of the amygdala as an alarm system. The first brain circuit involved simply takes in that sound as raw physical waves and transforms them into the language of the brain to startle you into alertness. This circuit goes from the ear to the brainstem and then to the thalamus. From there two branches separate: a smaller bundle of projections leads to the amygdala and the nearby hippocampus; the other, larger pathway leads to the auditory cortex in the temporal lobe, where sounds are sorted out and comprehended.

The hippocampus, a key storage site for memory, quickly sorts that "crash" against other similar sounds you've heard, to see if it is familiar—is this "crash" one that you immediately recognize? Meanwhile the auditory cortex is doing a more sophisticated analysis of the sound to try to understand its source—is it the cat? A shutter banging in the wind? A prowler? The auditory cortex comes up with its hypothesis—it might be the cat knocking a lamp off the table, say, but it might also be a prowler—and sends that message to the amygdala and hippocampus, which quickly compare it to similar memories.

If the conclusion is reassuring (it's only the shutter that bangs whenever it gets too windy) then the general alert does not escalate to the next level. But if you are still unsure, another coil of circuitry reverberating between amygdala, hippocampus, and the prefrontal cortex further heightens your uncertainty and fixates your attention, making you even more concerned about identifying the source of the sound. If no satisfying answer comes from this further keen analysis, the amygdala triggers an alarm, its central area activating the hypothalamus, the brainstem, and the autonomic nervous system.

The superb architecture of the amygdala as a central alarm system for the brain becomes evident in this moment of apprehension and subliminal anxiety. The several bundles of neurons in the amygdala each have a distinct set of projections with receptors primed for different neurotransmitters, something like those home alarm companies where operators stand at the ready to send out calls to the local fire department, police, and a neighbor whenever a home security system signals trouble.

Different parts of the amygdala receive differing information. To the amygdala's lateral nucleus come projections from the thalamus and auditory and visual cortices. Smells, via the olfactory bulb, come to the corticomedial area of the amygdala, and tastes and messages from the viscera go to the central area. These incoming signals make the amygdala a continual sentinel, scrutinizing every sensory experience.

From the amygdala projections extend out to every major part of the brain. From the central and medial areas a branch goes to the areas of the hypothalamus that secrete the body's emergency-response substance, corticotropin-releasing hormone (CRH), which mobilizes the fight-or-flight reaction via a cascade of other hormones. The amygdala's basal area sends out branches to the corpus striatum, linking into the brain's system for movement. And, via the nearby central nucleus, the amygdala sends signals to the autonomic nervous system via the medulla, activating a wide range of far-flung responses in the cardiovascular system, the muscles, and the gut.

From the amygdala's basolateral area, arms go to the cingulate cortex and

⊃ the fibers known as the "central gray," cells that regulate the large muscles of the skeleton. It is these cells that make a dog snarl or that arch the back of a cat threatening an interloper on its territory. In humans these same circuits tighten the muscles of the vocal cords, creating the high-pitched voice of fright.

Still another pathway from the amygdala leads to the locus ceruleus in the brainstem, which in turn manufactures norepinephrine (also called "noradrenaline") and disperses it throughout the brain. The net effect of norepinephrine is to heighten the overall reactivity of the brain areas that receive it, making the sensory circuits more sensitive. Norepinephrine suffuses the cortex, the brainstem, and the limbic system itself, in essence setting the brain on edge. Now even the ordinary creaking of the house can send a tremor of fear coursing through you. Most of these changes go on outside awareness, so that you are not yet aware you feel fear.

But as you begin to actually feel fear—that is, as the anxiety that had been unconscious pierces awareness—the amygdala seamlessly commands a wide-ranging response. It signals cells in the brainstem to put a fearful expression on your face, make you edgy and easily startled, freeze unrelated movements your muscles had underway, speed your heart rate and raise your blood pressure, and slow your breathing (you may notice yourself suddenly holding your breath when you first feel fearful, all the better to hear more clearly what it is you are fearful of). That is only one part of a wide, carefully coordinated array of changes the amygdala and connected areas orchestrate as they commandeer the brain in a crisis.

Meanwhile the amygdala, along with the interconnected hippocampus, directs the cells that send key neurotransmitters, for example, to trigger releases of dopamine that lead to the riveting of attention on the source of your fear—the strange sounds—and put your muscles at readiness to react accordingly. At the same time the amygdala signals sensory areas for vision and attention, making sure that the eyes seek out whatever is most relevant to the emergency at hand. Simultaneously cortical memory systems are reshuffled so that knowledge and memories most relevant to the particular emotional urgency will be most readily recalled, taking precedence over other less relevant strands of thought.

Once these signals have been sent, you are pitched into full-fledged fear: you become aware of the characteristic tightness in your gut, your speeding heart, the tightening of the muscles around your neck and shoulders or the trembling of your limbs; your body freezes in place as you strain your attention to hear any further sounds, and your mind races with possible lurking dangers and ways to respond. This entire sequence—from surprise to uncertainty to apprehension to fear—can be telescoped within a second or so. (For more information, see Jerome Kagan, *Galen's Prophecy*. New York: Basic Books, 1994.)

W. T. Grant Consortium: Active Ingredients of Prevention Programs

Key ingredients of effective programs include:

EMOTIONAL SKILLS

- Identifying and labeling feelings
- Expressing feelings
- Assessing the intensity of feelings
- Managing feelings
- Delaying gratification
- Controlling impulses
- Reducing stress
- Knowing the difference between feelings and actions

COGNITIVE SKILLS

- Self-talk—conducting an "inner dialogue" as a way to cope with a topic or challenge or reinforce one's own behavior
- Reading and interpreting social cues—for example, recognizing social influences on behavior and seeing oneself in the perspective of the larger community
- Using steps for problem-solving and decision-making—for instance, controlling impulses, setting goals, identifying alternative actions, anticipating consequences

- Understanding the perspective of others
- Understanding behavioral norms (what is and is not acceptable behavior)
- A positive attitude toward life
- Self-awareness—for example, developing realistic expectations about oneself

BEHAVIORAL SKILLS

- Nonverbal—communicating through eye contact, facial expressiveness, tone of voice, gestures, and so on
- Verbal—making clear requests, responding effectively to criticism, resisting negative influences, listening to others, helping others, participating in positive peer groups

SOURCE: W. T. Grant Consortium on the School-Based Promotion of Social Competence, "Drug and Alcohol Prevention Curricula," in J. David Hawkins et al., *Communities That Care* (San Francisco: Jossey-Bass, 1992).

APPENDIX E

The Self Science Curriculum

Main components:

- *Self-awareness:* observing yourself and recognizing your feelings; building a vocabulary for feelings; knowing the relationship between thoughts, feelings, and reactions
- *Personal decision-making:* examining your actions and knowing their consequences; knowing if thought or feeling is ruling a decision; applying these insights to issues such as sex and drugs
- *Managing feelings:* monitoring "self-talk" to catch negative messages such as internal put-downs; realizing what is behind a feeling (e.g., the hurt that underlies anger); finding ways to handle fears and anxieties, anger, and sadness
- *Handling stress:* learning the value of exercise, guided imagery, relaxation methods
- *Empathy:* understanding others' feelings and concerns and taking their perspective; appreciating the differences in how people feel about things
- *Communications:* talking about feelings effectively: becoming a good listener and question-asker; distinguishing between what someone does or says and your own reactions or judgments about it; sending "I" messages instead of blame
- *Self-disclosure:* valuing openness and building trust in a relationship; knowing when it's safe to risk talking about your private feelings
- *Insight:* identifying patterns in your emotional life and reactions; recognizing similar patterns in others
- *Self-acceptance:* feeling pride and seeing yourself in a positive light; recognizing your strengths and weaknesses; being able to laugh at yourself
- *Personal responsibility:* taking responsibility; recognizing the consequences of your decisions and actions, accepting your feelings and moods, following through on commitments (e.g., to studying)

- *Assertiveness:* stating your concerns and feelings without anger or passivity

- *Group dynamics:* cooperation; knowing when and how to lead, when to follow

- *Conflict resolution:* how to fight fair with other kids, with parents, with teachers; the win/win model for negotiating compromise

SOURCE: Karen F. Stone and Harold Q. Dillehunt, *Self Science: The Subject Is Me* (Santa Monica: Goodyear Publishing Co., 1978).

Social and Emotional Learning: Results

Child Development Project

Eric Schaps, Development Studies Center, Oakland, California.

Evaluation in schools in Northern California, grades K–6; rating by independent observers, comparing with control schools.

RESULTS:

- more responsible
- more assertive
- more popular and outgoing
- more pro-social and helpful
- better understanding of others
- more considerate, concerned
- more pro-social strategies for interpersonal problem-solving
- more harmonious
- more "democratic"
- better conflict-resolution skills

SOURCES: E. Schaps and V. Battistich, "Promoting Health Development Through School-Based Prevention: New Approaches," *OSAP Prevention Monograph, no. 8: Preventing Adolescent Drug Use: From Theory to Practice.* Eric Gopelrud (ed.), Rockville, MD: Office of Substance Abuse Prevention, U.S. Dept. of Health and Human Services, 1991.

D. Solomon, M. Watson, V. Battistich, E. Schaps, and K. Delucchi, "Creating a Caring Community: Educational Practices That Promote Children's Prosocial Development," in F. K. Oser, A. Dick, and J.-L. Patry, eds., *Effective and Responsible Teaching: The New Synthesis* (San Francisco: Jossey-Bass, 1992).

Paths

Mark Greenberg, Fast Track Project, University of Washington.

Evaluated in schools in Seattle, grades 1–5; ratings by teachers, comparing matched control students among 1) regular students, 2) deaf students, 3) special-education students.

Results:

- Improvement in social cognitive skills
- Improvement in emotion, recognition, and understanding
- Better self-control
- Better planning for solving cognitive tasks
- More thinking before acting
- More effective conflict resolution
- More positive classroom atmosphere

Special-needs students:

Improved classroom behavior on:

- Frustration tolerance
- Assertive social skills
- Task orientation
- Peer skills
- Sharing
- Sociability
- Self-control

Improved emotional understanding:

- Recognition
- Labeling
- Decreases in self-reports of sadness and depression
- Decrease in anxiety and withdrawal

Sources: Conduct Problems Research Group, "A Developmental and Clinical Model for the Prevention of Conduct Disorder: The Fast Track Program," *Development and Psychopathology* 4 (1992).

M. T. Greenberg and C. A. Kusche, *Promoting Social and Emotional Development in Deaf Children: The PATHS Project* (Seattle: University of Washington Press, 1993).

M. T. Greenberg, C. A. Kusche, E. T. Cook, and J. P. Quamma, "Promoting Emotional Competence in School-Aged Children: The Effects of the PATHS Curriculum," *Development and Psychopathology* 7 (1995).

Seattle Social Development Project

J. David Hawkins, Social Development Research Group, University of Washington

Evaluated in Seattle elementary and middle schools by independent testing and objective standards, in comparison to nonprogram schools.

RESULTS:

- More positive attachment to family and school
- Boys less aggressive, girls less self-destructive
- Fewer suspensions and expulsions among low-achieving students
- Less drug-use initiation
- Less delinquency
- Better scores on standardized achievement tests

SOURCES: E. Schaps and V. Battistich, "Promoting Health Development Through School-Based Prevention: New Approaches," *OSAP Prevention Monograph, no. 8: Preventing Adolescent Drug Use: From Theory to Practice.* Eric Gopelrud (ed.), Rockville, MD: Office of Substance Abuse Prevention, U.S. Dept. of Health and Human Services, 1991.

J. D. Hawkins et al., "The Seattle Social Development Project," in J. McCord and R. Tremblay, eds., *The Prevention of Antisocial Behavior in Children* (New York: Guilford, 1992).

J. D. Hawkins, E. Von Cleve, and R. F. Catalano, "Reducing Early Childhood Aggression: Results of a Primary Prevention Program," *Journal of the American Academy of Child and Adolescent Psychiatry* 30, 2 (1991), pp. 208–17.

J. A. O'Donnell, J. D. Hawkins, R. F. Catalano, R. D. Abbott, and L. E. Day, "Preventing School Failure, Drug Use, and Delinquency Among Low-Income Children: Effects of a Long-Term Prevention Project in Elementary Schools," *American Journal of Orthopsychiatry* 65 (1994).

Yale-New Haven Social Competence Promotion Program

Roger Weissberg, University of Illinois at Chicago

Evaluated in New Haven Public Schools, grades 5–8, by independent observations and student and teacher reports, compared with control group.

RESULTS:

- Improved problem-solving skills
- More involvement with peers
- Better impulse control
- Improved behavior
- Improved interpersonal effectiveness and popularity

- Enhanced coping skills
- More skill in handling interpersonal problems
- Better coping with anxiety
- Less delinquent behaviors
- Better conflict-resolution skills

SOURCES: M. J. Elias and R. P. Weissberg, "School-Based Social Competence Promotion as a Primary Prevention Strategy: A Tale of Two Projects," *Prevention in Human Services* 7, 1 (1990), pp. 177–200.

  M. Caplan, R. P. Weissberg, J. S. Grober, P. J. Sivo, K. Grady, and C. Jacoby, "Social Competence Promotion with Inner-City and Suburban Young Adolescents: Effects of Social Adjustment and Alcohol Use," *Journal of Consulting and Clinical Psychology* 60, 1 (1992), pp. 56–63.

Resolving Conflict Creatively Program

Linda Lantieri, National Center for Resolving Conflict Creatively Program (an initiative of Educators for Social Responsibility), New York City

  Evaluated in New York City schools, grades K–12, by teachers' ratings, pre- and post-program.

RESULTS:

- Less violence in class
- Fewer verbal put-downs in class
- More-caring atmosphere
- More willingness to cooperate
- More empathy
- Improved communication skills

SOURCE: Metis Associates, Inc., *The Resolving Conflict Creatively Program: 1988–1989. Summary of Significant Findings of RCCP New York Site* (New York: Metis Associates, May 1990).

The Improving Social Awareness–Social Problem Solving Project

Maurice Elias, Rutgers University

  Evaluated in New Jersey schools, grades K–6, by teacher ratings, peer assessments, and school records, compared to nonparticipants.

RESULTS:

- More sensitive to others' feelings
- Better understanding of the consequences of their behavior
- Increased ability to "size up" interpersonal situations and plan appropriate actions
- Higher self-esteem
- More prosocial behavior
- Sought out by peers for help
- Better handled the transition to middle school
- Less antisocial, self-destructive, and socially disordered behavior, even when followed up into high school
- Improved learning-to-learn skills
- Better self-control, social awareness, and social decision-making in and out of the classroom

SOURCES: M. J. Elias, M. A. Gara, T. F. Schuyler, L. R. Branden-Muller, and M. A. Sayette, "The Promotion of Social Competence: Longitudinal Study of a Preventive School-Based Program," *American Journal of Orthopsychiatry* 61 (1991), pp. 409–17.

M. J. Elias and J. Clabby, *Building Social Problem Solving Skills: Guidelines From a School Based Program* (San Francisco: Jossey Bass, 1992).

Notes

PART ONE: THE EMOTIONAL BRAIN

Chapter 1. What Are Emotions For?

1. Associated Press, September 15, 1993.

2. The timelessness of this theme of selfless love is suggested by how pervasive it is in world myth: The Jataka tales, told throughout much of Asia for millennia, all narrate variations on such parables of self-sacrifice.

3. Altruistic love and human survival: The evolutionary theories that posit the adaptive advantages of altruism are well-summarized in Malcolm Slavin and Daniel Kriegman, *The Adaptive Design of the Human Psyche* (New York: Guilford Press, 1992).

4. Much of this discussion is based on Paul Ekman's key essay, "An Argument for Basic Emotions," *Cognition and Emotion*, 6, 1992, pp. 169–200. This point is from P. N. Johnson-Laird and K. Oatley's essay in the same issue of the journal.

5. The shooting of Matilda Crabtree: *The New York Times*, Nov. 11, 1994.

6. Only in adults: An observation by Paul Ekman, University of California at San Francisco.

7. Body changes in emotions and their evolutionary reasons: Some of the changes are documented in Robert W. Levenson, Paul Ekman, and Wallace V. Friesen, "Voluntary Facial Action Generates Emotion-Specific Autonomic Nervous System Activity," *Psychophysiology*, 27, 1990. This list is culled from there and other sources. At this point such a list remains speculative to a degree; there is scientific debate over the precise biological signature of each emotion, with some researchers taking the position that there is far more overlap than difference among emotions, or that our present ability to measure the biological correlates of emotion is too immature to distinguish among them reliably. For this debate see: Paul Ekman and Richard Davidson, eds., *Fundamental Questions About Emotions* (New York: Oxford University Press, 1994).

8. As Paul Ekman puts it, "Anger is the most dangerous emotion; some of the main problems destroying society these days involve anger run amok. It's the least adaptive emotion now because it mobilizes us to fight. Our emotions evolved when we didn't have the technology to act so powerfully on them. In prehistoric times, when you had an instantaneous rage and for a second wanted to kill someone, you couldn't do it very easily—but now you can."

9. Erasmus of Rotterdam, *In Praise of Folly*, trans. Eddie Radice (London: Penguin, 1971), p. 87.

10. Such basic responses defined what might pass for the "emotional life"—more aptly, an "instinct life"—of these species. More important in evolutionary terms, these are

311

the decisions crucial to survival; those animals that could do them well, or well enough, survived to pass on their genes. In these early times, mental life was brutish: the senses and a simple repertoire of reactions to the stimuli they received got a lizard, frog, bird, or fish—and, perhaps, a brontosaurus—through the day. But this runt brain did not yet allow for what we think of as an emotion.

11. The limbic system and emotions: R. Joseph, "The Naked Neuron: Evolution and the Languages of the Brain and Body," New York: Plenum Publishing, 1993; Paul D. MacLean, *The Triune Brain in Evolution* (New York: Plenum, 1990).

12. Rhesus infants and adaptability: "Aspects of emotion conserved across species," Ned Kalin, M.D., Departments of Psychology and Psychiatry, University of Wisconsin, prepared for the MacArthur Affective Neuroscience Meeting, Nov., 1992.

Chapter 2. Anatomy of an Emotional Hijacking

1. The case of the man with no feelings was described by R. Joseph, op. cit. p. 83. On the other hand, there may be some vestiges of feeling in people who lack an amygdala (see Paul Ekman and Richard Davidson, eds., *Questions About Emotion*. New York: Oxford University Press, 1994). The different findings may hinge on exactly which parts of the amygdala and related circuits were missing; the last word on the detailed neurology of emotion is far from in.

2. Like many neuroscientists, LeDoux works at several levels, studying, for instance, how specific lesions in a rat's brain change its behavior; painstakingly tracing the path of single neurons; setting up elaborate experiments to condition fear in rats whose brains have been surgically altered. His findings, and others reviewed here, are at the frontier of exploration in neuroscience, and so remain somewhat speculative— particularly the implications that seem to flow from the raw data to an understanding of our emotional life. But LeDoux's work is supported by a growing body of converging evidence from a variety of neuroscientists who are steadily laying bare the neural underpinnings of emotions. See, for example, Joseph LeDoux, "Sensory Systems and Emotion," *Integrative Psychiatry*, 4, 1986; Joseph LeDoux, "Emotion and the Limbic System Concept," *Concepts in Neuroscience*, 2, 1992.

3. The idea of the limbic system as the brain's emotional center was introduced by neurologist Paul MacLean more than forty years ago. In recent years discoveries like LeDoux's have refined the limbic system concept, showing that some of its central structures like the hippocampus are less directly involved in emotions, while circuits linking other parts of the brain—particularly the prefrontal lobes—to the amygdala are more central. Beyond that, there is a growing recognition that each emotion may call on distinct brain areas. The most current thinking is that there is not a neatly defined single "emotional brain," but rather several systems of circuits that disperse the regulation of a given emotion to farflung, but coordinated, parts of the brain. Neuroscientists speculate that when the full brain mapping of the emotions is accomplished, each major emotion will have its own topography, a distinct map of neuronal pathways determining its unique qualities, though many or most of these circuits are likely to be interlinked at key junctures in the limbic system, like the amygdala, and prefrontal cortex. See Joseph LeDoux, "Emotional Memory Systems in the Brain," *Behavioral and Brain Research*, 58, 1993.

4. Brain circuitry of different levels of fear: This analysis is based on the excellent synthesis in Jerome Kagan, *Galen's Prophecy* (New York: Basic Books, 1994).

5. I wrote about Joseph LeDoux's research in *The New York Times* on August 15, 1989.

The discussion in this chapter is based on interviews with him, and several of his articles, including Joseph LeDoux, "Emotional Memory Systems in the Brain," *Behavioural Brain Research*, 58, 1993; Joseph LeDoux, "Emotion, Memory and the Brain," *Scientific American*, June, 1994; Joseph LeDoux, "Emotion and the Limbic System Concept," *Concepts in Neuroscience*, 2, 1992.

6. Unconscious preferences: William Raft Kunst-Wilson and R. B. Zajonc, "Affective Discrimination of Stimuli That Cannot Be Recognized," *Science* (Feb. 1, 1980).

7. Unconscious opinion: John A. Bargh, "First Second: The Preconscious in Social Interactions," presented at the meeting of the American Psychological Society, Washington, DC (June 1994).

8. Emotional memory: Larry Cahill et al., "Beta-adrenergic activation and memory for emotional events," *Nature* (Oct. 20, 1994).

9. Psychoanalytic theory and brain maturation: the most detailed discussion of the early years and the emotional consequences of brain development is Allan Schore, *Affect Regulation and the Origin of Self* (Hillsdale, NJ: Lawrence Erlbaum Associates, 1994).

10. Dangerous, even if you don't know what it is: LeDoux, quoted in "How Scary Things Get That Way," *Science* (Nov. 6, 1992), p. 887.

11. Much of this speculation about the fine-tuning of emotional response by the neocortex comes from Ned Kalin, op. cit.

12. A closer look at the neuroanatomy shows how the prefrontal lobes act as emotional managers. Much evidence points to part of the prefrontal cortex as a site where most or all cortical circuits involved in an emotional reaction come together. In humans, the strongest connections between neocortex and amygdala run to the left prefrontal lobe and the temporal lobe below and to the side of the frontal lobe (the temporal lobe is critical in identifying what an object is). Both these connections are made in a single projection, suggesting a rapid and powerful pathway, a virtual neural highway. The single-neuron projection between the amygdala and prefrontal cortex runs to an area called the *orbitofrontal cortex*. This is the area that seems most critical for assessing emotional responses as we are in the midst of them and making mid-course corrections.

The orbitofrontal cortex both receives signals from the amygdala and has its own intricate, extensive web of projections throughout the limbic brain. Through this web it plays a role in regulating emotional responses—including inhibiting signals from the limbic brain as they reach other areas of the cortex, thus toning down the neural urgency of those signals. The orbitofrontal cortex's connections to the limbic brain are so extensive that some neuroanatomists have called it a kind of "limbic cortex"—the thinking part of the emotional brain. See Ned Kalin, Departments of Psychology and Psychiatry, University of Wisconsin, "Aspects of Emotion Conserved Across Species," an unpublished manuscript prepared for the MacArthur Affective Neuroscience Meeting, November, 1992; and Allan Schore, *Affect Regulation and the Origin of Self* (Hillsdale, NJ: Lawrence Erlbaum Associates, 1994).

There is not only a structural bridge between amygdala and prefrontal cortex, but, as always, a biochemical one: both the ventromedial section of the prefrontal cortex and the amygdala are especially high in concentrations of chemical receptors for the neurotransmitter serotonin. This brain chemical seems, among other things, to prime cooperation: monkeys with extremely high density of receptors for serotonin in the prefrontal-amygdala circuit are "socially well-tuned," while those with low concentrations are hostile and antagonistic. See Antonio Damosio, *Descartes' Error* (New York: Grosset/Putnam, 1994).

13. Animal studies show that when areas of the prefrontal lobes are lesioned, so that they no longer modulate emotional signals from the limbic area, the animals become erratic, impulsively and unpredictably exploding in rage or cringing in fear. A. R. Luria, the brilliant Russian neuropsychologist, proposed as long ago as the 1930s that the prefrontal cortex was key for self-control and constraining emotional outbursts; patients who had damage to this area, he noted, were impulsive and prone to flareups of fear and anger. And a study of two dozen men and women who had been convicted of impulsive, heat-of-passion murders found, using PET scans for brain imaging, that they had a much lower than usual level of activity in these same sections of the prefrontal cortex.

14. Some of the main work on lesioned lobes in rats was done by Victor Dennenberg, a psychologist at the University of Connecticut.

15. Left hemisphere lesions and joviality: G. Gianotti, "Emotional behavior and hemispheric side of lesion," *Cortex,* 8, 1972.

16. The case of the happier stroke patient was reported by Mary K. Morris, of the Department of Neurology at the University of Florida, at the International Neurophysiological Society Meeting, February 13–16, 1991, in San Antonio.

17. Prefrontal cortex and working memory: Lynn D. Selemon et al., "Prefrontal Cortex," *American Journal of Psychiatry,* 152, 1995.

18. Faulty frontal lobes: Philip Harden and Robert Pihl, "Cognitive Function, Cardiovascular Reactivity, and Behavior in Boys at High Risk for Alcoholism," *Journal of Abnormal Psychology,* 104, 1995.

19. Prefrontal cortex: Antonio Damasio, *Descartes' Error: Emotion, Reason and the Human Brain* (New York: Grosset/Putnam, 1994).

PART TWO: THE NATURE OF EMOTIONAL INTELLIGENCE

Chapter 3. When Smart Is Dumb

1. Jason H.'s story was reported in "Warning by a Valedictorian Who Faced Prison," in *The New York Times* (June 23, 1992).

2. One observer notes: Howard Gardner, "Cracking Open the IQ Box," *The American Prospect,* Winter 1995.

3. Richard Herrnstein and Charles Murray, *The Bell Curve: Intelligence and Class Structure in American Life* (New York: Free Press, 1994), p. 66.

4. George Vaillant, *Adaptation to Life* (Boston: Little, Brown, 1977). The average SAT score of the Harvard group was 584, on a scale where 800 is tops. Dr. Vaillant, now at Harvard University Medical School, told me about the relatively poor predictive value of test scores for life success in this group of advantaged men.

5. J. K. Felsman and G. E. Vaillant, "Resilient Children as Adults: A 40-Year Study," in E. J. Anderson and B. J. Cohler, eds., *The Invulnerable Child* (New York: Guilford Press, 1987).

6. Karen Arnold, who did the study of valedictorians with Terry Denny at the University of Illinois, was quoted in *The Chicago Tribune* (May 29, 1992).

7. Project Spectrum: Principal colleagues of Gardner in developing Project Spectrum were Mara Krechevsky and David Feldman.

8. I interviewed Howard Gardner about his theory of multiple intelligences in "Rethinking the Value of Intelligence Tests," in *The New York Times Education Supplement* (Nov. 3, 1986) and several times since.

9. The comparison of IQ tests and Spectrum abilities is reported in a chapter, coauthored with Mara Krechevsky, in Howard Gardner, *Multiple Intelligences: The Theory in Practice* (New York: Basic Books, 1993).

10. The nutshell summary is from Howard Gardner, *Multiple Intelligences,* p. 9.

11. Howard Gardner and Thomas Hatch, "Multiple Intelligences Go to School," *Educational Researcher* 18, 8 (1989).

12. The model of emotional intelligence was first proposed in Peter Salovey and John D. Mayer, "Emotional Intelligence," *Imagination, Cognition, and Personality* 9 (1990), pp. 185–211.

13. Practical intelligence and people skills: Robert J. Sternberg, *Beyond I.Q.* (New York: Cambridge University Press, 1985).

14. The basic definition of "emotional intelligence" is in Salovey and Mayer, "Emotional Intelligence," p. 189.

15. IQ vs. emotional intelligence: Jack Block, University of California at Berkeley, unpublished manuscript, February, 1995. Block uses the concept "ego resilience" rather than emotional intelligence, but notes that its main components include emotional self-regulation, an adaptive impulse control, a sense of self-efficacy, and social intelligence. Since these are main elements of emotional intelligence, ego resilience can be seen as a surrogate measure for emotional intelligence, much like SAT scores are for IQ. Block analyzed data from a longitudinal study of about a hundred men and women in their teen years and early twenties, and used statistical methods to assess the personality and behavioral correlates of high IQ independent of emotional intelligence, and emotional intelligence apart from IQ. There is, he finds, a modest correlation between IQ and ego resilience, but the two are independent constructs.

Chapter 4. Know Thyself

1. My usage of *self-awareness* refers to a self-reflexive, introspective attention to one's own experience, sometimes called *mindfulness.*

2. See also: Jon Kabat-Zinn, *Wherever You Go, There You Are* (New York: Hyperion, 1994).

3. The observing ego: An insightful comparison of the psychoanalyst's attentional stance and self-awareness appears in Mark Epstein's *Thoughts Without a Thinker* (New York: Basic Books, 1995). Epstein notes that if this ability is cultivated deeply, it can drop the self-consciousness of the observer and become a "more flexible and braver 'developed ego,' capable of embracing all of life."

4. William Styron, *Darkness Visible: A Memoir of Madness* (New York: Random House, 1990), p. 64.

5. John D. Mayer and Alexander Stevens, "An Emerging Understanding of the Reflective (Meta) Experience of Mood," unpublished manuscript (1993).

6. Mayer and Stevens, "An Emerging Understanding." Some of the terms for these emotional self-awareness styles are my own adaptations of their categories.

7. The intensity of emotions: Much of this work was done by or with Randy Larsen, a former graduate student of Diener's now at the University of Michigan.

8. Gary, the emotionally bland surgeon, is described in Hillel I. Swiller, "Alexithymia: Treatment Utilizing Combined Individual and Group Psychotherapy," *International Journal for Group Psychotherapy* 38, 1 (1988), pp. 47–61.

9. *Emotional illiterate* was the term used by M. B. Freedman and B. S. Sweet, "Some Specific Features of Group Psychotherapy," *International Journal for Group Psychotherapy* 4 (1954), pp. 335–68.

10. The clinical features of alexithymia are described in Graeme J. Taylor, "Alexithymia: History of the Concept," paper presented at the annual meeting of the American Psychiatric Association in Washington, DC (May 1986).

11. The description of alexithymia is from Peter Sifneos, "Affect, Emotional Conflict, and Deficit: An Overview," *Psychotherapy-and-Psychosomatics* 56 (1991), pp. 116–22.

12. The woman who did not know why she was crying is reported in H. Warnes, "Alexithymia, Clinical and Therapeutic Aspects," *Psychotherapy-and-Psychosomatics* 46 (1986), pp. 96–104.

13. Role of emotions in reasoning: Damasio, *Descartes' Error.*

14. Unconscious fear: The snake studies are described in Kagan, *Galen's Prophecy.*

Chapter 5. Passion's Slaves

1. For details on the ratio of positive to negative feelings and well-being, see Ed Diener and Randy J. Larsen, "The Experience of Emotional Well-Being," in Michael Lewis and Jeannette Haviland, eds., *Handbook of Emotions* (New York: Guilford Press, 1993).

2. I interviewed Diane Tice about her research on how well people shake off bad moods in December 1992. She published her findings on anger in a chapter she wrote with her husband, Roy Baumeister, in Daniel Wegner and James Pennebaker, eds., *Handbook of Mental Control* v. 5 (Englewood Cliffs, NJ: Prentice-Hall, 1993).

3. Bill collectors: also described in Arlie Hochschild, *The Managed Heart* (New York: Free Press, 1980).

4. The case against anger, and for self-control, is based largely on Diane Tice and Roy F. Baumeister, "Controlling Anger: Self-Induced Emotion Change," in Wegner and Pennebaker, *Handbook of Mental Control.* But see also Carol Tavris, *Anger: The Misunderstood Emotion* (New York: Touchstone, 1989).

5. The research on rage is described in Dolf Zillmann, "Mental Control of Angry Aggression," in Wegner and Pennebaker, *Handbook of Mental Control.*

6. The soothing walk: quoted in Tavris, *Anger: The Misunderstood Emotion,* p. 135.

7. Redford Williams's strategies for controlling hostility are detailed in Redford Williams and Virginia Williams, *Anger Kills* (New York: Times Books, 1993).

8. Venting anger does not dispel it: see, for example, S. K. Mallick and B. R. McCandless, "A Study of Catharsis Aggression," *Journal of Personality and Social Psychology*

4 (1966). For a summary of this research, see Tavris, *Anger: The Misunderstood Emotion*.

9. When lashing out in anger is effective: Tavris, *Anger: The Misunderstood Emotion*.

10. The work of worrying: Lizabeth Roemer and Thomas Borkovec, "Worry: Unwanted Cognitive Activity That Controls Unwanted Somatic Experience," in Wegner and Pennebaker, *Handbook of Mental Control*.

11. Fear of germs: David Riggs and Edna Foa, "Obsessive-Compulsive Disorder," in David Barlow, ed., *Clinical Handbook of Psychological Disorders* (New York: Guilford Press, 1993).

12. The worried patient was quoted in Roemer and Borkovec, "Worry," p. 221.

13. Therapies for anxiety disorder: see, for example, David H. Barlow, ed., *Clinical Handbook of Psychological Disorders* (New York: Guilford Press, 1993).

14. Styron's depression: William Styron, *Darkness Visible: A Memoir of Madness* (New York: Random House, 1990).

15. The worries of the depressed are reported in Susan Nolen-Hoeksma, "Sex Differences in Control of Depression," in Wegner and Pennebaker, *Handbook of Mental Control*, p. 307.

16. Therapy for depression: K. S. Dobson, "A Meta-analysis of the Efficacy of Cognitive Therapy for Depression," *Journal of Consulting and Clinical Psychology* 57 (1989).

17. The study of depressed people's thought patterns is reported in Richard Wenzlaff, "The Mental Control of Depression," in Wegner and Pennebaker, *Handbook of Mental Control*.

18. Shelley Taylor et al., "Maintaining Positive Illusions in the Face of Negative Information," *Journal of Clinical and Social Psychology* 8 (1989).

19. The repressing college student is from Daniel A. Weinberger, "The Construct Validity of the Repressive Coping Style," in J. L. Singer, ed., *Repression and Dissociation* (Chicago: University of Chicago Press, 1990). Weinberger, who developed the concept of repressors in early studies with Gary F. Schwartz and Richard Davidson, has become the leading researcher on the topic.

Chapter 6. The Master Aptitude

1. The terror of the exam: Daniel Goleman, *Vital Lies, Simple Truths: The Psychology of Self-Deception* (New York: Simon and Schuster, 1985).

2. Working memory: Alan Baddeley, *Working Memory* (Oxford: Clarendon Press, 1986).

3. Prefrontal cortex and working memory: Patricia Goldman-Rakic, "Cellular and Circuit Basis of Working Memory in Prefrontal Cortex of Nonhuman Primates," *Progress in Brain Research*, 85, 1990; Daniel Weinberger, "A Connectionist Approach to the Prefrontal Cortex," *Journal of Neuropsychiatry* 5 (1993).

4. Motivation and elite performance: Anders Ericsson, "Expert Performance: Its Structure and Acquisition," *American Psychologist* (Aug. 1994).

5. Asian IQ advantage: Herrnstein and Murray, *The Bell Curve*.

6. IQ and occupation of Asian-Americans: James Flynn, *Asian-American Achievement Beyond IQ* (New Jersey: Lawrence Erlbaum, 1991).

7. The study of delay of gratification in four-year-olds was reported in Yuichi Shoda, Walter Mischel, and Philip K. Peake, "Predicting Adolescent Cognitive and Self-regulatory Competencies From Preschool Delay of Gratification," *Developmental Psychology,* 26, 6 (1990), pp. 978–86.

8. SAT scores of impulsive and self-controlled children: The analysis of SAT data was done by Phil Peake, a psychologist at Smith College.

9. IQ vs. delay as predictors of SAT scores: personal communication from Phil Peake, psychologist at Smith College, who analyzed the SAT data in Walter Mischel's study of delay of gratification.

10. Impulsivity and delinquency: See the discussion in: Jack Block, "On the Relation Between IQ, Impulsivity, and Delinquency," *Journal of Abnormal Psychology* 104 (1995).

11. The worried mother: Timothy A. Brown et al., "Generalized Anxiety Disorder," in David H. Barlow, ed., *Clinical Handbook of Psychological Disorders* (New York: Guilford Press, 1993).

12. Air traffic controllers and anxiety: W. E. Collins et al., "Relationships of Anxiety Scores to Academy and Field Training Performance of Air Traffic Control Specialists," *FAA Office of Aviation Medicine Reports* (May 1989).

13. Anxiety and academic performance: Bettina Seipp, "Anxiety and Academic Performance: A Meta-analysis," *Anxiety Research* 4, 1 (1991).

14. Worriers: Richard Metzger et al., "Worry Changes Decision-making: The Effects of Negative Thoughts on Cognitive Processing," *Journal of Clinical Psychology* (Jan. 1990).

15. Ralph Haber and Richard Alpert, "Test Anxiety," *Journal of Abnormal and Social Psychology* 13 (1958).

16. Anxious students: Theodore Chapin, "The Relationship of Trait Anxiety and Academic Performance to Achievement Anxiety," *Journal of College Student Development* (May 1989).

17. Negative thoughts and test scores: John Hunsley, "Internal Dialogue During Academic Examinations," *Cognitive Therapy and Research* (Dec. 1987).

18. The internists given a gift of candy: Alice Isen et al., "The Influence of Positive Affect on Clinical Problem Solving," *Medical Decision Making* (July–Sept. 1991).

19. Hope and a bad grade: C. R. Snyder et al., "The Will and the Ways: Development and Validation of an Individual-Differences Measure of Hope," *Journal of Personality and Social Psychology* 60, 4 (1991), p. 579.

20. I interviewed C. R. Snyder in *The New York Times* (Dec. 24, 1991).

21. Optimistic swimmers: Martin Seligman, *Learned Optimism* (New York: Knopf, 1991).

22. A realistic vs. naive optimism: see, for example, Carol Whalen et al., "Optimism in Children's Judgments of Health and Environmental Risks," *Health Psychology* 13 (1994).

23. I interviewed Martin Seligman about optimism in *The New York Times* (Feb. 3, 1987).

24. I interviewed Albert Bandura about self-efficacy in *The New York Times* (May 8, 1988).

25. Mihaly Csikszentmihalyi, "Play and Intrinsic Rewards," *Journal of Humanistic Psychology* 15, 3 (1975).

26. Mihaly Csikszentmihalyi, *Flow: The Psychology of Optimal Experience*, 1st ed. (New York: Harper and Row, 1990).

27. "Like a waterfall": *Newsweek* (Feb. 28, 1994).

28. I interviewed Dr. Csikszentmihalyi in *The New York Times* (Mar. 4, 1986).

29. The brain in flow: Jean Hamilton et al., "Intrinsic Enjoyment and Boredom Coping Scales: Validation With Personality, Evoked Potential and Attention Measures," *Personality and Individual Differences* 5, 2 (1984).

30. Cortical activation and fatigue: Ernest Hartmann, *The Functions of Sleep* (New Haven: Yale University Press, 1973).

31. I interviewed Dr. Csikszentmihalyi in *The New York Times* (Mar. 22, 1992).

32. The study of flow and math students: Jeanne Nakamura, "Optimal Experience and the Uses of Talent," in Mihaly Csikszentmihalyi and Isabella Csikszentmihalyi, *Optimal Experience: Psychological Studies of Flow in Consciousness* (Cambridge: Cambridge University Press, 1988).

Chapter 7. The Roots of Empathy

1. Self-awareness and empathy: see, for example, John Mayer and Melissa Kirkpatrick, "Hot Information-Processing Becomes More Accurate With Open Emotional Experience," University of New Hampshire, unpublished manuscript (Oct. 1994); Randy Larsen et al., "Cognitive Operations Associated With Individual Differences in Affect Intensity," *Journal of Personality and Social Psychology* 53 (1987).

2. Robert Rosenthal et al., "The PONS Test: Measuring Sensitivity to Nonverbal Cues," in P. McReynolds, ed., *Advances in Psychological Assessment* (San Francisco: Jossey-Bass, 1977).

3. Stephen Nowicki and Marshall Duke, "A Measure of Nonverbal Social Processing Ability in Children Between the Ages of 6 and 10," paper presented at the American Psychological Society meeting (1989).

4. The mothers who acted as researchers were trained by Marian Radke-Yarrow and Carolyn Zahn-Waxler at the Laboratory of Developmental Psychology, National Institute of Mental Health.

5. I wrote about empathy, its developmental roots, and its neurology in *The New York Times* (Mar. 28, 1989).

6. Instilling empathy in children: Marian Radke-Yarrow and Carolyn Zahn-Waxler, "Roots, Motives and Patterns in Children's Prosocial Behavior," in Ervin Staub et al., eds., *Development and Maintenance of Prosocial Behavior* (New York: Plenum, 1984).

7. Daniel Stern, *The Interpersonal World of the Infant* (New York: Basic Books, 1987), p. 30.

8. Stern, op. cit.

9. The depressed infants are described in Jeffrey Pickens and Tiffany Field, "Facial Expressivity in Infants of Depressed Mothers," *Developmental Psychology* 29, 6 (1993).

10. The study of violent rapists' childhoods was done by Robert Prentky, a psychologist in Philadelphia.

11. Empathy in borderline patients: "Giftedness and Psychological Abuse in Borderline Personality Disorder: Their Relevance to Genesis and Treatment," *Journal of Personality Disorders* 6 (1992).

12. Leslie Brothers, "A Biological Perspective on Empathy," *American Journal of Psychiatry* 146, 1 (1989).

13. Brothers, "A Biological Perspective," p. 16.

14. Physiology of empathy: Robert Levenson and Anna Ruef, "Empathy: A Physiological Substrate," *Journal of Personality and Social Psychology* 63, 2 (1992).

15. Martin L. Hoffman, "Empathy, Social Cognition, and Moral Action," in W. Kurtines and J. Gerwitz, eds., *Moral Behavior and Development: Advances in Theory, Research, and Applications* (New York: John Wiley and Sons, 1984).

16. Studies of the link between empathy and ethics are in Hoffman, "Empathy, Social Cognition, and Moral Action."

17. I wrote about the emotional cycle that culminates in sex crimes in *The New York Times* (Apr. 14, 1992). The source is William Pithers, a psychologist with the Vermont Department of Corrections.

18. The nature of psychopathy is described in more detail in an article I wrote in *The New York Times* on July 7, 1987. Much of what I write here comes from the work of Robert Hare, a psychologist at the University of British Columbia, an expert on psychopaths.

19. Leon Bing, *Do or Die* (New York: HarperCollins, 1991).

20. Wife batterers: Neil S. Jacobson et al., "Affect, Verbal Content, and Psychophysiology in the Arguments of Couples With a Violent Husband," *Journal of Clinical and Consulting Psychology* (July 1994).

21. Psychopaths have no fear—the effect is seen as criminal psychopaths are about to receive a shock: One of the more recent replications of the effect is Christopher Patrick et al., "Emotion in the Criminal Psychopath: Fear Image Processing," *Journal of Abnormal Psychology* 103 (1994).

Chapter 8. The Social Arts

1. The exchange between Jay and Len was reported by Judy Dunn and Jane Brown in "Relationships, Talk About Feelings, and the Development of Affect Regulation in Early Childhood," Judy Garber and Kenneth A. Dodge, eds., *The Development of Emotion Regulation and Dysregulation* (Cambridge: Cambridge University Press, 1991). The dramatic flourishes are my own.

2. The display rules are in Paul Ekman and Wallace Friesen, *Unmasking the Face* (Englewood Cliffs, NJ: Prentice Hall, 1975).

3. Monks in the heat of battle: the story is told by David Busch in "Culture Cul-de-Sac," *Arizona State University Research* (Spring/Summer 1994).

4. The study of mood transfer was reported by Ellen Sullins in the April 1991 issue of the *Personality and Social Psychology Bulletin*.

5. The studies of mood transmission and synchrony are by Frank Bernieri, a psychologist at Oregon State University; I wrote about his work in *The New York Times*. Much

of his research is reported in Bernieri and Robert Rosenthal, "Interpersonal Coordination, Behavior Matching, and Interpersonal Synchrony," in Robert Feldman and Bernard Rime, eds., *Fundamentals of Nonverbal Behavior* (Cambridge: Cambridge University Press, 1991).

6. The entrainment theory is proposed by Bernieri and Rosenthal, *Fundamentals of Nonverbal Behavior.*

7. Thomas Hatch, "Social Intelligence in Young Children," paper delivered at the annual meeting of the American Psychological Association (1990).

8. Social chameleons: Mark Snyder, "Impression Management: The Self in Social Interaction," in L. S. Wrightsman and K. Deaux, *Social Psychology in the '80s* (Monterey, CA: Brooks/Cole, 1981).

9. E. Lakin Phillips, *The Social Skills Basis of Psychopathology* (New York: Grune and Stratton, 1978), p. 140.

10. Nonverbal learning disorders: Stephen Nowicki and Marshall Duke, *Helping the Child Who Doesn't Fit In* (Atlanta: Peachtree Publishers, 1992). See also Byron Rourke, *Nonverbal Learning Disabilities* (New York: Guilford Press, 1989).

11. Nowicki and Duke, *Helping the Child Who Doesn't Fit In.*

12. This vignette, and the review of research on entering a group, is from Martha Putallaz and Aviva Wasserman, "Children's Entry Behavior," in Steven Asher and John Coie, eds., *Peer Rejection in Childhood* (New York: Cambridge University Press, 1990).

13. Putallaz and Wasserman, "Children's Entry Behavior."

14. Hatch, "Social Intelligence in Young Children."

15. Terry Dobson's tale of the Japanese drunk and the old man is used by permission of Dobson's estate. It is also retold by Ram Dass and Paul Gorman, *How Can I Help?* (New York: Alfred A. Knopf, 1985), pp. 167–71.

PART THREE: EMOTIONAL INTELLIGENCE APPLIED

Chapter 9. Intimate Enemies

1. There are many ways to calculate the divorce rate, and the statistical means used will determine the outcome. Some methods show the divorce rate peaking at around 50 percent and then dipping a bit. When divorces are calculated by the total number in a given year, the rate appears to have peaked in the 1980s. But the statistics I cite here calculate not the number of divorces that occur in a given year, but rather the odds that a couple marrying in a given year will eventually have their marriage end in divorce. That statistic shows a climbing rate of divorce over the last century. For more detail: John Gottman, *What Predicts Divorce: The Relationship Between Marital Processes and Marital Outcomes* (Hillsdale, NJ: Lawrence Erlbaum Associates, Inc., 1993).

2. The separate worlds of boys and girls: Eleanor Maccoby and C. N. Jacklin, "Gender Segregation in Childhood," in H. Reese, ed., *Advances in Child Development and Behavior* (New York: Academic Press, 1987).

3. Same-sex playmates: John Gottman, "Same and Cross Sex Friendship in Young Children," in J. Gottman and J. Parker, eds., *Conversation of Friends* (New York: Cambridge University Press, 1986).

4. This and the following summary of sex differences in socialization of emotions are based on the excellent review in Leslie R. Brody and Judith A. Hall, "Gender and Emotion," in Michael Lewis and Jeannette Haviland, eds., *Handbook of Emotions* (New York: Guilford Press, 1993).

5. Brody and Hall, "Gender and Emotion," p. 456.

6. Girls and the arts of aggression: Robert B. Cairns and Beverley D. Cairns, *Lifelines and Risks* (New York: Cambridge University Press, 1994).

7. Brody and Hall, "Gender and Emotion," p. 454.

8. The findings about gender differences in emotion are reviewed in Brody and Hall, "Gender and Emotion."

9. The importance of good communication for women was reported in Mark H. Davis and H. Alan Oathout, "Maintenance of Satisfaction in Romantic Relationships: Empathy and Relational Competence," *Journal of Personality and Social Psychology* 53, 2 (1987), pp. 397–410.

10. The study of husbands' and wives' complaints: Robert J. Sternberg, "Triangulating Love," in Robert Sternberg and Michael Barnes, eds., *The Psychology of Love* (New Haven: Yale University Press, 1988).

11. Reading sad faces: The research is by Dr. Ruben C. Gur at the University of Pennsylvania School of Medicine.

12. The exchange between Fred and Ingrid is from Gottman, *What Predicts Divorce*, p. 84.

13. The marital research by John Gottman and colleagues at the University of Washington is described in more detail in two books: John Gottman, *Why Marriages Succeed or Fail* (New York: Simon and Schuster, 1994), and *What Predicts Divorce*.

14. Stonewalling: Gottman, *What Predicts Divorce*.

15. Poisonous thoughts: Aaron Beck, *Love Is Never Enough* (New York: Harper and Row, 1988), pp. 145–46.

16. Thoughts in troubled marriages: Gottman, *What Predicts Divorce*.

17. The distorted thinking of violent husbands is described in Amy Holtzworth-Munroe and Glenn Hutchinson, "Attributing Negative Intent to Wife Behavior: The Attributions of Maritally Violent Versus Nonviolent Men," *Journal of Abnormal Psychology* 102, 2 (1993), pp. 206–11. The suspiciousness of sexually aggressive men: Neil Malamuth and Lisa Brown, "Sexually Aggressive Men's Perceptions of Women's Communications," *Journal of Personality and Social Psychology* 67 (1994).

18. Battering husbands: There are three kinds of husbands who become violent: those who rarely do, those who do so impulsively when they get angered, and those who do so in a cool, calculated manner. Therapy seems helpful only with the first two kinds. See Neil Jacobson et al., *Clinical Handbook of Marital Therapy* (New York: Guilford Press, 1994).

19. Flooding: Gottman, *What Predicts Divorce*.

20. Husbands dislike squabbles: Robert Levenson et al., "The Influence of Age and Gender on Affect, Physiology, and Their Interrelations: A Study of Long-term Marriages," *Journal of Personality and Social Psychology* 67 (1994).

21. Flooding in husbands: Gottman, *What Predicts Divorce*.

22. Men stonewall, women criticize: Gottman, *What Predicts Divorce*.

23. "Wife Charged with Shooting Husband Over Football on TV," *The New York Times* (Nov. 3, 1993).

24. Productive marital fights: Gottman, *What Predicts Divorce.*

25. Lack of repair abilities in couples: Gottman, *What Predicts Divorce.*

26. The four steps that lead to "good fights" are from Gottman, *Why Marriages Succeed or Fail.*

27. Monitoring pulse rate: Gottman, Ibid.

28. Catching automatic thoughts: Beck, *Love Is Never Enough.*

29. Mirroring: Harville Hendrix, *Getting the Love You Want* (New York: Henry Holt, 1988).

Chapter 10. Managing With Heart

1. The crash of the intimidating pilot: Carl Lavin, "When Moods Affect Safety: Communications in a Cockpit Mean a Lot a Few Miles Up," *The New York Times* (June 26, 1994).

2. The survey of 250 executives: Michael Maccoby, "The Corporate Climber Has to Find His Heart," *Fortune* (Dec. 1976).

3. Zuboff: in conversation, June 1994. For the impact of information technologies, see her book *In the Age of the Smart Machine* (New York: Basic Books, 1991).

4. The story of the sarcastic vice president was told to me by Hendrie Weisinger, a psychologist at the UCLA Graduate School of Business. His book is *The Critical Edge: How to Criticize Up and Down the Organization and Make It Pay Off* (Boston: Little, Brown, 1989).

5. The survey of times managers blew up was done by Robert Baron, a psychologist at Rensselaer Polytechnic Institute, whom I interviewed for *The New York Times* (Sept. 11, 1990).

6. Criticism as a cause of conflict: Robert Baron, "Countering the Effects of Destructive Criticism: The Relative Efficacy of Four Interventions," *Journal of Applied Psychology* 75, 3 (1990).

7. Specific and vague criticism: Harry Levinson, "Feedback to Subordinates" *Addendum to the Levinson Letter,* Levinson Institute, Waltham, MA (1992).

8. Changing face of workforce: A survey of 645 national companies by Towers Perrin management consultants in Manhattan, reported in *The New York Times* (Aug. 26, 1990).

9. The roots of hatred: Vamik Volkan, *The Need to Have Enemies and Allies* (Northvale, NJ: Jason Aronson, 1988).

10. Thomas Pettigrew: I interviewed Pettigrew in *The New York Times* (May 12, 1987).

11. Stereotypes and subtle bias: Samuel Gaertner and John Davidio, *Prejudice, Discrimination, and Racism* (New York: Academic Press, 1987).

12. Subtle bias: Gaertner and Davidio, *Prejudice, Discrimination, and Racism.*

13. Relman: quoted in Howard Kohn, "Service With a Sneer," *The New York Times Sunday Magazine* (Nov. 11, 1994).

14. IBM: "Responding to a Diverse Work Force," *The New York Times* (Aug. 26, 1990).

15. Power of speaking out: Fletcher Blanchard, "Reducing the Expression of Racial Prejudice," *Psychological Science* (vol. 2, 1991).

16. Stereotypes break down: Gaertner and Davidio, *Prejudice, Discrimination, and Racism.*

17. Teams: Peter Drucker, "The Age of Social Transformation," *The Atlantic Monthly* (Nov. 1994).

18. The concept of group intelligence is set forth in Wendy Williams and Robert Sternberg, "Group Intelligence: Why Some Groups Are Better Than Others," *Intelligence* (1988).

19. The study of the stars at Bell Labs was reported in Robert Kelley and Janet Caplan, "How Bell Labs Creates Star Performers," *Harvard Business Review* (July–Aug. 1993).

20. The usefulness of informal networks is noted by David Krackhardt and Jeffrey R. Hanson, "Informal Networks: The Company Behind the Chart," *Harvard Business Review* (July–Aug. 1993), p. 104.

Chapter 11. Mind and Medicine

1. Immune system as the body's brain: Francisco Varela at the Third Mind and Life meeting, Dharamsala, India (Dec. 1990).

2. Chemical messengers between brain and immune system: see Robert Ader et al., *Psychoneuroimmunology,* 2nd edition (San Diego: Academic Press, 1990).

3. Contact between nerves and immune cells: David Felten et al., "Noradrenergic Sympathetic Innervation of Lymphoid Tissue," *Journal of Immunology* 135 (1985).

4. Hormones and immune function: B. S. Rabin et al., "Bidirectional Interaction Between the Central Nervous System and the Immune System," *Critical Reviews in Immunology* 9 (4), (1989), pp. 279–312.

5. Connections between brain and immune system: see, for example, Steven B. Maier et al., "Psychoneuroimmunology," *American Psychologist* (Dec. 1994).

6. Toxic emotions: Howard Friedman and S. Boothby-Kewley, "The Disease-Prone Personality: A Meta-Analytic View," *American Psychologist* 42 (1987). This broad analysis of studies used "meta-analysis," in which results from many smaller studies can be combined statistically into one immense study. This allows effects that might not show up in any given study to be detected more easily because of the much larger total number of people being studied.

7. Skeptics argue that the emotional picture linked to higher rates of disease is the profile of the quintessential neurotic—an anxious, depressed, and angry emotional wreck— and that the higher rates of disease they report are due not so much to a medical fact as to a propensity to whine and complain about health problems, exaggerating their seriousness. But Friedman and others argue that the weight of evidence for the emotion-disease link is borne by research in which it is physicians' evaluations of observable signs of illness and medical tests, not patients' complaints, that determine the level of sickness—a more objective basis. Of course, there is the possibility that increased distress is the result of a medical condition, as well as precipitating it; for that reason the most convincing data come from prospective studies in which emotional states are evaluated prior to the onset of disease.

8. Gail Ironson et al., "Effects of Anger on Left Ventricular Ejection Fraction in Coronary Artery Disease," *The American Journal of Cardiology* 70 1992. Pumping efficiency, sometimes referred to as the "ejection fraction," quantifies the heart's ability to pump blood out of the left ventricle into the arteries; it measures the percentage of blood pumped out of the ventricles with each beat of the heart. In heart disease the drop in pumping efficiency means a weakening of the heart muscle.

9. Of the dozen or so studies of hostility and death from heart disease, some have failed to find a link. But that failure may be due to differences in method, such as using a poor measure of hostility, and to the relative subtlety of the effect. For instance, the greatest number of deaths from the hostility effect seem to occur in midlife. If a study fails to track down the causes of death for people during this period, it misses the effect.

10. Hostility and heart disease: Redford Williams, *The Trusting Heart* (New York: Times Books/Random House, 1989).

11. Peter Kaufman: I interviewed Dr. Kaufman in *The New York Times* (Sept. 1, 1992).

12. Stanford study of anger and second heart attacks: Carl Thoreson, presented at the International Congress of Behavioral Medicine, Uppsala, Sweden (July 1990).

13. Lynda H. Powell, Emotional Arousal as a Predictor of Long-Term Mortality and Morbidity in Post M.I. Men," *Circulation*, vol. 82, no. 4, Supplement III, Oct. 1990.

14. Murray A. Mittleman, "Triggering of Myocardial Infarction Onset by Episodes of Anger," *Circulation*, vol. 89, no. 2 (1994).

15. Suppressing anger raises blood pressure: Robert Levenson, "Can We Control Our Emotions, and How Does Such Control Change an Emotional Episode?" in Richard Davidson and Paul Ekman, eds., *Fundamental Questions About Emotions* (New York: Oxford University Press, 1995).

16. The angry personal style: I wrote about Redford Williams's research on anger and the heart in *The New York Times Good Health Magazine* (Apr. 16, 1989).

17. A 44 percent reduction in second heart attacks: Thoreson, op. cit.

18. Dr. Williams's program for anger control: Williams, *The Trusting Heart*.

19. The worried woman: Timothy Brown et al., "Generalized Anxiety Disorder," in David H. Barlow, ed., *Clinical Handbook of Psychological Disorders* (New York: Guilford Press, 1993).

20. Stress and metastasis: Bruce McEwen and Eliot Stellar, "Stress and the Individual: Mechanisms Leading to Disease," *Archives of Internal Medicine* 153 (Sept. 27, 1993). The study they are describing is M. Robertson and J. Ritz, "Biology and Clinical Relevance of Human Natural Killer Cells," *Blood* 76 (1990).

21. There may be multiple reasons why people under stress are more vulnerable to sickness, apart from biological pathways. One might be that the ways people try to soothe their anxiety—for example, smoking, drinking, or bingeing on fatty foods—are in themselves unhealthy. Still another is that constant worry and anxiety can make people lose sleep or forget to comply with medical regimens—such as taking medications—and so prolong illnesses they already have. Most likely, all of these work in tandem to link stress and disease.

22. Stress weakens the immune system: For instance, in the study of medical students facing exam stress, the students had not only a lowered immune control of the herpes virus, but also a decline in the ability of their white blood cells to kill infected cells, as well as an increase in levels of a chemical associated with suppression of immune

abilities in lymphocytes, the white blood cells central to the immune response. See Ronald Glaser and Janice Kiecolt-Glaser, "Stress-Associated Depression in Cellular Immunity," *Brain, Behavior, and Immunity* 1 (1987). But in most such studies showing a weakening of immune defenses with stress, it has not been clear that these levels were low enough to lead to medical risk.

23. Stress and colds: Sheldon Cohen et al., "Psychological Stress and Susceptibility to the Common Cold," *New England Journal of Medicine* 325 (1991).

24. Daily upsets and infection: Arthur Stone et al., "Secretory IgA as a Measure of Immunocompetence," *Journal of Human Stress* 13 (1987). In another study, 246 husbands, wives, and children kept daily logs of stresses in their family's life over the course of the flu season. Those who had the most family crises also had the highest rate of flu, as measured both by days with fever and flu antibody levels. See R. D. Clover et al., "Family Functioning and Stress as Predictors of Influenza B Infection," *Journal of Family Practice* 28 (May 1989).

25. Herpes virus flare-up and stress: a series of studies by Ronald Glaser and Janice Kiecolt-Glaser—e.g., "Psychological Influences on Immunity," *American Psychologist* 43 (1988). The relationship between stress and herpes activity is so strong that it has been demonstrated in a study of only ten patients, using the actual breaking-out of herpes sores as a measure; the more anxiety, hassles, and stress reported by the patients, the more likely they were to have herpes outbreaks in the following weeks; placid periods in their lives led to dormancy of the herpes. See H. E. Schmidt et al., "Stress as a Precipitating Factor in Subjects With Recurrent Herpes Labialis," *Journal of Family Practice,* 20 (1985).

26. Anxiety in women and heart disease: Carl Thoreson, presented at the International Congress of Behavioral Medicine, Uppsala, Sweden (July 1990). Anxiety may also play a role in making some men more vulnerable to heart disease. In a study at the University of Alabama medical school, 1,123 men and women between the ages of forty-five and seventy-seven were assessed on their emotional profiles. Those men most prone to anxiety and worry in middle age were far more likely than others to have hypertension when tracked down twenty years later. See Abraham Markowitz et al., *Journal of the American Medical Association* (Nov. 14, 1993).

27. Stress and colorectal cancer: Joseph C. Courtney et al., "Stressful Life Events and the Risk of Colorectal Cancer," *Epidemiology* (Sept. 1993), 4(5).

28. Relaxation to counter stress-based symptoms: See, for example, Daniel Goleman and Joel Gurin, *Mind Body Medicine* (New York: Consumer Reports Books/St. Martin's Press, 1993).

29. Depression and disease: see, e.g., Seymour Reichlin, "Neuroendocrine-Immune Interactions," *New England Journal of Medicine* (Oct. 21, 1993).

30. Bone marrow transplant: cited in James Strain, "Cost Offset From a Psychiatric Consultation-Liaison Intervention With Elderly Hip Fracture Patients," *American Journal of Psychiatry* 148 (1991).

31. Howard Burton et al., "The Relationship of Depression to Survival in Chronic Renal Failure," *Psychosomatic Medicine* (March 1986).

32. Hopelessness and death from heart disease: Robert Anda et al., "Depressed Affect, Hopelessness, and the Risk of Ischemic Heart Disease in a Cohort of U.S. Adults," *Epidemiology* (July 1993).

33. Depression and heart attack: Nancy Frasure-Smith et al., "Depression Following Myocardial Infarction," *Journal of the American Medical Association* (Oct. 20, 1993).

34. Depression in multiple illness: Dr. Michael von Korff, the University of Washington psychiatrist who did the study, pointed out to me that with such patients, who face tremendous challenges just in living from day to day, "If you treat a patient's depression, you see improvements over and above any changes in their medical condition. If you're depressed, your symptoms seem worse to you. Having a chronic physical disease is a major adaptive challenge. If you're depressed, you're less able to learn to take care of your illness. Even with physical impairment, if you're motivated and have energy and feelings of self-worth—all of which are at risk in depression—then people can adapt remarkably even to severe impairments."

35. Optimism and bypass surgery: Chris Peterson et al., *Learned Helplessness: A Theory for the Age of Personal Control* (New York: Oxford University Press, 1993).

36. Spinal injury and hope: Timothy Elliott et al., "Negotiating Reality After Physical Loss: Hope, Depression, and Disability," *Journal of Personality and Social Psychology* 61, 4 (1991).

37. Medical risk of social isolation: James House et al., "Social Relationships and Health," *Science* (July 29, 1988). But also see a mixed finding: Carol Smith et al., "Meta-Analysis of the Associations Between Social Support and Health Outcomes," *Journal of Behavioral Medicine* (1994).

38. Isolation and mortality risk: Other studies suggest a biological mechanism at work. These findings, cited in House, "Social Relationships and Health," have found that the simple presence of another person can reduce anxiety and lessen physiological distress in people in intensive-care units. The comforting effect of another person's presence has been found to lower not just heart rate and blood pressure, but also the secretion of fatty acids that can block arteries. One theory put forward to explain the healing effects of social contact suggests a brain mechanism at work. This theory points to animal data showing a calming effect on the posterior hypothalamic zone, an area of the limbic system with rich connections to the amygdala. The comforting presence of another person, this view holds, inhibits limbic activity, lowering the rate of secretion of acetylcholine, cortisol, and catecholamines, all neurochemicals that trigger more rapid breathing, a quickened heartbeat, and other physiological signs of stress.

39. Strain, "Cost Offset."

40. Heart attack survival and emotional support: Lisa Berkman et al., "Emotional Support and Survival After Myocardial Infarction, A Prospective Population Based Study of the Elderly," *Annals of Internal Medicine* (Dec. 15, 1992).

41. The Swedish study: Annika Rosengren et al., "Stressful Life Events, Social Support, and Mortality in Men Born in 1933," *British Medical Journal* (Oct. 19, 1993).

42. Marital arguments and immune system: Janice Kiecolt-Glaser et al., "Marital Quality, Marital Disruption, and Immune Function," *Psychosomatic Medicine* 49 (1987).

43. I interviewed John Cacioppo for *The New York Times* (Dec. 15, 1992).

44. Talking about troubling thoughts: James Pennebaker, "Putting Stress Into Words: Health, Linguistic and Therapeutic Implications," paper presented at the American Psychological Association meeting, Washington, DC (1992).

45. Psychotherapy and medical improvements: Lester Luborsky et al., "Is Psychotherapy

Good for Your Health?" paper presented at the American Psychological Association meeting, Washington, DC (1993).

46. Cancer support groups: David Spiegel et al., "Effect of Psychosocial Treatment on Survival of Patients with Metastatic Breast Cancer," *Lancet* No. 8668, ii (1989).

47. Patients' questions: The finding was cited by Dr. Steven Cohen-Cole, a psychiatrist at Emory University, when I interviewed him in *The New York Times* (Nov. 13, 1991).

48. Full information: For example, the Planetree program at Pacific Presbyterian Hospital in San Francisco will do searches of medical and lay research on any medical topic for anyone who requests it.

49. Making patients effective: One program has been developed by Dr. Mack Lipkin, Jr., at New York University Medical School.

50. Emotional preparation for surgery: I wrote about this in *The New York Times* (Dec. 10, 1987).

51. Family care in the hospital: Again, Planetree is a model, as are the Ronald McDonald houses that allow parents to stay next door to hospitals where their children are patients.

52. Mindfulness and medicine: See Jon Kabat-Zinn, *Full Catastrophe Living* (New York: Delacorte, 1991).

53. Program for reversing heart disease: See Dean Ornish, *Dr. Dean Ornish's Program for Reversing Heart Disease* (New York: Ballantine, 1991).

54. Relationship-centered medicine: *Health Professions Education and Relationship-Centered Care*. Report of the Pew-Fetzer Task Force on Advancing Psychosocial Health Education, Pew Health Professions Commission and Fetzer Institute at The Center of Health Professions, University of California at San Francisco, San Francisco (Aug. 1994).

55. Left the hospital early: Strain, "Cost Offset."

56. Unethical not to treat depression in heart disease patients: Redford Williams and Margaret Chesney, "Psychosocial Factors and Prognosis in Established Coronary Heart Disease," *Journal of the American Medical Association* (Oct. 20, 1993).

57. An open letter to a surgeon: A. Stanley Kramer, "A Prescription for Healing," *Newsweek* (June 7, 1993).

PART FOUR: WINDOWS OF OPPORTUNITY

Chapter 12. The Family Crucible

1. Leslie and the video game: Beverly Wilson and John Gottman, "Marital Conflict and Parenting: The Role of Negativity in Families," in M. H. Bornstein, ed., *Handbook of Parenting*, vol. 4 (Hillsdale, NJ: Lawrence Erlbaum, 1994).

2. The research on emotions in the family was an extension of John Gottman's marital studies reviewed in Chapter 9. See Carole Hooven, Lynn Katz, and John Gottman, "The Family as a Meta-emotion Culture," *Cognition and Emotion* (Spring 1994).

3. The benefits for children of having emotionally adept parents: Hooven, Katz, and Gottman, "The Family as a Meta-emotion Culture."

4. Optimistic infants: T. Berry Brazelton, in the preface to *Heart Start: The Emotional Foundations of School Readiness* (Arlington, VA: National Center for Clinical Infant Programs, 1992).

5. Emotional predictors of school success: *Heart Start*.

6. Elements of school readiness: *Heart Start*, p. 7.

7. Infants and mothers: *Heart Start*, p. 9.

8. Damage from neglect: M. Erickson et al., "The Relationship Between Quality of Attachment and Behavior Problems in Preschool in a High-Risk Sample," in I. Betherton and E. Waters, eds., *Monographs of the Society of Research in Child Development* 50, series no. 209.

9. Lasting lessons of first four years: *Heart Start*, p. 13.

10. The follow-up of aggressive children: L. R. Huesman, Leonard Eron, and Patty Warnicke-Yarmel, "Intellectual Function and Aggression," *The Journal of Personality and Social Psychology* (Jan. 1987). Similar findings were reported by Alexander Thomas and Stella Chess, in the September 1988 issue of *Child Development*, in their study of seventy-five children who were assessed at regular intervals since 1956, when they were between seven and twelve years old. Alexander Thomas et al., "Longitudinal Study of Negative Emotional States and Adjustments From Early Childhood Through Adolescence," *Child Development* 59 (1988). A decade later the children who parents and teachers had said were the most aggressive in grade school were having the most emotional turmoil in late adolescence. These were children (about twice as many boys as girls) who not only continually picked fights, but who also were belittling or openly hostile toward other children, and even toward their families and teachers. Their hostility was unchanged over the years; as adolescents they were having trouble getting along with classmates and with their families, and were in trouble at school. And, when contacted as adults, their difficulties ranged from tangles with the law to anxiety problems and depression.

11. Lack of empathy in abused children: The day-care observations and findings are reported in Mary Main and Carol George, "Responses of Abused and Disadvantaged Toddlers to Distress in Agemates: A Study in the Day-Care Setting," *Developmental Psychology* 21, 3 (1985). The findings have been repeated with preschoolers as well: Bonnie Klimes-Dougan and Janet Kistner, "Physically Abused Preschoolers' Responses to Peers' Distress," *Developmental Psychology* 26 (1990).

12. Difficulties of abused children: Robert Emery, "Family Violence," *American Psychologist* (Feb. 1989).

13. Abuse over generations: Whether abused children grow up to be abusing parents is a point of scientific debate. See, for example, Cathy Spatz Widom, "Child Abuse, Neglect and Adult Behavior," *American Journal of Orthopsychiatry* (July 1989).

Chapter 13. Trauma and Emotional Relearning

1. I wrote about the lasting trauma of the killings at Cleveland Elementary School in *The New York Times* "Education Life" section (Jan. 7, 1990).

2. The examples of PTSD in crime victims were offered by Dr. Shelly Niederbach, a psychologist at the Victims' Counseling Service, Brooklyn.

3. The Vietnam memory is from M. Davis, "Analysis of Aversive Memories Using the Fear-Potentiated Startle Paradigm," in N. Butters and L. R Squire, eds., *The Neuropsychology of Memory* (New York: Guilford Press, 1992).

4. LeDoux makes the scientific case for these memories being especially enduring in "Indelibility of Subcortical Emotional Memories," *Journal of Cognitive Neuroscience* (1989), vol. 1, 238–43.

5. I interviewed Dr. Charney in *The New York Times* (June 12, 1990).

6. The experiments with paired laboratory animals were described to me by Dr. John Krystal, and have been repeated at several scientific laboratories. The major studies were done by Dr. Jay Weiss at Duke University.

7. The best account of the brain changes underlying PTSD, and the role of the amygdala in them, is in Dennis Charney et al., "Psychobiologic Mechanisms of Posttraumatic Stress Disorder," *Archives of General Psychiatry* 50 (April 1993), 294–305.

8. Some of the evidence for trauma-induced changes in this brain network comes from experiments in which Vietnam vets with PTSD were injected with yohimbine, a drug used on the tips of arrows by South American Indians to render their prey helpless. In tiny doses yohimbine blocks the action of a specific receptor (the point on a neuron that receives a neurotransmitter) that ordinarily acts as a brake on the catecholamines. Yohimbine takes the brakes off, keeping these receptors from sensing the secretion of catecholamines; the result is increasing catecholamine levels. With the neural brakes on anxiety disarmed by the drug injections, the yohimbine triggered panic in 9 of 15 PTSD patients, and lifelike flashbacks in 6. One vet had a hallucination of a helicopter being shot down in a trail of smoke and a bright flash; another saw the explosion by a land mine of a Jeep with his buddies in it—the same scene that had haunted his nightmares and appeared as flashbacks for more than 20 years. The yohimbine study was conducted by Dr. John Krystal, director of the Laboratory of Clinical Psychopharmacology at the National Center for PTSD at the West Haven, Conn., VA Hospital.

9. Fewer alpha-2 receptors in men with PTSD: see Charney, "Psychobiologic Mechanisms."

10. The brain, trying to lower the rate of CRF secretion, compensates by decreasing the number of receptors that release it. One telltale sign that this is what happens in people with PTSD comes from a study in which eight patients being treated for the problem were injected with CRF. Ordinarily, an injection of CRF triggers a flood of ACTH, the hormone that streams through the body to trigger catecholamines. But in the PTSD patients, unlike a comparison group of people without PTSD, there was no discernible change in levels of ACTH—a sign that their brains had cut back on CRF receptors because they already were overloaded with the stress hormone. The research was described to me by Charles Nemeroff, a Duke University psychiatrist.

11. I interviewed Dr. Nemeroff in *The New York Times* (June 12, 1990).

12. Something similar seems to occur in PTSD: For instance, in one experiment Vietnam vets with a PTSD diagnosis were shown a specially edited 15-minute film of graphic combat scenes from the movie *Platoon*. In one group, the vets were injected with naloxone, a substance that blocks endorphins; after watching the movie, these vets showed no change in their sensitivity to pain. But in the group without the endorphin blocker, the men's pain sensitivity decreased 30 percent, indicating an increase in endorphin secretion. The same scene had no such effect on veterans who did not have PTSD, suggesting that in the PTSD victims the nerve pathways that regulate endorphins were overly sensitive or hyperactive—an effect that became apparent

only when they were reexposed to something reminiscent of the original trauma. In this sequence the amygdala first evaluates the emotional importance of what we see. The study was done by Dr. Roger Pitman, a Harvard psychiatrist. As with other symptoms of PTSD, this brain change is not only learned under duress, but can be triggered once again if there is something reminiscent of the original terrible event. For example, Pitman found that when laboratory rats were shocked in a cage, they developed the same endorphin-based analgesia found in the Vietnam vets shown *Platoon*. Weeks later, when the rats were put into the cages where they had been shocked—but without any current being turned on—they once again became insensitive to pain, as they originally had been when shocked. See Roger Pitman, "Naloxone-Reversible Analgesic Response to Combat-Related Stimuli in Posttraumatic Stress Disorder," *Archives of General Medicine* (June 1990). See also Hillel Glover, "Emotional Numbing: A Possible Endorphin-Mediated Phenomenon Associated with Post-Traumatic Stress Disorders and Other Allied Psychopathologic States," *Journal of Traumatic Stress* 5, 4 (1992).

13. The brain evidence reviewed in this section is based on Dennis Charney's excellent article, "Psychobiologic Mechanisms."

14. Charney, "Psychobiologic Mechanisms," 300.

15. Role of prefrontal cortex in unlearning fear: In Richard Davidson's study, volunteers had their sweat response measured (a barometer of anxiety) while they heard a tone followed by a loud, obnoxious noise. The loud noise triggered a rise in sweat. After a time, the tone alone was enough to trigger the same rise, showing that the volunteers had learned an aversion to the tone. As they continued to hear the tone without the obnoxious noise, the learned aversion faded away—the tone sounded without any increase in sweat. The more active the volunteers' left prefrontal cortex, the more quickly they lost the learned fear.

In another experiment showing the prefrontal lobes' role in getting over a fear, lab rats—as is so often the case in these studies—learned to fear a tone paired with an electric shock. The rats then had what amounts to a lobotomy, a surgical lesion in their brain that cut off the prefrontal lobes from the amygdala. For the next several days the rats heard the tone without getting an electric shock. Slowly, over a period of days, rats who have once learned to fear a tone will gradually lose their fear. But for the rats with the disconnected prefrontal lobes, it took nearly twice as long to unlearn the fear—suggesting a crucial role for the prefrontal lobes in managing fear and, more generally, in mastering emotional lessons. This experiment was done by Maria Morgan, a graduate student of Joseph LeDoux's at the Center for Neural Science, New York University.

16. Recovery from PTSD: I was told about this study by Rachel Yehuda, a neurochemist and director of the Traumatic Stress Studies Program at the Mt. Sinai School of Medicine in Manhattan. I reported on the results in *The New York Times* (Oct. 6, 1992).

17. Childhood trauma: Lenore Terr, *Too Scared to Cry* (New York: HarperCollins, 1990).

18. Pathway to recovery from trauma: Judith Lewis Herman, *Trauma and Recovery* (New York: Basic Books, 1992).

19. "Dosing" of trauma: Mardi Horowitz, *Stress Response Syndromes* (Northvale, NJ: Jason Aronson, 1986).

20. Another level at which relearning goes on, at least for adults, is philosophical. The eternal question of the victim—"Why me?"—needs to be addressed. Being the victim of trauma shatters a person's faith that the world is a place that can be trusted, and that what happens to us in life is just—that is, that we can have control over our destiny by

living a righteous life. The answers to the victim's conundrum, of course, need not be philosophical or religious; the task is to rebuild a system of belief or faith that allows living once again as though the world and the people in it can be trusted.

21. That the original fear persists, even if subdued, has been shown in studies where lab rats were conditioned to fear a sound, such as a bell, when it was paired with an electric shock. Afterward, when they heard the bell they reacted with fear, even though no shock accompanied it. Gradually, over the course of a year (a very long time for a rat—about a third of its life), the rats lost their fearfulness of the bell. But the fear was restored in full force when the sound of the bell was once again paired with a shock. The fear came back in a single instant—but took months and months to subside. The parallel in humans, of course, is when a traumatic fear from long ago, dormant for years, floods back in full force with some reminder of the original trauma.

22. Luborsky's therapy research is detailed in Lester Luborsky and Paul Crits-Christoph, *Understanding Transference: The CCRT Method* (New York: Basic Books, 1990).

Chapter 14. Temperament Is Not Destiny

1. See, for example, Jerome Kagan et al., "Initial Reactions to Unfamiliarity," *Current Directions in Psychological Science* (Dec. 1992). The fullest description of the biology of temperament is in Kagan, *Galen's Prophecy*.

2. Tom and Ralph, archetypically timid and bold types, are described in Kagan, *Galen's Prophecy*, pp. 155–57.

3. Lifelong problems of the shy child: Iris Bell, "Increased Prevalence of Stress-related Symptoms in Middle-aged Women Who Report Childhood Shyness," *Annals of Behavior Medicine* 16 (1994).

4. The heightened heart rate: Iris R. Bell et al., "Failure of Heart Rate Habituation During Cognitive and Olfactory Laboratory Stressors in Young Adults With Childhood Shyness," *Annals of Behavior Medicine* 16 (1994).

5. Panic in teenagers: Chris Hayward et al., "Pubertal Stage and Panic Attack History in Sixth- and Seventh-grade Girls," *American Journal of Psychiatry* vol. 149(9) (Sept. 1992), pp. 1239–43; Jerold Rosenbaum et al., "Behavioral Inhibition in Childhood: A Risk Factor for Anxiety Disorders," *Harvard Review of Psychiatry* (May 1993).

6. The research on personality and hemispheric differences was done by Dr. Richard Davidson at the University of Wisconsin, and by Dr. Andrew Tomarken, a psychologist at Vanderbilt University: see Andrew Tomarken and Richard Davidson, "Frontal Brain Activation in Repressors and Nonrepressors," *Journal of Abnormal Psychology* 103 (1994).

7. The observations of how mothers can help timid infants become bolder were done with Doreen Arcus. Details are in Kagan, *Galen's Prophecy*.

8. Kagan, *Galen's Prophecy*, pp. 194–95.

9. Growing less shy: Jens Asendorpf, "The Malleability of Behavioral Inhibition: A Study of Individual Developmental Functions," *Developmental Psychology* 30, 6 (1994).

10. Hubel and Wiesel: David H. Hubel, Thorsten Wiesel, and S. Levay, "Plasticity of Ocular Columns in Monkey Striate Cortex," *Philosophical Transactions of the Royal Society of London* 278 (1977).

11. Experience and the rat's brain: The work of Marian Diamond and others is described in Richard Thompson, *The Brain* (San Francisco: W. H. Freeman, 1985).

12. Brain changes in treating obsessive-compulsive disorder: L. R. Baxter et al., "Caudate Glucose Metabolism Rate Changes With Both Drug and Behavior Therapy for Obsessive-Compulsive Disorder," *Archives of General Psychiatry* 49 (1992).

13. Increased activity in prefrontal lobes: L. R. Baxter et al., "Local Cerebral Glucose Metabolic Rates in Obsessive-Compulsive Disorder," *Archives of General Psychiatry* 44 (1987).

14. Prefrontal lobes maturity: Bryan Kolb, "Brain Development, Plasticity, and Behavior," *American Psychologist* 44 (1989).

15. Childhood experience and prefrontal pruning: Richard Davidson, "Asymmetric Brain Function, Affective Style and Psychopathology: The Role of Early Experience and Plasticity," *Development and Psychopathology* vol. 6 (1994), pp. 741–58.

16. Biological attunement and brain growth: Schore, *Affect Regulation*.

17. M. E. Phelps et al., "PET: A Biochemical Image of the Brain at Work," in N. A. Lassen et al., *Brain Work and Mental Activity: Quantitative Studies with Radioactive Tracers* (Copenhagen: Munksgaard, 1991).

PART FIVE: EMOTIONAL LITERACY

Chapter 15. The Cost of Emotional Illiteracy

1. Emotional literacy: I wrote about such courses in *The New York Times* (March 3, 1992).

2. The statistics on teen crime rates are from the Uniform Crime Reports, *Crime in the U.S., 1991,* published by the Department of Justice.

3. Violent crimes in teenagers: In 1990 the juvenile arrest rate for violent crimes climbed to 430 per 100,000, a 27 percent jump over the 1980 rate. Teen arrest rates for forcible rape rose from 10.9 per 100,000 in 1965 to 21.9 per 100,000 in 1990. Teen murder rates more than quadrupled from 1965 to 1990, from 2.8 per 100,000 to 12.1; by 1990 three of four teenage murders were with guns, a 79 percent increase over the decade. Aggravated assault by teenagers jumped by 64 percent from 1980 to 1990. See, e.g., Ruby Takanashi, "The Opportunities of Adolescence," *American Psychologist* (Feb. 1993).

4. In 1950 the suicide rate for those 15 to 24 was 4.5 per 100,000. By 1989 it was three times higher, 13.3. Suicide rates for children 10 to 14 almost tripled between 1968 and 1985. Figures on suicide, homicide victims, and pregnancies are from *Health, 1991,* U.S. Department of Health and Human Services, and Children's Safety Network, *A Data Book of Child and Adolescent Injury* (Washington, DC: National Center for Education in Maternal and Child Health, 1991).

5. Over the three decades since 1960, rates of gonorrhea jumped to a level four times higher among children 10 to 14, and three times higher among those 15 to 19. By 1990, 20 percent of AIDS patients were in their twenties, many having become infected during their teen years. Pressure to have sex early is getting stronger. A survey in the 1990s found that more than a third of younger women say that pressure from peers made them decide to have sex the first time; a generation earlier just 13

percent of women said so. See Ruby Takanashi, "The Opportunities of Adolescence," and Children's Safety Network, *A Data Book of Child and Adolescent Injury*.

6. Heroin and cocaine use for whites rose from 18 per 100,000 in 1970 to a rate of 68 in 1990—about three times higher. But over the same two decades among blacks, the rise was from a 1970 rate of 53 per 100,000 to a staggering 766 in 1990—close to *13 times* the rate 20 years before. Drug use rates are from *Crime in the U.S., 1991*, U.S. Department of Justice.

7. As many as one in five children have psychological difficulties that impair their lives in some way, according to surveys done in the United States, New Zealand, Canada, and Puerto Rico. Anxiety is the most common problem in children under 11, afflicting 10 percent with phobias severe enough to interfere with normal life, another 5 percent with generalized anxiety and constant worry, and another 4 percent with intense anxiety about being separated from their parents. Binge drinking climbs during the teenage years among boys to a rate of about 20 percent by age 20. I reported much of this data on emotional disorders in children in *The New York Times* (Jan. 10, 1989).

8. The national study of children's emotional problems, and comparison with other countries: Thomas Achenbach and Catherine Howell, "Are America's Children's Problems Getting Worse? A 13-Year Comparison," *Journal of the American Academy of Child and Adolescent Psychiatry* (Nov. 1989).

9. The comparison across nations was by Urie Bronfenbrenner, in Michael Lamb and Kathleen Sternberg, *Child Care in Context: Cross-Cultural Perspectives* (Englewood, NJ: Lawrence Erlbaum, 1992).

10. Urie Bronfenbrenner was speaking at a symposium at Cornell University (Sept. 24, 1993).

11. Longitudinal studies of aggressive and delinquent children: see, for example, Alexander Thomas et al., "Longitudinal Study of Negative Emotional States and Adjustments from Early Childhood Through Adolescence," *Child Development,* vol. 59 (Sept. 1988).

12. The bully experiment: John Lochman, "Social-Cognitive Processes of Severely Violent, Moderately Aggressive, and Nonaggressive Boys," *Journal of Clinical and Consulting Psychology,* 1994.

13. The aggressive boys research: Kenneth A. Dodge, "Emotion and Social Information Processing," in J. Garber and K. Dodge, *The Development of Emotion Regulation and Dysregulation* (New York: Cambridge University Press, 1991).

14. Dislike for bullies within hours: J. D. Coie and J. B. Kupersmidt, "A Behavioral Analysis of Emerging Social Status in Boys' Groups," *Child Development* 54 (1983).

15. Up to half of unruly children: See, for example, Dan Offord et al., "Outcome, Prognosis, and Risk in a Longitudinal Follow-up Study," *Journal of the American Academy of Child and Adolescent Psychiatry* 31 (1992).

16. Aggressive children and crime: Richard Tremblay et al., "Predicting Early Onset of Male Antisocial Behavior from Preschool Behavior," *Archives of General Psychiatry* (Sept. 1994).

17. What happens in a child's family before the child reaches school is, of course, crucial in creating a predisposition to aggression. One study, for example, showed that children whose mothers rejected them at age 1, and whose birth was more complicated, were four times as likely as others to commit a violent crime by age 18. Adriane

Raines et al., "Birth Complications Combined with Early Maternal Rejection at Age One Predispose to Violent Crime at Age 18 Years," *Archives of General Psychiatry* (Dec. 1994).

18. While low verbal IQ has appeared to predict delinquency (one study found an eight-point difference in these scores between delinquents and nondelinquents), there is evidence that impulsivity is more directly and powerfully at cause for both the low IQ scores and delinquency. As for the low scores, impulsive children don't pay attention well enough to learn the language and reasoning skills on which verbal IQ scores are based, and so impulsivity lowers those scores. In the Pittsburgh Youth Study, a well-designed longitudinal project where both IQ and impulsivity were assessed in ten- to twelve-year-olds, impulsivity was almost three times more powerful than verbal IQ in predicting delinquency. See the discussion in: Jack Block, "On the Relation Between IQ, Impulsivity, and Delinquency," *Journal of Abnormal Psychology* 104 (1995).

19. "Bad" girls and pregnancy: Marion Underwood and Melinda Albert, "Fourth-Grade Peer Status as a Predictor of Adolescent Pregnancy," paper presented at the meeting of the Society for Research on Child Development, Kansas City, Missouri (Apr. 1989).

20. The trajectory to delinquency: Gerald R. Patterson, "Orderly Change in a Stable World: The Antisocial Trait as Chimera," *Journal of Clinical and Consulting Psychology* 62 (1993).

21. Mind-set of aggression: Ronald Slaby and Nancy Guerra, "Cognitive Mediators of Aggression in Adolescent Offenders," *Developmental Psychology* 24 (1988).

22. The case of Dana: from Laura Mufson et al., *Interpersonal Psychotherapy for Depressed Adolescents* (New York: Guilford Press, 1993).

23. Rising rates of depression worldwide: Cross-National Collaborative Group, "The Changing Rate of Major Depression: Cross-National Comparisons," *Journal of the American Medical Association* (Dec. 2, 1992).

24. Ten times greater chance of depression: Peter Lewinsohn et al., "Age-Cohort Changes in the Lifetime Occurrence of Depression and Other Mental Disorders," *Journal of Abnormal Psychology* 102 (1993).

25. Epidemiology of depression: Patricia Cohen et al., New York Psychiatric Institute, 1988; Peter Lewinsohn et al., "Adolescent Psychopathology: I. Prevalence and Incidence of Depression in High School Students," *Journal of Abnormal Psychology* 102 (1993). See also Mufson et al., *Interpersonal Psychotherapy*. For a review of lower estimates: E. Costello, "Developments in Child Psychiatric Epidemiology," *Journal of the Academy of Child and Adolescent Psychiatry* 28 (1989).

26. Patterns of depression in youth: Maria Kovacs and Leo Bastiaens, "The Psychotherapeutic Management of Major Depressive and Dysthymic Disorders in Childhood and Adolescence: Issues and Prospects," in I. M. Goodyer, ed., *Mood Disorders in Childhood and Adolescence* (New York: Cambridge University Press, 1994).

27. Depression in children: Kovacs, op. cit.

28. I interviewed Maria Kovacs in *The New York Times* (Jan. 11, 1994).

29. Social and emotional lag in depressed children: Maria Kovacs and David Goldston, "Cognitive and Social Development of Depressed Children and Adolescents," *Journal of the American Academy of Child and Adolescent Psychiatry* (May 1991).

30. Helplessness and depression: John Weiss et al., "Control-related Beliefs and Self-reported Depressive Symptoms in Late Childhood," *Journal of Abnormal Psychology* 102 (1993).

31. Pessimism and depression in children: Judy Garber, Vanderbilt University. See, e.g., Ruth Hilsman and Judy Garber, "A Test of the Cognitive Diathesis Model of Depression in Children: Academic Stressors, Attributional Style, Perceived Competence and Control," *Journal of Personality and Social Psychology* 67 (1994); Judith Garber, "Cognitions, Depressive Symptoms, and Development in Adolescents," *Journal of Abnormal Psychology* 102 (1993).

32. Garber, "Cognitions."

33. Garber, "Cognitions."

34. Susan Nolen-Hoeksema et al., "Predictors and Consequences of Childhood Depressive Symptoms: A Five-Year Longitudinal Study," *Journal of Abnormal Psychology* 101 (1992).

35. Depression rate halved: Gregory Clarke, University of Oregon Health Sciences Center, "Prevention of Depression in At-Risk High School Adolescents," paper delivered at the American Academy of Child and Adolescent Psychiatry (Oct. 1993).

36. Garber, "Cognitions."

37. Hilda Bruch, "Hunger and Instinct," *Journal of Nervous and Mental Disease* 149 (1969). Her seminal book, *The Golden Cage: The Enigma of Anorexia Nervosa* (Cambridge, MA: Harvard University Press) was not published until 1978.

38. The study of eating disorders: Gloria R. Leon et al., "Personality and Behavioral Vulnerabilities Associated with Risk Status for Eating Disorders in Adolescent Girls," *Journal of Abnormal Psychology* 102 (1993).

39. The six-year-old who felt fat was a patient of Dr. William Feldman, a pediatrician at the University of Ottawa.

40. Noted by Sifneos, "Affect, Emotional Conflict, and Deficit."

41. The vignette of Ben's rebuff is from Steven Asher and Sonda Gabriel, "The Social World of Peer-Rejected Children," paper presented at the annual meeting of the American Educational Research Association, San Francisco (Mar. 1989).

42. The dropout rate among socially rejected children: Asher and Gabriel, "The Social World of Peer-Rejected Children."

43. The findings on the poor emotional competence of unpopular children are from Kenneth Dodge and Esther Feldman, "Social Cognition and Sociometric Status," in Steven Asher and John Coie, eds., *Peer Rejection in Childhood* (New York: Cambridge University Press, 1990).

44. Emory Cowen et al., "Longterm Follow-up of Early Detected Vulnerable Children," *Journal of Clinical and Consulting Psychology* 41 (1973).

45. Best friends and the rejected: Jeffrey Parker and Steven Asher, "Friendship Adjustment, Group Acceptance and Social Dissatisfaction in Childhood," paper presented at the annual meeting of the American Educational Research Association, Boston (1990).

46. The coaching for socially rejected children: Steven Asher and Gladys Williams, "Helping Children Without Friends in Home and School Contexts," in *Children's Social Development: Information for Parents and Teachers* (Urbana and Champaign: University of Illinois Press, 1987).

47. Similar results: Stephen Nowicki, "A Remediation Procedure for Nonverbal Processing Deficits," unpublished manuscript, Duke University (1989).

48. Two fifths are heavy drinkers: a survey at the University of Massachusetts by Project Pulse, reported in *The Daily Hampshire Gazette* (Nov. 13, 1993).

49. Binge drinking: Figures are from Harvey Wechsler, director of College Alcohol Studies at the Harvard School of Public Health (Aug. 1994).

50. More women drink to get drunk, and risk of rape: report by the Columbia University Center on Addiction and Substance Abuse (May 1993).

51. Leading cause of death: Alan Marlatt, report at the annual meeting of the American Psychological Association (Aug. 1994).

52. Data on alcoholism and cocaine addiction are from Meyer Glantz, acting chief of the Etiology Research Section of the National Institute for Drug and Alcohol Abuse.

53. Distress and abuse: Jeanne Tschann, "Initiation of Substance Abuse in Early Adolescence," *Health Psychology* 4 (1994).

54. I interviewed Ralph Tarter in *The New York Times* (Apr. 26, 1990).

55. Tension levels in sons of alcoholics: Howard Moss et al., "Plasma GABA-like Activity in Response to Ethanol Challenge in Men at High Risk for Alcoholism" *Biological Psychiatry* 27(6) (Mar. 1990).

56. Frontal lobe deficit in sons of alcoholics: Philip Harden and Robert Pihl, "Cognitive Function, Cardiovascular Reactivity, and Behavior in Boys at High Risk for Alcoholism," *Journal of Abnormal Psychology* 104 (1995).

57. Kathleen Merikangas et al., "Familial Transmission of Depression and Alcoholism," *Archives of General Psychiatry* (Apr. 1985).

58. The restless and impulsive alcoholic: Moss et al.

59. Cocaine and depression: Edward Khantzian, "Psychiatric and Psychodynamic Factors in Cocaine Addiction," in Arnold Washton and Mark Gold, eds., *Cocaine: A Clinician's Handbook* (New York: Guilford Press, 1987).

60. Heroin addiction and anger: Edward Khantzian, Harvard Medical School, in conversation, based on over 200 patients he has treated who were addicted to heroin.

61. No more wars: The phrase was suggested to me by Tim Shriver of the Collaborative for the Advancement of Social and Emotional Learning at the Yale Child Studies Center.

62. Emotional impact of poverty: "Economic Deprivation and Early Childhood Development" and "Poverty Experiences of Young Children and the Quality of Their Home Environments." Greg Duncan and Patricia Garrett each described their research findings in separate articles in *Child Development* (Apr. 1994).

63. Traits of resilient children: Norman Garmezy, *The Invulnerable Child* (New York: Guilford Press, 1987). I wrote about children who thrive despite hardship in *The New York Times* (Oct. 13, 1987).

64. Prevalence of mental disorders: Ronald C. Kessler et al., "Lifetime and 12-month Prevalence of DSM-III-R Psychiatric Disorders in the U.S.," *Archives of General Psychiatry* (Jan. 1994).

65. The figure for boys and girls reporting sexual abuse in the United States are from Malcolm Brown of the Violence and Traumatic Stress Branch of the National Institute of Mental Health; the number of substantiated cases is from the National Committee for the Prevention of Child Abuse and Neglect. A national survey of children found the

rates to be 3.2 percent for girls and 0.6 percent for boys in a given year: David Finkelhor and Jennifer Dziuba-Leatherman, "Children as Victims of Violence: A National Survey," *Pediatrics* (Oct. 1984).

66. The national survey of children about sexual abuse prevention programs was done by David Finkelhor, a sociologist at the University of New Hampshire.

67. The figures on how many victims child molesters have are from an interview with Malcolm Gordon, a psychologist at the Violence and Traumatic Stress Branch of the National Institute of Mental Health.

68. W. T. Grant Consortium on the School-Based Promotion of Social Competence, "Drug and Alcohol Prevention Curricula," in J. David Hawkins et al., *Communities That Care* (San Francisco: Jossey-Bass, 1992).

69. W. T. Grant Consortium, "Drug and Alcohol Prevention Curricula," p. 136.

Chapter 16. Schooling the Emotions

1. I interviewed Karen Stone McCown in *The New York Times* (Nov. 7, 1993).

2. Karen F. Stone and Harold Q. Dillehunt, *Self Science: The Subject Is Me* (Santa Monica: Goodyear Publishing Co., 1978).

3. Committee for Children, "Guide to Feelings," *Second Step 4–5* (1992), p. 84.

4. The Child Development Project: See, e.g., Daniel Solomon et al., "Enhancing Children's Prosocial Behavior in the Classroom," *American Educational Research Journal* (Winter 1988).

5. Benefits from Head Start: Report by High/Scope Educational Research Foundation, Ypsilanti, Michigan (Apr. 1993).

6. The emotional timetable: Carolyn Saarni, "Emotional Competence: How Emotions and Relationships Become Integrated," in R. A. Thompson, ed., *Socioemotional Development/Nebraska Symposium on Motivation* 36 (1990).

7. The transition to grade school and middle school: David Hamburg, *Today's Children: Creating a Future for a Generation in Crisis* (New York: Times Books, 1992).

8. Hamburg, *Today's Children*, pp. 171–72.

9. Hamburg, *Today's Children*, p. 182.

10. I interviewed Linda Lantieri in *The New York Times* (Mar. 3, 1992).

11. Emotional-literacy programs as primary prevention: Hawkins et al., *Communities That Care*.

12. Schools as caring communities: Hawkins et al., *Communities That Care*.

13. The story of the girl who was not pregnant: Roger P. Weisberg et al., "Promoting Positive Social Development and Health Practice in Young Urban Adolescents," in M. J. Elias, ed., *Social Decision-making in the Middle School* (Gaithersburg, MD: Aspen Publishers, 1992).

14. Character-building and moral conduct: Amitai Etzioni, *The Spirit of Community* (New York: Crown, 1993).

15. Moral lessons: Steven C. Rockefeller, *John Dewey: Religious Faith and Democratic Humanism* (New York: Columbia University Press, 1991).

16. Doing right by others: Thomas Lickona, *Educating for Character* (New York: Bantam, 1991).

17. The arts of democracy: Francis Moore Lappe and Paul Martin DuBois, *The Quickening of America* (San Francisco: Jossey-Bass, 1994).

18. Cultivating character: Amitai Etzioni et al., *Character Building for a Democratic, Civil Society* (Washington, DC: The Communitarian Network, 1994).

19. Three percent rise in murder rates: "Murders Across Nation Rise by 3 Percent, but Overall Violent Crime Is Down," *The New York Times* (May 2, 1994).

20. Jump in juvenile crime: "Serious Crimes by Juveniles Soar," Associated Press (July 25, 1994).

Appendix B. Hallmarks of the Emotional Mind

1. I have written about Seymour Epstein's model of the "experiential unconscious" on several occasions in *The New York Times,* and much of this summary of it is based on conversations with him, letters to me, his article, "Integration of the Cognitive and Psychodynamic Unconscious" (*American Psychologist* 44 (1994), and his book with Archie Brodsky, *You're Smarter Than You Think* (New York: Simon & Schuster, 1993). While his model of the experiential mind informs my own about the "emotional mind," I have made my own interpretation.

2. Paul Ekman, "An Argument for the Basic Emotions," *Cognition and Emotion,* 6, 1992, p. 175. The list of traits that distinguish emotions is a bit longer, but these are the traits that will concern us here.

3. Ekman, op cit., p. 187.

4. Ekman, op cit., p. 189.

5. Epstein, 1993, p. 55.

6. J. Toobey and L. Cosmides, "The Past Explains the Present: Emotional Adaptations and the Structure of Ancestral Environments," *Ethology and Sociobiology,* 11, pp. 418–19.

7. While it may seem self-evident that each emotion has its own biological pattern, it has not been so for those studying the psychophysiology of emotion. A highly technical debate continues over whether emotional arousal is basically the same for all emotions, or whether unique patterns can be teased out. Without going into the details of the debate, I have presented the case for those who hold to unique biological profiles for each major emotion.

Acknowledgments

I first heard the phrase "emotional literacy" from Eileen Rockefeller Growald, then the founder and president of the Institute for the Advancement of Health. It was this casual conversation that piqued my interest and framed the investigations that finally became this book. Over the course of these years it has been a pleasure to watch Eileen as she has nurtured this field along.

Support from the Fetzer Institute in Kalamazoo, Michigan, has allowed me the luxury of time to explore more fully what "emotional literacy" might mean, and I am grateful for the crucial early encouragement of Rob Lehman, president of the Institute, and an ongoing collaboration with David Sluyter, program director there. It was Rob Lehman who, early on in my explorations, urged me to write a book about emotional literacy.

Among my most profound debts is to the hundreds of researchers who over the years have shared their findings with me, and whose efforts are reviewed and synthesized here. To Peter Salovey at Yale I owe the concept of "emotional intelligence." I have also gained much from being privy to the ongoing work of many educators and practitioners of the art of primary prevention, who are at the forefront of the nascent movement in emotional literacy. Their hands-on efforts to bring heightened social and emotional skills to children, and to re-create schools as more humane environments, have been inspiring. Among them are Mark Greenberg and David Hawkins at the University of Washington; David Schaps and Catherine Lewis at the Developmental Studies Center in Oakland, California; Tim Shriver at the Yale Child Studies Center; Roger Weissberg at the University of Illinois at Chicago; Maurice Elias at Rutgers; Shelly Kessler of the Goddard Institute on Teaching and Learning in Boulder, Colorado; Chevy Martin and Karen Stone McCown at the Nueva Learning Center in Hillsborough, California; and Linda Lantieri, director of the National Center for Resolving Conflict Creatively in New York City.

I have a special debt to those who reviewed and commented on parts of this manuscript: Howard Gardner of the Graduate School of Education at Harvard University; Peter Salovey, of the psychology department at Yale

University; Paul Ekman, director of the Human Interaction Laboratory at the University of California at San Francisco; Michael Lerner, director of Commonweal in Bolinas, California; Denis Prager, then director of the health program at the John D. and Catherine T. MacArthur Foundation; Mark Gerzon, director of Common Enterprise, Boulder, Colorado; Mary Schwab-Stone, MD, Child Studies Center, Yale University School of Medicine; David Spiegel, MD, Department of Psychiatry, Stanford University Medical School; Mark Greenberg, director of the Fast Track Program, University of Washington; Shoshona Zuboff, Harvard School of Business; Joseph LeDoux, Center for Neural Science, New York University; Richard Davidson, director of the Psychophysiology Laboratory, University of Wisconsin; Paul Kaufman, Mind and Media, Point Reyes, California; Jessica Brackman, Naomi Wolf, and, especially, Fay Goleman.

Helpful scholarly consultations came from Page DuBois, a Greek scholar at the University of Southern California; Matthew Kapstein, a philosopher of ethics and religion at Columbia University; and Steven Rockefeller, intellectual biographer of John Dewey, at Middlebury College. Joy Nolan gathered vignettes of emotional episodes; Margaret Howe and Annette Spychalla prepared the appendix on the effects of emotional literacy curricula. Sam and Susan Harris provided essential equipment.

My editors at *The New York Times* over the last decade have been marvelously supportive of my many enquiries into new findings on the emotions, which first appeared in the pages of that paper and which inform much of this book.

Toni Burbank, my editor at Bantam Books, offered the editorial enthusiasm and acuity that sharpened my resolve and thinking.

And my wife, Tara Bennett-Goleman, provided the cocoon of warmth, love, and intelligence that nurtured this project along.

Index

WORKING WITH
EMOTIONAL
INTELLIGENCE

*To those who have shown me what it means to work
with emotional intelligence:*

* *

my parents, Fay and Irving Goleman

my uncle, Alvin M. Weinberg

my professor, David C. McClelland

Contents

5

The Emotionally Intelligent Organization

Acknowledgments

The thinking that led to this book has many roots. One of the most important was an ongoing series of talks with my wife, Tara Bennett-Goleman, triggered by sitting through many frustrating business meetings together, particularly of boards of directors we sat on. I was often aware that, for some reason, things just were not working. Tara was able to tune in to the emotional currents beneath the surface of those meetings and identify the ones that diverted the group's focus and energy, keeping us from getting our business done.

Tara and I began working together on what eventually became the book *Emotional Intelligence*. Her thinking and work are bearing fruit in a book of her own, now in progress. She has been with me every step of the way on this intellectual journey.

Another main taproot of the thinking reflected here is my late friend David C. McClelland, formerly my professor at Harvard University. David's visionary sense of the nature of competence and his keen quest for truth have long been an inspiration for me, and a large portion of the evidence on which I build my case traces back to David's research. I was saddened to learn of David's death as I was finishing this book.

I was helped by many friends at the Boston office of Hay/McBer (the company David founded with David Berlew, now my business advisor): James Burrus, president; Mary Fontaine, vice president and general manager; Ruth Jacobs, senior consultant; and Jason Goldner and Wei Chen, researchers.

Richard Boyatzis, associate dean for executive education at the Weatherhead School of Management at Case Western Reserve University, a past president at Hay/McBer, a colleague of David McClelland, and a good friend since our graduate school days at Harvard, has been of enormous help. His books *The Competent Manager* and *Innovation in Education* are classic statements of the importance of emotional competencies and the best practices for cultivating them. Richard has generously shared his years of data on competence, as well as his wealth of insights and experience; I'm delighted to be working together with him in my new venture, Emotional Intelligence Services.

Lyle Spencer, director of research and technology worldwide at Hay/McBer, has been a font of data and wisdom about the competencies of star performance, and the value of stars for organizational performance. The book he coauthored, *Competence at Work,* remains definitive for professionals in the field.

Marilyn Gowing, director of the Personnel Resources and Development Center at the U.S. Office of Personnel Management, was especially helpful in sharing her groundbreaking research into the role of emotional competence in individual and organizational performance.

Particular gratitude goes to my other colleagues on the Consortium for Research on Emotional Intelligence in the Workplace: my cochair, Cary Cherniss, of the Graduate School for Applied Psychology at Rutgers University; Robert Caplan, professor of organizational psychology at George Washington University; Kathy Kram, director of the executive MBA program at Boston University School of Management; Rick Price, of the Institute for Social Research at the University of Michigan; and Mary Ann Re in Human Resources Governance at AT&T. Rob Emmerling and Cornelia Roche, researchers for the Consortium, provided invaluable assistance in scouring the research literature on training and development. Graduate students of Maurice Elias at Rutgers did an early background survey of the research terrain.

Deep appreciation goes to the Fetzer Institute for their support of the Consortium's work, and their ongoing interest in emotional intelligence initiatives.

My colleagues Rita and Bill Cleary, Judith Rodgers, Ken Rhee, and Thérèse Jacobs-Stewart at Emotional Intelligence Services have been instrumental in evolving the practical applications that flow from my analysis of working with emotional intelligence.

I owe an intellectual debt to Claudio Fernández-Aráoz of the Buenos Aires office of Egon Zehnder International, whose generosity of spirit, keen intellect, and prodigious energy enriched this book. And conversations with those at Egon Zehnder International, including the CEO, Daniel Meiland, Victor Loewenstein, the managing director, and Egon Zehnder himself—a pioneer in creating an emotionally intelligent organization—aided my case study.

Others who generously shared their thinking with me include Warren Bennis, Distinguished Professor of Business Administration at USC; John Seely Brown, chief scientist at Xerox Corporation; Rick Canada, director of leadership and organizational development for Motorola's Cellular Sector; Kate Cannon, director of leadership development, American Express

Financial Advisors; Richard Davidson, director of the Laboratory for Affective Neuroscience at the University of Wisconsin; Margaret Echols and Meg O'Leary, at Coopers & Lybrand; Susan Ennis, head of executive development at BankBoston; Joanna Foster, of British Telecom; Howard Gardner, professor at Harvard University; Robert E. Kelley, at Carnegie-Mellon University; Phil Harkin, president of Linkage; Judith Hall, psychologist at Northeastern University; Jed Hughes of Walter V. Clarke Associates; Linda Keegan, vice president for executive development at Citibank; Fred Kiehl, president of KRW Associates in Minneapolis; Doug Lennick, executive vice president at American Express Financial Advisors; Mark Loehr, managing director at Salomon Smith Barney; George Lucas, CEO, LucasFilm; Paul Robinson, director of Sandia National Laboratories; Deepak Sethi, executive education, AT&T; Erik Hein Schmidt, CEO of Rangjung Yeshe Publications; Birgitta Wistrand, of the Swedish Parliament; Nick Zeniuk, of Interactive Learning Labs; Dr. Vega Zagier of the Tavistock Institute, London; Shoshana Zuboff, of Harvard Business School; and Jim Zucco of Lucent Technologies.

Rachel Brod, my chief research assistant, tracked down the studies I needed to keep this book grounded in the most current findings. Miranda Pierce, my chief data analyst, analyzed hundreds of competence models to assess the potency of emotional intelligence in excellence at work. Robert Buchele, professor of economics at Smith College, performed a parallel analysis on federal employees and provided other helpful research in economics.

David Berman, computer consultant par excellence, offered timely crisis management and technical support. Rowan Foster, my assistant, kept my professional life running while writing consumed my time.

My deepest gratitude is to the hundreds of men and women from companies large and small around the world who have shared with me their experiences, stories, and thoughts. Many are cited by name in these pages, but many, many more are not. This book owes much to them for its insights into what it means to work with emotional intelligence.

1

....

Beyond
Expertise

1

The New Yardstick

The rules for work are changing. We're being judged by a new yardstick: not just by how smart we are, or by our training and expertise, but also by how well we handle ourselves and each other. This yardstick is increasingly applied in choosing who will be hired and who will not, who will be let go and who retained, who passed over and who promoted.

The new rules predict who is most likely to become a star performer and who is most prone to derailing. And, no matter what field we work in currently, they measure the traits that are crucial to our marketability for future jobs.

These rules have little to do with what we were told was important in school; academic abilities are largely irrelevant to this standard. The new measure takes for granted having enough intellectual ability and technical know-how to do our jobs; it focuses instead on personal qualities, such as initiative and empathy, adaptability and persuasiveness.

This is no passing fad, nor just the management nostrum of the moment. The data that argue for taking it seriously are based on studies of tens of thousands of working people, in callings of every kind. The research distills with unprecedented precision which qualities mark a star performer. And it demonstrates which human abilities make up the greater part of the ingredients for excellence at work—most especially for leadership.

If you work in a large organization, even now you are probably being evaluated in terms of these capabilities, though you may not know it. If you are applying for a job, you are likely to be scrutinized through this lens, though, again, no one will tell you so explicitly. Whatever your job, understanding how to cultivate these capabilities can be essential for success in your career.

If you are part of a management team, you need to consider whether your organization fosters these competencies or discourages them. To the degree your organizational climate nourishes these competencies, your organization will be more effective and productive. You will maximize your group's intelligence, the synergistic interaction of every person's best talents.

If you work for a small organization or for yourself, your ability to perform at peak depends to a very great extent on your having these abilities—though almost certainly you were never taught them in school. Even so, your career will depend, to a greater or lesser extent, on how well you have mastered these capacities.

In a time with no guarantees of job security, when the very concept of a "job" is rapidly being replaced by "portable skills," these are prime qualities that make and keep us employable. Talked about loosely for decades under a variety of names, from "character" and "personality" to "soft skills" and "competence," there is at last a more precise understanding of these human talents, and a new name for them: emotional intelligence.

A Different Way of Being Smart

had the lowest cumulative grade point average ever in my engineering school," the codirector of a consulting firm tells me. "But when I joined the army and went to officer candidate school, I was number one in my class—it was all about how you handle yourself, get along with people, work in teams, leadership. And that's what I find to be true in the world of work."

In other words, what matters is a different way of being smart. In my book *Emotional Intelligence,* my focus was primarily on education, though a short chapter dealt with implications for work and organizational life.[1]

What caught me by utter surprise—and delighted me—was the flood of interest from the business community. Responding to a tidal wave of letters and faxes, e-mails and phone calls, requests to speak and consult, I found myself on a global odyssey, talking to thousands of people, from

CEOs to secretaries, about what it means to bring emotional intelligence to work.

Over and over I heard what became a familiar litany. People like the high-performing business consultant with the low GPA told me they found emotional intelligence, not technical expertise or book learning, to be what mattered most for excellence. My book, they said, made it safe to speak up about the business costs of emotional ineptitude, and to question a narrow, expertise-is-all view of capabilities. They felt they now had a new way to think about what they wished for in their own workplaces.

People spoke with extraordinary candor about matters far beyond the reach of corporate PR radar. Many detailed what is *not* working (such tales of emotional ineptitude are retold here without revealing the person's or organization's identity). But many others told success stories, confirming the practical value of working with emotional intelligence.

And so began the two-year inquiry that has culminated in this book. The effort has woven together several professional strands from my own life. From the outset, I've relied on the methods of journalism to delve into the facts and to narrate my conclusions. I've also gone back to my professional roots as an academic psychologist, conducting an exhaustive review of the research that illuminates the place of emotional intelligence in high performance for individuals, teams, and organizations. And I've performed or commissioned several new scientific analyses of data from hundreds of companies to establish a precise metric for quantifying the value of emotional intelligence.

This search has taken me back to research I participated in while a graduate student, and then faculty member, at Harvard University. That research was part of an early challenge to the IQ mystique—the false but widely embraced notion that what matters for success is intellect alone. This work helped spawn what has now become a mini-industry that analyzes the actual competencies that make people successful in jobs and organizations of every kind, and the findings are astonishing: IQ takes second position to emotional intelligence in determining outstanding job performance.

Analyses done by dozens of different experts in close to five hundred corporations, government agencies, and nonprofit organizations worldwide have arrived independently at remarkably similar conclusions, and their findings are particularly compelling because they avoid the biases or limits inherent in the work of a single individual or group. Their conclusions all point to the paramount place of emotional intelligence in excellence on the job—in virtually any job.

To be sure, these ideas are not new to the workplace; how people manage themselves and relate to those around them is central to much classic management theory. What's new is the data: We now have twenty-five years' worth of empirical studies that tell us with a previously unknown precision just how much emotional intelligence matters for success.

Another strand: In the decades since my own research in psychobiology, I have been tracking cutting-edge findings in neuroscience. This has allowed me to propose a foundation in brain science for the emotional intelligence model. Many businesspeople are traditionally skeptical of "soft" psychology and wary of the pop theories that come and go, but neuroscience makes crystal clear why emotional intelligence matters so much.

The ancient brain centers for emotion also harbor the skills needed for managing ourselves effectively and for social adeptness. Thus these skills are grounded in our evolutionary heritage for survival and adaptation.

This emotional part of the brain, neuroscience tells us, learns differently from the thinking brain. That insight has been pivotal in my development of this book—and leads me to challenge much conventional wisdom in corporate training and development.

I'm not alone in this challenge. For the last two years I have been working as cochair of the Consortium for Research on Emotional Intelligence in Organizations—a group of researchers from business schools, the federal government, and industry. Our research reveals deplorable weaknesses in how businesses train people in skills from listening and leadership to team building and handling change.

Most training programs have embraced an academic model—but this has been a drastic mistake, wasting millions of hours and billions of dollars. What's needed is an entirely new way of thinking about what it takes to help people boost their emotional intelligence.

Some Misconceptions

As I've toured the world talking and consulting with people in business, I've encountered certain widespread misunderstandings about emotional intelligence. Let me clear up some of the most common at the outset. First, emotional intelligence does not mean merely "being nice." At strategic moments it may demand not "being nice," but rather, for example, bluntly confronting someone with an uncomfortable but consequential truth they've been avoiding.

Second, emotional intelligence does not mean giving free rein to feelings—"letting it all hang out." Rather, it means managing feelings so that they are expressed appropriately and effectively, enabling people to work together smoothly toward their common goals.

Also, women are not "smarter" than men when it comes to emotional intelligence, nor are men superior to women. Each of us has a personal profile of strengths and weaknesses in these capacities. Some of us may be highly empathic but lack some abilities to handle our own distress; others may be quite aware of the subtlest shift in our own moods, yet be inept socially.

It is true that men and women as groups tend to have a shared, gender-specific profile of strong and weak points. An analysis of emotional intelligence in thousands of men and women found that women, on average, are more aware of their emotions, show more empathy, and are more adept interpersonally.[2] Men, on the other hand, are more self-confident and optimistic, adapt more easily, and handle stress better.

In general, however, there are far more similarities than differences. Some men are as empathic as the most interpersonally sensitive women, while some women are every bit as able to withstand stress as the most emotionally resilient men. Indeed, on average, looking at the overall ratings for men and women, the strengths and weaknesses average out, so that in terms of total emotional intelligence, there are no sex differences.[3]

Finally, our level of emotional intelligence is not fixed genetically, nor does it develop only in early childhood. Unlike IQ, which changes little after our teen years, emotional intelligence seems to be largely learned, and it continues to develop as we go through life and learn from our experiences—our competence in it can keep growing. In fact, studies that have tracked people's level of emotional intelligence through the years show that people get better and better in these capabilities as they grow more adept at handling their own emotions and impulses, at motivating themselves, and at honing their empathy and social adroitness. There is an old-fashioned word for this growth in emotional intelligence: *maturity.*

Emotional Intelligence: The Missing Priority

More and more companies are seeing that encouraging emotional intelligence skills is a vital component of any organization's management philosophy. "You don't compete with products alone anymore, but how well you use your people," a manager at Telia, the Swedish telecommunications company, put it to me. And Linda Keegan, vice president for executive development at Citibank, told me, "Emotional intelligence is the underlying premise for all management training."

It's a refrain I hear time and again:

▪ The president of a hundred-person job shop in the aerospace industry tells me that one of the main companies he supplies, Allied-Signal, required that he and all his employees be trained in the ubiquitous "quality circle" approach. "They wanted us to work better as a team, which was great," he says. "But we've found it hard—how can you be a team if you're not a group first? And to bond as a group we needed to boost our emotional intelligence."

▪ "We've been very effective at increasing profitability through methods like reengineering and speeding up the turnaround cycle for new products. But even with some big successes, our curve of improvement is flattening," a manager at Siemens AG, the German conglomerate, tells me. "We see the need to use our people better—maximize our human assets—to make the curve rise again. So we're trying to make the company more emotionally intelligent."

▪ A former project manager at Ford Motor Company recounts how he used the "learning organization" methods developed at MIT's Sloan School of Management in redesigning the Lincoln Continental. He says that learning about emotional intelligence was a kind of epiphany for him: "Those are exactly the abilities we had to build up to make us an effective learning organization."

A 1997 survey of benchmark practices among major corporations, done by the American Society for Training and Development, found that four out of five companies are trying to promote emotional intelligence in their employees through training and development, when evaluating performance, and in hiring.[4]

If so, why write this book? Because many or most organizations' efforts to encourage emotional intelligence have been poor, wasting vast amounts of time, energy, and money. For instance, the most systematic study ever done of the return on investment in leadership training (as we will see in Part 4) found that one well-respected week-long seminar for top-level executives actually had a slight *negative* effect on their job performance.

Businesses are waking up to the fact that even the most expensive training can go awry, and often does. And this ineptness comes at a time when emotional intelligence in individuals and organizations is emerging as a missing ingredient in the recipe for competitiveness.

Why This Matters Now

A t a California biotech start-up, the CEO proudly enumerated the features that made his organization state-of-the-art: No one, including him, had a fixed office; instead, everyone carried a small laptop—their mobile office—and was wired to everyone else. Job titles were irrelevant; employees worked in cross-functional teams and the place bubbled with creative energy. People routinely put in seventy- and eighty-hour work weeks.

"So what's the downside?" I asked him.

"There is no downside," he assured me.

And that was the fallacy. Once I was free to talk with staff members, I heard the truth: The hectic pace had people feeling burned out and robbed of their private lives. And though everyone could talk via computer to everyone else, people felt that no one was truly listening to them.

People desperately felt the need for connection, for empathy, for open communication.

In the new, stripped-down, every-job-counts business climate, these human realities will matter more than ever. Massive change is a constant; technical innovations, global competition, and the pressures of institutional investors are ever-escalating forces for flux.

Another reality makes emotional intelligence ever more crucial: As organizations shrink through waves of downsizing, those people who remain are more accountable—and more visible. Where earlier a midlevel employee might easily hide a hot temper or shyness, now competencies such as managing one's emotions, handling encounters well, teamwork, and leadership, show—and count—more than ever.

The globalization of the workforce puts a particular premium on emotional intelligence in wealthier countries. Higher wages in these countries, if they are to be maintained, will depend on a new kind of productivity. And structural fixes or technological advances alone are not enough: As at the California biotech firm, streamlining or other innovations often create new problems that cry out for even greater emotional intelligence.

As business changes, so do the traits needed to excel. Data tracking the talents of star performers over several decades reveal that two abilities that mattered relatively little for success in the 1970s have become crucially important in the 1990s: team building and adapting to change. And entirely new capabilities have begun to appear as traits of star performers, notably change catalyst and leveraging diversity. New challenges demand new talents.

Churning and the New Dread

A friend at a Fortune 500 company, one that had just downsized, letting thousands of employees go, told me: "It was terrible—so many people I've known for years were booted out, demoted, or transferred. It was hard for everybody. I still have my job, but I'll never feel the same about this place.

"I've been here thirty years, and over that time we were given the sense that as long as we put in a decent work day, the company would stand by us. Then, out of the blue, we were told, 'No one is guaranteed a job here anymore.' "

It seems no one is guaranteed a job *anywhere* anymore. These are troubled times for workers. The creeping sense that no one's job is safe, even as the companies they work for are thriving, means the spread of fear, apprehension, and confusion.

One sign of this growing unease: An American headhunting firm reported that more than half of callers making inquiries about jobs were still employed—but were so fearful of losing those jobs that they had already started to look for another.[5] The day that AT&T began notifying the first of forty thousand workers to be laid off—in a year when its profits were a record $4.7 billion—a poll reported that a third of Americans feared that someone in their household would soon lose a job.

Such fears persist at a time when the American economy is creating more jobs than it is losing. The churning of jobs—what economists euphemistically call "labor market flexibility"—is now a troubling fact of work life. And it is part of a global tidal wave sweeping through all the leading economies of the developed world, whether in Europe, Asia, or the Americas. Prosperity is no guarantee of jobs; layoffs continue even amidst a booming economy. This paradox, as Paul Krugman, an MIT economist, puts it, is "the unfortunate price we have to pay for having as dynamic an economy as we do."[6]

There is now a palpable bleakness about the new landscape of work.

"We work in what amounts to a quiet war zone" is the way one midlevel executive at a multinational firm put it to me. "There's no way to give your loyalty to a company and expect it to be returned anymore. So each person is becoming their own little shop within the company—you have to be able to be part of a team, but also ready to move on and be self-sufficient."

For many older workers—children of the meritocracy, who were taught that education and technical skills were a permanent ticket to success—this new way of thinking may come as a shock. People are beginning to realize that success takes more than intellectual excellence or technical prowess, and that we need another sort of skill just to survive—and certainly to thrive—in the increasingly turbulent job market of the future. Internal qualities such as resilience, initiative, optimism, and adaptability are taking on a new valuation.

A Coming Crisis: Rising IQ, Dropping EQ

Since 1918, when World War I brought the first mass use of IQ tests on American army recruits, the average IQ score in the United States has risen 24 points, and there has been a similar rise in developed countries around the world.[7] The reasons include better nutrition, more children completing more schooling, computer games and puzzles that help children master spatial skills, and smaller family size (which generally correlates with higher IQ scores in children).

There is a dangerous paradox at work, however: As children grow ever smarter in IQ, their emotional intelligence is on the decline. Perhaps the most disturbing single piece of data comes from a massive survey of parents and teachers that shows the present generation of children to be more emotionally troubled than the last. On average, children are growing more lonely and depressed, more angry and unruly, more nervous and prone to worry, more impulsive and aggressive.

Two random samples of American children, age seven to sixteen, were evaluated by their parents and teachers—adults who knew them well. The first group was assessed in the mid-1970s, and a comparable group was surveyed in the late 1980s.[8] Over that decade and a half there was a steady worsening of children's emotional intelligence. Although poorer children started out at a lower level on average, the rate of decline was the same across all economic groups—as steep in the wealthiest suburbs as in the poorest inner-city slum.

Dr. Thomas Achenbach, the University of Vermont psychologist who did these studies—and who has collaborated with colleagues on similar assessments in other nations—tells me that the decline in children's basic emotional competencies seems to be worldwide. The most telling signs of this are seen in rising rates among young people of problems such as despair, alienation, drug abuse, crime and violence, depression or eating disorders, unwanted pregnancies, bullying, and dropping out of school.

What this portends for the workplace is quite troubling: growing deficiencies among workers in emotional intelligence, particularly among those newest to the job. Most of the children that Achenbach studied in the late 1980s will be in their twenties by the year 2000. The generation that is falling behind in emotional intelligence is entering the workforce today.

What Employers Want

A survey of American employers reveals that more than half the people who work for them lack the motivation to keep learning and improving in their job. Four in ten are not able to work cooperatively with fellow employees, and just 19 percent of those applying for entry-level jobs have enough self-discipline in their work habits.[9]

More and more employers are complaining about the lack of social skills in new hires. In the words of an executive at a large restaurant chain: "Too many young people can't take criticism—they get defensive or hostile when people give them feedback on how they're doing. They react to performance feedback as though it were a personal attack."

The problem is not just in new workers—it's true for some seasoned executives as well. In the world of the 1960s and 1970s, people got ahead by going to the right schools and doing well there. But the world is full of well-trained, once-promising men and women who have plateaued in their careers—or worse, derailed—because of crucial gaps in emotional intelligence.

In a national survey of what employers are looking for in entry-level workers, specific technical skills are now less important than the underlying ability to learn on the job. After that, employers listed:

- Listening and oral communication
- Adaptability and creative responses to setbacks and obstacles

- Personal management, confidence, motivation to work toward goals, a sense of wanting to develop one's career and take pride in accomplishments

- Group and interpersonal effectiveness, cooperativeness and teamwork, skills at negotiating disagreements

- Effectiveness in the organization, wanting to make a contribution, leadership potential[10]

Of seven desired traits, just one was academic: competence in reading, writing, and math.

A study of what corporations are seeking in the MBAs they hire yields a similar list.[11] The three most desired capabilities are communication skills, interpersonal skills, and initiative. As Jill Fadule, managing director of admissions and financial aid at the Harvard Business School, told me, "empathy, perspective taking, rapport, and cooperation" are among the competencies the school is looking for in those who apply.

Our Journey

My mission in writing this book is to act as a guide to the scientific case for working with emotional intelligence—as individuals, in groups, as organizations. At every step I have sought to validate the science with the testimony of people in jobs and organizations of all kinds, and their voices will be heard all along the way.

In Part 1 I make the case that emotional intelligence counts more than IQ or expertise for determining who excels at a job—*any* job—and that for outstanding leadership it counts for almost everything. The business case is compelling: Companies that leverage this advantage add measurably to their bottom line.

Part 2 details twelve specific job capabilities, all based on self-mastery—initiative, trustworthiness, self-confidence, and achievement drive among them—and describes the unique contribution each makes to star performance.

In Part 3 I turn to thirteen key relationship skills—such as empathy and political awareness, leveraging diversity, team capabilities, and leadership. These are the skills that let us, for instance, navigate the currents of an organization effortlessly while others founder.

Throughout, readers can get a rough sense of where they stand when it comes to working with emotional intelligence. As I will show in Chapter 3, star performance does not require us to excel in all these competencies, but rather that we be strong in enough of them to reach the critical mass for success.

Part 4 heralds the good news: Whatever competencies we may be weak in, we can always learn to be better. To help readers who want to improve their own emotional intelligence capabilities—and to avoid wasting time and money—I offer practical, scientifically grounded guidelines for the best ways of doing so.

Finally, Part 5 considers what it means for an organization to be emotionally intelligent. I describe one such company and show why such practices can help not just with business performance but also in making organizations satisfying and desirable to work for. I also show how companies that ignore the emotional realities of their employees do so at their own risk, while those organizations with emotional intelligence are best equipped to survive—and to do well—in the ever more turbulent years ahead.

Though my aim is to be helpful, this is not a self-help book. There are perhaps too many how-to books promising far too much about improving emotional intelligence. Though these books are no doubt well intended, they typically perpetuate misconceptions about what upgrading these most essential capacities truly demands. Instead of quick fixes, you will find here sound guidelines for the real work of becoming more emotionally competent. These guidelines represent a level-headed survey of new thinking, research findings, and model practices from organizations around the world.

We live in a time when our prospects for the future increasingly depend on managing ourselves and handling our relationships more artfully. My hope is to offer some practical guidance for the crucial personal and business challenges we all face in the coming century.

2

Competencies of the Stars

t was the dawn of the 1970s, at the height of worldwide student protests against the Vietnam War, and a librarian stationed at a U.S. Information Agency post abroad had received bad news: A student group was threatening to burn down her library. But the librarian had friends among the group of student activists who made the threat. Her response on first glance might seem either naïve or foolhardy—or both: She invited the group to use the library facilities for some of their meetings.

But she also brought Americans living in the country there to listen to them—and so engineered a dialogue instead of a confrontation.

In doing so, she was capitalizing on her personal relationship with the handful of student leaders she knew well enough to trust—and for them to trust her. The tactic opened new channels of mutual understanding, and it strengthened her friendship with the student leaders. The library was never touched.

The librarian exhibited the skills of a superb negotiator or peacemaker, able to read the currents of a tense, swiftly moving situation and manage a response that brings people together instead of setting them against each other. Her facility escaped the damage wreaked on other American outposts manned by those less adept at these human skills.

The librarian was among a group of young diplomats the State Department identified as "superstars," who were intensively interviewed by a team led by Professor David McClelland of Harvard.[1]

At the time, McClelland was my main advisor for my doctoral work, and he drew me into his research program. The results of his studies led McClelland to publish a paper that sparked a revolution in thinking about the roots of excellence.

In exploring the ingredients of superb job performance, McClelland was joining an enterprise that got its first scientific footing at the beginning of the twentieth century with the work of Frederick Taylor. Taylorist efficiency experts swept the world of work, analyzing the most mechanically efficient moves a worker's body could make. The measure of human work was the machine.

On the heels of Taylorism came another standard of evaluation: the IQ test. The correct measure of excellence, proponents argued, was the capacities of the human mind.

Then, with the rise of Freudian thinking, another wave of experts argued that in addition to IQ, personality was an ingredient in excellence. By the 1960s, personality tests and typologies—whether, for example, a person was outgoing or introverted, a "feeling" or "thinking" type—were part of the standard measures of work potential.

But there was a problem. Many of the personality tests had been designed for completely different reasons, such as diagnosing psychological disorders, and so were poor predictors of how well people actually performed on the job. IQ tests, too, were not infallible; people of high IQ often performed poorly at work, while those of moderate IQ did extremely well.

McClelland's 1973 paper "Testing for Competence Rather than Intelligence" shifted the terms of the debate. He argued that traditional academic aptitude, school grades, and advanced credentials simply did not predict how well people would perform on the job or whether they would succeed in life.[2] Instead, he proposed that a set of specific competencies including empathy, self-discipline, and initiative distinguished the most successful from those who were merely good enough to keep their jobs. To find the competencies that make for star performance at a given job, McClelland suggested, first look at the stars and determine what competencies they display.

His paper launched an entirely new approach to the measure of excellence, one that assesses people's competencies in terms of the specific job they are doing. A "competence," in this tradition, is a personal trait or set of habits that leads to more effective or superior job performance—in other words, an ability that adds clear economic value to the efforts of a person on the job.

That insight has, over the last quarter century, triggered research on hundreds of thousands of workers, from clerks to top executives, in organizations as vast as the U.S. government and AT&T, and as tiny as one-person enterprises. In all the findings, a common core of personal and social abilities has proven to be the key ingredient in people's success: emotional intelligence.

The Tuned-Out Programmer

Two computer programmers are explaining how they go about doing their job, designing programs to fill the pressing business needs of their clients. Recounts one: "I heard him say he needed all the data in a simple format that could fit on one page." So the programmer followed through to deliver just that.

The second, however, seems to have trouble getting to the point. Unlike the first programmer, he doesn't mention the needs of his clients. Instead he launches into a litany of technical talk: "The HP3000/30's BASIC compiler was too slow, so I went directly to a machine-language routine." In other words, he focuses on machines, not people.

The first programmer was identified as outstanding at his work, able to design programs that are user-friendly; the second is at best mediocre at this task—he has essentially tuned out his customers. The first computer programmer displays emotional intelligence; the other exemplifies its absence. Both were interviewed using a method developed by McClelland to detect the competencies that distinguish star performers in jobs of every kind.[3]

McClelland's original insight was rooted in work he had done for corporations and in organizations such as the U.S. State Department, where he had been asked to assess the capabilities of outstanding foreign-service officers, the young diplomats who represent America in other countries. Like sales staff or account managers in a large corporation, the real job of these officers is to "sell" America, to get people abroad to feel positively about the United States.

Selection for these diplomatic posts was a formidable hurdle, one only those with the best education could jump. The selection test gauged abilities higher officials in the State Department thought a diplomat needed—mainly a sound grounding in academic disciplines like American history and culture, language fluency, and specialized expertise in a field such as economics. The problem was that the exam reflected only how well candidates had done in their studies.

Their scores were a poor indicator of how adept these new diplomats were on their feet in Frankfurt, Buenos Aires, or Singapore.[4] In fact, their on-the-job performance ratings actually correlated *negatively* with how well they did on the very test used to select them; sheer mastery of academic topics was irrelevant (or worse, detrimental) to the competencies that count in that form of sales known as diplomacy.

What mattered, McClelland found, was another kind of competence altogether. When he interviewed the superstars—those the State Department had identified as their most brilliant and effective young diplomats—and compared them to peers who were mediocre, the most telling differences emerged in a set of basic human abilities that academic or IQ tests simply did not measure.

Among the radically different tests McClelland turned to was a clever assessment of the ability to read emotions, newly developed by a Harvard colleague. In this test people watch snatches of videotapes of people talking about emotional situations like going through a divorce or having an argument at work.[5] An electronic filter alters the sound, so what comes through is not the words themselves, but rather the tones and nuances that reveal what the person is feeling.

McClelland found that the stars scored much higher than the mediocre diplomats at accurately discerning the speakers' emotions. This translated into an ability to read emotional messages in people with backgrounds vastly different from their own, even when they couldn't understand the language being spoken—a competence crucial not only for diplomats but throughout today's work world for capitalizing on diversity.

Time after time in describing critical moments on the job, the foreign-service officers told tales of touchy situations similar to those of the peace-making librarian. But for the less socially astute diplomats the stories more often ended with events blowing up in their faces because of their inability to read or handle the people they dealt with.

Domains of Excellence: The Limits of IQ

Two of the smartest people I ever knew (at least in the academic sense) followed strikingly different career paths. One was a friend during my freshman year in college who had perfect scores on his college admissions tests—a pair of 800s on the verbal and math sections of the SAT, and a 5 on each of three advanced placement tests. But he was unmotivated in school, often skipped class, and got papers in late. He dropped out for a while, finally graduating after ten years. Today he reports he is satisfied working as a one-man computer consulting business.

The other was a math prodigy who entered my high school at ten, graduated at twelve, and got his doctorate in theoretical mathematics from Oxford at eighteen. In high school he was a bit short for his age, which, because he was so young, made him about a foot shorter than most of us. He was also about twice as bright as everyone else—and many students resented him for it. He was often taunted and bullied. But despite his diminutive stature, he didn't back down. Like a little bantam rooster, he stood his ground against the biggest hulks in school. He had assertiveness to match his intellect—which may explain why, last I heard, he's now the head of one of the most prestigious mathematics departments in the world.

Given how much emphasis schools and admissions tests put on it, IQ alone explains surprisingly little of achievement at work or in life. When IQ test scores are correlated with how well people perform in their careers, the highest estimate of how much difference IQ accounts for is about 25 percent.[6] A careful analysis, though, suggests a more accurate figure may be no higher than 10 percent, and perhaps as low as 4 percent.[7]

This means that IQ alone at best leaves 75 percent of job success unexplained, and at worst 96 percent—in other words, it does not determine who succeeds and who fails. For example, a study of Harvard graduates in the fields of law, medicine, teaching, and business found that scores on entrance exams—a surrogate for IQ—had zero or negative correlation with their eventual career success.[8]

Paradoxically, IQ has the least power in predicting success among that pool of people smart enough to handle the most cognitively demanding fields, and the value of emotional intelligence for success grows more powerful the higher the intelligence barriers for entry into a field. In MBA programs or in careers like engineering, law, or medicine, where professional selection focuses almost exclusively on intellectual abilities, emotional intelligence carries much more weight than IQ in determining who emerges as a leader.

"What you learned in school distinguishes superior performers in only a handful of the five or six hundred jobs for which we've done competence studies," says Lyle Spencer Jr., director of research and technology worldwide and cofounder of what is now Hay/McBer, the consulting firm McClelland started.[9] "It's just a threshold competence; you need it to get in the field, but it does not make you a star. It's the emotional intelligence abilities that matter more for superior performance."

This paradoxical importance of emotional intelligence in cognitively demanding disciplines is a consequence of the difficulty of entering them in the first place. In professional and technical fields the threshold for entry is typically an IQ of 110 to 120.[10] The result of having to jump such a high initial entry barrier is that since everyone is in the top 10 percent or so of intelligence, IQ itself offers relatively little competitive advantage.

We do not compete in our careers with people who lack the requisite intelligence to enter and stay in our field—but rather against the much smaller group of those who have managed to jump the hurdles of schooling, entry exams, and other cognitive challenges to get into the field in the first place.

Since emotional intelligence is not nearly as great a factor as IQ in selection for entering such fields, there is more variation in this "soft" domain than there is in IQ among these professionals. The difference between those at the high and low ends of the emotional intelligence scale is very large, and being at the top confers a major competitive advantage. Thus "soft" skills matter even more for success in "hard" fields.

The Second Domain: Expertise

Here's the dilemma: You're a cultural affairs officer at a U.S. embassy in North Africa, and you get a wire from Washington telling you to show a film featuring an American politician greatly reviled in that country.

If you show it, the locals will find it offensive. If you don't, headquarters back home will be upset.

What do you do?

This is not a hypothetical situation; it was the predicament faced by one of the foreign-service officers McClelland studied. The officer recalled, "I knew that if I showed the film, this place would be burned down the next day by about five hundred angry students. Yet Washington felt the film was great. What I had to do was figure out how to show the film so the embassy could tell Washington we had done as they wished, and yet not offend people in the country."

His solution? He screened the movie on a holy day, when he knew no one could come.

That brilliant bit of common sense exemplifies practical intelligence, a combination of technical expertise and experience.[11] Apart from IQ, our practical skills, along with the technical abilities we master, determine how well we perform on an everyday basis. Whatever our intellectual potential, it is expertise—our total body of specialized information and practical skills—that makes us good enough to do a particular job.

The most competent doctors, for example, are those who keep expanding their knowledge base by keeping up with current findings and who have a vast reservoir of hands-on experience, and can draw on all this in making diagnoses and treating their patients. This continued drive to keep up-to-date matters far more in how well they can help their patients than their scores on the entrance exam for medical school.

In large part, expertise is a combination of common sense plus the specialized knowledge and skill we pick up in the course of doing any job. Expertise comes from in-the-trenches learning. It shows up as an insider's sense of the tricks of a trade—the real knowledge of how to do a job that only experience brings.

Such down-to-earth abilities have been extensively studied by Yale psychologist Robert Sternberg, an authority on intelligence and success.[12] In tests with managers at Fortune 500 companies, Sternberg discovered that practical intelligence seems to account for at least as much on-the-job success as does IQ.[13]

On the other hand, practical intelligence is rarely the main factor in a star's outstanding job performance. "In the hundreds of rigorous studies we've done comparing star performers with merely average ones in companies around the world, expertise just never made the difference," says Ruth Jacobs, a senior consultant at Hay/McBer in Boston.

"Expertise is a baseline competence. You need it to get the job and get it done, but how you do the job—the other competencies you bring to your expertise—determines performance," Jacobs adds. "Are you able to translate your expertise into something that's marketable, that stands out? If not, it makes little difference."

Supervisors of technical and professional workers, for example, need to have some degree of expertise in their area; it would be nearly impossible to manage such work without a reasonable understanding of what people are doing. But that expertise is a *threshold* requirement; the abilities that distinguish the outstanding supervisors in technical fields are not technical, but rather relate to handling people.[14]

So to a degree, experience and expertise, like IQ, matter—but there is much more to the story when it comes to excellence.

The Third Domain: Emotional Intelligence

Sternberg tells a cautionary tale about two students, Penn and Matt. Penn was a brilliant and creative student, an exemplar of the best Yale had to offer.[15] The trouble with Penn was that he knew he was exceptional—and so was, as one professor put it, "unbelievably arrogant." Penn, despite his abilities, put people off, especially those who had to work with him.

Even so, he looked spectacular on paper. When he graduated, Penn was highly sought after: All the top organizations in his field offered him interviews for jobs, and he was a universal first pick—at least on the basis of his résumé. But Penn's arrogance came across all too clearly; he ended up with only one job offer, from a second-tier outfit.

Matt, another Yale student in Penn's field, wasn't as academically brilliant. But he was adept interpersonally; everyone who worked with him liked him. Matt ended up with seven job offers out of eight interviews and went on to success in his field, while Penn was let go after two years at his first job.

Penn lacked—and Matt had—emotional intelligence.

Emotional intelligence skills are synergistic with cognitive ones; top performers have both. The more complex the job, the more emotional intelligence matters—if only because a deficiency in these abilities can hinder the use of whatever technical expertise or intellect a person may have. Take, for example, an executive who had just been brought in to run a $65 million, family-owned business, the first president from outside the family.[16]

A researcher, using an interview method to assess the executive's ability to handle cognitive complexity, determined his capacity was the very highest—a "level six," someone smart enough, theoretically, to be CEO of a global firm or head of a country.[17] But during that interview the conversation turned to why he had to leave his previous job: He had been fired because he had failed to confront subordinates and hold them responsible for their poor performance.

"It was still an emotional trigger for him," the researcher told me. "His face got red and flushed, he started waving his hands—he was clearly agitated. It turned out that his new boss—the owner of the company—had criticized him that very morning for the same thing, and he went on and on about how hard it was for him to confront low-performing employees, especially when they had been with the company for a long time." And, the researcher noted, "While he was so upset his ability to handle cognitive complexity—to reason—plummeted."

In short, out-of-control emotions can make smart people stupid. As

Doug Lennick, an executive vice president at American Express Financial Advisors, put it to me, "The aptitudes you need to succeed start with intellectual horsepower—but people need emotional competence, too, to get the full potential of their talents. The reason we don't get people's full potential is emotional incompetence."

The Great Divide

It was Super Bowl Sunday, that sacrosanct day when most American men are to be found in front of their televisions. A departing flight from New York to Detroit was delayed two hours, and the tension among the passengers—almost entirely businessmen—was palpable. When they finally arrived in Detroit, a mysterious glitch with the boarding ramp made the plane stop about a hundred feet from the gate. Frantic about being late, passengers leaped to their feet anyway.

One of the flight attendants went to the intercom. How could she most effectively get everyone to sit down so that the plane could finish taxiing to the gate?

She did *not* announce, in a stern voice, "Federal regulations require that you be seated before we can move to the gate."

Instead, she warbled in a singsong tone, suggestive of a playful warning to an adorable small child who has done something naughty but forgivable, "You're staaan-ding!"

At that everyone laughed and sat back down until the plane had finished taxiing to the gate. And, given the circumstances, they got off the plane in a surprisingly good mood.

The great divide in competencies lies between the mind and heart, or, more technically, between cognition and emotion. Some competencies are purely cognitive, such as analytic reasoning or technical expertise. Others combine thought and feeling; these I call "emotional competencies."[18]

All emotional competencies involve some degree of skill in the realm of feeling, along with whatever cognitive elements are at play. This stands in sharp contrast to purely cognitive competencies, which a computer can be programmed to execute about as well as a person. A digitized voice could have announced: "Federal regulations require all passengers be seated before we proceed to the gate."

But the stilted tones of a computerized voice would never have had the artful effect of that flight attendant's wit. People might grudgingly comply with a robotlike directive, but they would undergo nothing like the mood shift the attendant accomplished. She was able to hit exactly the right emotional note—something human cognition alone (or for that matter, computers) cannot do (at least not yet).[19]

Take competence in communication. As I type this, for example, I can ask my software program to check what I'm writing for grammatical accuracy. But I cannot ask it to check what I'm writing for its emotional power, its passion, or its ability to engage and influence readers. These other, crucial elements of effective communication depend on emotional capacities: being able to gauge an audience's reactions, to fine-tune a presentation to have meaningful emotional impact.

The most convincing, powerful arguments speak to the heart as well as the head. This tight orchestration of thought and feeling is made possible by what amounts to a superhighway in the brain, a bundle of neurons connecting the prefrontal lobes, behind the forehead—the brain's executive decision-making center—with an area deep in the brain that harbors our emotions.[20]

Damage to this crucial connection leaves people emotionally incompetent, even though their purely intellectual abilities are untouched. In other words, such people would still score well on IQ tests and other measures of cognitive ability. But on the job—and in life generally—they would fail at the emotional arts that make people like the flight attendant so effective.

Thus the divide between those competencies that are purely cognitive, and those that depend on emotional intelligence as well, reflects a parallel division in the human brain.

Emotional Competence

An emotional *competence* is a learned capability based on emotional intelligence that results in outstanding performance at work.[21] Take the finesse shown by the flight attendant. She was superb at influence, an important emotional competence: getting others to respond in a desired way. At the heart of this competence are two abilities: empathy, which involves reading the feelings of others, and social skills, which allow handling those feelings artfully.

Our emotional *intelligence* determines our potential for learning the practical skills that are based on its five elements: self-awareness, motivation, self-regulation, empathy, and adeptness in relationships. Our emotional *competence* shows how much of that potential we have translated into on-the-job capabilities. For instance, being good at serving customers is an emotional competence based on empathy. Likewise, trustworthiness is a competence based on self-regulation, or handling impulses and emotions well. Both customer service and trustworthiness are competencies that can make people outstanding in their work.

Simply being high in emotional intelligence does not guarantee a person will have learned the emotional competencies that matter for work; it means only that they have excellent potential to learn them. A person might be highly empathic, for example, and yet not have learned the skills based on empathy that translate into superior customer service, top-flight coaching or mentoring, or the ability to bring together a diverse work team. The parallel in music would be someone with perfect pitch, say, who also had lessons in singing, and so became a superb operatic tenor. Without the lessons, there would be no opera career, despite the potential—a Pavarotti who never had the chance to blossom.

Emotional competencies cluster into groups, each based on a common underlying emotional intelligence capacity. The underlying emotional intelligence capacities are vital if people are to successfully learn the competencies necessary to succeed in the workplace. If they are deficient in social skills, for instance, they will be inept at persuading or inspiring others, at leading teams or catalyzing change. If they have little self-awareness, they will be oblivious to their own weaknesses and lack the self-confidence that comes from certainty about their strengths.

Table 1 shows the relationship between the five dimensions of emotional intelligence and the twenty-five emotional competencies.[22] None of us is perfect on this scale; we inevitably have a profile of strengths and limits. But, as we shall see, the ingredients for outstanding performance require only that we have strengths in a given number of these competencies, typically, at least six or so, and that the strengths be spread across all five areas of emotional intelligence. In other words, there are many paths to excellence.

These emotional intelligence capacities are:

- *Independent:* Each makes a unique contribution to job performance.

- *Interdependent:* Each draws to some extent on certain others, with many strong interactions.

- *Hierarchical:* The emotional intelligence capacities build upon one another. For example, self-awareness is crucial for self-

TABLE 1

The Emotional Competence Framework

Personal Competence

These competencies determine how we manage ourselves.

Self-Awareness

Knowing one's internal states, preferences, resources, and intuitions
(see Chapter 4)

- *Emotional awareness:* Recognizing one's emotions and their effects
- *Accurate self-assessment:* Knowing one's strengths and limits
- *Self-confidence:* A strong sense of one's self-worth and capabilities

Self-Regulation

Managing one's internal states, impulses, and resources
(see Chapter 5)

- *Self-Control:* Keeping disruptive emotions and impulses in check
- *Trustworthiness:* Maintaining standards of honesty and integrity
- *Conscientiousness:* Taking responsibility for personal performance
- *Adaptability:* Flexibility in handling change
- *Innovation:* Being comfortable with novel ideas, approaches, and new information

Motivation

Emotional tendencies that guide or facilitate reaching goals
(see Chapter 6)

- *Achievement drive:* Striving to improve or meet a standard of excellence
- *Commitment:* Aligning with the goals of the group or organization
- *Initiative:* Readiness to act on opportunities
- *Optimism:* Persistence in pursuing goals despite obstacles and setbacks

Social Competence

These competencies determine how we handle relationships.

Empathy

Awareness of others' feelings, needs, and concerns
(see Chapter 7)

- *Understanding others:* Sensing others' feelings and perspectives, and taking an active interest in their concerns
- *Developing others:* Sensing others' development needs and bolstering their abilities
- *Service orientation:* Anticipating, recognizing, and meeting customers' needs
- *Leveraging diversity:* Cultivating opportunities through different kinds of people
- *Political awareness:* Reading a group's emotional currents and power relationships

Social Skills

Adeptness at inducing desirable responses in others
(see Chapters 8 and 9)

- *Influence:* Wielding effective tactics for persuasion
- *Communication:* Listening openly and sending convincing messages
- *Conflict management:* Negotiating and resolving disagreements
- *Leadership:* Inspiring and guiding individuals and groups
- *Change catalyst:* Initiating or managing change
- *Building bonds:* Nurturing instrumental relationships
- *Collaboration and cooperation:* Working with others toward shared goals
- *Team capabilities:* Creating group synergy in pursuing collective goals

regulation and empathy; self-regulation and self-awareness contribute to motivation; all the first four are at work in social skills.

■ *Necessary, but not sufficient:* Having an underlying emotional intelligence ability does not guarantee people will develop or display the associated competencies, such as collaboration or leadership. Factors such as the climate of an organization or a person's interest in his or her job will also determine whether the competence manifests itself.

■ *Generic:* The general list is to some extent applicable to all jobs. However, different jobs make differing competence demands.

The list offers a way to inventory our strengths and to pinpoint competencies we may want to bolster. Parts 2 and 3 of the book give more detail and insight into each of the competencies, showing how they look when displayed in full power—or when they are lacking. Readers may want to turn directly to the competencies most relevant to their interests; the chapters describing them do build on one another to an extent (as do the competencies they describe), but they need not be read in a fixed order.

The Best: What It Takes

The same competencies can make people excel in different jobs. For instance, at a Blue Cross health insurance division, successful customer service representatives exhibit high self-control, conscientiousness, and empathy. For successful retail store managers, the key competencies include the same triumvirate—self-control, conscientiousness, and empathy—plus a fourth competence, service orientation.[23]

The competencies one needs for success may change as one rises through the ranks; in most large organizations, senior executives need a greater degree of political awareness than middle managers.[24] And certain positions require specific competencies.[25] For the best nurses, it's a sense of humor; for bankers, respecting customers' confidentiality; for outstanding school principals, seeking out ways to get feedback from teachers and parents. At the Internal Revenue Service, the best tax collectors are strong not just in accounting, but also in social skills. Among law enforcement officers, using the least amount of force necessary is, understandably, a valued ability.

Furthermore, key competencies match a given organization's reality. Each company and each industry has its own emotional ecology, and the most adaptive traits for workers will differ accordingly.

Such specifics aside, close to three hundred different company-sponsored studies show that across a wide array of jobs the recipe for excellence gives far more weight to emotional competencies than to cognitive abilities.[26] That the most important competencies among stars stem from emotional intelligence is no surprise for, say, salespeople. But even among scientists and those in technical professions analytic thinking ranks third, after the ability to influence and the drive to achieve. Brilliance alone will not propel a scientist to the top unless she also has the ability to influence and persuade others, and the inner discipline to strive for challenging goals. A lazy or reticent genius may have all the answers in his head, but they amount to little if no one knows or cares!

Take the "techies of the techies," whose usual title is "corporate consulting engineer." These brilliant troubleshooters are kept on hand by high-tech firms to rescue projects in danger of going off the track; they are so highly valued that annual reports list them along with corporate officers. What makes the best technology gurus so special? "What made the difference was not their brain power—most everyone at these companies is just as smart—but their emotional competence," Susan Ennis, of BankBoston and formerly of DEC, says. "It's their abilities to listen, to influence, to collaborate, and to get people motivated and working together well."

To be sure, many people have gotten to the top despite flaws in emotional intelligence; that's long been a reality of organizational life. But as work becomes more complex and collaborative, companies where people work together best have a competitive edge.

In the new workplace, with its emphasis on flexibility, teams, and a strong customer orientation, this crucial set of emotional competencies is becoming increasingly essential for excellence in every job and in every part of the world.[27]

3

The Hard Case for Soft Skills

■ At Lucent Technologies, the teams that stock raw material for manufacturing need more than technical know-how—they need skills in listening and understanding, flexibility, and teamwork. They also need the ability to energize others, commitment, and confidence in those they work with.

■ At the University of Nebraska Medical Center, technical expertise and analytical skills are invaluable, but so are emotional competencies like interpersonal skills, innovation, effective leadership, building partnerships, and networking.

■ At Amoco, the giant petrochemical firm, for superior performance in engineering or managing information technology, expertise and analytic thinking are, again, on the list. But so are self-confidence, flexibility, an achievement drive, service orientation, teamwork and cooperation, wielding influence, and developing others.[1]

These portraits of competence, drawn from hundreds of hours of on-the-job interviews and assessments, summarize the nitty-gritty reality of thousands of people at work. Poring over hundreds of such summaries, it struck me to ask a question that no one had thought to ask before: Exactly how important for excellence is emotional competence compared to technical skills and intellect?

The Ratio of Excellence

I was lucky enough to have access to competence models for 181 different positions drawn from 121 companies and organizations worldwide, with their combined workforce numbering in the millions. The models showed what management in each organization agreed captured the particular profile of excellence for a given job.[2]

My analysis was straightforward: I compared which competencies listed as essential for a given job, role, or field could be classed as purely cognitive or technical skills, and which were emotional competencies. For instance, fifteen key competencies were listed for information technology project managers at Amoco. Of these, four were purely cognitive or technical, while the rest fell in the emotional competence category. Simple math yields the finding: 73 percent of the abilities identified by Amoco as key to superior performance in this job were emotional competencies.

When I applied this method to all 181 competence models I had studied, I found that *67 percent*—two out of three—of the abilities deemed essential for effective performance were emotional competencies. Compared to IQ and expertise, emotional competence mattered *twice* as much. This held true across all categories of jobs, and in all kinds of organizations.

To make sure my findings weren't a fluke, I turned to Hay/McBer and commissioned them to do an independent study. (See Appendix 2 for more details of this and other corroborating research.) They reanalyzed raw data from forty different corporations to determine how much more of a given competence star performers demonstrated compared to average—a slightly different way to answer my question.

The Hay/McBer analysis was based on some of the very best data available anywhere, the results of in-depth interviews and extensive testing and evaluation of hundreds of workers. Again, emotional competencies were found to be *twice* as important in contributing to excellence as pure intellect and expertise.

The Leadership Edge

E motional competence is particularly central to leadership, a role whose essence is getting others to do their jobs more effectively. Interpersonal ineptitude in leaders lowers everyone's performance: It wastes time, creates acrimony, corrodes motivation and commitment, builds hostility and apathy. A leader's strengths or weaknesses in emotional competence can be measured in the gain or loss to the organization of the fullest talents of those they manage.

A manager for business research at a global technology company is in charge of two hundred researchers worldwide. Among their critical tasks: to meet with technical experts who have developed new product ideas and decide if the concept should be brought to market; to prod managers of products whose market share is dropping; to guide researchers who are floundering and need direction.

"Feelings run high in these meetings," the manager tells me. "You've got to be reasonable, quell any tense situation, keep your cool. People can be highly excitable when they want to bring a product they've been developing to market, or when they're having problems. But you've got to keep your perspective and present yourself in such a way that you will be trusted and respected.

"Most of our people are MBAs; they've learned the analytic tools," he observes. "But when people come at them with all their fears and problems, they have to be able to take it in stride and take a global perspective. They have the technical tools, but they have to be able to seize the creative idea or offer an actionable, practical path that will turn an idea into a useful product."

Handling an emotional situation demands troubleshooting skills: being able to establish trust and rapport quickly, to listen well, and to persuade and sell a recommendation. As he puts it, "You need capacities like self-awareness, perspective taking, a sense of presence, so you're the person at the table everyone is going to rely on."

Robert Worden, director of business research at Eastman Kodak, agrees: "It's not enough to be able to do a conjoint analysis or sit at your computer excited about a fantastic regression analysis if you're squeamish about presenting those results to an executive group. The ability to relate, to speak up and be heard, to be comfortable with yourself—these are the kinds of abilities that make the crucial difference."

Other ingredients for excellence at Kodak are, in Worden's words: "How well can you present your case? Drive—are you just there eight A.M. to five P.M. and need prodding, or do you have high energy and are willing to make some personal sacrifices? Are you difficult to work with, or are you seen as a natural leader? Then there's diplomacy—do you sense personal and organizational sensitivities? Are you able to take creative risks and adapt? Are you combative, undermining other people's self-confidence, or do you inspire and guide other people? And finally, there's proactivity: Are you action-oriented, following up to impact the business?"

Many top managers at Kodak have come up via market research, including the president, who spent seven years there. But the feel for the market that research gives people is just a start. "Half the skills you need are technical," says Worden. "But the other half are in that softer domain, emotional intelligence. And it's amazing how it's the latter that distinguishes the top performers."

The Rule of Thumb

W orden's observation is borne out by data. In studying hundreds of companies, it became clear to me that the importance of emotional intelligence increases, the higher you go in the organization.

My hunch was borne out in a systematic study of one very large organization—the U.S. government, with more than two million employees. It's one of the few organizations anywhere to have a detailed assessment of the competencies necessary for effective performance in virtually every job.[3] Working with Robert Buchele, a labor economist at Smith College, we found that, indeed, the higher the level of the job, the less important technical skills and cognitive abilities were, and the more important competence in emotional intelligence became.

But government might be a special case. So I again commissioned Hay/McBer to reanalyze their database, this time to assess the importance of emotional competence for executive and leadership positions in business. Based on their research with hundreds of top executives at fifteen global companies—including IBM, PepsiCo, and Volvo—the results were stunning.

Just one cognitive ability distinguished star performers from average: pattern recognition, the "big-picture" thinking that allows leaders to pick out the meaningful trends from the welter of information around them and to think strategically far into the future.[4]

But with this one exception, intellectual or technical superiority played no role in leadership success. At the top executive levels, everyone needs cognitive skills, to a certain extent, but being better at them does not make a star leader.

Rather, emotional competence made the crucial difference between mediocre leaders and the best. The stars showed significantly greater strengths in a range of emotional competencies, among them influence, team leadership, political awareness, self-confidence, and achievement drive. On average, close to *90 percent* of their success in leadership was attributable to emotional intelligence.

To sum up: For star performance in all jobs, in every field, emotional competence is twice as important as purely cognitive abilities.

For success at the highest levels, in leadership positions, emotional competence accounts for virtually the entire advantage.

The Value of Magic

atrick McCarthy is working his retail magic again, this time with Donald Peterson, the retired chairman of Ford Motor Company. Peterson is looking for a certain kind of sport coat in size 43 long, which is difficult to get. He calls McCarthy, a salesman in men's clothing at Nordstrom's flagship store in Seattle, who searches their stock but can't find the jacket. So Peterson keeps asking around at other men's clothing stores, only to find that no one has the jacket.

But a few days later McCarthy calls Peterson: He was able to make a special appeal to his supplier, and so the jacket in the right size is on its way to him.

At a chain famous for customer service, McCarthy is a legend who reigned as the number one sales associate for over fifteen years.[5] McCarthy nurtures his personal customer base of about six thousand shoppers by going beyond merely giving helpful service when they are in the store: He routinely takes it upon himself to call specific customers when merchandise comes in that he thinks they will like. He even phones the family of customers with gift suggestions when the customer has an upcoming birthday or anniversary.

Given that emotional competencies make up two thirds or more of the ingredients of such a standout performance, the data suggests that finding people who have these abilities, or nurturing them in existing employees, adds tremendous value to an organization's bottom line. How much? McCarthy's annual sales of over $1 million compare with an industry average of around $80,000.

The best estimate of the economic value added by such standouts comes from a landmark analysis of thousands of people in jobs ranging from postal clerks to partners in corporate law firms.[6] The study, by the experts in this area, John Hunter (at Michigan State University), Frank Schmidt, and Michael Judiesch (both at the University of Iowa), compared the economic value of top performers like Patrick McCarthy—those in the highest 1 percent—with that of average or poor performers.

That value, they found, increases with the complexity of the job:

- For simpler jobs, like machine operators or clerks, those in the top 1 percent produced three times more output than those in the bottom 1 percent—that is, they were worth three times more.

- For jobs of medium complexity, like sales clerks or mechanics, a top performer was twelve times more productive than those at the bottom. That is, a single person in the top 1 percent was worth twelve people in the bottom 1 percent.

- A different comparison was made for the most complex jobs, like insurance salespeople, account managers, lawyers, and physicians. Those at the top were measured against average performers, rather than against those at the bottom. Even in this case, the added value of a performer in the top 1 percent was 127 percent more.[7]

Competence Pays Most at the Top

A CEO at a subsidiary of a South American conglomerate was promoted to another position, leaving six top managers vying to succeed him. The six fell into a competition that undermined their unity as a management team. The conglomerate called in a consultant to sort out the strengths and weaknesses of the six and thus help them come to a decision.

Manager #1 had the most experience and was the smartest of the bunch; he probably would have been the choice by traditional standards. But Manager #1 had a drawback: He was widely known to lack the personal and social qualities of emotional intelligence.

Manager #2 looked like a strong candidate, too—fairly high in experience, and in emotional intelligence, and very bright. And Manager #3 was a contender, too—highest in emotional intelligence, slightly behind the other two leading candidates in IQ and experience.

The choice?

Manager #3. A key reason was that one chief task of the new CEO was to head the management team and make it work again, a job that demanded a high degree of interpersonal effectiveness. Says the consultant, "The new CEO's very strong emotional intelligence made it easier for the other five managers, who had all been competing for the CEO position, to accept his promotion." Under the new CEO's direction, he adds, the company "has become the most profitable in the country in its sector, and has achieved its highest profitability ever."

To the degree emotional competence spurs such outstanding accomplishment, it understandably pays off most at the top. Because of their financial leverage, executives' performance has a much greater dollar consequence than does that of the clerks who work for them. At the extreme, a brilliant CEO can multiply the earnings of a large company by millions, while a blundering one can sink a company.

In the lower reaches of job complexity there is a more or less direct ratio between a person's cognitive ability and performance, in that a smarter clerk or machine operator will do better than one who is not so bright. But at the higher levels of job complexity—in executive or managerial ranks, or among engineers and scientists, for example—IQ and expertise, as we saw in Chapter 2, do not predict who will be the standout performers; rather, they are largely entry-level barriers.

The immense difference in economic value between top and bottom performers in high-complexity jobs, the Hunter analysis suggests, makes emotional intelligence not simply additive with cognitive ability, but multiplicative: arguably, the hidden ingredient in star performance.

What Exactly Is a Star Worth?

A small group of account managers at RCA were able to increase the size of their accounts each year for tens of millions of dollars more in sales. How? It wasn't because they had more technical expertise than other account managers—it was because they had better people skills.

This case is one of thousands collected by a McClelland protégé, Lyle Spencer Jr., director of research and technology worldwide at Hay/McBer in Boston.[8] The reason for the astounding success of the account managers?

"Just-average account managers were content to spend a minimal amount of time with their clients, just enough to make sure the customers were satisfied," Spencer told me. "But these stars spent lots of time with them, wooing them, going out drinking, telling them about new technologies and product possibilities that would improve their clients' products—so they didn't just keep the account steady, but made more sales. What mattered was relationship building, sensing the client's hot buttons and enthusiasms and knowing how to play to them, and making the match between the client's needs and desires and their product."

One of the more surprising job arenas where emotional intelligence makes a competitive difference is computer programming, where the rate at which the top 10 percent exceed average performers in producing effective programs is 320 percent. And those rare superstars, in the top 1 percent of programmers, produce a boggling 1,272 percent more than the average.[9]

"It's not just computing skills that set apart the stars, but teamwork," says Spencer. "The very best are willing to stay late to help their colleagues finish a project, or to share shortcuts they discover rather than keep them to themselves. They don't compete—they collaborate."

The payoff from top levels of competence can be spectacular. In a study of salespeople in forty-four Fortune 500 firms, including AT&T, IBM, and PepsiCo, Spencer asked sales heads how much better than average their very best salespeople performed. He found that the top 10 percent of the sales force toted up $6.7 million in sales per person, compared to the norm of $3 million—more than twice the average. Given that the typical salary of the sales force at the time was around $42,000, that meant the top performers' value added of $3.7 million was about eighty-eight times their salary![10]

The Tipping Point

Competencies come in clusters. For top performance a person must master a mix of competencies, not just one or two. David McClelland found that stars are not just talented in, say, initiative or influence—they have strengths across the board, including competencies from each of the five emotional intelligence areas: self-awareness, self-regulation, motivation, empathy, and social skills.

Only when they reach a critical mass from the full spectrum do they emerge as outstanding—something akin to a chemical reaction achieving the moment of catalysis. McClelland calls this critical mass the "tipping point."

"Once you reach the tipping point, the probability of your performance being outstanding shoots up," Mary Fontaine of Hay/McBer explained to me about studies with executives at IBM and PepsiCo. "The critical point may be due to how frequently you show the key competencies, or your level of sophistication in them, or how well you can manifest them."

At PepsiCo, those executives who had reached the tipping point—possessing strengths in at least six competencies from across the entire spectrum—were far more likely to perform in the top third as reflected in salary bonuses for performance of the divisions they led. Of those leaders who were strong in six or seven competencies, 87 percent were in the top third.[11]

The competencies predicted success not just at the company's branches in the United States, but around the world; those who reached the tipping point were in the top third 82 percent of the time in Europe and 86 percent of the time in Asia.

Weaknesses in these competencies were often fatal flaws. In Europe, for example, those who lacked strengths in the key competencies had outstanding performance only 13 percent of the time, in Asia just 11 percent, and in America 20 percent.

The emotional competencies that most often led to this level of success were:

- Initiative, achievement drive, and adaptability.

- Influence, team leadership, and political awareness.

- Empathy, self-confidence, and developing others.

Division leaders with these strengths outperformed their targets by 15 to 20 percent; those who lacked them underperformed by almost 20 percent.

The tipping point is important not just for executives; it operates at every level in an organization. One of the more dramatic demonstrations was found at a national insurance company. Those insurance sales agents who were very weak in specific emotional competencies such as self-confidence, initiative, and empathy sold policies with an average premium of $54,000. But those who were very strong in at least five of eight key competencies had remarkable success by comparison, with the average size of policies they sold $114,000.

When Turnover Bleeds the Bottom Line

J ust as there is clear value added from emotional competence, a deficit in these competencies also carries a high price—in turnover. Lyle Spencer estimates that the real cost to a company from the turnover of an employee is the equivalent of one full year of pay. These hidden costs come not just from finding and training replacements, but in customer satisfaction and retention, and in lowered efficiency for everyone who works with the new hire.

When organizations lose many employees, even at low salary levels, the real costs can be substantial. Turnover rates in retail and insurance sales, for example, are estimated to exceed 50 percent per year, mostly among new hires.[12] When the employee who leaves is a highly placed executive, that expense can be enormous. The cost for a company to replace a derailed executive with someone from outside can run into the hundreds of thousands, even millions, of dollars.

At a global consumer beverage firm, when standard methods—which ignored emotional competence—were used to hire division presidents, 50 percent left within two years (most because they were performing poorly) at a total search cost of close to $4 million. But when the firm started to evaluate for competencies such as initiative, self-confidence, leadership, and the like, the retention rate was much greater, with only 6 percent of new division presidents leaving within two years.[13]

Consider three cases, all salespeople in very different kinds of industries.[14] At L'Oréal, the cosmetics giant, sales agents who were selected for their strengths in emotional competence had 63 percent less turnover during their first year than did those whose selection disregarded their competence profile. Among newly hired sales reps at a start-up computer company, those hired for emotional competence were 90 percent more likely to finish their training than those hired on other criteria. And at a national furniture retailer, salespeople hired because of strengths in key emotional competencies had half the dropout rate of those hired on the basis of other standards during their first year on the job.

The Case of the Derailed COO

A fter hearing me give a talk on emotional intelligence, the CEO of a company—one of the ten largest in its market—told me in confidence about why, instead of grooming his chief operating officer of many years to take his place as CEO, he fired him: "He was extraordinarily talented, brilliant conceptually, a very powerful mind. He was great on the computer, knew the numbers up, down, and backward. That's how he got to be chief operating officer.

"But he was not a brilliant leader, not even particularly likable. He was often brutally acerbic. In groups he was socially awkward; he had no social graces, or even a social life. At forty-five, he had nobody he was close to, no friends. He worked all the time. He was one-dimensional; that's why I finally let him go.

"But," the CEO added, "if he could have done just five percent of what you're talking about, he'd still be here."

This example fits well with the conclusions of a landmark study of top executives who derailed.[15] The two most common traits of those who failed:

- *Rigidity:* They were unable to adapt their style to changes in the organizational culture, or they were unable to take in or respond to feedback about traits they needed to change or improve. They couldn't listen or learn.

- *Poor relationships:* The single most frequently mentioned factor: being too harshly critical, insensitive, or demanding, so that they alienated those they worked with.

These traits proved fatal handicaps even to brilliant executives with strong technical expertise. One executive described a derailed colleague this way: "He's a great strategic thinker and he has high ethical standards, but he lashes out at people. He's very smart, but he achieves superiority through demeaning others. Many people have tried to help him work on this flaw, but it seems hopeless."[16]

The opposite of rigidity is adaptability. "Leadership agility, the ability to work with different styles and with people at all levels of the organization, from the sales rep on the street to top management, demands empathy and emotional self-management. You need agility in leadership and in learning," Patrick O'Brien, formerly vice president for North American sales at Johnson Wax, tells me. "We find an absence of this kind of agility is a top derailer for people we seek to develop."

Sharp differences emerged between the successful managers and those who derailed on most major dimensions of emotional competence.[17]

- *Self-control:* Those who derailed handled pressure poorly and were prone to moodiness and angry outbursts. The successful

stayed composed under stress, remaining calm and confident—
and dependable—in the heat of crises.

- *Conscientiousness:* The derailed group reacted to failure and
  criticism defensively—denying, covering up, or passing on the
  blame. The successful took responsibility by admitting their
  mistakes and failures, taking action to fix the problems, and
  moving on without ruminating about their lapse.

- *Trustworthiness:* The failures typically were overly ambitious,
  too ready to get ahead at the expense of other people. The
  successes had high integrity, with a strong concern for the needs
  of their subordinates and colleagues, and for the demands of the
  task at hand, giving these higher priority than impressing their
  own boss at any cost.

- *Social skills:* The failures lacked empathy and sensitivity, and so
  were often abrasive, arrogant, or given to intimidation of
  subordinates. While some were charming on occasion, even
  seeming concerned about others, the charm was purely
  manipulative. The successes were empathic and sensitive,
  showing tact and consideration in their dealings with everyone,
  superiors and subordinates alike.

- *Building bonds and leveraging diversity:* The insensitivity and
  manipulative manner of the failed group meant that they failed
  to build a strong network of cooperative, mutually beneficial
  relationships. The successes were more appreciative of diversity,
  able to get along with people of all kinds.

Talents for These Times: The Global View

Claudio Fernández-Aráoz, in charge of executive searches throughout
Latin America from Egon Zehnder International's Buenos Aires office,
compared 227 highly successful executives with 23 who failed in their
jobs.[18] He found that the managers who failed were almost always high in
expertise and IQ. In every case their fatal weakness was in emotional intelligence—arrogance, overreliance on brainpower, inability to adapt to the occasionally disorienting economic shifts in that region, and disdain for
collaboration or teamwork.

Parallel analyses of successful and failed managers in Germany and Japan revealed the same pattern: Those who failed had their largest deficit in the emotional intelligence competencies, and their failure came despite strengths in expertise and cognitive abilities. In Germany, three quarters of failed managers showed a major deficit in emotional intelligence; in Japan a little more than half did so.[19]

In Latin America a deficit in emotional intelligence seems to imply almost certain failure. That is not so strongly the case in Germany or Japan—yet. As Fernández-Aráoz told me, "Latin America has seen a huge rate of change in recent years—hyperinflation, political turmoil, shifts from controlled to open economies. Things change radically, sometimes almost every day. Your experience is not as crucial as your adaptability. You need close contact with everybody you work with, your customers, your suppliers—everyone—just to keep track of what's going on. There are new forms of organization, new mergers and coalitions, new technologies, new rules. We've found that a lack of emotional intelligence in such an unstable environment means certain failure. And that's everyone's future."

Or, as summed up by Kevin Murray, director of communications at British Airways: "Organizations going through the greatest change are those who need emotional intelligence the most."

The Peter Principle:
Too Much College, Too Little Kindergarten

A young engineer who had earned straight A's in school came to work at an environmental engineering company but was fired within a relatively short period of time. The reason? "He was brilliant at his work," his manager told me, "but he couldn't take direction. His supervisor would tell him how to do a design, and he'd do it his own way. When his supervisor would point out how the design didn't conform to the specifications, he'd get defensive. He couldn't take feedback—he acted as though it were a personal criticism.

"When other engineers would ask him to help, he'd turn them down, saying he was too busy with his own part of the project. He created so much animosity that when he needed some help, no one wanted to give it to him."

High IQ and technical expertise can have a paradoxical effect among seemingly promising people who fail. In a study of once-successful managers who failed, most were technically brilliant.[20] And their technical skills were often the very reason they were promoted into management in the first place.

But once they reached higher positions, their technical strength became a liability: Arrogance led some to offend their peers by acting superior, others to micromanage subordinates—even those with better technical expertise.

This is the Peter Principle at work: People are promoted to their level of incompetence. A person who is promoted because of expertise ("He's great with the numbers") finds himself at a new level, where many or most duties revolve around managing people—not technical skill. This means the working world is peppered with bad bosses.

The Peter Principle does much to explain why so many people who are abrasive, thoughtless, and otherwise interpersonally inept are in so many positions of power in organizations everywhere. The classic mistake is assuming that if someone has a special expertise, it necessarily means they also have the ability to lead. "I call it the Michael Jordan effect," Paul Robinson, director of Sandia National Laboratories, tells me. "I see it all the time in science labs: A top executive leaves and you immediately turn to the best scientist as the replacement.

"But it's as if the Chicago Bulls lost a coach and appointed Michael Jordon to replace him. He's a brilliant basketball player, of course, but the game comes so naturally to him that he may not be very good at coaching other players—he probably never even thinks about how he does what he does. So how well are the Bulls going to do as a team when Michael Jordan is on the bench, not on the court? It's the same with us—we need those outstanding scientists in the lab, not in the office."

To avoid the problem, "We set up two tracks, recognizing that some people are excellent technical professionals and like their work, but terrible managers and dislike management as a career," Ira Stepanian, retired CEO of BankBoston, told me. "Without the people skills they would never succeed at the top levels of management. We tried to spare them the failure of the Peter Principle by keeping them in a professional track."

Again, the principle applies to jobs of every sort. Take, for example, Patrick McCarthy, the star sales associate at Nordstrom. Early in his career McCarthy was promoted to department manager—a post he left after a year and a half to return to sales.[21] As he put it: "Sales was what I was good at and felt comfortable with."

The Computer Nerd: Trained Incapacity

People in information technology are notorious for having high levels of technical skills, but not getting along with people so well," an executive at Hitachi Data Systems told me. "They tend to lack certain skills, like empathy and social abilities. Folks in information tech divisions are famous in our industry for not getting along with people in other parts of their companies."

I used to think that such pronouncements reflected a cultural misperception, a negative stereotype of the "computer nerd." Underlying my assumption was my belief that emotional intelligence and IQ were essentially independent.

But a friend on the faculty at MIT argues that at the extreme high end of the IQ scale, there is often a lack of social skills. "Trained incapacity" is the term used by Stephen Rosen, himself a theoretical physicist, and now head of a project to study why some scientists' careers founder.[22] "The smarter they are, very often the less competent they are emotionally and in handling people. It's as though the IQ muscle strengthened itself at the expense of muscles for personal and social competence."

Mastery of these technical pursuits demands long hours spent working alone, often beginning in childhood or the early teen years—a period of life when, ordinarily, people learn vital social skills from interacting with friends. Self-selection plays a role, too. People who are attracted to fields typified by very high levels of cognitive effort, like computer science or engineering, are sometimes drawn "in part because you don't have to deal with your emotions," points out Robert E. Kelley, a psychologist at Carnegie-Mellon University. "This is why nerds are drawn to fields like engineering—you can be reclusive, get by with few social graces, as long as you do well on the cognitive side."

This does not mean, of course, that all high-IQ scientists are socially incompetent. But it does mean that emotional intelligence abilities will pay off with special strength in such careers, where the pool of potential standout managers—people with both high science skills and high social skills—may be relatively small.

In an unusual study begun at the University of California at Berkeley in the 1950s, eighty Ph.D. students in science went through an intensive battery of IQ and personality tests, as well as extensive interviews with psychologists who evaluated them on such qualities as emotional balance and maturity, integrity, and interpersonal effectiveness.[23]

Forty years later, when the former students were in their early seventies, researchers tracked them down again. In the 1994 follow-up, estimates were made of each person's career success on the basis of résumés, evaluations by experts in their own field, and sources like *American Men and Women of Science*. The result: Emotional intelligence abilities were about *four times* more important than IQ in determining professional success and prestige—even for these scientists.

As an engineer who formerly worked at Exxon told me, "What made the difference there wasn't your grade point average—everyone there had done well in school. The difference was in personal qualities like perseverance, finding a mentor, being willing to put in more hours and try harder." Or, as Ernest O. Lawrence, the Nobel laureate who founded the labs at Berkeley that bear his name, put it, "In scientific work, excellence is not about technical competence, but character."[24]

Help Wanted: Techies with Passion and Intuition

Such realizations have spurred a growing movement among graduate schools to ensure that budding engineers and scientists come into the working world with stronger emotional intelligence skills. Phil Weilerstein, director of the National Collegiate Inventors and Innovators Alliance, told me, "The skills engineers will need in the future are different from what they have been trained for: to sit in a cubicle at General Dynamics and design propeller blades. They need to be nimble enough to change jobs every three, four, five years. They need to know how to develop and execute ideas as a part of a team, how to sell an idea, take criticism and feedback, adapt. Engineering education has ignored this range of skills in the past. It can't afford to in the future."

As John Seely Brown, director of Xerox Corporation's Silicon Valley R&D facility, said to me, "I raise eyebrows when I tell people that we don't go out of our way to hire the brightest people—in all the years here, I've never looked at anyone's university transcript. The two competencies we look for the most are grounded intuitions and a passion for making an impact. We want people who are bold but grounded."

But what does it mean to be intuitive, passionate, bold but grounded—to display emotional intelligence? What *are* the human capabilities that matter most for on-the-job effectiveness?

Answering these questions in precise detail will be the next stop in our exploration of what it means to work with emotional intelligence.

Self-Mastery

4

·················

The Inner Rudder

A good friend, a physician, was once offered a business proposition: If he would leave his practice to become medical director of a fledgling condominium health resort and invest $100,000 of his own capital in the venture, his projected share of the business would amount to $4 million within three years. Or so the business plan promised.

My friend liked the vision of a resort where people could improve their health as they vacationed; coupled with the lure of a possibly fantastic pay-off, he couldn't resist. He sold his medical practice, invested in the resort, and became its medical director. But during that start-up year he found that there was no medical program to direct yet—he ended up spending his days essentially as a salesman, trying to interest people in buying time-share condos at the resort.

One day, as he was driving to work at his new job, he found himself—to his astonishment—pounding the dashboard of his car and yelling, "I can't do this! I can't do this!" Pulling over, my friend took a few moments to get a grip on his tumultuous feelings, calmed down, and drove on to work.

A year later the resort was bankrupt—and so was he.

He admits now that he had a gut feeling from the outset that there was something wrong with the proposition, that the projections in the business plan were too rosy, and that the scheme was really about real estate development, not preventive medicine. But at the time he had been craving a change. And the financial incentives looked so promising that he buried his misgivings—much to his later regret.

Life more often than not presents us with murky decisions, nothing like the clear, neat "if this, then that" matrices taught in classes on risk analysis and decision making. That approach is oversold as a way to make the real, day-to-day choices we face at work: which person to promote, which company to merge with, what marketing strategy to follow, or whether a proffered business deal should be accepted. When it comes to decisions like these, our gut feelings—our deepest sense of what *feels* right and what is "off"—provide critical information that we must not ignore, lest we regret our choices a month or a year down the road.

Beyond the Pros and Cons

The deal my friend accepted looked good—on paper. But far more important than the financial projections were intangibles such as the trustworthiness and abilities of the people he was allying himself with. Though there are no easily quantifiable ways of measuring such important aspects of a decision, we do nevertheless have an immense amount of relevant "data" in the form of hunches. And, as my friend did, we ignore such data at our own risk.

Of sixty highly successful entrepreneurs connected with companies having revenues ranging from $2 million to $400 million, just one said his business decisions were made using only the classic decision-tree methods—and even he added that his final decision was still made intuitively.[1] The others all either used their feelings to confirm (or disconfirm) a rational analysis or let their emotions guide them at the outset and subsequently looked for data or a rationale that supported their gut hunch.

One entrepreneur told me, "The first step is to work it out step by step, consciously and deliberately, very analytically . . . but at the same time the emotional side is doing something. I think you need both."

Another pointed to the fallacy of trying to make decisions purely rationally, what he called the "yellow pad theory": "When you do that and you're completely objective . . . all you really have are cold statistics. But inside, it's almost as if you had a meter that measures all of that data. . . . The needle is measuring feeling. Sometimes the brain says, 'Well, that's going to make a lot of people ticked off,' or whatever, and yet this sixth sense says, 'Yeah, but it feels right.' And I have learned to trust that."

The Source of Gut Feeling

The ability to read such subjective currents has primordial roots in evolution. The brain areas involved in gut feelings are far more ancient than the thin layers of the neocortex, the centers for rational thought that enfold the very top of the brain. Hunches start much deeper in the brain. They are a function of the emotional centers that ring the brain stem atop the spinal cord—most particularly an almond-shaped structure called the amygdala and its connected neural circuitry. This web of connectivity, sometimes called the extended amygdala, stretches up to the brain's executive center in the prefrontal lobes, just behind the forehead.[2]

The brain stores different aspects of an experience in different areas—the source of a memory is encoded in one zone, the sights and sounds and smells in other areas, and so on. The amygdala is the site where the emotions an experience evokes are stored. Every experience that we have an emotional reaction to, no matter how subtle, seems to be encoded in the amygdala.[3]

As the repository for everything we feel about what we experience, the amygdala constantly signals us with this information. Whenever we have a preference of any kind, whether for ordering the risotto rather than the sea bass special, or a compelling sense that we should dump our shares in a stock, that is a message from the amygdala. And via the amygdala's related circuitry, particularly nerve pathways that run into the viscera, we can have a somatic response—literally, a "gut feeling"—to the choices we face.

This capacity, like other elements of emotional intelligence, can grow stronger with the accumulating experiences life brings us. As one successful entrepreneur in a University of Southern California study described it: "It's a *kinesthetic* feel that some people have. I think that there are fewer people with strong intuitions at a young age than old, because life experiences add up. . . . It's like your gut tells you things and there's a chemical reaction that's going on in your body, which is triggered by your mind, and tightening your stomach muscles, so your gut is saying, 'This doesn't feel right.' "

The classic term for this strengthening of our guiding sensibility is *wisdom*. And, as we shall see, people who ignore or discount messages from this repository of life's wisdom do so at their peril.

The Lawyer Who Couldn't Decide

r. Antonio Damasio, a neurologist at the University of Iowa, had a patient who was a brilliant corporate lawyer. Some years earlier, this man had been diagnosed with a small tumor in his prefrontal lobes. Surgery was successful—except that the surgeon accidentally cut the circuits connecting the lawyer's prefrontal lobes with the amygdala. The results were puzzling—and dramatic. On the one hand, the lawyer had no discernible cognitive deficits. On the other, he became inept at work, lost his job, and was unable to keep another. He ended up out of work; his wife left him; he lost his house.[4]

The lawyer went to Damasio for help. Looking over the results of his neuropsychological tests, which were all normal, Damasio was baffled at first. Then one day he noticed that when he asked the innocent question, "When should we have our next appointment?" the lawyer was capable of giving him the rational pros and cons for every possible hour for the next two weeks—but had no idea which of those hours was best.

Damasio realized the flaw: The lawyer had no *feelings* about his thoughts, and so no preferences. Damasio's conclusion was that our minds are not designed like a computer, to give us a neat printout of the rational arguments for and against a decision in life based on all the previous times we've faced a similar situation. Instead, the mind does something much more elegant: It weighs the *emotional* bottom line from those previous experiences and delivers the answer to us in a hunch, a gut feeling.

This sense of rightness or wrongness deep in the body is part of a steady background flow of feeling that continues throughout the day. Just as there is a stream of thought, there is a parallel stream of feeling. The notion that there is "pure thought," rationality devoid of feeling, is a fiction, an illusion based on inattention to the subtle moods that follow us through the day. We have feelings about everything we do, think about, imagine, remember. Thought and feeling are inextricably woven together.

Such fleeting feelings are typically subtle, but important. Not that gut feeling outweighs the facts—but it should be weighed in *with* the facts. Attunement to feelings offers us crucial information for navigating through life. This sense of "rightness" or "wrongness" signals that what we are doing either does or does not fit our preferences, guiding values, and life wisdom.

The Power of Intuition: The First Thirty Seconds

Credit managers must sense when a deal might go bad even if the numbers look fine; executives have to decide whether a new product is worth the time and money it takes to develop; people must make an educated guess about who among a field of candidates for a job will have the best chemistry in a working group. All such decisions demand the capacity to fold into the decision-making process our intuitive sense of what is right and wrong.

Indeed, among three thousand executives in a study of decision making, those at the top in a wide range of fields were most adept at utilizing intuition in reaching their decisions.[5] As one highly successful entrepreneur put it, "An intuitive decision is nothing but a subconscious logical analysis. . . . Somehow the brain goes through these calculations and comes up with what we would call a weighted conclusion—it seems more right to do it this way than that way."[6]

Intuition may play its biggest role in work life when it comes to people. Bjorn Johansson, head of a Zurich executive search firm specializing in placing top-level executives with multinational firms, told me, "This business is intuition from A to Z. First you have to assess a company's chemistry—size up the CEO, his personal qualities and expectations, the tone he sets, and the resulting culture of the corporation. I have to understand how the management team works, how they deal with each other. There's what you might call a 'smell' to every corporation, a distinctive quality you can sense."

Having registered that "smell," Johansson then sizes up prospective job candidates accordingly. The key judgment is intuitive: "I know within thirty seconds of meeting someone whether this person's chemistry fits with my client. Of course I need to also analyze his career, his references, and the like. Still, if he doesn't pass the first barrier, my intuitive sense, I don't bother. But if my brains, heart, and gut all say this is the right person, that's who I recommend."

That fits with data from studies at Harvard: People can sense intuitively in the first thirty seconds of an encounter what basic impression they will have of the other person after fifteen minutes—or half a year. For instance, when people watch just thirty-second snatches of teachers giving a lecture, they can assess each teacher's proficiency with about 80 percent accuracy.[7]

Such instantaneous intuitive astuteness may be the remnant of an essential early warning system for danger, one that lives on today in feelings such as apprehension. Gavin deBecker, a specialist in security arrangements for celebrities, calls apprehension a "gift of fear."[8] This radar for danger alerts us with a primal feeling that something is "off."

■ ■ ■

Intuition and gut feeling bespeak the capacity to sense messages from our internal store of emotional memory—our own reservoir of wisdom and judgment. This ability lies at the heart of self-awareness, and self-awareness is the vital foundation skill for three emotional competencies:

- *Emotional awareness:* The recognition of how our emotions affect our performance, and the ability to use our values to guide decision making

- *Accurate self-assessment:* A candid sense of our personal strengths and limits, a clear vision of where we need to improve, and the ability to learn from experience

- *Self-confidence:* The courage that comes from certainty about our capabilities, values, and goals

■ EMOTIONAL AWARENESS ■

Recognizing One's Emotions and Their Effects

People with this competence

- Know which emotions they are feeling and why

- Realize the links between their feelings and what they think, do, and say

- Recognize how their feelings affect their performance

- Have a guiding awareness of their values and goals

He's a candidate to become a partner at a huge Wall Street investment banking firm. And he's in trouble.

"He's made it by virtue of conquering everything and everyone in his way," said the psychiatrist his company had him consult. "But he uses this warrior's ruthlessness when it just doesn't apply. He gets irritated way too easily, without any sense that his anger is making him treat people in an abrasive way. No one wants to work with him or for him. He just doesn't have any awareness at all of how his emotions are pushing him around."

That awareness—of how our emotions affect what we are doing—is the fundamental emotional competence. Lacking that ability, we are vulnerable, like the investment banker, to being sidetracked by emotions run amok. Such awareness is our guide in fine-tuning on-the-job performance of every kind, managing our unruly feelings, keeping ourselves motivated, tuning in with accuracy to the feelings of those around us, and developing good work-related social skills, including those essential for leadership and teamwork.

Perhaps it's no surprise that outstanding counselors and psychotherapists demonstrate this skill. "It's a focusing ability, knowing the internal meters and subtle signals that tell you what you're feeling, and using them as an ongoing guide to how you're doing," says Richard Boyatzis, who studied self-awareness in counselors.

The same skill comes into play in most jobs, particularly those that involve dealing with people about any sort of sensitive matter. For instance, at American Express Financial Advisors, financial advisors' awareness of their own emotions is a competence central to excellent performance in that job.[9] The interaction between a planner and client is delicate, dealing not only with hard questions about money, but also, when life insurance comes up, the even more sensitive issue of mortality.

The company found these interactions rife with feelings of distress, uneasiness, and distrust, all too often ignored in the haste to make a sale. American Express realized they would have to help their financial advisors tune in to this sea of feeling and handle it effectively in order to better serve their clients.

As we'll see in Chapter 11, when financial advisors at American Express were trained to be more emotionally self-aware and to have more empathy for their clients, they were better able to build long-term, trusting relationships. And those relationships translated into higher sales per customer.

Emotional awareness starts with attunement to the stream of feeling that is a constant presence in all of us and with a recognition of how these emotions shape what we perceive, think, and do. From that awareness comes another: that our feelings affect those we deal with. For financial planners, this means knowing that their own emotions can reverberate in the interaction with clients—for better or worse (more on this in Chapter 7).

A person excelling in this competence is aware of her emotions at any given moment—often recognizing how those emotions feel physically. She can articulate those feelings, as well as demonstrate social appropriateness in expressing them.

American Express Financial Advisors recognized that their planners needed not just an awareness of feelings, but also an ability to sense whether their own work-life, health, and family concerns are in balance, as well as the capacity to align work with personal values and goals—all, as we shall see, abilities that build on self-awareness.

The Stream of Feeling

Our background stream of feeling runs in perfect parallel to our stream of thought. We always feel some mood or other, though we typically do not tune in to the subtle moods that ebb and flow as we go through our daily routine: the sullen or cheery feeling we wake up with, the slight irritation that a frustrating commute to work triggers, the hundreds or even thousands of large and small emotions that come and go with the day's ups and downs.

In the rush and pressure of our work days, our minds are preoccupied by the stream of thought—planning the next thing, immersion in our present task, preoccupation with things undone. It takes a mental pause to become sensitive to the subterranean murmur of mood—a moment we rarely take. Our feelings are always with us, but we are too seldom with them. Instead, we typically become aware of emotions only when they build up and boil over. But if we are attentive, we can experience them at subtler levels long before they emerge so strongly.

The rhythm and pace of modern life give us too little time to assimilate, reflect, and react. Our bodies are geared to a slower rhythm. We need time to be introspective, but we don't get it—or don't take it. Emotions have their own agenda and timetable, but our rushed lives give them no space, no airtime—and so they go underground. All of this mental pressure crowds out a quieter inner voice that offers an inner rudder of conviction we could use to navigate through life.

People who are unable to know their feelings are at a tremendous disadvantage. In a sense, they are emotional illiterates, oblivious to a realm of reality that is crucial for success in life as a whole, let alone work.

For some, emotional "tone deafness" takes the form of obliviousness to the messages their bodies are trying to send—in the form of chronic headaches, lower back pain, anxiety attacks—that something is amiss. At the other extreme are those with alexithymia, the psychiatric term for people with a confused awareness of their own feelings. For such people, the outer world is clearer and more detailed than their own inner universe. Such people blur distinctions among emotions, whether benign or unpleasant, and have a constricted emotional range, particularly sparse in positive moods like happiness. For them the nuances of emotion are elusive, and so they are unable to use a gut sense to guide their thinking and action.

But self-awareness can be cultivated. Edward McCracken, former CEO of Silicon Graphics, who affirms the ability to include the intuitive in decision making, says, "In our industry very often we don't have time to think. You have to do all your homework, but then you have to go with your intuition without letting your mind get in the way." McCracken's method of allowing his intuitive feelings space? He's been meditating daily for a decade.[10]

His approach is a time-honored way to get in touch with our deeper, quieter voice of feeling: taking time out to "do nothing." Doing nothing productively means not only not working, but also not filling the time with idle time wasters: watching TV, say, or, even worse, doing something else while watching TV. Instead it means putting aside for the time being all other goal-oriented activities and doing something that opens our minds to a deeper, quieter sensibility.

Living by the Inner Rudder

Richard Abdoo has a resolution: No matter how busy his work gets, he reserves eight hours a week for solitary reflection.[11] As CEO of Wisconsin Energy, a $2-billion-a-year utility company, that resolution takes some effort. A devout Catholic, Abdoo often uses those hours for long walks. Or sometimes his contemplative time takes other forms, like working in his home shop—or riding his Harley. "You have to force yourself to spend some time away from the hustle and bustle of your job in order to get down to reality again," Abdoo explains. "If you don't spend enough time doing that, you can lose hold of the reins and get into all kinds of trouble."

What kind of trouble? Drifting away from our guiding values, for one. Personal values are not lofty abstractions, but intimate credos that we may never quite articulate in words so much as *feel*. Our values translate into what has emotional power or resonance for us, whether negative or positive.

Self-awareness serves as an inner barometer, gauging whether what we are doing (or are about to do) is, indeed, worthwhile. Feelings give the essential reading. If there is a discrepancy between action and value, the result will be uneasiness in the form of guilt or shame, deep doubts or nagging second thoughts, queasiness or remorse, and the like. Such uneasiness acts as an emotional drag, stirring feelings that can hinder or sabotage our efforts.

Choices made in keeping with this inner rudder, on the other hand, are energizing. They not only feel right but maximize the attention and energy available for pursuing them. In a study of "knowledge workers" (in this case, engineers, computer programmers, and auditors), the star performers made career choices that let them work with their own sense of meaning intact or enhanced, where they felt a sense of accomplishment and believed they made a contribution.[12]

While average workers were content to take on whatever project they were assigned, superior performers thought about what project would be invigorating to work on, which person would be stimulating to work under, which personal idea would make a good project. They knew intuitively what they did best and enjoyed—and what they did not. Their performance excelled because they were able to make choices that kept them focused and energized.

People who follow their inner sense of what is worthwhile minimize emotional static for themselves. Unfortunately, too many people feel that they cannot speak up for their deep values at work, that such a thing is somehow impermissible.

The silence about values skews the collective sense of what motivates people, making money alone seems to loom much larger than it actually is for many of us. In the University of Southern California study of sixty highly successful entrepreneurs, ostentatious displays of wealth were rare. What motivated these successful entrepreneurs more than money, the report concluded, were things like the excitement and challenge of starting a business, the freedom of being the boss, the chance to be creative, and the opportunity to help others by helping themselves.

Except for the financially desperate, people do not work for money alone. What also fuels their passion for work is a larger sense of purpose or passion. Given the opportunity, people gravitate to what gives them meaning, to what engages to the fullest their commitment, talent, energy, and skill. And that can mean changing jobs to get a better fit with what matters to us.

Managing Your Career

The drive to establish ourselves and make our mark in the world is most urgent in our twenties and thirties, and into our forties. But by our mid-forties or early fifties people typically reevaluate their goals, because they often come to the radical realization that life is limited. With this acknowledgment of mortality comes a reconsideration of what really matters.

"By midlife, there are many, many corporate executives and lawyers pulling down seven-figure salaries who wish instead they were doing social work or running a restaurant," says Stephen Rosen, who counsels professionals who are trying to find more fulfilling livelihoods—or who have no choice, having lost a job.

A consultant who has assessed top executives at firms such as General Electric, DEC, and Mobil Oil tells me that many at midlife are "highly excited about pet projects—being on a school board, a small business they're running on the side. But they're bored by their own job." One highly successful entrepreneur who had started a series of businesses found himself running one he hated: "This company is at the point where it controls me. I'm stuck. . . . I don't like what I'm doing. I'm much happier fixing the engine on my boat or something, but not this."[13]

As the saying goes, "If you don't know where you're going, any road will get you there." The less aware we are of what makes us passionate, the more lost we will be. And this drifting can even affect our health; people who feel their skills are not being used well on the job, or who feel their work is repetitive and boring, have a higher risk of heart disease than those who feel that their best skills are expressed in their work.[14]

Self-awareness offers a sure rudder for keeping our career decisions in harmony with our deepest values. "Some women executives have suppressed their self-awareness to get where they are," Kathy Kram, a professor of management at Boston University, told me. "These are high-achieving women who end up in senior management, but who suffer from relationship deprivation. Their connections are instrumental, goal-oriented—the pattern more typical of men. The cost for them is that their personal lives wither."

This problem is by no means limited to women. "Many executives, especially males, have never really thought it important to educate themselves about their interior landscape," Michael Banks, a New York–based executive coach with KRW International, tells me. "They never made the connection between how they behave under stress and their ability to retain loyalty and talent or meet the bottom line. They may be moving into their late forties and get an inkling that something's been missing. It might be triggered by a marriage falling apart or by finding they're making mistakes because of their inner turmoil." But these can be fruitful crises: "It starts to crack open their hard veneer—they start to feel emotions they never let themselves feel before, and to take a new look at that side of their lives."

Attention: Our Most Precious Resource

He was the managing partner of a prosperous corporate law firm, wealthy and accomplished. But at fifty, something was gnawing at him.

"He had always believed by the time he was fifty he would have more freedom and flexibility in his life," Shoshana Zuboff, a psychologist and professor at the Harvard Business School, told me about the lawyer. "But instead he saw himself a slave to billable hours, to the needs of his partners and demands of his clients. His success was his own prison."

That reality came home to him as he made the journey through Odyssey, a unique program of self-reflection.[15] Developed by Zuboff, the program was first offered only to alumni of the Harvard Business School, but by virtue of its popularity, it is now available to other businesspeople and professionals at midlife. The enthusiasm for Odyssey stems in large part from the chance it gives people to closely examine their lives by using their deepest feelings to find answers to questions like "Who am I?" "Where am I going?" and "What do I want?"

The people who participate, says Zuboff, tend to be very successful, having achieved the goals they set for themselves in their twenties and thirties. But they're looking forward to two or three decades more of productive work life and are asking, "What's next?"

The standard approach to that question "encourages us to look at our work lives from the outside—how to make yourself a more attractive commodity, how to market yourself—and to think in terms of external variables, like what's the salary or position or city a job is in, how am I doing compared to my peers? We take the opposite approach, looking from the inside out at our changing sense of self and what constitutes fulfillment," Zuboff says.

For many of those in Odyssey, their careers have become like a train—pulling them along without giving them the time or space to decide if they really want to be going down that track. Odyssey gives people a chance to look within and reflect on their journey. The first week of the program helps focus people on paying attention to their inner world, and how they feel about what they are doing or would like to do—followed by three weeks off, to further digest and reflect, and then another week where they and their spouse come back to work out a plan for the future.

"People have to stop thinking of their feelings as irrelevant and messy, and realize they are in fact highly differentiated, nuanced patterns of reaction, knowable sources of information," Zuboff explains. "We only will know what to do by realizing what feels right to us. Attention is our most precious resource. Feelings are the body's version of the situation; everything we want to know about our situation is revealed in our feelings. The big switch for businesspeople comes when they realize what they thought was soft is hard, and what they thought was hard is often arbitrary. In this sense, feelings are guides to the big issues, like 'Where am I going?'"

For the disgruntled lawyer, the week of reflection led to the realization, recounts Zuboff, that he no longer needed the law firm in the way he once did, though his partners still derived their main sense of identity from it. He was living for other people's expectations. His real pleasure came from a cattle-trading business he ran on the side with his son. Though the enterprise had started as a hobby, he found it engrossing, challenging, and fun.

With this self-knowledge, he resolved to reduce his billable hours by 50 percent over the course of two or three years and spend the other half of his time trading cattle. The result: Two years later he had done just that, plus started up two other businesses—and he made more from cattle sales in six months than he had in two years at the law firm.

More important, said Zuboff, "He's happy. He'd been someone who dreaded getting up in the morning and going to work. Now he's excited, reenergized, renewed."

■ ACCURATE SELF-ASSESSMENT ■

Knowing One's Inner Resources, Abilities, and Limits

People with this competence are

■ Aware of their strengths and weaknesses

■ Reflective, learning from experience

■ Open to candid feedback, new perspectives, continuous learning, and self-development

■ Able to show a sense of humor and perspective about
themselves

■ ■

Mort Meyerson's awakening started when he accepted an invitation to become CEO of Perot Systems, a computer services company. In the first six months at his new job he began to realize that, compared to the organizational world he had known years earlier as CEO of the computer services giant EDS, everything was different—not just the technology, the market, and the customers, but also the people who worked for him and their reasons for working.

He realized that he too must change. As he wrote about it in a surprisingly revealing and introspective article, "Everything I thought I knew about leadership was wrong. My first job as a leader was to create a new understanding of myself."[16]

Meyerson went through what he describes as a time of "intense self-examination," wrestling with questions that went to the heart of the leadership style he had prided himself on. He came to see that during his years running EDS, he had been both extremely successful and extremely ruthless. To be sure, under his stewardship EDS saw profits climb every quarter without exception, making many employees with equity wealthy, but in looking back, Meyerson also saw that he had created immense personal misery for his employees even as he made them rich. At EDS eighty-hour work weeks were typical, people were shuffled from place to place without a second thought about the disruptions it might cause in their lives—and no questioning was tolerated. The employees' term for assignments there was "death march"; the cultural tone was, as Meyerson put it, "young, male, and military."

While at EDS, Meyerson headed a fifty-person team designing the federal system for processing Medicare claims, with everyone working eighteen-hour days in order to meet a deadline. One day, despite a heavy snow, every member of the team made it in to work except for one, Max Hopper. Meyerson, furious, called him up and bawled him out. Hopper left the company at the first opportunity—and went on to revolutionize the airline reservation industry with his invention of the SABRE computerized reservation system.

Recalling his alienation of Hopper, a brilliant, talented employee, Meyerson admitted he was too quick to make harsh judgments, too slow to see things from other people's perspectives. Reflecting on the human cost of his old style years later, Meyerson came to realize that what he had considered strengths were now more clearly identifiable as weaknesses. For example, at EDS his communications with employees were in the old hierarchical model: "I showed up onstage every six months and delivered a pep rally speech." His memos went only to the top dozen people; he had virtually no contact with the rest of his employees.

With the realization that a leader today needs to be receptive to honest, direct messages from anywhere and everywhere in a company, Meyerson changed his ways. He got an e-mail address that received thousands of messages a month—all of which he read—from all over the company. He even fired off a congratulatory e-mail to a team that made a competitive sale— and did so within an hour of their victory.

"Before you can lead others, before you can help others, you have to discover yourself," says Joe Jaworski, formerly with Royal Dutch/Shell's scenario planning group.[17] "If you want a creative explosion to take place, if you want the kind of performance that leads to truly exceptional results, you have to be willing to embark on a journey that leads to an alignment between an individual's personal values and aspirations and the values and aspirations of the company."

Blind Spots

Harry was a top manager at a company that had begun a major campaign to flatten the corporate hierarchy and give employees the authority to make critical decisions. Harry had all the right rhetoric about "sharing power" and delegating authority—he just couldn't do it when any hint of a crisis arose.

When things were going well, Harry was actually fairly good about handing down responsibility to his staff, who were extremely competent. But at the least whiff of an emergency, Harry grabbed the reins, rebuffing anyone else's advice or efforts. This not only undermined the company's initiative to push power down the line, but it damaged the self-confidence of Harry's staff. And his incessant talk about the virtues of sharing power while actually taking it back corroded his credibility.

"Unfortunately, Harry couldn't see the contradiction, even when a subordinate had the nerve to point it out to him," says Robert E. Kaplan, formerly of the Center for Creative Leadership.[18] "The first step in improving one's performance is to identify a need for improvement, but, as in Harry's case, such self-knowledge can be extremely difficult to come by."

Being blind to our problem areas can put our career at risk. In a comparison of executives who derailed and those who did well, *both* groups had weaknesses; the critical difference was that those who did not succeed failed to learn from their mistakes and shortcomings.[19] The unsuccessful executives were far less open to acknowledging their own faults, often rebuffing people who tried to point them out. This resistance meant they could do nothing to change them.

Among several hundred managers from twelve different organizations, accuracy in self-assessment was a hallmark of superior performance, something poorer performers lacked.[20] It's not that star performers have no limits on their abilities, but that they are *aware* of their limits—and so they know where they need to improve, or they know to work with someone else who has a strength they lack.

Our Strengths—and Our Weaknesses

He was promoted to the top tier of a large manufacturing company, bringing with him a reputation as a kick-ass turnaround artist because of the ruthless reengineering and job cutting he had conducted in the past. "He never smiled—there was a scowl on his face all the time," Kathryn Williams, an executive coach with KRW International, told me. "He was always impatient and quick to anger. When people brought bad news, he would attack the messenger, so people stopped telling him things. He had no idea he frightened people. His gruff, intimidating demeanor may have worked while he was the turnaround artist, but now it was undermining him."

Williams was called in to consult with the executive. She videotaped him in action and then replayed the tape for him, pointing out the effect his habitual forbidding facial expression had on people. It was a revelation: "When he realized how he was coming across, he got tears in his eyes," Williams remembers.

That was the beginning of positive change for the once-gruff executive. But that is not always the case: People in high positions too often view their need to change as a sign of failure or weakness. The competitive striving that got them to the top can also stop them from admitting shortcomings, if only out of fear of their competitors in organizational politics.

We all share this tendency toward denial, an emotionally comfortable strategy that protects us from the distress that acknowledging the harsh truth would bring. Defensiveness takes many forms: minimizing the facts, filtering out crucial information, rationalizations and "good excuses"—anything to rob the facts of their emotional truth.

And people around us may tend to collude with our denial. Among the more difficult kinds of information to get in organizational life is honest, constructive feedback about how we are doing, especially about our lapses. Coworkers, subordinates, and bosses have an easier time complaining to each other out of earshot of a person than having an honest and open talk with that person about what's wrong. There is a Faustian bargain in this collusion to act as though everything is fine when in fact it is not, for we buy the illusion of harmony and effectiveness at the cost of the truth that could open the way to genuine improvement.

Whenever someone consistently mishandles a given situation, that is a sure sign of a blind spot. In the lower reaches of an organization, such problems can more easily be dismissed as "quirks." But at higher levels these problems are magnified in consequence and visibility; the adverse effects matter not just to the person who has them, but to the group as a whole.

Here is a list of some of the more common—and costly—blind spots from a study of forty-two otherwise highly successful executives studied by Robert E. Kaplan.[21] Those studied ranged from department heads to CEOs, but similar problems can arise in any position.

- *Blind ambition:* Has to win or appear "right" at all costs; competes instead of cooperates; exaggerates his or her own value and contribution; is boastful and arrogant; sees people in black-and-white terms as allies or enemies

- *Unrealistic goals:* Sets overly ambitious, unattainable goals for the group or organization; is unrealistic about what it takes to get jobs done

- *Relentless striving:* Compulsively hardworking at the expense of all else in life; runs on empty; is vulnerable to burnout

- *Drives others:* Pushes other people too hard, burning them out; micromanages and takes over instead of delegating; comes across as abrasive or ruthless and insensitive to the emotional harm to others

- *Power hungry:* Seeks power for his or her own interests, rather than the organization's; pushes a personal agenda regardless of other perspectives; is exploitative

- *Insatiable need for recognition:* Addicted to glory; takes credit for others' efforts and puts blame on them for mistakes; sacrifices follow-through in pursuit of the next victory

- *Preoccupation with appearances:* Needs to look good at all costs; is overly concerned with public image; craves the material trappings of prestige

- *Need to seem perfect:* Enraged by or rejects criticism, even if realistic; blames others for his or her failures; cannot admit mistakes or personal weaknesses

Such blind spots can actually motivate people to avoid self-awareness, since by knowing themselves they would have to admit to failings they cannot bear to acknowledge. This need to deny makes such people resistant to any and all feedback—and can make them a nightmare to work with and for.

All workplace competencies are *learned habits*—if we are deficient in one or another, we can learn to do better. The arrogant and impatient person *can* learn to listen and take other views into account; the workaholic *can* slow down and find more balance in life. But those improvements will never happen without the first step, which is to become aware of how these habits damage us and poison our relationships. With no glimmer of what these behaviors do to us and others, we have no motive to change them. As the head of executive development at a Fortune 500 company told me, "The biggest problem around here is the lack of self-awareness."

Among 184 midlevel managers in a leadership program at the Center for Creative Leadership, there were telling discrepancies between how managers rated themselves on abilities like listening and adaptability and how their peers rated them. In general, when there are such discrepancies, how our peers see us is the more accurate predictor of our actual job performance.[22] For the most part such discrepancies averaged out, with managers rating themselves more leniently than peers on some competencies, more harshly on others.

But some managers had only a rosy view of themselves—if they rated themselves significantly better on abilities such as being considerate and flexible, they would also see themselves as trustworthy and credible. At the extreme, this is the self-view of the narcissist, who admits no flaws, exaggerates his own abilities, and dodges feedback, not wanting to hear about any of his own deficiencies.

Roads to Improvement

A college professor tells about a small, inventive step he took to help himself become a more effective communicator.[23] One day a student was brave enough to tell him about what amounted to a verbal tic that distracted and confused his listeners: He ended sentences with the words "on it," much as some people pointlessly insert "you know" into sentences.

The professor was shocked when he started monitoring his own lectures—"on it" came up time and again without his having intended it or even realizing he was speaking the words. He had been utterly oblivious to this disquieting habit. But now, determined to change, he took a bold step, asking his students to raise their hands whenever they heard the words. And, he says, "With three hundred hands making me fully conscious of this habit, I changed in no time."

Superior performers intentionally seek out feedback; they *want* to hear how others perceive them, realizing that this is valuable information. That may be part of the reason people who are self-aware are also better performers.[24] Presumably their self-awareness helps them in a process of continuous improvement.

And self-awareness in itself is an invaluable tool for change, especially if the need to change is in line with the person's goals, sense of mission, or basic values—including the belief that self-improvement is good.

Knowing their strengths and weaknesses, and approaching their work accordingly, was a competence found in virtually every star performer in a study of several hundred "knowledge workers"—computer scientists, auditors, and the like—at companies including AT&T and 3M. Says Robert Kelley of Carnegie-Mellon University, who did the study with Janet Caplan, "Stars know themselves well."[25]

▪ SELF-CONFIDENCE ▪

A Strong Sense of One's Self-Worth and Capabilities

People with this competence

- ▪ Present themselves with self-assurance; have "presence"

- ▪ Can voice views that are unpopular and go out on a limb for what is right

- ▪ Are decisive, able to make sound decisions despite uncertainties and pressures

While he would never say so, his job performance was a profile in courage.

Brought in to head a privately owned airline in a small Latin American country, he found the business a quagmire. The falling revenues were due to a legacy of cronyism and favoritism: The main sales agent for the airline was a close friend of the owner, and his contract was far more favorable than his competitors', though his agency was weak in sales. The excessively generous contract for the pilots, who were part of one of the most politically powerful unions in the country, was a major cash drain for the company. Their pay was far above the industry standard.

What's more, two of the company's planes had crashed on the way to a resort, and the bad publicity cut their market share from 50 percent to 20 percent within days.

People cautioned the new head of the airline not to take on the union; people who did such things sometimes found their families threatened or their own lives in danger. But he waded in. He told the pilots that the company would go bankrupt and be out of business if they didn't renegotiate their contract. The pilots listened and upped the hours they worked without demanding more pay.

Then he went to the owner of the airline, bluntly detailing how the owner's close friend, the head of the ticket agency, was incompetent and didn't produce the revenue he should. "Get rid of that agency or I'm leaving," he said. The owner listened too, and canceled his crony's contract.

As a friend who knew this courageous executive put it, "He was willing to confront even when his own job or safety was at stake."

Such self-confidence is the sine qua non of superior performance—without it, people lack the conviction that is essential for taking on tough challenges. Self-confidence gives us the requisite self-assurance for plunging ahead or stepping in as a leader.

For those who lack self-confidence, every failure confirms a sense of incompetence. The absence of self-confidence can manifest itself in feelings of helplessness, powerlessness, and crippling self-doubt. Extreme self-confidence, on the other hand, can look like arrogance, especially if the person lacks social skills. And self-confidence is not to be confused with brashness; to have a positive impact, self-confidence must be aligned with reality. For this reason a lack of self-awareness is an obstacle to realistic self-confidence.

Self-confidence can reveal itself in a strong self-presentation, a projection of "presence." Highly self-confident people can seem to exude charisma, inspiring confidence in those around them. Indeed, among supervisors, managers, and executives, higher levels of self-confidence set apart the best performers from average ones.[26]

People with self-confidence typically see themselves as efficacious, able to take on challenges and to master new jobs or skills. They believe themselves to be catalysts, movers, and initiators, and feel that their abilities stack up favorably in comparison to others'. From such a position of inner strength, they are better able to justify their decisions or actions, staying unfazed by opposition. One trait of outstanding auditors, for example, is not being intimidated or easily pressured.

Self-confidence gives the strength to make a tough decision or follow a course of action one believes in despite opposition, disagreement, or even explicit disapproval from those in authority. People with self-confidence are decisive without being arrogant or defensive, and they stand by their decisions. As Lee Iacocca, who rebuilt Chrysler into a world-class auto company, put it, "If I had to sum up in one word the qualities that make a good manager, I'd say that it all comes down to decisiveness. . . . In the end you have to bring all your information together, set up a timetable, and act."[27]

Having Talent—and Believing It

W hen I was around nine or ten, I decided I wanted to earn money during the summer by mowing lawns. I lined up a mower, got my parents to agree to pay for the gas, and even had flyers printed. But when it came time for me to go door-to-door to solicit business, I lacked the confidence to approach even one house."

That poignant memory comes from a student as an explanation for why, having returned to an executive MBA program after a few years as a manager, he is determined to increase his self-confidence.[28] Even now, as an adult, he finds that "one of the most difficult things for me to do is to approach someone, on the phone or in person, to discuss opportunities in which I am interested—I lack the self-confidence."

This story ends happily: Over the course of several months of systematic efforts to be more assertive, he grew in self-confidence. While some people seem born with a natural self-assurance, even those who are shy and timid can become more bold with practice.[29]

Closely related to self-confidence is what psychologists call "self-efficacy," the positive judgment of one's own capacity to perform. Self-efficacy is not the same as the actual skills we have, but rather our *belief* about what we can do with the skills we have. Skill alone is not enough to guarantee our best performance—we have to *believe* in our skills in order to use them at their best.

Albert Bandura, the Stanford University psychologist who pioneered the study of self-efficacy, points out the contrast between those who doubt themselves and those who believe in their abilities when it comes to taking on a difficult task.[30] Those with self-efficacy gladly step up to the challenge; those with self-doubt don't even try, regardless of how well they might actually do. Self-confidence raises aspirations, while self-doubt lowers them.

Among 112 entry-level accountants studied, it was those with the highest sense of self-efficacy who ten months later were rated by their supervisors as having the best job performance. Their level of self-efficacy was a stronger predictor of job performance than the actual level of skill or training they had received before being hired.[31]

There is a tight link between self-knowledge and self-confidence. We each have an inner map of our proclivities, abilities, and deficiencies. For example, one young man who viewed himself as skilled at personal public relations, able to carry off a job interview or sales call with style, felt shy in his personal life, whether at a party or on a date.[32] Our sense of self-efficacy, then, is domain-specific: How well we think we can do on the job does not necessarily match how well we believe we might do in a parallel activity elsewhere in life.

Workers who believe in their abilities do better in part because that belief motivates them to work harder and longer and to persist through difficulties. We typically avoid situations or fields in which we fear we might fail; even if we actually have the abilities it takes to succeed at a job, if we lack the belief that we can handle its challenges, we can start to act in ways that doom us. The thought "I can't do this" is crippling.

One of the more common traits found in workers who lack self-confidence is the paralyzing fear of seeming inept. Another is too easily giving up on their own opinions and judgments—even their good ideas—when challenged. Others include chronic indecisiveness, especially under pressure; shying away from even the smallest risk; and failing to voice valuable ideas.

In a decades-long study of managers at AT&T, self-confidence early in a person's career predicted promotions and success in higher management years later.[33] And in a sixty-year study of more than a thousand high-IQ men and women followed from childhood through retirement, those most self-confident in their early years were most successful as their careers unfolded.[34]

The Courage to Speak Out

I t was out-of-control blood pressure—a result of neglecting to take his hypertension medication—that had led the elderly man to suffer a massive stroke. Now he was in intensive care in a hospital that specialized in brain injury, and the next few days would tell whether he would live or die. Frantic treatments focused on assessing the amount of brain damage and trying to control any further bleeding.

His visitor, a close friend who was a registered nurse working in the same hospital, happened to see the man's medical chart and noticed that of the many medications he was being given, none was for controlling blood pressure. Concerned, she asked the neurology resident poring over the results of a brain scan at her friend's bedside, "Is he taking his blood pressure medication?"

Irritated at the interruption, the brain specialist snapped, "We only treat them from the neck up here," and stalked out of the room.

Now alarmed that a medication crucial for her friend's recovery seemed to have been overlooked, the nurse marched into the office of the hospital's chief of medicine. She waited for him to finish a phone call, apologized for the interruption, and explained her concern. The order to resume the patient's blood pressure medication came immediately.

"I knew I was going outside proper channels by going to the chief of medicine," the nurse explained to me. "But I'd seen stroke patients die because their blood pressure wasn't properly controlled. It was too urgent to let protocol get in the way."

The attitude that the rules and standard procedures can be bent, and the courage to do so, are hallmarks of self-confidence. Indeed, in a study of 209 nurses at a large university hospital, those who had the strongest sense of self-efficacy were most likely to speak out when confronting inadequate or medically risky situations.[35] Nurses high in self-confidence would confront the physicians directly or, if that failed to correct things, go to their superior.

Such a confrontation or protest is an act of courage, especially given the low status of nurses in the hospital hierarchy. The self-confident nurses believed that if they dissented, their opinions would carry weight in changing the problem for the better. The nurses who lacked self-confidence had another inclination: Rather than protest or make efforts to right the wrong, they said they would quit.

Nursing may be a special case, because nurses as a rule are highly employable. In occupations where the job market is tighter—teaching, social work, or middle management, for instance—it may take a particularly high level of self-confidence to see a similar degree of courageous, open dissent. But no matter the kind of job or organization, it is those with the greatest self-confidence who will be most willing to take the risk of speaking up and pointing out problems or injustices that others only grumble about—or quit over.

5

....

Self-Control

Banish fear.
—W. Edwards Deming

It's every public speaker's worst nightmare. My friend, a psychologist, had flown from the East Coast to Hawaii to address a convention of police chiefs. Delayed planes and missed connections made him lose a night's sleep, leaving him both exhausted and jet-lagged, and his speech was first thing the next morning. My friend had been apprehensive about the talk to begin with, since he was taking a controversial stand. Now exhaustion was rapidly converting that apprehension to outright panic.

My friend began by telling a joke—but stopped just before the punch line. He had forgotten it. He froze, his mind a blank. Not only couldn't he remember the punch line, he couldn't remember his speech. His notes suddenly made no sense, and his attention fixed on the sea of faces, riveted on him. He had to apologize, excuse himself, and leave the podium.

Only after several hours' rest was he able to compose himself and give his lecture—including the complete joke—to great applause. Telling me later about his initial bout of panic, he said, "All I could think of was all those faces staring at me—but I couldn't for the life of me remember what I was supposed to say."

The single most striking finding from brain studies of people under stress—like giving a talk in front of a critical audience—shows the emotional brain at work in ways that undermine the workings of the brain's executive center, the prefrontal lobes, located just behind the forehead.

The prefrontal area is the site of "working memory," the capacity to pay attention and keep in mind whatever information is salient. Working memory is vital for comprehension and understanding, planning and decision making, reasoning and learning.

When the mind is calm, working memory functions at its best. But when there is an emergency, the brain shifts into a self-protective mode, stealing resources from working memory and shunting them to other brain sites in order to keep the senses hyperalert—a mental stance tailored to survival.

During the emergency, the brain falls back on simple, highly familiar routines and responses and puts aside complex thought, creative insight, and long-term planning. The focus is the urgent present—or the crisis of the day. For my friend, this emergency mode paralyzed his ability to recall his speech, while focusing his attention on the "threat" at hand—all those rapt faces in the audience waiting for him to speak.

While the circuitry for emergencies evolved millions of years ago, we experience its operation today in the form of troubling emotions: worries, surges of anxiety, panic, frustration and irritation, anger, rage.

The Three-Million-Dollar Amygdala Hijack

When Mike Tyson became enraged and bit off a chunk of Evander Holyfield's ear during their 1997 heavyweight boxing title match, it cost him $3 million—the maximum penalty that could be taken from his $30 million purse—and a year's suspension from boxing.

Tyson was, in a sense, a victim of the brain's alarm center. Located in the ancient emotional brain, the alarm circuitry centers on a series of structures that ring the brain stem, which are known as the limbic system. The structure that plays the key role in emotional emergencies—that makes us "snap"—is the amygdala.

The prefrontal area, the executive center, links to the amygdala through what amounts to a neural superhighway. These neural links between amygdala and prefrontal lobes act as the brain's alarm, a setup that has had immense survival value during the millions of years of human evolution.

The amygdala is the brain's emotional memory bank, repository for all our moments of triumph and failure, hope and fear, indignation and frustration. It uses these stored memories in its role as a sentinel, scanning all incoming information—everything we see and hear from moment to moment—to assess it for threats and opportunities by matching what's happening now to the stored templates of our past experiences.[1]

For Tyson, a head-butting by Holyfield flooded him with angry memories of Holyfield's doing the same eight months earlier, in a match that Tyson also lost—and about which he had complained vociferously. The upshot for Tyson was a classic amygdala hijack, an instantaneous reaction with disastrous consequences.

In evolution, the amygdala most likely used its memory templates to answer questions crucial for survival, such as "Am I its prey, or is it mine?" The answers to such questions required astute senses to take in the situation, and formulate an instantaneous, ready response. Not helpful: Pausing to reflect deeply or mull things over.

The brain's crisis response still follows that ancient strategy—it heightens sensory acuity, stops complex thought, and triggers the knee-jerk, automatic response—though this can have dramatic drawbacks in modern work life.

When Emotions Boil Over

I can't help but overhear the conversation of the woman on the phone next to me at O'Hare Airport—she's yelling. It's clear she's in the middle of a messy divorce, and that her ex is being difficult. "He's being a bastard about the house!" she shouts into the phone. "My lawyer beeped me out of a meeting to tell me we have to go back to court now. And I have to give a presentation this afternoon. . . . This is the worst possible time for this bullshit!" She slams down the receiver, gathers her bags, and stalks off.

It's always "the worst possible time" for the hassles and pressures that put us over the edge—or so it seems. When stresses pile one on top of the other, they are more than additive—they seem to *multiply* the sense of stress, so that as we near a breaking point, each additional burden seems all the more unbearable, the last straw. This is so even for small hassles that ordinarily wouldn't faze us but suddenly can seem overwhelming. As poet Charles Bukowski put it, "It's not the big things that send us to the madhouse, not the loss of a love, but the shoelace that breaks when there's no time left."

To the body, there is no division between home and work; stress builds on stress, no matter the source. The reason a small hassle can drive us over the brink if we are already overwrought is biochemical. When the amygdala hits the brain's panic button, it induces a cascade that begins with the release of a hormone known as CRF and ends with a flood of stress hormones, mainly cortisol.[2]

The hormones we secrete under stress are enough for a single bout of fight or flight—but once secreted, they stay in the body for hours, and each successive upsetting incident adds more stress hormones to the levels already there. The resulting buildup can make the amygdala a hair trigger, ready to hijack us into anger or panic at the least provocation.

One impact of stress hormones is on blood flow. As the heart rate shoots up, blood is shunted away from the brain's higher cognitive centers to other sites more essential for emergency mobilization. Levels of blood sugar available for fuel jump, less relevant body functions slow down, and heart rate climbs to prepare the body to fight or run. The overall impact of cortisol on brain function is to enforce that primitive strategy for survival: heightening the senses, dulling the mind, and doing what's most well rehearsed, even if that habit is yelling or freezing in panic.

Cortisol steals energy resources from working memory—from the intellect—and shunts them to the senses. When cortisol levels are high, people make more errors, are more distracted, and can't remember as well—even something they've just recently read.[3] Irrelevant thoughts intrude, and processing information becomes more difficult.

If stress is sustained, the likely end state is burnout or worse. When lab rats are put under constant strain, cortisol and related stress hormones reach toxic levels, actually poisoning and killing neurons. If the stress continues for a significant part of their lifespan, the effect on their brain is dramatic: an erosion and shrinkage of the hippocampus, a key center for memory.[4] Something similar goes on with people.[5] It's not just that acute stress can make us momentarily inept; sustained stress can have a lasting, dulling effect on intellect.

Of course stress is a given; it's often impossible to avoid the situations or people that swamp us. Take the message explosion. A study of workers at major corporations found that each received and sent an average of 178 messages a day; they were interrupted by a message three times or more an hour, each one with its (usually false) air of urgency.[6]

E-mail, instead of reducing information overload, has added to the total amount of messages coming by phone, voice mail, fax, letter, and so on. Being flooded with intermittent messages puts people in a reactive mode, as though they are continually putting out small brush fires. The biggest impact is on concentration: Each message serves as a distraction, making it all the harder to return with full focus to the interrupted task at hand. The cumulative effect of the message deluge is chronic distractedness.

Indeed, a study of daily productivity in jobs like engineering found that one major cause of low performance was frequent distractions. One outstanding engineer, though, found a strategy that let him stay focused: He wore headphones while working away at his keyboard.[7] Everyone thought he was listening to music, but he was actually listening to nothing—the headphones were just to keep the phone and coworkers from breaking his concentration! Such strategies may work to some extent, but we also need the inner resources to handle the feelings that stress triggers within us.

The Just-Say-No Neurons

The prefrontal lobes ordinarily keep the amygdala's urges in check, bringing to this raw impulse judgment, an understanding of the rules of life, and a sense of what response is most skillful and appropriate.[8] These "just-say-no" circuits reassure the frantic amygdala that we are not, in fact, in danger, and that a less desperate mode of response will do.

The basic design of the brain is built around a simple opposition: Some neurons initiate action, others inhibit that same action. From the finely tuned orchestration of these counterposed tendencies comes smooth execution, whether it be the delivery of a persuasive pitch or the precise incision made by a skilled surgeon. When people are too impulsive, the trouble seems to be in the operation of the prefrontal inhibitory circuitry for impulse rather than in the amygdala—such individuals are not overly eager to act so much as unable to stop once they've started.[9]

Because the amygdala is the brain's alarm, it has the power to override the prefrontal lobes within a split second to meet the emergency it proclaims. The prefrontal lobes, on the other hand, cannot quickly and directly override the amygdala. Instead, the prefrontal lobes have an array of "inhibitory" neurons capable of stopping the directives the amygdala so frantically sends—much like punching in the secret code that shuts down a home security system's false alarm.

Richard Davidson, the director of the Laboratory for Affective Neuroscience at the University of Wisconsin, conducted a landmark series of brain imaging studies that tested two groups of people: one identified as highly resilient to life's ups and downs, the other easily upset by them. Davidson tracked their brain function as they performed stressful tasks, such as writing about the most upsetting experience in their lives or performing difficult math problems under time pressure.

The resilient people had a remarkably rapid recovery from stress, with their prefrontal areas starting to calm the amygdala—and them—within seconds. The more vulnerable people, by contrast, saw a continued escalation of their amygdala's activity, and their distress, for several minutes after the stressful activity ended.

"The resilient people had already started to inhibit the distress during the stressful encounter," Davidson says. "These are optimistic, action-oriented people. If something goes wrong in their lives, they immediately start to think about how to make it better."

This inhibitory circuit between prefrontal lobes and amygdala underlies many of the self-regulation competencies, especially self-control under stress and the ability to adapt to change, both of which allow calm in the face of those existential facts of work life: crisis, uncertainty, and shifting challenges. The prefrontal lobes' ability to inhibit the amygdala's message preserves mental clarity and keeps our actions on a steady course.[10]

To go from the laboratory to reality, consider the cost to a business when a manager, the chief decision maker and people handler, does poorly at this most basic emotional skill. A study of store managers at a large American retail chain found that the managers who were most tense, beleaguered, or overwhelmed by job pressures ran stores with the worst performance, as measured four ways: by net profits, sales per square foot, sales per employee, and per dollar of inventory investment. And those who stayed most composed under the same pressures had the best per-store sales records.[11]

The Marshmallow Kids Grow Up and Go to Work

Six friends, all in college, were drinking and playing cards late into the night when an argument broke out. Mack and Ted's disagreement got louder and angrier until Mack flew into a rage, yelling and screaming—at which point Ted became noticeably cool and reserved. But Mack's temper was now out of control; he stood up and challenged Ted to a fight. Ted responded to Mack's goading very calmly, saying he'd consider fighting Mack, but only if they finished playing the card game.

Mack, though boiling with rage, agreed. During the several minutes it took to play out the game, everyone else took Ted's lead and finished the game as though nothing much had happened. This gave Mack time to settle down and collect his thoughts. At the end of the hand Ted calmly told Mack, "Now if you would like to discuss this further, I'll step outside." But Mack, who by now had had time to quiet down and think things over, apologized for his temper, and there was no fight.

They met again twenty years later, at their school reunion. Ted had a successful career in commercial real estate, while Mack was out of work and struggling with drugs and alcohol.[12]

The contrast between Mack and Ted is telling testimony of the benefits of being able to say no to impulse. The key circuitry here is an array of inhibitory neurons in the prefrontal lobes that can veto the impulsive messages that come from the emotional centers, primarily the amygdala, in moments of rage and temptation. For Ted, that circuit apparently operated well; for Mack, it too often failed.

The tale of Mack and Ted parallels neatly the life trajectory of two groups of children I wrote about in *Emotional Intelligence* who were part of an experiment at Stanford University known as the "marshmallow test." Briefly, four-year-olds in the Stanford preschool were brought into a room one by one, a marshmallow was put on the table in front of them, and they were told, "You can have this marshmallow now if you want, but if you don't eat it until after I run an errand, you can have two when I return."

Some fourteen years later, as they were graduating from high school, the children who ate the marshmallow right away were compared with those who waited and got two.[13] Those who grabbed, compared to those who waited, were more likely to fall apart under stress, tended to become irritated and pick fights more often, and were less able to resist temptation in pursuit of their goals.

Most surprising to the researchers, though, was a completely unanticipated effect: Those children who had waited for the marshmallow, compared to those who hadn't, had scores averaging a remarkable 210 points higher (out of a possible 1,600) on the SAT, the college entrance exam.[14]

My best guess as to why impulsivity should diminish learning ability harks back to the link between amygdala and prefrontal lobes. As the source of emotional impulse, the amygdala is the font of distraction. The prefrontal lobes are the site of working memory, the capacity to pay attention to what is on our mind at the moment.

To the extent we are preoccupied by emotionally driven thoughts, we have that much less attentional space left in working memory. For a schoolchild, this means less attention to pay to the teacher, to a book, to homework. If this persists over years and years, the result is the deficiency in learning that was revealed by the lower SAT scores. The same is true for someone at work—the cost of impulsivity and distractedness is a hampered ability to learn or adapt.

As the children in the Stanford study grew into adulthood and joined the workforce the differences became even more pronounced.[15] In their late twenties, those who had resisted the marshmallow in childhood were still more intellectually skilled, more attentive, and better able to concentrate. They were better able to develop genuine and close relationships, were more dependable and responsible, and showed better self-control in the face of frustration.

By contrast, those who grabbed the marshmallow at four were now, in their late twenties, less cognitively adept and strikingly less emotionally competent than those who had restrained themselves. They were more often loners; they were less dependable, more easily distracted, and unable to delay gratification in pursuing their goals. When stressed, they had little tolerance or self-control. They responded to pressure with little flexibility, instead repeating the same futile and overblown response time and again.

The story of the marshmallow kids holds larger lessons about the costs of out-of-control emotions. When we are under the sway of impulse, agitation, and emotionality, our ability to think—and work—suffers.

The Managed Heart

Emotional self-regulation includes not just damping down distress or stifling impulse; it can also mean intentionally eliciting an emotion, even an unpleasant one. Some bill collectors, I'm told, prime themselves for calls on people by getting themselves worked up into an irritable, ill-tempered state. Physicians who have to give bad news to patients or their families put themselves in a suitably somber, dour mood, as do morticians meeting with bereaved families. In retail and service industries, exhortations to be friendly to customers are virtually universal.

One school of thought argues that when workers are ordered to display a given emotion, they have to perform an onerous "emotional labor" in order to keep their job.[16] When the dictates of the boss determine the emotions a person must express, the result is an estrangement from one's own feelings. Retail clerks, flight attendants, and hotel staff are among the workers prone to such attempted management of the heart, which Arlie Hochschild, a sociologist at the University of California, Berkeley, calls a "commercialization of human feelings" that amounts to a form of emotional tyranny.

A closer look reveals this perspective to be only half the story. Critical in determining whether emotional labor is onerous or not is how much the person identifies with the job.[17] For a nurse who sees herself as a caring, compassionate person, taking a few moments to console a patient in distress represents not a burden but what makes her job more meaningful.

The notion of emotional self-control does not mean denying or repressing true feelings. "Bad" moods, for instance, have their uses; anger, sadness, and fear can become sources of creativity, energy, and connectedness. Anger can be an intense source of motivation, particularly when it stems from the urge to right an injustice or inequity. Shared sadness can knit people together. And the urgency born of anxiety—if not overwhelming—can prod the creative spirit.

Emotional self-control is not the same as *over*control, the stifling of all feeling and spontaneity. In fact, there is a physical and mental cost to such overcontrol. People who stifle their feelings, especially strong negative ones, raise their heart rate, a sign of increased tension. When such emotional suppression is chronic, it can impair thinking, hamper intellectual performance, and interfere with smooth social interactions.[18]

By contrast, emotional competence implies we have a choice as to *how* we express our feelings. Such emotional finesse becomes particularly important in a global economy, since the ground rules for emotional expression vary greatly from culture to culture. What is appropriate in one country may appear an unseemly outburst in another. For example, executives from emotionally reserved cultures, like those in northern Europe, can be seen as "cold" and aloof by Latin American business partners.

In the United States, being emotionally unexpressive often communicates a negative message, a sense of distance or indifference. One study of nearly two thousand supervisors, managers, and executives in American companies showed a strong link between lack of spontaneity and poor performance.[19] While superior managers were more spontaneous than their mediocre peers, executives as a group were more controlled in expressing their personal feelings than managers at lower levels; the executives apparently gave more consideration to the impact of expressing the "wrong" feeling in a given situation.

That measured approach in the top tiers speaks to the sense in which the workplace is a special case when it comes to emotions, almost a "culture" apart from the rest of life. Within the intimate zone of friends and family, we can bring up and mull over whatever weighs on our heart—and should. At work, a different set of emotional ground rules more often prevails.

■   ■   ■

Self-regulation—managing impulse as well as distressing feelings—depends on the working of the emotional centers in tandem with the brain's executive centers in the prefrontal areas. These two primal skills—handling impulse and dealing with upsets—are at the core of five emotional competencies:

- *Self-control:* Managing disruptive emotions and impulses effectively

- *Trustworthiness:* Displaying honesty and integrity

- *Conscientiousness:* Dependability and responsibility in fulfilling obligations

- *Adaptability:* Flexibility in handling change and challenges

- *Innovation:* Being open to novel ideas, approaches, and new information

■ SELF-CONTROL ■

Keeping Disruptive Emotions and Impulses in Check

People with this competence

- Manage their impulsive feelings and distressing emotions well

- Stay composed, positive, and unflappable even in trying moments

- Think clearly and stay focused under pressure

"Bill Gates is pissed. His eyes are bulging and his oversized glasses are askew. His face is flushed and spit is flying from his mouth. . . . He's in a small, crowded conference room at the Microsoft campus with 20 young Microsofties gathered around an oblong table. Most look at their chairman with outright fear, if they look at him at all.

"The sour smell of sweaty terror fills the room."

So begins the narrative of a demonstration of the high art of handling emotions.[20] While Gates continues his angry tirade, the hapless programmers fumble and stutter, trying to persuade or at least placate him. All to no avail. No one seems to be able to get through—except a small, soft-spoken Chinese-American woman, who seems to be the only person in the room who is unfazed by his tantrum. She looks him in the eye while everyone else avoids eye contact.

Twice she interrupts his tirade to address him in quiet tones. The first time, her words seem to calm him a bit before his shouting resumes. The second time, he listens in silence, thoughtfully gazing down at the table. Then his anger suddenly vanishes and he tells her, "Okay—this looks good. Go ahead." With that he ends the meeting.

What the woman said was not much different from what the others had been saying. But her unflappability may well have allowed her to say it better, to think clearly rather than being swamped by anxiety. Her manner was certainly part of her message, sending the signal that the tirade did not intimidate her, that she could take it without becoming unhinged, that there was no real reason to be so agitated.

This skill is, in a sense, largely invisible—self-control manifests largely in the *absence* of more obvious emotional fireworks. Signs include being unfazed under stress or handling a hostile person without lashing out in return. Another mundane example is time management: Keeping ourselves on a daily schedule demands self-control, if only to resist seemingly urgent but actually trivial demands, or the lure of time-wasting pleasures or distractions.

The ultimate act of personal responsibility at work may be in taking control of our own state of mind. Moods exert a powerful pull on thought, memory, and perception. When we are angry, we more readily remember incidents that support our ire, our thoughts become preoccupied with the object of our anger, and irritability so skews our worldview that an otherwise benign comment might now strike us as hostile. Resisting this despotic quality of moods is essential to our ability to work productively.

When Work Is Hell

Many years ago I had a newly promoted boss who struck me as vastly ambitious. His strategy for looking good in his new post was to hire fresh writers—"his people"—and make sure their work got prominent display in the publication. He would spend a great deal of time with the new folks, while studiously ignoring us old hands.

Perhaps my boss was under pressure from *his* boss—I never knew his motivation. But one day, to my surprise, he asked me to have a cup of coffee with him in the company cafeteria. There, after a few words of perfunctory small talk, he abruptly informed me that my work was not up to standards. Exactly how I didn't meet standards was vague—under a former boss my work had been nominated for major awards. But the consequence was clear: If I didn't improve, he would fire me.

Needless to say, that caused me tremendous, relentless anxiety. Over my head in debt and with children heading for college, I desperately needed that job. Worse, writing itself demands high levels of concentration, and those worries kept intruding, distracting me with vivid fantasies of career and financial catastrophe.

What saved my sanity was a relaxation technique I had learned years before, a simple meditation practice that I had done on and off for years. Though I had been lackadaisical in using it, now I became fanatical, allowing myself a half hour or even a full hour of calming centeredness every morning before I started my day.

It worked; I kept myself together and sane, doing my best to turn out workmanlike articles on demand. And then came relief: My unbearable boss got his promotion—to another department.

People best able to handle distress often have a stress management technique they call on when needed, whether it's a long bath, a workout, or a yoga session—as I did with meditation. Having such a relaxation method in our repertoire does not mean that we won't feel upset and distressed from time to time. But regular, daily practice of a relaxation method seems to reset the trigger point for the amygdala, making it less easily provoked.[21] This neural resetting gives us the ability to recover more quickly from amygdala hijacks while making us less prone to them in the first place. The net result is that we are susceptible to distress less often, and our bouts are shorter.

A Sense of Helplessness

The feeling of helplessness about work pressures is in itself pernicious. Among small-business owners and employees, those with a stronger sense that they control what happens to them in life are less likely to become angry, depressed, or agitated when faced with conflicts and strains on the job. But those who feel little control are more prone to getting upset or even quitting.[22]

In a study of 7,400 men and women in London civil service jobs, those who felt they had to meet deadlines imposed by someone else and had little say in how they did their work or with whom they did it had a 50 percent higher risk of developing symptoms of coronary heart disease than those with more job flexibility.[23] Feeling little control over the demands and pressures of the work we have to do holds as great a risk of heart disease as risk factors like hypertension.[24] That is why, of all the relationships we have at work, the one with our boss or supervisor has the greatest impact on our emotional and physical health. When volunteers at a British colds research unit were exposed to a cold virus and followed for five days to see who would get sick, it turned out that those entangled in social tensions were the most susceptible.[25] An isolated tough day at the office was not a problem, but having persistent trouble with a superior was stressful enough to lower immune resilience.

In the newly discovered anatomical links between brain and body that connect our mental state with physical health, the emotional centers play the critical role, with the richest web of connection to both the immune system and the cardiovascular system. These biological ties explain why distressing feelings—sadness, frustration, anger, tension, intense anxiety double the risk that someone with heart disease may experience a dangerous decrease in blood flow to the heart within hours of having these feelings. Such decreases can sometimes trigger a heart attack.[26]

It is no news to working mothers that they bear a unique physiological burden as ordinary work pressures are compounded by the mental strain of being "on call" for unexpected family problems, like a sick child. Single and married mothers alike who hold midlevel jobs where they have little control have substantially higher levels of cortisol, the stress hormone, than do their counterparts at work who do not have children at home.[27]

At low levels, cortisol can help the body fight a virus or heal damaged tissues, but when too much cortisol flows, it diminishes the effectiveness of the immune system.[28] As one researcher at the National Institute of Mental Health put it, "If you're sitting there watching the stock market crash, your cortisol from the psychological stress is going to be up. Then, if someone coughs in your face, you're going to be susceptible to getting the flu."[29]

How Self-Awareness Pays Off

A college professor with heart problems was given a portable heart rate monitor to wear, because when his heart rate exceeded 150 beats per minute, too little oxygen reached his heart muscle. One day the professor went to one of the regular, seemingly endless departmental meetings, which he felt were a waste of time.

But he learned from the monitor that, while he thought he was cynically detached from the discussions, his heart was pounding away at dangerous levels. He had not realized until then how emotionally upset he was by the daily tussle of departmental politics.[30] Self-awareness pays off as a key skill in handling stress. Without careful attention, we can—like the college professor—be surprisingly oblivious to just how stressful our work life really is.

Simply bringing simmering feelings into awareness can have salutary effects. When sixty-three laid-off managers participated in a study at Southern Methodist University, many were, understandably, angry and hostile. Half were told to keep a journal for five days, spending twenty minutes writing out their deepest feelings and reflections on what they were going through. Those who kept journals found new jobs faster than those who didn't.[31]

The more accurately we can monitor our emotional upsets, the sooner we can recover from distress. Consider an experiment in which people watch a graphic anti-drunk-driving film depicting bloody automobile accidents.[32] During the half hour after the film, viewers report feeling distressed and depressed, with their thoughts repeatedly going back to the troubling scenes they've just witnessed. The quickest to recover are those with the greatest clarity about their feelings. Emotional clarity, it seems, enables us to manage bad moods.

Unflappability, however, does not necessarily mean we have done the job. Even when people seem unflappable, if they are actually seething inside, they still need to handle their troubled feelings. Some cultures, particularly those in Asia, encourage this pattern of masking negative feelings. While this may keep relationships tranquil, it can have a cost to the individual. A psychologist teaching emotional intelligence abilities to flight attendants in Asia said, "Imploding is the problem there. They don't explode—they hold it in and suffer."

Emotional implosion has several drawbacks: Imploders often fail to take any action to better their situation. They may not show outward signs of an emotional hijack, but they suffer the internal fallout anyway: headaches, edginess, smoking and drinking too much, sleeplessness, endless self-criticism. And they have the same health risks as those who explode, and so need to learn to manage their own reactions to distress.

Self-Control in Action

I t's a classic Manhattan street scene: A man stops his Lexus in a No Stopping zone on a busy street, hurries into a shop, makes a few purchases, and rushes out—only to find a traffic cop has not only written out a ticket, but also called a tow truck, to which his Lexus is now being hitched.

"Goddamn!" the man explodes in rage, screaming at the traffic cop. "You are the lowest form of human slime!" he yells, pounding the hood of the tow truck with his fist.

The cop, visibly ruffled, somehow manages a calm response: "It's the law. If you think it's wrong, you can appeal." And with that, he turns and walks away.

Self-control is crucial for those in law enforcement. When facing someone who is in the throes of an amygdala hijack, like the abusive motorist, the odds of the encounter ending in violence will escalate rapidly if the officer involved gets hijacked by his amygdala, too. Indeed, Officer Michael Wilson, who teaches at New York City's police academy, says these situations make many officers struggle to handle their visceral response to disrespect, an attitude they see not just as an idle threat, but as signaling a shift in power in the interaction, which could pose a danger to their life.[33] As Wilson puts it, "Initially, when someone gives you major grief, your body wants to react. But there is this little person inside your head saying, 'It's not worth it. I put my hands on this person, I lose.' "

The training of police (at least in the United States, which, sadly, has one of the highest levels of violence in the world) requires a careful titration of the use of force in amounts that correspond to the situation at hand. Threats, physical intimidation, and drawing a gun are last resorts, since each of these is itself likely to incite an amygdala hijack in the other person.

Competence studies in law enforcement organizations find outstanding officers use the least force necessary, approach volatile people calmly and with a professional demeanor, and are adept at de-escalation. A study of New York City traffic cops found that those who managed a calm response even when faced with angry motorists had the fewest incidents escalate into outright violence.[34]

The principle of remaining calm despite provocation applies to anyone who routinely faces obnoxious or agitated people on the job. Among counselors and psychotherapists, for example, superior performers respond calmly to a personal attack by a patient.[35] So do outstanding flight attendants faced with disgruntled passengers.[36] And among managers and executives, superior performers balance their drive, ambition, and assertiveness with self-control, harnessing their personal needs in the service of the organization's goals.[37]

Resilience—Thriving on Stress

Compare two executives at one of America's regional telephone companies, a company where stress has soared as the entire industry undergoes wrenching changes. One of the executives is plagued by tension: "My life seems like a rat race. I'm always trying to catch up, meet deadlines imposed on me, but most aren't even important. They're just routine. So even though I'm nervous and tense, I'm also bored a lot of the time."

The other executive says, "I'm almost never bored. Even when there's something I have to do that doesn't strike me as interesting at first, usually once I get into it, I find it worthwhile in a way that teaches me something. I'm always out there straining to make a difference, to shape a productive work life for myself."

The first executive was identified as low in—and the second high in—a quality called "hardiness," the ability to stay committed, feel in control, and be challenged rather than threatened by stress. The study found that those who react to stress with hardiness, seeing work as strenuous but exciting and change as a chance to develop rather than as an enemy, bear the physical burden of stress much better, coming through with less illness.[38]

A paradox of work life is that a situation can be seen by one person as a devastating threat but by another as an invigorating challenge. With the right emotional resources, what seems threatening can be taken instead as a challenge, and met with energy, even enthusiasm. There is a crucial difference in brain function between "good stress"—the challenges that mobilize and motivate us—and "bad stress," the threats that overwhelm, paralyze, or demoralize us.

The brain chemicals that generate enthusiasm for a challenge are different from those that respond to stress and threat. They are at work when our energy is high, our effort maximal, and our mood positive. The biochemistry of these productive states revolves around activating the sympathetic nervous system and the adrenals to secrete chemicals called catecholamines.

The catecholamines, adrenaline and noradrenaline, arouse us to action in a more productive way than the frantic urgency of cortisol. Once the brain goes into its emergency mode, it starts pumping out cortisol as well as vastly elevated levels of catecholamines, but we do our best work at a lower level of brain arousal, when only the catecholamine system is engaged. (And it doesn't take a threat to our job or a negative comment from the boss to activate cortisol; boredom, impatience, frustration, even tiredness will do it.)

In a sense, then, there are two kinds of stress—good and bad—and two distinct biological systems at work. There is also a balance point when the sympathetic nervous system is pumping (but not too much), our mood is positive, and our ability to think and react is optimal. Here lies our peak performance.

▪ TRUSTWORTHINESS AND CONSCIENTIOUSNESS ▪

Maintaining Integrity and Taking Responsibility for Personal Performance

▪▪

People with this competence

For Trustworthiness

▪ Act ethically and are above reproach

▪ Build trust through their reliability and authenticity

▪ Admit their own mistakes and confront unethical actions in others

▪ Take tough, principled stands even if they are unpopular

For Conscientiousness

▪ Meet commitments and keep promises

▪ Hold themselves accountable for meeting their objectives

▪ Are organized and careful in their work

▪▪

The inventor of a promising new product, a two-chamber air mattress that had the competitive advantage of preserving body heat, tells of talking to a businessman who offered to manufacture and sell the mattresses, giving the inventor a royalty. The businessman, over the course of their conversation, revealed with some pride that he never paid any taxes.[39]

"How do you do it?" the inventor asked, incredulous.

"I keep two sets of books," the businessman replied smugly.

"So which set of books will you use to record the sales of my mattresses to compute the royalty you owe me?" the inventor asked.

To that question there was no reply. End of deal.

Credibility stems from integrity. Stars know that trustworthiness at work translates into letting people know one's values and principles, intentions and feelings, and acting in ways that are reliably consistent with them. They are forthright about their own mistakes, and confront others about their lapses.

Workers with integrity are frank, even acknowledging their feelings—"I was getting a little nervous about that"—which contributes to their aura of authenticity. By contrast, those who never admit a lapse or imperfection or who "hype" themselves, their company, or a product undermine their credibility.

Integrity—acting openly, honestly, and consistently—sets apart outstanding performers in jobs of every kind. Take those in sales roles that depend on the strength of ongoing relationships. In such a job, someone who hides crucial information, breaks promises, or fails to fulfill commitments undermines the trust so vital to repeat business.

"Of the general managers for sales who've worked for me and washed out, the single thing they lacked most was trustworthiness," a senior vice president at a division of Automatic Data Processors told me. "In sales, it's trade-offs—I'll give you this if you give me a concession on that. It's an ambiguous situation, where you have to take someone's word for it. A field like finance—that's more science than art, it's more clear-cut. But in sales it's grays, so being trustworthy is all the more important."

Douglas Lennick, executive vice president of American Express Financial Advisors, concurs: "Some people have the mistaken impression you can succeed in business by cheating people or pressuring them into buying something they don't need. That may work for you in the short term, but it will undermine you in the long run. You'll be far more successful if you stay in alignment with your personal values."

When Business Is Business

met her on a plane, my seatmate for a few hours on a flight out West. We'd been chatting for a while when she found out I was writing about emotions at work. Then her story spilled out: "We do safety testing for the chemical industry, assessing their materials and how they handle them for risks like combustibility. We verify that their procedures for handling these substances meet federal safety standards. But my boss doesn't care if the report is accurate; he just wants it done on time. His motto is, Get the job done quick as you can and get the money.

"I recently found that the calculations for one job were wrong, so I redid them. But the boss gave me grief about it because it took more time than he wanted. I have to do what this guy tells me, even though I know he's incompetent. So I'm always redoing calculations at home, on my own time. Everyone's unhappy that the boss pushes us this way."

Why does she put up with it?

She tells me about a messy divorce, having to take care of her two children on her own, being stretched. "I'd leave if I could, but I need the work. Jobs are tight just now. . . ."

After a long, reflective silence, she continues. "He signs all the work, even what we do. At first it bothered me that he was taking all the credit, but now I'm relieved—I don't want my name on those reports. It doesn't feel right to me. There haven't been any accidents, like fires or explosions, but there might be someday."

Shouldn't she speak up, report what's going on?

"I've thought about saying something to someone, but I can't say anything because I signed a secrecy agreement when I was hired. I'd have to leave the company and then be able to prove in court what I said—that would be a nightmare."

As our plane taxis in for a landing, she seems at once relieved and nervous about what she's revealed—so anxious, she won't tell me her name or that of her company. Still, she takes my name and number, saying she has more to say. She'll call me.

She never does.

The Ethics Officers Association commissioned a survey of 1,300 workers at all levels in American companies, and what they found is startling: About half admitted to engaging in unethical business practices.[40]

For the most part, breaches of trust or codes of morality were relatively minor, such as calling in sick when they want time off, or taking home supplies from the company cabinet. But 9 percent admitted lying or deceiving a customer, 6 percent have falsified numbers in reports or documents, and 5 percent have lied to superiors on serious matters or withheld critical information. And 4 percent admitted to having taken credit for someone else's work or idea. Some of the breaches are extremely serious: 3 percent have engaged in a copyright or software infringement, and 2 percent have forged someone's name on a document. One percent have reported false information when filing government forms, such as tax returns.

By contrast, a study of outstanding accountants at one of America's largest firms discovered that one distinction was a competence called "courage": They were willing to stand up to their clients and against pressures at their own accounting firms, to risk losing an account, to insist people do what was right. And the best accountants had the courage to speak up against even massive resistance to be sure the rules were followed—a stance requiring immense integrity and self-confidence. (There was a good news/bad news edge to this finding: The good news was that their best accountants had this kind of courage; the bad news was that most of their accountants did not.)

Impulse Control: An Emotional Fault Line

■ A corporate comptroller was fired because he sexually harassed the women who worked for him. He was also intensely aggressive in dealing with people generally.

■ An executive at another company was by nature outgoing, talkative, friendly, and spontaneous—but also had little self-restraint. He was fired for leaking company secrets.

■ The head of a small industrial company was charged with criminal behavior in managing his company's funds. He had selected a chief financial officer (an accomplice) who shared with him both a lack of conscience and little apprehension about the consequences of what they were doing.

These case studies of wrecked careers come from the files of a consulting company that assessed each of these executives in the course of testing 4,265 people, from company heads to blue-collar workers.[41] They all had a lack of impulse control, with little or no ability to delay gratification. With self-restraint, people can think through the potential consequences of what they are about to do and assume responsibility for their words and deeds.

The consulting firm that did the study of self-restraint in professions, recommends that, in general, "When selecting people for industrial jobs—at all levels—it is wise to reject candidates who are low or very low" in self-restraint, since "the odds of them creating problems of some kind are extremely high." (It does note, though, that people can be helped to handle their impulsivity better—poor impulse control need not be a sentence to a dead-end career.)

Even among football players, whose very role would seem to demand a certain level of spontaneous aggressiveness, restraint pays. In a study of more than seven hundred pros, NFL draft choices, and college players, those with higher levels of restraint were rated by their coaches as being more motivated, having better abilities as football players, being better leaders, and being easier to coach.[42] On the other hand, those with low levels of restraint were rated as showing little respect for teammates and coaches and were unwilling to listen or take direction. They were cavalier about their agreements or contracts, used insulting "trash talk" with opponents, and indulged in show-offish end-zone dancing. Take two football players with very low levels of restraint: One was found to be using drugs, and the other was a troublemaker who punched and knocked out a teammate during practice.

Quiet Virtue: The Conscientious

B y contrast, the everyday signs of conscientiousness—being punctual, careful in doing work, self-disciplined, and scrupulous in attending to responsibilities—are hallmarks of the model organizational citizen, the people who keep things running as they should. They follow the rules, help out, and are concerned about the people they work with. It's the conscientious worker who helps orient newcomers or updates people who return after an absence, who gets to work on time and never abuses sick leaves, who always gets things done on deadline.

Conscientiousness is a taproot of success in any field. In studies of job performance, outstanding effectiveness for virtually all jobs, from semi-skilled labor to sales and management, depends on conscientiousness.[43] It is particularly important for outstanding performance in jobs at the lower levels of an organization: the mailroom clerk who never misplaces a package, the secretary whose message taking is impeccable, the delivery truck driver who is always on time.

Among sales representatives for a large American appliance manufacturer, those who were most conscientious had the largest volume of sales.[44] Conscientiousness also offers a buffer against the threat of job loss in today's ever-churning market, because employees with this trait are among the most valued. For the sales reps, their level of conscientiousness mattered almost as much as their sales in determining who stayed on.[45]

There is an aura of sorts around highly conscientious people that makes them seem even better than they actually are. Their reputation for reliability biases supervisors' ratings of their work, giving them higher evaluations than objective measures of their performance would predict.

But conscientiousness in the absence of empathy or social skills can lead to problems. Since conscientious people demand so much of themselves, they can hold other people to their own standards, and so be overly judgmental when others don't show the same lofty levels of exemplary behavior. Factory workers in Great Britain and the United States who were extremely conscientious, for example, tended to criticize coworkers even about mundane lapses that seemed trivial to those they criticized, which strained their relationships.[46]

When conscientiousness takes the form of a relentless conformity to expectations, it can put a damper on creativity. In creative callings like art or advertising, openness to wild ideas and spontaneity are at a premium. Success in such occupations calls for a balance, however; without enough conscientiousness to follow through, people become mere dreamers, with nothing to show for their imaginativeness.

■ INNOVATION AND ADAPTABILITY ■

Being Open to Novel Ideas and Approaches, and Being Flexible in Responding to Change

■■

People with this competence

For Innovation

- Seek out fresh ideas from a wide variety of sources

- Entertain original solutions to problems

- Generate new ideas

- Take fresh perspectives and risks in their thinking

For Adaptability

- Smoothly handle multiple demands, shifting priorities, and rapid change

- Adapt their responses and tactics to fit fluid circumstances

- Are flexible in how they see events

■■

It was a subtle signal. Sometime in the mid-1970s there was a shift in how Intel managers were treated by their peers in Japan. Where before they had been shown lavish respect, now they came back with the vague feeling that they were being viewed with a newfound derision. Something had changed.

That report from the front lines was a harbinger of the coming Japanese supremacy in the market for computer chips, at the time Intel's main business. The story is told by Andrew S. Grove, Intel's chairman, as an example of how hard it can be for executives to adapt to shifts in an industry.[47]

It took Intel's top management, Grove confesses, several more years to realize that Japanese companies had used their strength in precision manufacturing to beat Intel at its own game, making and selling memory chips.

Such moments, when changing circumstances turn a winning strategy sour, are crucial in the history of any company. These moments amount to what Grove calls a "valley of death": If a company is not nimble enough to rethink its strategy while it still has the assets and strength to change and adapt, it is doomed to wither or die.

In facing such make-or-break moments, the emotional capabilities executives bring to bear make a crucial difference. The ability to be flexible, to take in new, even painful, information without tuning out in self-protection, and to respond nimbly is essential.

Too often corporate inertia takes over instead, with top management failing to read the signs of the coming sea change—or fearing to act on the implications—even as the rules of the game are mutating.

At Intel the dominant assumption into the 1980s was that they were a "memory company," selling chips, even though by then their share of that market had shrunk to around 3 percent. Barely noticed was the sideline work that would become their new core business: microprocessors, or what we all now know as "Intel Inside."

The high-tech industry, perhaps the fastest-changing of all, is littered with the remains of companies whose management failed to adapt to market shifts. An engineer who had worked at Wang Laboratories during its heyday in the 1980s, when the company surged to $3 billion in sales—and was there to see the company fail—said, "I've seen what success does—it breeds arrogance. You stop listening to your customers and employees. You get complacent about your business, and finally get leapfrogged by competitors."

Change Is the Constant

Grove contends a company's ability to survive such a looming valley of death depends on one thing: "How the top management reacts emotionally." When their very status and well-being—and that of their company—face a great threat, when their most cherished assumptions about their mission and their business are being undermined, what emotions take over?

At Intel adaptability was crucial in facing two major crises: the loss of the memory chip market and, more recently, the disaster when a flaw in the company's then-new Pentium processor made millions of computer owners lose faith in the product. While the latter corporate drama took only about a month to unfold, beginning to end, that short period telescoped a classic management adaptation to challenging new realities: a cycle of initial denial followed by unavoidable facts, followed by a flood of distress, all of which was resolved when Grove and his top executives came to grips with reality and finally made a wrenching, costly concession—the promise to replace Pentium processors for all who asked, even though it would cost the company $475 million.

The half a billion dollars the replacements cost the company was the price for establishing Intel as a commercial brand name. The "Intel Inside" campaign was intended to make computer buyers perceive that the microprocessor inside the computer *is* the computer. This built customer loyalty to Intel that went beyond whatever brand of PC they might buy.

For any organization to reinvent itself, basic assumptions, visions, strategies, and identities have to be questioned. But people hold emotional attachments to all these elements of their work life, making change all the harder.[48] Consider the disaster at the Schwinn bicycle company, America's number one manufacturer of bicycles from the mid-1950s through the 1970s.[49] A family-owned company, Schwinn failed to spot the motocross and mountain-biking trends of the 1980s and was slow to match competition from abroad for the booming market in upscale bikes for adults. Top management, oblivious to the changing tides of bikers' tastes, was far too slow in rethinking their marketing strategy. One sales manager even dismissed the new, lightweight bikes with the derisive comment, "Are you gonna ride it or carry it?"

Its overseas suppliers—including Giant Bicycles of Taiwan, which Schwinn had inadvertently helped build into a bicycle manufacturing titan—were among the creditors that eventually forced Schwinn into bankruptcy in 1992.

Such changes in market realities, of course, are an inevitable part of competition in business large and small. An executive at a company that processes data for auto dealers tells me, "One of our main competitors made four hundred million dollars a year supplying forms to auto dealers. Then we introduced a way for auto dealers to use computers and laser printers to do away with the forms. We grew to sixty million dollars per year, all business taken from that competitor. Just this month they finally woke up and introduced a computerized system competitive to ours—but it took them four years and cost them a huge piece of their business."

Surviving Change: The Emotional Prerequisites

H e was brilliant, no question about it: a CPA who also had a master's in economics, an MBA, and additional advanced course work in finance, all from an Ivy League university. He had been a standout as a credit officer and risk manager for a major global bank for many years.

And now he was being fired.

The reason: He could not adjust to his new job. His success had won him a place on a team the bank had put together to find promising companies to invest in. Their mandate was to recoup the value of government bonds in countries where they had been devalued up to 80 percent. Within the countries themselves, the bonds could still be invested at full face value. But instead of helping his team think through the *positive* scenarios that might make a company a good buy, this former risk manager simply continued with his old naysaying approach.

"He kept insisting on analyzing for weakness, for what the downside might be—killing businesses instead of building them," I was told by the executive recruiter he saw when he lost his job. "His boss finally got fed up and fired him. He just couldn't adapt to the new goal."

At work these days, the constant is change. "We used to be very rigid in how we operated. You did it by the book, A, B, C, D—no other way," an advertising sales rep for a major publication told me. "But now we make those decisions ourselves; there's no set formula for how you work. We're encouraged to take risks, work as teams. The atmosphere has changed. But some people seem at a loss. They just have a hard time with the new way of doing things."

People who lack adaptability are ruled by fear, anxiety, and a deep personal discomfort with change. Many managers are having trouble adapting to the trend toward diffusing responsibility and decision making throughout organizations. As an executive at Siemens AG, the German conglomerate, explained, "People have old habits of authority. The new model empowers individuals to make decisions themselves, delegating responsibility downward in the hierarchy, closer to the customer. But when things go poorly—say, profitability is down for a month—some managers panic, fall back on their old ways, and tighten up control again. When they do, it undermines the new way of doing things."

If there is any competence these times call for, it is adaptability. Stars in this competence relish change and find exhilaration in innovation.[50] They are open to new information and—like the management team at Intel—can let go of old assumptions, and so adapt how they operate. They are comfortable with the anxiety that the new or unknown often brings and are willing to take a gamble on a new way of doing things.

Adaptability requires the flexibility to take into account multiple perspectives on a given situation. This flexibility depends, in turn, on an emotional strength: the ability to stay comfortable with ambiguity and remain calm in the face of the unexpected. Another competence that supports adaptability is self-confidence, particularly the sureness that allows someone to quickly adjust their responses, even dropping everything without reservation as realities shift.

The openness to change that typifies adaptability ties this competence to another that is increasingly prized in these turbulent times: innovation.

The Innovators

Levi Strauss, the huge garment manufacturer, faced a dilemma regarding two sewing subcontractors in Bangladesh who were using child laborers. International human rights activists were pressuring Levi Strauss to stop allowing contractors to use underage workers. But company investigators discovered that if the children lost their jobs, they would be impoverished and maybe driven into prostitution. Should the company fire them, in a principled stand against child labor? Or keep them on, to protect them from a worse fate?

The creative solution: neither. Levi Strauss decided to keep the children on the payroll while they went to school full time, and then, when they reached fourteen—the local age of maturity—hire them back.[51]

That innovative response offers a model of creative thinking for multinationals seeking to be socially responsible. Coming to such an original resolution demands entertaining ideas that may seem too radical or risky at first glance, yet having the courage to pursue them anyway.

The emotional foundation of the innovator at work is taking pleasure in originality. Creativity on the job revolves around applying new ideas to achieve results. People who have this knack can quickly identify key issues and simplify problems that seem overwhelmingly complex. Most important, they can find original connections and patterns that others overlook.

People who lack a flair for innovation, by contrast, typically miss the larger picture and get enmeshed in details, and so deal with complex problems only slowly, even tediously. Their fear of risk makes them shy away from novel ideas. And when they try to find solutions, they often fail to realize that what worked in the past is not always the answer for the future.

Deficits in this competence can go beyond mere lack of imagination. People who are uncomfortable with risk become critics and naysayers. Defensive and cautious, they may constantly deride or undermine innovative ideas.

The creative mind is, by its very nature, a bit unruly. There is a natural tension between orderly self-control and the innovative urge. It's not that people who are creative are out-of-control emotionally; rather, they are willing to entertain a wider range of impulse and action than do less adventurous spirits. That is, after all, what creates new possibilities.

Self-control—in the sense of following the rules—predicts outstanding performance in large organizations, especially where a bureaucratic sense of doing the right thing is rewarded. But in entrepreneurial companies and in creative jobs like advertising, being *overly* controlled predicts failure.

A German venture capitalist decries the lack of support in his country for the innovative thinking and risk taking at the heart of entrepreneurial ventures. I hear the same concern voiced in Japan. The German venture capitalist tells me, "Many countries, like my own, are worrying about how to encourage the entrepreneurial skills that create jobs." Risk taking and the drive to pursue innovative ideas are the fuel that stokes the entrepreneurial spirit.

Old and New Paradigms for Innovation

The act of innovation is both cognitive and emotional. Coming up with a creative insight is a cognitive act—but realizing its value, nurturing it, and following through calls on emotional competencies such as self-confidence, initiative, persistence, and the ability to persuade. And throughout, creativity demands a variety of self-regulation competencies, so as to overcome the internal constraints posed by emotions themselves. As Yale psychologist Robert Sternberg observes, these involve fluctuations in emotions from depression to elation, apathy to enthusiasm, and distractedness to focus.[52]

The nineteenth-century mathematician Jules-Henri Poincaré proposed a model of the basic four stages of the creative act that more or less holds true today. The first stage is *preparation*—immersing ourselves in the problem, gathering a broad range of data and information. This first stage more often than not leads to a sometimes frustrating impasse: lots of possibilities, but no insights.

In the next phase, *incubation,* the information and possibilities simmer on a mental back burner. We let the mind play: daydreaming, free-associating, brainstorming, harvesting ideas as they float up. Then, with some luck, comes the third phase, *illumination*—that "aha!" moment where the breakthrough insight comes. This is a thrilling moment, a culmination. But illumination is not enough: The working world is littered with promising ideas never pursued. The final phase is *execution,* following through with action. This demands a dogged persistence despite all the objections, setbacks, trials, and failures that typically arise with any innovation.

"There's a huge difference between someone who actually invents something and makes it real, and someone who just dreams about it," says Phil Weilerstein, director of the National Collegiate Inventors and Innovators Alliance. Those who can follow through and execute their ideas, he tells me, "tend to have a high emotional intelligence level. They see that a variety of elements—most of them human—have to come together to make something new happen. You've got to communicate with people and persuade them, solve problems with them, collaborate."

Ray Kurzweil, an inventor of voice recognition software, agrees: "Courage is essential if you're going to get a creative project off the ground," he told me. "And not just courage, but salesmanship."

Today the very paradigm of invention, even in science, is changing its focus from the individual to collaboration. "In fields of complex modern technology and business we are clearly in an era where the ideas of a single person seldom lead to significant progress," I heard Alex Broer, vice chancellor of Cambridge University and a former director of research at IBM, tell a London briefing on emotional intelligence for British Telecom.

"The ideas of an individual must fit into a matrix of innovation that spreads across a group of researchers around the world," Dr. Broer added. "You have to *talk* to everybody. So today you need more emotional intelligence than before to know how and from whom to get relevant ideas," let alone to form the coalitions and collaborations that will bring those ideas to fruition.

Angel's Advocates and Voices of Doom

New ideas are fragile and all too easily killed by criticism. Sir Isaac Newton is said to have been so sensitive to criticism that he withheld the publication of a paper on optics for fifteen years, until his main critic died. Managers who work with creative groups can help nurture these tendrils of new possibility by protecting them from too-withering criticism that comes too early.

"We have a standing rule that whenever someone offers a creative idea, the people who speak up about it first have to be angel's advocates, people who support and defend it," Paul Robinson, director of Sandia National Laboratories, told me. "Only then can we hear the inevitable criticisms that otherwise might kill an idea in the bud."

Marvin Minsky, the pioneer in artificial intelligence at MIT, observes that the problem in capitalizing on creativity is not just creating ideas, but choosing the ones to bet on. He told me that in the late 1970s Xerox had created six prototypes of the laser printer, the first of their kind, and loaned one to his group at MIT to try out. As Minsky recalls it, "We at MIT said, 'This is fabulous'—and some vice president at Xerox ignored our opinion and decided not to pursue the technology. Canon was the first to bring it to market, and Xerox lost a crucial head start on a billion-dollar market."

Just as chilling as the voice of doubt is its close cousin, the voice of indifference. Engineers have a term for it: NIH, "not invented here"—if it's not our idea, we're not interested. Teresa Amabile, a psychologist at the Harvard Business School, describes four "creativity killers," each of which constricts working memory, the mental space in which brainstorms occur and creativity flourishes, and squelches risk taking:[53]

- *Surveillance:* Hovering and constant scrutiny. This stifles the essential sense of freedom needed for creative thinking.

- *Evaluation:* A critical view that comes too soon or is too intense. Creative ideas should be critiqued—not all are equally good, and promising ones can be refined and honed by helpful criticism—but evaluation is counterproductive when it leads to a preoccupation with being judged.

- *Overcontrol:* Micromanaging every step of the way. Like surveillance, it fosters an oppressive sense of constriction, which discourages originality.

- *Relentless deadlines:* A too-intense schedule that creates panic. While some pressure can be motivating, and deadlines and goals can focus attention, they can kill the fertile "off time" where fresh ideas flourish.

Collective Creativity

A dapting nimbly to shifting market realities requires a collective creativity, a comfort with uncertainty at every level of a company. Consider SOL, a highly successful industrial cleaning business in Finland. When it was spun off from a larger family-owned conglomerate in 1992, it had two thousand employees, fifteen hundred customers, and annual revenues of $35 million. Just four years later it had doubled its customer base, almost doubled its employees, and reached revenues of $60 million.[54]

Employees there have extraordinary freedom in how they do their work. It's a workplace with no titles, individual offices, executive perks, or even secretaries. Nor are there set working hours, a radical innovation for Finland, where an eight-to-four work day is almost universal. SOL has freed its employees to be creative about how they do their business—and what business they do.

This autonomy has allowed SOL to shine for its nimble innovation in an otherwise stodgy, low-end business. At some hospitals, for instance, SOL cleaners saw a niche and so have taken on some night nursing duties, like helping patients get to the bathroom or notifying doctors about emergencies. At several grocery chains, SOL cleaners use their nighttime hours to stock shelves.

Creativity tends also to be enhanced in organizations that, like SOL, have less formality, allow more ambiguous and flexible roles, give workers autonomy, have open flows of information, and operate in mixed or multidisciplinary teams.[55]

Just as with creativity in individuals, there are several stages to the flourishing of innovation in organizations. Two crucial ones are *initiation,* coming up with the bright idea in the first place, and *implementation,* getting the idea enacted.

In an organization, the idea generators and those who champion the innovation are typically different people, from different groups. A study of thousands of people in the R&D arms of engineering firms shows that the idea generators tend to have strengths in a narrow range of expertise and find pleasure when immersed in abstract ideas.[56] They also prefer to work alone.

By contrast, those who are effective champions of the resulting innovations are particularly adept at influence and political awareness: selling the ideas and finding support and allies. While it goes without saying that the relevant technical expertise is vital to generating innovative ideas, when it comes to putting those ideas to practical use, navigating the web of influence that permeates an organization makes all the difference. So an organization that values innovation needs to support both kinds of competence in its key people.

6

What Moves Us

Joe Kramer can fix anything. A welder who helps assemble railroad cars in a South Chicago plant, Joe is the guy everyone calls on when any piece of machinery breaks down.

Joe loves the challenge of finding out what makes a machine work. He started as a boy, fixing his mother's toaster, and he continues to seek out new mechanical challenges. When he decided to put in a sprinkler system at home, he couldn't find one that had a mist fine enough to make rainbows. So he designed his own and built it on his basement lathe.

Joe also knows every aspect of how the plant operates, and he can fill in for any of the two hundred or so others who work there. Almost sixty, Joe has been doing his job for close to forty years, and he still loves what he does. "If I had five more like Joe," the manager says, "I'd have the most efficient railroad shop in the business."

Joe is an example of people who find their work exhilarating—and who perform at their best. The key to that exhilaration is not the task itself—Joe's job is often routine—but the special state of mind Joe creates as he works, a state called "flow." Flow moves people to do their best work, no matter what work they do.

Flow blossoms when our skills are fully engaged and then some—say, by a work project that stretches us in new and challenging ways. The challenge absorbs us so much we lose ourselves in our work, becoming so totally concentrated we may feel "out of time." In this state we seem to handle everything effortlessly, nimbly adapting to shifting demands. Flow itself is a pleasure.[1]

Flow is the ultimate motivator. Activities we love draw us in because we get into flow as we pursue them. Of course, what gives people such pleasure varies: a machinist may love the challenge of a difficult weld; a surgeon gets contentedly absorbed in a complex operation; an interior designer finds delight in the creative play of pattern and color. When we work in flow, the motivation is built in—work is a delight in itself.

Flow offers a radical alternative to the widely held ideas about what motivates people at work. This is not to say that incentives don't matter; they are key as prods or ways to "keep score." There is, of course, value in reviews and promotions, stock options and bonuses—as there is with basic salary. But the most powerful motivators are internal, not external.

For instance, when people kept a journal of how they felt while they performed a range of tasks throughout the day, one result was clear: They felt better doing work they loved rather than work they did only because they were rewarded for it. When doing a task for the pleasure of it, their mood was upbeat, both happy and interested. When doing something simply for the pay, they were bored, disinterested, even mildly irritated (and most unhappy if the tasks were stressful and onerous). It feels better to do what we have passion for, even if the rewards are greater elsewhere.

When all is said and done and a job has been pursued to its end, what are the ultimate sources of satisfaction? That question was asked of more than seven hundred men and women in their sixties, most of whom were nearing the end of successful careers as professionals or business executives.[2] Most rewarding was the creative challenge and stimulation of the work itself, and the chance to keep learning. The next three sources of reward: pride in getting things done, work friendships, and helping or teaching people on the job. Much lower on the list came status, and even lower was financial gain.

Traditional incentives miss the point when it comes to getting people to perform at their absolute best. To reach the top rung, people must love what they do and find pleasure in doing it.

Motive and *emotion* share the same Latin root, *motere,* "to move." Emotions are, literally, what move us to pursue our goals; they fuel our motivations, and our motives in turn drive our perceptions and shape our actions. Great work starts with great feeling.

Loving What Pays Off

People in flow often make the difficult look easy, an external appearance that mirrors what is happening in their brain. Flow poses a neural paradox: We can be engaged in an exceptionally demanding task, and yet our brain is operating with a minimal level of activity or expenditure of energy. The reason seems to be that when we are bored and apathetic, or frenzied with anxiety, our brain activity is diffused; the brain itself is at a high level of activation, albeit poorly focused, with brain cells firing in far-flung and irrelevant ways. But during flow, the brain appears efficient and precise in its pattern of firing. The result is an overall lowering of cortical arousal—even though the person may be engaged in an extremely challenging task.[3]

And work is the main arena in life that gives people the chance for flow. Mihalyi Csikzentmihalyi, the University of Chicago psychologist who pioneered the study of flow, outfitted 107 people in positions from management and engineering to the assembly line with a beeper that periodically reminded them to note what they were doing and how they felt. The results were surprising.[4] They reported, on average, being in flow about half the time while on the job—and less than 20 percent of the time during their leisure hours. The most common emotional state reported during leisure time was apathy!

But there was also a wide variation in just how much of the time people were in flow at work. Those with complex, challenging jobs, who had more flexibility in how they approached each task, were most likely to be in flow. Managers and engineers had more flow time than those in routine jobs. More control means more opportunity to maximize flow. Control can take many forms—even putting something off until the last minute as a way to up the challenge, creating a pressured "rush" period that adds adrenaline to an otherwise easy task.

For top performers, there is an especially tight calibration of flow and task; flow occurs in the work that is most critical to their goals and productivity, rather than in fascinating diversions or irrelevancies.[5] For the stars, excellence and pleasure in work are one and the same.

Psychological Presence

A project manager at an architectural firm notices a draftsman struggling over a simple aspect of a blueprint. The project deadline looms, and they are all under tremendous pressure. As she approaches her colleague, the project manager notices that her hands are clenched, her thoughts are fixed on angry feelings about the difficult deadline, and she feels frustrated because the draftsman is not further along.

She relaxes a bit and asks the draftsman, "What's going on—is something wrong?" His response is a litany of frustrations of his own—about not having enough information to finish the drawing, about how much he was asked to do in so little time.

Sympathetic, the project manager asks the draftsman more detailed questions about what he's up against. Her speech is lively, animated, her gaze direct. She lets him know she feels overwhelmed by the pressure, too.

Her line of questioning leads him to see that he actually has more information than he thought, and that he can, in fact, finish the drawing. He is buoyed, eager again to get back to the task. The project manager even makes a joke about how everyone was missing some data on this project—especially the vice president who had made such a crazy commitment in the first place. They both laugh and get on with the work at hand.

What did the project manager do that was so right? She was *present*.

This encounter, though nothing extraordinary, exemplifies the quality of being emotionally present at work. When people are present in this sense, they are fully attentive and completely involved in their work—and so perform at their best. Others experience them as accessible and engaged, and they contribute their creative ideas, energy, and intuitions fully.

The opposite, a psychological absence, is all too familiar from people who go through their work routines by rote, obviously bored, or otherwise disconnected. In a sense, they may as well not have shown up. The receptionist at the same architectural firm, who hates her job, puts it like this: "Sitting up here in front and smiling and typing and being friendly, it's all bullshit. It's just a role, and there isn't any satisfaction in it for me. This eight or nine hours is a waste."

Being present requires "not being disabled by anxiety, and so being open to others rather than closed," says William A. Kahn, the psychologist at Boston University School of Management who cites the project manager as a model.[6] Such presence shares a key attribute of flow: a total attention to, or immersion in, the task at hand. In contrast, the enemies of presence (and of flow) are the twin afflictions of apathy and anxiety.

Presence begins with self-awareness. The project manager, in Kahn's analysis, was attuned to her feelings; her clenched hands cued her to the anger she was feeling about the situation. And her empathy made her receptive to picking up the draftsman's sense of frustration without taking it as a reflection on herself.

The project manager's ability to be comfortable with these distressing feelings let her deal with them effectively rather than avoid them. Instead of dismissing the draftsman's frustration or preemptively criticizing his performance, she drew him out. And she was able to highlight information that transformed the frustration to enthusiasm, ending the encounter with a joke that put the onus where they both felt it to be—an emotional judo move that tightened the bond between them.

When fully present, we are more attuned to those around us and to the needs of the situation, and we fluidly adapt to what is needed—in other words, we are in flow. We can be thoughtful, funny, or self-reflective, drawing on whatever capacity or skill we need at the moment.

Getting Better and Better

A college professor describes why she loves her job: "I enjoy the fact that in the position I'm in, I'm continuously learning new things. It's continuous stimulation. I have to keep on my toes because things are always changing. You have to keep up."[7]

Our learning edge is at the point that most fully engages our maximum skill—and that precisely matches the zone of flow. Flow naturally propels self-improvement, for two reasons: People learn best when they are fully engaged in what they are doing, and the more people practice a task, the better they get. The result: continual motivation (enjoying flow) to master new challenges.

When a job lacks flow, even success can bring a curious malaise: What was once exciting can become boring. When a job has been mastered, the danger of stagnation rises sharply. That may explain why midlife is a notorious time for career changes.

"You get restless in midlife and midcareer, and that restlessness can have huge repercussions for your career," says a psychologist who counsels executives. "You start answering calls from headhunters even though you don't really want a new job. You start devoting your time and attention to a small business you start on the side. Or you get irritable and grouchy, or start collecting something like sports cars, or have affairs."

A main cause of such boredom is that people are no longer finding a challenge to their abilities; their work, so familiar and easy, has gone stale. The psychologist adds, "A healthy response might be to take on a new, challenging project within the company, because you need to find a way to keep yourself engaged in your work."

Good Stress: The Engaged Challenge

Remember the stormy tirade by Bill Gates that the unflappable woman handled so well? One school of thought holds that the well-timed use of such controlled outbursts can be motivating—that they can be a way of raising the temperature of a group. Gates is famous for his confrontational, explosive style; at Microsoft it's a kind of badge of honor to be a target of his attacks.

As one friend told me, "My boss knew who could take it; he never yelled at me. He'd do it in a meeting where everyone was low-energy. He'd suddenly tear into someone and everyone would wake up."

Flow occurs in that middle zone between boredom and immobilizing anxiety. A *moderate* amount of anxiety in the air, a sense of urgency, mobilizes us. Too little urgency and we are apathetic; too much and we are overwhelmed. The message "This matters" can be compelling.

Eustress, or "good" stress, refers to the pressure that mobilizes us to action. Its neurochemistry is revealing. When we are positively engaged by a challenge, our brain is being soaked in a bath of catecholamines and other substances triggered by the adrenal system. These chemicals prime the brain to stay attentive and interested, even fascinated, and energized for a sustained effort. Intense motivation is, literally, an "adrenaline rush."

A German study shows this relationship between motivation and the brain chemistry of eustress rather neatly.[8] Volunteers were given a taxing mental challenge, 120 arithmetic problems that they had to solve in an ever-shorter span of time, until they were wrong one in every four times. Whenever they felt confident that their answers were correct, they were checked; if right, they got a cash reward, and if wrong, they were penalized the same amount.

Those volunteers highest in hope of success—a variant of the need to achieve—were best able to keep their mobilization at a level that produced mostly catecholamines, rather than letting it rise to the emergency mode, where cortisol kicks in. But those who were motivated by a fear of failure were swamped with cortisol.

This proved to be a self-reinforcing effect. Those with lower levels of cortisol were better able to think and pay attention during the math challenge. Their heart rates showed they were no more anxious during the challenge than before it started; they stayed alert, calm, and productive. The effect on their performance was dramatic: They won more than twice as much as their peers.

Affiliation: The People Motive

Eugenia Barton, in her twelfth year as a high-school teacher, still adores her students: "I think I like them more every year. As I get to know them and have them in two or three classes, I become very close to them."

In an evaluation of a large group of teachers, Barton rated among the most compassionate and caring.[9] The pleasure she gets from her connection with her students bespeaks the many avenues people have for getting into flow.

There is a saying in India, "When a pickpocket meets a saint, all he sees are the pockets." Our motives shape how we see the world; all attention is selective, and what matters to us most is what we automatically scan for. Someone who is motivated to get results notices ways to do better, to be entrepreneurial, to innovate, or to find a competitive advantage. People like Barton, who is motivated by the pleasure of her relationships with her students, seek out opportunities for connection.

The need for achievement is one of the most frequently occurring competencies in star performers. The need for *affiliation,* by contrast, shows up less often, except in the helping professions, like nursing, medicine, and teaching. But affiliative interest—a genuine appreciation and enjoyment of other people—is also a key element of success not just for top nurses and teachers, but also for client-relations managers.[10]

Affiliation as a motive becomes an end in itself—a goal, if you will—not a means to something else. This sounds quite positive, but when it is excessive or the main motivator, it can be detrimental to managerial performance. For instance, successful managers and supervisors often have relatively low affiliative needs—and so are freer to refuse requests or set limits, despite objections.[11]

Too high an affiliative drive can become distracting, even a hindrance.[12] "Affiliation—liking people—is fine when it serves to strengthen relationships in the course of getting the task done," Richard Boyatzis, who studied

affiliation in managers, told me. "If you're too caught up with personal relationships at work, you can lose sight of the manager's task."

Affiliation as a motive may play its most basic role in determining one's
career choice. Those with high affiliation needs gravitate toward "people"
jobs, like teaching and nursing. In this way, it operates as a threshold competence and can set people on very fulfilling career paths, where relating—
not managing and delegating—is a top priority.

The Neurology of Motivation

D ifferent motives presumably involve differing mixes of brain chemicals,
though we don't know which.[13] We *do* know that the amygdala houses
the general brain circuitry that undergirds motivation. The emotional learning that predisposes someone to take pleasure in one set of activities rather
than another, as well as the repertoire of memory, feelings, and habits associated with those activities, is stored in the emotional memory banks of the
amygdala and its related circuits.

One frustration for computer scientists trying to build robotlike devices
that can see and hear like humans is that computers lack the guiding hand of
emotion.[14] Without an emotional memory bank that can instantly recognize
what matters to us—what data arouses *feeling*—computers haven't a clue.
They give equal value to all they see and hear, and so fail to pick out what
in each moment is most salient. Computers lack the guiding force that our
emotions and motivations allow us.

Our motives guide our awareness toward the opportunities they seek
out. The amygdala is part of a "neural doorway" through which whatever we
care about—whatever motivates us—enters and is weighed in terms of its
value as an incentive.[15] A guide to what matters most to us, it is the clear-
inghouse for our priorities in life.

People who suffer brain diseases or trauma that deprive them of their
amygdala (but leave the rest of the brain intact) suffer from a disorder of
motivation. They are unable to distinguish between what matters most to
them and what is irrelevant, between what moves them and what leaves
them cold. Every act is of the same emotional valence, and so neutral. The
result is paralyzing apathy, or an indiscriminate, uncontrollable indulgence
in appetites.

This motivational circuitry—our navigator through life—connects to
the prefrontal lobes, the brain's executive center, which brings a sense of

context and appropriateness to the amygdala's surges of passionate interest. The prefrontal area houses an array of inhibitory neurons that can veto or tone down the amygdala's impulses, adding caution to the circuitry of motivation: While the amygdala wants to leap, the prefrontal lobes want to look first.

Three motivational competencies typify outstanding performers:

- *Achievement drive:* Striving to improve or meet a standard of excellence
- *Commitment:* Embracing the organization's or group's vision and goals
- *Initiative and optimism:* Twin competencies that mobilize people to seize opportunities and allow them to take setbacks and obstacles in stride

■ ACHIEVEMENT DRIVE ■

Striving to Improve or Meet a Standard of Excellence

People with this competence

- Are results-oriented, with a high drive to meet their objectives and standards
- Set challenging goals and take calculated risks
- Pursue information to reduce uncertainty and find ways to do better
- Learn how to improve their performance

"There are three hundred American companies selling auto insurance, and we're the sixth largest," Peter Lewis, CEO of Progressive Insurance, told me when I visited his Cleveland headquarters. "Our objective is to triple in size and be number three by the year 2000." And Progressive just may do it: Only fifteen years ago it was ranked forty-third. Their rapid climb has been marked by the introduction of several innovations that have raised the bar for the rest of what has traditionally been a stodgy, risk-averse industry.

For example, Progressive promises to get one of its people to an accident scene within two hours of being notified. And the agents, using laptop computers to price replacement parts and estimate repair costs, write a check on the spot. No other major insurer offers this swift, on-the-scene claims service.

Even more radical is 1–800–AUTOPRO, a twenty-four-hour toll-free service that quotes auto insurance rates—Progressive's and those of the top three other insurers in the local market—for people shopping around. Progressive's rates often, though not always, come out lowest. This open, easy comparison of rates is unheard-of in the industry (and came about at the suggestion of a college classmate of Lewis's, consumer advocate Ralph Nader).

Another sign of the company's success: Progressive is one of the few insurance companies that is profitable just from its premiums.

Lewis is blunt about his drive to do even better, to capture a larger and larger market share, and what that means for the people who work for him: "We demand a very high standard, but the rewards can be great—people can earn up to double their salary in bonuses. It's an aristocracy of performers: We pay the best, but we demand the most—and we fire people who don't produce."

Despite this perform-or-leave policy, the company has a turnover rate of around 8 percent, about par for the industry. The reason: Those who gravitate to the company share Lewis's commitment to achievement. As Lewis put it, "One of our core values is doing better than you did before. It's an enormous challenge, but these are people who love it."

Progressive's statement of core values reads in part like a credo for the achievement competence: *"Excellence.* We strive constantly to improve in order to meet and exceed the highest expectations of our customers, shareholders and people."

Success demands this drive to achieve. Studies that compare star performers in executive ranks to average ones find the stars show the following signs of the achievement competence: They talk about and take more calculated risks; they urge and support enterprising innovations and set challenging goals for their employees; and they throw their support behind others' entrepreneurial ideas. The need to achieve is the single strongest competence that sets apart star from average executives.[16]

For those at higher levels of management, the obsession with getting results can express itself through the working of an entire department or company—Progressive Insurance is the vehicle for Peter Lewis's competitive drive no less than Microsoft is for Bill Gates's.[17] A study of the hundred wealthiest Americans throughout history—including Gates and John D. Rockefeller—shows that what they all share is their competitive drive: a single-minded passion for their business.[18]

The Calculated Risk

I t seems like an innocent enough challenge: Toss a ring over an upright peg. The catch is that the farther away the peg is, the more points you make, and you get to set the peg yourself. People who are too grandiose in their thinking typically set the peg beyond their throwing range. Those who are too cautious set the peg too close and score too few points.

The ring-toss game is a metaphor for calculated risk taking in life. It was used by David McClelland, then my professor at Harvard, to assess the ability to set risky but manageable challenges. Entrepreneurial drive demands that people be comfortable taking risks but know how to calculate them carefully. This skill at taking smart risks is a mark of the successful entrepreneur.

McClelland found outstanding performers set more challenging goals for themselves; they routinely calculated a placement for the peg that brought them around a 50 percent success rate.

This risk strategy in high achievers alerts them to specific performance benchmarks; they can tell you, "When I took over, efficiency was 20 percent—now it's 85 percent." Their decisions are often based on a careful cost-benefit analysis that frees them to take calculated risks.

High achievers—those willing to commit to something new—are restless in positions that stifle that urge. "When we trained assembly line workers at Ford to raise their need to achieve, most ended up leaving and starting their own business," Lyle Spencer Jr., a longtime colleague of McClelland, tells me. "The same thing happened with a group of computer engineers at IBM."

What seems absurdly risky to others will seem possible to entrepreneurs. When Leif Lundblad, the Swedish inventor of an automatic cash dispensing device for tellers, made a deal with Citibank to deliver the first batch of machines, he felt perfectly confident he could fulfill the order—his first ever. But, Lundblad told me, after he had met the delivery date "the people at Citibank told me that they thought there was only a ten percent chance that I would succeed."

The drive to do better shows up as a constant theme in entrepreneurs' thoughts, and a continuous improvement in performance. Consider a study of fifty-nine entrepreneurs, most of them research scientists, each of whom had taken advantage of an innovative technology to found a high-tech firm.[19] Five years after establishing their firms, those who were highest in achievement traits (like seeking out feedback on their performance and setting goals) were the most likely to have flourished—they had an average increase in sales of $1 million a year, increased the number of employees by fifty or more, or sold their company for a substantial profit.

By contrast, those founders who were low in achievement competence had done poorly. They had four or fewer employees, had sold the business for a loss—or had simply given up.

A Passion for Feedback

When a major customer of the Donnelly Corporation, which supplies glass to the auto industry, kept rejecting large numbers of their products for being substandard, three Donnelly production workers drove four hundred miles to learn why the customer was unhappy with their product.

Their startling discovery: The customer was offering its own employees a bonus for finding less-than-perfect parts from Donnelly. Rising to this challenge, the Donnelly workers raised their own quality control standards, being sure to ship only perfect parts.[20]

Those enterprising workers at Donnelly exemplify the spirit of striving to improve that lies at the heart of the achievement motive. Whenever a working group meets regularly to find ways to improve performance, they embody a collective drive to achieve.

By contrast, when it comes to setting goals or standards for themselves, people low in achievement competence are lackadaisical or unrealistic, seeking work that is either too easy or unrealistically ambitious. Likewise, supervisors who lack this skill create a work climate where goals are fuzzy and people are unsure about their own responsibilities, the limits of their authority, and even their job objectives. They don't give employees feedback on how they're doing or what is expected of them.

Those driven by the need to achieve seek ways to track their success. For many, this means money—though they often say that money is less important for what it can buy than as feedback on how well they are doing. As one California entrepreneur put it, "Money was never a big issue with me; it was just a way of keeping score." Another called it "a report card."[21]

Even those with moderate levels of achievement competence rely on performance measures like sales quotas or company quality standards. They may create their own measures of performance, setting goals like outperforming peers, doing a job more quickly, or beating some competitor.

In a small business such as a restaurant, performance feedback comes daily; those who manage stock portfolios get it almost by the minute. But for many people getting performance feedback can be frustratingly difficult because of the unquantifiable nature of their work. Such people have to develop a strong self-critical sense, to provide the feedback themselves. And top performers seek out the feedback they need at the point when it is most useful to them.

The Pursuit of Information and Efficiency

Nathan Myhrvold, Microsoft's chief technology officer, is a prodigious reader, a collector of knowledge for its own sake, a tracker of data of every sort.[22] He has to be. As Microsoft's in-house visionary, he never knows what random bit of data will be the seed of the next billion-dollar idea. He typifies the information addict, someone whose thirst for knowledge is limitless and feeds into a keen sense of innovativeness—and competitiveness.

In the chaotic modern world of work, the sheer volume of data—and the queasy feeling that we are falling behind in tracking it—can be a source of gnawing anxiety. One way to alleviate that anxiety is to monitor relentlessly what's going on, like Myhrvold—and so reduce the level of uncertainty.[23] People with an intense need to achieve are voracious in seeking out new ideas and information, particularly as it pertains (even peripherally) to their goals. They regularly call on others to get their perspective, and recruit others into an ongoing network of informants to get fresh intelligence and essential feedback.

People who lack this competence settle for whatever information comes their way or consult only the obvious and readily available sources of data. For executives this need to know can take the form of "management by walking around" or encouraging impromptu contacts or informal meetings with people at all levels. Such wide information gathering minimizes unpleasant surprises and maximizes the likelihood of spotting and seizing potential opportunities.

The craving for data runs in parallel to an urge to make things ever more efficient. When this tendency takes the form of obsessive, rule-bound, by-the-book supervision, it signifies poor performance. When high-level executives exhibit too much concern for detail and order, it can be a sign that they are focused on a smaller scale than their job demands. This is the micromanager who bird-dogs subordinates while paying too little attention to the bigger picture.

However, this drive to handle uncertainty can also foster meticulous attention to the details that matter. Superior performers are adept at putting into place systems that track progress or ensure a better quality and flow of data. One sales manager, frustrated by the long interval between reports from his large sales team, developed an automated phone system that beeped every salesperson at the end of the day, prompting them to punch in the sales they had made. This meant he had vital information not in two weeks but in eight hours!

■ COMMITMENT ■

Aligning with the Goals of a Group or Organization

People with this competence

- Readily make sacrifices to meet a larger organizational goal

- Find a sense of purpose in the larger mission

- Use the group's core values in making decisions and clarifying choices

- Actively seek out opportunities to fulfill the group's mission

On learning that the American Airlines national office was about to become their neighbor, enterprising employees at a Dallas branch of Herman Miller, the office furniture company, wrote a letter asking the airline to consider furnishing their new office with Herman Miller products.

Their initiative paid off in a sizable order. But the week before the airline office opened, the employees who went over to check that the order had been delivered properly found that the packing crates had crushed the plush on the fabric of hundreds of chairs. So the employees formed teams to work around the clock and over the weekend to raise the plush with steam irons.[24]

The essence of commitment is making our goals and those of our organization one and the same. Commitment is emotional: We feel a strong attachment to our group's goals when they resonate strongly with our own. Those who value and embrace an organization's mission are willing not just to make an all-out effort on its behalf, but to make personal sacrifices when needed. These are the staff who choose to work late into the night or over a weekend to get a project done on deadline, and the managers willing to leave town on a few hours' notice when an urgent mission comes along.

Commitment can even express itself in unpopular decisions that are made to benefit the larger group, even if these decisions rouse opposition or controversy. The truly committed are willing to make short-term sacrifices if they are for the larger good of the group. In short, the committed are the "patriots" of a company, natural boosters.

Among the competencies that Johnson Wax seeks to instill in its award-winning sales team is an unselfish strategic vision—doing what's right for the long term, even if there are no immediate rewards. "It might take the organization two or three years to catch up with what you are doing and reward you fully for it, but if it's right for the long term, you go ahead and trust that management will support you," an executive there tells me.

High levels of commitment are, of course, more likely in companies where people see themselves as "shareholders" (or actually *are* shareholders) rather than simply as employees. But workers who are inspired by a shared goal often have a level of commitment that is greater than any financial incentive. As Patricia Sueltz, an IBM vice president who is leading a drive to make her company a major presence on the Internet, puts it, "I get called by headhunters all the time. They say, 'We can make you very rich.' But they don't get it. I am going to change the world with this. I'm making a difference."[25]

Companies or organizations that lack a well-formulated mission—or whose mission statements are little more than public-relations ploys—offer people little to commit to. Employees need a clear sense of an organization's core values to form an allegiance to them.

Self-awareness is a building block of commitment. Employees who know their own guiding values or purpose will have a clear, even vivid sense about whether there is a "fit" with an organization. When they feel a match, their commitment is spontaneous and strong.

I remember a woman who sold advertising space for *The New York Times* telling me about an after-hours conversation among people in her department: "We realized that we in advertising provide the diesel fuel for the rest of the *Times* to work, that we're crucial to the paper's mission. We were talking about the time the paper ran a pictorial editorial on the crisis in Rwanda, triggering a flood of news coverage, and how the U.S. government sent aid over right afterward. That made us all feel really good about what we do."

Organizational Citizenship

The committed are the model citizens of any organization. They go the extra mile. And like pebbles in a pond, committed workers send ripples of good feeling throughout an organization.

Employees who feel strong organizational commitment will put up with highly stressful job conditions if need be—long hours, deadline pressure, and the like—out of devotion to collective goals. High levels of commitment allow employees to thrive under challenges and pressures that those who feel no particular loyalty to the organization find only stressful and onerous. At one federal agency, those administrators who felt the greatest organizational commitment suffered the least from the high stress typical of their jobs and reported the most satisfaction with their work.[26]

But if employees are not treated fairly and respectfully, no organization will gain their emotional allegiance. The more support employees feel from their organization, the more trust, attachment, and loyalty they will feel, and the better organizational citizens they will be.[27]

Organizational commitment grows from such emotional bonding. In a study of workers like teachers, clerks, insurance reps, and police officers, the key to how much effort they put into their work was how *emotionally attached* they felt to their organization—how proud to work there, how large their job figures in their sense of identity, how much they feel "part of the family."[28]

The Uncommitted

set it up so they got the credit—it really motivated the team, and our unit did quite well," a manager reports about how he got his team to surpass their goal.

By contrast, a consultant boasts, "I made sure I got the juiciest assignment, did it well, and got the kudos. The others were envious, which is their problem."

The manager used his position of power to share credit and so boost the morale of—and motivate—his team; the consultant could care less about the impact of his self-serving manipulation on his peers or the organization—he just wants the glory.[29]

Employees who see themselves as visitors rather than organizational residents show little commitment. But the same attitude can be found among workers who may have been in an organization for years. Employees who feel bitter about being underpaid or otherwise taken advantage of by an organization are certain to feel little commitment to its overall goals. So do those who see themselves as isolated and disconnected from decisions that impact their work.

These disaffected people are most prone to using the resources of the organization solely for their own benefit. The opportunistic among them see their current position mainly as a step on the way to somewhere else. Those who feel disconnected aren't even interested in moving up; instead their dissatisfaction manifests itself as a lack of integrity (doctoring expense accounts, for example, or stealing supplies).

An attitude of self-interest is, understandably, growing more common among once-committed employees who now confront downsizing and other changes that make them feel their organization is no longer loyal to *them*. This sense of betrayal or distrust erodes allegiance and encourages cynicism. And once lost, trust—and the commitment that stems from it—is hard to rebuild.

Tom Peters points to an emerging balance between people's needs to manage their own career and to commit to shared goals at work.[30] As he puts it, the emerging nature of loyalty balances allegiance to one's own goals and to the web of one's working relationships. This variety of loyalty, he says, "isn't blind loyalty to the company. It's loyalty to your colleagues, loyalty to your team, loyalty to your project, loyalty to your customers, and loyalty to yourself."

▪ INITIATIVE AND OPTIMISM ▪

Displaying Proactivity and Persistence

People with this competence

For Initiative

▪ Are ready to seize opportunities

▪ Pursue goals beyond what's required or expected of them

▪ Cut through red tape and bend the rules when necessary to get the job done

▪ Mobilize others through unusual, enterprising efforts

For Optimism

▪ Persist in seeking goals despite obstacles and setbacks

▪ Operate from hope of success rather than fear of failure

▪ See setbacks as due to manageable circumstance rather than a personal flaw

On several college campuses across America booths appeared selling snow cones with a difference—and a message. Instead of the standard heaps of colorful, sweetly flavored crushed ice, these snow cones came only in black—a political protest against oil drilling in Alaska's Arctic Wildlife Refuge. The snow cones were the brainchild of Adam Werbach, whose first political action came when he was just seven: He circulated a petition to his fellow second-graders urging the ouster of then Secretary of the Interior James Watt, an antienvironmentalist. By high school Werbach was organizing a drive to buy a truck for recycling the school's trash, and in his senior year Werbach founded the Sierra Student Coalition, an organization of young environmental activists which, through his college years, he built into a thirty-thousand-member organization. He gave the environmentalist message a new immediacy for city dwellers by making lead poisoning of children the group's signature issue. And he organized "dorm-storming" activists to sweep through college dormitories, encouraging students to use their computers to e-mail their legislators about environmental issues. At twenty-four, Werbach was elected the youngest-ever president of the Sierra Club, America's largest environmentalist group.[31]

Initiative often takes this form of being unusually enterprising. Take the shipping clerk who realized his company did enough business with Federal Express to get not just a volume discount, but a dedicated computer to track shipping orders. The clerk took it on himself to approach the CEO as he was leaving work and pitch the idea—and saved the company $30,000.[32]

At PNC Bank in Pittsburgh, a credit supervisor did a back-of-the-envelope calculation of the amount of electricity being eaten up by the bank's hundreds of personal computers left on by people after they had gone home. Those sixteen hours of idle time, he calculated, cost the bank $268,000 each year.

But when he went to higher-ups with his bright idea, they put him off, saying that switching computers on and off would decrease the life of the PCs. Undaunted, he did more research, finding that most business computer systems became obsolete and were routinely replaced years before the components wore out. The bank finally bought the idea—at a savings that would have required about $2 million in new revenues to have the equivalent bottom-line impact.[33]

Ways to Seize the Day

Those with initiative act before being forced to by external events. This often means taking anticipatory action to avoid problems before they happen, or taking advantage of opportunities before they are visible to anyone else. And the higher up the executive ladder, the larger the window of anticipation; for a midlevel supervisor or manager, it may mean being able to see days or weeks ahead; a visionary corporate leader sees years or even decades ahead.[34]

Possessing this farsightedness may mean taking steps when no one else sees the need to. This takes a certain courage, especially when others object. Star performers in federal research agencies, for example, plead with a skeptical Congress for basic research funds that, far into the future, might pay off with new cures for diseases.[35]

Constantly reacting to events rather than being prepared for them marks those who lack initiative. The failure to anticipate what's coming means operating in crisis mode. Such workers tend to fall behind and are continually forced to handle emergencies they did not foresee. All of this—as well as procrastination and not taking action in a timely way—indicates a basic failure to plan for or anticipate what lies ahead.

In contrast, proactivity pays off. Real estate agents can simply wait for the phone to ring, or they can scour classified ads for houses being sold by owners and approach them to list the house with their agency. They can screen prospective buyers to ensure they spend their time with those most serious about purchasing a house. Such acts of initiative result in a greater number of listings, a greater number of houses sold, and larger commissions.[36]

Seizing new opportunities is crucial for success in fields like consulting, where there is no revenue without initiative. At Deloitte & Touche Consulting, star performers stay alert to opportunities for "add-ons" that might extend a short-term project into a larger one, and take advantage of serendipity and unexpected opportunities to develop new business.[37]

Sometimes initiative simply means sheer hard work. One salesman with initiative said, "I was up at two o'clock this morning finishing my proposal—I'm calling stores during the day and preparing my programs and presentations at night."[38] Or take the tale of two trust officers: One exhibited high levels of initiative by selling an account to his doctor while he was in the hospital for a severe illness, while the other asked the researcher at the end of their interview if he had a will, since to the trust officer *everyone* was a potential client!

Hope and Perseverance

My seatmate seems right at home in the first-class cabin on our flight to Houston. A well-dressed, thirtyish organic chemist with an MBA, he's an account manager for a top chemical company.

But he tells me something surprising: "I grew up in Newark, New Jersey, on welfare. My parents had divorced, and I lived with my grandparents in a neighborhood where more kids went to jail than to college. I went back to visit there last month and saw one of my old friends—he's just been sentenced to three and a half years for dealing drugs. He told me, 'That's all we knew how to do.' And it's true. We never had any models for a way out."

So what made the difference between this account manager and his drug-dealing old buddy? "I was lucky. After high school my grandparents sent me to Texas to live with an aunt. I got a part-time job helping out with some research. And I started to see that these Ph.D.s I was working for weren't much different from me. I thought, 'I could do this, too.' So I started to go to night school, and finally got my B.A. in chemistry. Once you know what you want and see that it's feasible, you can figure out the steps you have to take. Then it's just persistence that gets you there."

And his old friends? "Those other kids gave up on themselves. They thought they didn't have what it takes to go to college. The only way they knew how to get respect was with a handgun."

A lack of initiative typifies those who feel a certain hopelessness—that their best efforts won't really make a difference. So, like the chemist's childhood friends, they don't push themselves. They see themselves as victims or passive pawns in the game of life, rather than master of their fate. The chemist's resilience may have owed more than he realized to the character lessons learned from his grandparents and aunt, but whatever its roots, those with initiative feel their own actions determine their future. These attitudes, in turn, determine how well we can deal with hardships and vicissitudes on the job. For example, among midlevel managers at a large corporation, those who saw themselves as masters of their fate were less fazed by difficult challenges and more positive in the face of stresses than were those who saw their destiny as being outside their control.[39]

Those who lack initiative are most likely to give up on themselves—and their jobs. This attitude can be seen in workers who need someone to direct them in performing their assignments. When it comes to going the extra mile—for example, staying late to get a priority project finished on time, or putting their own work aside to help someone else—such workers will often take a "not-my-job" line of resistance.

Too Much Initiative

While initiative is generally laudable, it needs to be balanced with social awareness in order to avoid unintended negative consequences.

Take the vice president of marketing at a large consumer products company, who discovered that one of his sales reps was unable to close a sale with a large national account.[40] The VP had made many presentations to that same account in the past, and so on his own initiative he called and set up a meeting there. Then he phoned the sales rep with instructions to meet him at the account's office the next day.

One result of the VP's initiative was that they made the sale. Another, unintended result was that the sales rep was deeply humiliated.

Feeling he had been made to look foolish and incompetent in front of his client, the rep protested, and his two bosses—the regional and the national sales managers—fired off irate memos to the vice president, claiming he had stepped out of bounds in going over their heads and humiliating their staffer.

But the warning had no effect. The same pattern continued for two years, with the VP acting high-handedly with other sales reps, until the president of the company, worried about a slump in sales, blamed it on the VP's demoralization of the company's sales force. The net result: The president gave the VP a choice—leave the company or step down to take a regional sales job.

Bosses who micromanage—who take control over small details best left to subordinates—may *seem* to have initiative, but they lack a basic awareness of how their actions affect other people. Initiative without empathy—or a sense of the bigger picture—can be destructive and typifies managers who perform poorly.[41]

Persisting—and Bouncing Back

Two executives were both refused a promotion because of negative evaluations from a superior.[42] One reacted to the setback with rage and fantasies of killing his boss; he complained to anyone who would listen and he went on a drinking binge. "It seemed like my life was over," he said later.

He avoided his boss, lowering his head when they passed in the hall. "Even though I was angry and felt cheated," he adds, "deep down I feared that he was right, that I am sort of worthless, that I had failed, and there was nothing I could do to change that."

The other passed-over executive was also stunned and angry. But he had a more open-minded perspective: "I can't say I was surprised, really. He and I have such different ideas, and we've argued a lot."

This executive went home and talked over the setback with his wife to figure out what had gone wrong and what he could do about it. Engaging in some introspection, he realized he hadn't been giving his maximum effort. With that knowledge his anger faded, and he resolved to talk with his boss. The result: "I had some discussions with him and things went very well. I guess he was troubled about what he had done, and I was troubled about not working up to potential. Since then, things have been better for both of us."

The key competence here is optimism, which hinges on how we *interpret* our setbacks. A pessimist, like the first executive, sees a setback as confirming some fatal flaw in himself that cannot be changed. The net result of such a defeatist attitude is, of course, hopelessness and helplessness: If you're doomed to fail, why try?

Optimists, by contrast, see a setback as a result of factors they have the power to do something about, not some flaw or deficiency in themselves. Like the second executive, optimists can deal with a setback by finding a positive response.

Consider how optimism helps people recover from failure.

Anne Busquet, once head of American Express's Optima Card division, was demoted in 1991 when five of her employees were revealed to have hidden $24 million in bad debt. Busquet, though not responsible, was accountable, and so lost her position as general manager of the division. Though devastated by the setback, Busquet felt a basic confidence in her abilities and rallied to another challenge she was offered at a lower level: salvaging merchandising services, a failing division of American Express.[43]

Optimists can more readily make a realistic assessment of a setback and admit how they contributed to it. Busquet, for example, reexamined her perfectionist, sometimes overly critical management style—even considering that it might have cowed her employees into hiding losses. She underwent executive coaching to soften her style, becoming more patient and a better listener. And under her direction, the failing merchandising services division reached profitability within two years.

Or take Arthur Blank, whose personality clashes with his boss at Handy Dan's, a Los Angeles hardware chain, led to his being fired in 1978. Blank's mother had kept the mail-order drug company his father had founded going after his death when Blank was young, and Blank himself, having witnessed how she overcame adversity, learned to keep trying instead of giving up when things went badly in life. So when an investor approached him, he jumped at the chance to found Home Depot, the no-frills, high-service, huge-selection home improvement chain that has grown to be a retailing giant.

Arthur Blank didn't give up; he reacted like an optimist, using the insider's expertise he had acquired in his years at Handy Dan's to invent a business that could outcompete his former employer. He saw himself as having the ability to change things for the better. For an optimist, a failure is just a lesson to learn from for the next round.

"Mistakes are treasures," as a German manager put it to me, "a chance to improve." But he added, "many managers have to realize they should be more tolerant of people's mistakes—not punish them for it, but help them learn from it."

Optimism and Hope

Classic studies of how optimism bolstered sales productivity at MetLife, an insurance company, were done by Martin Seligman, a University of Pennsylvania psychologist.[44] Seligman found that optimists sold 29 percent more insurance in the first year than did their more pessimistic peers, and 130 percent more their second year.

The value of an optimistic outlook has been proven in many organizations. At American Express Financial Advisors, a pilot test of optimism training helped produce a rise in sales after just three months, big enough to convince the company to make it a standard part of training. Other studies of superior managers show that they look at their failures as due to a correctable mistake and take steps to ensure that the problem won't crop up again.[45]

The near cousin of optimism is hope: knowing the steps needed to get to a goal and having the energy to pursue those steps. It is a primal motivating force, and its absence is paralyzing. Competence studies show that top performers in the human services—everything from health care and counseling to teaching—express hope for those they seek to help.[46]

The power of hope was shown in a study of caseworkers whose task it is to help people with the most severe mental disabilities—chronic schizophrenia, severe retardation—carve out a life for themselves in supervised homes.[47] The first year in such jobs is the toughest: Clients don't get better, things go wrong, people can be ungrateful, caseworkers burn out and quit. But those caseworkers who were the most hopeful—optimistic about their clients' potential for improvement and their own ability to help—fared the best. After a year on the job, those who began with high levels of hope survived with the most satisfaction, were less emotionally exhausted, and were most likely to stay in their jobs.

In jobs like these, where stress is high and frustrations common, a rosy outlook may get better results. Hopefulness is crucial when anyone undertakes a tough task; positive expectations may be especially beneficial in the toughest jobs, where high optimism may be a pragmatic job strategy.[48]

A caveat: There is something very American about these upbeat competencies. They reflect a frontier ideology that does not translate to all other cultures. In research done among top executives in a global food and beverage company, for instance, optimism was found to predict star performance in America—but not in Asia or Europe.

"In many Asian countries, like Japan, Taiwan, and India, the can-do attitude is seen as too bold or too individualistic," Mary Fontaine, managing director of the Hay/McBer Innovation and Research Center, told me. "In those cultures optimism typically manifests in more low-key ways, with the attitude, 'This is a very difficult challenge, and I'm trying, even though I may not be able to do it.' You don't hear people saying, 'I know I can do it, I know I'm good.' And in Europe, what Americans see as optimism can simply seem like arrogance."

3

....

People
Skills

7

Social Radar

The major account was underperforming, baffling the sales team at Johnson Wax: Why were the sales on a key product far softer there than at other retailers'?

The sales rep responsible for the account thought he knew the reason: The chain's buyer wanted to place bigger orders, but he was powerless: A battle between managers of two different departments at the retailer meant that the product was being sold in the wrong part of the stores—and so faring poorly. The department manager who was selling the product refused to give it up to the other department, and the buyer did not have the power to break the deadlock.

To solve the problem, Johnson Wax's sales team called for the retail equivalent of a bilateral diplomatic commission: a meeting with three levels of executives above the sales rep and the buyer. At that meeting, Johnson Wax shared data with the executives from the chain showing that if they handled the product differently, it could bring them $5 million more in profits annually. That hit home.

"When they saw they were passing up a five-million-dollar opportunity because of battles between departments, they decided they had to break down the walls," says Patrick O'Brien, then vice president for North American sales. "All three levels got behind the buyer. It had taken a year to have the discussion—but once they saw they wanted to do it, it took just days to make the change."

That sales strategy exemplifies one of the marks of empathy: being able to see a sales situation from the standpoint of the customer in order to help *the customer* succeed. Such sensitivity demands being able to read the political currents and realities of someone else's organization.

"The best approach is to have a deep understanding of a buyer's business needs and objectives, and work toward that end," O'Brien comments. "The key is probing and listening to hear what's important for that person's success. It's been one of the fundamentals of sales success for the last century."

When I spoke with O'Brien, he was flush with two triumphs: His sales team had just been named Vendor of the Year by both Wal-Mart and Target, two of America's largest retail chains.

One of the changing barometers for retail sales is "category management," where retailers at a grocery store, for example, will treat all their snacks or air fresheners as a single category, and make judgments on which brands to carry collectively, rather than on a one-by-one basis. Paradoxically, this by-the-numbers approach has made personal relationships between sales reps and category managers all the more important.

"Our sales stars have the ability to balance the world of fact with the interpersonal world," O'Brien notes. "The sales profession has gone from rapport selling to number-based sales; the field has been shifting from the traditional social skills of sales to a model of managers who work their numbers, not their contracts; but you have to balance these. You need the interpersonal side because these are still individual decisions."

Empathy takes many forms. One is the kind of astute awareness the people at Johnson Wax had of their client's needs. But it also can be seen in the company that has a realistic, accurate sense of its own people, its customers and clients, its competitors and market, and other stakeholders, from unions to shareholders. Being able to see reality from their perspective, to sense how they are reacting to the company's actions, offers a powerful set of readings for effective management.

The head of a private bank in Switzerland tells me, "My job is something like a family priest or doctor. You can't be in private banking without using your emotional intelligence, especially empathy. You have to sense what your client hopes for, fears—even if he can't express it in words."

Empathy Begins Inside

As Freud observed, "Mortals can keep no secret. If their lips are silent, they gossip with their fingertips; betrayal forces its way through every pore." The nervous fidgeting of a negotiator belies her deadpan expression; the studied disinterest of a customer dickering over prices in an auto showroom is contradicted by the excited way he gravitates toward the convertible he covets. Being able to pick up on such emotional clues is particularly important in situations where people have reason to conceal their true feelings—a fact of life in the business world.

Sensing what others feel without their saying so captures the essence of empathy. Others rarely tell us in words what they feel; instead they tell us in their tone of voice, facial expression, or other nonverbal ways. The ability to sense these subtle communications builds on more basic competencies, particularly self-awareness and self-control. Without the ability to sense our own feelings—or to keep them from swamping us—we will be hopelessly out of touch with the moods of others.

Empathy is our social radar. A friend tells me about her early sense of a colleague's unhappiness: "I went to my boss and said, 'Something's up with Kathleen—she's not happy here.' She wasn't making eye contact with me, she stopped sending me her usual witty e-mails. Then she announced she was leaving for another job."

Lacking such sensitivity, people are "off." Being emotionally tone deaf leads to social awkwardness, whether from misconstruing feelings or through a mechanical, out-of-tune bluntness or indifference that destroys rapport. One form this lack of empathy can take is responding to other people as stereotypes rather than as the unique individuals they are.

At the very least, empathy requires being able to read another's emotions; at a higher level, it entails sensing and responding to a person's unspoken concerns or feelings. At the highest levels, empathy is understanding the issues or concerns that lie behind another's feelings.

The key to knowing others' emotional terrain is an intimate familiarity with our own, shown in research by Robert Levenson at the University of California at Berkeley.[1] Levenson has married couples come into his physiology lab for two discussions: a neutral "How was your day?" talk and a fifteen-minute discussion of something the couple disagrees about. During this small battle Levenson records their responses in every way, from heart rate to changes in their facial expression.

After the disagreement, one partner leaves. The one who stays then watches a replay of the talk while narrating the hidden dialogue of what he or she was actually feeling but did not express. Then that partner leaves, and the other returns to narrate the same scene from the *other* partner's perspective.

Partners adept at empathizing do something quite extraordinary physiologically: Their own body mimics their partner's while they empathize. If the heart rate of the partner in the videotape goes up, so does the heart rate of the partner who is empathizing; if the heart rate slows down, so does that of the empathic spouse.[2] This mimicry involves a biological phenomenon called entrainment, a sort of intimate emotional tango.[3]

Such highly attuned rapport demands we put aside our own emotional agendas for the time being so that we can clearly receive the other person's signals. When we are caught up in our own strong emotions, we are off on a different physiological vector, impervious to the more subtle cues that allow rapport.[4]

Charles Darwin proposed that the twin abilities to send and read feelings have played an enormous role in human evolution, both in creating and maintaining the social order. In evolution, negative emotions—fear and anger— no doubt had immense survival value, impelling a threatened animal to fight or flee. In a sense this evolutionary holdover is still with us today; during our own amygdala hijacks, we read and respond more strongly to someone else who is also in a bad mood than to someone in a good one. This can be a recipe for emotional disaster, creating a feedback loop of negativity or rage.

The prerequisite for empathy is self-awareness, recognizing the visceral signals of feelings in one's own body. Among counselors, for instance, the most effective and empathic were best able to tune in to their body's own signals for emotion—an essential for any job where empathy matters, from teaching to sales and management.[5]

A Subtle Dance

We had a woman who could clear a room in minutes," the marketing manager of a California-based educational software firm tells me. "She wouldn't listen first and then join the conversation. She'd launch into a monologue—some complaint or attack that had nothing to do with what was being talked about—and she'd go on and on, oblivious to the yawns. She didn't know when to stop. She didn't have a clue."

The smoothness in any social interaction depends to a great extent on spontaneous entrainment. When two people start to talk with each other, they immediately begin to fall into a subtle dance of rhythmic harmony, syn chronizing their movements and postures, their vocal pitch, rate of speaking, and even the length of pauses between one person's speaking and the other's response.[6]

This mutual mimicry goes on outside conscious awareness, and seems to be controlled by the most primitive parts of the brain. These mechanisms kick in with breathtaking rapidity, as quickly as a fifticth of a second. If this automatic coordination is missing, we feel slightly uncomfortable.

One of the main mutual adjustments is in facial expression. When we see a happy face (or an angry one), it evokes the corresponding emotion in us, albeit subtly.[7] To the degree we take on the pace, posture, and facial expression of another person, we start to inhabit their emotional space; as our body mimics the other's, we begin to experience emotional attunement.[8]

Our nervous system is automatically set to engage in this emotional empathy (again, the amygdala plays the key role in this attunement).[9] But how well we use this capacity is largely a learned ability that depends on motivation. Animals—and people—who have been raised in extreme social isolation are poor at reading emotional cues in those around them not because they lack the basic circuitry for empathy but because, lacking emotional tutors, they have never learned to pay attention to these messages and so haven't practiced this skill.

Our first lessons in empathy begin in infancy, when we are held in our mother's or father's arms. These primary emotional bonds lay the groundwork for learning how to cooperate and be welcomed into a game or group. The extent to which we master this emotional curriculum determines our level of social competence. Take children on the playground who don't pick up the crucial cues for smooth interaction; when they want to join a game, they'll often just wade in and thereby disrupt it.

More socially skilled children, on the other hand, wait and watch awhile. They tune in to the game first and then enter seamlessly at a natural opening. It's the same with adults: Picking up the social rhythm and timing of those we work with is essential.

Because of differences in how well we have learned the basic skills of social awareness, there are corresponding differences among us in workplace competencies that build on empathy. Empathy represents the foundation skill for all the social competencies important for work. These include:

- *Understanding others:* Sensing others' feelings and perspectives, and taking an active interest in their concerns

- *Service orientation:* Anticipating, recognizing, and meeting customers' needs

- *Developing others:* Sensing others' development needs and bolstering their abilities

- *Leveraging diversity:* Cultivating opportunities through diverse people

- *Political awareness:* Reading the political and social currents in an organization

UNDERSTANDING OTHERS

Sensing Others' Feelings and Perspectives, and Taking an Active Interest in Their Concerns

People with this competence

- Are attentive to emotional cues and listen well

- Show sensitivity and understand others' perspectives

- Help out based on understanding other people's needs and feelings

An assistant at a large design firm describes the poisonous feelings emanating from a temperamental partner like this: "With a glance he became a closed door; he put up this don't-bother-me sign, so I knew to stay away from him. But if I have to deal with him at some of those times, I keep it short. I don't joke or anything—I did once and he went nuts. So I get monotonic, almost moronic, with him."[10]

The key phrase here is "with a glance he became a closed door"; that was the cue that told the assistant how to act around the temperamental design partner. At work we constantly pick up such emotional cues and adjust our behavior accordingly. Lacking such radar, we are vulnerable to shipwreck in the shoals created by the rocky emotions of those we work with.

Empathy is essential as an emotional guidance system, piloting us in getting along at work.

Beyond mere survival, empathy is critical for superior performance wherever the job focus is on people. Whenever an artful reading of a person's feelings matters, from sales and organizational consulting to psychotherapy and medicine, as well as leadership of every kind, empathy is crucial to excellence.

Medicine is a field newly awakened to the benefits of empathy, in part for some compelling economic reasons. In a day of heightened competition for patient loyalty, those physicians who are better at recognizing emotions in their patients are more successful in treating them than their less sensitive colleagues.[11] Physicians, of course, need to sense the anxiety and discomfort of their patients so they can treat them effectively, but a study found how rarely they listen. Patients usually had an average of four questions in mind to ask, but during the visits they were able to ask just one or two. Once a patient started speaking, the first interruption by the physician occurred, on average, within eighteen seconds.[12]

Physicians who don't listen get sued more—at least in the United States. Among primary-care physicians, those who had never had a malpractice suit were shown to be far better communicators than their lawsuit-prone peers. They took time to tell their patients what to expect from a treatment, to laugh and joke, to ask the patients' opinion and check their understanding, and to encourage the patients to talk.[13] And the time needed for a doctor to be successfully empathic? Just three minutes.

Empathic Design

Empathy has come to R&D. Researchers watch customers use a company's products—at home or at work—much as an anthropologist might observe another culture.[14] This peek into the customer's world offers a fuller understanding than can be gained through the typical round of focus groups and market surveys.

Such intimate exploration into a customer's life, combined with a company's openness to change, is a potent mix for innovation. When Kimberly-Clark sent observers to watch parents and toddlers use diapers, they realized that toddlers needed a first step toward "grown-up" dressing. That insight led to the creation of Huggies Pull-Ups, which toddlers can pull on themselves—and to $400 million in annual sales before competitors caught up.

The ability to read customers' needs well comes naturally to the best managers of product development teams. Being able to read what the market wants means empathizing with customers and then developing a product that suits their needs.[15]

At Ford Motor Company, empathic design was used in a makeover of the Lincoln Continental. The engineers, for the first time, were given intensive contact with owners of the car they were all trying to reinvent.

Instead of the old method, where market researchers would lead focus groups of car owners and distill the results, engineers spent a week talking to people who had bought Continentals. Their task: Get a sense of what owners loved about the car.

"Customers sense and feel distinctive qualities they value in a product," Nick Zeniuk, then one of the project managers, told me. "So we had to tune in to our customers' feelings. To do this, we had to be empathic. I told the design managers, 'Forget about the data you've seen from market research. Go out and talk to the people we're building this for. Listen, feel, sense. Look into their eyes, get a gut sense of what they want.' "

This personal approach brought a strong sense of the customer into the room with the automotive engineers as they created their specifications. Zeniuk remembers, "They'd come back with a video of a customer and say, 'You can't see it, but right here he was feeling very strongly about what he was saying.' We had to first get a sense of how all this needed to feel, and then figure out what that would look like in engineering terms—the technical specifications that would make the car feel comfortable or more responsive."

The Art of Listening

When you're desperate to make a sale you don't listen as well," the director of sales at a Wall Street brokerage firm told me. "There's nothing better in selling than when someone objects to something and you can say, 'You're absolutely right—we should consider that.' You do much better if you can listen and sympathize with their viewpoint."

A finely tuned ear is at the heart of empathy. Listening well is essential for workplace success. The U.S. Department of Labor estimates that of the total time we spend in communication, 22 percent is devoted to reading and writing, 23 percent to speaking—and 55 percent to listening.[16]

Those who cannot or do not listen come across as indifferent or uncaring, which in turn makes others less communicative. And listening is an art.

The first step is giving the sense that one is open to listening in the first place; managers with an "open door" policy, who appear approachable or go out of their way to hear what people have to say, embody this competence. And people who seem easy to talk to are those who get to hear more.

Listening well and deeply means going beyond what is said by asking questions, restating in one's own words what you hear to be sure you understand. This is "active" listening. A mark of having truly heard someone else is to respond appropriately, even if that means making some change in what you do. But just how far we should go in adjusting our actions based on what another says is itself a matter of some controversy.

In sales circles some view empathy quite narrowly, arguing that taking the customer's perspective will kill sales of products or services customers don't really want or need.[17] This, of course, implies a somewhat cynical or naïve view of the salesperson's task, as though it is only about making the sale, not building or improving a relationship with the customer.

A more enlightened view of sales, though, sees the task as being able to listen well and understand what the customer or client needs, and then find a way to meet those needs. This lesson, that empathy is at the heart of effective selling, was borne out by a survey of a random sample of buyers for both large and small American retailers, who were asked about apparel sales reps.[18]

The old stereotype that sales go to the highly affable, outgoing salesperson did not hold up. It wasn't enough to be a fast-talking extrovert; the buyers' consensus favored the reps who were most empathic—who cared about their needs and concerns.[19] That was especially true if the empathy went hand in hand with the sense that the sales rep could be trusted.

When Empathy Lacks Integrity

want to assure you at the outset that the most important thing is the kids— they come first. I know some of you are worried. But if we find anything that might harm the kids, we'll stop."

So began the warm, reassuring presentation of the president of an outfit that specialized in recovering metals from the ash left by industrial burning. He had come to talk to the parents and teachers of a grammar school in the small town where his company was relocating; the plant would be down the street from the school, pending final approval by the town government.

As the company president ran through what would go on at the plant—the jobs it would bring, the benefits for the local economy—his sincerity and concern for the well-being of the children and their community were winning over his audience. He seemed so understanding, so empathic.

But then came the question-and-answer period. One of the parents, a chemist, asked, "But aren't you going to be processing ash that contains dioxin? And isn't dioxin highly carcinogenic? How will you protect our children from that?"

With that question, the president became flustered, defensive, even antagonistic—especially when other parents, now not so trusting, challenged him on why he had failed to mention this unsettling fact earlier.

The meeting ended with the parents deciding to consult an expert on industrial toxins and to ask the town manager to hold public hearings before approving the plant.

Empathy can be used as a tool for manipulation. This manifests frequently as pseudoempathy, a social pose that disintegrates quickly if recognized. A friend complained to me about the salespeople in a pricey clothing store she likes to browse in: "They always say how nice it is to see me, and follow me around trying to make small talk. I just want them to leave me alone until I have a question." Then one day, in an unguarded moment, one of the salespeople confessed that her boss had instructed them to strike up a friendly conversation with customers who had made expensive purchases before. But this forced friendliness just didn't ring true—it actually put off my friend.

We may have natural safeguards against such artificial empathy—the capacity to sense, as my friend did, when empathy is not sincere. And researchers who have assessed manipulative people find that those who are most motivated by a Machiavellian urge to use people for their own gain tend to be poorest at empathy. By contrast, those who are trusting—who believe that people are basically good—tend to be more highly attuned to feelings.[20]

Empathy Avoidance

S am was emotionally tone deaf. He picked up the phone, heard a sobbing voice ask to speak with his wife, Marcy, and handed her the phone with a cheery, "Marcy, it's for you!"

Elaine Hatfield, the University of Hawaii psychologist who knows him, says, "Sam was oblivious to emotional messages because he couldn't care less."[21]

It's not enough to have the potential to empathize—we have to care. But some people who seem to lack empathy may actually be doing so strategically and intentionally; they may avoid caring in order to hold to a hard line and to resist the urge to help.[22] And in the right measure, this is not necessarily a bad thing in the workplace.

Managers who go overboard in focusing on relationships or catering to people's emotional needs at the expense of organizational requirements perform poorly.[23] In situations where the perceived cost of empathy is thought to be too high —for example, in a negotiation over wages—people on both sides of the issue may have to blunt their sympathy. Lawyers, too, are notorious for their studied indifference to the concerns of the other side during litigation (though, as we shall see in Chapter 8, an extreme shutdown of empathy is not a fruitful negotiation strategy).

There may be some wisdom in tempering empathy, particularly when it comes to allocating tight resources in an organization. When we identify too strongly with someone else's need, we are more prone to go to extremes in helping them, even when that decision harms the collective good.[24]

By the same token, the head alone, without the heart, can make decisions that will backfire—as has been the case with many companies that ruthlessly downsized, then found themselves loathed or distrusted by the dispirited employees who were left. And some managers tune out the feelings of those they work with simply to avoid having to take those feelings into account—a tactic that can make them seem imperious or cold.

A lack of empathy may account for what happened with the surgeon who was going to treat a friend of mine for a blood clot in her leg. When he explained to her that one risk of the surgery was that she might lose her leg, my friend burst into tears.

His response: "If you're going to cry, you'll have to find another physician to treat you."

So she did.

Empathy Distress

She had been a pediatric nurse for seven years, but now she was asking for a transfer to a different service at the medical center. Why?

"I just can't take holding another little kid who is going to die of cancer. It's too hard on me."

The nurse's anguish offers a case study in "empathy distress," where one person "catches" another person's upset. Instead of helping the children out of their pain and distress, the nurse found herself joining it.

Empathy distress is most common when we find ourselves deeply upset that someone we care about is in pain. For example, concern for a troubled friend—say, a coworker who fears being laid off—may stir the same troubling feelings in us. This phenomenon occurs when someone who is highly empathic is exposed to another person's negative moods and doesn't have the self-regulation skills to calm their own sympathetic distress.

Medical residents "toughen" themselves to handle empathy distress; their joking about patients near death as "crispy critters" or "goners" is part of this emotional shell, a way to deal with their own sensitivities. The danger, of course, is that they will end up like the insensitive surgeon who drove my friend away. A new generation of medical school programs has begun to teach students ways to manage their own distress more effectively without forfeiting empathy.

Workers such as customer service representatives, who regularly deal with people in bad moods, are also in danger of empathy distress. This problem often plagues people in the helping professions, who are exposed day after day to people in dire circumstances. The alternative is to stay open to feelings, but to be adept in the art of emotional self-management, so that we are not overwhelmed by the distress we catch from those we deal with.

The Politics of Empathy

There is a politics of empathy: Those with little power are typically expected to sense the feelings of those who hold power, while those in power feel less obligation to be sensitive in return. In other words, the studied lack of empathy is a way power-holders can tacitly assert their authority.

During the days of the civil rights movement, Martin Luther King Jr. expressed surprise at how little insight whites had into the feelings of blacks; blacks, he said, had to be much more sensitized to how whites felt, if only to survive in a racist society. A parallel argument holds that to the degree women are oppressed in a society, they have had to be more empathic than men (for a review of the data on gender differences in empathy, see Appendix 3).

Research in the 1970s and 1980s suggested a negative correlation between being in positions of power and empathic abilities.[25] But that may hold less true today, since organizations are becoming more team-oriented and less stiffly hierarchical. The demands of modern leadership now include competence at empathy; the authoritarian style of the past just doesn't work as well as it once did.

Those who still dismiss empathy as out of place in business, or as too "soft," do so mainly because of two common misunderstandings. One is confusing empathy with psychologizing; the other is the mistaken belief that empathizing with people is the same as *agreeing* with them.

Richard Boyatzis told me, "At a major computer manufacturer I was assessing managers for empathy by asking them to describe a time they had helped someone with a problem. I found that some people would tell about deeply exploring the other person's psychological state and explaining it to them in terms of its childhood roots or some pop-psych theory like codependency. But that is psychologizing, not empathy—you're actually *dismissing* the problem by talking about its supposed causes."

Psychologizing, Boyatzis found, was related to mediocre performance in managers. The top performers listened and understood the others' feelings, and offered advice, without imposing their own "diagnosis" of what was behind the problem. Such psychological theorizing may be of interest, even helpful, over a cup of coffee between friends—but it is not appropriate at work. And while it may masquerade as empathy, it is not the same.

Similarly, understanding someone's point of view or perspective—knowing why they feel as they do—does not inevitably mean embracing it. Particularly in business dealings, understanding how someone feels need not lead to giving in, but to more skillful negotiation and management. As a result, tough decisions may generate less resentment and lasting ill will.

I remember talking with leaders of management teams at Lockheed Martin, an aerospace company that had gone through a period of major cutbacks. Many of the managers had laid off hundreds of workers—a process some described as the hardest thing they had ever had to do. I mentioned that some managers fear empathy will make them too softhearted to make the hard decisions of business life, and I asked them if they thought empathy mattered. "Absolutely," was one reply. "When you have to let thousands of people go, everyone else who stays is watching." They had to go through with the layoffs despite the pain—but, they told me, if they hadn't gone about the process with empathy, it would have demoralized or antagonized everyone.

Consider how employees were treated when plants closed at two companies. At GE, workers had two years' notice that the plant would be closed, and the company made an intense outplacement effort to help them find other jobs. The other company announced the closing with just one week's notice, and made no effort to help workers locate other employment.

The results? Almost a year later, the majority of the former GE workers said it had been a good place to work, and 93 percent lauded the transition services offered them.[26] At the other company, only 3 percent said it had been a good place to work. GE preserved a large pool of goodwill, while the other firm left a legacy of bitterness.

▪ DEVELOPING OTHERS ▪

Sensing Others' Development Needs and Bolstering Their Abilities

People with this competence

- Acknowledge and reward people's strengths and accomplishments

- Offer useful feedback and identify people's needs for further growth

- Mentor, give timely coaching, and offer assignments that challenge and foster a person's skills

It was a small lesson, but one with lasting impact. As a high-profile, fast-track editor at a national magazine, she had a problem: "I was prone to snap decisions, committing to projects in a moment of enthusiasm, then having to suffer through a torturous series of rewrites with authors that ended in their articles being killed. It was emotionally draining for me, and it created too much animosity and just plain pain.

"But then," she told me, "my editor in chief taught me a phrase that has helped immensely."

What was the phrase?

" 'I'll think about it.' "

That simple bit of advice exemplifies coaching, which lies at the heart of developing others. Excellence in this competence is emerging as second only to team leadership among superior managers.[27] For sales managers, developing others is even more important—the competence most frequently found among those at the top of the field.[28]

This is a person-to-person art; the heart of coaching and developing is the act of counseling. And the effectiveness of counseling hinges on empathy and the ability to focus on our own feelings and share them.[29]

In a study of supervisors, managers, and executives in twelve large organizations, the impact of developing others was greatest among supervisors, suggesting that this skill is crucial in managing those involved in front-line work—salespeople, line workers, and the like.[30] As the realm of a manager or executive's influence increases, the direct opportunities for developing others may diminish, while other competencies, like leadership, may emerge as more relevant.

Even so, "The head of an organization is essentially a teacher," Harry Levinson, a pioneer in consulting psychology, tells me. He adds, "People these days need to have the sense they are getting increasingly competent as they go on—or else they won't stay."

Strong coaching or mentoring helps employees perform better, enhances loyalty and job satisfaction, leads to promotions and pay increases, and lowers rates of turnover.[31]

An open, trusting relationship is the foundation of success in on-the-job coaching. That was the clear conclusion when fifty-eight top managers, all vice presidents or above at companies with annual sales of $5 billion or more, were asked about their own experiences.[32] These executives focus on helping people they see as having high potential. As one high-level executive puts it, "I'm nice to those whom I just expect to do their jobs, but I really lean on the talented ones—I push them to transcend themselves."

They spent most of their coaching time trying to boost performance, mainly by giving feedback and offering tips on developing needed skills. By and large their comments were positive; they spent only about 5 percent of their time confronting poor performance.

The key to success as coaches? The best coaches show a genuine personal interest in those they guide, and have empathy for and an understanding of their employees. Trust was crucial—when there was little trust in the coach, advice went unheeded. This happened also when the coach was impersonal and cold, or the relationship seemed too one-sided or self-serving. Coaches who showed respect, trustworthiness, and empathy were the best. But when employees resisted change or were difficult, then the experience was so unrewarding for the coaches that they tended to drop the effort.

"In retrospect, one of my biggest failures in business was not looking for coaching in my early years," a vice president at a large media conglomerate told me. "I was so afraid to seem inadequate that I didn't ask for advice on how to handle things. So I shut down many potential coaching relationships. Now a young associate of mine will appear in my doorway asking me to coach her on how to approach our president about something, or how to handle some situation. She's being smart."

The standard image of coaching or mentoring is a seasoned hand helping a favored younger person along. But people who are gifted at helping others can do so with anyone—even superiors. Managing upward—helping a superior do a better job—is part of this art. A chief petty officer in the U.S. Navy, for example, recounted how he had to "teach junior officers how to lead me. I tell them, 'You're running the ship and I'm watching all this equipment for you; you've got a right to know how it's running. Ask me. And ask me to help you when I can.' "[33]

The Art of the Critique

When it comes to giving feedback, perhaps no one is better than Shirley DeLibero, head of the New Jersey Transit Authority, which under her direction emerged as the most efficient transit company in America. DeLibero shows people she appreciates them, while giving them a consistent stream of positive and constructive performance feedback. "I spend lots of time praising people—I send personal notes to people throughout the company when they do a good job," DeLibero told me. "But I also let people know when they goof up. You do a disservice to people if you don't evaluate their performance honestly. You have to let them know *what* they need to improve."

Like DeLibero, the helpful coach gives specific information about what is wrong, combined with corrective feedback and a positive expectation of the person's ability to improve. By contrast, the worst way to give feedback is during an amygdala hijack, when the result is inevitably a character attack.

While that has a pernicious effect, so does another common failing: neglecting to give any performance feedback at all.

In a study of the effects of performance feedback on self-confidence, MBA students either were praised, were criticized, or received no feedback on their performance in a simulation of creative problem solving. They had been told that their efforts would be compared with how well hundreds of others had done on the same task. Those who heard nothing about how well they did suffered as great a blow to their self-confidence as those who were criticized.[34] The report cautions that "when organizations deprive employees of specific job-related information, they may unknowingly inhibit their performance."

People hunger for feedback, yet too many managers, supervisors, and executives are inept at giving it or are simply disinclined to provide any. And in some cultures—especially in Asia and Scandinavia—there is a tacit prohibition against expressing criticism openly, particularly in front of others. An executive at a Saudi company told me, "We have twenty-seven different nationalities working together in our organization. Most come from countries where people were brought up not to say bad things about the people they work with. So it's hard to get honest performance feedback."

On the other hand, giving brutal feedback can be a cover for pure competitive aggression—an attack disguised as "helpfulness." An executive at a bank in the Netherlands says, "Some people here give feedback to score in a macho game of one-upmanship; they pay no attention to the impact on the person receiving it, they're far too blunt. But it's not authentic help—it's part of a game. They need more empathy."

The Power of Pygmalion

They were a burden to their shipmates—sailors who were constantly in trouble, or simply did not do their jobs. "Undermotivated problem sailors" was the term the U.S. Navy used for them; the military acronym was "LP," for "low performer."

But their supervisors were given a set of tactics to change the LPs' behavior. The supervisors were taught something new: to expect the best of these low performers despite their abominable histories.

The supervisors let the LPs know they believed in their ability to change, and they treated them more like winners. That positive expectation proved powerful: The LPs began to do better on every front, receiving fewer punishments, showing better overall performance, even improving their personal appearance.[35] It was the Pygmalion effect in action: Expecting the best from people can be a self-fulfilling prophecy.

Athletic coaches and good managers alike have long known they can boost a person's performance by giving them a suitable challenge coupled with a vote of confidence.

One way to promote positive expectations is to let others take the lead in setting their own goals, rather than dictating the terms and manner of their development. This communicates the belief that employees have the capacity to be the pilot of their destiny, which is a core tenet held by those who take initiative.

Another technique that encourages people to perform better is to point to problems without offering a solution; this implies they can find the solution themselves. Outstanding tutors use this strategy with their students. They initiate what amounts to a Socratic dialogue, leading the person through a series of questions. This lets students find their own way to the answers, which will bolster their confidence in decision making.[36]

At a higher level of development, the coach or mentor arranges an ongoing assignment that will give the person needed training, experience, or challenges. This might take the form of delegating responsibilities, or putting the person in charge of a project that will call forth new skills. Doing this well demands a sensitivity to the readiness of the person being coached—if the assignment is too easy, little will be learned; if it's too difficult, the person may experience a setback. The skill lies in arranging successful "stretch" experiences that increase capability and confidence. The ultimate support comes in the form of promoting employees to appropriate positions—as a genuine acknowledgment of their newly achieved level of competence, and a new proving ground for yet another level of skill.

Still, the urge to help develop someone's abilities can go overboard, conflicting with the better interests of the organization. Putting too much emphasis on coaching and development at the expense of other needs is a danger. Supervisors and managers who devote too much time and effort to coaching and too little to leading or managing end up doing a mediocre job at best.[37]

▪ SERVICE ORIENTATION ▪

Anticipating, Recognizing, and Meeting Customers' Needs

▪▪▪

People with this competence:

▪ Understand customers' needs and match them to services or products

▪ Seek ways to increase customers' satisfaction and loyalty

▪ Gladly offer appropriate assistance

▪ Grasp a customer's perspective, acting as a trusted advisor

▪▪▪

To visit Stéphane & Bernard, a clothing boutique on the island of St. Barts, is to experience customer service as high art. The eponymous owners attend visitors with a combination of Gallic charm, wit, and undivided attention.

For two hours one lazy January afternoon, my wife and I luxuriated in that attention. My wife and Bernard talked about her life and her clothes, with Bernard running back and forth to the racks to find her the perfect piece. But he also took twenty minutes to carefully annotate a map of the island for me while regaling me with highlights of its restaurants, beaches, and snorkeling spots.

"My business is first of all to make people feel good here, to make everyone comfortable," Bernard explains, indicating their store, which crams clothes from fifteen top designers into just 450 square feet. Their tiny shop earns five times more per square foot than other such retailers—most of it in the four winter months of the tourist season.

The key to this success lies in their philosophy of customer service. "I have to know my customers to help them—how they like to dress, what they like to do, what part of their body they're dissatisfied with," Stéphane tells me.

They eschew the commission approach to sales, "where the salespeople don't care if it looks good or not. They just want to make the sale, so they tell you that whatever you've picked is perfect." Stéphane continues, "If I don't like how something looks on a customer, I tell her so—and why. I don't want to sell her something that's not right for her. I act as an advisor to my customers."

That is exactly what they are to their three hundred or so regular customers. These clients are so familiar to them that when Stéphane and Bernard travel on buying trips, many purchases are made with a specific customer in mind. "We build relationships," says Bernard. "We keep a complete file on each customer, follow what they bought, what they're looking for, and over the years we help them build a wardrobe."

Stéphane and Bernard exemplify the highest level of customer service, which means being able to identify a client's real, underlying—and often unstated—needs, and then matching them to one's products or services. It also means taking a long-term perspective and so sometimes trading off immediate gains in order to protect and preserve the relationship.

The service ideal of top performers transcends the ordinary customer service model altogether. Sales or continued patronage is no longer the sole goal of the relationship, but rather a natural by-product of servicing the client's needs.

Superlative customer service entails being a trusted advisor, as Stéphane and Bernard realize. This stance can mean occasionally taking a position that runs against the immediate interests of one's own organization but is the correct action for the client. This kind of trust-based relationship will only grow over time.

At the ultimate level of service, one acts as the client's advocate. This can lead to benefits in the long run—for example, advising a client not to overextend credit on purchases may mean fewer sales in the short term, but it ensures that the account will stay viable into the future. It might even mean on occasion suggesting a competitor's product, which may lose an immediate sale but cement a long-term relationship.

A Broader View

In the modern organization, everyone has "customers." Any colleague we need to assist or whose needs our own job affects is a client of sorts. Star performers go out of their way to make themselves available to serve their clients, especially during crucial moments. Stars also help their clients look good: for example, doing something that creates a visible success for the client (or coworker).

For those in the compensation and benefits arm of Sandoz Pharmaceuticals, outstanding customer service took forms like spending extra hours working closely with the head of sales to determine incentive targets, or giving a home phone number to a department head going through a critical period of reorganization, being available day or night to help out.[38] It also meant occasionally letting another person take credit for a job well done.

To shine at service we need to monitor the satisfaction of customers, not waiting to hear complaints but freely offering information that might be helpful without self-interest motivating the gesture. This lays the groundwork for a trusting relationship, one where the client or coworker will feel a positive regard and start to see us as a source of reliable and helpful information—elevating the relationship above one simply of buyer and seller.

That, of course, takes empathy. Consider the results from a study of the sales force of an office supply and equipment company that sells to industrial organizations and government agencies. The most successful members of the sales force were able to combine taking the customer's viewpoint with appropriate assertiveness to steer them toward a choice that satisfied both their needs.[39]

If a salesperson takes too much control, it can lead to resentment. Successful salespeople empathize at the outset of the interaction, sensing the buyer's viewpoint, and fine-tuning their sense of what the buyer wants as the interaction continues—for instance, noting signs of discomfort in response to a suggestion, and expressing empathic concern before going on.

The shift toward making the customer's needs the center of the relationship goes hand in glove with having a friendly emotional tone. This is crucial in handling disgruntled customers. "A customer was having some difficulty getting a refund check," a manager in a large retail store recalls.[40] "She came to me because she said our operations manager was rude to her. I'm sure that was just a misunderstanding, but I apologized, helped her get the check, and sent her on her way. It took only a few minutes to straighten out the problem, and she left feeling better than when she came in."

That last line bears repeating: "She left feeling better than when she came in." How customers *feel* when they interact with an employee determines how they feel about the company itself. In a psychological sense, the "company" as experienced by the customer *is* these interactions. Loyalty is lost or strengthened in every interaction between a company and its customers. To paraphrase business maven Peter Drucker, the purpose of business is not to make a sale, but to make and keep a customer.

The Costs of Cost-Cutting

Nancy Cohen walked into a Pier 1 store intending to buy a new set of kitchen chairs. The store had the chairs, but she walked out empty-handed and furious.

"I was presold," she told a colleague of mine.[41] "But I couldn't get anyone to help me. The sales help were too busy chatting among themselves. I said to the woman who finally faced me, 'I am interested in the chairs in the window. Do you have any in stock and do you have any other colors?' "

The reply: a vague gesture to a corner of the store filled with glassware, and the even vaguer, almost mystifying response, "I think it comes in that color."

And with that, the saleswoman walked away—from an $800 sale.

That salesclerk was absolutely incompetent at customer service, the critical ability for anyone who works at the interface between a company and its clientele.[42] And such incompetence is on the rise in American department and discount stores; a 1996 survey of four thousand consumers by Yankelovich Partners rated such retailers eleventh out of twenty consumer services, behind telephone companies, restaurants, and even the U.S. Post Office.[43] One villain seems to be too-sharply reduced staffing on sales floors; another, curtailing training; the American retail industry now spends less on training salespeople than any other business.

One of the worst signs of incompetence at customer service is an us-against-them mind-set, where the customer or client is targeted as an enemy and viewed only as someone to be manipulated. This stance hampers salespeople's effectiveness at selling because they don't really see the customer. This can lead to a misguided hard sell, where a salesperson comes on too strong in a way that is utterly at odds with the customer's needs.

■ LEVERAGING DIVERSITY ■

Cultivating Opportunities Through Different Kinds of People

People with this competence

■ Respect and relate well to people from varied backgrounds

- Understand diverse worldviews and are sensitive to group differences

- See diversity as opportunity, creating an environment where diverse people can thrive

- Challenge bias and intolerance

■ ■

I often tell the story about my encounter with an outgoing bus driver in New York City who managed to keep up an upbeat patter with his passengers as he navigated the streets of the city. By the time people got off that bus, their bad moods had been lifted by exposure to his sheer exuberance. It was a breathtaking demonstration of social adeptness.

I used to describe the bus driver as "a black man around sixty." But after one lecture, an African-American woman came up and challenged me: "Why did you mention he was black? Would you have mentioned it if he had been Jewish or Japanese?"

I was stunned by her question. Thinking it over, I realized that, for me, mentioning the bus driver's race was implicitly part of a rejoinder I was making to the book *The Bell Curve,* which had argued that IQ is the key to life success and that African-Americans had a disadvantage relative to other groups in this area. In my analysis the book was based on flawed data, and besides, IQ was but one part of a spectrum of factors that led to life success, with emotional intelligence playing a major role.[44] I wanted to make the point that this African-American man was gifted in that domain.

But the woman retorted that I hadn't made any of that explicit, and to her ears I seemed to be describing someone who gets along by being overly eager to please white people. At any rate, his race was irrelevant, she argued.

And she was right. In the context in which I told the story, the man's race *was* irrelevant. To call attention to his race was to raise a difference that was beside the point. I dropped any mention of his race from then on.

Calling attention to someone's group affiliation when that identity is irrelevant can invoke a stereotype about that group in the minds of all concerned. And group stereotypes can have an *emotional* power that negatively affects performance.

The destructive power of stereotypes—particularly for members of minority groups in an organization—has been revealed in an elegant series of studies by Claude Steele, a psychologist at Stanford University. Steele should know: He's one of very few African-American members of that university's mostly white faculty.

While Steele's experiments dealt with academic performance, the implications for the workplace are direct: Negative stereotypes can cripple work performance. To be successful on a job, people need to feel they belong there and are accepted and valued, and that they have the skills and inner resources needed to achieve, even prosper. When negative stereotypes undermine these assumptions, they hamper performance.

"Stereotype threat" is the term Steele coined to refer to a kind of emotional land mine, an expectation of low performance that, though unspoken, permeates an organization, creating an atmosphere that negatively affects someones work abilities.[45] Such expectations have the potential to cause levels of anxiety that seriously impair cognitive ability. As we saw in Chapter 5, the aroused amygdala can shrink the space available in working memory, and stereotype threat is certainly capable of activating the amygdala.

A Threat in the Air

The test Steele devised was straightforward enough: College men and women who were strong in math were asked to solve problems taken from the qualifying exam for graduate school. They took the test in two groups. The first group was told that the test usually showed differences in ability between men and women. The others were told nothing.

The women's scores on the test were appreciably lower than the men's—but *only* when they had been told the test was sensitive to gender differences. The women who had not been reminded about gender issues did just as well as the men!

The same performance-lowering effect occurred when black test takers were given a similarly threatening message. Steele's experiments offer dramatic evidence of the power of even suggesting stereotypes. The active ingredient in lowering the women's scores, Steele found, was debilitating anxiety. Though they had the potential to perform well, the anxiety triggered by the threatening stereotype impaired their performance.

Steele contends that this anxiety is worsened by the interpretive framework the stereotype creates. The usual anxieties of a challenging task are seen as confirming that they cannot perform, which amplifies their own anxieties so they do, indeed, perform poorly.

Those most likely to feel the effects of stereotype threat are those at the *vanguard* of a group—the first women to become jet pilots, say, or the first minority group member to enter a law firm or brokerage house. Despite having the skills and self-confidence to enter this new territory, once there they can feel the full effect of stereotype threat and so, for the first time, may experience emotionally induced performance lapses.

Women who are at the higher reaches of executive ranks offer a case in point. A survey of women—and their CEOs—revealed that the CEOs believed women's lack of management experience and tenure was what prevented them from advancing to corporate leadership positions. The women executives, though, named as the number one and two reasons stereotyping and exclusion from informal networks in the organization.[46]

The stereotype threat for women executives seems to come into play in specific circumstances. A review of sixty-one studies on workplace prejudice against women managers found that bias comes into play most when women work in jobs that traditionally have been held by men, or are evaluated by men rather than women.[47]

How Stereotypes Threaten

Steele argues that stereotype threat may be one reason women are underrepresented in math, engineering, and the physical sciences. While American girls show no difference from boys in math abilities through elementary and middle school, once they enter high school their scores on math tests start to lag, and the gap widens through college and graduate school. At the start of their college careers, women drop out of math, science, and engineering programs at two and a half times the rate of men. American women earn just 22 percent of college degrees in these fields and only 13 percent of the Ph.D.s—and hold just 10 percent of the jobs (where, incidentally, they earn only three quarters of the salary paid to men in comparable positions).[48]

This failure to perform has nothing to do with skill. It has much to do with the presence of disabling stereotypes. Steele points to instances of underperformance by blacks and women despite high test scores as evidence of the role of emotional threat once people enter a domain where a threatening stereotype exists. At that point, he argues, people are particularly vulnerable to doubting their own abilities, questioning their talents and skills—thus undermining their own sense of capability. Their anxiety acts as a spotlight, both for themselves and (at least in their minds) those who are watching to see how well—or how poorly—they will do.

Black students, for example, are affected by "rumors of inferiority," such as those put forth in the book *The Bell Curve.* That same kind of wrong thinking afflicts oppressed minorities around the world. Through long exposure, such negative social stereotypes take hold, Steele argues, and so intimidate those who belong to such groups. That intimidation becomes emotionally potent and destructive in the workplace.

Success Through Others

One of the watchwords at the Harvard Business School these days is "Success through others who are different from yourself." There is strength in difference, and this makes the ability to leverage diversity an increasingly crucial competence.

The vastly greater variety of people working in organizations of every kind demands a greater awareness of the subtle distortions that stereotypes and bias bring to working relationships. Among managers, for example, being able to read people accurately, without the distortions of emotionally laden stereotypes, sets superior performers apart from average.[49]

We generally have difficulty reading the subtle nonverbal signals of emotion in those who belong to groups very different from our own—whether a different gender, race, nationality, or ethnic group.[50] Every group has its own norms for expressing emotion, and to the extent we are unfamiliar with those norms, empathizing grows more difficult. As we have seen, a failure of empathy can throw any interaction off-key, making both people uncomfortable and creating an emotional distance, which in turn encourages us to view the other person through the lens of a group stereotype rather than see him or her as an individual.

The missing ingredient in many diversity programs is that they fail to take advantage of diversity by using it to help participants learn how to do their business better. It's all well and good to make people of diverse backgrounds feel comfortable and welcome at work, but we can go further, *leveraging* diversity to heighten performance across the board.

Beyond zero tolerance for intolerance, the ability to leverage diversity revolves around three skills: getting along well with people who are different, appreciating the unique ways others may operate, and seizing whatever business opportunity these unique approaches might offer.

These principles point the way to what David Thomas and Robin Ely contend, in a *Harvard Business Review* article, can be the potential benefits of leveraging diversity: heightened profitability, enhanced organizational learning, flexibility, and rapid adaptation to shifting markets.[51]

To go that extra step requires questioning the widespread assumption that the only goal of diversification is simply to raise the numbers of different kinds of people in a workforce, channeling them to jobs specializing in dealing with customers like themselves. This assumes, Thomas and Ely argue, that the main special contribution minority group members can make to a company is in using their insider's sensibility to help the company market better to members of their group.

That is a decent goal so far as it goes, but it fails to reap the true benefits of diversity. Thomas and Ely propose that diverse people "bring different, important, and competitively relevant knowledge and perspectives about how to actually *do work*—how to design processes, reach goals, frame tasks, create effective teams, communicate ideas, and lead."[52] And this knowledge can improve an organization.

Consider the case of a public-interest law firm in the northeastern United States. In the 1980s, the law firm's all-white staff became concerned that their main clients, women in workplace disputes, were also all white. They felt obligated to diversify their client base.

So the firm hired a Hispanic lawyer, hoping she would bring in Hispanic clients. But something *more* happened: She brought in a new way of thinking about the basic business of the law firm itself. One result was that the firm expanded its practice beyond women's issues, also pursuing precedent-setting litigation challenging English-only policies.

As the firm began to take on more nonwhite lawyers, says one of its principal partners, "it affected our work by expanding our notions of what are relevant issues and framing them in creative ways that would have never been done with an all-white staff. It's really changed the substance—and in that sense enhanced the quality—of our work."[53]

When leaders of organizations value the insights brought to work by people of diverse backgrounds, it can lead to organizational learning that boosts competitiveness. Take a financial services company whose sales model had focused on rapid-fire cold calls, until it realized that its most successful salespeople were women who used a sales approach more in keeping with their gender style: the slow, sure building of relationships. This company now takes a more flexible approach to sales, encouraging and rewarding the differing styles that work better for salespeople of different backgrounds. The company was able to use the insight offered by the women's success to question its own assumptions, learn, and change—and so do better by leveraging diversity.

▪ POLITICAL AWARENESS ▪

Reading Social and Political Currents

People with this competence

- ▪ Accurately read key power relationships

- ▪ Detect crucial social networks

- ▪ Understand the forces that shape views and actions of clients, customers, or competitors

- ▪ Accurately read organizational and external realities

An outstanding diplomat tells of being posted to an oil-rich African nation and quickly learning that it was "the prime minister's executive assistant's mistress's nephew" who actually called the shots on that nation's petroleum policy. So the diplomat immediately arranged to get invited to a party where he could meet, befriend, and eventually lobby the nephew.[54]

The ability to read political realities is vital to the behind-the-scenes networking and coalition building that allows someone to wield influence—no matter what their professional role. Mediocre performers lack such social acumen and so betray a distressingly low level of political savvy.

A director of training and development at a Fortune 500 company asked me to help design a program for managers there, because, as she candidly put it, "You can describe many of the managers here as practically unconscious, oblivious to what's going on around them."

Every organization has its own invisible nervous system of connection and influence. Some people are oblivious to this below-the-radar world, while others have it fully on their own screen. Skill at reading the currents that influence the *real* decision makers depends on the ability to empathize on an organizational level, not just an interpersonal one.

People who maintain rich personal networks in an organization typically are savvy about what is going on, and this social intelligence extends to understanding the larger realities that affect the organization. For example, knowing how to read the currents in the client organization typifies people outstanding in corporate sales. One politically savvy star performer gave this example: "An executive VP who was relatively new on the board was a rising star and a 'favorite son' of the president of the corporation we sell to. He was really the decision maker: He had carte blanche from the president. We found that fostering a relationship with him was very much to our benefit and the key to the sale."[55]

Outstanding performers in most organizations share this ability. Among managers and executives generally, this emotional competence distinguishes superior performers; their ability to read situations objectively, without the distorting lens of their own biases or assumptions, allows them to respond effectively—and the further up the organizational ladder, the more this matters.[56]

Executives continually are put in the predicament of having to balance seemingly conflicting points of view or interests, whether from within or from the world at large. Without this political astuteness, managers are at a loss to balance the multitudinous perspectives of peers, bosses, subordinates, customers, and competitors.

People who do this well are able to distance themselves a bit, setting aside their own emotional involvement in events to see with more objectivity. For example, when faced with a conflict within their organization, they can take multiple perspectives, describing with some accuracy the position of each person involved. This is true despite the fact that all of us encounter few events—especially emotionally loaded ones—about which we have no opinion or feeling. This emotional competence builds on both emotional self-control and empathy, allowing people to see clearly rather than be swayed by their own point of view.

Political Savvy

The vice chairman of a large American oil company went to China during the rule of Deng Xiaoping. While there, he gave a talk to a small group of Chinese officials and made some comments critical of President Clinton.[57]

His audience sat listening in a frozen silence, and when he finished, no one said a word. The next day someone came to the offices of the oil company to apologize, saying with some delicacy, "We are sorry we were not able to carry on a conversation in a more interactive way yesterday. But you understand that many of the topics your vice chairman brought up are foreign to us."

The employee who received the message said later, "I considered them very gracious. What they did not say to my face was, 'Your vice chairman can criticize Clinton and feel that's okay. But if one of us did the same thing to our head of state, he'd probably be in jail the next day.' "

The oil company vice chairman lacked sensitivity to the ground rules of the culture he was dealing with. And as with national cultures, every organization has its implicit ground rules for what is acceptable and what is not. Empathizing at the organizational level means being attuned to the climate and culture of an organization.

The inevitable politics of organizational life create competing coalitions and power struggles. A sensitivity to these political fault lines of alliance and rivalry makes a person more understanding of the underlying issues and better able to address what really matters to key decision makers. At an even higher level of competence, this awareness extends to the larger forces in the world—competitive or regulatory pressures, technological opportunities, political forces, and the like—that determine the global opportunities and constraints of the organization.

A caution: While "political animals," those who live to play the game of organizational politics in pursuit of their own interest and advancement, eagerly study the invisible web of power, their weakness lies in the fact that their motive for doing so is pure self-interest. They ignore information that does not bear on their personal agenda, and this can create blind spots. It also means they tune out the feelings of those around them except when pertinent to their own ambition—and so political animals often come across as uncaring, insensitive, and self-centered.

Disdain of (or disinterest in) organizational politics is also a liability. Whatever the reason, those who lack political astuteness more often blunder in trying to mobilize others to their cause because their attempts at influence are misdirected or inept. An accurate understanding of the formal structure of the organizational chart is not enough; what's needed is a keen sense of the informal structure and the unspoken power centers in the organization.

8

The Arts of Influence

The merger of Salomon Brothers and Smith Barney created one of the world's largest financial firms. In the business press the event was heralded as a crowning achievement of Smith Barney's CEO, Sanford ("Sandy") Weill, who engineered the merger (and who, months later, would go on to yet another, with Citicorp).

Within weeks of the announcement, a series of meetings were held throughout the two firms, detailing just how the two heavyweight companies would morph into a single giant. As is usually the case in such mergers, hundreds of employees would lose their jobs, since many functions were duplicated between the companies.

But how can that news be delivered without rendering this already worrisome reality all the more so?

One department head did it the worst way. He gave a gloomy, even menacing, speech, saying essentially, "I don't know what I'm going to do, but don't expect me to be nice to you. I have to fire half the people here, and I'm not exactly sure how I'm going to make that decision, so I'd like each of you to tell me your background and qualifications so I can start."

His counterpart at the other company did much better. His message was upbeat: "We think this new company will be a very exciting platform for our work, and we're blessed with talented people from both organizations to work with. We'll make our decisions as quickly as we can, but not until we're positively sure we've collected enough information to be fair. We'll update you every few days on how we're doing. And we'll decide both on the basis of objective performance data plus qualitative abilities, like teamwork."

Those in the second group, Mark Loehr, a managing director at Salomon Smith Barney, told me, "became *more* productive, because they were excited about the potential. And they knew even if they didn't end up with a job, it would be a fair decision."

But in the first group, he observed, "Everyone was unmotivated. They heard 'I'm not being treated fairly,' and it triggered a collective amygdala attack. They were bitter, demoralized. People were saying, 'I don't know if I even *want* to work for this jerk anymore, let alone the company.' Headhunters connected with his people and recruited some of the best away—but not those in the other group."

Said Loehr, "When Lehman didn't fully integrate Shearson when they merged, there was a massive failure. But when Smith Barney took over Shearson, they were able to make it work. It's how you treat people immediately after the merger that makes all the difference. It allows the roots of trust between the two cultures to start growing. Sandy Weill's genius is his ability to integrate firms quickly so they don't die."

The art of influence entails handling emotions effectively in *other* people. Both department heads were, in this sense, influential—but in opposite ways. Star performers are artful at sending emotional signals, which makes them powerful communicators, able to sway an audience—in short, leaders.

Emotions Are Contagious

All these abilities take advantage of a primal fact: We influence each other's moods. Influencing another person's emotional state for better or worse is perfectly natural; we do it constantly, "catching" emotions from one another like some kind of social virus. This emotional exchange constitutes an invisible interpersonal economy, part of every human interaction, but it is usually too subtle to notice.

Even so, the transmission of mood is remarkably powerful. When three strangers, all volunteers for a study of mood, sat quietly in a circle for two minutes, the most emotionally expressive person transmitted his or her mood to the two others over the course of the two minutes.[1] In every such session, the mood the most expressive person had going in was also the mood the other two felt coming out—whether happy, bored, anxious, or angry.

Emotions are contagious. As the Swiss psychoanalyst C. G. Jung put it, "In psychotherapy, even if the doctor is entirely detached from the emotional contents of the patient, the very fact that the patient has emotions has an effect upon him. And it is a great mistake if the doctor thinks he can lift himself above it. He cannot do more than become conscious of the fact that he is affected. If he does not see that, he is too aloof and then misses the point."

What holds in the intimate exchange of psychotherapy is no less true on the shop floor, in the boardroom, or in the emotional hothouse of office life. We transmit moods among us with such ease because they can be vital signals for survival. Our emotions tell us what to focus on, when to be ready to act. Emotions are attention grabbers, operating as warnings, invitations, alarms, and the like. These are powerful messages, conveying crucial information without necessarily putting that data into words. Emotions are a hyperefficient mode of communication.

In a primitive human band, emotional contagion—the spread from person to person of fear—presumably acted as an alarm signal, quickly focusing everyone's attention on an imminent danger, like a stalking tiger.

Today that same collective mechanism operates whenever word spreads of an alarming drop in sales, a coming wave of layoffs, or a new threat from a competitor. Each person in the chain of communication activates the same underlying emotional state in the next, and so passes on the message to be alert.

Emotions as a signaling system need no words—a fact evolutionary theorists see as one reason emotions may have played such a crucial role in the development of the human brain long before words became a symbolic tool for humans. This evolutionary legacy means that our radar for emotions attunes us to those around us, helping us interact more smoothly and effectively.

The *emotional* economy is the sum total of the exchanges of feeling among us. In subtle (or not so subtle) ways, we all make each other feel a bit better (or a lot worse) as part of any contact we have; every encounter can be weighted along a scale from emotionally toxic to nourishing. While its operation is largely invisible, this economy can have immense benefits for a business or for the tone of organizational life.

The Group Heart

A group of managers are negotiating how to distribute a limited amount of bonus money. Each presents a worthy candidate from his or her own department, making the arguments for what size bonus each candidate will get. It's a discussion that can turn acrimonious or end in harmony, depending.

Depending on what? It turns out that what makes the difference are the *moods* that spread among the managers as they talk. The moods people catch from each other at work are a crucial—yet often unnoticed—ingredient in how *well* they work.

One dramatic scientific demonstration of how the emotions rippling through a group can impact performance was done by Sigal Barsade, a professor at the Yale University School of Management.[2] A group of volunteers from the business school were brought together to act the part of managers allocating bonuses. Each volunteer had two goals: to get as large a bonus as possible for their candidate, and to help the committee as a group make the best use of the pool of funds for the company as a whole.

What they did not know was that among them was a plant who had been coached by Barsade. A trained actor, this manager always went first, and always made identical arguments. But he did it in one of four emotional keys: with cheerful, ebullient enthusiasm; with a relaxed, serene warmth; with a depressed sluggishness; or with an unpleasant and hostile irritability. His real role was to infect the group with one or another of these emotional states, like spreading a virus among unknowing victims.

The emotions *did* spread like a virus. When the actor argued with cheerfulness or warmth, those feelings rippled through the group, making people more positive as the meeting went on. And when he was irritable, people felt grumpier. (Depression, on the other hand, spread little, perhaps because it manifests as a subtle social withdrawal—indicated, for instance, by little eye contact—and so has little amplification.)

Good feelings spread more powerfully than bad ones, and the effects were extremely salutary, boosting cooperation, fairness, collaboration, and overall group performance. The improvement was more than just a glow from good feelings: Objective measures showed the groups were more effective—in this case, better able to distribute the bonus money fairly and in ways that would most benefit the company.

In the world of work, no matter the business at hand, emotional elements play a crucial role. Emotional competence requires being able to pilot through the emotional undercurrents always at play rather than being pulled under by them.

Handling the Other Person's Emotions

I t's the end of a long, tiring, muggy day at Walt Disney World, and a bus-load of parents and children are starting the twenty-minute ride back to their hotel. The children are overstimulated and cranky, and so are the parents. Everyone is whiny.

It's a bus ride from hell.

Then, rising above the miasmic drone of complaining children and parents, comes a thin, persistent warble: The bus driver has started to sing the song "Under the Sea," from the movie *The Little Mermaid*. Everyone begins to quiet down and listen. Eventually a little girl chimes in, then several more children. By the end of the ride everyone is singing "The Circle of Life" from the movie *The Lion King*. The bus ride from hell has become the plea-surable, song-filled end to a full day.

That bus driver knew just what he was doing. In fact, the singing drivers are part of an intentional strategy to help keep customers mellow. I still re-member (with some delight) the driver of a Mickey Mouse bus breaking into the theme song for the then-popular *Mickey Mouse Club* TV show when I visited Disneyland as a child way back in the 1950s; it remains my most vivid memory of that holiday trip.

This strategy takes clever advantage of emotional contagion. We are all part of each other's emotional tool kits, for better or worse; we continually prime others' emotional states, just as they do ours. This fact offers a pow-erful argument against the uninhibited expression of toxic feelings at work: They poison the well. On the flip side, our positive feelings about a company are to a large extent based on how the people that represent the organization make us feel.

The most effective people in organizations know this innately; they nat-urally use their emotional radar to sense how others are reacting, and they fine-tune their own response to push the interaction in the best direction. As Tom Pritzker, president of Hyatt Hotels, told me, "The lady at the front desk who wins over the customer with her smile can't be quantified, but you can sense the advantage." (It happens that smiles are the most contagious emo-tional signal of all, having an almost irresistible power to make other people smile in return. And smiling in and of itself primes positive feelings.)[3]

The same brain mechanisms that underlie empathy and allow for emo-tional attunement also create the pathway for emotional contagion. But in addition to the circuitry emanating from the amygdala, the basal areas (in-cluding the brain stem), which regulate reflexive, automatic functions, are also involved. These areas operate to create a tight loop of biological connectedness, re-creating in one person the physiological state of the other—and this seems to be a pathway emotions follow in traveling from one person to another.[4]

This is the system at work when someone is skilled at swaying an audience. As Howard Friedman, a psychologist at the University of California at Irvine, observes, "The essence of eloquent, passionate, spirited communication seems to involve the use of facial expressions, voices, gestures and body movements to transmit emotions." Friedman's research shows that people who have this emotional adeptness are better able to move and inspire others, and to captivate their imagination.[5]

In a sense, emotional display is like theater. We all have a backstage, the hidden zone where we feel our emotions, and a stage front, the social arena where we present the emotions we choose to reveal. This private split between our public and private emotional lives is analogous to the concept of the front of the store and the back office. Emotional displays are more often carefully stage-managed when interacting with customers, and less well managed backstage, and this discrepancy can be unfortunate. As one organizational consultant put it, "Many an executive who appears highly charismatic out of the office comes back and acts like a jerk with his employees." Or as the director of a large Sunday school complained to me about her minister, "He's just too impassive, completely unexpressive. He's so hard to read, I don't know how to take much of what he says to me—it's very difficult to work with him." Being poor at managing and appropriately expressing emotions can be a major handicap.

Social skills, in the essential sense of handling *another person's* emotions artfully, underlie several competencies. These include:

- *Influence:* Wielding effective tactics of persuasion
- *Communication:* Sending clear and convincing messages
- *Conflict management:* Negotiating and resolving disagreements
- *Leadership:* Inspiring and guiding
- *Change catalyst:* Initiating, promoting, or managing change

▪ INFLUENCE ▪

Wielding Effective Tactics for Persuasion

People with this competence

- ▪ Are skilled at winning people over

- ▪ Fine-tune presentations to appeal to the listener

- ▪ Use complex strategies like indirect influence to build consensus and support

- ▪ Orchestrate dramatic events to effectively make a point

A representative of an American company in Tokyo was taking his visiting boss to a series of meetings with their Japanese counterparts. On the way to the first meeting the representative, who spoke Japanese fluently, advised his American boss not to ask him to translate in front of the Japanese, but to rely instead on the translator. His boss readily agreed.[6]

Why?

"They'll think I'm just a mouthpiece to send things back to New York. I wanted to make sure they saw me as having real power to make decisions on the spot. I wanted to be seen as the person who did most of the talking. I had the answers, not New York."

That sensitivity to the impact of such a seemingly trivial matter bespeaks competence at influence. At the most basic level, influence and persuasion hinge on arousing specific emotions in the other person—whether that be respect for our power, passion for a project, enthusiasm for outdoing a competitor, or appropriate outrage over some unfairness.

People adept at influence are able to sense or even anticipate their audience's reaction to their message and can effectively carry everyone along toward an intended goal. Star performers at Deloitte & Touche Consulting, for example, know that a simple good argument may not be enough to win clients over, and they have the ability to sense what kinds of other appeals will persuade key decision makers.[7] Critical in these skills is being able to notice when logical arguments are falling flat and when appeals that are more emotional may add impact.

This emotional competence emerges over and over as a hallmark of superior performers, particularly among supervisors, managers, and executives.[8] At every level, however, a sophisticated understanding of influence is called for. "In entry-level positions, being too highly power-driven and overly concerned with having an impact can trip you up, especially if you try to put on airs and take on the trappings of power," Richard Boyatzis tells me. "If you were just made sales manager and you try to impress people by imposing distance or by feigning status—you start wearing expensive three-piece suits or tell subordinates to stop calling you by your first name, for example—you can alienate people."

The stratagems used by top performers include impression management, appeals to reason and facts, dramatic arguments or actions, building coalitions and behind-the-scenes support, emphasizing key information—and on and on. For instance, one outstanding manager was put in charge of quality control at a large manufacturer. The first thing he did was to change the name to quality *services,* a subtle but crucial shift of emphasis: "The image I wanted to create was that it's not just a policeman organization, but it provides technical input, too. Now we have an iron grip on tracking down quality complaints from customers, and the production people don't get defensive right away."[9]

Dramatic action can capture attention and arouse emotion; if well done, this is among the most effective of influence strategies. "Dramatic" does not necessarily mean having flashy visuals in presentations; sometimes the effect is felt through the most prosaic means. One outstanding salesman wowed a prospective account by spending the better part of a day with his sleeves rolled up, using one of his products to fix a piece of equipment— equipment that had been purchased from a competitor!

What got him the account was his dramatic demonstration of the level of service his prospective client could expect.[10] As he put it, "They were amazed."

First, Build Rapport

Empathy is crucial for wielding influence; it is difficult to have a positive impact on others without first sensing how they feel and understanding their position. People who are poor at reading emotional cues and inept at social interactions are very poor at influence. The first step in influence is building rapport.

For a business analyst at a global American oil company, that meant changing the way he approached the representatives of a South American bank.[11] He said, "I have a lot of funds going back and forth and the bank plays an important role, and in South America friendship ties mean a lot when you're doing business. I wanted to be able to call a commercial rep and say, 'Hey, I've got a problem,' and have them be willing to work with us to get our work done." His tactic: a long, leisurely meeting over coffee with several key representatives, where they talked about themselves, their families, their lives—not just business.

Similarly, a manufacturer's rep told me, "When you walk into a customer's office, the first thing you do is scan the room to pick up on something he's enthusiastic and excited about—that's where you start the conversation." His approach takes for granted that building rapport necessarily precedes persuasion. As one outstanding salesman put it, "Sometimes it means I go in without a briefcase and say, 'Hey, how ya doin' today? Want a hot dog from the guy across the street? Let's go out and get it together.' And I know that if I'm going to call on the man in the jeans and the flannel shirt, I won't wear my three-piece suit."[12]

Similar persuasion skills are seen in the executive who is trying to recruit someone to take a job that requires moving to another city. He knows the prospect loves sailing, and so shows her the local marina. Or he capitalizes on the prospect's spouse's love of riding by introducing him to friends who are equestrians, so that he will be on board for the move, too.

Persuasion is lubricated by identifying a bond or commonality; taking time to establish one is not a detour but an essential step. An announcement made by a remote and largely invisible CEO may have less immediate persuasive power than the same message delivered by someone workers have day-to-day contact with. One strategy for spreading change in a large and far-flung organization, then, is to use networks of local leaders, the individuals within a working group that everyone knows, likes, and respects.[13]

At the highest levels of effectiveness, the influential rely on indirect strategies, so that their hand is virtually invisible. They have a third party make the crucial argument, establishing chains of influence; they set up effective behind-the-scenes coalitions for support, or shape the presentation of information in subtle ways so that everyone easily and fluidly arrives at the desired consensus.

The rule of thumb is that consensus building is crucial, but this is ignored to a surprising degree. In a study of strategic decisions at 356 American companies, more than half were never adopted, were implemented only partially, or were abandoned at the outset.[14]

The single most common reason for the failure of these plans was that the lead executives were imperious, trying to impose their ideas instead of building a supporting consensus. When the imperious approach was employed, 58 percent of the time the result was failure. But when executives first conferred with colleagues to rethink their long-term priorities, strategic plans were adopted 96 percent of the time. As Paul McNutt, the Ohio State University professor of management who did the study, says, "If you involve people in at least some of the steps of the process, they will become missionaries for you."

The Failure to Convince

The benefit was for a good cause—a new preschool for children of poor, single working mothers. A local artist of some national prominence had invited about a hundred friends to a special show of her newest work and a buffet dinner contributed by several local restaurants. After the meal, the hostess gathered everyone together on the lawn and introduced the head of the organization that ran the preschool, who began with a detailed rundown of the events in her life that had led her to take her present job. Then she gave a blow-by-blow account of how the preschool got started. After that she proceeded to run through the entire history of the preschool, in what turned out to be excruciating detail.

A talk that might have been effective had it lasted for ten minutes went on for almost an hour. And she hadn't even introduced some mothers and teachers, each of whom was going to say a few words.

The audience, all sympathetic at the beginning, began to drift off. Dusk had arrived, and with it swarming mosquitoes.

Finally the hostess's husband, a somewhat cantankerous older gentleman, got up conspicuously, ambled straight for the cake table, and bellowed, "Too much detail! The cakes are falling!"

With that, all semblance of an attentive audience collapsed, and everyone headed for dessert.

People who, despite their good intentions, fail to connect emotionally with their audience fall at the bottom of the influence competence hierarchy: They may mean well, but they lack the means to get their message across. The blunt critique by the hostess's husband captured the mood of the audience at that moment far better than the speech by the long-winded school head.

Those who rely too heavily on the persuasive effects of aids such as elaborate overhead projections or elegant statistical analyses of data also can miss the boat. An audience must be emotionally engaged, but mediocre presenters rarely go beyond the same dry litany of facts, however flashily displayed, and never take into account the emotional temperature of the audience. Without an accurate reading of how a listener is taking in an idea, that idea is in danger of falling on deaf, indifferent, or even hostile ears.

No matter how intellectually brilliant we may be, that brilliance will fail to shine if we are not persuasive. That is particularly true in fields where entry has high hurdles for cognitive abilities, like engineering and science, medicine and law, and executive ranks in general. As the director of research at one of Wall Street's largest brokerage firms put it to me, "To get into our business you need to be highly adept at numbers. But to make things happen, that's just not enough—you have to be able to persuade."

Signs of weakness in the ability to persuade include:

- Failure to build a coalition or get "buy-in"

- Overreliance on a familiar strategy instead of choosing the best one for the moment

- Bullheaded promotion of a point of view, no matter the feedback

- Being ignored or failing to inspire interest

- Having a negative impact

The Machiavellian Manipulator

For him, appearance was all. He married a woman from a noble family, and he himself was extremely polished socially. As a highly placed manager in a German industrial dynasty, he was in charge of a division with revenues of more than $1 billion annually. But on the job he focused all his considerable charm upward, toward his own boss, and outward, to impress those who met him. When it came to those who reported to him, he was a petty tyrant mistreating his serfs.

"When you met him he could be quite beguiling, but people who worked for him were afraid of him," I was told by an outside consultant who was hired to do an impartial appraisal of the manager. "He had no respect for the people under him. If there was low performance, he shouted at people; if high, he said nothing. He demoralized his subordinates. His CEO finally asked him to leave—but, because he makes such a good first impression, he landed another high-level job immediately."

The slick German manager exemplifies a type who can thrive in organizations that are more politically oriented than performance oriented. Such people are "effective upward, but poor downward, because they don't really care," the consultant told me. "They are often self-centered, don't like people, and feel an obligation only to themselves, not to the organization."

Charm and social polish in themselves do not add up to competence at influence; social skill in the service of oneself, and to the detriment of the group as a whole, is sooner or later recognized as a charade. True influence as a positive competence is very different from a Machiavellian drive for personal success at all costs. The power exhibited in the influence competence is socialized and harmonious with the collective goal, rather than exclusively for selfish gain.

As one analyst of influence in close to three hundred organizations put it, "We have not found the best performers pursuing their own status, prestige, or gain at the expense of others or of the organization."[15]

▪ COMMUNICATION ▪

Listening Openly and Sending Convincing Messages

People with this competence

▪ Are effective in give-and-take, registering emotional cues in attuning their message

▪ Deal with difficult issues straightforwardly

▪ Listen well, seek mutual understanding, and welcome sharing of information fully

▪ Foster open communication and stay receptive to bad news as well as good

For Bill Gates at Microsoft, it's an e-mail address; for Martin Edelston, president of the Boardroom, Inc., it's an old-fashioned suggestion box. And for Jerry Kalov, CEO of Cobra Electronics, it's a phone extension known only to his employees. Any call on that confidential number is a priority; he picks it up whenever it rings.

Each of these conduits of communication represents one way of resolving every boss's dilemma: "Are they telling me only what they want me to hear instead of what I need to know?" Kalov got the idea for his phone line long before he became an executive.[16] "Very often I had things I wanted to say, but my immediate boss didn't let me, because he wanted to take the credit," Kalov remembers. "Or maybe he didn't agree with it. So I felt like I had good ideas or things to say but I couldn't get through. . . . Who knows where the next brilliant idea is going to come from?"

The phone line, Kalov adds, works better than management by walking around, because people may be intimidated to be seen talking to the chief executive or may be too shy even to approach him. The phone line offers discretion and confidentiality, which adds to open—even daring—communication.

Such open channels pay. A note in Edelston's suggestion box from a low-level employee —someone who ordinarily would never speak to him— saved the company half a million dollars a year. The suggestion from a shipping clerk was to keep company mailings under a four-pound postal rate limit. By reducing by one eighth the size of the books the company mailed out, the cumulative savings were hugely significant.

Creating an atmosphere of openness is not a trivial gesture. The biggest single complaint of American workers is poor communication with management; two thirds say it prevents them from doing their best work.[17]

"I'd say you're unlocking the value of a person when you communicate openly with them," Mark Loehr, a managing director at Salomon Smith Barney, observed to me. "When you communicate openly, you open the possibility of getting the best out of people—their energy, creativity. If you don't, then they just feel like cogs in a machine, trapped and unhappy."

Mood and Meaning

My boss withholds her emotions," an advertising account manager at a $2-billion-a-year media company complains to me. "She never praises anything I do. I just convinced a really big account to go from around three hundred thousand dollars a year in billings to almost double that. Her response when I told her wasn't 'You did a great job' but 'Sure they took your offer—it's a great deal.' There was no feeling whatsoever in her voice, no warmth or enthusiasm. Then she just walked away. When I told other sales managers about my coup, they complimented me. It was the biggest sale I'd ever made, and my boss just didn't acknowledge all the work I'd done to get the deal."

The account manager continues: "I started to feel that something must be wrong with me, but lots of other people feel the same about her: She never shows any positive feelings or gives any encouragement—not with little things, not with big things. . . . Our team is productive, but there's no sense of any bond with her."

Being an adept communicator is the keystone of all social skills. Among managers, communications competence strongly distinguishes star performers from average or poor ones; the lack of this ability, as seen in the account manager's boss, can torpedo morale.

Listening well, the key to empathy, is also crucial to competence in communicating. Listening skills—asking astute questions, being open-minded and understanding, not interrupting, seeking suggestions—account for about a third of people's evaluations of whether someone they work with is an effective communicator.[18] Understandably, listening is among the most frequently taught business skills.

Being in control of our own moods is also essential to good communication. A study of 130 executives and managers found that how well people handled their own emotions determined the degree to which those around them preferred to deal with them.[19] In dealing with peers and subordinates, calmness and patience were key. Bosses likewise preferred dealing with employees who were not overly aggressive with them.

It doesn't matter what mood we're in—the challenge is to stay cool and collected. Aiming for a neutral mood is the best strategy in anticipation of dealing with someone else, if only because it makes us an emotional clean slate and allows us to adapt to whatever the situation calls for.[20] It's like putting a car into neutral so that you can more readily shift into reverse, low, or high gear, as the emotional terrain demands. A neutral mood leaves us ready to be more fully involved, present rather than emotionally removed.

Keeping Cool

Being caught up in a strong consuming mood is a roadblock to smooth interaction. If we enter into a conversation while preoccupied by a strong mood, the other person is likely to experience us as being unavailable, or what the sociologist Irving Goffman has called "away"—just going through the motions of the conversation while obviously distracted.[21]

The ability to "keep cool" helps us to put preoccupations aside for the time being, staying flexible in our own emotional responses. This trait is admired worldwide, even in cultures that prefer agitation over calm in certain situations.[22] People who can stay collected in an emergency or in the face of someone else's panic or distress have a reassuring sense of self-control, enter smoothly into a conversation and stay effectively involved. In contrast, people who are burdened by their emotions are much less available for whatever the present moment demands.

A study of middle- and upper-level managers found that those rated best as communicators shared the ability to adopt a calm, composed, and patient manner, no matter what emotional state they were in.[23] They were able to put aside the imperatives of their own feelings, even when turbulent, in order to make themselves fully available for the person they were with. As a result, these managers were able to take the time needed to gather essential information and find a way to be helpful, including giving constructive feedback. Instead of being dismissive or attacking, they tended to be specific about what went right, what went wrong, and how to keep the good things going while fixing what was off. They exercised emotional control, keeping cool so as to stay open to what they were hearing, fine-tuning their responses instead of taking a one-size-fits-all approach.

Being socially outgoing and extroverted is not in itself a guarantee of being skilled at communication. And what constitutes effective communication in one culture or social setting can fail miserably in another.

Sometimes effective interaction means underplaying one's presence. Among the staff at an elite resort in the southwestern United States, effectiveness correlated *negatively* with being highly extroverted. In such a posh setting, those who were too loquacious and outgoing were experienced by guests as being intrusive. The guests were there for privacy, so the resort required its staff to be friendly and helpful as needed, but otherwise to be utterly inconspicuous.[24]

■ CONFLICT MANAGEMENT ■

Negotiating and Resolving Disagreements

People with this competence

- Handle difficult people and tense situations with diplomacy and tact

- Spot potential conflict, bring disagreements into the open, and help de-escalate

- Encourage debate and open discussion

- Orchestrate win-win solutions

"A banker wanted to sell a copper company to investors, and he needed a research person expert in mining to write about it so he could convince people in sales to pitch the deal. But the researcher refused outright, upsetting the banker. I was director of research, so the banker complained to me," says Mark Loehr, of Salomon Smith Barney.

"I went to the researcher, who told me he was overwhelmed. He was already working seventy to eighty hours a week, had to finish analyses of eighteen companies by the end of the month, make a hundred phone calls, run off to meetings in Boston—and this report would have taken him another forty hours to do. After we talked, he went back to the banker and explained how swamped he was, but added, 'If you want me to do it, I will.'

"Once the banker understood the researcher's predicament, he decided to find another way to get the job done. But there could have been a blowup. Everyone is so busy and overwhelmed, their listening abilities dwindle to nothing. And they tend to just assume that no one is as busy as they are, so they make imperious demands.

"It's so hard to get people to take the time to be good listeners. It's not just about being nice—until you're a good enough listener, until you can sense what the other person is going through, you won't be able to make a reasonable suggestion, to come up with something they'll buy."

One talent of those skilled at conflict resolution is spotting trouble as it is brewing and taking steps to calm those involved. Here, as Loehr points out, the arts of listening and empathizing are crucial: Once the investment banker understood the researcher's perspective, he became more accommodating—and the conflict ended.

Such diplomacy and tact are qualities essential for success in touchy jobs like auditing, police work, or mediation—or *any* job where people depend on each other under pressure. One of the competencies sought in tax auditors by the U.S. government is the ability to present an unpopular position in a way that creates little or no hostility and preserves the other person's sense of dignity. The word for this skill is *tact*. At American Express, the ability to spot potential sources of conflict, take responsibility for one's own role, apologize if need be, and engage openly in a discussion of each person's perspective is prized in their financial advisors.

Reading the Signs

Charlene Barshefsky had finally gotten the Chinese government, after months and months of negotiation, to agree to clamp down on the piracy of American movies, compact discs, and computer software. How? Barshefsky had refused to accept their "final" offer, just another in an ongoing series, all of which she felt were inadequate. But this time, the head of the Chinese delegation thanked her for her work, told her he would respond at a later date, and then moved his shoulders back in a slight shrug. That simple and subtle gesture indicated she had won their cooperation.

Barshefsky had been closely studying the faces across the table from her that day, and she had sensed far less acrimony than before in the endless, tedious meetings. That day, reactions were muted and questions few—a striking change from the combative, sharply challenging dialogue that had marked the early rounds of the negotiations.

Barshefsky's reading of those subtle signals proved right: That was the day the Chinese delegation stopped fighting and started moving toward the trade agreement the countries later signed.[25]

The ability to read the feelings of the opposition during a negotiation is critical to success. As one of my lawyers, Robert Freedman, says about negotiating contracts, "It's mainly psychological. Contracts are emotional—it's not just what the words say, but how the parties think and *feel* about them, that matters."

Those who have mastered the art of the deal realize the emotionally charged nature of any negotiation. The best negotiators can sense which points matter most to the other party and gracefully concede there, while pressing for concessions in points that do not carry such emotional weight. And that takes empathy.

Skill at negotiation obviously matters for excellence in professions like law and diplomacy. But to some extent everyone who works in an organization needs these abilities; those who can resolve conflict and head off trouble are the kind of peacemakers vital to any organization.

In a sense, a negotiation can be seen as an exercise in joint problem solving, since the conflict belongs to both parties. The reason for the negotiation, of course, is that each side has its own competing interests and perspective and wants to convince the other to capitulate to its wishes. But the very act of agreeing to negotiate acknowledges that the problem is a shared one and that there may be a mutually satisfying solution available. In this sense negotiation is a cooperative venture, not just a competitive one. Indeed, as Herbert Kelman, a Harvard psychologist who specializes in negotiations, points out, the process of negotiation itself restores cooperation between conflicting parties. Solving their problems together transforms their relationship.[26]

That resolution requires that each side be able to understand not just the other's point of view, but their needs and fears. This empathy, Kelman observes, makes each side "better able to influence the other to their own benefit, by being responsive to the other's needs—in other words, to find ways in which both parties can win."

Negotiating Channels

Negotiations, mostly informal, happen all the time. Take the negotiation between a manufacturer and the retail stores that sell its products, like this one: "I've been cut off from carrying one of our main lines of women's jewelry," a boutique owner explained. "I wanted to negotiate a better deal with the distributor—we've been a good outlet for them. But he got a better offer from a store across town. So I made a counterproposal. But the other store got the account—and the company only wants one outlet in a town this size. So now I'm out of luck."

Such channels of distribution are essential for manufacturers' very survival, just as the retailers depend on the manufacturers for their stock. But each party has an array of choices. The result is an ongoing negotiation over such issues as how large markups will be, the terms of payment, and timeliness of deliveries.

Most "channel relationships" are long-term and symbiotic. And in any long-term relationship, problems simmer and boil to the surface from time to time. When they surface, those involved on either side of manufacturer-retailer disputes typically use one of three styles of negotiation: problem solving, in which both parties try to find the solution that works best for each side; compromise, where both parties give in more or less equally regardless of how that serves their needs; and aggression, where one party forces unilateral concessions from the other side.

In a survey of retail buyers in department store chains, each of whom handled merchandise worth $15 million to $30 million, the style of negotiating was an accurate barometer of the health of the manufacturer-retailer relationship.[27] Predictably, when negotiations were typically aggressive, revolving around threats and demands, it boded poorly for the future of the relationship; buyers ended up embittered and dissatisfied and often dropped the product line. But for those relationships in which aggressiveness was ruled out in favor of problem solving or compromise, the longevity of the relationship increased.

Threats and demands poison the waters of negotiation. As the survey showed, even when one party is far more powerful than the other, a magnaminous spirit may be a winning strategy in the long run, particularly when the parties will have continued dealings. And this is why even when a retailer was completely dependent on a single manufacturer, negotiations were most often noncoercive; given the desire for a long-term relationship and their mutual dependence, a spirit of cooperation always worked best.

Resolving Conflict—Creatively

One evening Linda Lantieri was walking down a desolate, dangerous block lined with abandoned, boarded-up buildings when suddenly, out of nowhere, she was surrounded by three boys about fourteen years old. One pulled out a knife with a four-inch blade as they pressed in around her.

"Give me your purse! Now!" the boy with the knife hissed.

Though frightened, Lantieri had the presence of mind to take some deep breaths and reply coolly, "I'm feeling a little uncomfortable. You know, guys, you're a little into my space. I'm wondering if you could step back a little."

Lantieri studied the sidewalk—and, to her amazement, she saw three pairs of sneakers take a few steps back. "Thank you," she said, then continued, "Now, I want to hear what you just said to me, but to tell you the truth, I'm a little nervous about that knife. I'm wondering if you could put it away."

After what seemed an eternity of silence and uncertainty, the knife went back into a pocket.

Quickly reaching into her purse, Lantieri took out a $20 bill, caught the eye of the one with the knife, and asked, "Who should I give it to?"

"Me," he said.

Glancing at the other two, she asked if they agreed. One of the two nodded.

"Great," she said, handing the leader the $20 bill. "Now here's what's going to happen. I'm going to stay right here while you walk away."

With puzzled looks on their faces, the boys slowly started to walk away, glancing over their shoulders at Lantieri—and then they broke into a run. *They* were running from *her.*

In a sense, that small miracle of turning the tables is no surprise: Lantieri is the founder and director of the New York City–based Resolving Conflict Creatively Program, which teaches these skills in schools. Lantieri has immersed herself in the crafts of negotiation and handling conflict amicably.[28] While she learned her trade as a teacher—for a while in a Harlem school not far from that desolate block—she now trains others in more than four hundred schools throughout the United States.

Lantieri does more than just promote education in conflict resolution— she first convinces skeptical school boards to approve her program. In fact, when the school board of one California town was paralyzed by two bitterly bickering factions, both sides were so impressed by her negotiating skills they asked Lantieri to come in and help them heal the split.

Lantieri's maestro performance on the street illustrates some classic moves for cooling down conflicts:

- First, calm down, tune in to your feelings, and express them.

- Show a willingness to work things out by talking over the issue rather than escalating it with more aggression.

- State your own point of view in neutral language rather than in an argumentative tone.

- Try to find equitable ways to resolve the dispute, working together to find a resolution both sides can embrace.

These strategies parallel those espoused for win-win solutions by experts at Harvard's Center for Negotiation. But while following these strategies may seem simple, implementing them as brilliantly as Lantieri did requires the prerequisite emotional competencies of self-awareness, self-confidence, self-control, and empathy. Remember, empathy need not lead to sympathetically giving in to the other side's demands—knowing how someone feels does not mean agreeing with them. But cutting off empathy to hold a hard line can lead to polarized positions and deadlocks.

▪ LEADERSHIP ▪

Inspiring and Guiding Individuals and Groups

People with this competence

- ▪ Articulate and arouse enthusiasm for a shared vision and mission
- ▪ Step forward to lead as needed, regardless of position
- ▪ Guide the performance of others while holding them accountable
- ▪ Lead by example

Here's an extraordinarily instructive contrast in leadership: Ronald W. Allen, former CEO of Delta Air Lines, and Gerald Grinstein, a former CEO of Western Airlines and the Burlington Northern railway.[29]

Grinstein, a lawyer by training, is a virtuoso at establishing rapport with his employees and using that emotional attunement to persuade. As CEO of Western Airlines, an ailing company when he took it over in 1985, he spent hundreds of hours in cockpits, behind check-in counters, and in the baggage-handling pits getting to know his employees.

The rapport he built was crucial in convincing Western Airlines' workforce to agree to concessions on work rules and to take pay cuts, all for his promise of a solvent company in which they would have a bigger stake. With those concessions in hand, Western Airlines landed solidly in the black, and Grinstein was able to sell the airline to Delta for $860 million after just two years.

In 1987 he became CEO of Burlington Northern, another money-losing company, and again Grinstein worked his interpersonal magic. He flew a selected group of maintenance workers, secretaries, and train crews from all over the country to company headquarters in Fort Worth to dine with him. He rode the railroad's routes and talked with crews, all the while working—successfully—toward convincing them to buy into his cost-cutting plans.

A close friend of Grinstein observed of his leadership style, "You don't have to be an SOB to be tough."

Though the railroad was laden with $3 billion of debt when he took it over, Grinstein turned it around. And in 1995 he created the largest U.S. rail network when Burlington Northern bought Santa Fe Pacific.

Now let's look at Ronald W. Allen, who was fired by his board as CEO of Delta Air Lines in April of 1997, even as the company was enjoying record profits.

Allen had moved up through the ranks to become CEO in 1987, taking the helm just as the airline industry was deregulated. His strategic plan was to become more globally competitive; in 1991 he bought just-bankrupt Pan American World Airways, for access to its European routes. That turned out to be a miscalculation, loading Delta with a huge debt burden just as the industry saw profits plummet. Delta, always profitable in the past, plunged $500 million more into debt over each of the three years following the Pan Am purchase.

However, it was not this disastrous financial decision that cost Allen his job. Allen reacted to the hard times by becoming a tough, almost ruthless boss. He gained a reputation for humiliating underlings by berating them in front of other employees. He silenced opposition among top executives, even moving to replace the chief financial officer, the one person who had openly disagreed with him on the acquisition of Pan Am. Another top executive (with whom Allen had competed to become CEO) announced he was leaving to become president of Continental Airlines, and Allen is said to have responded by demanding the keys to the executive's company car on the spot, leaving him to find another way home.

Such pettiness aside, Allen's main failing was his heartless downsizing. Allen hacked away twelve thousand jobs, about a third of the total Delta workforce—some positions fat, no doubt, but many others the muscle, sinew, and nerves of the organization. With the deep cuts came a precipitous drop in the airline's once-enviable customer service ratings. Complaints about Delta suddenly skyrocketed—everything from dirty planes and late departures to missing baggage. Allen had squeezed the spirit out of the company along with the fat.

Delta employees were in shock; the company had never treated them so harshly before. Insecurity and anger were rampant. Even after the cuts put the airline into the black again, a company-wide survey of the twenty-five thousand remaining employees revealed a skeptical, frightened workforce, half of them hostile to Allen's leadership.

In October 1996 Allen publicly admitted that his draconian cost-cutting campaign had had devastating effects on Delta's workforce. But his comment was, "So be it." And that became the battle cry for the employees' protest; pins with the phrase "So be it" sprouted on the uniforms of pilots, flight attendants, and mechanics alike.

With Allen's contract up for renewal, the Delta board looked beyond the numbers to the overall health of the company. Delta's reputation for outstanding service was tarnished; talented managers were leaving the company. And, worst of all, morale among employees was abysmal.

So the board—led by none other than Gerald Grinstein—acted. Allen, the man whose power had once been so great that he held the titles of chairman, CEO, and president, was out at age fifty-five, largely because he was killing the company's soul.

Leadership as Giving Energy

The twin tales of Robert W. Allen and Gerald Grinstein demonstrate that the art of leadership lies in *how* a person implements change, not just in the change itself. Both men went through the painful process of cutting costs, but one did so in a way that kept employees' loyalty and spirits high, while the other demoralized and alienated an entire workforce.

The artful leader is attuned to the subtle undercurrents of emotion that pervade a group, and can read the impact of her own actions on those currents. One way leaders establish their credibility is by sensing these collective, unspoken feelings and articulating them for the group, or acting in a way that tacitly shows they are understood. In this sense, the leader is a mirror, reflecting back to the group its own experience.

However, the leader is also a key *source* of the organization's emotional tone. The excitement emanating from a leader can move an entire group in that direction. As Birgitta Wistrand, the CEO of a Swedish company, put it, "Leadership is giving energy."

This transmission of emotional energy lets leaders be the pilots of an organization, setting its course and direction. For example, when Lou Gerstner was brought in as CEO of IBM, he knew he had to transform the culture of the company to save it. And that, Gerstner said, "is not something you do by writing memos. You've got to appeal to people's emotions. They've got to buy in with their hearts and bellies, not just their minds."[30]

The ability of leaders to get that buy-in hinges in part on how emotions flow within a group. We've already seen how emotions spread from the most expressive person in a group. But this ability to transmit emotions is amplified for leaders, since people in groups spend more time looking at the leader than at anyone else. This attention magnifies the impact of the leader's mood on the group; a small change in the facial expression or tone of voice of a powerful figure can have more impact than dramatic shows of feeling by someone in a lesser position of power.

People not only pay more attention to leaders, they also tend to mimic them. Lore has it that at Microsoft people rock back and forth as they are pondering or arguing a point in a meeting, a nonverbal homage to Bill Gates's habit. Such mimicry is an unconscious way of showing allegiance and attunement to the most powerful person in a group.

During his presidency Ronald Reagan was known as "the Great Communicator." A professional actor, the emotional power of Reagan's charisma was shown in a study of how his facial expressions affected those of his listeners during an election debate with his opponent, Walter Mondale. When Reagan smiled, people who watched him—even on videotape—tended to smile, too; when he frowned, so did viewers. Mondale, who lost the election, had no such emotional impact, even on viewers who were sympathetic to his views.[31]

The ease with which emotions spread from a leader through the group has a downside, too. As the old saying holds, "A fish rots from the head down." Brutish, arrogant, or arbitrary leadership demoralizes a group. Birgitta Wistrand uses the term "emotional incontinence" for the leakage of destructive emotions from the top down: "With disturbing emotions a leader saps other people's energy by making them anxious, depressed, or angry," she says.

On the other hand, extremely successful leaders exhibit a high level of positive energy that spreads throughout the organization. And the more positive the mood of a group leader, the more positive, helpful, and cooperative are those in the group.[32]

In general, emotional charisma depends on three factors: feeling strong emotions, being able to express those emotions forcefully, and being an emotional sender rather than a receiver. Highly expressive people communicate through their facial expression, their voice, their gestures—their whole body. This ability allows them to move, inspire, and captivate others.[33]

The ability to convey emotion convincingly, from the heart, requires that a leader be sincere about the message being delivered; truly believing the emotional message is what separates the charismatic leader from the self-serving, manipulative one. Manipulative leaders may be able to play-act for a time, but they can less readily convince followers of their sincerity. Cynicism undermines conviction; to be a charismatic messenger, the leader must act from authentic belief.[34]

The Leader's Competence Tool Kit

Each emotional competency interacts with others; this applies to the leadership competence more than most. The task of the leader draws on a wide range of personal skills. My analysis of myriad jobs found that emotional competence makes up about two thirds of the ingredients of star performance in general, but for outstanding *leaders* emotional competencies—as opposed to technical or cognitive cues—make up 80 to 100 percent of those listed by companies themselves as crucial for success.[35]

Mathew Juechter, chairman of the American Society for Training and Development, agrees. "Leadership is almost all emotional intelligence, especially in distinguishing between what managers do and what leaders do—things like taking a stand, knowing what's important to you, pursuing your goals in partnership with others."

For the most effective CEOs, there are three main clusters of competence. The first two fall under the emotional intelligence heading; the first includes personal competencies like achievement, self-confidence, and commitment, while the second consists of social competencies like influence, political awareness, and empathy. This broad band of capabilities typified high-performing CEOs in Asia, the Americas, and Europe, suggesting that the traits of outstanding top leaders transcend cultural and national boundaries.[36]

The third cluster of competencies in the CEOs was cognitive: They think strategically, seeking out information with a broad scan, and apply strong conceptual thinking. As with the analysis of leaders in fifteen major corporations in Chapter 2, what distinguished standouts was the ability to see the big picture, to recognize telling patterns amidst the clutter of information, and to think far into the future.

But great leaders go a step further, integrating emotional realities into what they see, and so instilling strategy with meaning and resonance. Their emotional intelligence allows the blending of all of these elements into an inspired vision.

The best leaders, says Robert E. Kaplan of the Center for Creative Leadership, "have an almost magical ability to turn a phrase and articulate their agenda for the organization graphically, compellingly, memorably."[37] In other words, leadership entails exciting people's imaginations and inspiring them to move in a desired direction. It takes more than simple power to motivate and lead.

Nice Guys Finish First

An analysis of the power of a leader to set a positive—or negative—emotional tone in an organization was undertaken within the U.S. Navy, where the standards for superior performance are cut-and-dried: Annual awards are given to the most efficient, safest, and most prepared squadrons.[38] In an extensive comparison of superior and just-average commands, a striking difference in the *emotional* tone the commanding officers set was revealed. The very best commands, it turned out, were run not by Captain Ahab types who terrorized their crews, but by, well . . . nice guys.

The superior leaders managed to balance a people-oriented personal style with a decisive command role. They did not hesitate to take charge, to be purposeful, assertive, and businesslike. But the greatest difference between average and superior leaders was in their emotional style. The most effective leaders were more positive and outgoing, more emotionally expressive and dramatic, warmer and more sociable (including smiling more), friendlier and more democratic, more cooperative, more likable and "fun to be with," more appreciative and trustful, and even gentler than those who were merely average.

By contrast, the mediocre navy leaders reflected the classic stereotype of the military taskmaster. They were legalistic, negative, harsh, disapproving, and egocentric. Compared to the superior commanders, the average ones were more authoritarian and controlling, more domineering and tough-minded, more aloof and self-centered, and needed to show they were right more often. They led by the book, through the rules and the assertion of the raw power of their position. And it did not work, *even in the military,* where this emotional style might seem to find its natural home.

The Leadership Ripple Effect

The emotional tone set by any leader ripples downward with remarkable precision.[39] When successive levels from top to bottom of an organization are analyzed, the effect is very much like a set of Russian dolls, one stacked inside the other, with the leader containing all the rest.

This is most easily seen in military hierarchies, where—as was found in the navy study—the most effective leaders were warm and outgoing, emotionally expressive, democratic, and trusting—and so were leaders on down through the ranks, though not to the same extent as the top commander. By contrast, less effective officers were harsher and more disapproving, distant and irritable, legalistic and uncooperative—and so their subordinates were also.

While average leaders tend to be invisible, the best leaders frequently walk around and strike up conversations with their staff, asking about their families and other personal matters. They also let it be known that they want to be informed, creating an atmosphere of openness that makes it easier for communication to take place. This two-way channel encourages people at all levels to keep their superiors informed.

In mediocre military commands, junior-level people were reluctant to send news upward, especially bad news, because the top commanding officers so often "went ballistic" when given bad news, and, instead of delegating authority to the lowest possible level, stepped in to micromanage.

To be sure, the best officers were highly task-oriented and firm in swiftly reprimanding people whose actions threatened performance standards. But they were flexible when it came to trivial rules. The mediocre commanders made no distinction between meaningful and trivial regulations, holding instead to a legalistic, inflexible standard that did nothing to boost morale or performance.

Realizing that unity and cohesiveness are built from personal bonds, the best officers organize downtime events like softball games and awards celebrations—and make a point of attending themselves. From this shared downtime, with the attendant in-jokes and warm social climate, comes a strong sense of shared identity, which in turn pays off in superior on-the-job performance. By contrast, the mediocre officers are more concerned with whether the equipment is functioning than they are with their people.

When to Be Tough

To be sure, leadership does demand a certain toughness—at times. The art of leadership entails knowing when to be assertive—for example, confronting someone directly about their performance lapses—and when to be collegial and use less direct ways to guide or influence.

Leadership demands tough decision making: Someone has to tell people what to do, hold people to their obligations, be explicit about consequences. Persuasion, consensus building, and all the other arts of influence do not always do the job. Sometimes it comes down to simply using the power of one's position to get people to act.

A common failing of leaders, from supervisors to top executives, is the failure to be emphatically assertive when necessary. One obstacle to such assertiveness is passivity, as can happen when someone is more concerned with being liked than with getting the job done right, and so tolerates poor performance rather than confronting it. People who are extremely uncomfortable with confrontation or anger are also often reluctant to take an assertive stance even when it is called for.

Incompetence here can show up in something as commonplace as failing to take the helm in a meeting and so letting it meander rather than steering it directly to key agenda items. Another deficiency in leadership in this area is the inability to be clear and firm. This results in workers not knowing what's expected of them.

One sign of an assertive leader is the ability to say no firmly and definitively. Another is to set an expectation of high standards for performance or quality and insist people meet them, even publicly monitoring performance if necessary.

When people fail to perform, the leader's task is to give helpful feedback rather than let the moment—and the lapse—go unnoted. And when someone consistently performs poorly, despite all attempts at helpful feedback and development, the lapse has to be confronted directly and openly.

Take the manager who says, "My predecessor didn't establish any discipline about meetings. The first meeting I ran, people straggled in late and weren't prepared. So when it happened a third time I put my foot down. I said, 'Ladies and gentlemen, I can't accept this behavior. I'm postponing this meeting for two days. Be on time and be prepared, or there'll be hell to pay.' "[40]

This does not describe the petty tyrant or office bully, however. This is a strategy that comes into play only when other, less severe approaches have failed—not as a first response. If the tone described above typifies a manager's everyday style, then there is something wrong with his abilities to build rapport and influence people. In other words, constant toughness is a sign of weakness, not a sign of strong leadership.

The glorification of leaders who are oafish, arrogant, and brash ignores the cost to the organization. To be sure, a certain decisiveness in making hard decisions is necessary, but if that decision is carried out with imperious ruthlessness, the boss who did it will end up hated—and a failure as a leader.

During hard times, leaders need to call on whatever reserve of goodwill they may have built up over time. This is when the Attila the Huns are often undone. "At our company one manager was pushy and abrasive, even re-sented by his people—but he got things done," Muhammad-Amin Kashgari, an executive vice president at the Savola Company, Saudi Arabia's largest food manufacturer, told me. "But when things changed and the market got tougher, and we all had to work harder to maintain our market share," he added, "that manager's autocratic style defeated him." The star manager that emerged then was someone people liked and who inspired everyone to work harder. "But the imperious manager just kept pushing in the same old way—and his people abandoned him."

Having the ability to keep raw, unrestrained lust for power under control is one mark of a mature leader. A classic long-term study at AT&T found that, particularly in large organizations, managers who combined self-control with the ability to have a high impact were promoted as time went on, while those who had great impact but lacked the basics of self-control foundered.[41] In top-performing managers and executives, the drive of per-sonal ambition is held in check by strong self-control, and focused toward collective goals.[42]

The Virtual Leader

It's a fogged-in, desperate day at the San Francisco airport. Flight after flight is being canceled, and the lines at the airlines' service desks are snaking out of sight. Tension has been building by the hour, with people sniping at the airline representatives—and at each other. David Kolb, a pro-fessor of management at Case Western Reserve University, who tells this story, decided to try to change the mood of the mob—at least of those near him. So he announced, "I'm going to get some coffee—anyone else want some?"

He took down orders from a building chorus of frustrated fellow passengers, trundled off, and returned with a stack of drinks. And that was enough to trigger a rippling cascade of good feeling.

Kolb, at that moment, emerged as the natural leader of this inchoate group. His spontaneous rise speaks to the fluid nature of leadership itself.

Someone's formal position on the organizational chart and her actual role as leader don't always match up. People may come forward to take a leadership role for a time, as some special need arises—it can be in something as small as taking a supplier to task for a sloppy job—then fade back into the group. Such assertiveness can also be directed upward, as when a lower-level employee challenges a higher-level one on difficult issues or truths vital to the well-being of the organization.

For instance, higher-ups at an oil company that was establishing offices in a South American city chose to rent space in a brand-new high-rise tower in the most expensive part of town. But the manager of that branch, when talking with a local minister, was told sarcastically, "That sounds like something a company like yours would do."

Puzzled, the manager asked around and finally realized that locating their offices in that part of town had sent a message that the company was more interested in making an impression than in doing business. With that information in hand, he took it upon himself to abandon the original plan and look for offices in a growing business district, a location that would send the signal they were serious. Then he called his bosses back in the United States and told them what he had done and why.

His bosses' response: "We disagree with you, but we're not down there—you decide what's best."

Such a move, of course, requires self-confidence and initiative, both emotional competencies essential to leadership. The surfacing of such virtual leaders is becoming a standard mode of operating in high-tech fields, where very junior people may be very senior in terms of newly emergent areas of expertise.

At Finland's Nokia Telecommunications Group, about 70 percent of the employees are engineers, with an average age of thirty-two. A large percentage of these engineers are fresh out of university and are more familiar with newer technologies than are their fortyish bosses. Veli-Pekka Niitamo, head of competence management and recruitment there, says, "We've redefined the nature of leadership. Everyone has leadership—a young engineer takes leadership as necessary. Our model is that you are your own boss inside the Nokia world. The old static structure of managers and subordinates is outdated."

Indeed, all static structures are outdated in today's business climate. Which gets us to the next competence: leading change.

▪ CHANGE CATALYST ▪

Initiating or Managing Change

People with this competence

▪ Recognize the need for change and remove barriers

▪ Challenge the status quo to acknowledge the need for change

▪ Champion the change and enlist others in its pursuit

▪ Model the change expected of others

The personal epiphany came late in 1993 for John Patrick. And it took him just twenty-four months to transform that inspired insight into company policy.

The company is IBM; 1993 marked the year Lou Gerstner came to the helm and began the organization's turnaround. But massive, deep change happens not just from the top down; in Patrick's case, his minirevolution was a grassroots victory.

It all revolved around the Internet. That day in 1993, Patrick, then a senior strategist for the company, was fiddling with a program called Gopher, an Internet software utility. As he tells it, "I became captivated by the idea of sitting at home and cruising around in someone else's computer. Being remotely connected was hardly a new idea at IBM. But being *inside* someone else's computer, no matter what kind of computer either of us had—a light went off."[43]

At that point, IBM was a company focused on computer hardware. The burgeoning Internet was beneath its radar, and the company had virtually no products or plans for the Web. Gerstner was about to change that—but it was people like Patrick, dispersed throughout the company, who made it reality.

Patrick created the manifesto "Get Connected," in which he argued that Internet-like connections would reinvent the nature of organizations, industries, and work. He offered some practical suggestions to buttress his idea: Give an e-mail address to everyone in the organization, encourage newsgroups within the company in order to build communities of mutual interest, and put up an IBM website.

While those ideas are widely accepted now, at the time—and especially at IBM—they were radical. But the audience was there, spread throughout the company. As soon as he distributed his manifesto, Patrick started hearing from people by fax, e-mail, and phone, from every corner of IBM. So Patrick started a mailing list and used it to stitch together a kind of virtual organization within IBM that cut across its formal groups.

The members of this new group were from around the world. They had no formal status, authority, or budget. And though they were still undetected by the organizational radar, they got things done. Their first project was up and running by May 1994. It involved putting up IBM's company website, one of the first such by any major corporation.

That same month, Patrick committed the company to participate in the next Internet World forum—without permission from IBM. This moment of risk taking took courage and vision—and perhaps a bit of simple faith as well.

That faith paid off. Patrick approached various divisions of the company for funding, collecting $5,000 here, $5,000 there, and by the time Internet World rolled around, fifty-four people from twelve different units had signed on to represent IBM. The effort still had no formal status within the company, nor any budget.

But with this momentum, IBM developed a formal Internet strategy, convened a task force, and created its Internet division. That division came into being on December 1, 1995. Its task, defining and pursuing the company's Internet initiatives, was to be led by John Patrick, vice president in charge and chief technology officer. What was once a loose-knit virtual team was now a formal division with six hundred people.

One of its projects was a wildly successful website for the 1996 Olympics in Atlanta; the site averaged eleven *million* hits each day. The IBM team, using software in development to handle all that traffic, found the experience a natural R&D opportunity. They realized that they had developed software that could handle massive amounts of traffic, and rolled it over into what became commercial software—one of many product lines for the Net that are the fruit of Patrick's original epiphany.

The Change Catalyst: Key Ingredients

Today, organizations are reshuffling, divesting, merging, acquiring, flattening hierarchies, going global. The acceleration of change through the 1990s has made the ability to lead it a newly ascendant competence. In earlier studies in the 1970s and 1980s, being a change catalyst was not highly valued. But as we approach the millennium, more and more companies are putting a premium on people who can lead through change.

What are the qualities that make someone an effective change catalyst? "When we work with a company to help them transform their business, the personal abilities of the leader of their team count immensely," John Ferreira, a partner at Deloitte & Touche Consulting, tells me. "Say we're helping them cut the time it takes to fill orders. To do that, you have to work across the separate silos of the organization, and you need someone who's not at too high a level—not a theorist, but someone with enough hands-on expertise that they're close enough to what's going on that they can cut across all the functions involved and see the real situation. It's often a second-level manager."

Beyond technical expertise, the change catalyst needs a host of other emotional competencies. "You want the kind of second-level manager who has the ability to go into a vice president's office and lay on the table what that VP needs to do, without being intimidated by the fact that he's just a second-line manager," Ferreira adds.

For example, at a large financial services company going through the turmoil of deregulation and a newly competitive market, the leaders who were most confident in their abilities led divisions that flourished despite the changes.[44]

In addition to high levels of self-confidence, effective change leaders have high levels of influence, commitment, motivation, initiative, and optimism, as well as an instinct for organizational politics. As Ferreira puts it: "You need someone who takes this as a mission, not just a job—who is passionate about the change, gets up in the morning thinking about it. It's something like the difference between a renter and an owner—owners are dedicated. That's crucial, because it also takes perseverance—you get lots of smoke screens thrown up, lots of resistance. You need to know how to use us, the consultants, to help make your case to the right people at the right time. And you have to keep presenting your case, building coalitions of support, until you reach a critical mass that gets it over the top."

The Transformational Leader

hange *leaders* are not necessarily *innovators*. While leaders recognize the value of a new idea or way of doing things, they often are not the ones who originated the innovation. For organizations riding the waves of change (and what organization is *not* these days?), traditional management is not enough. In times of transformation, a charismatic, inspiring leader is called for.

The model of "transformational leadership" goes beyond management as usual; such leaders are able to rouse people through the sheer power of their own enthusiasm. Such leaders don't order or direct; they inspire. In articulating their vision, they are intellectually and emotionally stimulating. They show a strong belief in that vision, and they excite others about pursuing it with them.[45] And they are committed to nurturing relationships with those they lead.

Unlike more rational modes of leadership, in which leaders use standard rewards like pay and promotions to encourage their workers, the transformational leader goes to another level, mobilizing people for organizational change by arousing their emotions about the work they do. In doing so, such leaders appeal to people's sense of meaning and value. Work becomes a kind of moral statement, a demonstration of commitment to a larger mission that affirms people's sense of sharing a valued identity.[46]

Doing this requires the leader to articulate a compelling vision of the new organizational goals. Even though the goals may be somewhat utopian, committing to them can be emotionally satisfying in itself. Arousing people's emotions in this way and harnessing them in pursuit of lofty or noble goals gives a leader a powerful force for change. Indeed, studies show that this kind of leadership brings greater efforts and better performance from subordinates, making their work more effective.[47]

The Emotional Craft

test of this transformational leadership style came at a large Canadian financial services company that was struggling with immense market turbulence and high levels of uncertainty brought on by deregulation.[48] What had once been a staid and successful company in a protected market now had to be nimble to keep a place in a market it had once dominated.

A group of senior managers from the company's top four levels were followed for a year as they led their units through these chaotic times. At the end of that period each was evaluated in terms of productivity improvement, premium income, and salary-to-budget ratio. There was a wide range of success: Some leaders met as little as 17 percent of the targeted goals, while others achieved up to 84 percent of the targets.

Those who relied on the transformational style had the greatest success. Indeed, those who practiced standard management were seen as trying to control and restrict workers.

The successful leaders were rated by people who worked for them as highly charismatic and flexible. They seemed to spread their own sense of confidence and competence, and they inspired people to be more imaginative, adaptive, and innovative.

This study echoes what John Kotter, a Harvard Business School leadership expert, cites as the difference between "management" and "leadership."[49] In the way he uses the words, *management* refers to the ways complex enterprises are kept orderly, nonchaotic, and productive. *Leadership,* by contrast, refers to effectively handling the changes that the competitiveness and volatility of the times have wrought.

As Kotter puts it, "Motivation and inspiration energize people, not by pushing them in the right direction as control mechanisms but by satisfying basic human needs for achievement, a sense of belonging, a feeling of control over one's life, and the ability to live up to one's ideals. Such feelings touch us deeply and elicit a powerful response." Leadership of this kind, then, is an emotional craft.

9

Collaboration, Teams, and the Group IQ

None of us are as smart as all of us.

—Japanese proverb

t was a seminal moment in the early history of Silicon Valley. At a 1982 meeting of the Silicon Valley Computer Club, with hundreds of engineers packing the room, a writer for the *San Jose Mercury* asked the assembly, "How many of you plan to start your own companies?"

Two out of three hands shot up.[1]

Since then thousands of companies, including Silicon Graphics, Oracle, and Cisco Systems, have popped up. The common theme of all these enterprises is the conviction that a great idea or innovative technology can make a difference. But there is something else that's needed if a great idea is to become the seed of a great business: collaboration.

The quest for superb teams represents a modern grail of sorts for business. "In the world today there's plenty of technology, plenty of entrepreneurs, plenty of money, plenty of venture capital. What's in short supply is great teams." So says John Doerr, a legendary Silicon Valley venture capitalist who has backed industry-changing start-ups from Lotus and Compaq to Genentech and Netscape.[2]

Doerr's company, Kleiner Perkins Caulfield and Byers, gets twenty-five hundred business plans each year from hopeful entrepreneurs. Of these, they pick about a hundred to consider seriously, and they invest in about twenty-five. Says Doerr, "A team thinks it's selling us on the technology and the product or service. But actually we're thinking about *them*—the team members. We want to understand who they are, how they will work together." During his meetings with prospective start-ups, he probes the group's dynamic: how they might manage themselves, agree on priorities, measure whether they're doing their jobs well, handle someone who isn't working out. "I'm checking their instincts, their navigation system, their values."

Crucial to such a team is the right mix of intelligence and expertise—or what Doerr calls "really smart people"—and (though he doesn't use the phrase) emotional intelligence. Doerr cautions the two must be balanced—not all brilliance and experience, nor just drive, energy, and passion. "Getting that mix right is the difference between ventures that achieve greatness and start-ups that are merely successful, or worse."

Survival of the Social

Humans are the primordial team players: Our uniquely complex social relationships have been a crucial survival advantage. Our extraordinarily sophisticated talent for cooperation culminates in the modern organization.

Some evolutionary thinkers see the key moment for the emergence of interpersonal skills as the point when our ancestors moved from treetops to life on the broad savannas—when social coordination in hunting and gathering paid huge dividends. Learning the essential skills for survival meant children needed "schooling" in that critical period, up to age fifteen or so, during which the human brain becomes anatomically mature. Cooperation provided this advantage, and with it came a complex social system—and a new challenge to human intelligence.[3]

This view of the crucial role of cooperation in evolution is part of a radical rethinking of just what the famous phrase "survival of the fittest" means.[4] In the late nineteenth century social Darwinists seized on that phrase to argue that "fitness" meant the strong and ruthless would inevitably triumph over the weak. They used that as a rationale to celebrate unbridled competition and to ignore the plight of the poor and disenfranchised.

Today that idea has been overturned in evolutionary theory by the simple insight that evolutionary fitness is measured not by toughness, but by reproductive success: how many of one's children survive to pass on one's genes to future generations. That genetic legacy is the true sense of "survival" in evolution.

From that perspective, the *group* working together—foraging for food, nurturing children, fending off predators—has been the key to human survival, not the ruthlessness of lone rogues. And, indeed, Darwin himself first proposed that human groups whose members were ready to work together for the common good survived better and had more offspring than those whose members were self-serving, or those who were not part of any group at all.

Even today the benefits of a close-knit band are evident in the few remaining human groups that subsist as hunters and gatherers, the mode of living throughout the millions of years during which our brain took on its present architecture. In such groups, one of the main determinants of children's health is whether they have a living grandmother or other elderly relative who can supplement the mother and father's efforts to garner food.[5]

One modern legacy of this past is the radar for friendliness and cooperation most of us have; people gravitate to those who show signs of these qualities. We also have a strong early-warning system that alerts us to someone who may be selfish or untrustworthy. An experiment at Cornell University had groups of strangers mix and meet for thirty minutes and then rate each other on how selfish or cooperative the others were. Those ratings held up when compared with how the people actually performed in a game where they could choose selfish or cooperative strategies for winning. Likewise, people are drawn to others who are as cooperative and friendly as they are; groups made up of cooperative strangers are as altruistic and helpful to each other as are members of the same family.[6]

Socializing Shapes the Brain

One great anatomical legacy of the human need to band together is the neocortex, the brain's topmost layers, which gives us the capacity to think.

The adaptive challenges that matter most to the survival of a species are what lead to evolutionary changes in that species. Operating in a coordinated band—whether it be a working corporate team or a roving group of protohumans—demands a high level of social intelligence, skill in reading and handling relationships. If the more socially intelligent have the greatest number of surviving offspring—and therefore are the most "fit"—then nature would select for changes in the human brain that better handle the complexities of living in groups.[7] In evolution, as today, group members had to balance the advantages of cooperation in fending off enemies, hunting and foraging, and caring for children with the disadvantages of competition within the group for food, mates, or other limited resources, particularly in times of scarcity. Add to that having to compute hierarchies of dominance, social and kinship obligations, and quid pro quo exchanges, and the result was a staggeringly large amount of social data to track and use well.

Therein lies the evolutionary pressure to develop a "thinking brain" with the capacity to make all these social connections instantly. In the animal kingdom, only mammals have a neocortex at all. Among primates (including us humans), the ratio of neocortex to total brain volume increases in direct proportion to the size of the group typical of that species.[8] For early humans, that group could number in the dozens or hundreds (and in today's organizational life it can be in the thousands).

In this view, social intelligence made its appearance well before the emergence of rational thought; the abstract thinking abilities of the human species piggybacked later onto a neocortex that had initially expanded to deal with the immediate interpersonal world.[9] The neocortex, however, evolved from more ancient structures in the emotional brain, like the amygdala, and so is heavily laced with circuitry for emotion.

The neocortex, with its sophisticated understanding of group dynamics, must interpret its data in attunement with emotional signals. Indeed, every mental act of recognition ("That's a chair") has embedded within it an emotional reaction (". . . and I don't like it").

This same brain circuitry lets us know immediately, for instance, whom among those standing near us in an elevator we should greet and whom not ("The boss looks like she's in a bad mood today—I think I won't bother her"). And it forges every detail of the cooperative working relationships that are the key to survival in today's organizations.

Even as we pass the driest information back and forth, our neural monitors for emotional nuance are reading innumerable tacit cues—tone of voice, choice of words, subtleties of posture, gesture, timing—for the textured messages that give that information its emotional context. These emotional signals have the power to keep the conversation—or the group—on track or not. Smooth coordination depends on this emotional channel as much as on the explicit, rational content of what is said and done.

The Art of Collaboration

John Seely Brown, chief scientist at Xerox Corporation and a cognitive theorist himself, points out that the crucial nature of social coordination is perhaps nowhere more evident than in today's scientific enterprises, where cutting-edge knowledge grows through orchestrated, collaborative efforts.

Brown explains, "Many theorists think of learning from a purely cognitive viewpoint, but if you ask successful people to reflect on how they learned what they currently know, they'll tell you: 'We learned most all we know from and with each other.' That takes social intelligence, not just cognitive ability. Many people have trouble because they don't understand how you become part of a human situation, part of a relationship. It's easy to focus on cognitive ability and ignore social intelligence. But it's when you bring those together that you can create magic."

At Xerox Corporation's legendary Silicon Valley R&D facility, which Brown directs, he tells me, "Everything is done collaboratively, like everywhere in today's high-tech world. There are no lone geniuses anywhere. Even Thomas Edison was a brilliant knowledge manager. We traffic in human capital; ideas don't come from a lone head, but from collaboration in a deep sense."

Social intelligence matters immensely for success in a world where work—especially research and development—is done in teams. "One of the most important skills in management is the ability to read the human context, to be aware of what's in play," says Brown. "Power in management is the ability to make things happen. But how do you let the world do some of the work for you? It takes what amounts to organizational judo—being able to read the situation, the human currents, and move accordingly. The more we operate in less controlled environments, the more we need to be able to read human energies."

Brown continues, "There are some people who are blind to the dynamics of a group. I'll walk out of a meeting with one researcher, and he won't have a clue about what went on, while another researcher will have read the dynamics in the room perfectly: knowing when to step in, how to put things, what matters. That person can carry ideas beyond work out into the world."

The art of "making an impact through people," Brown adds, "is the ability to pull people together, to attract colleagues to the work, to create the critical mass for research. Then, once you've done that, there's the next question: How do you engage the rest of the corporation? And then, how do you get the message out and convert the rest of the world? To communicate is not just a matter of pushing information at another person. It's creating an experience, to engage their gut—and that's an emotional skill."

Team Advantage: The Group Mind

In today's workplace, this is a fundamental fact: Each of us has only a part of the information or expertise we need to get our jobs done. Robert Kelley, of Carnegie-Mellon University, has been asking people working at a wide variety of companies the same question for many years: What percentage of the knowledge you need to do your job is stored in your own mind?

In 1986 the answer was typically about 75 percent. But by 1997 the percentage had slid to between 15 and 20 percent.[10] This no doubt reflects the explosive growth of information. More knowledge has been generated in the twentieth century, it is said, than in all of history before, and the rate of increase continues to accelerate as we enter the twenty-first.

Given this fact, the network or team of people to whom we can reach out for information and expertise is increasingly vital. We've come to depend on the group mind as never before.

"My intelligence does not stop at my skin" is how Howard Gardner, the influential Harvard theorist, puts it. Rather, he points out, it encompasses his tools, such as his computer and its databases, and, just as important, "my network of associates—office mates, professional colleagues, others whom I can phone or to whom I can dispatch electronic messages."[11]

There's no doubt the group mind can be far more intelligent than the individual; the scientific data on this point is overwhelming. In one experiment, students studied and worked in groups while taking a college course. For their final exam, they first took a portion of the exam individually. Then, after they turned in their answer sheets, they were given an additional set of questions to answer as a group.

Results from hundreds of groups showed that 97 percent of the time the group scores were higher than those of the best individuals.[12] This same effect has been found over and over again, even for extremely short-lived groups, ones that were formed solely for the purposes of an experiment. When teams of strangers listen to a narrative about the ups and downs of someone's career, the more people on the team, the better their collective memory: Three people did better than two, four better than three, and so on.[13]

"As a math major, I believed that the whole is equal to the sum of its parts—until I worked with teams," Chuck Noll, the legendary former coach of the Pittsburgh Steelers, told me. "Then when I became a coach I saw the whole is never the sum of its parts—it's greater or lesser, depending on how well the individuals work together."

Lubricating the mechanisms of the group mind so that it can think and act brilliantly demands emotional intelligence. Superb intellect and technical talents alone do not make people great team members.

That was shown in a compelling series of experiments at a business school at Cambridge University. Researchers there put together 120 simulated management teams to make decisions for a mock business. Some of the teams were composed entirely of people who were highly intelligent. But despite this obvious advantage, the high-IQ teams performed worse than other teams whose members were not all so brilliant.[14] And observation of the teams in action tells why: High-IQ members spent too much of their time in competitive debate, and the debating became an unending session of academic showmanship.

Another weakness of the high-IQ teams was that all the members opted for the same kind of task: applying their critical abilities to the intellectually intriguing parts of the job at hand, engaging in analysis and counteranalysis. No one got around to other necessary parts of the job: planning, collecting and exchanging practical information, keeping track of what had been learned, coordinating a plan of action. Everyone was so busy trying to be the intellectual star that the team flopped.

The Group IQ

They're lost on a desert, the sun beating down mercilessly, mirages shimmering, not a recognizable landmark in sight. Their water is running low, and they have no compass or map. Their only hope is to set out in search of rescue—but their supplies are too heavy. They have to choose what to take and what to leave in order to survive.

It's a life-and-death scenario, but not life-threatening—it's a simulation used to test the teamwork skills of participants. The scenario allows each person to be rated on his or her individual choices, and for those choices to be compared to those made by the group as a whole.

The conclusion, from hundreds and hundreds of trials, is that groups fall into one of three performance levels. At the worst, frictions within the group make it fail as a team, with performance that is *poorer* than the average individual score. When the team works reasonably well, the group score will be greater than the *average* individual score. But when the team has real synergy, its score far exceeds even the *best* individual score.

For example, in terms of technical expertise and experience, the members of the management team at the auto division of one of Europe's largest automakers outmatched those on the equivalent team in the truck division. Yet the management group for the truck division operated better as a team.

"It made no sense when you looked at the profiles and backgrounds of the individuals in the truck division—you'd think they would be mediocre compared to that other team," the management consultant who worked with the teams told me. "Yet when they operated as a unit, they were superb."

What makes a team perform better than the best person on it? That question is key. Outstanding team performance raises the "group IQ"—the sum total of the best talents of each member on a team, contributed to their fullest.[15] When teams operate at their best, the results can be more than simply additive—they can be *multiplicative,* with the best talents of one person catalyzing the best of another and another, to produce results far beyond what any one person might have done. The explanation of this aspect of team performance lies in the members' *relationships*—in the chemistry between members.

In a classic study of group IQ by Wendy Williams and Robert Sternberg at Yale, the interpersonal skills and compatibility of the group members emerged as key to their performance (a result found time and again).[16] Williams and Sternberg found that those who were socially inept, out of tune with others' feelings, were a drag on the whole effort—especially if they lacked the ability to resolve differences or communicate effectively. Having at least one high-IQ member was essential for good performance but not sufficient; the group had to click in other ways, too. Another potential liability was the "eager beaver," a member who was too controlling or domineering to allow the full contribution of the others.

Motivation mattered greatly. If members cared and were committed to the goals, they tried harder and so did better. All in all, the *social* effectiveness of the group predicted how well it would do, more than did the individual IQs of its members. The conclusion: Groups perform better when they foster a state of internal harmony. Such groups leverage the full talent of their members.

A study of sixty work teams in a large American financial services company found that many elements mattered to some extent for the teams' effectiveness. But the single dimension that mattered most was the human element—how members interacted with each other and those the team connected with.[17]

■ ■ ■

Several competencies of star performers are rooted in the basic human talents for social coordination:

■ *Building bonds:* Nurturing instrumental relationships

■ *Collaboration and cooperation:* Working with others toward shared goals

■ *Team capabilities:* Creating synergy in working toward group goals

■ BUILDING BONDS ■

Nurturing Instrumental Relationships

People with this competence

■ Cultivate and maintain extensive informal networks

■ Seek out relationships that are mutually beneficial

■ Build rapport and keep others in the loop

■ Make and maintain personal friendships among work associates

Jeffrey Katzenberg is furiously making connections. Three headset-wearing secretaries function as his antennae, probing and searching the entertainment industry for his next point of contact—incessantly ringing people to arrange times, calling back to reschedule or with a reminder of the upcoming call—all so that Katzenberg can be continuously on the phone during any and all free moments, reaching out to the hundreds of people he stays in touch with as a matter of routine.[18]

Katzenberg, one of the three founders of the Hollywood creative company Dreamworks SKG, is a networker without equal. The motive for his manic flurries of calls is, mainly, just to stay in touch—not explicitly to "do business." But his telephone routine primes these relationships, keeping them fresh, so that when the business need comes along, he can call on them seamlessly: make a proposal, pin down a deal.

In the entertainment industry, relationships are the key to doing business, because the projects—a film, a TV series, an interactive CD-ROM—are all short-term, goal-focused, and time-limited. They require knitting together an instant organization, a pseudofamily of director, producers, actors, and production people, all of whom dissolve back at the end into a loose network of potential players. Katzenberg keeps a weblike thread of connection out to everyone so that he can reel them in as needed.

This talent for connecting epitomizes stars in almost every kind of job. For instance, studies of outstanding performers in fields like engineering, computer science, biotechnology, and other "knowledge work" fields find the building and maintenance of networks crucial for success.[19] Even in fields like technology, the networks are linked the old-fashioned way, face-to-face and by phone, as well as through e-mail.

But what cements a connection is not physical proximity (though it helps) so much as *psychological* proximity. The people we get along with, trust, feel simpatico with, are the strongest links in our networks

The networks of top performers are not random; they are carefully chosen, with each person being included because of a particular expertise or excellence. These networks traffic expertise and information back and forth in an artful, ongoing give-and-take. Each member of a network represents an immediately available extension of knowledge or expertise, accessible with a single phone call.

People who work a network well also have an immense time advantage over those who have to use broader, more general sources of information to find answers. One estimate indicates that for every hour a star puts into seeking answers through a network, an average person spends three to five hours gathering the same information.[20]

The Art of Networking

Weblike connectivity is the secret of success in many industries where people spend less of their careers in a single organization and more in short-lived, high-intensity relationships. Entertainment is certainly one such field. But this pattern, some predict, will come to typify many or most fields in the years to come. In such a fluid reality, where virtual organizations form to do projects, then dissolve once the project is complete, the key to success is not whom you have worked *for* but whom you have worked *with*—and whom you are still in touch with.

The electronics industry offers a case study in the crucial role of human networks in entrepreneurship. One estimate of the growth in value of the personal computer industry from 1981 to 1990 puts it going from virtually nothing to nearly $100 billion—an immense accumulation of wealth spurred by the alliances forged between enterprising technical wizards and equally enterprising venture capitalists.[21] Two thirds of high-tech firms were backed by venture capitalists, a breed of investors that has had a symbiotic relationship with America's high-tech industry since its earliest days, long before banks, let alone financial markets, would invest a penny.

Venture capitalists in Silicon Valley do far more than just spot a promising idea and put money into the start-up—they stay involved with the company they invest in. Their involvement typically includes giving the fledgling company access to the people they know in management, finance, and the high-tech industry itself, and even helping recruit key talent.

For example, just about all of the start-ups funded by the venture capital firm of Kleiner Perkins Caulfield and Byers were sent to them by someone they knew and trusted. John Doerr, a lead partner at the firm, talks about this rich web of relationships this way: "Think of Silicon Valley as an effective system for getting people, projects, and capital together." Such a system of connections can spawn vast wealth—and the absence of such a system can take a dire toll, especially during hard times.

Social Networks, Personal Capital

It was the 1980s on Wall Street, when just about anything went. He was only twenty-four, yet he managed a $3 billion money market fund, and his earnings were spectacular. But his investments were almost entirely in junk bonds, and the fund lost virtually all its value in the crash of October 1987. He lost his job.

"That was when he learned relationships are everything in business," his wife tells me. "There was no one there to protect him. He had gotten so cocky and full of himself, he hadn't bothered to cultivate the kind of friendships that might have led someone to say, 'Let's keep him.' Then, when he tried to look for a new job, he didn't know anyone who would help him find something at another company."

After six months—and five hundred fruitless phone calls—he finally landed another, far less prestigious job, from which he began to work his way up the ladder again. But his basic attitude has changed.

"Now he's the president of his local professional society, and he knows all the other key people in the business," his wife says. "The question we ask ourselves is, If he lost his job tomorrow, how many phone calls would it take for him to get a new job? Today it would take just one."

Networks of personal contacts are a kind of personal capital. Doing well in our jobs depends to a greater or lesser extent on the work of a web of others. As one executive put it, while it may *seem* that he has control over how well he does his job, "in reality, in addition to my direct subordinates, there are hundreds of people whom I have no direct control over but who can affect the performance of my job. At least two dozen of these people are crucial."[22]

One of the virtues of building relationships is the reservoir of goodwill and trust that arises. Highly effective managers are adept at cultivating such relationships, whereas less effective managers generally fail to do so.[23] This is particularly crucial for advancement from the lower rungs of an organization to the higher levels; these human links are the routes through which people come to be known for their abilities.

These networks may be quite distinct from the web of friendships we cultivate primarily for pleasure. Relationship building has a motive; these are friendships with a purpose. People skilled at networking often mix their private life and their work life, so that many or most of their personal friendships are made through work, though it takes clarity and discipline to keep work and private agendas from becoming entangled.

People who are shy, introverted, or reclusive are, of course, poor at cultivating such relationships. And people who merely accept the invitations they are extended but make none themselves or restrict their conversation to work matters do little to enlarge their web of relationships.

Another common failing is that people are too protective of their own work time and agendas, turning down requests to help or to work cooperatively; the result is often resentment and a stunted network. But people who can't say no whenever anyone makes a request of them are in danger of taking on so much that their own work suffers. Outstanding performers are able to balance their own critical work with carefully chosen favors, building accounts of goodwill with people who may become crucial resources down the line.[24]

Rapport building is central to developing strong, useful relationships. Rapport hinges on empathy and typically emerges naturally in the course of casual conversation about family, sports, children, and the stuff of life. Finally, the building of a close work friendship means establishing an alliance, a relationship that can be counted on. Those highly adept at relationship building, like Katzenberg or Doerr, can call on an extensive—and ever-expanding—network of friends.

Bring In the Relationship Managers

arks & Spencer, the huge British retail chain, gives an unusual gift to its regular suppliers: a special key card that lets them into the chain's head offices anytime. Although they still have to make appointments, the key card makes them feel like members of the Marks & Spencer family.

That is exactly the point. The key card is part of an intentional effort by Marks & Spencer to nurture a relationship of trust and cooperation with its suppliers. That effort also includes trips with suppliers to trade shows and to other countries to visit sources of raw materials. The goal: to strengthen mutual understanding, as well as to spot new possibilities for products they can develop jointly.

The Marks & Spencer program exemplifies a trend among suppliers and retailers to build collaborative relationships, rather than simply playing one potential partner against another. That cooperative strategy has tangible payoffs: An analysis of 218 retailers carrying the products of a replacement auto parts manufacturer showed those retailers who trusted the manufacturer, compared to those who distrusted it, were 22 percent less likely to have alternative sources of supply, and to have 78 percent higher sales of the products.[25]

While links between such large organizations may seem abstract, they boil down to the day-to-day connections of sales reps, account managers, product managers, and the like. These people-to-people coalitions across companies have concrete benefits for both sides: They can share mutually important proprietary information and allocate people and resources to customize business. Those from one company can sometimes act as de facto consultants for another. For example, a sales team from Kraft Foods took it on itself to do a six-month study of a retailer's dairy case. The Kraft team then came up with recommendations for reorganizing shelf space and stocking new items that reflect recent buying trends. The result: Sales for the retailer—and of Kraft products to that retailer—increased by about 22 percent.[26]

Another example: Procter & Gamble used to pay its sales managers on the basis of the total amount of inventory they got retailers to take, even if that inventory ended up back in the warehouse. But that meant P&G salespeople were rewarded for a strategy that, in the end, hurt retailers and eroded business relationships. Now P&G has shifted its policy to compensate its salespeople for maximizing *both* P&G's results and those of the stores that sell its products.

Since a company-to-company relationship is nothing more than the ties between the people from each, the interpersonal chemistry is crucial. For that reason, Sherwin-Williams, the paint manufacturer, actually invites managers from Sears, Roebuck, one of its main retailers, to help choose the representatives who will handle the Sears account.

As Nirmalya Kumar, writing about this approach in the *Harvard Business Review,* put it, "The trust game has implications for the type of people that a company recruits to work with [its] partners. . . . Traditional manufacturers, salespeople, and retail buyers have had a volume or price focus. They need to be replaced by *relationship managers* with appropriate bedside manners."[27]

■ COLLABORATION AND COOPERATION ■

Working with Others Toward Shared Goals

■■■

People with this competence

■ Balance a focus on task with attention to relationships

■ Collaborate, sharing plans, information, and resources

■ Promote a friendly, cooperative climate

■ Spot and nurture opportunities for collaboration

■■■

Intel, the hugely successful computer processor manufacturer, had a paradoxical problem: Its success was, in a sense, killing it. An extremely task-focused organization, the company's concentration on product development, staying ahead of the curve in creating new technologies, and improving turn-around for new product introduction paid off in huge market share and profit. Yet for too many people, it just wasn't fun anymore.

That, at any rate, is how a consultant to a division at Intel, who was called in for some advice, put it to me.

"They wanted a workshop on how to attend to the relationship side of their business, because it was becoming increasingly unenjoyable," the consultant told me. "At the personal level they liked each other, but they were so intensely task-oriented, their working relationships were suffering. They needed to let supervisors know it's not enough just to get the job done if you destroy the relationships within the working group. They needed management to appreciate that neglecting the soft side has hard consequences."

This interpersonal crisis at Intel points to the value of a collaborative, cooperative spirit. Groups that have fun together—who enjoy being in each other's company, who can joke together and share good times—have the emotional capital not just to excel in good times, but to get through hard times as well. Groups who do not share this emotional bond are more likely to become paralyzed or dysfunctional or to disintegrate under pressure.

Even those who subscribe to the tough-minded business-is-war ideology and see no point in cultivating a humane tone may do well to ponder the immense effort put into cultivating esprit de corps at the platoon level in armies. The sophisticated understanding of what makes a unit work well under extraordinary pressures has always been that emotional bonds are crucial to morale, effectiveness, and the unit's very survival.

The Organizational Marriage

Everyone knew the meeting was a personal disaster for Al, a fledgling vice president at a large urban medical center. To be sure, all agreed the meeting was for a good purpose: to create a vision and strategy for a failing community program Al had been brought in to run. But Al sabotaged both himself and the meeting. As he admitted afterward, "I got my behind kicked."

Al's first mistake was calling the meeting of the hospital's already over-scheduled senior management group on too short notice, selecting a day when he knew the VP of the nursing unit—someone with a crucial contribution—was usually out of the hospital. The consultant to the management team also couldn't make it. Al's second mistake was failing to offer a pre-meeting briefing or preparation of any kind—he was winging it, even though this was his debut as a new vice president. His third and perhaps biggest mistake was to rebuff an offer from Sarah, his boss and the president of the medical center, to help design a meeting that would be lively and more effective.

As the meeting unfolded it was painfully evident to everyone that Al was unprepared and flustered, and those who came felt the session was a waste of their time. Sarah felt Al's disastrous performance reflected poorly on her judgment in bringing him into the job.

What went so wrong?

James Krantz, a professor at the Yale School of Organization and Management, who observed Al and Sarah on the job, says the failed meeting was yet another symptom of something deeply amiss in their working relationship.[28] With surprising rapidity, they had settled into a pattern that brought out the worst in each other. Privately, Al admitted to feeling that Sarah was overbearing and hypercritical of him, chronically dissatisfied with whatever he did; Sarah said Al seemed passive, inept, and sullen with her. At the emotional level, the two of them acted and looked like a couple trapped in a miserable marriage—except that this was work, not private life.

But, Krantz observes, it could happen anywhere—and with alarming ease. Any superior and subordinate can slip into a destructive emotional dynamic, because each needs the other in order to succeed. A subordinate can make a boss seem effective—or pathetic—to the boss's own boss, since the superior is accountable for how well the subordinate does. And, of course, the subordinate depends on the superior for promotions, raises, and simply keeping a job—all of which makes the subordinate emotionally vulnerable to the boss.

Therein lies the blessing or the curse. This interdependence ties a subordinate and superior together in a way that can become highly charged. If both do well emotionally—if they form a relationship of trust and rapport, understanding and inspired effort—their performance will shine. But if things go emotionally awry, the relationship can become a nightmare and their performance a series of minor and major disasters.

The Vertical Couple

The power of a subordinate to make a boss look good to *her* boss is, potentially, tremendous. But for Sarah, Al had become a magnet for some of her deepest anxieties about her own performance. She was embarrassed by the failure of the program Al had been brought in to run—she felt it reflected poorly on her own abilities as president and threatened her professional reputation. She now doubted Al's ability to save the unit—and thus her reputation—and so was angry about his performance.

Al, for his part, had been perfectly capable at his previous job, but the promotion to vice president left him unsure of himself. He feared the others on the management team would see him as incompetent; at his worst moments, he felt like an impostor. And, to make everything worse, Al sensed Sarah's lack of confidence in him, which only compounded his anxieties and his ineptitude.

Each secretly felt the other was the cause of their problems: Al saw Sarah as undermining his confidence by being overly controlling as well as doubting his competence. Sarah, for her part, had started to see Al (just as he feared) as lacking both the confidence and competence to do the job she needed him to do, and so she felt obliged to be responsible, even aggressive, for both of them. The result was a downward spiral in which Al became more passive, unsure, and inept, and Sarah micromanaged, becoming more critical and controlling, finally trying to do Al's job for him.

Krantz invokes a ponderous term for this dynamic between Sarah and Al: "projective identification." Each of them projected onto the other their worst fears and doubts in an emotional self-fulfilling prophecy.[29] Any close working relationship can take on such hidden undertones, though the one between a boss and subordinate is most prone to such emotional sabotage.

These unconscious agreements serve a rather sinister psychological function: They keep people from facing or even recognizing problems, bad news, or conflicts. If a boss can blame some defect of his own—and the resulting problems in the organization—on a subordinate, then he never needs to face the real source of trouble: himself. One symptom of this kind of projection—"the problem is with him, not me"—is a boss who can never find or name a replacement, even as retirement looms. No one is good enough; every candidate has fatal flaws.

Kiss Up, Kick Down

Sycophancy by subordinates, and a corresponding arrogance in the superior, is another all-too-common symptom of projection. The subordinates see the boss as having special power or ability; the boss buys into the projections and his sense of himself becomes inflated to the point where he feels the rules of decency no longer apply.

This pattern seems particularly common in some cultures. I'm told by Deepak Sethi, an expert in executive education, that in India, his country of origin, the rule is "Kiss up and kick down." As Sethi says, "There's a lack of empathy downward in most old-style Indian companies. You see it in bosses who are openly angry at people. There's no stigma to it; it's completely acceptable to yell at your subordinates there."

A major reason subordinates put up with it, Sethi says, is that so many Indian companies are privately held by powerful families, and there are many more highly qualified people than there are good jobs available, "So even if you're a professional manager, you're at the mercy of the owners."

An understandable result of the kiss-up–kick-down relationship is a large pool of resentment "that's never expressed upward, but passed on downward, in a chain of angry rudeness." This leads workers to sabotage the company's success in passive ways, like not getting things done on time—which, of course, makes the boss yell at everyone all over again.

That bitter cycle echoes the stalemate between Sarah and Al: Sarah felt she couldn't trust Al to do his job well enough, so she kept pushing him to do tasks while hovering over him, expecting the worst. This, in turn, made Al feel demeaned—and undermined his abilities.

The saga of Sarah and Al, fortunately, had a happy resolution. Sarah was acutely aware that something was off track in her relationship with Al, if only because it stood in such stark contrast to the effective ties she had to everyone else on the management team. Once the diagnosis was made, Sarah was able to stop micromanaging and show Al that she had some faith in his capabilities. She also clarified his responsibilities. No longer shadowed by the fear that she saw him as unfit for his job, Al was now able to take initiative and show his competence.

Their story is one with wide implications. Virtually everyone who has a superior is part of at least one vertical "couple"; every boss forms such a bond with each subordinate. Such vertical couples are a basic unit of organizational life, something akin to human molecules that interact to form the latticework of relationship that *is* the organization. And while vertical couples have all the emotional overlay that power and compliance bring to a relationship, peer couples—our relationships with coworkers—have a parallel emotional component, something akin to the pleasures, jealousies, and rivalries of siblings.

If there is anywhere emotional intelligence needs to enter an organization, it is at this most basic level. Building collaborative and fruitful relationships begins with the couples we are a part of at work. Bringing emotional intelligence to a working relationship can pitch it toward the evolving, creative, mutually engaging end of the continuum; failing to do so heightens the risk of a downward drift toward rigidity, stalemate, and failure.

■ TEAM CAPABILITIES ■

Creating Group Synergy in Pursuing Collective Goals

People with this competence

■ Model team qualities like respect, helpfulness, and cooperation

■ Draw all members into active and enthusiastic participation

■ Build team identity, esprit de corps, and commitment

■ Protect the group and its reputation; share credit

Teamwork is of utmost importance to companies like Owens-Corning, a building materials manufacturer, which found itself with about two hundred incompatible software systems, each tailored to a specific task like tracking shingle counts or invoices for insulation. To help their salespeople sell the company's whole line, rather than just insulation or roofing, Owens-Corning needed a single, unified software system.

So Michael Radcliff, their chief information officer, turned to SAP, a German industrial-applications software company, which installed a system at Owens-Corning that connects all the information in the entire operation. When a sales rep sends in an order, the system automatically allocates the raw materials for its manufacture, schedules its production and delivery, and takes care of billing—all with a single data entry.

But there's a risk—the SAP system is notoriously complex, and a small glitch can create company-wide chaos. Owens-Corning—and all SAP's other manufacturing customers worldwide—need to trust that they can rely on SAP to keep them running.[30]

"Before," an SAP account rep tells me, "I sometimes would have a hard time getting people from other divisions within our company to help me with a one-two punch—to come together with a unified solution for a customer's problem. After all, if our software goes down, they can't get their product out the door; they need to be assured they can count on us." Hence the formation of teamSAP, the shorthand term for the teams of SAP employees available to all their customers at all times.

Similar teams seem to be everywhere in business these days—management teams, task forces, quality circles, learning groups, self-managed work teams, and so on. And then there are the instant, ad hoc teams called into being over the course of a meeting, or as a short-lived virtual group working together on a one-time project. While people at work have always helped each other out and coordinated their efforts, the ascendance of work teams in large organizations puts a new premium on team skills.

About half the Fortune 1,000 companies in a General Accounting Office survey said they were using self-managed work teams, and expected to expand their use in coming years.[31] The advantages begin at the personal level—people feel the combination of cooperation and increased autonomy offered by a self-managed work team offers more enjoyment and fulfillment. When teams work well, turnover and absenteeism decline, while productivity tends to rise.[32]

Perhaps the most compelling strength of teams for business is their pure economic potential. Just as individuals who are superior performers can add tremendous financial value, so it is with teams. The top work teams at a polyester fiber plant achieved an astonishing productivity advantage when compared to teams doing the exact same work. Each of the top ten teams produced 30 percent more fiber per year—in total, about seven million pounds more.[33] At a market price of $1.40 per pound, that meant an economic value added of $9.8 million!

As analyst Lyle Spencer Jr. told me, "There's a huge leverage from better working teams. When you look at the economic value added, it's out of all proportion to the salaries of team members. Data like this give the lie to people who dismiss these competencies or things like team building as 'touchy-feely'—the benefits are quite real."

Spencer adds, benefits from high-performing teams at the top offer even greater payoffs. "At the highest levels, the scope of thinking is bigger—people are projecting five and ten years out—and the economic advantages of a high-performance executive team for a company can be vast."

Strong groups are essential in a climate of corporate upheaval. I visited AT&T in 1996, shortly after it had announced its intention to split into three separate companies and lay off forty thousand employees. An executive in a division that is now part of Lucent Technologies told me: "The pain is not being felt everywhere. In a lot of the tech units where people work in tight teams, and where they find great meaning in what they do together, they're fairly impervious to the turmoil."

He added, "Whenever there's a strong self-managed team, with clarity about its mission, high standards for its product, and a clear sense of how to do its work, you just don't see fears and uncertainty the way you do in other parts of the organization. Members put their trust in their teammates, not just in the organization or its leaders."

The Team Achievement Drive

A friend who manages a team of software engineers in Silicon Valley tells me, "With a single phone call, any of the people I work with could get a job across town for twenty thousand dollars more a year. But they don't."

Why?

"I keep it fun."

The ability to make everyone on a team love what they are doing together is at the heart of team building and team leadership. Studies of the highest-performing self-managing work groups find that a critical mass of their members love working in a group. This "team achievement" outlook is a combination of a shared competitive drive, strong social bonds, and confidence in each other's abilities. Taken together, these elements add up to what Spencer summarizes as "fast, focused, friendly, self-confident, fun teams."[34]

People on such teams tend to share a common motivational pattern. They are competitive and evenhanded in matching members to the best role for their talents. They have a strong affiliative need—they like people for their own sake—which makes them more harmonious, better able to handle conflicts and offer mutual support. And rather than seeking power that is purely self-interested, they wield power in the best interests of the group—they share a commitment to the group goal.

These are the kind of teams, Spencer notes, that are increasingly widespread in entrepreneurial high-tech organizations, where quick product development is vital to meeting the competitive pressure of an industry in which the shelf life of a product line is measured in weeks and months.

Just twenty years ago team skills were only threshold abilities, not a trait that defined outstanding leaders. In the 1990s, though, team skills are a defining quality of star performers. At IBM, 80 percent of the time a person's strength as a team leader predicts "whether someone is a top performer or just average," Mary Fontaine, of Hay/McBer, told me. "These are people who can create compelling visions, conceptualize their business in an exciting way, articulate it simply and emphatically," and so inspire others with enthusiasm in their work together.

In a study by the Center for Creative Leadership of top American and European executives whose careers derailed, the *inability* to build and lead a team was one of the most common reasons for failure.[35] Team skills, which had been of little consequence in a similar study in the early 1980s, had emerged as a key mark of leadership ten years later. By the 1990s, teamwork became the most frequently valued managerial competence in studies of organizations around the world.[36]

"The number one challenge for leadership here is getting the heads of our units to play together, to collaborate," an executive at a Fortune 500 company tells me. That is the great challenge at any level, in any organization. Team abilities come into play anytime people work together toward a common goal, whether in an informal group of three or in an entire corporate division. The demand for team skills will only grow in the coming years, as work revolves more and more around ad hoc groups and virtual organizations, around spontaneous teams that arise and dissolve as the need for them comes and goes—and as tasks become so complex that no one person has all the skills needed to accomplish them.

The Value of Star Teams

A s with individuals, so with groups: Emotional intelligence is key to excellence. Of course intellect and expertise matter—but what sets star teams apart has much to do with their emotional competence. Studies at companies like GE, Abbott Laboratories, and Hoechst-Celanese asked: What competencies distinguish highly effective teams from mediocre ones?[37]

To find that answer, Vanessa Drukat, now a professor at the Weatherhead School of Management at Case Western Reserve University, analyzed 150 self-managed teams at a huge American polyester fiber plant run by Hoechst-Celanese, the German chemical company (and where Spencer's data also came from). On the basis of objective performance data, she compared the ten most outstanding teams with average ones doing the same jobs.

These emotional competencies emerged as distinguishing capabilities of the ten star teams:[38]

- Empathy, or interpersonal understanding

- Cooperation and a unified effort

- Open communication, setting explicit norms and expectations, and confronting underperforming team members

- A drive to improve, so that the team paid attention to performance feedback and sought to learn to do better

- Self-awareness, in the form of evaluating their strengths and weaknesses as a team

- Initiative and taking a proactive stance toward solving problems

- Self-confidence as a team

- Flexibility in how they went about their collective tasks

- Organizational awareness, in terms of both assessing the need of other key groups in the company and being resourceful in using what the organization had to offer

- Building bonds to other teams

A case in point for how such competencies let teams work better can be seen in a study of strategic decision making in forty-eight top management teams at food-processing companies across the United States. CEOs were asked to identify the most recent strategic decision their company had made. Researchers then contacted the members of the management team who had been involved in that decision.[39]

Making team decisions presents a paradox: On one hand, the wisdom holds that the more freewheeling and intense the debate, the better the final decision; on the other hand, open conflict can corrode the ability of a team to work together.

Research on decision making in management teams shows that having people who possess the three qualities of high cognitive capabilities, diverse perspectives, and expertise leads to higher-quality decision making. But intellect and expertise are not enough; members also have to mix in a healthy interaction, one that furthers rigorous, open debate and critical examination of people's assumptions.

Achieving this level of openness can be a delicate, emotionally loaded matter. Too easy a consensus risks a low-quality decision, while too much contention results in a lack of unity and resolve. What allows a management team to argue heatedly but end up with a strong consensus? The presence of emotional intelligence.

And what makes a group go off track, with healthy debate devolving into open war? When disagreement is couched as personal attack, or when debate is in the service of political gamesmanship, or when a dispute triggers acrimony in a group member.

The central finding: If arguments become emotionally loaded, the quality of decisions suffers. As one consultant told me, "The image of the well-coordinated management team is a myth when amygdala hijacks, conflicts, and other undealt-with emotional static interfere with their abilities to plan, decide, and learn together." On the other hand, debate free of bad feelings—carried out in a positive spirit of mutual inquiry, with everyone feeling the process is fair and open, and holding a shared concern for the organization rather than their narrow self-interest—led to the best decisions.

In sum, there is a middle way: Teams can use intellectual battle to upgrade the quality of decisions, provided they keep debates free of the emotionality that might alienate or sabotage commitment to the decision by some team members. The key lies in emotional competencies such as self-awareness, empathy, and communication—that is, in how well team members argue.

The Glue People

The ability to keep a group working well together is a valuable talent in itself. Every high-functioning group almost certainly has at least one member with this talent. The greater the complexity of the group's task, the more crucial such people are to its success. This is most evident in science and technology, where the mission is to discover or create. Take neuroscience: "Biomedical research is increasingly interdisciplinary and high-tech; no one can know everything," says Dr. Jerome Engel, a neurobiologist and professor of neurology who directs the Seizure Disorder Center at UCLA. "It's all research teams now. People who are great motivators and collaborators, who are gifted in making a medical project work, are the glue that holds it all together. The future of research depends on having people like that on your team."

Yet, at least in the academic world, these skills are sadly undervalued. "When people come up for tenure review, the value of their contribution to the group gets no consideration," Dr. Engel adds. "These good collaborators tend to publish with other people, usually their supervisor, and tenure committees blindly assume it's the superior's work—though these people are key. It's a disaster. I find myself fighting for the reviewers to understand that the collaboration is in itself a skill worth keeping someone for—it's essential to biomedical research. But academics from disciplines like math and history, where research is a solitary pursuit, don't understand."

The result: "There's a counterreaction among younger researchers, who are sometimes afraid to collaborate because of this—which can mean they go off alone and do trivial or unimportant research," says Dr. Engel. "It's creating an atmosphere of paranoia, an unwillingness to share data or work together, that's undermining a scientific generation's ability to collaborate."

Where academia has been slow to recognize the value of a talent for cooperation and teamwork, business has not. Richard Price, a psychologist at the Institute for Social Research at the University of Michigan, calls these superbly nurturing types who are the cornerstone of strong work teams "health-engendering people," or HEPs. "They're crucial to a team," says Price. "It doesn't mean everyone has to be a social-emotional leader, but if one HEP is there, the team will work ten times better."

One legendary team, the engineering group at Data General whose efforts were memorialized in the best-selling book *The Soul of a New Machine,* had two HEPs on board.[40] The team's second in command, Carl Alsing, was everyone's confidant and emotional support. Alsing, who had planned to be a psychotherapist before heading into electronic engineering, became a group sounding board; everyone felt comfortable talking to him.

The second team nurturer was Rosemarie Seale, their secretary, who acted as a kind of den mother, seeing that everyone's material needs were taken care of and handling the minor crises of the day like a paycheck gone astray, or making sure people joining the team were shown around.[41] While such secretarial tasks may seem routine and mundane, they are crucial because they let people at work feel protected, supported, and cared for—and this, some say, is why secretaries or their equivalent will always be invaluable, despite technologies that would seem to render them obsolete.

The Competent Team Leader

An American pharmaceutical firm had an expensive problem: Once a new drug was identified and patented, testing and development took an investment of around $100 million and up to thirteen years to get the FDA approval that allowed marketing. Because the patent on a new drug's basic chemical compound lasts just seventeen years, that gave the company about a four-year window to recoup its investment and turn a profit before the drug became available as a generic.

A task force looking into the dilemma recommended a new structure: project teams focused on specific drugs, headed by project leaders reporting directly to the head of R&D—leaders who would be trained in the team leadership competencies. Such leaders could both be product champions within the company and bring entrepreneurial energy, enthusiasm, and collaboration to the team itself.

When these teams were compared three years later to others where the leaders had no such training, they not only had higher morale and esprit de corps, but had cut product development time by 30 percent, thereby doubling the time the company would have the drug exclusively.[42]

The designated leader is something like a parent in a family. Like a parent, leaders have to be sure that their actions are perceived by everyone on the team as fair, and, like a parent, a good team leader will look out for the team members, defending them—for example, when their reputation comes under attack—in the organization at large and providing for them by getting the practical support they need, in budgets, personnel, or time.

The best team leaders are able to get everyone to buy into a common sense of mission, goals, and agenda. The ability to articulate a compelling vision that serves as the guiding force for the group may be the single most important contribution of a good team leader. A charismatic leader can hold a team on course when all else fails.

Apart from molding the crucial emotional tone of a team, the leader provides coordination, which is the secret of cooperation and consensus. When people were put together in a leaderless group and told to work on solving a tough problem together, the more effective teams were those that spontaneously developed a structure where one person orchestrated their efforts, so they could solve a tough problem as efficiently as possible. Groups that operated in a leaderless mode, with everyone communicating with everyone else willy-nilly, were less effective.[43]

But strong team leaders do not act as the group's "brains," or autonomous decision makers, so much as consensus builders. When team leaders express their own opinion too early in a decision-making discussion, the group generates fewer ideas, and so makes poorer decisions. But when team leaders hold back, acting mainly as facilitators of the group's process without imposing their views, not expressing them until toward the end of a discussion, the outcome is a better decision.[44]

In this sense, team leaders lead best when they lead least. This is especially true for self-managed work teams, where the supervisors of the teams are not team members and the teams can perform autonomously.

In a study of self-managing customer service teams at a major American telephone company, the teams faltered when the supervisors gave suggestions and even "encouraging" advice.[45] The "advice" seems to have been read by the team in two ways: either as a demoralizing message that they were doing poorly and so needed extra help, or as meddling that got in the way of the team doing its best work.

The dynamic was very different in customer service teams that were self-managing but directly run by a supervisor. In these more traditional teams the supervisors' feedback had a positive effect on performance. The difference in the impact of supervisory control seems to revolve around the team's charter. When a team has a mandate to run itself, a supervisor, no matter how well-intentioned, may undermine team performance.[46] So when it comes to self-managed teams, the best leadership seems to be little or no leadership at all.

The Team and Organizational Politics

They've got these separate silos of authority and creativity, but no one talks across the boundaries," a consultant called in by one of America's largest food manufacturers tells me. "People who handle one brand won't cooperate with people who manage another, let alone try to innovate new products or marketing approaches together. But to stay competitive, they've got to create teams that transcend these boundaries."

Organizations of all kinds have come to the realization that the success of the whole demands that talents be orchestrated in teams that cut across traditional boundaries. This can be seen in ad hoc project teams and teams for planning, improving processes, developing products, and troubleshooting. All such teams are unified around a focused task, with members coming from discrete parts of the organization.

Such cross-functional teams are a special case, a kind of pseudo-team that brings together a mix of people who have their feet in two camps: their home base within the organization and their common meeting point as a team. Because they represent diverse parts of the organization, they have the potential for wider impact and coordination than would a team that is partitioned off. As these teams work together for the larger good of the organization, each member remains beholden to a constituency back home.

But overallegiance to the home base can have disastrous effects for the team. At an American automaker, for example, a cross-functional steering committee working on a new prototype held a meeting to work out their mutual electrical needs. The car's electrical power serves twenty different subsystems, including stereo, dashboard, headlights, and engine. The prototype for each of these subsystems, in turn, was being developed by a separate team, and when they met, they found that their combined solutions would consume 125 percent of the electrical power available. And since many members of the steering team were sent to the meeting with instructions from their own bosses to make *no* compromises, the meeting was a disaster.[47]

How can teams like this do their work effectively? An analysis of forty-three such teams at a global automaker—the same study that tracked the electrical power meeting—suggests several answers. The first lies in the organizational context, in which resources and power are given to the team itself and its members are rewarded based on the team's performance.

Another solution lies in raising the collective level of emotional intelligence. This might include delegating someone as a "process leader," who can track whether the group's work exemplifies collaboration, mutual respect, openness to diverse perspectives, listening, empathy, and the other hallmarks that raise a group's IQ. If the team process is on track, then members should feel the work is exciting, challenging, and important. Lacking these emotional intelligence team basics, the alternative is, as one member of a dysfunctional cross-functional team put it, "a fiasco."

The Team as Hero

The world's attention was captured for several weeks in 1997 by the spectacle of Sojourner, the spunky rover that sputtered along the rock-strewn landscape of Mars.

The television coverage of the tiny rover pluckily threading its way through Mars's jagged terrain like the Little Engine That Could was drama enough. But the real miracle was the remarkable team effort behind getting Sojourner there at all.

The project as originally conceived by NASA was a full-scale exploration of Mars. It suffered a near-fatal setback in 1992, when Congress froze funding, leaving barely enough to build a tiny, scaled-down demo model that had been planned only as a preliminary step in the larger plan.

So the project members were faced with converting what was to have been a nonworking scale model into a fully operational, miniaturized version of the probe.

Anthony Spear, the director of the Pathfinder project that delivered Sojourner, let Donna Shirley, the program manager, model a team on "Skunkworks," the name of the famed R&D team at Lockheed that sequestered itself and produced a stream of pioneering aviation prototypes, from America's first supersonic jet fighter to the Stealth bomber.

Shirley assembled a small, sleek team that would accomplish only the work necessary for the mission. Spear made the team even more efficient by doing away with layers of bureaucracy that had typified past NASA space projects. With the Pathfinder, one group would do everything, from design to operation.

The team shared the whole task, often in creative problem-solving sessions that wore on into the night. These were open forums, where everyone, no matter their ostensible rank, was given an equal hearing.

Though the challenge was daunting, the spirit was playful. Al Sacks, data systems manager, recalls someone asking for more money—yet again. So Sacks pulled a rubber dart gun from under the table and shot his teammate. "This was serious business," says Sacks, "but we turned it into fun."

The team had to be nimble; new challenges and surprises were constant. For instance, as Sojourner was being loaded into the Pathfinder spacecraft that would carry it to Mars, the engineers noticed—during a televised news conference, no less—that the large metal folding petals designed to protect the rover once on Mars were not shutting all the way. They were horrified.

Sending the press home, the team scrambled frantically to find the problem and solve it. Since they had never before put the whole rover together, they had not considered the possibility that the latches that closed the petals would sag under the weight of all the parts.

So team members pulled parts off an engineering model, made slight modifications, hand-carried them from their facility in California to the launch site at Cape Canaveral, and replaced them. It worked.

The team worked around the clock for six months before the launch. What kept everyone on track despite the grueling pace was the grandeur of their goal. Said Bridget Landry, deputy uplink systems engineer, "The idea that what we're building and testing right now will be used when we land on Mars was really exciting. I tried to think of that when the fourth revision in the last hour for the same sequence came in!" Yet, she added, "There are few jobs that are all glamour and no dirt; the good ones, like mine, are those where the glamour, excitement, and emotional rewards make up for the scut work."

That scut work produced a marvel. The six-wheeled rover had a surprisingly modest brain: While the best Pentium computers have more than five million transistors, there are under seven thousand in the rover's.

And when Sojourner was finally launched, the project was not only a spectacular success, it was also $7,000 under budget. The team had invented at least twenty-five new devices or processes and had produced a spacecraft in one fourth the usual time. While the Mars Observer, lost in 1991 before reaching the planet, cost $1 billion, Sojourner was successful and came in at a quarter of that cost.

As one team member says, "It was like we caught fire—nothing could stop us." The Sojourner team was in flow.

Group Flow

When I've asked seasoned executives and managers what it's like when teams they've been on or run have caught fire and outdone themselves—and achieved flow—the same characteristics come up time and again.[48]

■ *A daunting challenge or a noble mission.* "One of the reasons group goals often fail is they're too materialistic," a vice president of space launch systems at Lockheed Martin told me. "I look for superordinancy—goals big enough that the whole group can get behind them." Such work has compelling meaning and motivation; working toward something monumental deserves everyone's best effort.

The late Nobel Prize–winning physicist Richard Feynman remembered how differently people worked on the Manhattan Project before and after they knew what their effort was for. Originally strict security meant the whole team was kept in the dark, so they often worked slowly, and not always very well.

Then Feynman convinced Robert Oppenheimer to tell the team of technicians what they were actually working on—it was during the darkest days of World War II, and their project was a weapon that might stop the Axis enemy, who were at the time ascendant. From that point on, Feynman recalled, "*Complete* transformation. *They* began to invent ways of doing it better. . . ."[49] He calculated that their work went ten times as fast after they understood the goal.

■ *Intense group loyalty.* "When extraordinary teams talk about what made them so successful, you often hear them say it's because they really love and care about each other," says Daniel Kim, cofounder of MIT's Center for Organizational Learning, and now with Pegasus Communications. "If people were honest about what makes great teams in an organization, they'd say part of it is the emotional connections that allow both openness and caring."

■ *Diverse range of talents.* The stronger the array of capabilities a team brings to its task, the more flexible it can be in meeting changing demands. Diversity begins with technical demands, but extends also to emotional competence—including a "glue person."

■ *Trust and selfless collaboration.* People in successful teams feel they can count on each other. When Bob Taylor assembled the team at Xerox PARC that developed the prototype of the user-friendly computer (eventually the basis for the first Apple computer when Xerox failed to follow through), he looked for people who could work collaboratively, and encouraged everyone to help out with other people's work. "You could spend forty percent of your time working as 'hands' on somebody else's project," recalls Alan Kay, one of the first computer scientists asked to join.

■ *Focus and passion.* The demands of meeting a great goal inherently provide focus; the rest of life can seem not just mundane, but trivial by comparison. For the duration, the details of life are on hold. Focus can be sharpened by creating a working space for the group, separate from the rest of the organization, both in function and in place. The Manhattan Project was carried on at top-secret sites accessible only to project members; the Skunkworks at Lockheed was in a windowless, signless building that was off-limits to everyone else at the company.

■ *Work that is intrinsically fun and rewarding.* Such intense focus is in itself a kind of high. Members work less for external perks like money, promotion, or prestige than for the inner rewards of the work itself. Whether that thrill comes from the drive to achieve or a need to make an impact, there is an intense emotional payoff from outdoing all others as part of a group. As a member of the Data General software team put it, "There's a big high in here somewhere for me that I don't fully understand. . . . The reason I work is to win."[50]

The Team as Learning Lab: The Five Secrets

Burt Swersey's bright idea came to him when an article I wrote for the *New York Times* back in September 1995 caught his eye. It was about the Bell Labs study in which stars in an engineering division seemed to owe their success more to emotional intelligence skills than to technical ones, and it inspired Swersey to try something new with his engineering students at Rensselaer Polytechnic Institute.

He started his class by telling them about the Bell Labs study and what he called the "five simple secrets of success": rapport, empathy, persuasion, cooperation, and consensus building. And, he announced, instead of spending the first day of class reviewing engineering basics, they would conduct a learning lab on the five secrets.

"How would you go about establishing rapport with someone you don't know?" Swersey asked.

As the class, somewhat baffled and tentative at first, offered suggestions, Swersey listed them on the blackboard: "Introduce yourself, look at the person while you talk, ask them a question about themselves, shake hands, tell them about yourself, listen carefully . . ."

"These sound like the right answers," Swersey told them. "Now pick someone you don't know and take three minutes to establish some rapport."

The students pitched in enthusiastically; the room was filled with their chatter and banter. Swersey had a hard time getting them to stop and focus on the next "secret," the art of being empathic.

Asking them what *empathy* meant, he wrote these answers on the board: "Caring, listening, being supportive . . ." A young man wearing a baseball cap backward, his feet on the desk, muttered, "Showing you give a damn."

"That seems to capture it pretty well," said Swersey. "Now I want you to come up with something in your lives you feel you need some support for, and tell it to your partner. Partners, your job is to empathize." The buzz in the room made it clear that this was going well, too.

So Swersey upped the ante: "Now make up something that directly negatively impacts your partner. If you're the listener, no matter how hard it is to take, resist the temptation to tear the person apart—just be empathic." So the role-playing began and students spun out earnestly enacted, antagonizing tales: "I smashed your car." "I killed your goldfish." "I slept with your girlfriend."

For the empathizers, Swersey insisted they go beyond a stoic "Okay" and put themselves in the shoes of their partner, saying something like, "I feel so bad for you; you must be so upset." That led to a classwide discussion of a more realistic situation: someone on an engineering team who fails to deliver their promised part of a project on time. The students talked about taking the other person's perspective—and began to understand the importance of being supportive rather than angry.

They went on to practice persuasion and consensus building, taking three minutes to decide as a group which was the single best flavor of ice cream in the world, and why (one consensus-building answer: Neapolitan, a combination of three favorite flavors).

The results of this small social experiment?

"These sections turned out to be the best teams I've had in years of teaching Introduction to Engineering Design," says Swersey now. "They not only worked better together than any students I've had, but they produced extremely ambitious, innovative devices. I attribute a good part of their success to the time spent working on the five secrets."

Swersey's humble experiment speaks to a larger problem in organizations, particularly ones that are laden with technical experts. "When I work with companies that have to manage engineers, the main problem in team building is that as a profession, engineers don't view people skills as relevant," Daniel Kim, formerly at MIT, tells me. "Now these companies are waking up to the cost of not having emotional competence."

That awakening can be seen, too, at professional schools like the Harvard Business School and the MIT Sloan School of Management. "These days more of the curriculum is becoming team based," Kim adds. "This is in response to criticism from companies that MBAs have been trained to excel as individuals, but they need to learn how to work well in teams, too."

What many team enthusiasts fail to see is that every team itself can become a learning lab for the very capabilities people need in order to perform better as team members. "Every member of a team brings unique strengths and skills to the group, some technical, some in emotional and social capabilities," observes Kathy Kram, a director of Boston University's executive MBA program. "It's a great opportunity for mutual learning, if the team can make that learning an explicit goal or part of their contract together."

That opportunity is typically wasted, she adds, "because too often a focus on how team members relate is seen as a distraction from achieving the team's goal, instead of a way to help them work better together. But using teams for learning team skills makes great sense, especially in team-based organizations."

And that brings us to the next point: Whether through a team or on our own, each of us can strengthen and develop any of these emotional competencies—if we know how.

4

A New
Model of
Learning

10

....

The Billion-Dollar Mistake

lready the country's fastest-growing major life insurance company, "We saw a way to do even better," says Jim Mitchell, president of IDS Life, American Express's insurance division. Mitchell saw an opportunity—a big opportunity. Despite clients' financial plans showing they should purchase life insurance, more than two out of three declined to buy it. This large loss of potential sales was no temporary blip; sales for several years running yielded the same conclusion.

The potential for more sales was so great that Mitchell, set up his own "Skunkworks" operation in order to find a "breakthrough that could make life insurance more compelling to clients."[1]

Their first step was an investigation of how planners and clients really felt about selling and buying life insurance. The answer, in a word: terrible.

The investigation tapped a startling outpouring of negative feeling from clients and planners alike. While the team expected to find some major flaws in the life insurance *products* the company was offering, they found instead that the problem was with the sales *process* itself. It boiled down to emotional incompetence.

Clients said they distrusted the sales relationship with advisors, that the prospect of buying insurance made them feel "powerless, uninformed, inadequate, and suspicious." The negativity was prevalent even among those clients who *did* buy insurance. The problem wasn't a fear of death, the expense, or any feature of the policies; in fact, clients said they were perfectly satisfied with the products offered. Rather, it was the sales interaction that soured them. Small wonder: Many advisors confessed feeling "unqualified, incompetent, untruthful, and selfish" while proposing life insurance. Some said a sense of pressure to "make the sale" led them to act in ways that challenged their personal ethics. They yearned to feel more confident and more principled. Many said that working under the general bad reputation of insurance salespeople and making cold calls was building up a reservoir of helplessness and depression.

When a client displayed anxiety or uneasiness, the common wisdom in the insurance industry held that the best response was not empathy but a rational argument. So the advisors were left trying to shut out the client's emotions as well as their own. "Our advisors had been taught that if there was an emotional reaction in a client, it was a form of resistance—so you needed to explain it logically, with more numbers, and ignore their feelings," explained Kate Cannon, who was a member of the Skunkworks team and who is now responsible for emotional competence programs at American Express Financial Advisors.

In short, the feelings roiling within clients and planners alike set a miserable emotional tone for their encounter; as a final report put it, "A mountain of emotional negativity stood between our sales process and our bottom line."

Advisors could set a more positive emotional tone, but they had to deal with their own rocky emotional state first. As one planner put it, "We can spend millions on product research and development, but if the delivery of these products is impaired due to our self-limitations, what have we accomplished?"

Remedying the Yuck Factor

The remedy began (as we saw in Chapter 4) with heightening the advisors' emotional self-awareness. And that unearthed what became known as the "yuck." "We analyzed the 'yuck' in the business—the emotional battles people faced daily that were distasteful and painful," Cannon told me.

The yuck list was formidable. Among the items:

- The rejections were demoralizing. A stream of rejections might lead to catastrophic thinking like "I can't do this—I'll lose my job. . . . I'll never be able to make a living."

■ The sheer volume of information on products left some advisors overwhelmed.

■ The entrepreneurial nature of the advisors' task, where their income depended on their sales, was scary for many advisors, who feared not being able to support themselves.

■ Confusion about reconciling the needs of clients tormented some.

■ The long hours needed to get a foothold in the business left a number of advisors anguished about the imbalance between work and family.

But for every emotional quandary there was a remedy—a skill to be acquired, an attitude to be changed. The solution was, in essence, to bolster the advisors' levels of emotional competence.

An emotionally competent advisor, in the words of one company analysis, "maintains confidence, has resilience in adversity, and acts from core principles and values." The rationale: Advisors who were driven by their own principles, not sales pressure, would relate to clients in a way that elicited trust. With their hearts in their work, they would be more convincing. And with better control over their own fears and frustrations, they would be able to persist despite setbacks. Sales would be a natural result of better meeting clients' needs.

Advisors themselves agreed; many said emotional competence was the hidden ingredient in their success or failure.

The evaluation team decided to focus on only a few emotional competencies at the outset. They knew advisors couldn't set the right tone or deal with their clients' emotions well until they could manage their own.

Building Emotional Competence—and Sales

'm a hothead," Sharmayne Williams, a financial advisor at American Express's Chicago office, confides. "I was extremely emotional—I'd take everything to heart and react strongly. It badly affected my relationships with people in the office: If they didn't see things my way, I'd get mad. It was my way or no way. I couldn't see it from their perspective, I wouldn't compromise."

That lack of emotional self-control worked against Williams. "It prevented me from moving up; it got in the way of making decisions," she told me. "If I was upset about something, I couldn't move on to the next project. It cost me money."

Williams had been a licensed stockbroker for eight years before joining American Express Financial Advisors, and when she had her first training session in emotional competence a year later, it was a revelation: "I'd never encountered anything like this before. This was the missing piece."

The program, she says, has changed her life. "I see how my emotions were controlling me. Now if something is bothering me, I talk it over with my business partner, write it in my journal, talk to my field vice president right away. I let them know I'm upset—I don't let it fester. I'm more accepting. I realize you can have all kinds of emotions, but you don't have to let them run you."

She has found ways to handle the tension. "Now when I feel it building up, I go to a ballet studio in my building and work out. The physical relaxation cools me out for days."

And now Williams, always a high performer, is doing even better. In her first year at American Express she made about $1,700,000 in sales. In her second year, Williams tells me, she reached $2,400,000, and is on track for advancement.

That improvement is just the point. In the first pilot of the emotional competence program, financial advisors who went through the training had sales gains of 8 to 20 percent over the previous year—significantly more than comparison groups who did not get the training, and more than the average company-wide.

"We were pleased enough with the outcome to make it part of our standard training for new salespeople, as well as offering it to managers and other people in leadership positions," Doug Lennick, an executive vice president at American Express Financial Advisors, told me. And it represents a personal triumph for Lennick, who championed the emotional competence program.

When Lennick became head of the American Express Financial Advisors sales force, he had the emotional competence program expanded and offered to a broader range of people. Now training covers two days—concentrating on self-awareness, interpersonal, and coping skills—with another three-day session a few weeks or months later. And the program is available to all incoming financial advisors and new supervisors, as well as to sales management teams and other team leaders and those directly under them.

For Lennick, the success of emotional competence training dovetails with a vision he has long held that the financial advisor's role should be less that of the traditional salesperson and more that of a trusted consultant in a long-term relationship.

"I never thought clients wanted a relationship with five or six advisors, but rather an ongoing relationship with one advisor," says Lennick. "The advisors with the best relationships with their clients do more than just help them achieve their financial objectives: They help with life planning. That's a radical revision of their role, encompassing not just helping the client stay financially fit, but also live in alignment with their sense of purpose."

Says Lennick, "We've proven that if you help people deal with their emotions, they will have more professional success without compromising their personal values."

As Sharmayne Williams puts it, "Being a trustworthy person and in control helps me with my clients." Emotionally intelligent relationships pay off.

The Good News

At Promega, a biotech company in Madison, Wisconsin, a group of scientists gather daily to practice mindfulness, a method for focusing and relaxing they learned in an eight-week training program. The scientists say they feel more calm, concentrated, and creative using the method.

Well and good. But even more impressive is that researchers documented positive changes in the scientists' *brain function* as a direct result of the mindfulness training. Their left prefrontal lobes—the brain area that suppresses amygdala hijacks and generates positive feelings—have become significantly more active than before the program.[2] The scientists' sense of greater alertness and relaxation is no mere illusion: It stems from an underlying change in the brain. This brain change duplicates that found in those individuals who are most resilient and adaptable under stress (as we saw in Chapter 5). The finding suggests that as a competence such as self-control strengthens, so do the corresponding circuits in the brain.

All emotional competencies can be cultivated with the right practice. Consider the people who did poorly on the empathy tests described in Chapter 2. They floundered when they were asked to read the feelings of videotaped men and women having spontaneous reactions—joy, rage, and so on—but with the words indistinct. But when they were given feedback after each of their guesses on what the people portrayed were actually feeling, their empathic accuracy improved markedly.[3] Even a small amount of immediate feedback on emotional accuracy has a surprisingly large carryover to empathy in other situations.[4]

The good news about emotional intelligence, then, is that—unlike IQ itself—*it can improve throughout life.* In a serendipitous fashion, life offers chance after chance to hone our emotional competence. In the normal course of a lifetime, emotional intelligence tends to increase as we learn to be more aware of our moods, to handle distressing emotions better, to listen and empathize—in short, as we become more mature. To a large extent, maturity itself describes this process of becoming more intelligent about our emotions and our relationships.

In a comparison of several hundred adults and adolescents by John D. Mayer, a University of New Hampshire psychologist who developed the pioneering theory of emotional intelligence with Yale's Peter Salovey, the adults were better at it across the board.[5] And an evaluation by Reuven Bar-On of emotional intelligence in more than three thousand men and women—ranging from teenagers to people in their fifties—found small but steady and significant increases as people go from age group to age group, with a peak occurring in the forties.[6] As Mayer concludes, "Emotional intelligence develops with age and experience from childhood to adulthood."

When it comes to cultivating emotional competence, maturity remains an advantage; it may be slightly harder to "teach young dogs new tricks." In a study of how well students in an MBA program were able to master new levels of emotional competence—with the age of students ranging from early twenties to fifties—the most improvement occurred in those twenty-nine or older, compared to those students under twenty-five.[7]

Whether that finding will generalize to other groups remains an open question. But it does show that, given the motivation, older workers can be as able or better than younger ones when it comes to mastering new levels of these capabilities.

Men and women seem equally able to increase their emotional intelligence. While women tend to be stronger in competencies based on empathy and social skills, with men doing better in those based on self-regulation, the same study of MBA students discovered that men and women can improve to the same extent, no matter where they start out on a given competence.

This improvement puts emotional intelligence in sharp contrast to IQ, which remains largely unchanged throughout life. While purely cognitive capacities remain relatively fixed, emotional competence can be learned at any point in life. No matter how insensitive, shy, hot-tempered, awkward, or tuned-out people may be, with motivation and the right effort they can cultivate emotional competence.

But how?

Understanding Is Not Enough

Consider Henry and Lai, who started out as electrical engineers at Bell Labs about the same time, with roughly the same credentials: Both had 3.8 grade point averages from top-flight universities with effusive recommendations from professors, and both had spent summers interning at computer companies.

But the moment they arrive at Bell Labs, all similarities fall away. Henry acts as though he hasn't left graduate school. He stays glued to his computer screen, voraciously devouring technical documents and learning new software programs. His new colleagues rarely see him except at staff meetings; he's a recluse. His thinking: "It's my technical proficiency that will matter most for me on this job."

Lai takes a different approach. She makes sure to devote adequate time to her work. But her spare time is dedicated to getting to know her coworkers, finding out about their interests, projects, concerns. When they need a helping hand, she offers one—when everyone needed to install a new, cumbersome software tool, for example, she volunteered to do it. Her thinking: "One of the best ways for me to be accepted into the team is to help out."

After six months on the job, Henry has done a slightly better job technically—but Lai is seen as someone who can work well on a team and take initiative, and is already marked for the fast track. Henry has failed to realize that building bonds is a crucial competence for his job; he's more comfortable as a loner. His coworkers see that he is technically adept, but they have little trust he can work well on a team.

Lai shows excellence in several emotional intelligence competencies—but if Henry's technical gifts are to be put to best use, he needs to master these competencies, too. How do you help someone like Henry change for the better?

Robert Kelley, of Carnegie-Mellon University, who offers this case study, points out that Lai has learned strategies typical of star performers, like building bonds and taking initiative.[8] But there is more to what she does than simply knowing about a winning strategy—the ability to *execute* a strategy such as networking and cooperation depends on the requisite emotional competence. For someone like Henry to make the necessary changes, it's not enough for him to have the *intellectual* understanding that they would be useful. Merely knowing that he should build relationships may not be enough to budge him from his cubicle—or to make him adept at it if he tries.

There is a crucial difference between *declarative* knowledge, knowing a concept and its technical details, and *procedural* knowledge, being able to put those concepts and details into action. Knowing does not equal doing, whether in playing the piano, managing a team, or acting on essential advice at the right moment.

A study of management training in a supermarket chain found very little correlation between managers' knowledge of the competencies they were trained in and how they actually behaved once back at their stores. Many trainees came out of the program with high levels of understanding about what they *should* do back on the job—they just failed to do it when they got there. Intellectual understanding of a competence may be necessary, but it is not sufficient in itself to result in behavior change.[9]

Having a cognitive realization about what to do says nothing about someone's readiness to begin to act differently, nor about his motivation or capacity to do so, nor about the method by which he can gain a new level of mastery of the new capability. Helping people master an emotional competence demands a new understanding of how we learn.

As one of the most frequently cited sources on training and development puts it, those who study training "have tended to consider all training the same, without regard to the purpose of the training or the type of learning involved."[10] For cognitive and technical competence, declarative knowledge may be sufficient—but not for emotional intelligence. It is time to stop lumping all training together; we need to use our new understanding of the brain's workings to make meaningful—and practical—distinctions and promote the real learning of emotional competence.

The Ultimate Test

Teaching *about* a competence—that is, having workers get an intellectual grasp of the concepts involved—may offer the easiest training approach, but compared to other approaches I'll discuss shortly, it has the least effect on actually changing performance. Intellectual understanding is a threshold process, necessary for learning, but not sufficient for lasting improvement.

Deep change requires the retooling of ingrained habits of thought, feeling, and behavior.

Consider Henry, the reticent engineer at Bell Labs who doesn't venture out of his office and engage his coworkers. Why does he behave this way?

Henry's isolation might be due to shyness, to social ineptness, or simply to being unskilled in the art of teamwork. Whatever the specific cause of his isolation, he is the victim of a learned habit. And what has been learned can be *un*learned—and a more effective habit learned instead—with effort and time. This unlearning and learning occur at the level of the brain connections themselves.

As we acquire our habitual repertoire of thought, feeling, and action, the neural connections that support this repertoire are strengthened, becoming dominant pathways for nerve impulses. While connections that are unused become weakened or even lost, those we use over and over grow increasingly strong.[11]

Given a choice between two alternative responses, the one that has the richer, stronger network of neurons will win out. And the more a response occurs, the thicker the neural pathways grow to support it. When habits have been well learned, through countless repetitions, then the underlying neural circuitry becomes the brain's default option—we act automatically and spontaneously.

Competencies can be seen as a coordinated bundle of habits—what we think, feel, and do to get a job done. When such a habit is dysfunctional, replacing it with a more effective one requires enough practice of the better habit—and inhibition of the poor one—that the neural circuitry for the old behavior finally withers (psychologists call this "extinguishing") and the circuitry for the better behavior grows stronger. Eventually the better habit will replace the old one as the automatic response in key situations.

The test of this kind of learning—of such rewiring—for an emotional competence lies in how a person automatically reacts in the salient moment. The proof of whether someone like Henry has mastered the fundamentals of making connections and cooperation comes in situations where he has a critical choice: either to remain in his cubicle grinding away alone or to consult several coworkers who have helpful information and expertise. If he spontaneously steps out of his cubicle to approach a colleague—and does so effectively—this would indicate that a new habit has been mastered.

A Different Model of Learning

Agovernment researcher at the U.S. Office of Personnel Management is briefing me on the results of a massive analysis of the competencies required for a wide range of government jobs. "Training for the technical part of jobs is easy—but it's much harder to train people to be flexible, to have integrity, be conscientious, or be skilled interpersonally."

Technical training *is* easy compared to developing emotional intelligence. Our entire system of education is geared to cognitive skills. But when it comes to learning emotional competencies, our system is sorely lacking. Capacities like empathy or flexibility differ crucially from cognitive abilities; they draw on different areas of the brain.

Purely cognitive abilities are based in the neocortex, the "thinking brain." But with personal and social competencies, additional brain areas come into play, mainly the circuitry that runs from the emotional centers—particularly the amygdala—deep in the center of the brain up to the prefrontal lobes, the brain's executive center. Learning emotional competence retunes this circuitry.

Because intellectual learning differs from behavior change in fundamental ways, the models of education for each are significantly different. For intellectual skills, the classroom is an appropriate setting, and simply reading about or hearing a concept once can be enough to master it. Strategic thinking and computer programming can be taught effectively in this mode, removed from the give-and-take of life on the job. For behavior change, on the other hand, life itself is the true arena for learning, and this takes practice over an extended period of time.

Learning in school is, in essence, adding information and understanding to the memory banks of the neocortex. The neocortex learns by fitting new data and insights into existing frameworks of association and understanding, extending and enriching the corresponding neural circuitry.

But learning an emotional competence involves that and more—it requires that we also engage our emotional circuitry, where our social and emotional habits are stored. Changing such habits—learning to approach people positively instead of avoiding them, to listen better, or to give feedback skillfully—is a more challenging task than simply adding new facts to old. Emotional learning demands a more profound change at the neurological level: both weakening the existing habit and replacing it with a better one.

Understanding this difference in underlying brain function is crucial to designing ways to teach emotional competencies. One common mistake made by organizations is trying to instill an emotional competence like a service orientation or leadership, using the same techniques that effectively teach how to create a business plan. This is not enough: Changing a habit based on emotional intelligence demands an entirely new kind of learning strategy. Some schools, corporations, and even governments are finally beginning to understand this.

Many of the standard learning principles for training and development in organizations derive from trivial studies of college students practicing basic motor skills or engaged in simple cognitive tasks like memorizing lists of words.[12] But these principles are insufficient for the more complicated task of upgrading emotional competencies. Cultivating emotional competence requires an understanding of the fundamentals of behavior change. The failure to take this into account wastes an immense investment in development and training each year. As I write this, millions upon millions of dollars are being wasted on training programs that have no lasting impact—or little effect at all—on building emotional competence. It amounts to a billion-dollar mistake.

"Spray and Pray"

The CEO of one of America's leading pharmaceutical firms was impatient. He had seen a huge growth in training costs at the company and wanted to know one thing: What were they getting for their money?

A reasonable request—and, coming from the CEO, one that got an immediate response. Soon he was presented with a hastily drawn-up report—based on anecdotes.

That was not acceptable: The CEO, an M.D. by training with a Ph.D. in biomedical statistics, and a former research scientist himself, wanted hard data. So those involved went back to the drawing board and came up with a more thorough plan for evaluating the dollar value and long-term strategic worth of training. They called in outside experts—Charley Morrow, from the consulting firm Linkage, and Melvin Rupinski, of Tulane University. The result was a rarity in the organizational world: a rigorous, four-year project using the quantitative methods of science to assess whether the company's training actually justified its cost.[13]

That this is a rarity in the business world is itself a paradox. Despite the billions of dollars spent on corporate training programs globally, the effectiveness of these programs is rarely evaluated by the companies that pay for them—nor by anyone else. Estimates of the extent to which skills taught in company training programs carry over into day-to-day practice on the job are as low—and gloomy—as a mere 10 percent. But no one knows for sure what the true rate of improved job performance is, because the data are rarely collected.[14]

In October 1997 the American Society for Training and Development surveyed a select group of thirty-five highly regarded "benchmark" companies. Twenty-seven said they tried in some way to promote emotional competence through training and development.[15] But of these, more than two thirds had never attempted to evaluate the impact of their efforts. Those who did, for the most part, relied on soft measures like reactions to training sessions and employee opinion surveys.

A larger ASTD survey found that only 13 percent of companies evaluated their training in terms of on-the-job performance.[16] "The only hard measure we've had of development training is the number of bodies on chairs—we only know that people go through the training, not that they get anything out of it," the head of human resources at one of the world's largest financial services companies confided. "Sometimes we call it 'spray and pray': expose everybody to the training and hope it sticks to some."

The Bottom Line

The executives who gathered for a seminar in a secluded mountain resort were from the top tiers of management at a giant pharmaceutical company. The week focused largely on "people skills" and looking at ways to more effectively lead other managers in an increasingly competitive and dynamic business environment.

The topics included a range of emotional competencies, including how to model "effective people management," how to motivate subordinates and evaluate their strengths and weaknesses, and how to give performance feedback, manage teams, handle conflict, and lead innovation. There was also time set aside for some reflection on the executives' own behavior and its impact on the people they deal with.

It was a full five-day menu of development—one fairly representative of thousands of such executive and management courses given in organizations around the world. But was it worth the cost, as the CEO had wondered?

No.

Not only was there no improvement, but those executives who attended were rated by their bosses as, on average, *less* effective in these competencies than before the seminar. "Comparing pre- and postseminar ratings of their managerial behavior, there was a slight negative shift," one of the evaluators told me. "They were a little less capable."

This was one of the more disappointing among the dozen or so management programs evaluated by the pharmaceutical company's study. Overall, results were mixed; while some programs proved themselves definitely worth the effort, several did not.

The training programs were very different in focus, in audience, and in results. The competencies they aimed to bolster ranged from teaching top executives to motivate their employees, to helping managers communicate more effectively, resolve conflicts, and manage change, to improving supervisors' ability to give feedback and foster positive relations with workers.

All the programs were evaluated on the basis of their observable effects on the performance of those who went through them, with pre- and post-program assessments by bosses, peers, or subordinates, as appropriate. A clever statistical technique allowed these results to be turned into calculations of return on investment, and the methods used offer a state-of-the-art model for such training evaluations—a model that should be widely imitated.[17]

The results of this very careful—and too-rare—evaluation are sobering, particularly for those in the business of management training. Three of the eleven programs focusing on interpersonal capabilities essential for management were found to be utterly worthless. These included the five-day mountain retreat, a training for lab chiefs in managing individual performance, and a program in team building.

Calculation of the time for these three programs to pay back their cost—that is, just to break even—showed it would take seven years for the team-building program to pay for itself, providing the effects could last that long (a dubious assumption). The time to pay back for the other two: *never.* Neither produced a strong enough impact on job performance to justify its cost!

Five of the eleven programs, the evaluation revealed, would take more than a year to pay for themselves, again assuming their results would last. Those five programs, so ineffective in retrospect, cost a total of nearly $700,000 for the 147 employees evaluated.

The news was better for the five other leadership and management trainings.[18] The return on investment for these ranged from 16 percent to 492 percent. And another program on time management (a stress-management skill that calls on impulse control and other self-regulation competencies) had a spectacularly short payback period—about three weeks—and a return on investment in the first year of 1,989 percent. In terms of return on investment, this home-grown course, developed in-house, outperformed a well-known time-management course by far—largely because it cost just $3,000, compared to $68,000 for the nationally prominent course.

In short, when programs work, they pay for themselves, most within the first year or so, and are justified by quantifiably improving on-the-job performance. When programs fail, they waste time and money.

Was the four-year project to evaluate training at the pharmaceutical firm worth the time and money? Undoubtedly. For one thing, it was a relative bargain: The entire effort cost $500,000—during a period when the company was spending $240 million on training. In other words, the evaluation represented only .02 percent of the training budget.[19]

Since then the company has completely revamped its training and development programs; none of the money-losing programs is offered anymore. And the study itself stands as a benchmark, setting the standard for how companies could go about getting an empirically sound reading of the value of their own training programs.

When the Hard-Nosed Become Soft

After searching far and wide for corporate training programs in emotional competencies that had been evaluated using impartial outcome measures and a comparison group—the golden mean of evaluation—Cary Cherniss, a psychologist at Rutgers University (and cochair with me of the Consortium for Research on Emotional Intelligence in Organizations), noted with amazement, "Few companies actually test the training programs they're making million-dollar bets on. When it comes to human relations, hard-nosed companies become very soft; they just don't insist on demonstrated results. There are lots of executives who don't seem to realize you can design studies to test the programs you are spending so much on."

Sometimes this is a result of naïveté, and sometimes organizational politics are at fault. Cherniss tells of a high-tech company that invested over a million dollars in a training program for working better in teams. Yet they made no attempt to evaluate its effectiveness. Why? "It was a pet project of an executive vice president. No one wanted to know if it *worked*—just if people liked it. Companies don't evaluate outcomes to see if the programs have any real impact on performance."

When they do, the results can be disturbing. "We just tried to assess the benefits of a training program we've used for years and spent millions of dollars on," an executive at a Fortune 100 company lamented. "We've found zero correlation with productivity on any measure."

Too often the only real effect of training, no matter what it's for, is that people get a short-term "buzz" of energy that lasts no more than a few days or weeks, after which attendees fall back into whatever their habitual mode was before the training. The most general effect of training seminars—no matter the ostensible content—is that they increase people's self-confidence—at least for a while.[20]

But if all that has been boosted is the trainee's confidence, then these expensive programs are like the magic feather in the old Disney cartoon *Dumbo*. When the timid baby elephant with the huge ears gets a magic feather from his mentor, a wily field mouse, he clutches it tightly in his trunk, flaps his ears—and starts to fly.

Of course, Dumbo loses his feather one day, and learns he still can fly. For emotional competencies it's not always that simple. While enthusiasm and a can-do spirit are helpful, they can only work to the degree that people have the underlying skills and learn the competencies to *make* them work. If you don't have empathy or are socially inept, or haven't learned to manage conflict or take a customer's perspective, sheer enthusiasm is no replacement—and can lead to well-intended blunders.

The world of training seems prone to whims and infatuated with fads. So laments a review of the current state of training and development, which concludes that too many programs are "adopted on the basis of a persuasive salesperson, a slick brochure, or testimonials from previous participants."[21]

When it comes to evaluation, rigor gives way to impression. Hard-nosed evaluations like the ones done at the pharmaceutical firm are extremely rare. Rather than an objective assessment of the effects of training, the typical evaluation comes in the form of "happy sheets," feedback from participants about whether trainees liked the program, and what about it they liked the most—a rating system that patently favors slick, fun experiences over substantive ones. Having a good time becomes the mark of excellence, a valuing of entertainment over education.

This lack of data feeds the endless waves of "hot" programs that sweep through the corporate seas. In the 1960s and early 1970s companies sent thousands of employees off to "encounter groups" and "sensitivity training"—unstructured sessions where people vented their rawest feelings (an often futile exercise in emotionality, as opposed to being intelligent *about* emotion). They did so despite the lack of any evidence that such sessions helped people in their jobs, and in the face of emerging data that such groups, when poorly led, could have negative repercussions.

Emotional Competencies: Guidelines for Learning

When heads of development at Fortune 500 companies were asked what makes it difficult for them to evaluate their own training programs, the most common complaint was the lack of standards and yardsticks available for training in the so-called soft skills like emotional competencies.[22]

To help change this, I cofounded the Consortium for Research on Emotional Intelligence in Organizations, a coalition of researchers and practitioners from business schools, the federal government, consulting firms, and corporations.[23] Our consortium has searched the scientific findings on behavior change and studied exemplary training programs, to create basic guidelines for the best practices in teaching competencies based on emotional intelligence.[24]

The resulting guidelines are summarized in Table 2. Two key points:

- Each element is necessary for effective learning, but not sufficient by itself.

- The impact of each element increases to the degree it is part of a process that includes the others.

TABLE 2
Guidelines for Emotional Competence Training

Assess the job. Training should focus on the competencies needed most for excellence in a given job or role.

Caveat: Training for irrelevant competencies is pointless.
Best Practice: Design training based on a systematic needs assessment.

Assess the individual. The individual's profile of strengths and limitations should be assessed to identify what needs improving.

Caveat: There's no point in sending people for training in competencies they already have or do not need.
Best Practice: Tailor training to the individual's needs.

Deliver assessments with care. Feedback on a person's strengths and weaknesses carries an emotional charge.

Caveat: Inept feedback can be upsetting; skillful feedback is motivating.
Best Practice: Use emotional intelligence in delivering initial evaluations of a person's emotional competence.

Gauge readiness. People are at differing levels of readiness.

Caveat: When people lack readiness, training is more likely to be wasted.
Best Practice: Assess for readiness, and if someone is not yet ready, make cultivating readiness an initial focus.

Motivate. People learn to the degree they are motivated—for example, by realizing that a competence is important to doing their job well—and making the competence a personal goal for change.

Caveat: If people are unmotivated, training will lack effectiveness.
Best Practice: Make clear how training will pay off on the job or for the individual's career, or be otherwise rewarding.

Make change self-directed. When people direct their learning program, tailoring it to their needs, circumstances, and motivation, learning is more effective.

Caveat: One-size-fits-all training programs fit no one specifically.
Best Practice: Have people choose their own goals for development and help them design their own plan for pursuing them.

Focus on clear, manageable goals. People need clarity on what the competence is and the steps needed to improve it.

Caveat: Poorly focused or unrealistic programs for change lead to fuzzy results or failure.
Best Practice: Spell out the specifics of the competence and offer a workable plan to get there.

Prevent relapse. Habits change slowly, and relapses and slips need not signal defeat.

Caveat: People can become discouraged by the slowness of change and the inertia of old habits.
Best Practice: Help people use lapses and slip-ups as lessons to prepare themselves better for the next time.

Give performance feedback. Ongoing feedback encourages and helps direct change.

Caveat: Fuzzy feedback can send the training off track.
Best Practice: Design into the change plan feedback from supervisors, peers, friends—anyone who can help coach, mentor, or give appropriate progress reviews.

Encourage practice. Lasting change requires sustained practice both on and off the job.

Caveat: A single seminar or workshop is a beginning, but not sufficient in itself.
Best Practice: Use naturally arising opportunities for practice at work and at home, and try the new behaviors repeatedly and consistently over a period of months.

Arrange support. Like-minded people who are also trying to make similar changes can offer crucial ongoing support.

Caveat: Going it alone makes change tougher.
Best Practice: Build a network of support and encouragement. Even a single buddy or coach will help.

Provide models. High-status, highly effective people who embody the competence can be models who inspire change.

Caveat: A do-what-I-say-not-what-I-do attitude in superiors undermines change.
Best Practice: Encourage supervisors to value and exhibit the competence; make sure trainers do, too.

Encourage. Change will be greater if the organization's environment supports the change, values the competence, and offers a safe atmosphere for experimentation.

Caveat: When there is no real support, particularly from bosses, the change effort will seem hollow—or too risky.
Best Practice: Encourage change that fits the values of the organization. Show that the competence matters for job placement, promotion, performance review, and the like.

Reinforce change. People need recognition—to feel their change efforts matter.

Caveat: A lack of reinforcement is discouraging.
Best Practice: Be sure the organization shows it values the change in a consequential way: praise, a raise, or expanded responsibility.

Evaluate. Establish ways to evaluate the development effort to see if it has lasting effects.

Caveat: Many or most development programs go unevaluated, and so mistakes or pointless programs go unchanged.
Best Practice: Find measures of the competence or skill as shown on the job, ideally before and after training, and also several months (and, if possible, a year or two) later.

Teaching the Skills That Matter

She was an accountant in the health care industry—and she had a real problem. She couldn't take criticism; when she felt her ideas—or her character—were being attacked, her anger flared and she said things she felt ashamed about later.

But she was determined to do something about it. Now enrolled in an executive MBA program, she had an opportunity to cultivate emotional self-control, a competence she knew she needed to improve.

Her plan for doing so was multipronged:

- Learn and master steps for better self-control, such as anticipating hot-button situations and preparing herself so that she won't "lose it." Remind herself that what she sees as "criticism" or an "attack" is most often feedback that is meant to be helpful.

- Practice those responses at every opportunity. Mentally rehearse them twice a month.

- Recruit fellow students to role-play troubling situations with her so she can try out new self-control strategies.

- Have a fellow member of her learning team agree to signal her when he sees her being stubborn, inflexible, or otherwise overreacting, to remind her to exercise self-control.

This set of learning tactics, so well-suited to cultivating emotional intelligence, may seem out of place in an MBA program. But they are part of the curriculum at the Weatherhead School of Management at Case Western Reserve University in Cleveland, a leader in preparing its students in these crucial capabilities.

Weatherhead took to heart a number of common criticisms of MBA graduates—including that they are too analytical and lack interpersonal, communication, and team skills. So the school embarked on a plan to reinvent business education, developing an innovative course, Managerial Asessment and Development, that incorporates many (if not most) of the Consortium guidelines.[25]

The course, spearheaded by Richard Boyatzis, an associate dean, offers students tools for lifelong learning: methods for assessing and developing the personal abilities they need for management throughout their career.

Since 1990 it has been offered to several different groups of students. Most are men and women in their twenties and thirties who have decided to go back to business school for an MBA after several years on the job. It is also offered to physicians, lawyers, and other professionals, most of them in their forties and fifties, who attend a special one-year, nondegree program at Weatherhead.

The course begins with a period of self-examination during which students reflect on their values, aspirations, and goals. They then go through a range of assessments of their competencies, identifying their strengths and weaknesses.

The course provides a map of the emotional competencies similar to Table 1 in Chapter 2.[26] From this map, and in light of their own assessment results and their career needs, each student chooses a set of competencies to strengthen. Instead of the one-size-fits-all approach so familiar in organizational training, students construct an individualized learning plan for themselves.

The class meets for one three-hour session a week. The first two weeks focus on assessment; the next seven weeks reflect on the results. Only then, when the assessments and their implications have been fully digested, do students spend up to five weeks developing their learning plans—like that of the hot-tempered financial advisor, who needed to cultivate self-control.

Does it work? To find out, successive graduating classes of Weatherhead students have been put through a set of rigorous assessments, using objective measures common in industry.[27] Compared to similar ratings on entering the school, they showed improvement in 86 percent of the abilities assessed. And follow-ups three years after they had finished the program showed these gains holding on the job.[28]

The moral for business education: Students can master the emotional intelligence capabilities the working world demands—if they are given the right tools for learning.

Getting Back to Work

One of the more innovative workplace applications of emotional intelligence training is not to be found in any company: It's a program for people who have *lost* their jobs, and it's designed to help them cultivate the inner resources that will help them find a new one.

Because people are shaken after losing a job, uncertain about their future, frightened about finances, and haunted by self-doubt, the job search it-self can be made easier by boosting their emotional competence. That was the strategy used in a strikingly successful reemployment project, the Michigan JOBS program, set up by a group at the University of Michigan after a wave of job cuts in the state's auto industry.

The program was a huge success—and another model application of the Consortium guidelines. People who went through the program got jobs about 20 percent more quickly—and higher-quality jobs—than did comparable people who had not.

"This works for everyone—the laid-off vice president as well as the guy who used to empty the VP's ashtrays," says Robert Caplan, head of the organizational behavior program at George Washington University and co-founder of the JOBS program with Richard Price, a psychologist at the University of Michigan.

The underlying principle is simple: Many of the same emotional competencies that make people excel at work also make them more adept at finding a new job. Helping people boost those competencies helps them get back to work sooner—and do better once they're there.

"If you're shy, as well as pessimistic and depressed after losing your job, you're in double jeopardy," Caplan says. "It's a paralyzing combination."

Yet the JOBS program found that job seekers who faced the worst odds in finding new employment benefited the most from the training. "This works even for those who are clinically depressed, as many people are after they've lost their job," Caplan asserts.

JOBS instills two sets of abilities in job seekers: practical skills (like identifying marketable talents and networking to hear about opportunities) and the inner resiliencies that let them capitalize on their marketability.

In a simple five-session format, two trainers work with groups of fifteen to twenty participants, most recruited through corporate outplacement programs.[29] The sessions focus on action learning, employing tools like mental rehearsals, dramatizations, and role-playing of key skills.

One of these skills is optimism. Given the uncertainties and setbacks that job seekers confront, they need an inoculation against defeatism in the face of failure. Rejections are an inevitable part of any job search. Discouragement can bleed into hopelessness and despair. And despair is not a marketable attitude.

Small wonder depression, drinking problems, and marital strife escalate among those who remain out of work—and abate once the person finds a rewarding job.[30] In the program, people are taught to anticipate rejection and rehearse what they should tell themselves when it happens. Anticipating such difficult moments and having a workable internal response lessens the emotional toll and speeds up the bounce-back time.

Among other capabilities the program bolstered:

- Perspective taking, to help job seekers think like an employer

- Self-confidence, the crucial sense that one can succeed, which is critical to making the effort in the first place

- Networking, since most jobs are found through personal contacts

- Decision making for career management—the first offer that comes is not necessarily the one to take, and any job needs to be measured against a person's values and career goals

- Emotional self-control, so that distressing feelings don't overwhelm and paralyze the person, making it difficult to put in the hard effort that is needed

All these emotional intelligence capabilities, of course, are likely to pay off *after* landing a job as well. That's what happened with JOBS: Midway into their second year of working, JOBS grads outearned similar job seekers who did not go through the program by $6,420 (and had estimated lifetime earnings that were $48,000 greater).[31]

The JOBS program, like those at Weatherhead and American Express, offers a model of how to help people strengthen emotional competence.

11

Best Practices

Since the 1995 publication of my book *Emotional Intelligence,* programs bearing the same title have taken their place in the lineup of trendy trainings. I regularly get reports from various parts of the world that someone or other is offering a program in what purports to be "emotional intelligence"—often only a repackaging or slight remodeling of a program they had offered before under another name.

If such programs follow the guidelines outlined here, well and good. If not, let the buyer beware.

All too often development programs for emotional intelligence are poorly designed, executed, and evaluated—and so have disappointingly little impact on people's effectiveness back on the job. Thus the need for the guidelines elaborated on in this chapter.

Though almost every program includes at least a few of these "best practices," optimal impact comes from their added potency when used in combination.

It will be tempting for those involved in training and development to read through the guidelines with a mental checklist in mind, ticking off those they already follow. More helpful—and challenging—however, is to highlight those that are *not* part of the routine at one's own organization, and to consider including them.

Few, if any, training programs follow every one of these guidelines, but to the degree a program follows many or most, it should be discernibly more effective in producing on-the-job performance improvements.

The goal: to use this new understanding of best practices to put the entire enterprise of improving "soft skills" on a sounder, more scientific footing. These guidelines offer a state-of-the-art blueprint for teaching—and learning—emotional intelligence.

Assess the Job

One basic question needs to be asked and answered before any training is undertaken: What does it take to do this job superbly? The answers to that question are not always readily apparent.

Take strategic planners. The going theory holds that the sharper the intellect of a strategic planner, the better the performance; planning, after all, is a purely cognitive task—or so the thinking goes. And when experts—strategic planners themselves, or those executives they report to—were polled, they pretty much agreed that the single key for successful planning is "analytic and conceptual thinking."[1]

True, a strategic planner can't do the job without the requisite cognitive skills, but it turns out there's more to success as a planner than brainpower. Emotional skills are essential as well.

Studies reveal that the *outstanding* strategic planners are not necessarily superior in their analytic skills. Instead, the skills that raise them above the crowd are those of emotional competence: astute political awareness, the ability to make arguments with emotional impact, and high levels of interpersonal influence.[2]

The "experts" had overlooked a simple fact of organizational life: Everything is political. A more objective analysis revealed that planners' effectiveness depended on knowing how to involve key decision makers in the planning process at every step, making sure these people bought into the plan's assumptions and goals and were therefore willing to adopt it.

No matter how brilliant a strategic plan is, without allies and supporters it is doomed, given the politics of organizational life. And even the smartest strategic planners can be blind to the true role of emotional competence in their success.

When Coopers & Lybrand, one of the Big Six accounting and consulting firms, decided to offer their partners training in the key skills for their role, they did not assume they knew what that training should focus on. Ever methodical, in the style of their firm, they wanted data.

"Our charge was to identify the competencies required for success in our firm," said Margaret Echols, the senior manager in charge of competency development at the time, who directed the initiative at Coopers & Lybrand. "So we started by creating a competency model for partners."

Their team started out by having partners nominate those among them who were outstanding in their performance. Once that pool of standouts was identified, they and a comparison group of average performers were studied in depth, using structured interviews in which, for instance, they were asked to describe in detail "critical incidents"—occasions when they had done superbly, and some where their performance had been disappointing.

Transcripts of those interviews were then coded and analyzed to detect common themes and the patterns of thinking, feeling, and acting that were at the heart of their success. From those results, the list of competencies that mattered most were identified. Then these competencies were tested to see if they actually distinguished average from star performers, to be sure they held up. In short, Coopers & Lybrand followed a state-of-the-art methodology for developing a competence model.[3]

Such a systematic, objective method is needed to get a true picture of the competencies that matter most for a given role. That's why assessing the competencies that make someone outstanding at a particular job has become something of a mini-industry, with practitioners using a range of well-validated methods to tease out the ingredients of star performance.[4]

Training strategies also need to take into account the ways one set of capabilities supports another. People rarely need to improve just one competence; emotional capabilities are interwoven, not independent. And, as we have seen, many higher-order competencies like change catalyst or leadership are actually constructed from others.

There are some elements of emotional intelligence that are so basic as to constitute "meta-abilities," which are essential for most other competencies. These basics include self-awareness, self-regulation, motivation, empathy, and social skills. These primary capabilities are essential for supporting the emotional competencies that flow from them. For instance, a manager who tries to shift his or her leadership style may also need to improve in self-awareness in order to make the other change.

In studies of a European airline, what set apart superior flight attendants were two clusters of emotional intelligence attributes: a self-mastery cluster, including emotional self-control, achievement, and adaptability, and an interpersonal cluster, including influence, service, and teamwork.[5] So when an American airline asked me and my colleague, Thérèse Jacobs-Stewart, to help design a training program for them, we focused on self-management and on handling people well.

But we added two supporting emotional intelligence capabilities, each of which makes people better at those needed competencies. One is self-awareness, which helps people recognize when they are about to become victims of an amygdala hijack—and so become better able to short-circuit the hijack before they find themselves out of control. The other is empathy, which allows them to do the same for someone else—pick up the early warning signs of irritation, frustration, or anxiety that mark a person as being at risk for a hijack. The reason is simple: The best strategy for avoiding destructive encounters is to prevent them.

The flight attendants also needed empathy training with an international twist. Every culture puts a unique stamp on how people express emotions; the less familiar we are with a given group, the more likely we are to misinterpret their feelings. So we focused on developing empathy with a diverse range of people.[6]

Assess the Individual

Are we the best judge of our own strengths and weaknesses? Not always. Consider an irony about empathy. When you ask people how accurate they are at reading other people's feelings, there is no correlation between their answers and how well they actually perform on objective tests.[7] In contrast, when people who know them well rate someone on empathy, there is a very high level of accuracy. In short, there are many ways in which other people know us better than we know ourselves—particularly when it comes to how adept we are in our relationships.

In general, the ideal evaluation relies not on any one source but on multiple perspectives. These may include self-reports as well as peer, boss, and subordinate feedback. The "360-degree" evaluation method offers feedback from all these sources and can be a powerful source of data targeting the competencies that need to be improved. There are several 360-degree methodologies that assess at least some of the emotional competencies.[8]

Ideally, an evaluation would also include more objective indexes of work performance, such as the "assessment center" methods, which gauge how people do in simulations of work situations. While any method individually is fallible, used in combination they can paint a more accurate, if complex, picture of our profile of emotional competence. (See Appendix 5 for more on evaluation methods.)

As Susan Ennis, head of executive development at BankBoston, observes, "Multiple perspectives on yourself are extremely powerful ways to build self-awareness—and get you ready to do something about it."

At the Weatherhead School of Management, for instance, students get information on themselves from three very different sources. First they do a self-evaluation of their strengths and limits, as well as their values. Then there is feedback from others, including members of a working team they belong to as part of the course, peers and a boss at work, and family and friends. Finally they get results from a battery of assessment tests and simulation exercises.

They are forewarned, however, that none of these sources is in itself better or more accurate than any of the others, or less prone to distortion. Each simply adds different kinds of data and perspectives offering a different eye, ear, and voice. The students themselves—with guidance—interpret the data and from this find a path to self-development.

The JOBS program borrowed a method from the entertainment industry to assess the emotional competence of people they were screening to hire as trainers—they held auditions. "We wanted to observe them in a situation that would draw on all the social and emotional competencies they'd need as trainers," Robert Caplan tells me. "So we asked each one to come and teach us something—how to budget our money, how to interview, *anything*—for just fifteen minutes. You could see how competent people were from the very first few moments."

The auditions were telling, Caplan recalls. "One prospect would start in a businesslike way, passing out budget forms and putting up a slide, starting out by saying, 'I want you to put how much you spent in column A.' No engagement, nothing personal. Deadly. But one we hired started out in a very genuine tone, 'It's really good to see you here; I know what a difficult time this has been for you. I'd like to hear about each of you before I begin.' You immediately felt the empathy, that you liked and trusted this person."

Deliver Assessments with Care

A health plan in the Southwest decided to evaluate employees using the 360-degree method, and then have them coached as needed by their supervisors.[9] The trouble began when someone decided to simply send all the results to both the employees and their supervisors at the same time, with no warning or interpretation.

The result was a disaster: Some supervisors called employees in at once, before the employees had a chance to digest the evaluations, so many felt they were being called on the carpet rather than being helped. Some employees were enraged—especially when the supervisor's ratings were lower than those by peers—and went storming in to demand an explanation or even an apology.

Feedback is too often given ineptly, with predictably bad consequences. But used artfully, feedback on competencies can be a priceless tool for self-examination—and for cultivating change and growth. Used poorly, it can be an emotional bludgeon.[10]

"I don't hear good things from people about their experiences with 360-degree feedback," a manager at one company tells me. "The people giving the feedback lack empathy, self-awareness, and sensitivity themselves—so the experience can be brutal for those getting it."

Much better is the report from a computer software giant, where an executive development specialist tells me that he delivers 360-degree feedback results strictly in confidence, one-on-one. "No one else sees their results, and they never have to share them with anyone. I don't even keep a copy when I'm done with them. We want this to be a development tool, not a hammer for someone else to use."

A common mistake is simply devoting too little time to the feedback. "People will spend two or three days in an assessment center, going through complex simulations, taking inventory after inventory, getting all kinds of performance measures done on them," a consultant tells me. "Then, after it's all done, they'll spend an hour or two going over the results in what amounts to a data dump. People end up confused, not more self-aware."

If there ever was a task that called for emotional intelligence, giving people the results of 360-degree evaluations is it; empathy, sensitivity, and delicacy are essential. One common mistake is focusing on people's weaknesses and failing to note their strong points. This can be demoralizing rather than motivating.

"You've got to celebrate the strengths a person has, as well as show them where their limits are," Boyatzis says. "Too often the focus is on someone's deficiencies. But you want to help the person recognize the core of their strengths, to affirm what they value about themselves. For instance, people can gain much resolve from the belief that they have the capacity to change."

At Weatherhead, great care is taken to help students interpret the results of their competence evaluations and use the information to shape a genuinely helpful learning plan. The program for executive MBAs devotes four three-hour sessions, plus individual counseling, to interpreting and absorbing the data from the competence evaluations. Then four more three-hour sessions focus on using the information to create individual learning plans.

Gauge Readiness

A large number of people at our training seminars feel like prisoners of the human resource department," a management trainer at a multinational bank tells me. "They just don't want to be here. And their resistance is infectious."

Willingness is crucial, but many organizations pay no attention to whether the people they send for training really want to learn or change. The director of executive development at a Fortune 100 company remarked to me that trainees fall into three groups: the "eager beavers," who are ready to change; the "vacationers," who are happy to get out of work for a day or two; and the "prisoners," who were told by their manager they had to come.

One rule of thumb is that only about 20 percent of a group are ready to put in the work to change at any given point, though the vast majority of development programs are designed as though 100 percent are.[11] There is no reason to let that low percentage stand. Interest, motivation, and readiness to change—the prerequisites for attending and benefiting from training—can be assessed (see Appendix 5 for details); if people aren't really ready to change, then that fact itself can become a first focus for them. Anything else will be a waste of time. If people are not ready to take action, forcing them will lead to disaster: the sham of going through the motions only to satisfy others, resentment rather than enthusiasm, quitting.

To avoid such a waste of time and money, a first step is to help people assess their own readiness. There are four levels of readiness: obliviousness or outright resistance, contemplating a change at some vague point in the future, ripeness to formulate a plan, and readiness to take action.[12]

At American Express Financial Advisors, before a team comes for its training in emotional competence, one of the training staff meets with the team leader, who in turn discusses the program in team meetings to gauge how people feel about going through it. In addition, "Before they come to the first session we try to talk to each person about any concerns they might have," Kate Cannon says.

Those not ready may benefit from exploring their own values and vision for themselves, to see if they want to change at all. Which brings us to the next step.

Motivate

The feeling 'I can do it' is the motor that drives change," Robert Caplan says, and in the JOBS program this is visibly true. "When it comes to job seeking, if you don't make the call and keep the appointment, you won't get the job. And to get people to make the effort, you have to raise their expectation of success, pump them up."

That applies in general: People learn to the degree they are motivated. Motivation influences the entire learning process, from whether or not someone signs up to whether they actually apply what they've learned in their jobs.[13] And we are most moved to pursue change that fits with our values and hopes. As Weatherhead's Boyatzis puts it: "People have to be grabbed by their values, their goals, their dreams of what's possible for them. If you focus at the outset on people's values and visions, on what they want to do with their life, then they see themselves as using the training opportunity for their own development—not just the company's."

Windows of opportunity for development—moments when we are most motivated to upgrade our capabilities—come at predictable points in a career.[14]

- Added responsibility, like a promotion, can make a weakness in emotional intelligence glaringly apparent.

- Life crises, like trouble at home, career doubts, or a "midlife crisis" about direction, can offer a fruitful motivation to change.

- Job troubles, like interpersonal difficulties, disappointment with an assignment, or feeling unchallenged, can motivate efforts to boost competencies.

For most of us the simple realization that cultivating a given capacity will help us do better increases our enthusiasm. "Because people here realize these competencies matter for their performance, motivation for training is usually high," Kate Cannon at American Express tells me. When people understand that training can increase their competitiveness in the job market or within the organization—that is, when they see it as an opportunity—their motivation increases. And the more motivated people are to learn, the greater the effectiveness of the training for them.[15]

Make Change Self-Directed

The assembly-line approach, where everyone in a particular job or role at a company gets sent through an identical program, may work when the content is purely cognitive. But when it comes to emotional competencies, this one-size-fits-all approach represents the old Taylorist efficiency thinking at its worst. Particularly in this domain of education, tailoring—not "Tayloring"—maximizes learning.

We change most effectively when we have a plan for learning that fits our lives, interests, resources, and goals.[16] At American Express, everyone designs their own action plan. One financial planner working to boost initiative had a personal goal of making twenty cold calls a week. His plan included writing out the scenario of a successful call and rehearsing it before he dialed each number. "That method and focus worked very well—for him," says Cannon. "But I wouldn't advise all the planners to try it. It might be inappropriate or irrelevant."

Plans also need to be fine-tuned to the individual's level of development. "We've set it up so that each person can grow and develop from wherever their starting point is," says Cannon. "For example, some people simply don't realize that what you say to yourself—your thoughts about what you're doing—affects your results. Others have a more sophisticated understanding."

Ideally, trainees should be able to consult a menu of techniques and be encouraged to contribute ideas of their own. One weakness of many prepackaged development seminars is their reliance on a single, generic approach.

"The standard training program, where everyone goes through a cookie-cutter experience, turns out to have the worst return on investment," Charley Morrow, of the consulting firm Linkage, tells me. From evaluation research he's conducted at Fortune 500 companies, Morrow concludes, "When people *have* to go, there are many kinds of problems. Some people may already have the skills they're being sent to learn, others don't need them. Others simply resent having to go, or are just unmotivated—they don't care."

Giving people the power to tailor their learning plans to their own needs and aspirations overcomes many of these problems. The guiding principle behind self-directed learning at Weatherhead, says Richard Boyatzis, is "You place control of the change process in the hands of the students. After all, they are in control anyway. This approach merely avoids the delusion of faculty control."[17]

Focus on Clear, Manageable Goals

He had moved to Ohio from the East Coast to participate in the Weatherhead MBA program, and he needed a part-time job. But he lacked self-confidence, particularly in approaching people he didn't know. At Weatherhead he was shown how to break his larger goal—developing this kind of self-confidence—into smaller, realistic action steps. The first, updating his résumé, was easy. But the next steps were more challenging, so he first made these promises to himself: "I will call the chairman of the University Finance Department by next month and request a meeting to discuss any available opportunities there. If not, I'll ask about other people to approach." He planned to do the same with his mentor, a local executive. On top of that, he committed himself to searching the local want ads and calling to apply for promising jobs. And he resolved, "I will be confident and assertive in these conversations." The concrete payoff of this strategy: He had a part-time job by the beginning of the next term.

The task seems mundane enough; thousands of people go through similar motions daily. But for this Weatherhead student, these methodical steps were part of a larger plan. They put him in situations that challenged him to practice self-confidence. And each completed step increased his confidence to undertake the next.

While a grand goal beckons, the practical focus needs to stay on the immediate, manageable steps—and the operative word is *manageable.* Those who attempt changes in whopping doses set themselves up for failure. Breaking goals into smaller steps offers easier challenges—and successes.[18]

Because we are buoyed by frequent small successes, we stay motivated and engaged, propelled by a growing sense of self-efficacy. And the more ambitious the goal, the greater the resulting change. A Japanese strategy takes these two principles into account: In *kaizen,* or continuous improvement, people start with goals that are only moderately difficult, and then gradually raise the challenge as the process continues. Making a change in such manageable steps lets us feel we are making at least a bit of progress toward our goal, and so keeps our spirits—and hope for success—high.[19]

Without clear goals, it is easy to wander off course. In the American Express program, seasoned psychologists work with each person to help them create clear personal goals for change. One common goal, for example, is to learn to handle distressing feelings better. But that goal is too global and fuzzy to be useful. "People start by realizing they need to take better care of themselves emotionally," Kate Cannon tells me. "But when they explore the trouble they have managing their feelings, they realize that it's due to being too stressed—and that often leads them to focus on specific helpful steps, like better time management."

But "better time management" is itself a fuzzy goal. It needs to be broken down into specifics: for example, spending twenty minutes a day meeting with subordinates to delegate responsibilities, eliminating time wasted watching junk TV, and setting aside three hours each week for relaxation.

Goal setting should also include the specific steps it will take to get there. For example, if the goal is to become more optimistic, taking setbacks and rejections in stride (an extremely useful competence for someone in sales), the analysis can be fine-grained: "You might start by noting your hot buttons, the events that trigger the unhelpful habit, and precisely what you think, feel, and do," says Kate Cannon. "You might identify pessimistic self-talk, like 'I can't do this,' 'This proves I'm not good at this.' " Or a pattern: First you get angry, then you withdraw, then you act up. You diagram the pattern or habit, familiarize yourself with what it is you do that you're trying to change and with the better way to think and act at those times. And each time you encounter one of those hot-button moments, you try to break the old pattern. The closer to the beginning you break it, the better."

In a sense, setting a goal defines what amounts to a "possible self": a vision of what we will be like after we have changed.[20] Just imagining this potential self has a certain power: Seeing ourselves as able to master the hoped-for change raises our motivation to take the steps to get there.

Prevent Relapse

Cultivating a new skill is gradual, with stops and starts; the old ways will reassert themselves from time to time. This is particularly true at the beginning, when the new habit feels strange and unfamiliar, and the old habit still feels natural.

Training can disintegrate—at least temporarily—in the face of stiff challenges. Such temporary lapses are only to be expected, and that fact can be used to advantage in relapse prevention.[21]

The key to using slips constructively is to realize that a step backward is not the same as a total relapse. People need to be warned at the outset of training that they are likely to experience bad days, when they revert to their old habits. Showing them how to learn valuable lessons from these slips provides a vaccination of sorts against despair or demoralization at such moments. Otherwise they might interpret the lapse with pessimism—as a total failure that means they are forever flawed and cannot change. Relapse prevention training prepares them to react like optimists, using slips in an intelligent way to gather critical information about their vulnerabilities and habits.

Take a manager who, under time pressure, slides back into dictatorial habits of leadership. He might learn that under pressure his own anxiety makes him susceptible to falling back on an autocratic style. Once the manager learns to recognize his trigger situations, he can prepare himself to act differently by rehearsing what to do—for example, asking for help instead of barking orders. This will up the odds that he will choose a better response, even under high stress.

Of course, developing such an early warning system requires self-awareness and the ability to monitor the incident (or, more likely, to do a postmortem afterward). Tracking the exact events that triggered the relapse, and the thoughts and feelings that went along with it, gives us added awareness of the moments in which we need to be particularly watchful and consciously recruit our new emotional competence.

Seeing the consequences of the lapse—a missed business opportunity, ruffled feelings in a colleague or customer—can also fuel our motivation to pursue change with more vigor.

Give Performance Feedback

A golf pro was prone to unpredictable rages that were ruining both his marriage and his career. While going through a program to reduce the intensity and frequency of his outbursts, he kept a "score" of sorts, tracking each time he got angry, how long it lasted, and how intensely he felt it.

Several months into the program, he blew up as intensely as ever, his rage completely out of control. The episode left him demoralized, despairing that all his efforts to change had led nowhere. But he was reinspired when he looked at his record. He realized that his rages had decreased markedly, from several times a week to just this one episode in the past two months.

Feedback lies at the heart of change. Knowing how we are doing keeps us on track. In its most basic form, feedback means that someone notices whether—or how well—the new competence is being used and lets us know.

When we are doing well, there can be a "feedforward" effect, where positive feedback buttresses our self-confidence to try out the emotional competence we are working to improve. This heightened self-confidence helps us do even better.[22]

When feedback is given poorly, too harshly, or not at all, it can demoralize and demotivate (as we saw in Chapter 8). The best results come when those giving feedback know how to do so productively and are encouraged or rewarded for doing so—and are open to feedback themselves on the quality of their feedback.

At American Express Financial Advisors, much of the feedback for emotional competence is woven into the fabric of work. "We pay as much attention to *how* you do your work as to how well you achieve goals," says Kate Cannon. "There are regular meetings with your direct supervisor. It's a relationship business—not just with our clients, but among ourselves. So people routinely get feedback about their emotional competence, even though it's probably called something else like teamwork or communication."

Encourage Practice

An international hotel chain was getting poor ratings from customers on the quality of staff hospitality. So they gave all employees who come into face-to-face contact with customers training designed to bolster their emotional intelligence. The training allowed them to practice being more aware of their feelings and showed them how to use that awareness to short-circuit their own amygdala hijacks. It also taught them how to tune in to the feelings of the hotel guests and influence their moods positively.

But the director of training and development complained that there was no benefit—that things even seemed to get a little worse.

How long did the training program last?

Just one day.

Therein lies the problem. Emotional competence cannot be improved overnight, because the emotional brain changes its habits over weeks and months, not hours and days. The old paradigm for development tacitly assumes change occurs dramatically and immediately: Send people through a two-day seminar, and—*voilà*—they are transformed. As a result of this misguided assumption, people are sent through brief trainings that have little lasting effect—and then may end up blaming themselves (or being blamed by supervisors) for some lack of will or determination when the promised improvements fail to materialize. A single seminar or workshop is a beginning, but it is not sufficient in itself.

People learn a new skill more effectively if they have repeated chances to practice it over an extended period of time than if they have the same amount of practice lumped into a single, intensive session.[23] Yet this simple rule of thumb is ignored time and again in training. Another mistake is to spend too much time merely talking about the competence, with not enough time devoted to actually practicing it in a controlled situation. In a study of training programs for managers and salespeople, Lyle Spencer Jr. and Charley Morrow analyzed how training time was divided between information about the competence learning, and actual practice. Practice sessions had double the impact on job performance as the presentation of concepts alone. And the return on investment for practice during training was *seven times* greater than for the didactic sessions.[24]

"If you use simulations to teach a competence like giving feedback—instead of just outlining the five principles of effective feedback without any opportunity for practice—the impact of training is far stronger," Spencer notes.

Reaching the point where a new habit replaces the old takes extensive practice. As one manager in a government agency put it, "People here get sent to a training, then go right back to work with no chance to try it out. So they revert to their old ways—the training never has a chance to transfer back to the job." But "overlearning," when people practice a new habit far beyond the point when they can do it well, greatly reduces the likelihood they will revert to the old habit under pressure.[25] Clinical studies of behavior change find that the longer people work at changing, the more durable the change will be. Weeks are better than days; months are better than weeks. For complex habits like emotional competence, the practice period for maximal effect may be three to six months, or longer.[26] (For more on practice issues, see Appendix 5.)

One rule of thumb for improving emotional competence: Capabilities that are being improved on or added to a person's repertoire—like becoming a better listener—can be developed in less time than is needed for remedial learning. Long-established habits, like having a short temper or being a perfectionist, are deeply ingrained. In such cases, we need to work both at *unlearning* the old, automatic habit and at *replacing* it with the new, improved one.

Exactly how long it will take a given person to master an emotional competence depends on a variety of factors. The more complex the competence, the longer mastery takes; time management, which draws on just a few competencies (self-control, which is necessary to resist the temptation of time-wasting activities, and achievement drive, which spurs a desire to improve by becoming more efficient, are two essentials for time management), can be mastered more quickly than, say, leadership, a higher-order competence that builds on more than half a dozen other competencies.

An effective program will encourage practice on our own time as well. Though we may have work reasons for cultivating a competence like listening, most are relevant in our private lives, too. Consider this provocative set of figures: Students in a two-year, full-time MBA program typically spend 2,500 hours in classes and doing assignments. But, assuming they average seven hours of sleep a night, they are awake about 10,500 hours during those two years. The question is, "What are they learning during the other 8,000 hours?"

That question was posed by Richard Boyatzis and the other designers of the Weatherhead course. It led to the proposition that self-directed learning can and should go on whenever and wherever the opportunity arises. Likewise, we don't spend all our waking hours at work (though it may *seem* we do). Especially when it comes to emotional competence, all of life can be the arena for change; life itself is the best classroom.

That attitude promotes "positive spillover," where the skills honed for work pay off elsewhere in life. A supervisor, for instance, learns to listen more effectively to employees, and brings it back home in talking with her kids. This positive spillover is seen as an explicit benefit at some companies, such as 3M, where a program designed to lower health costs purposely aims to bolster resiliency competencies for employees both at work and at home.

Arrange Support

A vice president at one of America's largest food companies had both a bachelor's degree in engineering and an MBA, as well as an IQ somewhere above 125. The president of the company would have liked to promote him. But this vice president had hit a ceiling: He wouldn't get the promotion unless he changed his style.

Unsociable and introverted, he was more comfortable sending e-mail or memos than dealing with colleagues face-to-face. In meetings he was often belligerent, combative, and dictatorial. "He would not get promoted unless he stopped doing this," recalled the executive coach brought in to help the otherwise promising vice president.

The coach went to work one-on-one with the VP. "I helped him to recognize his trigger points, so he can avoid situations where he's more likely to lose it. I taught him how to use self-talk, like athletes do, to prepare for situations where he's prone to get angry—he'll remind himself going in, 'I'm not going to let this happen to me, I'm not going to lose my temper.'

And I showed him a technique to short-circuit anger when he feels it building in his body: tighten all the muscles in his body, then let go all at once. It's a quick muscle-relaxation method."

The coaching sessions continued for months, until the VP was finally able to manage his anger. Such one-on-one lessons in the essentials of emotional competence are increasingly common in American business, particularly for highly valued employees. Coaching is one of many forms that sustained support can take. Mentors can serve much the same purpose.

While the standard view of mentoring is that it's a way to foster career development, mentoring can also serve as a coaching forum for boosting emotional competence. As Kathy Kram, director of the executive MBA program at the Boston University School of Management, found in her landmark study of mentors, people can get two kinds of benefits from mentors: help with their careers (such as protection, visibility, and sponsorship) and counseling and coaching.[27]

Much learning occurs in the natural course of relationships at work, whether it is deemed "coaching" or not. As Judith Jordan, a Harvard psychologist, points out, every relationship is an opportunity for both individuals to practice their personal competencies, and so grow and improve together.[20]

Such reciprocal learning can come naturally in peer relationships, where people can spontaneously alternate between the roles of mentor and learner, depending on their strengths and limits. "Some companies, like Bell Atlantic, have experimented with mentoring circles," Kathy Kram tells me. "They tried bringing together groups of midlevel women executives and attaching them to a more senior executive, to talk over common problems at work. They would tell each other about their experiences, rehash how they could have been handled, and so widen their own repertoire of how to deal with those same situations. The net effect was to build up their social and emotional competence."

For those who lack a formal mentor, one strategy is to find a temporary coach, someone adept at a specific skill or competence who will consult for a limited time. This arrangement differs from full-fledged mentoring by virtue of its temporary, task-oriented nature. As Kram has found, any relationship with someone who has greater experience or competence can be an opportunity for learning. And people who develop multiple relationships with a range of coworkers in varying areas of competence stand to improve the most.

As part of the American Express Financial Advisors emotional competence training, participants often choose a "learning partner," someone who teams with them for continued encouragement over several months once back on the job. "People agree to offer mutual support, to meet regularly for lunch, or to call routinely," says Kate Cannon. "They can discuss whatever habit they're trying to change—like worrying too much about things, being more assertive. They update each other, give advice, cheerlead."

Such buddy systems increase the transfer of learned emotional intelligence skills to the job.[29] And coaching can be very helpful on the spot: "If your partner knows that a particular person pushes your hot buttons, he might help you by giving you a reminder signal to ready yourself just before you go into the encounter," says Cannon. Such on-the-spot support happens more readily when, as is the case at American Express, an entire work group goes through the training together.

Weatherhead students are grouped in teams of ten to twelve, each with a facilitator and a corporate executive who serves as advisor. In addition, each student gets a mentor who is a midlevel manager or advanced professional. The combination of peer group, advisor, and mentor at Weatherhead offers students a variety of people to turn to for support as they strengthen their target competencies.

Provide Models

In learning a new behavior, having access to someone who exemplifies the competence at its best is immensely helpful. We learn by watching others; if someone can demonstrate a competence, they create a living classroom for us.[30]

For that reason, those who teach emotional competence should embody it. Here the medium is the message: Trainers who merely talk about these competencies but act in ways that make it clear they don't possess them undermine the message. When it comes to teaching someone how to use a computer program, the trainer's warmth is of relatively little importance. But it's crucial when it comes to helping someone be more expressive and empathic in their dealings with clients, or to control their temper in management meetings.

In the JOBS program, "It was clear we needed trainers who embody social and emotional competence," Robert Caplan told me. "That was the basic principle that guided our selection of trainers as well as their own training. And to maintain their level of competence, we gave them ongoing evaluation and feedback on these competencies. It has to permeate the culture of the group giving the training."

In general, we pattern our behavior after high-status people in our organization—which means we can take on their negative habits as well as positive ones.[31] When workers are exposed to an intemperate supervisor—say, one who arbitrarily reprimands people—they tend to become less tolerant and more harsh in their own leadership style.[32]

At Eastman Kodak, a manager told me, "In the old days, everyone was in the same place, here in Rochester, sitting next to each other. You'd see someone every day, get to know their style, get mentored or just be exposed to good role models—people who knew how to establish rapport, listen well, build trust, be respected. But now people are scattered all over, isolated in smaller units. You don't have the same chance to learn these soft skills."

Because there is less chance for these competencies to be modeled and passed on, the manager adds, he feels the need to be more intentional in seeing that people in his unit learn them. "We have a development plan to be sure we groom people in the skills that make people successful, not just the technical or analytic abilities, but the leadership skills like self-awareness, persuasion, reliability."

Encourage and Reinforce

Take two aides at a nursing home. One was callous and brusque with patients, occasionally even to the point of cruelty. The other was a model of compassionate care.[33] The callous aide, however, always finished tasks on schedule and followed orders; the kind aide sometimes bent the rules to help a patient, and, largely because she spent more time talking with patients, often finished late. Supervisors gave the cold aide top ratings, while the caring one was frequently in trouble and her ratings were far lower. How could this be when the stated mission of the nursing home was to provide compassionate care?

Such gaps between the espoused mission and values of an organization and what actually goes on become glaring when people are being encouraged to cultivate emotional competencies that, in day-to-day practice, are simply not supported. The result is employees who are more emotionally competent than their jobs require or than is appreciated in their organization.

An organization can help people upgrade their emotional competencies not just by offering programs to do so, but by creating an atmosphere that rewards and even celebrates such self-improvement. After all, our attempts to change are most effective in an atmosphere that makes us feel safe.[34] To develop, a competence must be meaningfully flexed—and for that to happen, it needs to be valued at work, as reflected in the criteria for selection, job placement, promotion, performance review, and the like. That might mean, for example, rewarding people's efforts at mentoring, and building coaching and training in emotional competencies into the performance appraisal process; opportunities for 360-degree feedback and competency training.

A fledgling competence needs to be expressed during the actual situation at work in order to take hold. Lack of connection between the new learning and on-the-job reality means the learning will wither. As a "training high" evaporates, our enthusiasm for following through on what we've learned often fades. And whether or not an organization has a supportive climate is cited over and over by people going through training programs as determining the extent to which they can transfer what they learned to their job.[35]

Perhaps the optimal supportive climate for training occurs when an entire work group focuses on cultivating competencies together, as happens with some management teams at American Express Financial Advisors. In these teams everyone, including the leader, makes a commitment to emotional competence training. Feedback and support are built into staff meetings, and time is set aside to talk about how people are doing with their emotional competence goals.

In addition, the talent assessment for executives there uses a checklist that includes emotional competencies. "Each senior executive completes the checklist on those in a unit, and each vice president does the same on himself or herself," says Cannon. "Then they have a dialogue over those areas where they differ. The conclusions are presented to the company president. Things like relationship skills, motivating yourself and others, self-management skills, really matter here."

Shortly after taking the helm at Banker's Trust New York, the new chairman and CEO, Frank Newman, worked with a consulting firm to make top managers more aware of the human skills the company needed to stay competitive.[36] The result was a program showing it was no longer enough simply to focus on the bottom line: Management skills would matter as much as financial performance for promotions and compensation.

How could Newman get his bankers and traders to pay attention? He went to at least part of each training session himself, where members of the bank's management committee are among the teachers. As the bank's head of development puts it, "This way no one is saying, 'My manager told me it isn't important.' "

Evaluate

The recommendation: first, establish sound outcome measures, especially for the competencies that were targeted in training, and include job performance measures. The best designs use pre- and post-training measurements, plus a long-term follow-up several months after training ends, and control groups with participants randomly assigned. While this ideal may be hard to meet, there are alternatives, such as using people's baseline measurements in lieu of a control group, or comparing an individual's changes on targeted competencies with changes in those not targeted. And if a program falls short, that information should be used to improve the next round of training.

But almost nowhere are these simple principles followed. Instead, there is a distressing gap between what research shows should be done and how training is actually conducted and evaluated. A survey of Fortune 500 companies found that chief training officers believe the number one reason to evaluate training is to determine if there is a payoff. Yet there was little or no hard evaluation of their training programs.[37]

The most common source of data was student evaluation sheets, followed by continuing demand for the training— more like popularity polls than hard indicators of performance change. Research suggests no correlation between trainees' reports of satisfaction and their learning or demonstrated improvement on the job—as one review puts it, "Liking does not imply learning."[38]

The best method for evaluation—an objective pre- and post-training look at the impact on job performance—was not used routinely by a single corporation. Ten percent did report having used such a design on occasion, though many of those assessments focused only on people's change in attitudes rather than on any change in their on-the-job performance.

But this is slowly changing. One of the most ambitious training evaluation projects anywhere is under way at the Weatherhead School of Management.[39] There the students who have gone through the managerial skills training program are asked to become part of an ongoing follow-up research project to see what advantage, if any, the cultivation of these capabilities gives them in their careers. The project is envisioned to go on for the next fifty years.

The Emotionally Intelligent Organization

12

·····················

Taking the Organizational Pulse

t an international business conference I attended recently, people were asked, "Does your organization have a mission statement?" About two thirds raised their hands.

Then they were asked, "Does the mission statement describe the day-to-day reality of life there?" All but a few hands went down.

When there is a glaring gap between the espoused vision of an organization and the actual reality, the inevitable emotional fallout can range from self-protective cynicism to anger and even despair. Companies whose profitability is won at the price of violating the implicit shared values of those who work there pay an emotional price: a burden of shame and guilt, a sense of tainted rewards.

An emotionally intelligent organization needs to come to terms with any disparities between the values it proclaims and those it lives. Clarity about an organization's values, spirit, and mission leads to a decisive self-confidence in corporate decision making.

An organizational mission statement serves an emotional function: articulating the shared sense of goodness that allows us to feel what we do together is worthwhile. Working for a company that measures its success in the most meaningful ways—not just the bottom line—is itself a morale and energy raiser.

Knowing what those shared values are requires what amounts to emotional self-awareness at the organizational level. Just as each person has a profile of strengths and weaknesses in the different areas of competence and has a certain level of awareness of these, so with organizations. For any organizational competence, these profiles can be mapped at every level: division by division, and down through each smaller unit to each working team.

But few organizations take stock of themselves in this way. How many companies know where, for instance, blundering managers infect their people with rancor and fear, or where the pockets of enterprise are among their salespeople? Many organizations may *think* they are making these assessments through internal surveys of job satisfaction, commitment, and the like. But these standard tools may miss the mark.

Some of the most widely used organizational measures were assessed by the Personnel Resources and Development Center at the U.S. Office of Personnel Management, under the direction of Marilyn Gowing.[1] The question: To what extent do these surveys assess emotional intelligence at the organizational level?

There were, as Gowing puts it, "some amazing gaps" in what was measured. These gaps point to missed possibilities in thinking about what makes an organization effective—and to ways of diagnosing performance lapses. Among the most notable gaps:[2]

- *Emotional self-awareness:* Getting a reading of the emotional climate as it impacts performance

- *Achievement:* Scanning the environment for crucial data and opportunities for enterprise

- *Adaptability:* Flexibility in the face of challenges or obstacles

- *Self-control:* Performing effectively under pressure rather than reacting out of panic, anger, or alarm

- *Integrity:* The reliability that breeds trust

- *Optimism:* Resilience in the face of setbacks

- *Empathy:* Understanding the feelings and perspective of others, whether clients and customers or internal constituencies

- *Leveraging diversity:* Utilizing differences as opportunities

- *Political awareness:* Understanding salient economic, political, and social trends

- *Influence:* Adeptness at persuasion strategies
- *Building bonds:* The strength of personal links between far-flung people and parts of an organization

The importance for any organization of these competencies seems self-evident. As I write this, Microsoft's top executives are publicly bemoaning their organization's lack of political awareness, a deficit that has put them at a seeming disadvantage in their struggle with the Justice Department over charges of monopolistic practices.

Still, the extent to which each of these collective competencies predicts better organizational performance remains to be seen. But that is just the point: No one seems to be looking.

Imagine the advantage for companies that cultivate these competencies—and the problems for those that don't. Let me make my point by sketching the differences for organizations, for better and worse, that three kinds of competencies can make: self-awareness, managing emotions well, and the drive to achieve.

Blind Spots

At the beach on a hot August day a family of four has packed up their towels, toys, and beach gear and is trudging through the sizzling sand when the younger child, a girl of about five, starts whining, "I want some *water.* Gimme some *water.*"

Her father, annoyed at her whining tone, complains to the mother, "Where'd she learn to talk like that?"

Then, to his whiny daughter, he says curtly, "Nobody hears you when you sound like that"—and walks on, pointedly ignoring her plaintive plea.

Through countless exchanges like this—often more covert and implied—each of us learned in our family of origin a set of rules about attention and emotions.

The first rule: Here's what we notice.
The second: Here's what we call it.
The third: Here's what we don't notice.
The fourth: Since we don't notice it, we don't call it anything.

So it is with organizations. Each has a distinctive zone of collective experience—of common feeling and shared information—that goes unvoiced (or is spoken of only in private, not openly), and so falls into the abyss of what amounts to an organizational blind spot.

Those zones of inattention can harbor potential dangers. At the Barings Bank branch in Singapore, for example, the fact that a renegade trader was in charge of both the front and back office operations—and so had no one supervising his trades—allowed him to lose hundreds of millions of dollars, sinking the company. For Archer Daniels Midland, the agricultural giant, a high-level collusion winked at price fixing that, when exposed, resulted in indictments of several top executives.

The Organizational Family

The rules that tell us what we can and cannot express at work are part of the implicit contract each organization imposes. Honoring these rules is the cost of being a member of the organizational family. We won't notice, say, that the manager here is a washed-out alcoholic who years ago had a better position but was parked here to get him out of the way of top management. We'll just deal with his assistant (who actually does his job), the way everyone else does.

Fear—which is not unreasonable—binds people to silence. Take the fate of whistle-blowers, people in an organization who publicly reveal its misdeeds. Studies of whistle-blowers in business find they are typically motivated not by vengeful or selfish motives, but by a lofty one: loyalty to the ethics of their profession or to the organization's avowed mission and principles. Yet most are victimized by the organization—fired, persecuted, sued—rather than thanked.

They commit the ultimate sin: speaking the unspeakable. And their expulsion from the organization sends a tacit signal to everyone else: "Go along with the collusion here lest you, too, lose your membership." To the extent that such collusion keeps questions vital to organizational effectiveness from being asked, it threatens the organization's survival.

It also contributes to frustrating group charades, like this example from a study observing top executive decision-making meetings:

> The subordinates were in agreement that too much time was spent in long presentations in order to make the president happy. The

president, however, confided that he did not enjoy listening to long, and, at times, dry presentations (especially when he had seen most of the data anyway). However, he felt that it was important to go through this because it might give the subordinates a greater sense of commitment to the problem![3]

Business Is Business

I n the early 1990s Carl Frost, an American business consultant, was meeting in Sweden with work teams at Volvo.[4] The talk was about the extralong vacations everyone was anticipating that year. But Frost was disturbed by an ominous fact underlying the length of those days off: Vacations were being extended because sales were down. Volvo had a huge amount of excessive inventory on its hands, and with demand low, assembly lines were idle.

The managers, Frost found, were quite comfortable, even happy about the decision to extend their holidays. But Frost felt the need to raise questions, to bring to the surface facts that the people at Volvo seemed oblivious to. The fundamental fact was that Volvo was losing the race in global competition for the auto market: Volvo's manufacturing costs exceeded those of every other major automaker in the world, it took Volvo workers twice as long to make a car as it took Japanese autoworkers, and Volvo's overseas sales had shrunk in recent years by 50 percent.

The company was in crisis, its future—and the jobs of these workers—in jeopardy. And yet as Frost tells it, everyone acted as though nothing were wrong. No one seemed to see a connection between the vacations they were about to take and the troubled company's future.

This blasé attitude, Frost felt, was a sign of a troubling failure of communication, one that let workers at Volvo ignore any link between their situation and the larger fate of their company. This lack of connection, he claims, meant they took little responsibility for helping their company become more competitive.

The inoculation against such collusion entails making an organization more honest and more open in its internal communications. This requires an atmosphere that values the truth, no matter how anxiety-provoking it may be, and that seeks to hear all sides of a question. But such real debate is only possible if people feel free enough to speak their minds without fear of punishment, retribution, or ridicule.

In a Coopers & Lybrand survey of Fortune 500 companies, only 11 percent of CEOs believed that "messengers of bad news take a real risk in my company." But among middle managers in those companies, a third said bearers of bad news put themselves at risk. Among nonmanagement workers, about half felt there was real risk in bearing bad news.[5]

This disparity between those at the top and those most in touch with what is going on day to day means that top decision makers may labor under the illusion they are getting all the data they need, while those who have the data—especially troubling facts—feel too anxious to share it. Leaders who fail to set a tone that encourages people to bring up all their misgivings and questions, including unsettling news, are setting themselves up for trouble. Then, says William Jennings, who led the Coopers & Lybrand survey, "It is easy for employees to view internal controls as an impediment to productivity, and to jettison them in a misguided effort to 'make the numbers.'"[6]

Lore has it that some years back, whenever new executives were hired at PepsiCo, then-president Wayne Calloway interviewed them. He would tell them, the story goes, "There are two ways to get fired here. One: not meet your numbers. Two: lie. But the fastest way to get fired is to lie about your numbers."

"If you withheld information, especially about a business disaster, he was unforgiving," a former colleague of Calloway told me. "But if you were immediately forthcoming, he was very gracious. The result was a culture where people were very candid, very genuine and open about the truth."

Contrast that with what I'm told about one high-tech company by an executive: "Telling the truth around here is career-eliminating behavior."

Managing Emotions Well

One largely ignored pulse of an organization's viability can be read in the typical emotional states of those who work there. Systems theory tells us that to ignore *any* significant category of data is to limit understanding and response. Sounding the depths of emotional currents in an organization can have concrete benefits.

Consider a gas plant division at Petro Canada, the country's largest oil and gas refining company. "Guys in the gas plants were having a wave of accidents, some fatal," I was told by a consultant who was called in to help.

"I found that in the macho culture of the petrochemical industry, guys never acknowledged their feelings. If someone came to work hung over, preoccupied over a sick child, or upset by a spat with his wife, his workmates would never ask how he was doing that day or if he was okay enough to be sharp on the job. The result would be that the guy would be inattentive and cause an accident."

With this basic insight into the human cost of ignoring emotions on the job, the company initiated a series of workshops for crews "to get them to see that how they are feeling has consequences—that *this matters*. They saw that they had to look out for each other, and they were doing themselves and everyone else a favor if they checked in about how they were doing. If someone was off that day, they needed to say to him, 'I don't think I can work with you today.' And their safety record improved."

This is not to argue for making organizations a place where people simply bare their feelings or souls to each other, in some nightmarish vision of the office as a kind of emotional salon or ongoing sensitivity group. That would be utterly counterproductive, a blurring of the distinction between work and private life that itself signifies poor emotional competence.

From the perspective of work, feelings matter to the extent that they facilitate or interfere with the shared goal. The paradox, though, is that our interactions at work are relationships like any others; our passions operate here also. As leadership expert Warren Bennis put it: "People feel alone with their pain—the hurts, the loneliness, the closed doors, the things left unsaid and unheard. It's not permissible to discuss this."

In too many organizations, the ground rules that marginalize emotional realities guide our attention away from such emotional static as though it did not matter. These blinders propagate endless problems: decisions that demoralize; difficulty managing creativity and making decisions; ignoring the crucial value of social skill; the inability to motivate, let alone inspire; hollow mission statements and empty slogans of the day; leadership by the book, lacking zest or energy; drudgery instead of spontaneity; a lack of esprit de corps; teams that don't work.

Burnout? Blame the Victim

As one executive at a high-growth company—where the turnover rate was recently at 40 percent—told me, "People at the top work all the time; many are candidates for divorce. We get huge rewards, but if you don't do better each year than the one before, you get fired. Job security doesn't exist here."

Such plaintive reports are the new downside of a technological and competitive landscape that has escalated demands of every kind. "It's constant white water," I'm told by a manager at a hugely successful company. "There's so much turbulence today, just from the sheer complexity of the business environment. You used to be able to come home and rest, but if you work for a global company, now you have to be available twenty hours a day—calling Europe at four in the morning, Asia until midnight."

One way his company gets people to challenge themselves relentlessly is by making the rewards so great: They pay more than anyone else, with many employees getting huge performance bonuses. It's a winning strategy for the company, but it often carries a high personal cost. Companies like this one can turbocharge productivity—to a point. The most driven workers will reap benefits, but if they are kept at this frenzied level, their personal lives, their morale, or their health—or all of these—will surely suffer.

Few organizations address the extent to which they themselves generate the stress. More usual is a form of blaming the victim. "Burnout is really a problem for the individual," one CEO told researchers.[7] "It does not have any real impact on the organization's productivity. It's a soft problem, not a clear-cut matter of finance or strategic management. If people want to use the EAP program or take their vacation days to get a good rest, that's fine. That's what those things are there for. There's not much else the organization can do."

The CEO's glaring errors: assuming that there's little an organization can do, and that such emotional exhaustion has no effect on an organization's productivity. One of the defining signs of burnout is a drop in efficiency and the ability to accomplish even routine tasks. If that occurs not just in a few individuals but among broad swaths of employees, the organization's performance inevitably suffers.

A study of burnout among nurses makes the point. In a large medical center, the extent to which nurses on inpatient units had classic burnout symptoms like cynicism, exhaustion, and frustration with working conditions correlated with patients' reports of dissatisfaction with their hospital stay. The more content nurses were with their jobs, the better patients rated their medical care overall.[8] Since patients are consumers who make choices about where to spend their health care dollars, such human realities can make a large difference in the competitiveness of the hospitals those nurses work for.

Consider, too, the risk when things go wrong. In a study of twelve thousand health care workers, those departments and hospitals where workers complained most about on-the-job stress had the highest rates of medical malpractice claims against them.[9]

How to Lower Performance

Companies can do much to protect themselves— and their employees— from the costs of burnout. This is evident in a twenty-year series of studies of the causes of burnout in several thousand men and women, from hundreds of organizations.[10] While most studies of burnout focus on the individual, this one looked at the practices and patterns in the organizations the people worked for. It pinpointed six primary ways organizations demoralize and demotivate employees:

- *Work overload:* Too much work to do, with too little time and support. Job cutbacks require supervisors to handle more employees, nurses more patients, teachers more students, bank tellers more transactions, managers more administrative duties. As the tempo, complexity, and demands of work escalate, people feel overwhelmed. Escalating work erodes the downtime during which people can recover. Exhaustion accumulates, work suffers.

- *Lack of autonomy:* Being accountable for work but having little say in how to go about it. Micromanagement means frustration when workers see ways to do their work better but are held back by rigid rules. This lessens responsibility, flexibility, and innovation. The emotional message to workers: The company lacks respect for their judgment and innate abilities.

- *Skimpy rewards:* Getting too little pay for more work. With cutbacks, wage freezes, and trends toward contract work and cutbacks in fringe benefits like health coverage, people lose their expectation that their salary can increase as their career continues. Another loss of reward is emotional: Work overload combined with too little control and job insecurity robs work of its intrinsic pleasure.

■ *Loss of connection:* Increasing isolation on the job. Personal relationships are the human glue that makes teams excel. Shuffled job assignments lower a sense of commitment to the work group. As relationships fragment, the pleasures that come from a sense of community with workmates erodes. That growing sense of alienation fuels conflict, even as it erodes the common history and emotional connections that can help heal such rifts.

■ *Unfairness:* Inequities in how people are treated. Lack of fairness breeds resentment, whether due to unequal pay or workloads, disregard for grievances, or policies that seem high-handed. Rapid escalation of top executive pay and bonuses while salaries in the bottom tiers rise little or not at all undermines people's trust in those who run the organization. Resentments breed in the absence of honest talk. The result: cynicism and alienation, along with a loss of enthusiasm for the organization's mission.

■ *Value conflicts:* A mismatch between a person's principles and the demands of their job. Whether this pushes workers into lying to make a sale, skipping a safety check to get things done on time, or simply using Machiavellian tactics to survive in a viciously competitive environment, the cost is to their moral sense. Jobs at odds with their values demoralize workers, leading them to question the worth of the work they do. So do lofty mission statements when belied by the day-to-day reality of operations.

The net result of these organizational malpractices is to breed chronic exhaustion, cynicism, and a loss of motivation, enthusiasm, and productivity.[11]

Now consider the advantages for a company of raising its collective emotional intelligence.

The Spirit of Achievement

The manufacturing company was losing a race with its competitors, who were getting price quotes for potential jobs to customers in twenty days, while those same quotes took this manufacturer forty days to get out the door.

So they reengineered. They changed the quote-generating process by adding more control points, computerizing parts of it, and making other such structural changes. Result: The turnaround time for quotes escalated from forty to fifty-five days.

Then they turned to outside expertise, bringing in consultants who were specialists in reengineering. The time for quotes ballooned to seventy days— and the error rate increased to 30 percent.

Desperate, they brought in experts in the methods of the "learning organization." Today the time it takes them to get a quote to customers is down to five days, and the error rate is down to 2 percent.

How did they do it? They changed their working relationships, not the technology or structure. "It's futile to try to solve with technology or structure a problem that is really a people problem," Nick Zeniuk, president of Interactive Learning Labs, who led the company through the learning process, tells me.

Zeniuk should know. He won fame in the world of learning organizations for his pivotal role in a triumph of the method when he, with Fred Simon, led the launch of the 1995 Lincoln Continental, and their case is cited as a classic success story by Peter Senge, of MIT's Learning Center.[12]

There's no question the redesigned 1995 Lincoln Continental was a spectacular success story. Independent ratings of quality and owner satisfaction pegged the '95 Lincoln at the top of the Ford line, better than every American car in its class, and on a par with the best foreign competition, from the Mercedes to the Infiniti. Customer satisfaction increased 9 percent, to 85 percent (Lexus, the highest-scoring car, had an 86 percent rating).

Equally impressive: Though the redesign effort started four months late, the car arrived on the market a month ahead of schedule. And on every metric of production success, the new Lincoln met or exceeded goals, a prodigious feat for a process that involved more than a thousand people, a core team of three hundred, and a budget of $1 billion.

The challenge could easily have been viewed as entirely technical—a cognitive puzzle par excellence that could be solved only by the smartest people with the most expertise. Auto design demands meshing hundreds of sometimes contradictory demands, from engine torque to braking, acceleration to fuel economy. The most intricate and difficult part of designing a new car is coming up with final engineering specifications for its components—a task akin to figuring out the size and shape of each piece of an immense jigsaw puzzle, and crafting the parts as you go, during the very act of trying to solve it.

Understandably, auto design teams typically have to backtrack and rework many of their design specifications after a prototype is assembled, because with the first prototype unanticipated problems become obvious. At this point—once hot metal has been poured to make a working model—such reworking is quite expensive: The job requires redoing the machine tooling for every part involved, typically at costs of millions of dollars.

Yet the Continental design team, with a budget of $90 million for these retooling needs, used only a third that amount, bucking an industry-wide trend to overspend the retooling budget. The design effort was as efficient as the Continental's engine itself: Engineering drawings for components were out a month early, rather than the usual three or four months late, with 99 percent of the parts in final shape rather than the standard 50 percent.

Hard Results, Soft Means

The challenge facing the Continental redesign team was to get hard results—a better car—through approaches that many managers in the auto industry felt were just too soft to matter, like openness, honesty, trust, and smooth communications.[13] The culture of that industry traditionally disregarded such values: It was hierarchical and authority-based, with the guiding assumption that the boss knows best and makes all key decisions.

Compounding this cultural problem was a dense emotional fog. There was a pervasive sense of frustration at starting four months late, and a host of barriers to trust and openness. One of the main roadblocks was at the very top of the team; Zeniuk recalls that the tensions between himself and the finance manager were so great, he couldn't talk to him "in less than a high-decibel range." That tension was a symptom of a deep hostility and mistrust between those in charge of producing the new model and those whose duty was to control costs.

To tackle these problems, the core management team used many learning organization methods, including one that helps people unlearn defensive habits of conversation.[14] The method is simple: Instead of arguing, the parties agree to mutually explore the assumptions that undergird their points of view.

A classic example of how people jump to conclusions is when you see someone yawn in a meeting, leap to the assumption he is bored, and then skip to the more damaging overgeneralization that he doesn't care about the meeting, anyone else's thoughts, or the entire project. So you tell him, "I'm disappointed in you."

In this learning organization method, that comment gets listed under a heading: "What Was Said or Done." The more critical data, though, is in another column, "Unspoken Thoughts and Feelings": that the yawn meant he was bored and doesn't care about the meeting, anyone else, or even the entire project. In that column, too, go our own feelings of hurt and anger.[15]

Once these hidden assumptions surface, they can be tested against reality by talking about them. For instance, we may discover the yawn was not from boredom but rather exhaustion due to getting up in the night with a cranky infant.

This exercise in learning to articulate what we are thinking and feeling—but not saying aloud—allows us to understand the hidden feelings and assumptions that can create otherwise inexplicable resentments and puzzling impasses.

Beyond requiring self-awareness to retrieve those hidden thoughts and feelings, this task demands other emotional competencies: empathy, to listen to the other person's point of view with sensitivity, and social skills, to collaborate productively in exploring the hidden differences—and loaded feelings—that surface.

In a sense, the *real* conversations are the inner ones, if only because they reveal how people actually think and feel about what's going on. The inner dialogue, especially if it is emotionally turbulent, often seeps out in a truculent tone of voice, say, or an averted gaze. But we can miss these signals, in others as well as in ourselves, when things move fast or we are pressured or distracted. The net result: The inner dialogue is ignored, even though it is rife with crucial information— misgivings, resentments, fears, and hopes.

As Zeniuk puts it, we don't know what to do with this real conversation, "So we ignore it. It's like toxic waste—what do you do with it? Dump it? Bury it? Whatever we do with this toxic waste is corrosive—it pollutes the conversation. If we confront people, they pull out their defenses." And so conversations at work go on as though there were no inner dialogue, even though everyone is utterly engaged in this mute exchange. The roots of conflict as well as the start of true collaboration are to be found in this deep level of discourse.

When used at the start of the Lincoln Continental project, the dialogue exercise revealed two bitterly opposed camps. The finance people thought those managing the program didn't care at all about controlling costs; the program managers thought the finance people "didn't have a clue" about what it took to build a quality car. The net result of this mutual exploration of hidden feelings and assumptions was to make glaringly clear that the project was hobbled by a lack of trust and openness. The core issues:

- Fear of being wrong led people to withhold information.

- The bosses' need to control got in the way of people on the team using their best capabilities.

- Suspicion was widespread—people saw each other as unhelpful and not to be trusted.

Here emotional intelligence becomes essential. To have a working group that can go beyond fear, power struggles, and distrust takes a reservoir of trust and rapport. The task ahead focused as much on strengthening the level of trust in the relationships between people as on surfacing their hidden assumptions. And that took a great deal of social engineering. As Fred Simon put it, "If I wanted to improve the quality of this car, my greatest leverage was in helping my team members develop better personal relationships and see each other more as people."

Starting at the Top

At first people had a deep resentment and despair about their inability to do the work they needed to—they started with a blame-the-bosses attitude," Zeniuk recalls. "But as the bosses engaged, really listening to what they had to say, it switched to 'Okay, I can do it. But leave me alone to do my job.' But no such thing: We're interconnected in our work, and we had to go the next step—learn to be interconnected. So the bosses became facilitators and coaches. The role of the leader was no longer just controlling and telling, but listening, providing resources and stewardship."

To facilitate these changes, the entire three-hundred-person design team was brought together in groups of twenty to work on the real problems they faced together on the job, such as reconfiguring the interior of the car. As they talked through their problems, facilitators like Daniel Kim, then at MIT, taught them the basic conceptual tools of collaborative learning. But the key was, as Zeniuk puts it, "emotional awareness, empathy, and building relationships. Fostering emotional intelligence wasn't a direct goal, but it evolved naturally as we tried to reach our goals."

Consider again the challenge involved: fifteen different design teams, each oriented around the parts of the car that performed a given function, like the car's chassis and power train, each working independently. But in the final design for the car, their efforts had to mesh seamlessly—yet they weren't talking enough to each other. Traditionally each team would work in isolation to produce what it considered the best design and then try to force designs for other parts to change to fit their own requirements. It was out-and-out turf warfare.

"If I make a design mistake in sheet metal and then have to go back and retool to correct it, that can cost nine million dollars," Zeniuk observes. "But if I spot the mistake before I get to the sheet metal–tooling stage, it costs nothing to fix. If something's not going to work, we need the bad news early."

In the typical design of a new model, there might be hundreds of small adjustments made to parts specifications down the line. That's why the Continental team had a budget of $90 million to cover the costs of these changes, a budget that usually is exceeded in the American auto industry. But in Japan, Zeniuk knew, most such changes were being made up front, before the specifications were set in the tooling machinery, when they would become so expensive to adjust.

"We found we didn't know about these changes up front because the engineers feared being embarrassed or attacked," Zeniuk tells me. "They'd hope someone else would admit the mistake first and take the blame. They'd think, 'Well, I can fix my dashboard mistake when they fix their side panel problem and no one will notice I goofed.' How do you get people to share the painful truth when they have such fear?"

But the crucial shift showed up, for example, in a new style for meetings. Says Zeniuk, "We made sure everyone had a chance to share what was on their minds" instead of letting the old habits take over, where "management walks into a situation thinking they have all the answers and are hesitant to admit when they don't know something." Instead, "We'd put out a decision and ask, 'How do you *feel* about this?' "

Rather than the usual political jockeying and trying to look good that so often sets the tone of group meetings, this more direct approach took hold, in effect raising the group's level of collective self-awareness. When someone was uncomfortable with a decision that was being made, they would stop the meeting and use the methods they had learned to engage in a careful, respectful inquiry into the feelings and assumptions that fed that unease.

"There is a high probability that there was a reason for that discomfort, and that reason could frequently change the entire decision," Zeniuk says. "It took a while for us to reach that level of honesty and openness."[16]

He notes one concrete payoff for this more emotionally intelligent approach: "We saw the teams stop competing to meet cost and quality objectives at the other guy's expense, and start working together. Instead of working in isolated islands, there was a constant back-and-forth. Once they saw the bigger picture, that my work is part of the other guy's, there were many, many trade-offs among the various teams. We even had some design teams give up part of their budget to let others add to the cost and quality of their part—something that just never happens in auto design."

The bottom line? "We got seven hundred changes in specifications eighteen months before production, instead of the usual wave of costly changes at the very last minute. That let us save sixty million dollars in retooling costs out of a budget of ninety million, and finish ahead of schedule by a month, despite starting four months late."

13

....

The Heart of Performance

ppliance sales at GE had slowed alarmingly, and the manager was dismayed. Studying a chart showing a steady dip in sales, he and his colleagues realized the appliance division was having serious trouble with marketing. The conversation quickly turned to seeking a solution. Should they concentrate on pricing? On advertising? On some other change in marketing?

Then someone from the company's financial services arm, GE Capital, displayed a chart showing that consumer debt was reaching saturation levels—it wasn't that the company was failing in its marketing, but that people were having more trouble paying for big-ticket items like appliances.

"Suddenly, everyone had a whole new angle on the problem," one meeting attendee noted. This fresh information led the discussion away from marketing to financing—searching for ways to help customers pay for such a large purchase.[1]

It was a moment when crucial information—a look at the bigger picture—arrived in time to avert the corporate equivalent of a minor shipwreck.

This example illustrates the way in which an organization as a whole has an "intelligence" of sorts, just as do the groups and teams within it.[2] *Intelligence,* in one of its most basic senses, is the capacity to solve problems, meet challenges, or create valued products.[3] In this sense, *organizational* intelligence represents that capacity as it emerges from the complex interplay of people and relationships, culture and roles within an organization.

Knowledge and expertise are distributed within an organization, and no one person can master all the information the group needs to run efficiently—the financial officer has one type of key expertise, the salespeople another, those in research and development still another. The organization itself will only be as "smart" as the timely and appropriate distribution and processing of these diverse elements of information.

Any organization is "cybernetic," which means being engaged in continuous and overlapping feedback loops, gathering information from within and without and adjusting operations accordingly. Systems theory tells us that in an environment of turbulent change and competition, the entity that can take in information most widely, learn from it most thoroughly, and respond most nimbly, creatively, and flexibly will be the most adaptive.

That principle applies to both the smallest corner business and the largest global firm. It points to the crucial role of information flow throughout an organization in determining its viability. Some discuss this in terms of how companies must use "intellectual capital": their patents and processes, management skills, technologies, and accumulated knowledge of customers, suppliers, and business practices. The sum of what everybody in a company knows and knows how to do gives a company much of its competitive edge—if it is mobilized well.

Maximizing the Organization's Intelligence

The "tech reps," who repaired copy machines for Xerox, were wasting huge amounts of time. Or so it seemed when Xerox analyzed how they went about doing their job.

They discovered the reps spent a good deal of time with each other rather than out helping customers. They'd regularly get together at the local parts warehouse and exchange stories from the field over a cup of coffee.

From an efficiency-minded perspective, this was an obvious waste of time. But that's not how John Seely Brown, Xerox's head scientist, saw it. Brown had sent a trained anthropologist to tag along with the reps, and this researcher believed the downtime was not wasted but rather was central to the reps' ability to do their jobs well.

As Brown puts it, field service "is a *social* activity. Like most work, it involves a community of professionals. The tech reps weren't just repairing machines; they were also coproducing insights about how to repair machines better."[4]

The reps are knowledge workers, and their conversations are where their knowledge is transferred and built upon. As Brown observes, "The real genius of organizations is the informal, impromptu, often inspired ways that real people solve real problems in ways that formal processes can't anticipate."

Both work and learning are social. Organizations, as Brown describes them, "are webs of participation." Key to successful performance with knowledge workers—with *any* workers—is instilling enthusiasm and commitment, two qualities that organizations can earn but not compel. "Only workers who choose to opt in—who voluntarily make a commitment to their colleagues—can create a winning company," says Brown.

That's where emotional intelligence comes into play. An organization's collective level of emotional intelligence determines the degree to which that organization's intellectual capital is realized—and so its overall performance. The art of maximizing intellectual capital lies in orchestrating the interactions of the people whose minds hold that knowledge and expertise.

When it comes to technical skill and the core competencies that make a company competitive, the ability to outperform others depends on the *relationships* of the people involved. In Brown's words, "You can't divorce competencies from the social fabric that supports them."

Just as maximizing the IQ of a small working group depends on the effective knitting together of the people within the group, so with organizations as a whole: Emotional, social, and political realities can enhance or degrade what the organization potentially can do. If the people in the organization cannot work well together, if they lack initiative, connection, or any of the other emotional competencies, the collective intelligence suffers as a result.

This need for smooth coordination of widely distributed knowledge and technical expertise has led some corporations to create a new role: that of "chief learning officer," or CLO, whose job it is to direct knowledge and information within an organization. But it's all too easy to reduce an organization's "intelligence" to its databases and technical expertise. Despite the ever greater reliance on information technology in organizations, it's put to use by *people*. Organizations that have such learning officers might do well to expand the CLO's (or *someone's*) duties to include maximizing the collective emotional intelligence.

Emotionally Intelligent Organizations: The Business Case

- "We're a ten-billion-dollar-a-year telecommunications company, but our past leader was very autocratic; the group he left behind was like an abused family," a senior vice president confides in me. "Now we're trying to heal the organization, make it more emotionally intelligent—so we can grow another ten billion dollars."

- "We've just gone through wrenching changes, and there will be more of them ahead," a director of a European airline reports. "We have an immense need for trust from our employees, and empathy and understanding from our managers—for a greater sense of 'we.' What we need throughout the company is emotionally intelligent leadership."

- "Our company culture has its roots in engineering and manufacturing," a corporate director at a high-tech company observes. "We want to build an atmosphere of trust, openness, and teamwork that touches on people's ability to deal with emotions in a direct and honest way. But we find many of our managers are just not skilled in dealing with this emotional side. We need to make ourselves more emotionally intelligent."

The quest to make companies more emotionally intelligent is one more and more organizations are embarking on, whether they use the term or not. An organization's collective emotional intelligence is no mere soft assessment; it has hard consequences.

Mitchell Kapor, the founder and former CEO of Lotus Development Corporation, now an investor in high-tech start-ups, told me that before his group puts its money into any company, they try to determine the company's level of emotional intelligence.

"We want to know if anyone is angry or resentful toward the company, if they harbor a grudge against it," Kapor said. "Companies have styles, like people. If they've been arrogant or duplicitous to their vendors, employees, or customers, those karmic debts can come back to haunt them. The more people they've angered while starting up, the more likely they are to be sued once they become successful."

Perhaps the strongest argument for the economic advantage of emotional intelligence in organizations can be read in data generated by Jac Fitz-Enz at the Saratoga Institute, in a project sponsored by the Society for Human Resource Management. Since 1986 the institute has collected data from nearly six hundred companies in more than twenty industries, detailing policies and practices. They analyzed top companies, selected for profitability, cycle times, volume, and other similar indices of performance.[5]

Searching for what these outstanding companies held in common, the institute identified the following basic practices in managing "human assets"—their people:[6]

- A balance between the human and financial sides of the company's agenda

- Organizational commitment to a basic strategy

- Initiative to stimulate improvements in performance

- Open communication and trust-building with all stakeholders

- Building relationships inside and outside that offer competitive advantage

- Collaboration, support, and sharing resources

- Innovation, risk taking, and learning together

- A passion for competition and continual improvement

This list is intriguing because of the clear similarities between these organizational practices and the emotional competencies that typify top-performing individuals. The last, for example, describes a motivational competence, the achievement drive, described at the personal level in Chapter 6. Likewise with innovativeness, comfort with risk, collaboration, building relationships, open communication, trustworthiness, initiative, commitment— we've seen in earlier chapters how each of these emotional competencies is an ingredient of star performance in individuals.

But here these same capabilities have ended up on a list generated by observing top-performing *companies,* not individuals.[7] Just as with individuals, organizational competencies can be thought of as falling into three domains: cognitive abilities, in the sense of managing knowledge well; technical expertise; and managing human assets, which requires social and emotional competence.

But what does an emotionally intelligent organization look like? Consider the case of Egon Zehnder International, a global executive search firm.[8]

A Global Team

Victor Loewenstein had a dilemma—a global dilemma. Asked by the World Bank to locate a candidate for a newly opened vice presidency, he was told to search the world for the right person. It had to be someone with sophisticated financial expertise, of course—and because the World Bank was trying to diversify, preferably not an American, a nationality over-represented in the bank's ranks. And Loewenstein, managing partner of the New York City office of Egon Zehnder International, was planted squarely in midtown Manhattan.

Undaunted, Loewenstein called into action the firm's worldwide offices. "I sent a memo to about twenty different offices in the countries most likely to have pools of people with the required high level of expertise in finance—mostly in Europe, but also in Hong Kong, Japan, Singapore, and Australia."

From these offices Loewenstein received twenty profiles of possible candidates; he asked that the eight he saw as most promising be interviewed by people in those offices to see if they indeed had the requisite technical competence. This eliminated two more.

"Beyond professional qualifications," says Loewenstein, "the person needed personal qualities and competencies that would mesh with the unique environment of the World Bank—and as the one who had dealt with the bank, only I could make that final determination." So with the field winnowed to six, Loewenstein himself crisscrossed the globe to visit the remaining candidates.

"The World Bank is a highly collegial environment," he observes. "You need to be able to work in a team, make decisions by consensus, cooperate; you can't be a prima donna. One candidate, for instance, was an investment banker; he was aggressively ambitious for center stage—it just wasn't appropriate in such a collegial organization, so he was out."

The ultimate choice, from the Netherlands, was a senior partner of a major auditing firm—one of two candidates Loewenstein felt had the right mix of expertise and personal chemistry to be a winning fit with the organization. Had he been on his own, Loewenstein might well have never found him—but by calling on his worldwide web of connections, the search was a success.

The story typifies the operations of Egon Zehnder International, which has knit its far-flung partners into a single global working team, fluidly sharing contacts and leads. When a Japanese auto manufacturer wanted a car stylist from Europe, Egon Zehnder International's offices in the United

Kingdom, France, Germany, and Italy scoured the auto industries in those countries, with the Tokyo office coordinating the search. When a global firm with a European base asked Egon Zehnder International to find a new head of human resources, the most promising candidate was identified by someone from the New York office who was on assignment in Asia. So the candidate was interviewed by the Hong Kong office, and was finally presented to the client by the firm's London office.

One for All: The Economics of Collaboration

Such seamless collaboration is a watchword at Egon Zehnder International. Perhaps the key reason the firm can operate so smoothly as a worldwide collaborative team lies in an innovation made early on in its history: It treats the global firm as a single team, with everyone paid on the basis of overall performance. The hundred or so partners share a pool of profits distributed according to a uniform formula. A person's share is calculated the same way whether their contribution to the firm's earnings that year was great or little. The entire firm operates as a single profit center.

Most search firms tie compensation to a mix of firmwide, office, and individual performance; stars usually earn a direct percentage of the fees they generate. But this is not the case at Egon Zehnder International. Says CEO Daniel Meiland, "The strength of our firm is that we do not have a 'star' concept."

From this equality in earnings and power stems an all-for-one, one-for-all spirit. This stands in contrast to the industry as a whole, where "headhunters" live up to their nickname by operating on a bounty system, with the successful recruiter receiving a proportion of the salary of the post filled.

As one executive at another search firm put it to me, "I hoard my information and contacts, because I get compensated on the basis of my listings. If I find a hot candidate in the course of a search for one position, I tuck that name away to keep it for myself for another search instead of sharing it with a colleague. I don't even know if I'll be working with the same company in another year—why should I give away my resources?"

At Egon Zehnder International, people of thirty-nine different nationalities and eight religions in forty-eight offices spread across thirty-nine countries operate as a single unit. "The fundamental difference between our firm and others is that we find ourselves all on the same ship," says Loewenstein. "We don't have differing agendas or vested interests to pull business our way. Instead, the more we collaborate, the more efficient we are—and the sooner we can get on with the next assignment."

The compensation model was a radical departure for its industry when Egon Zehnder instituted it. And even now, only a handful of competitors have begun to imitate it. Also, the firm is owned equally and entirely by its partners (consultants typically are elevated to partnership after about six years). Even Zehnder himself, who at one time owned the firm entirely, now holds just one share, like every other partner.

"I understood that if I did that, I could retain the best partners," Zehnder tells me. "It made us all entrepreneurs together.

"How do we work so well together? Because we've decoupled individual performance from money," Zehnder says. "No one is being evaluated by how big a billing volume they have. So a partner in Germany taking the time to help a partner in Tokyo with a search counts as much as getting a new client. Nobody cares who gets the credit for a success, because there's a single profit center that everyone shares in equally. An office that loses money gets as much as the office that made the most."

"We work in networks, sharing our expertise and trust," says Claudio Fernández-Aráoz, of the Buenos Aires office. "From Argentina I'm happy to share anything with my colleagues anywhere in the world, and I know they would help me in the same way, because our earnings depend on the total profits of the firm."

The company's egalitarian payment scheme reflects an insight Zehnder had about the nature of teamwork. "I realized that people who didn't make placements but did other things, like trying to get a new client or running the Harvard alumni association of Germany, were worth as much as the one who happens to be lucky in placing someone. I don't want stars—I want everyone to help everyone else be a star."

A Need to Achieve

That team approach pays off; Egon Zehnder International's performance as a business is extraordinary. As an executive search firm that specializes in finding CEOs and others in the top tiers of the corporate ranks, it is the most profitable search firm per capita in the world. And as of 1997 Egon Zehnder International's profitability had increased each year for the last six in a row.

According to the Economist Intelligence Unit, in 1995 the average net revenue per consultant for the top twenty such firms worldwide was $577,000.[9] For Egon Zehnder International, however, the equivalent figure was $908,000—making the company about 60 percent more productive than the industry average for top firms. By 1997, despite having increased its staff of consultants 27 percent (it typically takes new consultants three to five years to become fully productive), the revenue had risen to more than $1 million per consultant.

Egon Zehnder International's service is of tremendous importance to companies. Apart from the costs of replacing top executives who fail (a minimum of $500,000 for a top executive search is one standard estimate), the real value has to do with the impact, for better or worse, of these executives on an organization's performance.

As we saw in Chapter 3, the higher the levels of a job's complexity and authority, the greater the impact of outstanding performance on the bottom line. The implication for selection is clear: The higher the level of job, the more it pays to put great care into searching for the right person for the position. "Time after time we see cases where a company's poor performance is a reason to come to us to look for a new CEO," Claudio Fernández-Aráoz tells me. "Once he or she takes charge, if the search was properly conducted, results typically change dramatically."

The changes are not just in improved profitability, but also in "hard" areas like productivity, increased sales, and lowered costs, as well as in "soft" areas like increased morale and motivation, greater cooperation, and lower turnover and loss of talent. In short, as he puts it, "top managers can add or destroy huge economic value, and the higher the level, the higher the leverage—so the stronger the impact."

Building with Integrity

Zehnder himself was instrumental in introducing the executive search industry to Europe, where his company is still the leading executive search firm. In the 1950s, shortly after he finished his MBA at Harvard, Zehnder joined the American search firm Spencer Stuart, setting up offices for them first in Zurich, then London, Frankfurt, and Paris.

Integrity is a hallmark of the firm's culture, a value reflected, for instance, in the change Zehnder made in how he charged clients after he left Spencer Stuart to start his own firm in 1964.

"I didn't like the system where you were paid a percentage of the current salary of the person you were searching for, and only got paid if you found someone the client hired," Zehnder explains. "That created a pressure to only 'find' people who would demand the highest salary, whether or not they happened to be the most qualified, so you'd get the biggest fee."

Zehnder restructured compensation to make sure a candidate's fitness for the job was the only criterion. From the beginning Egon Zehnder International has charged clients only a flat fee calculated up front on the basis of the complexity of the search.

Zehnder's fixed fees free its consultants to search for the most qualified candidate rather than the highest-paid one. Their fees also mean that, at times, they "leave money on the table," getting less than the client would ordinarily pay for a given search done by another firm. For CEO Daniel Meiland, that loss of revenue pays back in client trust. As he puts it, "Clients pay based on their trust in the consultant and the firm. But as a professional firm, we must be consistent. We can't have one policy for setting fees seventy percent of the time and another policy the rest of the time."

It also pays back in repeat business and long-term ties with clients. Lee Pomeroy, of the New York office, describes a search for director of research at a large American bank. The search was relatively simple, so the fee was $110,000. But the first-year salary for the position was over a million dollars—and so would have commanded a fee of over $330,000 from another firm.

Pomeroy commented, "While the fee was low compared with what we could have charged if we had gone by industry standards, we started getting more business from this bank and we charged fees of a hundred and fifty thousand dollars each for the next two searches, which were international and a bit more complex in nature."

The firm balances its quest for profit with contributions to society. Partners are encouraged to do pro bono searches for charitable groups, hospitals, universities, and governments. "Monetary reward cannot be the sole incentive or objective of the firm," Victor Loewenstein comments. As of this writing the New York office is undertaking the pro bono initiative of finding high-caliber minority candidates for its longtime customers.

There is an indirect payoff from such pro bono activities. In the course of such work, the firm's consultants are "helping in ways that demonstrate their personal competence as well as dedication to serve others," Egon Zehnder points out. "Nothing is more important for attracting new clients than to see top talent like ours contributing unselfishly."

That speaks to Egon Zehnder International's tactic for growing its business through a naturally expanding web of relationships. In ordinary terms, the business seems to lack a marketing strategy; the firm never advertises, and partners are often reluctant to be quoted in the popular press. But in lieu of standard promotional efforts, the partners and consultants build networks of contacts through their day-to-day business, as well as through work in their communities. The company's people are networkers par excellence.

The Cardinal Sin

Loyalty marks the relationship between Egon Zehnder International's people and the firm itself. The company has yet to close an office where earnings lag. In the early 1990s, for example, some smaller offices were underperforming, but the company kept them going as part of its general policy of not laying people off—a stark contrast to the rest of the industry, where layoffs in hard times are routine.

As Meiland puts it, "Other search firms drop lots of consultants when the market sinks. They come to our people and ask them to leave, but we don't ever recruit from them. We don't buy Rolodexes. So how do we keep our people? People here say, 'This is the nicest firm I could be with. I have a good feeling here.' It's safe here and people know it."

With security comes obligation. There is, of course, a danger in the combination of what amounts to job tenure and a compensation system that rewards everyone regardless of their specific efforts. That's why loafing is a cardinal sin. As Zehnder tells me, "The system only works if all of us give our all. The crime is freeloading, not lack of success if you're working hard."

In such a close-knit group, "peer pressure and embarrassment," in the words of one partner, offer a major prod for people who fail to do their share of the work. When people seem to be loafing, they are given a warning. "I can tell someone, 'You aren't showing commitment in the hours you're putting in, the number of clients you talk to,' " Meiland says.

If there is still no improvement, people are put on a kind of probation by having their pay rate docked. For a ten-year veteran, their share for the year might be brought down to that of a five-year veteran, pending improvement. If there is no improvement that year, then it might be lowered again to the level of a three-year partner. But it very rarely comes to this, because of what partners describe as an intense loyalty and sense of obligation to each other and to their shared enterprise.

Because people join the firm to stay, there is a palpable sense of the company as a family. As one partner put it, "We know that we will be working together for many years, and therefore we are prepared to invest time and effort into building relationships."

Relationship building is a focus at the twice-yearly meetings, where all partners and consultants gather, and in which newly hired consultants are introduced to the firm. That meeting begins with a ritual: a slide show of the life of each fledgling consultant, with photos and stories from their infancy onward. "This gives us all a start at getting to know them," explains Fernández-Aráoz. "That's crucially important—our people are our only asset."

All this builds emotional bonds. "The best billers don't leave us," says Zehnder. "They stay because they love the culture. It's like a family. We understand the difficulties partners have in their lives—the crises in their families, illnesses, worries about children."

When a consultant in the New York office took a maternity leave, several colleagues volunteered to take on and complete the assignments she had not yet brought to a close, "helping out a colleague and a friend," as one of them put it. When Victor Loewenstein had a serious illness requiring an emergency operation, the whole firm got daily updates on his condition. And when a newly hired consultant in Canada was diagnosed with cancer during his first physical before joining the firm, he was hired anyway and kept on the payroll during the three years he battled the disease, until his death.

"We all feel a high level of personal concern for each other," Fernández-Aráoz tells me. That concern applies, too, to the balance between work and the rest of life. While the firm performs at the top of its industry, its culture discourages out-and-out workaholics, whose relentless hours destroy any hope of a sane family life.

"Twenty or thirty years ago people were willing to give up everything—family, marriage, private time—for their company's success," Zehnder recounts. "Now if someone says they're willing to pay everything for success, that's the wrong answer."

The familylike tone of the company stems in part from the democratization of power. As one partner puts it, "What we do at the top is what we do at the bottom." That is, no matter how long a person has been there, or what their title may be, everyone does more or less the same work. This sharing of work "cements relationships vertically in a very strong way, while the stability and reward structure cements relationships horizontally," as Philip Vivian, of the London office, puts it. The company chart is more web than hierarchy.

When Help Is Wanted

The operating style of Egon Zehnder International requires an extraordinary level of collaboration and cooperation, open communication, a knack for leveraging diversity, and a talent for teamwork. Its strategy for growth relies on its ability to network and develop relationships, and its collective drive to improve performance.

The firm's egalitarian approach to salary works only if everyone acts with both integrity and conscientiousness. Its very business, finding just the right person for a company, demands skill at empathy, intuitive accuracy, and organizational awareness. And nurturing long-term relations with clients demands a continued orientation to their needs. Small wonder Daniel Meiland tells me, "In what we do, emotional intelligence is essential."

How does the explicit focus on emotional intelligence look in operation? Consider how the firm goes about hiring people. Its business centers on gauging the chemistry between an organization and a prospective consultant. And the care they put into assessing prospective employees offers an exemplar for taking emotional intelligence into account in hiring.

While search firms typically put a premium on recruiting people from other search firms who can bring in business from the start, for Egon Zehnder International this is irrelevant: They never recruit people who have worked for search firms. "When we recruit a new consultant, our principal criteria are their personal qualities, rather than their ability to generate revenue on day one," a consultant said.

Prerequisites start with intellect and expertise. As with any job involving such a high level of cognitive complexity, IQ matters. And everyone hired has a prior record of success in another industry and *two* advanced degrees (mostly MBAs and law degrees from top schools, though about 25 percent have Ph.D.s). No one lacking this level of qualification need apply—but this high hurdle for intellect and experience merely gets people into the candidate pool.

A Human Radar

Typically a prospective consultant is interviewed by twenty, and sometimes as many as forty, of the firm's one hundred or so partners, in up to five different countries. Zehnder himself meets with around 150 prospects a year. He has no special veto power, but says that once or twice he has vigorously objected to what otherwise seemed strong candidates after he met them.

"We need a radar in this business, but that only develops with experience," Zehnder observes. "Our people need to be diligent in doing their research and homework, but the intuition develops the more they evaluate candidates."

Each partner who meets with prospective consultants evaluates them on four major dimensions. The first is purely cognitive—abilities like problem solving, logical reasoning, and analytic capability. But the other three reflect emotional intelligence. These include:

- *Building working relationships:* Being a team player; having self-confidence, presence, and style; being empathic and a good listener; having the ability to sell an idea; maturity and integrity

- *Getting things done:* Being a self-starter, with drive, energy, and a sense of urgency that gets results; showing judgment and common sense; being independent, entrepreneurial, and imaginative; having leadership potential

- *Personal fit:* Having the qualities of a friend, colleague, and partner; being honest and adhering to one's values; being motivated; being sociable, with "sparkle" and a sense of humor; modesty; having a full personal life and outside interests; understanding the firm and its values

The bar here is high, for good reason. "It's like joining a family," says Fernández-Aráoz. "We have to think in the long term. We don't want someone hiring just anybody because there's a heavy workload in their office and they need help—we want people who could someday become partners."

Egon Zehnder is more blunt: "We only have places in our ranks for zealous family members." That is not hollow rhetoric; the record suggests that about 90 percent of those hired as consultants go on to become partners. The number of those who leave is around 3 percent, compared to about 30 percent for the rest of the industry—a field in which anyone with a Rolodex thick enough can quit to start their own company.

Says Zehnder, "I meet with every single consultant for a two-hour talk before they are hired. I want to see what's important to them. Do they go to the opera? What kind of books do they read? What are their values? Are they too willing to give in, not able to stand up for their values?"

There's a personal motive beyond this business objective. Zehnder is candid: "I want to have fun doing my work. I want the kind of people I can sit over dinner with on a weekend. In my profession you need to be able to trust your people. I want the kind of people I like in my heart—people who I can still like when I'm exhausted at three A.M."

Some Final Thoughts

An organization is like an organism, with a moment of birth, growth through several distinct stages of development, maturation, and finally an end. Companies have life spans; if the past is prologue to the future, forty years from now up to two thirds of Fortune 500 companies will no longer exist.[1]

The adept ones likely will survive. And the ingredients of an effective organization, as we have seen, include a healthy dose of emotional intelligence.

Of course, there are numerous pathogens that can prove fatal to a company: seismic shifts in markets, myopic strategic vision, hostile takeovers, unforeseen competitive technologies, and the like. But a failure in emotional intelligence can be crucial in rendering a company vulnerable to the others—the corporate equivalent of a weakened immune system.

By the same token, emotional intelligence can be an inoculation that preserves health and encourages growth. If a company has the competencies that flow from self-awareness and self-regulation, motivation and empathy, leadership skills and open communication, it should prove more resilient no matter what the future brings.

And that, in turn, places a premium on people who themselves are emotionally intelligent.

Old ways of doing business no longer work; the increasingly intense competitive challenges of the world economy challenge everyone, everywhere, to adapt in order to prosper under new rules. In the old economy, hierarchies pitted labor against management, with workers paid wages depending on their skills, but that is eroding as the rate of change accelerates. Hierarchies are morphing into networks; labor and management are uniting into teams; wages are coming in new mixtures of options, incentives, and ownership; fixed job skills are giving way to lifelong learning as fixed jobs melt into fluid careers.

As business changes, so do the traits needed to survive, let alone excel. All these transitions put increased value on emotional intelligence. The ratcheting upward of competitive pressures puts a new value on people who are self-motivated, show initiative, have the inner drive for outdoing themselves, and are optimistic enough to take reversals and setbacks in stride. The ever-pressing need to serve customers and clients well and to work smoothly and creatively with an ever more diverse range of people makes empathic capabilities all the more essential.

At the same time, the meltdown of old organizational forms from a hierarchical wiring diagram into the mandala of a web, along with the ascendance of teamwork, increases the importance of traditional people skills such as building bonds, influence, and collaboration.

Then there is the challenge of leadership supply: The capabilities needed for leaders in the next century will differ radically from those valued today. Competencies like change catalyst, adaptability, leveraging diversity, and team capabilities weren't on the radar a decade ago. Now they matter more each day.

Our Children and the Future of Work

How can we best educate young people for the new world of work? For our children, this includes an education in emotional literacy; for those already at work, it means cultivating our emotional competence. All this, of course, demands rethinking the notion of the "basics" in education: Emotional intelligence is now as crucial to our children's future as the standard academic fare.

Parents around the world are waking up to the need for a broader preparation for life than the traditional school curriculum has offered. The Collaborative for Social and Emotional Learning at the University of Illinois at Chicago reports that more than 150 different emotional literacy programs are being used today by thousands of American schools. And from all parts of the world—Asia, Europe, the Middle East, the Americas, Australia—comes news of similar programs springing up.

Perhaps the most visionary approach can be seen in pioneering coalitions among local governments, schools, and businesses aimed at boosting the collective level of emotional intelligence in the community. The State of Rhode Island, for example, has begun an initiative to boost emotional intelligence in sites as varied as schools, prisons, hospitals, mental health clinics, and job retraining programs.

Farsighted companies are realizing that they, too, have a stake in how well the schools are educating their future workers. I can envision coalitions of companies encouraging emotional literacy programs as both a goodwill gesture and as a practical investment. If schools fail to help students master these human fundamentals, then companies will have to do it remedially when those students become employees. Such a concerted focus on helping schools teach these capabilities can help improve both the civility of life in our communities and their economic prosperity.

Tomorrow's Company:
The Virtual Organization

The premium on emotional intelligence can only rise as organizations become increasingly dependent on the talents and creativity of workers who are independent agents. Even now 77 percent of American "knowledge workers" say they decide what to do on the job, rather than being told by someone else.[2]

The rising popularity of telecommuting is accelerating this trend. Autonomy can work only if it goes hand in hand with self-control, trustworthiness, and conscientiousness. And as people work less "for the company" and more for themselves, emotional intelligence will be required to maintain the relationships vital for workers' survival.

Such free agents suggest a future for work somewhat akin to the functioning of the immune system, where roaming cells spot a pressing need, spontaneously collect into a tightly knit, highly coordinated working group to meet that need, and dissipate into free agency once again as the job finishes. In an organizational context, such groups, each with a specialized mix of talent and expertise, may arise within and across organizational boundaries as demands require, then cease to exist once their task is accomplished.

That mode already typifies the entertainment industry, where a pseudo-organization coalesces for the duration of a project, then disbands. This, many suggest, will be a standard mode for work in the future.

Such virtual teams can be especially agile because they are headed by whoever has the requisite skills, rather than by someone who happens to have the title "manager." Ad hoc project groups and task forces are proliferating within many organizations; other companies are creating the latent capacity for such groups by linking people together to chat and to share information and ideas.

The question for us all is whether the new world of work will become increasingly grim, with relentless job pressures and apprehensions robbing us of both a sense of security and a place in our lives for even the simple pleasures—or whether, even in the face of this new reality, we can find ways to work that excite, fulfill, and nurture us.

The Bottom Line

The good news is that emotional intelligence can be learned. Individually, we can add these skills to our tool kit for survival at a time when "job stability" seems like a quaint oxymoron.

For businesses of all kinds, the fact that emotional competencies can be assessed and improved suggests another area in which performance—and so competitiveness—can be upgraded. What's needed amounts to an emotional competence tune-up for the corporation.

At the individual level, elements of emotional intelligence can be identified, assessed, and upgraded. At the group level, it means fine-tuning the interpersonal dynamics that make groups smarter. At the organizational level, it means revising the value hierarchy to make emotional intelligence a priority—in the concrete terms of hiring, training and development, performance evaluation, and promotions.

To be sure, emotional intelligence is no magic bullet, no guarantee of more market share or a healthier bottom line. The ecology of a corporation is extraordinarily fluid and complex, and no single intervention or change can fix every problem. But, as the saying goes, "It's all done with people," and if the human ingredient is ignored, then nothing else will work as well as it might. In the years to come, companies in which people collaborate best will have a competitive edge, and so to that extent emotional intelligence will be more vital.

But apart from the emotional intelligence of the organizations we work for, having these capabilities offers each of us a way to survive with our humanity and sanity intact, no matter where we work. And as work changes, these human capacities can help us not just compete, but also nurture the capacity for pleasure, even joy, in our work.

Appendix 1

·····································

Emotional Intelligence

"Emotional intelligence" refers to *the capacity for recognizing our own feelings and those of others, for motivating ourselves, and for managing emotions well in ourselves and in our relationships.* It describes abilities distinct from, but complementary to, academic intelligence, the purely cognitive capacities measured by IQ. Many people who are book smart but lack emotional intelligence end up working for people who have lower IQs than they but who excel in emotional intelligence skills.

These two different kinds of intelligence—intellectual and emotional—express the activity of different parts of the brain. The intellect is based solely on the workings of the neocortex, the more recently evolved layers at the top of the brain. The emotional centers are lower in the brain, in the more ancient subcortex; emotional intelligence involves these emotional centers at work, in concert with the intellectual centers.

Among the most influential theorists of intelligence to point out the distinction between intellectual and emotional capacities was Howard Gardner, a Harvard psychologist, who in 1983 proposed a widely regarded model of "multiple intelligence."[1] His list of seven kinds of intelligence included not just the familiar verbal and math abilities, but also two "personal" varieties: knowing one's inner world and social adeptness.

A comprehensive theory of emotional intelligence was proposed in 1990 by two psychologists, Peter Salovey, at Yale, and John Mayer, now at the University of New Hampshire.[2] Another pioneering model of emotional intelligence was proposed in the 1980s by Reuven Bar-On, an Israeli psychologist.[3] And in recent years several other theorists have proposed variations on the same idea.

Salovey and Mayer defined emotional intelligence in terms of being able to monitor and regulate one's own and others' feelings, and to use feelings to guide thought and action. While they have continued to fine-tune the theory, I have adapted their model into a version I find most useful for understanding how these talents matter in work life. My adaptation includes these five basic emotional and social competencies:

- *Self-awareness:* Knowing what we are feeling in the moment, and using those preferences to guide our decision making; having a realistic assessment of our own abilities and a well-grounded sense of self-confidence

- *Self-regulation:* Handling our emotions so that they facilitate rather than interfere with the task at hand; being conscientious and delaying gratification to pursue goals; recovering well from emotional distress

- *Motivation:* Using our deepest preferences to move and guide us toward our goals, to help us take initiative and strive to improve, and to persevere in the face of setbacks and frustrations

- *Empathy:* Sensing what people are feeling, being able to take their perspective, and cultivating rapport and attunement with a broad diversity of people

- *Social skills:* Handling emotions in relationships well and accurately reading social situations and networks; interacting smoothly; using these skills to persuade and lead, negotiate and settle disputes, for cooperation and teamwork

Appendix 2

Calculating the Competencies of Stars

There are two levels of job competence, and so two kinds of job competence models. One assesses the *threshold* competencies, those that people need in order to get the job done. These are the minimal skills needed to carry out the tasks associated with a given position. Most organizational competence models I've seen fit into this category.

The other kind of job competence model describes *distinguishing* competencies, the capabilities that set star performers apart from average ones. These are the competencies people already in a job need in order to perform superbly.

For example, anyone in information technology needs a high level of technical expertise simply to do their job at all; such expertise is a threshold competence. But the two competencies that carry most weight in making someone outstanding in that field are the drive to improve and skill at persuasion and influence—and these are emotional competencies.

Lists of competencies in themselves do not tell exactly how much each of these ingredients contributes to outstanding performance, though they are good general indicators. The absolute best data comes from competence studies that analyze the *relative weight* each competence carries in distinguishing the stars from the average. That's because a single cognitive competence, say, might turn out to be three times as important as a given single emotional competence—or vice versa—in contributing to star performance.

To get a more precise understanding of the contribution of emotional competence to excellence, I turned to Ruth Jacobs and Wei Chen, researchers at Hay/McBer in Boston. They reanalyzed their own raw data from competence studies at forty companies to assess the relative weight of a given competence in setting star performers apart from average performers.

The results: Greater strengths in purely cognitive capacities were 27 percent more frequent in the stars than in average performers, while greater strengths in emotional competencies were 53 percent more frequent. In other words, emotional competencies were *twice* as important in contributing to excellence as were pure intellect and expertise.

That estimate fits my own finding (reported in Chapter 2), and I feel comfortable with that number as a conservative rule of thumb for the general value of emotional competence in star performance.

These findings on the importance of emotional competence fit a general pattern revealed in other empirical studies of on-the-job excellence. The data come from a multitude of sources. All suggest that, in general, emotional competencies play a far larger role in superior job performance than do cognitive abilities and technical expertise.

For example, a classic study of more than two thousand supervisors, middle managers, and executives at twelve different organizations was done by Richard Boyatzis, of the Weatherhead School of Management at Case Western Reserve University.[1] Of the sixteen abilities that distinguished stars from average performers, all but two were emotional competencies.

Those results were duplicated in a larger analysis of the distinctive qualities of star performers done by Lyle Spencer Jr., director of research and technology worldwide at Hay/McBer. Spencer's analysis includes competence studies at 286 organizations, two thirds in the United States, one third in twenty other countries. Jobs for which the competencies of star performers were analyzed included managerial positions, from supervisor to CEO; sales and marketing staff; scientific and technical professions; health care, government, and education—even religious organizations.

Of twenty-one generic competencies Spencer identified, all but three were based on emotional intelligence. Of the other three purely cognitive competencies, two were intellectual: analytic skills and conceptual thinking. The third was technical expertise. In other words, the vast majority—more than 80 percent—of general competencies that set apart superior from average performers depend on emotional intelligence, not on purely cognitive ability.

Marilyn Gowing, director of the personnel resources and development center for the U.S. Office of Personnel Management, oversaw a thorough analysis of the competencies deemed to set superior performers apart from barely adequate ones for virtually all federal jobs. Analyzing that data at my request, Robert Buchele, a labor economist at Smith College, calculated the ratio of technical competence to interpersonal skills that distinguished outstanding performers for jobs from lowest to highest levels.

For lower level positions (like purchasing clerks and clerical assistants), there was a higher premium on technical abilities than on interpersonal ones. But at higher levels (professional or managerial positions), the interpersonal abilities mattered more than technical skills in setting star performers apart. And for these upper level occupations, the more people advanced in their position, the more important became the interpersonal skills (but not the technical ones) in distinguishing superior from average performance.

At my request, another study of emotional competence in leadership was done at Hay/McBer in Boston by Lyle Spencer Jr. with Wei Chen. Their analysis of more than three hundred top-level executives from fifteen global companies showed that six emotional competencies distinguished stars from the average: influence, team leadership, organizational awareness, self-confidence, the drive to achieve, and leadership itself.

As was found with David McClelland's analysis of star performers at the highest executive levels (described in Chapter 3), these competencies represent strengths in a wide spectrum of emotional intelligence, from self-awareness and motivation to social awareness and social skill. The only emotional intelligence capability not represented was self-regulation—but adaptability, from this cluster, was 57 percent more common in stars (and, in other samples, has emerged as one of the distinguishing competencies, too).

While neither technical expertise nor intellectual ability distinguished stars from average leaders, one set of cognitive abilities— pattern recognition and "big-picture" thinking—was 13 percent greater among the stars. But deductive, if-then reasoning abilities were not strongly represented among the best leaders— they displayed it in their work 12 percent *less* than did average leaders. In other samples, big-picture thinking has also emerged as significant, as some researchers have noted.[2]

Appendix 3

....

Gender and Empathy

Women generally have had more practice at some interpersonal skills than men, at least in cultures like the United States, where girls are raised to be more attuned to feelings and their nuances than are boys. So does this mean women are more empathic than men?

Often—but not inevitably. The popular assumption that women are naturally more attuned than men to the feelings of others has a scientific basis—but there are two notable exceptions of particular significance for the workplace. For one, there is no sex difference in cases where people are trying to conceal their true feelings, nor is there one when the challenge is to sense the unstated thoughts of someone in an ongoing encounter.

A caveat about sex differences in general: Whenever large groups like men and women are compared on *any* psychological dimension, there are far more similarities between the groups than differences; the bell curves for the two groups have immense overlap, and an edge where they differ. This means, for example, that while on average women may be better than men at some emotional skills, some men will still be better than most women, despite there being a statistically significant difference between the groups.

Now, the data on empathy. The results from dozens and dozens of studies on the question are both mixed and clarifying.[1] For one, whether women do better than men depends on what is meant by "empathy." There is one sense in which women—at least in Western cultures—*are,* on average, more empathic: having the same feeling another person does—that is, when one person feels distress or delight, so does the other. The data shows women *do* tend to experience this spontaneous matching of feeling with others more than do men.[2]

Women are also better than men at *detecting* another person's fleeting feelings, as was shown in a test called the Profile of Nonverbal Sensitivity (PONS), which was developed by one of my professors at Harvard, Robert Rosenthal, with Judith Hall, now at Northeastern University. The test consists of dozens of short video clips in which someone is having an emotional reaction (having been told, for example, they just won a lottery, or that a beloved pet has just died). The clips are filtered, so that the words cannot be heard distinctly, though the facial expression and the tone of voice are clear. Through hundreds of studies, Rosenthal and Hall found that 80 percent of the time women performed better on average than men at the task of guessing what emotion the person was actually feeling.[3]

However, the gender gap in reading emotions closed when the clips included emotional cues that are less easy to control than facial expression. People are better at controlling their overall facial expression than their tone of voice, body language, or fleeting "microemotions" that flit across the face for just a split second. The more emotional leakage, the better men become at reading emotion in others. Being able to pick up such emotional leakage is particularly important in situations where people have reason to conceal their true feelings—a fact of life in the business arena. And so sex differences in empathy tend to disappear in many everyday business situations, like sales or negotiation, where most people simply cannot control all the body's channels for expressing emotion.

And when it comes to another dimension of empathy—being able to sense someone's specific thoughts—there appears to be no sex difference at all. This more complicated task, called *empathic accuracy,* integrates cognitive and affective skills. The experimental methods used to assess empathic accuracy go beyond showing a snippet of an emotional response and asking people to guess the emotion; rather, subjects watch an entire videotape of a conversation and evaluate a person's hidden thoughts—as well as feelings—throughout. Those guesses are then compared with the target person's own narrative. On this task women generally did no better than men in a series of seven different experiments—there was no evidence of a "female intuition" advantage.[4] The significant exception was in a special subset of tests in which women were subtly prompted to prove themselves empathic by the researcher's suggestion that empathy is a hallmark of feminine identity. With that prompt, the female advantage in empathy emerged once again. In other words, the motivation to *seem* empathic made women more so (presumably because they made more effort).[5]

Indeed, a major review of data on male-female sex differences argues that men have as much latent ability for empathy, but less motivation to be empathic, than do women. To the extent men tend to see themselves in terms of something like machismo, the argument goes, they have less motivation to seem sensitive, because that could be seen as a sign of "weakness."[6] As William Ickes, one of the main researchers on empathy, puts it, "If men appear at times to be socially insensitive, it may have more to do with the image they wish to convey than with the empathic ability they possess."[7]

Appendix 4

....

Strategies for Leveraging Diversity

There has been a backlash from some earlier well-intended diversification initiatives that put minority workers in high positions only to see them fail—in no small part, no doubt, victims of stereotype threat, as we saw in Chapter 7. But several approaches can help.

Claude Steele, the Stanford psychologist who studied the power of stereotype threat, offers some. From his understanding of the emotional dynamics that undermine performance in minority group members, Steele created a program of "wise strategies" that change those dynamics for the better. Results have been heartening—for example, black students at the University of Michigan who went through his ten-week program did far better in their freshman year than did comparable black students.[1] Here are some aspects of Steele's program that match strategies used by companies to make the workplace congenial for people of all kinds:

- *Optimistic leaders:* Mentors or supervisors affirm the ability of people who might otherwise suffer the stigma of threatening stereotypes.

- *Genuine challenges:* Challenging work conveys respect for the person's potential and demonstrates he or she is not seen through the lens of a debilitating stereotype. These challenges are calibrated to the person's skill and offer a manageable "stretch," not an overly daunting demand that is a setup for failure nor a too easy assignment that reinforces the worst fears of the stereotyped: that they are seen as unable to do the work.

- *Emphasis on learning:* Emphasis is placed on the idea that expertise and ability grow through on-the-job learning and that competence increases incrementally. This challenges the cruelest stereotype, that a person's inherent capacity is limited by virtue of their belonging to a certain group.

- *Affirming the sense of belonging:* Negative stereotypes create a sense of "I don't really belong here," casting doubt on one's suitability for a job. The affirmation of belonging, though, must be based on a person's true capabilities for the job.

- *Valuing multiple perspectives:* A variety of contributions are explicitly valued in the organizational culture. This tells those threatened by stereotypes that this is an organization where such stereotypes are not allowed.

- *Role models:* People from the person's own group who have been successful in this kind of job carry the implicit message that the threatening stereotype is not a barrier here.

- *Building self-confidence through Socratic feedback:* Instead of judgmental responses to performance, an ongoing dialogue helps direct the person, with minimal attention to whether they did well or poorly. This strengthens the mentor relationship while minimizing the emotional cost of early failures, a strategy that allows self-efficacy to build gradually along with successes large or small.

Appendix 5

·····································

Further Issues in Training

More On: Assessing Emotional Competence

No evaluation measure is perfect. Self-evaluations are vulnerable to skews from people wanting to look good. And when it comes to assessing emotional competence, there is the question of whether someone low in self-awareness can be trusted to accurately evaluate her own strengths and weaknesses. While self-evaluations can be helpful (and candid) if people trust that the results will be used for their own good, without this trust they can be less reliable.

Those who design self-evaluation tools usually build in a "lie scale," a series of questions that catch people who are trying to look "too good to be true"—for example, by agreeing with the statement "I never tell a lie." But here's the catch: While lie scales can usually catch intentional deception, they may not detect a *self*-deception due to a lack of self-awareness that makes people poor observers of themselves.

"The usefulness of self-evaluations depends on the purpose," Susan Ennis, head of executive development at Bank Boston, tells me. "One key question is, 'What's the company's role, and how will the data be stored and used?' The wish to look desirable is bound to influence people's answers. You want to look good."

Says Ennis, "When a self-evaluation is purely between you and your coach, confidential, not seen or kept by your company, then you'll be more candid, or as candid as you can be, given whatever other limit you may have on self-awareness."

On the other hand, evaluations by other people are susceptible to another set of skews. When office politics are involved, for example, 360-degree feedback may not always offer a pure reflection of the person being evaluated, since these evaluations can be used as weapons in office political wars or as a way for friends to exchange favors by giving inflated "grades" to each other.

Organizational politics can make it particularly difficult for executives in the topmost tiers to get candid evaluations, if only because the power they yield gets in the way—and, as we saw in Chapter 4, success itself can sometimes foster a narcissistic sense that one has no weak points. Executives tend to be insulated from evidence to the contrary partly because they are isolated, partly because subordinates fear offending them.

To some extent, any evaluation reflects the evaluator. For that reason, getting evaluations from multiple sources is a way to correct any distortions, since presumably one individual's emotional or political agenda would be balanced by other evaluations.

More On: Gauging Readiness

Extensive research (on more than thirty thousand people) by James Prochaska, a University of Rhode Island psychologist, establishes four levels of readiness people go through during a successful behavior change.

- *Oblivious:* As G. K. Chesterton, the British pundit, put it, "It isn't that they can't see the solution—they can't see the problem." People at this stage aren't ready at all; they deny they have any need to change in the first place. They resist any attempt to help them change—they just don't see the point.

- *Contemplation:* People at this stage see that they need to improve and have begun to think about how to do so. They are open to talking about it but not quite ready to pursue development wholeheartedly. Ambivalence is rampant; some wait for a "magic moment" of readiness, while others leap into action prematurely but meet failure because they are halfhearted. People at this stage are as likely to say they intend to take some action "next month" as they are to say they'll do it "in the next six months." Prochaska notes that it's not unusual for people "to spend years telling themselves that someday they are going to change." They substitute thinking for acting. Prochaska cites the case of an engineer who spent five years analyzing the factors that had made him passive and shy—but didn't think he understood the problem well enough to do anything about it.

- *Preparation:* Here people have begun to focus on the solution— on how to improve. They are on the verge, eager to develop an action plan. They are aware of the problem, see that there are ways to solve it, and palpably anticipate doing so. People are sometimes propelled to this heightened stage of readiness by a dramatic event—a heart-to-heart talk with a supervisor, a disaster on the job, a crisis in their personal life. One executive was jolted into bolstering his self-control competence when the police stopped him on the way home from a business dinner and arrested him for driving drunk. At this point people are ripe for change; this is the time for formulating a specific, detailed plan of action.

- *Action.* Visible change begins. People embrace the plan, start practicing its steps, and actually change how they act—their emotional patterns, the way they think about themselves, and all the other facets of transforming a long-standing habit. This stage is what most people think of as "making the change," though it builds on the earlier steps in getting ready.

More On: Practice

At the neurological level, cultivating a competence means extinguishing the old habit as the brain's automatic response and replacing it with the new one. The final stage of mastering a competence comes at the point when the old habit loses its status as the default response and the new one takes its place. At that point, the behavior change has stabilized, making a relapse to the old habit unlikely.

Generally, underlying deep attitudes and related values are harder to change than work habits. For example, an ethnic stereotype is less readily altered than is what a person says and does in the presence of someone from that group. Motives like the need for achievement and personality traits like affability can be upgraded or modified, but the process is lengthy.[1] So, too, with building underlying capacities like self-awareness, managing distressing emotions, empathy, and social skill.

Beyond the complexity of the competence being learned, the distance from the person's baseline behavior to the new matters immensely. For people who are already fairly empathic, learning to give performance feedback artfully or to attune themselves to customers' needs may come quite easily, since these competencies represent specific applications of a capability they already have. But for those who struggle to empathize, this mastery requires a more determined and lengthy effort.

Training programs that offer people a chance to practice the desired competence through well-focused simulations, games, role-playing, and other such methods can offer a strong beginning for practice. But with more complicated simulated job tasks, computerized business games, role-playing, team problem-solving exercises, and large-scale simulations of an entire organizational reality, the results tend to be mixed.

It is often unclear precisely what skills such simulations are meant to cultivate; there typically is little or no attention paid to exactly what competencies are being practiced. Moreover, merely taking part in a game or an exercise is not the same as learning. The overall recommendation for such simulations and games is that they be carefully planned, focus on specific competencies that are clearly described to participants, and end with a debriefing of the experience. They should also be used in conjunction with (rather than as a replacement for) coaching and feedback, reinforcement, and on-the-job practice.[2]

Computer-aided instruction, a current vogue in training, has limits when it comes to offering practice for emotional competence. While they have real promise in terms of individualized instruction, self-pacing, private opportunities for rehearsal and practice, immediate feedback on progress and remedial assistance, and the like, computer-aided techniques are generally better suited for training in technical skills than for developing personal and interpersonal capabilities.

"People say you can sit at your computer, assess yourself, and find out how to develop a competency," observes Richard Boyatzis, of Case Western Reserve University. "But you can't do this without relationships—you can't learn this in isolation."

Enthusiasm is high in many quarters for converting training to high-tech media like intelligent computer-based tutoring systems, virtual reality, interactive CD-ROMs, and so on. While these technologies may offer economies of cost by using machines instead of people as trainers, and more flexibility for the people who use them, there may be much of importance that gets lost if they are the only tool used. As one psychologist put it, "High-tech training media may have many virtues, but they tend to score rather low on emotional intelligence." To be sure, there may be a place for

such high-tech teaching aids in the overall design of an emotional competence training program (one example might be for individual practice sessions with video segments for feedback on empathic accuracy). Another
possibility might be on-line affinity groups, a kind of virtual support and
coaching group.

But an overemphasis on technology at the expense of essential human
contact—especially when it comes to practicing competencies—could be a
great mistake. One review of training trends observes wryly: "It is often the
mundane and low-technology factors of a training system that make the difference between a successful training program and wasted organizational resources"—and these low-tech factors are people with the essential
competencies of emotional intelligence.[3]

Notes

Chapter 1 / The New Yardstick

1. Daniel Goleman, *Emotional Intelligence* (New York: Bantam Books, 1995). See Appendix 1 for details on the nature of emotional intelligence.

2. Emotional intelligence in men and women: Reuven Bar-On, *Bar-On Emotional Quotient Inventory: Technical Manual* (Toronto: Multi-Health Systems, 1997).

3. No sex differences: Reuven Bar-On, a pioneer in assessing emotional intelligence and the researcher who did the study, tells me he finds the identical pattern of strengths and weaknesses for men and women worldwide—among the Igbu in Nigeria and Tamils in Sri Lanka, in Germany, Israel, America—everywhere he's looked. Bar-On's conclusions are based on studying the emotional intelligence of more than fifteen thousand people in a dozen countries on four continents.

4. Four out of five companies surveyed: ASTD Benchmarking Forum, Member-to-Member Survey results, American Society for Training and Development, Alexandria, Virginia, October 1997.

5. Job search by the employed: data from Challenger, Gray, and Christmas, reported in Bob Herbert, "Separation Anxiety," *New York Times,* January 19, 1996.

6. Krugman: quoted in Stephen Lohr, "On the Road with Chairman Lou," *New York Times,* June 26, 1994.

7. The rise in average IQ scores: Ulric Neisser (ed.), *The Rising Curve* (Washington, DC: American Psychological Press, 1997).

8. The decline in children's emotional intelligence: Thomas Achenbach and Catherine Howell, "Are America's Children's Problems Getting Worse? A 13-Year Comparison," *Journal of the American Academy of Child and Adolescent Psychiatry,* November 1989.

9. Survey of American employers: The Harris Education Research Council, "An Assessment of American Education," New York City, 1991.

10. What employers seek in entry-level hires: Anthony P. Carnevale et al., "Workplace Basics: The Skills Employers Want," U.S. Department of Labor Employment and Training Administration, 1989. By 1996, employers said the three most highly sought-after skills in new hires are oral communications, interpersonal abilities, and teamwork abilities.

11. Karen O. Dowd and Jeanne Liedtka, "What Corporations Seek in MBA Hires: A Survey," *The Magazine of the Graduate Management Admission Council,* Winter 1994.

Chapter 2 / Competencies of the Stars

1. The study of foreign-service officers and the beginnings of the competence-testing movement are described by David C. McClelland in his introduction to Lyle M. Spencer Jr. and Signe M. Spencer, *Competence at Work: Models for Superior Performance* (New York: John Wiley and Sons, 1993).

2. See David C. McClelland, "Testing for Competence Rather than Intelligence," *American Psychologist* 46 (1973). McClelland's landmark paper has continued to stir debate even after a quarter century.

3. The two computer programmers: Spencer and Spencer, *Competence at Work.*

4. Academic tests failed to predict best diplomats: Kenneth Clark found that scores by applicants on the selection test for foreign-service officers did not predict success as rated by their later on-the-job performance evaluations. Results of this study are reported by D. C. McClelland and C. Dailey, "Improving Officer Selection for the Foreign Service," McBer, Boston, 1972.

5. The test is the Profile of Nonverbal Sensitivity, or PONS, developed at Harvard by Robert Rosenthal. See, e.g., Robert Rosenthal, "The PONS Test: Measuring Sensitivity to Nonverbal Cues," in P. McReynolds (ed.), *Advances in Psychological Assessment* (San Francisco: Jossey-Bass, 1977).

6. The higher estimate of IQ and job performance: e.g., John B. Hunter and F. L. Schmidt, "Validity and Utility of Alternative Predictors of Job Performance," *Psychological Bulletin* 96 (1984); F. L. Schmidt and John B. Hunter, "Employment Testing: Old Theories and New Research Findings," *American Psychologist* 36 (1981).

7. A more careful view of IQ and job performance: Robert Sternberg, *Successful Intelligence* (New York: Simon & Schuster, 1996).

8. Harvard graduates entrance exam scores and later-life success: Dean K. Whitla, "Value Added: Measuring the Impact of Undergraduate Education," Office of Instructional Research and Evaluation, Harvard University, 1975;

cited in David C. McClelland, "The Knowledge-Testing-Educational Complex Strikes Back," *American Psychologist* 49 (1994).

9. Originally called McBer, the firm was also founded with David Berlew, another of McClelland's former students.

10. IQ in professional and highly complex technical fields: Spencer and Spencer, *Competence at Work*. As they put it, cognitive abilities alone are not the mark of top performers, since "in higher level technical, marketing, professional, and managerial jobs, almost everyone has an IQ of 120 or above and an advanced degree from a good university. What distinguishes superior performers in these jobs is motivation, interpersonal skills, and political skills."

11. See Robert J. Sternberg and Richard K. Wagner, *Practical Intelligence: Nature and Origins of Competence in the Everyday World* (Cambridge: Cambridge University Press, 1986).

12. See Sternberg, *Successful Intelligence*.

13. Practical intelligence and managerial success: R. K. Wagner and R. J. Sternberg, "Practical Intelligence in Real-World Pursuits: The Role of Tacit Knowledge," *Journal of Personality and Social Psychology* 49 (1985).

14. Technical skills as threshold abilities: Spencer and Spencer, *Competence at Work*.

15. The tale of Penn and Matt is told by Robert Sternberg in *Successful Intelligence*.

16. The tale of the president was told by Ann Graham Ehringer, director of the Family Business Program at the Marshall School of Business at the University of Southern California.

17. The measure of capacity to handle cognitive complexity was developed by Elliott Jacques; see Elliott Jacques, *Requisite Organization* (Arlington, VA: Cason Hall, 1989).

18. The term "emotional competence" has been used in this sense by several other theorists and researchers; see, e.g., Carol Saarni, "Emotional Competence: How emotions and relationships become integrated," in R. A. Thompson (ed.), *Nebraska Symposium on Motivation,* vol. 36, 1988; Carol Saarni, "Emotional Competence and Self-regulation in Childhood," in Peter Salovey and David J. Sluyter (eds.), *Emotional Development and Emotional Intelligence* (New York: Basic Books, 1997). By highlighting emotional competencies, I do not mean to imply that expertise and cognitive abilities are irrelevant; these abilities are part of a complex system, and in any such interacting system all parts make their contribution. My aim is to give emotional competencies—so easily discounted or overlooked—their due.

19. There is a nascent effort to translate emotional skills into software that will "humanize" computers. See Roz Picard, *Affective Computing* (Cambridge: MIT Press, 1998).

20. Damage to the brain's cortex impairs our abilities to think and perceive; damage to key subcortical areas destroys our ability to register emotions. Damage to circuits centering on the amygdala have the most devastating impact on the ability to register emotion. (See Joseph LeDoux, *The Emotional Brain* [New York: Simon & Schuster, 1996].) Cutting central links between the brain's topmost layers and these same emotional centers sabotages the emotional competencies, all of which depend on the tight orchestration of thought and feeling. The specific circuitry between neocortex and subcortex that is crucial for integrating thought and emotion runs from the amygdala in the limbic system, the brain's subcortical center for emotion, and the ventromedial area of the prefrontal lobes, the brain's neocortical executive center. This circuitry is described in detail in Antonio Damasio, *Descartes' Error: Emotion, Reason, and the Human Brain* (New York: Grosset/Putnam, 1994). Damasio, a neurologist at the University of Iowa Medical School, has done the best research on the brain basis of competence. When I sent him the list of emotional competencies, his conclusion was that all of them (though not cognitive abilities) would be impaired in people who had brain damage that cut the connections between the crucial prefrontal and emotional centers. In the logic of neurology, the capacities impaired in people with damage to a particular brain site suggest that this same area of the brain regulates those capacities in people whose brains are intact. In other words, the underlying neural circuitry for emotional competence—as opposed to intellectual competence—connects the prefrontal area with the emotional centers. The main clue is that damage to these areas impairs the personal and social abilities that allow effective job performance, even though cognitive abilities are intact.

21. The term "emotional competence" includes both social and emotional competencies, just as Howard Gardner uses the term "personal intelligence" to subsume both intra- and interpersonal abilities.

22. This generic competence framework distills findings from: MOSAIC competencies for professionals and administrators (developed by the U.S. Department of Personnel, 1996); Spencer and Spencer, *Competence at Work;* Richard Boyatzis, *The Competent Manager: A Model for Effective Performance* (New York: John Wiley and Sons, 1982); and competence studies published in Richard H. Rosier (ed.), *The Competency Model Handbook,* Vols. 1–3 (Lexington: Linkage, 1994–1996).

23. The specific competencies for Blue Cross reps, shoe store managers, brokers, and life insurance sales: Walter V. Clarke Associates, "Activity Vector

Analysis: Some Applications to the Concepts of Emotional Intelligence," June 1996.

24. Political awareness: Ann Howard and Douglas W. Bray, *Managerial Lives in Transition* (New York: Guilford Press, 1988).

25. Job-specific competencies: these can account for as much as 20 percent of those needed for superior performance. See Spencer and Spencer, *Competence at Work.*

26. Spencer and Spencer, *Competence at Work.*

27. These emotional competencies are to a large extent applicable to top performance in virtually every job. One estimate is that generic competencies cover 80 to 98 percent of behaviors typical of star performers, depending on the specific job. That estimate includes three that are purely cognitive—analytical thinking, conceptual thinking, and job-specific expertise—and so do not fall among the emotional intelligence group. See Spencer and Spencer, *Competence at Work,* for a more detailed discussion.

Chapter 3 / The Hard Case for Soft Skills

1. The Lucent Technologies, University of Nebraska, and Amoco competence models. Richard H. Rosier (ed.), *The Competency Model Handbook,* vol. 1 (Lexington, MA: Linkage, 1994).

2. In the best of the competence models, average performers are compared with those who rank in the top of their field. The pool of top performers is typically chosen on the basis of sales or other hard criteria of excellence, or on the basis of confidential 360-degree ratings, where bosses, peers, employees, and customers all rate the performance of a given person. Each nominee—and a comparable pool of average performers—goes through a rigorous interview about their job performance, including, for example, detailed narratives of what they actually did in three incidents of great on-the-job success and three instances of failure or missteps. The narratives are then analyzed and coded for clues to the competencies the person displayed in these actual samples of their behavior. A less precise method, though one commonly used to save time and money, asks expert panels to generate the competencies they have found typify star performers.

3. The U.S. government competency models are in a CD-ROM, "Personnel Manager." Personnel Resources and Development Center, U.S. Office of Personnel Management, Washington, DC, 1997.

4. While the best leaders relied more on big-picture thinking, they relied less than other leaders on deductive, if-then reasoning abilities.

5. Patrick McCarthy, star sales associate: Robert Spector and Patrick D. McCarthy, *The Nordstrom Way* (New York: John Wiley, 1995).

6. The landmark study of the value of top workers: John E. Hunter, Frank L. Schmidt, and Michael K. Judiesch, "Individual Differences in Output Variability as a Function of Job Complexity," *Journal of Applied Psychology* 75, 1 (1990).

7. By contrast, for low-level jobs the top 1 percent compared to the average, showed an advantage of 52 percent more value, and for medium-level jobs the added value was 85 percent more—still impressive. See Hunter, Schmidt, and Judiesch, "Individual Differences."

8. See his landmark book, Lyle M. Spencer Jr. and Signe M. Spencer, *Competence at Work: Models for Superior Performance* (New York: John Wiley and Sons, 1993).

9. Computer programmers, the stars and superstars: J. Martin, *Rapid Application Development* (New York: Macmillan, 1990); C. Jones, *Programming Productivity* (New York: McGraw-Hill, 1986). Both were cited by Lyle Spencer Jr. in his presentation to the annual meeting of the International Personnel Management Association, Boston, June 25, 1996.

10. The value-added of sales stars: S. Sloan and Lyle M. Spencer, "Participant Survey Results," Hay Salesforce Effectiveness Seminar, Atlanta, 1991.

11. Top executives and competencies: The six or seven that made for the tipping point were from among a set of twelve (ten of which are emotional competencies) that were especially important for success at a specific company. David C. McClelland, "Behavioral event interviews as an alternative to traditional ability tests as a way to identify personal competencies associated with top executive success," *Psychological Science,* in press, 1998. McClelland shared additional data with me.

12. Turnover rates: Spencer and Spencer, *Competence at Work.*

13. Division presidents cost of turnover: Hay/McBer Research and Innovation Group, 1997; McClelland, "Behavioral Event Interviews."

14. The three cases: Hay/McBer Research and Innovation Group, 1997.

15. Executive derailment meant getting fired, being forced to quit, or reaching a plateau in a dead-end position. Done originally in the early 1980s by researchers at the Center for Creative Leadership, the study was updated in 1996 in interviews with sixty-two executives at fifteen Fortune 500 multinational corporations in North America or the equivalent in ten European countries. Jean Brittain Leslie and Ellen Van Velsor, "A Look at Derailment Today: North America and Europe," Center for Creative Leadership, Greensboro, NC, 1996.

16. Leslie and Van Velsor, "A Look at Derailment Today."

17. Strengths and weaknesses of the successful versus failed managers were first identified in the original data set, and largely confirmed in the follow-up in 1996. Leslie and Van Velsor, "A Look at Derailment Today."

18. Comparison of 23 failed executives with 227 successes in Latin America: Claudio Fernández-Aráoz, personal communication, 1997.

19. The studies of failed executives were done in Japan by Ken Whitney and Tomo Watanabe in the Tokyo office of Egon Zehnder International and in Germany by Horst Bröcker of the Munich office of Egon Zehnder International.

20. Managers who failed: Leslie and Van Velsor, "A Look at Derailment Today."

21. Patrick McCarthy: Spector and McCarthy, *The Nordstrom Way.*

22. Stephen Rosen is director of the Science and Technology Advisory Board in New York City, a project of the Alfred P. Sloan Foundation. See Stephen Rosen and Celia Paul, *Career Renewal: Tools for Scientists and Technical Professionals* (New York: Academic Press, 1997).

23. Emotional intelligence in scientific careers: Gregory J. Feist and Frank Barron, "Emotional Intelligence and Academic Intelligence in Career and Life Success," presented at the Annual Convention of the American Psychological Society, San Francisco, June 1996.

24. Ernest O. Lawrence: His comment was in a conversation to Alvin M. Weinberg, former director of Oak Ridge National Laboratory, who repeated it to me.

Chapter 4 / The Inner Rudder

1. Decision making in entrepreneurs: Ann Graham Ehringer, *Make Up Your Mind* (Santa Monica, CA: Merritt Publishing, 1995).

2. The circuitry of the extended amygdala, which I refer to simply as the "amygdala," is described in James D. Duffy, "The Neural Substrates of Emotion," *Psychiatric Annals,* January 1997.

3. The amygdala as the storehouse for emotional memory—if only in terms of the emotional valence (liking or disliking) of what we experience: See Joseph LeDoux, *The Emotional Brain* (New York: Basic Books, 1996).

4. Bad decisions: Gretchen Vogel, "Scientists Probe Feelings Behind Decision-making," *Science,* February 28, 1997. Like the brilliant lawyer, Damasio's other patients with prefrontal deficits made disastrous financial, professional, or ethical decisions, even though perfectly capable of describing the rational

pros and cons of a decision. They drifted in and out of marriages, squandered money in foolish financial decisions, and at work would inadvertently offend or antagonize their coworkers.

5. Top executives and decision making: Weston Agor, *The Logic of Intuitive Decision-making* (New York: Quorum Books, 1986).

6. Ehringer, *Make Up Your Mind.*

7. Nalini Ambady, "Half a Minute: Predicting Teacher Evaluations from Thin Slices of Nonverbal Behavior and Physical Attractiveness," *Journal of Personality and Social Psychology* 64 (1993). Almost the same level of accuracy has been found from brief observations in forty-four other studies, including one of people's interactions with bosses, peers, and subordinates: Nalini Ambady and Robert Rosenthal, "Thin Slices of Expressive Behavior as Predictors of Interpersonal Consequences: A Meta-analysis," *Psychological Bulletin* 111 (1992).

8. Gavin deBecker, *The Gift of Fear: Survival Signs That Protect Us from Violence* (New York: Little, Brown, 1997).

9. "Awareness of One's Emotional Experience," one of several emotional competencies identified at American Express Financial Advisors, was shared with me by Kate Cannon, director of leadership development there.

10. The new introspectionism: Stratford Sherman, "Leaders Learn to Heed the Voice Within," *Fortune,* August 22, 1994.

11. Richard Abdoo: Sherman, "Leaders Learn to Heed the Voice Within."

12. Satisfying work and outstanding performance: Robert E. Kelley, *How to Be a Star at Work* (Times Books, 1998).

13. The unhappy entrepreneur: Ehringer, *Make Up Your Mind.*

14. Engaging skills at work and heart disease: see Leonard Syme, "Explaining Inequalities in Heart Disease," *The Lancet,* July 26, 1997.

15. One of the main self-awareness methods Zuboff uses is "focusing," developed by Eugene T. Gendlin at the University of Chicago, and The Focusing Institute, Spring Valley, New York. See Eugene T. Gendlin, *Focusing* (New York: Bantam Books, 1981).

16. Mort Meyerson recants: Mort Meyerson, "Everything I Thought I Knew About Leadership Is Wrong," *Fast Company,* special edition, May 1997.

17. Joe Jaworski: quoted in Allen M. Webber, "Destiny and the Job of the Leader," *Fast Company,* June/July 1996.

18. The case of Harry: Robert E. Kaplan, *Beyond Ambition: How Driven Managers Can Lead Better and Live Better* (San Francisco: Jossey-Bass, 1991).

19. Lack of self-awareness and derailment: Morgan W. McCall Jr. and Michael Lombardo, "Off the Track: Why and How Successful Executives Get Derailed," technical report no. 21, Center for Creative Leadership, Greensboro, NC, 1983; A. M. Morrison et al., *Breaking the Glass Ceiling: Can Women Reach the Top of America's Largest Corporations?* (Reading, MA: Addison-Wesley, 1987).

20. Accurate self-assessment in managers: Richard Boyatzis, *The Competent Manager: A Model for Effective Performance* (New York: John Wiley and Sons, 1982).

21. Common executive blind spots: Kaplan, *Beyond Ambition.*

22. How others see us as a more accurate predictor of job performance: e.g., Dianne Nilsen, "Understanding Self-observer Discrepancies in Multi-rater Assessment Systems," presented at the annual meeting of the American Psychological Association, San Francisco, 1991.

23. A small, inventive step: James O. Prochaska et al., *Changing for Good* (New York: Avon, 1994).

24. Self-awareness and superior performance: Dianne Nilsen and David P. Campbell, "Self-observer Rating Discrepancies: Once an Overrater, Always an Overrater?" *Human Resource Manager,* Summer/Fall 1993.

25. Self-awareness in star performers: Kelley, *How to Be a Star at Work.*

26. Boyatzis, *The Competent Manager.*

27. Lee Iacocca, *Iacocca: An Autobiography* (New York: Bantam Books, 1984).

28. The tale of the shy lawnmowing entrepreneur: cited in David Leonard, "The Impact of Learning Goals on Self-directed Change in Education and Management Development," Ph.D. thesis, Weatherhead School of Management, Case Western Reserve University, 1996.

29. People can learn to become more self-confident: see, for example, Jerome Kagan, *Galen's Prophecy* (New York: Basic Books, 1994).

30. Self-efficacy: see Albert Bandura, *Social Foundations of Thoughts and Action* (Englewood Cliffs, NJ: Prentice-Hall, 1986); Albert Bandura, "Organizational Applications of Social Cognitive Theory," *Australian Journal of Management,* December 1988.

31. Self-efficacy and job performance in new accountants: Alan M. Saks, "Longitudinal Field Investigation of the Moderating and Mediating Effects of

Self-efficacy on the Relationship Between Training and Newcomer Adjustment," *Journal of Applied Psychology* 80 (1995).

32. Inner maps of self-efficacy: Daniel Cervone, "Social-cognitive Mechanisms and Personality Coherence: Self-knowledge, Situational Beliefs, and Cross-situational Coherence in Perceived Self-efficacy," *Psychological Science* 8 (1997).

33. Self-confidence early in career predicts success later at AT&T: Ann Howard and Douglas W. Bray, *Managerial Lives in Transition* (New York: Guilford Press, 1988). Study after study finds that self-confidence distinguishes successful, effective workers from those who perform poorly; see, for example, Boyatzis, *The Competent Manager.*

34. Self-confidence in high-IQ people and career success: Carole K. Holahan and Robert R. Sears, *The Gifted Group in Later Maturity* (Stanford: Stanford University Press, 1995).

35. Self-confidence and dissent in nurses: Louise E. Parker, "When to Fix It and When to Leave: Relationships Among Perceived Control, Self-efficacy, Dissent, and Exit," *Journal of Applied Psychology* 78 (1993).

Chapter 5 / Self-Control

1. The amygdala: the best description of the emotional role of the amygdala is Joseph LeDoux, *The Emotional Brain: The Mysterious Underpinnings of Emotional Life* (New York: Simon & Schuster, 1996).

2. More specifically, the release of CRF triggers another brain chemical, called ACTH, which in turn causes a flood of hormones known as corticosteroids; in humans the main one is cortisol.

3. Cortisol and working memory: see, for example, O. M. Wolkowitz et al., "Cognitive Effects of Corticosteroids," *American Journal of Psychiatry* 147, 10 (1990).

4. Stress shrinks the hippocampus: Bruce McEwen and R. M. Sapolsky, "Stress and Cognitive Function," *Current Opinions in Neurobiology* 5 (1995).

5. Cortisol and memory impairment: M. Mauri et al., "Memory Impairment in Cushing's Disease," *Acta Neurologica Scandinavia* 87 (1993).

6. Deluge of messages: Alex Markels, "Memo 4/8/97, FYI: Messages Inundate Offices," *The Wall Street Journal,* April 8, 1997.

7. Engineer: Robert E. Kelley, *How to Be a Star at Work* (Times Books, 1998).

8. For example, a man who had an injury to his prefrontal cortex when an exploding tire drove part of the tire rim into his forehead was suddenly

transformed from a pious churchgoer to someone who would hurl a glass of orange juice at a waitress because it was warm. People with frontal lobe damage are prone to such fits of explosive, uncontrollable impulse, their primal feelings of fear or rage unchecked; Vietnam veterans with frontal-lobe damage were found to be up to six times as violent and aggressive as similar vets without such damage. Such clinical reports are telling for the rest of us: Whenever injury to a neural circuit results in dramatic changes in behavior, it suggests that normal variations in the operation of that circuit cause parallel variations in that same range of behavior. I review the evidence for the role of the prefrontal lobe, particularly the orbitofrontal cortex, in inhibiting impulse in more detail in *Emotional Intelligence* (New York: Bantam Books, 1995).

9. Impulsivity: Gordon D. Logan et al., "Impulsivity and Motor Control," *Psychological Science,* January 1997.

10. As these inhibitory circuits calm the amygdala, they allow the intellect to operate more effectively, even under stress. For example, in one laboratory experiment, people were given a fairly good analogue of the stress operating in a wide variety of jobs: They had to solve tough arithmetic problems under ever-increasing time pressure. People whose cortisol levels remained the lowest had the most accurate answers, and stayed accurate longer despite the tension of the situation; those with high cortisol had the most anxiety, anger, depression, and fatigue—and the poorest intellectual performance. J. Lehmann et al., "Differences in Mental Task Performance and Slow Potential Shifts in Subjects Differing in Cortisol Level," *International Journal of Psychophysiology* 13 (1992).

11. Tense managers and poor store performance: Robert F. Lusch and Rapy Serpkenci, "Personal Differences, Job Tension, Job Outcomes, and Store Performance: A Study of Retail Managers," *Journal of Marketing,* January 1990.

12. The story of the fight that didn't happen was passed on to me by Roger Grothe, then manager of in-flight training at Northwest Airlines.

13. The marshmallow kids grow up: The data collection and analysis of the children in the teen years and twenties was conducted by Philip Peake, a psychologist at Smith College, who shared the findings with me.

14. As the people at the Educational Testing Service in Princeton, who make the test, told me, a 210-point advantage is as great as that seen between children from the wealthiest and poorest homes, or between children whose parents have no high-school diploma and those with a parent who has a master's degree or better.

15. The follow-up was directed by Philip Peake.

16. Emotional labor: Arlie Hochschild, *The Managed Heart: The Commercialization of Human Feeling.* Berkeley: University of California Press, 1983.

17. Identity and emotional labor: Blake E. Ashforth and Ronald H. Humphrey, "Emotional labor in service roles: The influence of identity," *Academy of Management Review,* 18, 1993.

18. The costs of emotional suppression: James J. Gross and Robert W. Levenson, "Hiding Feelings: The Acute Effects of Inhibiting Negative and Positive Emotion," *Journal of Abnormal Psychology* 106 (1997).

19. Spontaneity in supervisors, managers, and executives: Richard Boyatzis, *The Competent Manager: A Model for Effective Performance* (New York: John Wiley and Sons, 1982).

20. The tale of Bill Gates's tirade: Fred Moody, "Wonder Women in the Rude Boys' Paradise," *Fast Company,* June/July 1996.

21. Relaxation as a stress buffer: My own research at Harvard offered some of the first evidence for this effect; see Daniel Goleman and Gary E. Schwartz, "Meditation as an Intervention in Stress Reactivity," *Journal of Clinical and Consulting Psychology* 44 (1976). Many other studies have found the same effect in the years since; see Daniel Goleman and Joel Gurin (eds.), *Mind/Body Medicine* (New York: Consumer Reports Books, 1994).

22. Stress and strain: M. Afzalur Rahim and Clement Psenicka, "A Structural Equations Model of Stress, Locus of Control, Social Support, Psychiatric Symptoms, and Propensity to Leave a Job," *Journal of Social Psychology* 136 (1996).

23. Little control over job, more heart disease: see Leonard Syme, "Explaining Inequalities in Heart Disease," *The Lancet,* July 26, 1997.

24. Lack of job control and heart disease: R. Karasek and T. Theorrell, *Healthy Work: Stress, Productivity, and the Reconstruction of Working Life* (New York: Basic Books, 1990).

25. Colds and bad bosses: Sheldon Cohen, paper delivered at the Third International Congress of the International Society for Neuroimmunomodulation, Bethesda, MD, November 1996. Reported in *Science,* November 29, 1996.

26. Distressing feelings and the heart: E. C. Gullete et al., "Effects of Mental Stress on Myocardial Ischemia During Daily Life," *Journal of the American Medical Association* 227 (1997).

27. Higher cortisol levels in working mothers: L. J. Luecken et al., "Stress in Employed Women: Impact of Marital Status and Children at Home on Neurohormone Output and Home Strain," *Psychosomatic Medicine* 59 (1997).

28. Cortisol and immune suppression: see Christine Blank, "Anticortisols Can Help Many," *Drug Topics,* December 8, 1997.

29. Cortisol and work stress: Kathleen Fackelman, "The Cortisol Connection," *Science News,* November 29, 1997.

30. The stressed professor: Richard Lazarus, *Emotion and Adaptation* (New York: Oxford University Press, 1991).

31. The self-aware laid-off managers: James Pennebaker, personal communication.

32. The experiment on self-awareness and handling stress well: Peter Salovey, John D. Mayer et al., "Emotional Attention, Clarity, and Repair: Exploring Emotional Intelligence Using the Trait Meta-mood Scale," in James W. Pennebaker (ed.), *Emotion, Disclosure, and Health* (Washington, DC: American Psychological Press, 1995).

33. Officer Wilson: in Deborah Sontag and Dan Barry, "Disrespect as Catalyst for Brutality," *The New York Times,* November 19, 1997.

34. The unflappable traffic agents: Elizabeth Brondolo et al., "Correlates of Risk for Conflict Among New York City Traffic Agents," in Gary R. VandenBos and Elizabeth Q. Bulatao (eds.), *Violence on the Job: Identifying Risks and Developing Solutions* (Washington, DC, American Psychological Association, 1996).

35. Calm counselors are superior: Richard A. Boyatzis and James A. Burrus, "The Heart of Human Resource Development: Counseling Competencies," unpublished manuscript, July 1995.

36. Unflappable flight attendants: Lyle M. Spencer Jr. and Signe M. Spencer, *Competence at Work: Models for Superior Performance* (New York: John Wiley and Sons, 1993).

37. Self-control in managers and executives: Boyatzis, *The Competent Manager.*

38. Hardiness and stress resilience: Salvatore R. Maddi and Suzanne C. Kobasa, *The Hardy Executive: Health Under Stress* (Homewood, IL: Dow Jones-Irwin, 1984).

39. The inventor and the man with two sets of books: the story is told in Stanley Foster Reed, *The Toxic Executive* (New York: HarperBusiness, 1993).

40. Survey of unethical business practices: reported in Henry Fountain, "Of White Lies and Yellow Pads," *The New York Times,* July 6, 1997.

41. The assessment of 4,265 people is reported in "Activity Vector Analysis: Some Applications to the Concepts of Emotional Intelligence," Walter V. Clarke Associates, Pittsburgh, June 1996.

42. Ratings of football players: "Activity Vector Analysis."

43. Conscientiousness and outstanding performance: M. R. Barrick and M. K. Mount, "The Big Five Personality Dimensions and Job Performance: A Meta-analysis," *Personnel Psychology* 44 (1991).

44. Conscientiousness and appliance sales: Murray R. Barrick, Michael K. Mount, and Judy P. Strauss, "Conscientiousness and Performance of Sales Representatives: Test of the Mediating Effects of Goal Setting," *Journal of Applied Psychology* 78 (1993).

45. Lack of conscientiousness and firing: Murray R. Barrick, M. K. Mount, and J. P. Strauss, "Antecedents of Involuntary Turnover Due to a Reduction in Force," *Personnel Psychology* 47 (1994).

46. Overconscientiousness and critical attitudes: Dennis W. Organ and Andreas Lingl, "Personality, Satisfaction, and Organizational Citizenship Behavior," *The Journal of Social Psychology* 135 (1995).

47. Andrew S. Grove: Robert A. Burgelman, and Andrew S. Grove, "Strategic Dissonance," *California Management Review* 38, 2 (1996).

48. Reactions of top management to crises is like the stages of coping with catastrophe: These ideas are developed in Burgelman and Grove, "Strategic Dissonance."

49. The Schwinn saga: Judith Crown and Glenn Coleman, *The Rise and Fall of the Schwinn Bicycle Company, an American Institution* (New York: Henry Holt, 1996).

50. Managers and flexibility: Boyatzis, *The Competent Manager.*

51. Innovative solution at Levi Strauss: Stratford Sherman, "Levi's: As Ye Sew, So Shall Ye Reap," *Fortune,* May 12, 1997.

52. Internal constraints: Robert Sternberg (ed.), *Handbook of Human Intelligence* (Cambridge: Cambridge University Press, 1988).

53. Creativity killers: Teresa Amabile, "The Intrinsic Motivation Principle of Creativity," in Barry Staw and L. L. Cummings (eds.), *Research in Organizational Behavior,* vol. 10 (Greenwich, CT: JAI Press, 1988).

54. Gina Imperato, "Dirty Business, Bright Ideas," *Fast Company,* February/March 1997.

55. Factors that boost organizational creativity: Amabile 1988.

56. Innovators versus implementers in engineering R&D: E. B. Roberts and A. R. Fusfeld, "Staffing the Innovative Technology-Based Organization," *Sloan*

Management Review 22 (1981); C. M. Beath, "Supporting the Information Technology Champion," *MIS Quarterly* 15 (1991).

Chapter 6 / What Moves Us

1. The classic description of flow: Mihalyi Csikszentmihalyi, *Flow: The Psychology of Optimal Experience* (New York: Harper and Row, 1990).

2. The real rewards of work: based on a survey of 1,528 men and women who had been followed at five-year intervals or so through the course of their lives, into the 1990s. See Carole K. Holahan and Robert R. Sears, *The Gifted Group in Later Maturity* (Palo Alto, CA: Stanford University Press, 1995).

3. The brain in flow: Jean Hamilton et al., "Intrinsic Enjoyment and Boredom Coping Scales: Validation with Personality, Evoked Potential and Attention Measures," *Personality and Individual Differences* 5 (1984).

4. Flow at work and leisure: Judith LeFevre, "Flow and Quality of Experience During Work and Leisure," in Mihalyi Csikszentmihalyi and Isabella S. Csikszentmihalyi (eds.), *Optimal Experience: Psychological Studies of Flow in Consciousness* (Cambridge: Cambridge University Press, 1988).

5. Flow and outstanding performers: Robert E. Kelley, *How to Be a Star at Work* (Times Books, 1998).

6. Being fully present: William A. Kahn, "To Be Fully There: Psychological Presence at Work," *Human Relations* 45 (1992); William A. Kahn, "Psychological Conditions of Personal Engagement and Disengagement at Work," *Academy of Management Journal* 33 (1990).

7. The professor and the factory worker: Maria T. Allison and Margaret C. Duncan, "Women, Work and Flow," in Csikszentmihalyi and Csikszentmihalyi (eds.), *Optimal Experience.*

8. The neurochemistry of motivation undoubtedly entails many neurochemicals, since the brain is continually secreting larger or smaller amounts of the more than two hundred neurotransmitters. But the catecholamines have been most studied, and they figure prominently in the underlying brain chemistry of motivation. See, e.g., U. Lundberg, "Catecholamine and Cortisol Excretion Under Psychologically Different Laboratory Conditions," in J. Usdin, T. Kvetnanski, and D. Kopin (eds.), *Catecholamines and Stress: Recent Advances* (North Holland: Elsevier, 1980).

9. Eugenia Barton, the compassionate teacher: in Cary Cherniss, *Beyond Burnout* (New York: Routledge, 1995).

10. Affiliation: see Richard Boyatzis, *The Competent Manager: A Model for Effective Performance* (New York: John Wiley and Sons, 1982); Lyle M.

Spencer Jr. and Signe M. Spencer, *Competence at Work: Models for Superior Performance* (New York: John Wiley and Sons, 1993).

11. Managers low in affiliation: Spencer and Spencer, *Competence at Work.*

12. Managers and affiliation: Boyatzis, *The Competent Manager.*

13. In a series of studies in which underlying brain chemistry was assessed in people ranked high in various motives, David McClelland deduced that norepinephrine is involved when the need for power is aroused, while the need for affiliation—wanting to feel close and connected to people—seems associated with dopamine, a brain chemical involved in pleasure, among other moods (see David C. McClelland et al., "The Relationship of Affiliative Arousal to Dopamine Release," *Motivation and Emotion* 11 [1987]; David C. McClelland et al., "The Need for Power, Brain Norepinephrine Turnover, and Memory," *Motivation and Emotion* 9 [1985]). And the need to achieve seemed to involve, among other brain chemicals, a pituitary hormone, vasopressin (see David C. McClelland, "Achievement Motivation in Relation to Achievement Related Recall, Performance, and Urine Flow, a Marker Associated with Release of Vasopressin," *Motivation and Emotion* 19 [1995]). But such specific connections between motives and brain chemistry are highly speculative at this point.

14. Computers and emotion: see Roz Picard, *Affective Computing* (Cambridge, MA: MIT Press, 1998).

15. The amygdala and motivation: see James D. Duffy, "The Neural Substrates of Emotion," *Psychiatric Annals,* January 1997.

16. In an analysis of 286 studies from organizations in twenty-one countries, the achievement motive turned up as the single most frequent distinguishing competence among superior executives. Spencer and Spencer, *Competence at Work.*

17. In Gates's industry, software development, as in most other technical and professional specialties, the need to achieve distinguishes star performers from average more than any other competency. Spencer and Spencer, *Competence at Work.*

18. Qualities of the wealthiest: Michael Klepper and Robert Gunther, *The Wealthy 100: A Ranking of the Richest Americans, Past and Present* (New York: Carol Publishing Group, 1997).

19. The study of fifty-nine high-tech entrepreneurs: John B. Miner et al., "Role of Entrepreneurial Task Motivation in the Growth of Technologically Innovative Firms: Interpretations from Follow-up Data," *Journal of Applied Psychology* 79 (1994).

20. The enterprising workers at Donnelly: in Carl F. Frost, *Changing Forever: The Well-Kept Secret of America's Leading Companies* (East Lansing: Michigan State University Press, 1996).

21. Money as keeping score: Ann Graham Ehringer, *Make Up Your Mind* (Santa Monica, CA: Merritt Publishing, 1995).

22. Nathan Myhrvold: Ken Auletta, "Annals of Communication," *The New Yorker,* May 12, 1997.

23. The description of the concern for efficiency is based largely on Spencer and Spencer, *Competence at Work.*

24. The Herman Miller raise-the-plush weekend: Frost, *Changing Forever.*

25. Patricia Sueltz: quoted in *Fast Company,* October/November 1997.

26. Commitment to the organization and thriving under stress: C. S. Leong et al., "The Moderating Effect of Organizational Commitment on the Occupational Stress Outcome Relationship," *Human Relations,* October 1996.

27. Attachment makes good organizational citizens: see, for example, Arthur Brief and S. J. Motowidlo, "Prosocial Organizational Behaviors," *Academy of Management Review* 11 (1986).

28. Organizational support and loyalty: Robert Eisenberger et al., "Perceived Organizational Support and Employee Diligence, Commitment and Innovation," *Journal of Applied Psychology* 75 (1990).

29. The glory-sharing manager and the glory-seeking consultant: in Spencer and Spencer, *Competence at Work.*

30. The new shape of loyalty: Tom Peters, "The Brand Called You," *Fast Company,* August/September 1997.

31. Adam Werbach: "We Can Sit Here Bemoaning Beavis and Butthead or We Can Learn from Their Appeal," *Time,* June 27, 1997.

32. The enterprising shipping clerk: The tale is told by Spencer and Spencer, *Competence at Work.*

33. The PNC Bank computer savings: Kelley, *How to Be a Star at Work.*

34. The extended time horizon as a mark of success: Elliott Jacques, *Requisite Organization* (Arlington, VA: Cason Hall, 1989).

35. Initiative in government: Boyatzis, *The Competent Manager.*

36. Initiative in real estate sales: J. Michael Crant, "The Proactive Personality Scale and Objective Job Performance Among Real Estate Agents," *Journal of Applied Psychology* 80 (1995).

37. Deloitte & Touche Consulting competency model: in Richard H. Rosier (ed.), *The Competency Model Handbook,* vol. 3 (Boston: Linkage, 1996).

38. The hardworking salesman: cited in Spencer and Spencer, *Competence at Work.*

39. The whims of fate and difficulty in managers: Ferdinand A. Gul et al., "Locus of Control, Task Difficulty, and Their Interaction with Employees' Attitudes," *Psychological Reports* 75 (1994).

40. The tale of the too-brash vice president of marketing is told in Boyatzis, *The Competent Manager.*

41. Too-eager managers perform poorly: Boyatzis, *The Competent Manager.*

42. The case of the two executives refused a promotion is described in Salvatore E. Maddi and Suzanne C. Kobasa, *The Hardy Executive: Health Under Stress* (Homewood, IL: Dow Jones-Irwin, 1984).

43. The cases of Anne Busquet and Arthur Blank: Patricia Sellers, "So You Fail. Now Bounce Back," *Fortune,* May 1, 1995.

44. Martin Seligman's studies of optimism and pessimism among insurance sales agents are detailed in Peter Schulman, "Explanatory Style and Achievement in School and Work," in G. Buchanan and Martin Seligman (eds.), *Explanatory Style* (Hillsdale, NJ: Lawrence Erlbaum, 1995).

45. Superior managers: Boyatzis, *The Competent Manager;* Spencer and Spencer, *Competence at Work.*

46. Hope in human services: Spencer and Spencer, *Competence at Work.*

47. Hopefulness in caseworkers: Stuart Kirk and Gary Koeske, "The Fate of Optimism: A Longitudinal Study of Case Managers' Hopefulness and Subsequent Morale," *Research in Social Work Practice,* January 1995.

48. The utility of unrealistic optimism: Shelley Taylor and J. D. Brown, "Illusion and Well-being: A Social Psychological Perspective on Mental Health," *Psychological Bulletin* 183 (1988).

Chapter 7 / Social Radar

1. Empathy in couples: Robert W. Levenson and Anna M. Ruef, "Physiological Aspects of Emotional Knowledge and Rapport," in William Ickes (ed.), *Empathic Accuracy* (New York: Guilford Press, 1997).

2. The physiological mirroring found in married couples has a paradoxical wrinkle. In couples who get along the least well, there is a strong tendency for

physiological linkage during the viewing of the video of their disagreement: The spouse viewing the video gets upset along with the spouse being viewed. This amygdala tango does not help the marriage, however, because though spouses have high empathy for what the other is feeling, they do not act on that knowledge in a constructive way. Though they have a raw empathy with their partner, they lack full empathic accuracy, in that they are clueless about what caused those feelings, what to do about them to make things better, and how to keep them from recurring in the future. See Robert Levenson and Anna Ruef, "Emotional Knowledge and Rapport," in William Ickes (ed.), *Empathic Accuracy* (New York: Guilford Press, 1997).

3. The physiological linkage was strongest for the high-arousal negative emotions, like anger, fear, disgust, and contempt. When partners were in rapport with positive emotions, the empathic physiological stance was to have low heart rate, an indicator of an amygdala in equipoise rather than in attack mode.

4. The insensitivity effect increases to the extent one's own strong emotions differ from those of the person one is with. Two angry people can still resonate with each other, but not an angry person and a sad one. See Levenson and Ruef, "Emotional Knowledge and Rapport."

5. Tuning in to one's own feelings as basis for empathy: Richard Boyatzis and James Burrus, "Validation of a Competency Model for Alcohol Counselors in the U.S. Navy," McBer, Boston, 1977.

6. The silent synchrony: Elaine Hatfield et al., *Emotional Contagion* (New York: Cambridge University Press, 1994).

7. Seeing an emotional face evokes the corresponding feeling in us: the data is reviewed in Hatfield et al., *Emotional Contagion*.

8. Coordination leads to emotional attunement: Hatfield et al., *Emotional Contagion*.

9. Neurons in the amygdala automatically register the emotions in the people around us. Studies with primates show that they have amygdala neurons that fire only in response to specific emotional expressions, like a grimace of fear or a threatening baring of teeth. See Leslie A. Brothers in *Science News,* January 18, 1997; and her "A Biological Perspective on Empathy," *American Journal of Psychiatry* 146 (1989). People with damage to the amygdala fail to display or register emotional distress, whether anger or fear, and have trouble recognizing cues for happiness and sadness. Ross Buck and Benson Ginsburg, "Communicative Genes and the Evolution of Empathy," in William Ickes (ed.), *Empathic Accuracy* (New York: Guilford Press, 1997).

10. The temperamental designer: William A. Kahn, "Psychological Conditions of Personal Engagement and Disengagement at Work," *Academy of Management Journal* 33 (1990).

11. Empathic physicians: Howard Friedman and Robert DiMatteo, *Interpersonal Issues in Health Care* (New York: Academic Press, 1982).

12. Interruptions by physicians: H. B. Beckman and R. M. Frankel, "The Effect of Physician Behavior on the Collection of Data," *Annals of Internal Medicine* 101 (1984).

13. Doctors who are sued don't listen: Wendy Levinson et al., "Physician-Patient Communication: The Relationship with Malpractice Claims Among Primary Care Physicians and Surgeons," *Journal of the American Medical Association,* February 19, 1997.

14. Empathic design: Dorothy Leonard and Jeffrey F. Rayport, "Spark Innovation Through Empathic Design," *Harvard Business Review,* November/December 1997.

15. Product development and customer service: Spencer and Spencer, *Competence at Work.*

16. Listening: Anthony P. Carnevale et al., *Workplace Basics: The Skills Employers Want* (American Society for Training and Development, Arlington, VA, and U.S. Department of Labor, Washington, DC, 1989).

17. Empathy limits sales: R. B. Marks, *Personal Selling* (Boston: Allyn and Bacon, 1991).

18. Sales and empathy: Bruce K. Pilling and Sevo Eroglu, "An Empirical Examination of the Impact of Salesperson Empathy and Professionalism and Merchandise Salability on Retail Buyers' Evaluations," *Journal of Personal Selling and Sales Management,* Winter 1994.

19. Extroverted glad-handing does not make for better sales: see also Murray R. Barrick, Michael K. Mount, and Judy P. Strauss, "Conscientiousness and Performance of Sales Representatives: Test of the Mediating Effects of Goal Setting," *Journal of Applied Psychology* 78 (1993).

20. Machiavellians lack empathy, those who trust have it: Mark Davis and Linda Kraus, "Personality and Empathic Accuracy," in Ickes, *Empathic Accuracy.*

21. Sam's emotional tone deafness: Hatfield et al., *Emotional Contagion.*

22. Avoiding empathy to resist caring: Laura Shaw et al., "Empathy Avoidance: Forestalling Feeling for Another in Order to Escape the Motivational Consequences," *Journal of Personality and Social Psychology* 67 (1994).

23. Managers who care too much: see, e.g., Richard Boyatzis, *The Competent Manager: A Model for Effective Performance* (New York: John Wiley and Sons, 1982).

24. Empathy and the collective good: C. Daniel Batson et al., "Empathy and the Collective Good: Caring for One of the Others in a Social Dilemma," *Journal of Personality and Social Psychology* 68 (1995).

25. The powerful don't empathize: see, for example, Hatfield et al., *Emotional Contagion.*

26. The GE plant closing follow-up: Deborah Sholl Humphreys, "Decline as a Natural Resource for Development," presented at the annual meeting of the Academy of Management, 1987.

27. Developing others is the second most frequent managerial competence: Spencer and Spencer, *Competence at Work.*

28. Sales managers and developing others: Spencer and Spencer, *Competence at Work.*

29. Competence of counselors: Richard Boyatzis and James Burrus, "The Heart of Human Resource Development: Counseling Competencies," unpublished manuscript, 1995; also Boyatzis and Burrus, "Validation of a Competency Model."

30. Developing others—supervisors, managers, executives: Boyatzis, *The Competent Manager.*

31. Career coaching pays off: Christopher Orpen, "The Effect of Mentoring on Employees' Career Success," *Journal of Social Psychology* 135 (1995); David Laband and Bernard Lentz, "Workplace Mentoring in the Legal Profession," *Southern Economic Journal,* January 1995.

32. Coaching by top executives: David Peterson et al., "Management Coaching at Work: Current Practices in Fortune 250 Companies," presented at the annual conference of the American Psychological Association, Toronto, August 1996.

33. Teaching superiors: Spencer and Spencer, *Competence at Work.*

34. Silence damages self-confidence as much as negative feedback: Paulette A. McCarty, "Effects of Feedback on the Self-confidence of Men and Women," *Academy of Management Journal* 29 (1986).

35. The low-performing sailors: K. S. Crawford et al., "Pygmalion at Sea: Improving the Work Effectiveness of Low Performers," *Journal of Applied Behavioral Science* 16 (1980).

36. Socratic coaching: Mark Lepper et al., "Motivational Techniques of Expert Human Tutors," in S. P. Lajoie and S. J. Derry (eds.), *Computers as Cognitive Tools* (Hillsdale, NJ: Lawrence Erlbaum, 1993).

37. Too much coaching, too little managing: Boyatzis, *The Competent Manager.*

38. Sandoz Pharmaceuticals: in Richard H. Rosier (ed.), *The Competency Model Handbook,* vol. 2 (Boston: Linkage, 1995).

39. Empathy in successful sales: Donald McBane, "Empathy and the Salesperson: A Multidimensional Perspective," *Psychology and Marketing* 12 (1995).

40. The helpful manager: Spencer and Spencer, *Competence at Work.*

41. The tale of Nancy Cohen: Jennifer Steinhauer, "Whatever Happened to Service?" *The New York Times,* March 4, 1997.

42. Customer service orientation: for more details, see Spencer and Spencer, *Competence at Work.*

43. Yankelovich survey of customer satisfaction: reported in Steinhauer, "Whatever Happened to Service?"

44. Flaws in *The Bell Curve:* The book ignores data showing that the black-white difference found in IQ scores among Americans does not hold in Caribbean cultures, where blacks are not an oppressed group, and that in every society where there is a privileged class and an oppressed group the same spread in IQ scores is found as that between American blacks and whites, suggesting the effect is due to economic and social conditions, not race. The book also neglects to mention data showing that when members of an oppressed group migrate to a culture where they are not victims of oppression, the IQ difference disappears in a single generation. See Ulric Neisser (ed.), *The Rising Curve: Long-Term Gains in IQ* (Washington, DC: APA Press), 1998.

45. Stereotype threat: Claude M. Steele, "A Threat in the Air: How Stereotypes Shape Intellectual Identity and Performance," *American Psychologist,* June 1997.

46. Reasons women are prevented from advancing to corporate leadership: "Women in Corporate Leadership: Progress and Prospects," *Catalyst*, New York, 1996.

47. Workplace prejudice against women leaders: The research by Alice Eagly, at Northwestern University, was reported in *The American Psychological Association Monitor,* August 1997.

48. Women in math, engineering, and science: N. M. Hewitt and E. Seymour, "Factors Contributing to High Attrition Rates Among Science and Engineering Undergraduate Majors," report to the Alfred P. Sloan Foundation, 1991.

49. Managers: Boyatzis, *The Competent Manager.*

50. People have more difficulty reading a person's emotions when that person is from a group they are not so familiar with. For example, when people from other nations try to read emotions from Americans on the PONS, they do more poorly the more dissimilar their own culture is from that of the United States: Robert Rosenthal, Judith Hall, et al., *Sensitivity to Nonverbal Communications: The PONS Test* (Baltimore: Johns Hopkins University Press, 1979).

51. David A. Thomas and Robin J. Ely, "Making Differences Matter: A New Paradigm for Managing Diversity," *Harvard Business Review,* September/October 1996.

52. Thomas and Ely, "Making Differences Matter."

53. Thomas and Ely, "Making Differences Matter."

54. The politically aware diplomat is described by David McClelland in his introduction to Spencer and Spencer, *Competence at Work.*

55. Key to the sale: Spencer and Spencer, *Competence at Work.*

56. Objective perception in superior managers and executives: Boyatzis, *The Competent Manager.*

57. The oil executive and the silent Chinese group: told in Richard Rosier, *The Competency Model Handbook,* vol. 3.

Chapter 8 / The Arts of Influence

1. Transmission of mood over two silent minutes: Howard Friedman and Ronald Riggio, "Effect of Individual Differences in Nonverbal Expressiveness on Transmission of Emotion," *Journal of Nonverbal Behavior* 6 (1981).

2. Sigal Barsade. "The ripple effect: emotional contagion in groups." Working paper, Yale School of Management, 1998; Sigal Barsade and Donald E. Gibson, "Group emotion: A view from the top and bottom," in D. Gruenfeld et al. (eds.) *Research on Managing Groups and Teams* (Greenwich, CT: JAI Press, in press, 1998).

3. Smiling the most contagious facial expression, and simply smiling primes happiness: Robert Levenson and Anna Ruef, "Emotional Knowledge and Rapport," in William Ickes (ed.), *Empathic Accuracy* (New York: Guilford Press, 1997).

4. Pathway of emotional transmission: Hatfield et al., 1994, op. cit.

5. Emotional adeptness and impact: Howard Friedman et al., "Understanding and Assessing Non-verbal Expressiveness: The Affective Communication Test," *Journal of Nonverbal Behavior* 6 (1981).

6. The rep who would not translate: Cited in Richard H. Rosier (ed.), *The Competency Model Handbook,* vol. 3 (Boston: Linkage, 1996).

7. Deloitte & Touche competency model for top-performing management consultants: In Rosier (ed.), *The Competency Model Handbook,* vol. 3.

8. Impact on supervisors, managers, and executives: Richard Boyatzis, *The Competent Manager: A Model for Effective Performance* (New York: John Wiley and Sons, 1982).

9. Quality services: Boyatzis, *The Competent Manager.*

10. The dramatic service call: Lyle M. Spencer Jr. and Signe M. Spencer, *Competence at Work: Models for Superior Performance* (New York: John Wiley and Sons, 1993).

11. The oil executive and the leisurely cup of coffee: cited in Rosier (ed.), *The Competency Model Handbook,* vol. 3.

12. Rapport in sales: Spencer and Spencer, *Competence at Work.*

13. Use local leaders: Sander Larkin, reply in *Harvard Business Review,* September-October 1996.

14. When strategic decisions are ignored: Paul C. Nutt, professor of management, Ohio State University, reported in *Fast Company,* October/November, 1997.

15. Power at the expense of others is a negative: Spencer and Spencer, *Competence at Work.*

16. Jerry Kalov's open phone line: Michelle Conlin, "The Truth," *Forbes,* February 10, 1997.

17. Poor communications: *Newsweek,* August 12, 1996.

18. Listening and effective communication: John Haas and Christa Arnold, "An Examination of the Role of Listening in Judgments of Communication Competence in Co-workers," *The Journal of Business Communication,* April 1995.

19. Self-regulation and communication: Walter V. Clarke Associates, Pittsburgh, April 1997.

20. The virtues of being an emotional clean slate for social interaction: see Ralph Eber et al., "On Being Cool and Collected: Mood Regulation in Anticipation of Social Interaction," *Journal of Personality and Social Psychology* 70, (1996).

21. "Away": Goffman cited as the primary example of someone who is away people with mental illness, who display their private moods in public places. Irving Goffman, *Behavior in Public Places* (New York: Free Press, 1963).

22. The universal appreciation of composure: see S. M. Lyman and M. B. Scott, "Coolness in Everyday Life," in S. M. Lyman and M. B. Scott (eds.), *The Sociology of the Absurd* (Pacific Palisades, CA: Goodyear, 1968).

23. Effective communicators are composed: "Activity Vector Analysis: Some applications to the concepts of emotional intelligence," Walter V. Clarke Associates, Pittsburgh, June 1996.

24. Extroversion not an asset in all settings: Greg L. Stewart and Kenneth P. Carson, "Personality Dimensions and Domains of Service Performance: A Field Investigation," *Journal of Business and Psychology* 9 (1995).

25. Charlene Barshefsky in negotiation: Elsa Walsh, "The Negotiator," *The New Yorker*, March 18, 1996.

26. Negotiation as cooperation: Herbert Kelman, "Negotiation as Interactive Problem-solving," *International Negotiation* 1 (1996).

27. Vendor-retailer relations and negotiation style: Shankar Ganesan, "Negotiation Strategies and the Nature of Channel Relationships," *Journal of Marketing Research*, May 1993.

28. The confrontation in Harlem: Linda Lantieri and Janet Patti, *Waging Peace in Our Schools* (Boston, Beacon Press, 1996).

29. The twin tales of Ronald W. Allen and Gerald Grinstein: Martha Brannigan and Joseph B. White, "Why Delta Air Lines Decided It Was Time for CEO to Take Off," *Wall Street Journal*, May 30–31, 1997; Phyllis Berman and Roula Khalaf, "Sweet-talking the Board," *Forbes*, March 15, 1993.

30. Lou Gerstner: quoted in Stephen Lohr, "On the Road with Chairman Lou," *New York Times*, June 26, 1994.

31. The power of Ronald Reagan's smile: G. J. McHugo et al., "Emotional Reactions to a Political Leader's Expressive Displays," *Journal of Personality and Social Psychology* 49 (1985). There was a downside to Reagan's emotional intelligence capabilities, as he displayed a certain lack of self-awareness, if not outright self-deception. At times he seems not to have known the difference between films he had seen or stories he heard and the actual facts. Reagan once brought tears to the eyes of Yitzhak Shamir, then prime minister of Israel, with a story about his days with the U.S. Signal Corps recording the atrocities of the German death camps at the end of World War II. The problem: Reagan spent the entire war in Hollywood recruiting for the army's film units. He had, however, seen footage from the liberated camps and, apparently, convinced himself he'd been there. See Michael Korda, "Prompting the President," *The New Yorker*, October 6, 1997.

32. Positive leader, positive group mood: J. M. George and K. Bettenhausen, "Understanding Prosocial Behavior, Sales Performance, and Turnover: A Group Level Analysis in a Service Context," *Journal of Applied Psychology* 75 (1990).

33. Expressiveness: Howard S. Friedman et al., "Understanding and Assessing Non-verbal Expressiveness: The Affective Communication Test," *Journal of Nonverbal Behavior* 6 (1981).

34. Sincerity and charisma: Patricia Wasielewski, "The Emotional Basis of Charisma," *Symbolic Interaction* 8 (1985).

35. In my (unweighted) analysis of leadership competence models from organizations around the world, the proportion of emotional intelligence-based competencies listed to cognitive abilities and expertise was about 80 percent. But in many corporate competence models for leadership, 100 percent of the ingredients listed derive from emotional intelligence. A weighted analysis, done by Hay/McBer, puts the value of emotional competence in contributing to outstanding leadership at just below 90 percent. See Appendix 2.

36. Cross-cultural comparison of CEO competencies: Lyle Spencer Jr. et al., *Competency Assessment Methods: History and State of the Art* (Boston: Hay/McBer, 1997). CEOs studied were in Japan, China, the Philippines, Canada, the United States, Mexico, Venezuela, the United Kingdom, Belgium, France, Germany, Spain, and Italy. This recipe for excellence in leadership seems roughly the same worldwide; differences from region to region are in nuances of how the competencies play out in a given culture.

37. Robert E. Kaplan, *Beyond Ambition: How Driven Managers Can Lead Better and Live Better* (San Francisco: Jossey-Bass, 1991).

38. Commands in the U.S. Navy: Wallace Bachman, "Nice Guys Finish First: A SYMLOG Analysis of U.S. Naval Commands," in Richard Brian Polley et al. (eds.), *The SYMLOG Practitioner: Applications of Small Group Research* (New York: Praeger, 1988).

39. Navy command emotional style: Polley et al. (eds.), *The SYMLOG Practitioner.*

40. The manager who put his foot down: Spencer and Spencer, *Competence at Work.*

41. Self-control and managers: David C. McClelland and Richard Boyatzis, "The Leadership Motive Profile and Long-term Success in Management," *Journal of Applied Psychology* 67 (1982).

42. Self-control and organizational goals: Boyatzis, *The Competent Manager.*

43. John Patrick's epiphany at IBM: the tale is told in Eric Ransdell, "IBM's Grassroots Revival," *Fast Company,* October/November 1997.

44. Self-confidence and flourishing in change: Jane Howell and Bruce Avolio, "Transformational Leadership, Transactional Leadership, Locus of Control, and Support for Innovation: Key Predictors of Consolidated-Business-Unit Performance," *Journal of Applied Psychology* 78 (1993).

45. Transformational leadership: M. B. Bass, *Bass and Stodgill's Handbook of Leadership: Theory, Research and Applications,* 3rd ed. (New York: Free Press, 1990).

46. Transformational leadership: see the discussion in Blake E. Ashforth and Ronald H. Humphreys, "Emotion in the Workplace: An Appraisal," *Human Relations* 48 (1995).

47. Transformational leadership marshals greater efforts: R. J. House et al., "Charismatic and Non-charismatic Leaders: Differences in Behavior and Effectiveness," in J. A. Conger et al. (eds.), *Charismatic Leadership: The Elusive Factor in Organizational Effectiveness* (San Francisco: Jossey-Bass, 1988).

48. Test of transformational leadership at a Canadian financial services company: Howell and Avolio, "Transformational Leadership."

49. Management versus leadership: John Kotter, "What Leaders Really Do," *Harvard Business Review,* May/June 1990.

Chapter 9 / Collaboration, Teams, and the Group IQ

1. The 1982 meeting: John Markoff, "The Soul of a New Economy," *New York Times,* December 29, 1997.

2. John Doerr: interviewed by Michael S. Malone, "John Doerr's Startup Manual," *Fast Company,* February/March 1997.

3. The need for cooperation as a force in shaping the brain in evolution was perhaps first proposed by Alison Jolly in "Lemur Social Behaviour and Primate Intelligence," *Science* 153 (1966).

4. The main theorist here is David S. Wilson, "Incorporating Group Selection into the Adaptationist Program: A Case Study Involving Human Decision-making," in J. Simpson and D. Kendrick (eds.), *Evolutionary Social Psychology* (Hillsdale, NJ: Lawrence Erlbaum, 1997). While some evolutionary psychologists focus on the human ability to deceive others as a source of competitive advantage, they slight the larger benefits accrued to the survival of a group by the more widespread acts of cooperation and mutual help that are essential to the group's very survival.

5. The evolutionary advantage of cooperation in human evolution can be glimpsed among chimpanzee bands; Jane Goodall reports those females who have particularly strong cooperative alliances with other females have a higher rate of infant survival, faster maturing daughters, and produce offspring most rapidly. Anne Pusey, Jennifer Williams, and Jane Goodall, "The Influence of Dominance Rank on Reproductive Success of Female Chimpanzees," *Science,* August 8, 1997.

6. Cooperation and a radar for selfishness: described in Bruce Bower, "Return of the Group," *Science News,* November 18, 1995.

7. The human brain evolved to handle the challenge of group life: The main proponent of this theory is Denise Cummins, an evolutionary psychologist, and author of *Human Reasoning: An Evolutionary Perspective* (Cambridge, MA: Bradford/MIT Press, 1997).

8. Neocortex is larger the bigger the group: T. Sawaguchi and H. Kudo, "Neocortical Development and Social Structures in Primates," *Primates* 31 (1990).

9. Social pressures drove brain evolution: see Cummins, *Human Reasoning.*

10. What percent of knowledge is stored in your own mind?: Robert E. Kelley, *How to Be a Star at Work* (New York: Times Books, 1998).

11. Intellect not in my skin: Howard Gardner, *Frames of Mind* (New York: Basic Books, 1993).

12. Groups outscore individuals: G. W. Hill, "Group Versus Individual Performance: Are N+1 Heads Better Than One?" *Psychological Bulletin* 91 (1982).

13. Collective memory in teams: Roger Dixon, *Interactive Minds* (New York: Cambridge University Press, 1996).

14. Simulated management teams: R. Meredith Belbin, *Management Teams: Why They Succeed or Fail* (London: Halstead Press, 1982); R. Meredith Belbin, *Team Roles at Work* (London: Butterworth-Heinemann, 1996).

15. The concept of group IQ was first developed in Wendy M. Williams and Robert J. Sternberg, "Group Intelligence: Why Some Groups Are Better Than Others," *Intelligence* 12 (1988). They define group intelligence as "the functional intelligence of a group of people working as a unit."

16. The classic study: Williams and Sternberg, "Group Intelligence."

17. Critical elements for effectiveness: Michael A. Campion et al., "Relations Between Work Team Characteristics and Effectiveness: A Replication and Extension," *Personnel Psychology* 49 (1996).

18. Jeffrey Katzenberg, as observed by Nathan Myhrvold of Microsoft, and described in Ken Auletta, "The Microsoft Provocateur," *The New Yorker,* May 1997.

19. Knowledge workers and networks: Kelley, *How to Be a Star at Work.*

20. Time saved through good networks: Kelley, *How to Be a Star at Work.*

21. The power of the alliance between high-tech start-ups and venture capitalists: "Venture Capitalists," *The Economist,* January 25, 1997.

22. People on whom performance depends: quoted in John Kotter, *Power in Management* (New York: AMACOM, 1979).

23. Superior managers effective at building bonds: Richard Boyatzis, *The Competent Manager: A Model for Effective Performance* (New York: John Wiley and Sons, 1982); Robert E. Kaplan, *Beyond Ambition: How Driven Managers Can Lead Better and Live Better* (San Francisco: Jossey-Bass, 1991).

24. Carefully chosen favors: Kelley, *How to Be a Star at Work.*

25. Marks and Spencer and other retailers are forging bonds of trust with suppliers: Nirmalya Kumar, "The Power of Trust in Manufacturer-Retailer Relationships," *Harvard Business Review,* November/December 1996.

26. Kraft Foods: Ken Partch, "Partnering: A Win-Win Proposition . . . or the Latest Hula Hoop in Marketing?" *Supermarket Business,* May 1991.

27. Kumar, "The Power of Trust."

28. The working relationship as a "couple": James Krantz, "The Managerial Couple: Superior-Subordinate Relationships as a Unit of Analysis," *Human Resource Management,* Summer 1989.

29. Projective identification: The best work on this insidious process is the classic by Thomas Ogden, *Projective Identification and Psychotherapeutic Technique* (New York: Jason Aronson, 1991).

30. Owens Corning and SAP: "Owens Corning: Back from the Dead," *Fortune,* May 26, 1997.

31. Self-managed work teams: cited in Lawler et al., *Employee Involvement and Total Quality Management: Practices and Results in Fortune 1,000 Companies* (San Francisco: Jossey-Bass, 1992).

32. Advantages of self-managed work teams: Richard Moreland et al., "Training People to Work in Groups," in R. S. Tinsdale (ed.), *Applications of Theory and Research on Groups to Social Issues* (New York: Plenum, 1997).

33. The value of a top team in a polyester fiber plant was 31 million pounds per year, while average teams produced 24 million pounds per year. The value of

the fiber from average teams was $33.6 million, that from superior teams $43.4 million. The total salary for a team was just $270,000. Source: Lyle Spencer Jr., presentation at International Family Business Programs Association, Northampton, MA, July 1997.

34. Team achievement profile: Lyle Spencer Jr. et al., *Competency Assessment Methods: History and State of the Art* (Boston: Hay/McBer, 1997).

35. Jean Brittain Leslie and Ellen Van Velsor, "A Look at Derailment Today: North America and Europe," Center for Creative Leadership, Greensboro, NC, 1996.

36. Team leadership most frequent competence in managers: Lyle M. Spencer Jr. and Signe M. Spencer, *Competence at Work: Models for Superior Performance* (New York: John Wiley and Sons, 1993).

37. The team studies were presented by Lyle Spencer Jr. and Charles Morrow at the International Conference on Competency-based Tools and Applications to Drive Organizational Performance, London, October 1997.

38. There were different ways teams could translate their competencies into team effectiveness; not every star team excelled in every one. One winning combination, for example, combined the drive to improve with a strong interpersonal focus, ensuring the team was cohesive and harmonious in working together. Another way to excel combined the drive to improve with an external outlook, emphasizing serving the needs of and building bonds with other parts of the company.

39. Strategic decision making in management teams: Allen C. Amason, "Distinguishing the Effects of Functional and Dysfunctional Conflict in Strategic Decision Making: Resolving a Paradox for Top Management Teams," *Academy of Management Journal* 39 (1996).

40. The Data General engineering team: Tracy Kidder, *The Soul of a New Machine* (Boston: Little, Brown, 1981).

41. The analysis of the Data General team: Lee Bolman and Terrence E. Deal, "What Makes a Team Work?" *Organizational Dynamics,* vol. 23, 1992.

42. The pharmaceutical R&D teams: Richard E. Boyatzis et al., "Entrepreneurial Innovation in Pharmaceutical Research and Development," *Human Resource Planning* 15 (1990).

43. The de facto leader: See Wilson, "Incorporating Group Selection."

44. Team leaders need to hold back: see, for example, L. E. Anderson and W. K. Balzer, "The Effects of Timing of Leaders' Opinions on Problem-solving Groups: A Field Experiment," *Group and Organizational Studies* 16 (1991).

45. Self-managing work teams: Susan G. Cohen et al., "A Predictive Model of Self-managing Work Team Effectiveness," *Human Relations* 49 (1996).

46. A meta-analysis of studies with hundreds of self-managing teams found that those without supervisors performed better than those that had supervisors: R. I. Beekun, "Assessing the Effectiveness of Sociotechnical Interventions: Antidote or Fad?" *Human Relations* 47 (1989).

47. The disastrous cross-functional meeting: Daniel R. Denison et al., "From Chimneys to Cross-functional Teams: Developing and Validating a Diagnostic Model," *Academy of Management Journal* 39 (1996).

48. The signs of group flow are seen in what Warren Bennis calls "Great Groups" in his landmark study of a half dozen remarkable teams. These groups display the hallmarks of people in a collective state of flow. That figures; flow is the state exhibited by people who are outdoing themselves, and so emerges with truly outstanding groups. Warren Bennis and Patricia Ward Biederman, *Organizing Genius: The Secrets of Creative Collaboration* (Reading, MA: Addison-Wesley, 1997).

49. Feynman quoted in Bennis and Biederman.

50. "I work to win.": Kidder, *The Soul of a New Machine.*

Chapter 10 / The Billion-Dollar Mistake

1. The case study of emotional competence at American Express was made available to me by Kate Cannon, director of leadership development at American Express Financial Advisors.

2. Brain changes at Promega were measured by the state-of-the-art method, a functional MRI before and after training. Those who went through the training were compared to a randomized control group of peers who had not yet had the training. The data was collected by Richard Davidson, director of the Laboratory for Affective Neuroscience at the University of Wisconsin. The mindfulness training was given by Jon Kabat-Zinn, director of the Stress and Relaxation Program at the University of Massachusetts Medical School in Worcester.

3. Training in empathy: see, for example, H. J. Smith et al., "Just a Hunch: Accuracy and Awareness in Person Perception," *Journal of Nonverbal Behavior* 15 (1991). While women on average do better than men on some tests of empathy, what gender differences exist can be erased by training men to be as accurate in reading emotions as women; see William Ickes (ed.), *Empathic Accuracy* (New York: Guilford Press, 1997).

4. Empathy training carryover: William Ickes et al., "Studying empathic accuracy in a clinically relevant context," in Ickes (ed.), *Empathic Accuracy.*

5. Adults are better at emotional intelligence than adolescents: John D. Mayer, David R. Caruso, and Peter Salovey, "Emotional Intelligence Meets Traditional Standards for an Intelligence," unpublished manuscript, 1997.

6. Emotional intelligence increases with age: Reuven Bar-On, *Bar-On Emotional Quotient Inventory: Technical Manual* (Toronto: Multi-Health Systems, 1997).

7. Most improvement in those over twenty-five: Ronald Ballou et al., "Fellowship in Lifelong Learning: An Executive Development Program for Advanced Professionals," unpublished manuscript, Weatherhead School of Management, 1997.

8. The case of Henry and Lai: Kelley, *How to Be a Star at Work* (Times Books, 1998).

9. Little correlation between knowledge of competence and on-the-job behavior: Bruce Tracey et al., "Applying Trained Skills on the Job: The Importance of the Work Environment," *Journal of Applied Psychology* 80 (1995). A more general review of correlations between what people learn in training programs and what they actually take back with them to daily life found that more than half of reported correlations between learning and behavior were disappointingly low—that is, it is common for people not to execute what they have learned. See G. M. Alliger and E. A. Janak, "Kirkpatrick's Levels of Training Criteria: Thirty Years Later," *Personnel Psychology* 42 (1989).

10. Consider all training the same: Scott I. Tannenbaum and Gary Yukl, "Training and Development in Work Organizations," *Annual Review of Psychology* 43 (1992).

11. Habits strengthen neural pathways: Gerald Edelman, *Neural Darwinism: The Theory of Neuronal Group Selection* (New York: Basic Books, 1987).

12. Learning principles based on trivial experiments: Tannenbaum and Yukl, "Training and Development."

13. The enlightened CEO's demand: Charley C. Morrow et al., "An Investigation of the Effect and Economic Utility of Corporate-wide Training," *Personnel Psychology* 50 (1997).

14. The gloomy estimate of transfer of skills to the job in corporate trainings: Timothy T. Baldwin and J. Kevin Ford, "Transfer of Training," *Personnel Psychology,* 41 (1988).

15. Two thirds of companies did not evaluate the impact of emotional competence training: Benchmarking Forum member-to-member survey results, American Society for Training and Development, Alexandria, Virginia, October 1997.

16. The ASTD survey: Laurie J. Bassi et al., "The Top Ten Trends," *Training*, November 1996.

17. The state-of-the-art training evaluation: see Morrow et al., "An Investigation of the Effect."

18. Two programs for managers were on cognitive or technical topics, not emotional competence.

19. While the pharmaceutical company evaluation cost was a trivial part of the total training budget, it did not evaluate all the trainings given there. However, as a pilot effort it established methods for ongoing evaluation that presumably could be adopted as a routine practice at a much lower cost.

20. The main effect of corporate training seminars is to increase self-confidence: Richard Boyatzis, "Consequences and Rejuvenation of Competency-based Human Resource and Organization Development," *Research in Organizational Change and Development* 9, 1993.

21. The current review of training and development: Robert Dipboye, "Organizational Barriers to Implementing a Rational Model of Training," in M. A. Quinones and A. Ehrenstein (eds.), *Training for a Rapidly Changing Workforce: Applications of Psychological Research* (Washington, DC: American Psychological Association, 1996).

22. Survey of Fortune 500 companies: William H. Clegg, "Management Training Evaluation: An Update," *Training and Development Journal*, February 1987.

23. The Consortium for Research on Emotional Intelligence in Organizations can be reached through my cochair, Dr. Cary Cherniss, in the Graduate School of Applied and Professional Psychology, Rutgers University, Piscataway, New Jersey 08855–0819.

24. The final report from the Consortium can be obtained from Dr. Cary Cherniss (see note 23), or the website: Http://www.EIConsortium.org

25. The Weatherhead initiative and details of the Managerial Assessment and Development course are detailed in Richard Boyatzis et al., *Innovation in Professional Education: Steps on a Journey from Teaching to Learning* (San Francisco: Jossey-Bass, 1995).

26. The competencies include self-confidence, initiative, flexibility, self-control, empathy, persuasiveness, networking, negotiating, team leadership, and developing others, among others. Analytic and technical skills are also included.

27. Assessments: Boyatzis et al., *Innovation in Professional Education*.

28. Three-year follow-up: Ronald Ballou et al., "Fellowship in Lifelong Learning"; Richard Boyatzis and Robert Wright, "Competency Development in Graduate Education: A Longitudinal Perspective," presented at First World Conference on Self-Directed Learning, Boston, September 1997.

29. Details of the JOBS program: J. Curran, *A Manual for Teaching People Successful Job Search Strategies* (Ann Arbor: Michigan Prevention Research Center, Institute for Social Research, University of Michigan, 1992).

30. The toll of the job search: Richard H. Price, "Psychosocial Impact of Job Loss on Individuals and Families," *Current Directions in Psychological Science* 1 (1992).

31. JOBS program: Robert Caplan, A. D. Vinokur, and Robert Price, "Field Experiments in Prevention-focused Coping," in George Albee and Thomas Gullotta (eds.), *Primary Prevention Works* (Thousand Oaks, CA: Sage, 1997).

Chapter 11 / Best Practices

1. Strategic planning is a purely cognitive task: see, for example, Chris Argyris and S. A. Schon, *Theory in Practice: Increasing Professional Effectiveness* (San Francisco: Jossey-Bass, 1974).

2. Strategic planners need competence beyond intellect: David C. McClelland, "Assessing Competencies Associated with Executive Success Through Behavioral Interviews," unpublished manuscript, 1996.

3. State-of-the-art methodology: the methods are detailed in several sources, e.g., Lyle M. Spencer Jr. and Signe M. Spencer, *Competence at Work: Models for Superior Performance* (New York: John Wiley and Sons, 1993).

4. Assessing competence models: see, for example, Spencer and Spencer, *Competence at Work;* David Dubois, *Competency-Based Performance Improvement: A Strategy for Organizational Change* (Amherst, MA: HRD Press, 1993).

5. Flight attendant competence study: Spencer and Spencer, *Competence at Work.*

6. Empathic accuracy for people very different from ourselves, like any other emotional competence, can be learned. We included training in reading feelings from faces of people from cultures that flight attendants were unfamiliar with. We also adapted the way empathy was approached to fit the cross-cultural realities of the job. The result: six months later, the attendants at a large overseas hub who had had the worst record of passenger complaints now had none.

7. People are poor evaluators of their own level of empathy: Mark Davis and Linda Kraus, "Personality and Accurate Empathy," in William Ickes (ed.), *Empathic Accuracy* (New York: Guilford Press, 1997).

8. One measure of the full spectrum of emotional intelligence capabilities I've co-developed is the Emotional Competence Inventory—360 (ECI-360), available from Emotional Intelligence Services, Sudbury, MA, 01776, e-mail: EISGlobal@AOL.com.

9. The Southwest health plan: in Mark R. Edwards and Ann J. Ewen, *360° Feedback* (New York, AMACOM, 1996).

10. Using 360-degree feedback as an emotional bludgeon: see, for example, "Performance Review Input by Peers Catches on at More Firms," *Los Angeles Times,* April 17, 1997.

11. The 20 percent rule is based on data from a wide range of behavior change programs, but its conclusion seems apt for development and training in organizations. See James O. Prochaska et al., *Changing for Good* (New York: Avon, 1994).

12. Questions to gauge readiness: In Prochaska et al., *Changing for Good.*

13. Motivation: Miguel Quinones, "Contextual Influences on Training Effectiveness," in M. A. Quinones and A. Ehrenstein (eds.), *Training for a Rapidly Changing Workforce: Applications of Psychological Research* (Washington, DC: American Psychological Association, 1996).

14. Windows of opportunity: Ellen Van Velsor and Christopher Musselwhite, "The Timing of Training, Learning, and Transfer," *Training and Development Journal,* August 1986.

15. Motivation and effectiveness of training: see, for example, Miguel Quinones, "Pretraining Context Effects: Training Assignment as Feedback," *Journal of Applied Psychology* 80 (1995).

16. Adapting training to the individual: see, for example, Scott I. Tannenbaum and Gary Yukl, "Training and Development in Work Organizations," *Annual Review of Psychology* 43 (1992).

17. Boyatzis: Richard Boyatzis et al., *Innovation in Professional Education: Steps on a Journey from Teaching to Learning* (San Francisco: Jossey-Bass, 1995).

18. Break large goals into smaller goals: C. R. Snyder, *The Psychology of Hope* (New York: Free Press, 1993).

19. Keep hopes high: Snyder, *The Psychology of Hope.*

20. Possible selves: Hazel Markus and Peter Nurius, "Possible Selves," *American Psychologist* 41 (1989).

21. The basic principles of relapse prevention are in Alan Marlatt and Judith Gordon (eds.), *Relapse Prevention* (New York: Guilford Press, 1985). The adaptation for organizational training and development is described in Robert D. Marx, "Relapse Prevention for Managerial Training: A Model for Maintenance of Behavior Change," *Academy of Management Review* 7 (1982) and Robert D. Marx, "Improving Management Development Through Relapse Prevention Strategies," *Journal of Management Development* 5 (1993).

22. Positive feedback enhances self-confidence and transfer of skills to job: Quinones, "Contextual Influences on Training Effectiveness."

23. Practice better when extended through time: F. N. Dempster, "The Spacing Effect: A Case Study in the Failure to Apply the Results of Psychological Research," *American Psychologist* 43 (1990).

24. Power of practice: Lyle Spencer and Charley Morrow did the analysis of data, reported in Lyle Spencer, "Competency Assessment Methods: what works; assessment development and measurement" (Hay/McBer, 1997).

25. Overlearning: See, for example, Timothy T. Baldwin and J. Kevin Ford, "Transfer of Training," *Personnel Psychology* 41 (1988).

26. Much of the research on the benefits of longer periods of effort in behavior change has been done by Kenneth Howard, a psychologist at Northwestern University. See, for example, Kenneth Howard et al., "The Dose-Effect Relationship in Psychotherapy," *American Psychologist* 41 (1986); Kenneth Howard et al., "Evaluation of Psychotherapy," *American Psychologist* 51 (1996).

27. Kathy E. Kram, "A Relational Approach to Career Development," in Douglas T. Hall and Associates, *The Career Is Dead—Long Live the Career* (San Francisco: Jossey-Bass, 1996).

28. Judith Jordan et al. (eds.), *Women's Growth in Connections* (New York: Guilford Press, 1991). As the title suggests, the relational mode of mutual learning comes more readily to women than men (at least in the United States).

29. Buddy systems: see, for example, R. K. Fleming and B. Sulzer-Azaroff, "Peer Management: Effects on Staff Teaching Performance," presented at the Fifteenth Annual Convention of the Association for Behavioral Analysis, Nashville, Tennessee, 1990. Cited in Tannenbaum and Yukl, "Training and Development."

30. Models: there is a rich documentation of the power of positive models in behavior change, dating from Albert Bandura's pioneering work. See, for example, Albert Bandura, "Psychotherapy Based on Modeling Principles" in

A. E. Bergin and S. L. Garfield (eds.), *Handbook of Psychotherapy and Behavior Change: An Empirical Analysis* (New York: John Wiley and Sons, 1971).

31. Imitation focuses on high-status people: see, for example, H. M. Weiss, "Subordinate Imitation of Supervisor Behavior: The Role of Modeling in Organizational Socialization," *Organizational Behavior and Human Performance* 19 (1977).

32. Taking on bad habits of the high-status person: Charles C. Manz and Henry P. Sims, "Beyond Imitation: Complex Behavioral and Affective Linkages Resulting from Exposure to Leadership Training Models," *Journal of Applied Psychology* 71 (1986).

33. The callous and compassionate aides: cited in Cary Cherniss, *Beyond Burnout* (New York: Routledge, 1995).

34. Psychological safety: David Kolb and Richard Boyatzis, "Goal Setting and Self-directed Behavior Change," *Human Relations* 23, 1970.

35. Supportive climate determines transfer: see, for example, Van Velsor and Musselwhite, "The Timing of Training."

36. Banker's Trust New York: reported in *Business Week,* October 20, 1997.

37. Survey of training evaluation in Fortune 500 companies: William H. Clegg, "Management Training Evaluation: An Update," *Training and Development Journal,* February 1987.

38. Liking does not imply learning: Tannenbaum and Yukl, "Training and Development."

39. The Weatherhead follow-up is under the direction of Richard Boyatzis.

Chapter 12 / Taking the Organizational Pulse

1. Analysis of organizational assessment surveys: Mary York, U.S. Office of Personnel Management, unpublished report, November 1997. Among the assessment instruments and models for high-performing organizations included in this analysis: S. M. Arad and M. A. Hanson, "High Performance Workplaces: A Construct Definition." Presented at the Twelfth Annual Conference of the Society for Industrial and Organization Psychology, St. Louis, MO; David Campbell, *The Campbell Organizational Survey: For Surveying Employee Attitudes about Organizational Issues.* National Computer Systems, 1988; James Collins and J. I. Porras, *Built to Last: Successful Habits for Visionary Companies.* (New York: HarperCollins Publishers, 1994); D. R. Denison, *Organizational Dynamics: Bring Corporate Culture to the Bottom Line.* (New York: American Management Association,

1984); D. R. Denison and A. K. Mishra, "Toward a Theory of Organizational Culture and Effectiveness," Organization Science, vol. 6 (2), 1995; D. R. Denison and W. S. Neale, *DENISON: Organizational Culture Survey, Linking Organizational Culture to the Bottom Line.* AVAIT, 1994; Jac Fitz-enz, *The 8 Practices of Exceptional Companies: How Great Organizations Make the Most of Their Human Assets,* (New York: American Management Association, 1997). D. J. Kravetz, *The Human Resource Revolution: Implementing Progressive Management Practices for Bottom-Line Success.* (San Francisco: Jossey-Bass Publishers, 1988); United States Office of Personnel Management, *Building a Model Agency: Changing OPM's Culture to Support Workplace Partnership and Diversity Initiatives, Organizational Assessment Survey,* (Washington, DC: US Office of Personnel Management, 1995).

2. Gaps: in the preliminary analysis, only one—or, more often, none—of the lists of key dimensions for organizational effectiveness matched on emotional competence at the collective level.

3. See Chris Argyris, "Interpersonal Barriers to Decision Making," *Harvard Business Review,* March/April 1966.

4. Volvo and the workers' vacations: Carl F. Frost, *Changing Forever: The Well-Kept Secret of America's Leading Companies* (East Lansing: Michigan State University Press, 1996).

5. Bearing bad news: William Jennings, "A Corporate Conscience Must Start at the Top," *New York Times,* December 29, 1996.

6. Jennings, "A Corporate Conscience."

7. The CEO and burnout: Christina Maslach and Michael P. Leiter, *The Truth About Burnout: How Organizations Cause Personal Stress and What to Do About It* (San Francisco: Jossey-Bass, 1998).

8. Nurse burnout and patient satisfaction: Michael P. Leiter et al., "The Correspondence of Nurse Burnout and Patient Satisfaction," *Social Science and Medicine,* in press, 1998.

9. Stress and malpractice: John W. Jones et al., "Stress and Medical Malpractice: Organizational Risk Assessment and Intervention," *Journal of Applied Psychology* 73 (1988).

10. The study of organizational factors in burnout: Michael P. Leiter and L. Robichaud, "Relationships of Occupational Hazards with Burnout: An Assessment of Measures and Models," *Journal of Occupational Health Psychology* 2 (1997); Maslach and Leiter, *The Truth About Burnout.*

11. Net result: Maslach and Leiter, *The Truth About Burnout.*

12. Peter Senge et al., *The Fifth Discipline Fieldbook: Strategies and Tools for Building a Learning Organization* (New York: Doubleday Currency, 1994).

13. Much of my account of the emotional turmoil faced in the 1995 Lincoln Continental launch, and how these problems were solved, comes from the documentation by George Roth and Art Kliener in "The Learning Initiative at the AutoCo Epsilon Program, 1991–1994," distributed by the Center for Organizational Learning at MIT, 1995. While the document describes how the principles of the learning organization were implemented, it also inevitably describes the emotional and social dynamics at work, since the two streams are intimately intertwined in life.

14. For more on the method, see Chris Argyris, *Overcoming Organizational Defenses* (New York: Prentice-Hall, 1990).

15. For more on the two-column method, see Peter Senge et al., *The Fifth Discipline Fieldbook.* While the two-column method is always explained as bringing to the surface hidden thoughts and feelings, in practice the emotions that accompany hidden thoughts seem often to be ignored, though in theory they are as important as the thoughts.

16. Zeniuk, in a presentation with Fred Simon to the Council for Continuous Improvement, "Learning to Learn: A New Look at Product Development," 1996.

Chapter 13 / The Heart of Performance

1. The meeting at GE is described in L. B. Ward, "In the Executive Alphabet You Call Them C.L.O.'s," *New York Times,* February 4, 1996.

2. The seminal article on organizational intelligence: Mary Ann Glynn, "Innovative Genius: A Framework for Relating Individual and Organizational Intelligences to Innovation," *Academy of Management Review* 21 (1996). Glynn offers this somewhat cumbersome definition: "Organizational intelligence is an organization's capability to process, interpret, encode, manipulate, and access information in a purposeful, goal-directed manner, so it can increase its adaptive potential in the environment in which it operates."

3. This definition of intelligence is a variant of that offered by Howard Gardner in his groundbreaking book *Frames of Mind* (New York: Basic Books, 1993).

4. The tech reps' rap sessions: John Seely Brown and Estee Solomon Gray, "The People Are the Company," *Fast Company,* November 1995.

5. Top 25 percent of companies: Jac Fitz-Enz, "The Truth About Best Practices: What They Are and How to Apply Them," *Human Resources Management,* Spring 1997.

6. Practices: Jac Fitz-Enz, *The Eight Practices of Exceptional Companies* (New York: American Management Association, 1997).

7. Of course, the collective emotional intelligence is but one set among the innumerable complex forces at play in determining business performance.

8. Egon Zehnder International: in addition to helpful sources at the firm, I have used the Harvard Business School case study done of the firm, "Egon Zehnder International," by Eunice Lai and Susan Harmeling under the direction of Professor Michael Y. Yoshino, Harvard Business School (N9–395–076), November 2, 1994.

9. Egon Zehnder International data: Nancy Garrison-Jenn, Economist Intelligence Unit, 1996.

Some Final Thoughts

1. Death rate of Fortune 500 companies: of those companies listed in 1955, 325 had disappeared by 1995. See Charles J. Bishop, 1995 annual report of the Industrial Research Institute, cited in Philip H. Abelson, "The Changing Frontiers of Science and Technology," *Science,* July 26, 1996.

2. The survey of American knowledge workers: this study was done by Michael Hair of Frank N. Magid Associates, Los Angeles, and reported in Dudley Buffa and Michael Hair, "How knowledge workers vote," *Fast Company,* October/November 1996.

Appendix 1

1. Multiple intelligence model: see Howard Gardner, *Frames of Mind* (New York: Basic Books, 1983). In addition to the standard cognitive abilities like mathematical reasoning and verbal fluency (as well as intelligences in domains like movement and music), Gardner proposed that there are "personal intelligences": one for managing oneself and another for handling relationships. But in Gardner's descriptions of the personal intelligences, he emphasized the cognitive elements of these personal intelligences, little exploring the crucial role of emotions in these realms.

2. Peter Salovey and John D. Mayer, "Emotional Intelligence," *Imagination, Cognition, and Personality* 9 (1990).

3. Reuven Bar-On's theory of emotional intelligence first appeared in his doctoral dissertation, which with further research was summarized in Reuven Bar-On,

"The Development of a Concept and Test of Psychological Well-being," unpublished manuscript, 1992. In essence, his model describes emotional intelligence as "an array of personal, emotional and social abilities that influence one's ability to succeed in coping with environmental demands and pressures." The fifteen key abilities fall into five general clusters: intrapersonal capacities (the ability to be aware of one's self, to understand one's emotions, and to assert one's feelings and ideas); interpersonal skills (the ability to be aware of and understand others' feelings, to be concerned about people in general, and to establish emotionally close relationships); adaptability (the ability to verify one's feelings, to accurately size up the immediate situation, to flexibly change one's feelings and thoughts, and to solve problems); stress management strategies (the ability to cope with stress and to control strong emotions); and motivational and general mood factors (the ability to be optimistic, to enjoy oneself and others, and to feel and express happiness).

Appendix 2

1. The classic study of competence among supervisors, managers, and executives: Richard E. Boyatzis, *The Competent Manager: A Model for Effective Performance* (New York: John Wiley and Sons, 1982).

2. Top leaders need more conceptual thinking: see, for example, Elliott Jacques, *Requisite Organization* (Arlington, VA: Cason Hall, 1989).

Appendix 3

1. Scientific studies of sex differences in empathy: see, for example, Tiffany Graham and William Ickes, "When Women's Intuition Isn't Greater than Men's," in William Ickes (ed.), *Empathic Accuracy* (New York: Guilford Press, 1997).

2. Women match emotions better than men: Graham and Ickes, "When Women's Intuition Isn't Greater than Men's."

3. Women better than men at decoding emotion: see Judith Hall, *Nonverbal Sex Difference* (Baltimore: Johns Hopkins University Press, 1984).

4. Men did as well as women in empathic accuracy: Graham and Ickes, "When Women's Intuition Isn't Greater than Men's."

5. Women become more empathic when motivated to be so: Graham and Ickes, "When Women's Intuition Isn't Greater than Men's."

6. Empathy as a sign of nurturance—or weakness: Graham and Ickes, "When Women's Intuition Isn't Greater than Men's."

7. Ickes, quoted in *Science News,* March 23, 1996.

Appendix 4

1. The remedial program for threatening stereotypes: Claude M. Steele, "A Threat in the Air: How Stereotypes Shape Intellectual Identity and Performance," *American Psychologist,* June 1997.

Appendix 5

1. Rules of thumb: adapted from Lyle Spencer Jr. et al., *Competency Assessment Methods: History and State of the Art* (Boston: Hay/McBer, 1997).

2. Simulations: Scott I. Tannenbaum and Gary Yukl, "Training and Development in Work Organizations," *Annual Review of Psychology* 43 (1992).

3. High-tech should not replace basic guidelines for training: Miguel Quinones, "Contextual Influences on Training Effectiveness," in M. A. Quinones and A. Ehrenstein (eds.), *Training for a Rapidly Changing Workforce: Applications of Psychological Research* (Washington, DC: American Psychological Association, 1996).

Index

Contacting Daniel Goleman

This book represents an ongoing exploration for me into emotional intelligence and its practical implications. I welcome thoughts, stories, and reactions from readers, though I am not always able to respond to every letter. My personal e-mail address is: goleman@javanet.com

For those people in organizations seeking to implement the ideas presented here, development tools, media products, and services are available through my consulting group, Emotional Intelligence Services. Among the tools EIS offers is the "Emotional Competence Inventory," which profiles the entire spectrum of emotional competencies. The ECI can be used as a needs assessment tool, or in a "360" form as a first step in developing emotional competence—both as a motivator for self-development and for targeting the competencies most in need of improvement. Other services include design and implementation of development programs in emotional competence, and training of trainers for organizations. To contact EIS:

Emotional Intelligence Services
142 North Road
Sudbury, MA 01776
Phone: (978) 371–5922 Fax: (978) 371–5903
e-mail: EISGlobal@AOL.com
website: www.EISGlobal.com

For a complete copy of the technical report on the development guidelines described in Chapter 11, visit the website of the Consortium for Research on Emotional Intelligence in Organizations: http://www.eiconsortium.org

A Note on the Author

Daniel Goleman, Ph.D., is the author of the international bestsellers *Emotional Intelligence*, *Working with Emotional Intelligence* and *Destructive Emotions*, and is co-author of *Primal Leadership*. Nominated twice for the Pulitzer Prize for his journalistic work covering the brain and behavioural sciences published in the *New York Times*, he is currently co-chair of the Consortium for Research on Emotional Intelligence at Rutgers University and a Fellow of the American Association for the Advancement of Science.

ALSO AVAILABLE BY DANIEL GOLEMAN

VITAL LIES, SIMPLE TRUTHS

- The mind can protect itself against anxiety by dimming awareness
- This mechanism creates a blind spot: a zone of blocked attention and self-deception
- Such blind spots occur at each major level of behaviour from the psychological to the social

Vital Lies, Simple Truths is a penetrating analysis of the ways in which we deceive ourselves. Daniel Goleman draws on evidence of all kinds – from brain function to social dynamics – to reveal how we must distort our most intimate relationships and our day-to-day lives by burying painful insights and memories. This self-deception is our means of psychological self-preservation, the currency of survival in which society transacts.

But although self-deception is sometimes benign, it can also be dangerous and life-diminishing. This important book both illuminates and raises challenging questions about a subject central to our psychological existence.

*

'A creative, challenging and groundbreaking book that entices the reader to question, to think and to see in new ways'
PSYCHOLOGY TODAY

'An ambitious undertaking ... accomplished without seeming effort. His lucid prose is enlivened by descriptions of intriguing experiments and case histories'
NEW YORK TIMES

*

BLOOMSBURY

DESTRUCTIVE EMOTIONS

AND HOW WE CAN OVERCOME THEM

A dialogue with the Dalai Lama

- Why do seemingly rational, intelligent people commit acts of cruelty and violence?
- What are the root causes of destructive behaviour?
- How can we control the emotions that drive these impulses?

In March 2000 a week-long discussion took place between the Dalai Lama and a panel of distinguished scientists and philosophers about human behaviour. Daniel Goleman's illuminating account of this meeting offers fresh insights into how we can recognise and change the emotions that pose grave danger to our individual and collective fate.

Goleman weaves a compelling account of what these destructive emotions are. He discusses where they come from, how the human mind is shaped, how these impulses can be transformed and how otherwise they will threaten our safety and our future.

*

'This book is one of the most absorbing and entertaining reports of brainstorming in the public interest since Plato wrote up those symposia of Socrates'
BOOKLIST

'Extraordinary ... A myriad of creative and positive results ... This essential volume offers a fascinating account of what can emerge when two profound systems for studying the mind and emotions, Western science and Buddhism, join forces'
PUBLISHERS WEEKLY

*

B L O O M S B U R Y

FOCUS

THE HIDDEN DRIVER OF EXCELLENCE

ARE YOU PAYING ATTENTION? Are you completely focused on this book in your hand? Or have you already distracted yourself by quickly checking your watch, e-mails, messages, Facebook stream, Twitter feed, etc? Still resisted the urge to let your mind drift? Then well done, because a reader's mind typically wanders up to 40% of the time when perusing a text. And what are the benefits of paying attention for sustained periods of time? One word: success. In this brilliantly argued book, Daniel Goleman shows why the cornerstone of success in all areas of your life hinge on your ability to FOCUS.

*

'Goleman is the guru'
DAILY TELEGRAPH

'A highly readable manifesto for turning our smartphones off once in a while'
FINANCIAL TIMES

*

ORDER YOUR COPY: BY PHONE 01256 302 699; BY EMAIL: DIRECT@MACMILLAN.CO.UK
DELIVERY IS USUALLY 3–5 WORKING DAYS. FREE POSTAGE AND PACKAGING FOR ORDERS OVER £20
ONLINE: WWW.BLOOMSBURY.COM/BOOKSHOP
PRICES AND AVAILABILITY SUBJECT TO CHANGE WITHOUT NOTICE.

WWW.BLOOMSBURY.COM/DANIELGOLEMAN

B L O O M S B U R Y